Conflict in the Early Americas

Conflict in the Early Americas

AN ENCYCLOPEDIA OF THE SPANISH EMPIRE'S AZTEC, INCAN, AND MAYAN CONQUESTS

Rebecca M. Seaman, Editor

ABC-CLIO

Santa Barbara, California • Denver, Colorado • Oxford, England

Library of Congress Cataloging-in-Publication Data

Conflict in the early Americas : an encyclopedia of the Spanish empire's Aztec, Incan, and Mayan conquests / Rebecca M. Seaman, editor.

    pages cm

  Includes bibliographical references and index.

  ISBN 978-1-59884-776-5 (hardcopy : alk. paper) — ISBN 978-1-59884-777-2 (ebook) 1. America—Discovery and exploration—Spanish—Encyclopedias. 2. Conquerors—America—History—Encyclopedias. 3. Conquerors—Spain—History—Encyclopedias. 4. Mexico—History—Conquest, 1519–1540—Encyclopedias. 5. Peru—History—Conquest, 1522–1548—Encyclopedias. 6. Yucatán Peninsula—History, Military—Encyclopedias. 7. Aztecs—History—16th century—Encyclopedias. 8. Incas—History—16th century—Encyclopedias. 9. Mayas—History—16th century—Encyclopedias. 10. Mayas—History—17th century—Encyclopedias. I. Seaman, Rebecca M., editor.

  E123.C729   2013

  970.01'5003—dc23   2013009363

ISBN: 978-1-59884-776-5
EISBN: 978-1-59884-777-2

17 16 15 14 13   1 2 3 4 5

This book is also available on the World Wide Web as an eBook.
Visit www.abc-clio.com for details.

ABC-CLIO, LLC
130 Cremona Drive, P.O. Box 1911
Santa Barbara, California 93116-1911

This book is printed on acid-free paper ∞

Manufactured in the United States of America

To Maureen Kelley O'Melveny: for inspiring an early love of languages and the study of differing cultures.

Contents

List of Entries

Preface

The study of the Spanish conquest of the Aztec, Inca, and Maya has intrigued people for centuries. The discoveries of archaeological sites in the 19th century, and the translation of the hieroglyphs over the following century spurred interpretations by historians, anthropologists, archaeologists, and others. These works were accompanied by the rediscovery and translation of numerous primary and early historical works from the 16th and early 17th century. The late 20th and early 21st century refocus upon pre-conquest, conquest, and post-conquest America owes a debt to the discussions prompted by the 500th anniversary of Christopher Columbus's discovery of America, as well as the growing ethnohistorical approach to studying indigenous populations.

This single volume edition sought to avail itself of the new historical research, correct some misconceptions, and add newly available information. Thanks to the new discoveries and analyses, a clearer picture of the science, math, social, and political structures of the Aztec, Incas, and Mayas emerged throughout this text. Additionally, the age-old view of the Spanish as a superior, civilizing influence on the Americas is revisited, balanced with information regarding the plunder, massacres, and slaving expeditions. Even the spread and impact of transmitted diseases receives a fresh examination. Additional features of this volume that add to the depth of content include background information regarding the Spanish at the point of conquest, pre-conquest information regarding indigenous societies, and a careful look using new data and interpretations regarding the impacts of the interactions of the competing societies.

The exploration of Spanish, Aztec, Inca, and Mayan cultures at the point and immediately following contact could easily fill multiple volumes. However, in the interest of capturing the key events, personalities, ideas, historical works, and issues that provide a clear understanding of the cultural interactions and outcomes, a single volume of approximately 280 terms has been developed. A variety of Native American, Latin American, and colonial specialists, as well as world historians, have contributed their expertise to provide concise but valuable insight into each culture before, during, and after the period of conquest.

Trying to thank all the people who have been instrumental is an impossible task. A general and heartfelt thanks goes out to all the contributors who spent long hours digging through old and new research to present new insights for this volume. Additionally, I need to give a great deal of credit to Pat Carlin, the Manager of Editorial Development for Military History, Security Issues, and Geography/World Cultures for ABC-CLIO. Without his encouragement and guidance, this volume would not have been produced. I would also like to give a special thanks to my colleagues and peers from the Department of History and Political Science at Elizabeth City State University for their continued support and understanding over the past year.

Finally, I cannot say enough for the support given by my very patient husband, Jack, who willingly stepped in to provide support from the home front.

Rebecca M. Seaman
Professor of History
Chair, Department of History &
Political Science
Elizabeth City State University

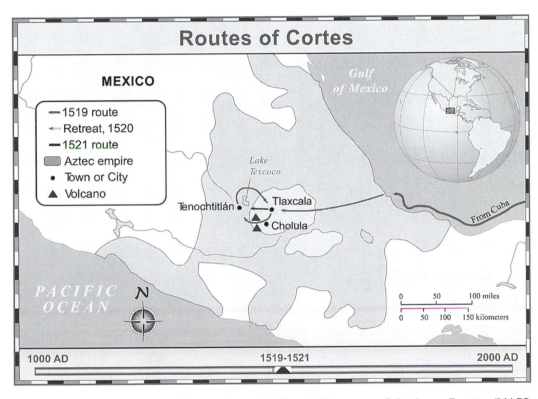

Exploration routes of Hernán Cortés during the Spanish Conquest of the Aztec Empire. (MAPS
.com/Corbis)

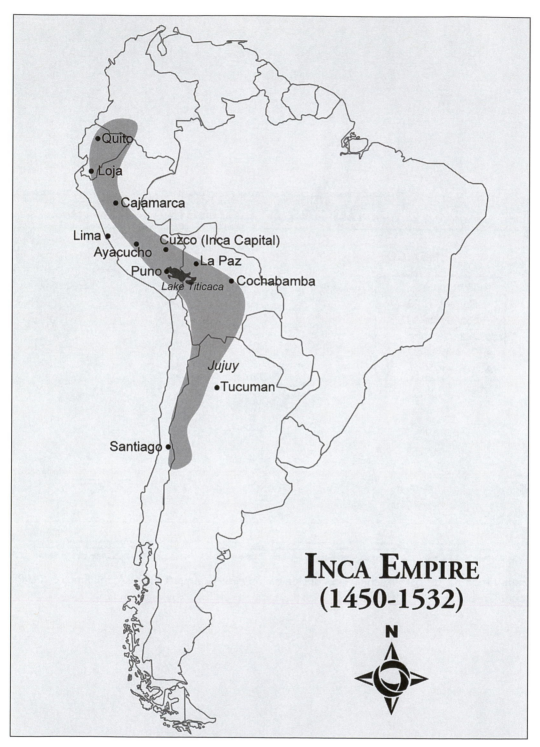

A map of the Inca Empire for the period from 1450 to 1532, highlighting the core inhabited areas under Inca control and the main cities of the Empire.

Map of the Maya Empire in relation to modern political states of the region.

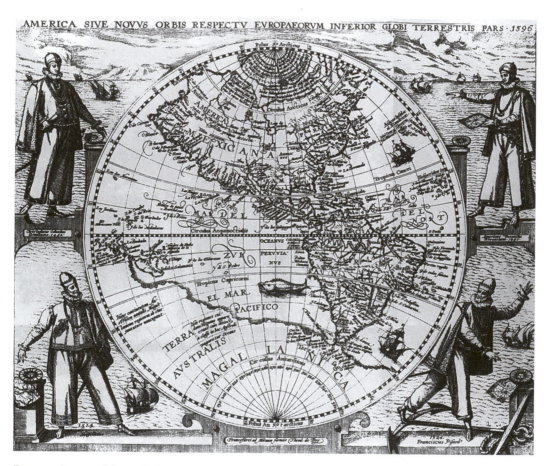

Engraved map of Spanish America, including portraits of the famous explorers: Columbus, Vespucci, Magellan, and Pizarro. (MAPS.com/Corbis)

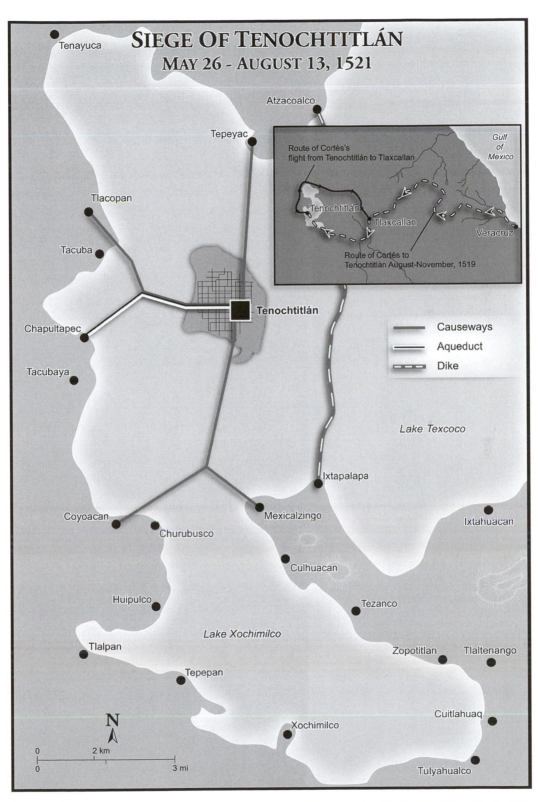

SIEGE OF TENOCHTITLÁN
MAY 26 - AUGUST 13, 1521

Tenayuca

Atzacoalco

Tepeyac

Route of Cortés's
flight from Tenochtitlán to Tlaxcallan

Gulf
of
Mexico

Tlacopan

Tenochtitlán

Tlaxcallan

Veracruz

Tacuba

Route of Cortés to
Tenochtitlán August-November, 1519

Chapultepec

Tenochtitlán

Causeways

Aqueduct

Dike

Tacubaya

Lake Texcoco

Ixtapalapa

Coyoacan

Mexicalzingo

Ixtahuacan

Churubusco

Culhuacan

Huipulco

Tezanco

Lake Xochimilco

Tlalpan

Zopotitlan

Tlaltenango

Tepepan

N

Cuitlahuaq

Xochimilco

0   2 km
0   3 mi

Tulyahualco

Map of the siege of Tenochtitlán, depicting the various cities involved in the conflict, the capital
city within Lake Texcoco, with the causeways used in the siege.

A

Acobamba, Treaty of

The Treaty of Acobamba was an agreement negotiated between the Spanish governor of Peru, Don Diego de Castro, and Titu Cusi Yupanqui, the Sapa Inca of the remaining Inca kingdom. The Spanish purpose for the treaty was to pull the Inca out of the mountainous refuge in the isolated northern region of Vilcabamba. However, the effort proved unsuccessful. Although the agreement, laid out by Castro after years of repeated negotiations and Spanish compromises, was eventually "ratified" by the Sapa Inca, Titu Cusi still refused to emerge from his distant capital.

Castro's intermediary in this long drawn out process was Rodriguez de Figueroa, who served as Corregidor. Initial negotiations began in the early 1560s and were renewed with increased Inca demands in 1565 and again in 1567. One such demand was for the Spanish to approve the marriage of Titu Cusi's son to his first cousin, Beatrice Clara Coya. This specific request necessitated approval from the highest authorities within the Catholic Church, which was delayed until 1569.

While Castro and his intermediary, Figueroa, are seen as instrumental in negotiating the treaty conditions with Titu Cusi, the instigating force behind the scene was Juan de Matienzo. A jurist and entrepreneur, Matienzo systematically attempted to ensure a base of moral integrity as a framework for Spanish colonial rule. While supporting Spanish conquest against what he viewed as the inferior natives of Peru, Matienzo also emphasized the need to protect the Incas against abuses. Key to this structure was the encomendero system, which not only organized the labor and economy under colonial rule, but also ensured the indoctrination of the natives into the Catholic faith. It was at Chuquichaca that Matienzo negotiated the terms for Titu Cusi to receive a substantial repartimiento and for the Spanish to allow Titu Cusi's son to marry his first cousin, all in return for the Sapa Inca to descend from his refuge at Vilcabamba.

The treaty promised great opportunity for the Spanish to spread the Catholic faith to the Inca Empire. A portion of the constantly renegotiated treaty provided for admission of the Christian faith into the kingdom of Vilcabamba, and in theory to Titu Cusi, himself. The Sapa Inca had received the sacrament of baptism as a child, taking the name of Diego. However, he had little recollection of the ceremony and was baptized again as an adult, providing an Inca accommodation in the treaty process. The Inca emperor did admit two priests into the Vilcabamba kingdom for an extended period of time and allowed them to baptize his son, Quispe Titu. While the treaty provided for the admission of priests into the remote kingdom, it did not provide for their sustenance, which came completely from the Spanish governor's treasury.

An interesting aspect of the Treaty of Acobamba was that it forbade the practice of Indians, who retained their traditional faith, to perform rites and ceremonies to their idols, specifically when such practice came in the view of the Catholic priests. This provision placed serious limits on the movements of the missionaries admitted to the remote kingdom of Vilcabamba. While they were allowed to reside and preach in areas such as Vitcos, the priests and all Christians were banned from admission into the capital city of Vilcabamba, where traditional Inca rites and ceremonies were practiced on a daily basis.

After nearly 40 years of Inca resistance to Spanish control of Peru, and after almost 10 years of extended negotiations by Castro, Titu Cusi Yupanqui finally acquiesced in 1566 and asserted that he agreed to the conditions of the Treaty of Acobamba. However, the delay in receiving official approval of his son's marriage to Beatrice Clara Coya (the approval papers arrived with Francisco de Toledo in 1569), the reluctance of the Inca to emerge from his remote refuge, repeated shifts in treaty demands, and the replacement of Castro as viceroy by Toledo in 1569, all cast doubt on the viability of the treaty. With Toledo's assumption of the office of viceroy, rapid changes in policies resulted in the Inca's insistence on renewing negotiations. Frustrated by the intransigence of the indigenous emperor, Toledo abandoned efforts to renegotiate and instead undertook a strategy of undermining Inca authority through the drafting of official reports to the Crown and the development of an official *History of the Incas* by his historian, Pedro Sarmiento de Gamboa.

Rebecca M. Seaman

See also: Castro, Diego de; *Corregidores;* Matienzo, Juan de; Sapa Inca; *Sarmiento's History of the Incas;* Titu Cusi Yupanqui; Toledo, Francisco de; Vilcabamba.

Resources

Jacobs, James. "Tupac Amaru: The Life, Times, and Execution of the Last Inca." *The Andes Web Ring.* http://www.jqjacobs.net /andes/tupac_amaru.html (accessed May 20, 2012).

Stern, Steve J. *Peru's Indian Peoples and the Challenge of Spanish Conquest: Huamanga to 1640.* 2nd ed. Madison: University of Wisconsin Press, 1993.

Titu Cusi Yupanqui. *The Conquest of Peru: An Inca Account of the Conquest of Peru.* Translated, Introduced, and Annotated by Ralph Bauer. Boulder: University Press of Colorado, 2005.

Adelantado

The Spanish used the term *adelantado* to designate a governor or local administrator of a specific district. Beginning from the medieval period, these local administrators usually held military significance and were responsible for organizing military units for the defense of their districts. Though the term declined in use in the 16th century, along the frontiers in America these regional military governors were crucial to the successful defense of Spanish territories. Appointed by the Crown, the powers of an *adelantado* were outside the jurisdictions of other colonial authorities such as the viceroys and/ or *audiencias.* Instead, they answered to the king, and the Council of the Indies (the highest civil government in the colonies).

Examples of *adelantados* in Spanish America include Bartolomé Colón, brother of Christopher Columbus, who held the post in Hispaniola during Columbus's absences. Diego Velázquez de Cuéllar was appointed in that role over Cuba in 1518, and Ponce de León briefly held the title for his intended colony in Florida. Hernán Cortés sought and received the appointment as a means of breaking free of the authority of Velázquez. Indeed, Cortés was granted both, the title of *adelantado* and governor by Carlos I (a.k.a. Charles V of the Holy Roman Empire). As late as 1565, Philip II bestowed the title of *adelantado* upon Pedro Menéndez de Avilés to govern over the newly established Spanish outpost of St. Augustine in Florida. Other *adelantados* of note include Francisco de Garay, Lucas Vázquez de Ayllón, Pánfilo de Narváez, and Hernando de Soto.

In Peru, the office of *adelantado* was also employed. Though the conquest of the Incas is typically associated with Francisco Pizarro, he collaborated with his partner, Diego de Almagro. Tensions between these partners increased over the years, until Carlos I divided the new colony of Peru between them. Pizarro was assigned the northern section of Peru, along with the title of governor, while Almagro was awarded the southern section, including the still unconquered region of Chile. As *adelantado*, Almagro used his military forces and native allies to conquer sections of Chile before returning to a native uprising within the city of Cuzco.

Intended as military leaders with the requisite judicial and governing authority for distant frontier settlements, the title of *adelantado* often was bestowed upon conquistadors. The *adelantados* wielded great powers with few checks, including from the very distant Spanish monarchy. Very quickly, these powerful positions were replaced with civil authorities, such as the alcaldes mayores and cabildos, who often governed towns with the authorities of magistrates.

Rebecca M. Seaman

See also: Almagro, Diego de; Cabildo; Charles V (HRE) or Carlos I of Spain; Cortés, Hernán; Narváez, Pánfilo de; Pizarro, Francisco; Soto, Hernando de, in Peru.

Resources

Hugh, Thomas. *Conquest: Montezuma, Cortés, and the Fall of Old Mexico.* New York: Simon & Schuster, 1993.

MacQuarrie, Kim. *Last Days of the Inca.* New York: Simon & Schuster, 2007.

Weber, David J. *The Spanish Frontier in North America.* New Haven: Yale University Press, 1992.

Agriculture and Economy, Pre-Conquest Mexico

Agricultural and economic origins of Mexico can be traced back to the period of the Olmec rule. Evidence of maize, squash, and beans as gradually domesticated crops in the region of Mexico is consistent over the years. Specialized goods and trade also helped complete the economic picture for the Aztec Empire prior to Spanish domination.

Maize was the foremost crop in Mexico and was grown throughout most areas of the empire. Beans were instrumental, not only as a source of protein in a society with few domesticated animals, but also for the nitrogen they returned to the soil. Additional edible crops that increased in importance included the avocado pear, a wide variety of chilies for seasoning, amaranth, and chia (for use in porridge). Other crops, harvested for their fibers and other qualities, included cotton, agave, yucca, and maguey cactus. The latter plant not only provided fiber for cloth; its spikes were harvested for use as needles and juice from the plant was fermented into the alcoholic beverage of pulque.

From these early agricultural products, one can gain a basic understanding of some of the trade commodities exchanged throughout much of Mexico. Cotton materials, especially quilted cotton fabric, was considered of high quality and reserved for use by the elite members of Aztec society. Coarser materials, typically woven from fibers of the agave and maguey cactus, were readily available to other societal ranks. Similarly, the alcoholic beverage of pulque had a limited usage. Used as a ceremonial drink of cleansing, the beverage was restricted to ritual use only. Intoxication outside of ritual usage was severely punished.

Agriculture in distant rural regions was practiced in irrigated fields surrounding villages. Aqueducts, bearing necessary water for maintaining fields, were developed. Farmers in these rural areas probably boasted better standards of living than their urban counterparts, or even artisans in the urban areas. With easy access to their fields, rural farmers could easily travel the short distances to and from their places of work, carrying their limited tools such as digging sticks and returning with burdens of farm produce.

Aqueducts also supplied the major urban areas with water for drinking and supported the urban agricultural efforts. Among these were impressive botanical gardens, unparalleled in Europe of the time. The task of creating and protecting the larger fields of produce for markets in the Valley of Mexico was more complex and crucial for the survival of the large urban populations. Efforts were undertaken to develop dikes that separated the freshwater lakes from the salt stretches to the east of the valley. Additionally, swamps were drained to reclaim rich soils for farming. Floating fields or islands of farmlands were developed, some as small as 2 by 20 meters while others were as large as 20 by 100 meters. These fields, or *chinampas,* were created by either digging drainage ditches that created the appearance of islands, or by the use of baskets of mud and aquatic plants that built up the islands in the midst of the lakes and swamps. Trees, planted along the perimeters of the floating fields, helped to retain the soil as well as contribute to additional agricultural crops.

Additionally, urban farmers had a greater distance to travel to access their fields. In an era and a region with no beasts of burden, and with increased quantities of crops needed to supply the urban populace, these farmers often traveled miles carrying produce on their backs. In comparison to their rural counterparts, the urban farmers experienced harsher conditions and lower standards of living.

Agriculture throughout much of Mexico was supplemented by hunting and fishing. Rabbits and deer were choice game hunted by the Aztecs, and the meat and peltry were used widely in society. In comparison, domesticated dogs and turkeys were primarily consumed by the more elite ranks of society. Fishing, in the lakes and canals, provided additional protein for urban diets.

Pre-conquest Mexico's economy was also affected by the artisans' guilds. Examples of guilds that controlled the quality and production of specialized goods included the goldsmiths, lapidaries, featherworkers, carvers, potters, obsidian-workers, and tailors. Among the religious ranks, persons tasked with writing and painting religious manuscripts and governmental documents joined the ranks of skilled craftsmen. The products of these artisans were sold in markets or as specifically commissioned works.

Merchants were an integral part of the Mexica economy. Some merchants, or *pochtecas,* even higher in rank from the commoners than the artisans, were capable of owning lands. The constant travel associated with the merchant lifestyle resulted in the acquisition of military skills (to defend their goods) and the practice of the empire using them as virtual spies. Allowed to enter the lands of potential enemies for the purpose of trade, the merchants often spoke the language of the opposition and donned dress that enabled them to disguise their origins. These merchants were strategic to the acquisition of needed raw materials not otherwise available to the empire and its people. Indeed, the necessity of acquiring trade goods to support the extensive population of cities such as Tenochtitlán was tied directly to trade and wars; where one method failed, the other emerged to fill the gap and provide the needs of the general populace and the empire.

Directly related to the economy and trade was the role of products familiarly used as accepted currency. Cotton and feathered mantels fell into this category. Other commonly exchanged items included coca beans, copper items, and gold quills. In total, the economy was driven locally by agriculture and throughout the empire by collected tributes and trade.

A final consideration to any discussion of pre-conquest agriculture and economy in Mexico is the inclusion of religion. Conversations about Aztec religion typically center upon the polytheistic and violent nature of Mexica practices. However, a central theme to most religious rituals was the safeguarding of crop cycles. To this end, favored gods were related to fertility and the maize deities. Unlike practices of farming, crafts and trade today, the Mexica incorporated religious rites into the protection of all aspects of their economy, seeking to sustain their society and maximize their productivity.

Rebecca M. Seaman

See also: Maize; Pochtecas.

Resources

Davies, Nigel. *The Ancient Kingdoms of Mexico: A Magnificent Re-creation of Their Art and Life.* London: Penguin Books, 1982.

Eakin, Marshall C. *The History of Latin America: Collision of Cultures.* New York: Palgrave Macmillan, 2007.

Stark, Barbara L. and Philip J. Arnold, III. *Olmec to Aztec: Settlement Patterns in the Ancient Gulf Lowlands.* Tucson: University of Arizona Press, 1997.

Agriculture and Economy, Pre-Conquest Peru

Peru is best known for being the heart of the ancient Inca Empire, but the region was home to many earlier indigenous cultures before the Inca absorbed them by conquest or assimilation. Despite the variety of tribes and cultures incorporated into the empire, Inca subjects had one trait in common: they were almost all farmers, shepherds, or fishermen. The economic system of the Inca did not use currency. Limited trade existed between the empire and outside regions, but there was no internal market system. Individuals paid taxes in the form of *mita* labor to the government, and in return, basic necessities were provided.

The Inca Empire invested heavily in farming infrastructure, developing sophisticated agricultural techniques to support its large population. Unusable land was transformed with terracing, raised beds, irrigation, fertilizing, and dredging to maximize the amount of arable land for crops. Inca farmers had extensive engineering skill. Terracing was a sophisticated technology that served a number of functions. It stabilized slopes, prevented erosion, created level ground for building, and provided additional land for agriculture. Terraces were created by building retaining walls on bedrock. They were backfilled with medium gravel and then covered with fine gravel and sand. The sand was topped off with a layer of fertilized topsoil, carried up in countless basket loads from lower elevations. The resulting terrace provided a level, well-drained, rich layer of earth for crops. Channels cut into the ground collected and circulated rainwater. The stone walls absorbed heat from the sun during the day and radiated that heat during the night, preventing the temperature from dropping below freezing on cold mountain slopes and protecting frost-sensitive crops such as maize.

Farmers also mastered crop irrigation to maximize food production. Channels and conduits diverted rainwater throughout the terraces to keep plants watered. Aqueducts and cisterns were carved into rock to store and divert water. Miles of canals and channels diverted rivers to extend agriculture into the desert. Human and animal manure were used to fertilize crops. In the mountains, it was mostly collected from llamas, alpacas, and other camelids. Along the coast, sea bird droppings (guano) and decayed fish parts were used.

The Inca Empire encompassed steep mountains, coastlines, deserts, and jungle. The empire began and expanded throughout the series of ranges making up the Andes Mountains and spanned four distinct climate zones; the yunga, the quechua, the suni, and the puna. The yunga zone reaches from the Andes foothills up to about 5,000 feet. Warmer and drier than many areas of the empire, the Inca built raised fields separated by irrigation ditches that supported a wide range of crops, including grains, corn, potatoes, beans and fruits. The quechua zone begins at 5,000 feet and reaches up to 11,500 feet. Cultures prior to the Inca cleared these forested regions for farming. With moderate temperatures and plenty of rain, many varieties of corn, potatoes, amaranth, quinoa, lima beans, squash, and fruit were produced. The suni, soaring over 11,500 feet, supported only the hardiest varieties of corn, potatoes, oca (another root vegetable), and grains. This climate zone was used more frequently for herding llamas and alpacas. The highest zone, the puna, is a cold barren region where few crops grow. The eastern slopes of the Andes dropped into the Amazon rain forest, where many unusual crops—sweet potatoes, pineapples, avocados, and guavas—prized

by the Incas grew. The empire also reached westward to the Pacific Ocean, where fishermen along the coast provided fish and seafood for the empire. Along with beans, meat provided protein to the Inca. The vast majority of meat came from llamas and alpacas. Guinea pigs were also raised as a food source, but they were more for festivals and parties, and provided more fat than protein.

All able-bodied individuals participated in farming activities that served as the backbone of Andean life. Even artisans only worked at their crafts part-time due to the obligations of offering tribute to the state and the idea of reciprocal exchange that drove the economy. All lands were divided into three parts. While everyone participated in farming, one third of all crops were worked for the state, one third for the religious establishment, and one third for the farmers' personal consumption. The state stored and distributed harvested crops to villages as the need arose.

Farming the steep and rocky slopes was backbreaking work. Inca farmers did not have domesticated animals suitable for agricultural tasks and did not have the wheel. All farming was done by hand with tools suited to the narrow platforms of the terraces. Teams of equal numbers of men and women worked in line to prepare the fields for planting. The men used sharp wooden foot plows to break up the soil. The women followed, removing stones and breaking the clumps of soil further. They would then sow the seeds. The work was done in unison, accompanied by singing or chanting.

The Inca Empire may be the only advanced civilization in history to have no currency, commerce, or class of traders. Everything families needed they produced for themselves. If a natural disaster destroyed the crops, provisions were provided by the state. The only exception was some limited trade between the empire and outsiders for goods that could not be produced within the boundaries of the empire.

With no form of currency, every household was required to provide labor as a tax. This *mita* labor benefited the state directly, by serving in the army or building roads, bridges, and canals. Indirectly, the *mita* served the state by supplying the harvest from state-owned fields.

Historians find it remarkable that a wealthy, sophisticated culture could evolve without ever inventing a market economy. Given the difficult terrain and climate challenges, it is possible that all their focus had to be on subsistence. Technological innovations revolved around increasing food production rather than economics and acquiring material goods. The Inca Empire was optimized to support its people. It is remarkable that an empire could achieve so much without ever spending a single coin.

Jill M. Church

See also: Government, Pre-Conquest Inca; Inca Roads; *Mita.*

Resources

Baudin, Louis. *Daily Life in Peru: Under the Last Incas.* London: George Allen & Unwin, 1961.

D'Altroy, Terence N. "Andean Land Use at the Cusp of History." In *Imperfect Balance: Landscape Transformations in the Precolumbian Americas,* edited by David L. Lentz, 357–390. New York: Columbia University Press, 2000.

D'Altroy, Terence N. *The Incas.* Oxford: Blackwell, 2002.

Erickson, Clark L. "The Lake Titicaca Basin: A Precolumbian Built Landscape." In *Imperfect Balance: Landscape Transformations in the Precolumbian Americas,* edited by David L. Lentz, 311–356. New York: Columbia University Press, 2000.

McEwan, Gordon. *The Incas: New Perspectives.* New York: W.W. Norton and Company, 2006.

Morris, Arthur. "The Agricultural Base of the Pre-Incan Andean Civilizations." *The Geographical Journal* 165 (1999): 286–295.

Aguilar, Fr. Gerónimo de

Born in the last decades of the 1400s in Ecija, Spain, Gerónimo de Aguilar received a religious education and took the vows of the Franciscan Order. After coming to the New World as a young man, the friar accompanied a Spanish explorer, Valdivia, on his way to San Domingo. En route Jamaica the ship went aground, resulting in the loss of all but 20 men aboard. Shipwrecked off the coast of the Yucatán Peninsula in 1511, the initial survivors struggled in a small boat for 13 days. Approximately half of the survivors perished from hunger and thirst before reaching the shore. Once ashore, the shipwrecked crew was taken hostage and five, including the leader Valdivia, were sacrificed and eaten by their captors. One of two Spaniards to survive the hazards of starvation, exposure, and captivity, Aguilar managed to flee inland where he was accepted by a Mayan society.

After years of living among the Mayans, it is not surprising that Aguilar and his companion, Gonzalo Guerrero, assimilated into the local culture, learning the Mayan language. However, at this point, part of the story differs depending on the author. Some historians record that the friar remained loyal to his religious vows, shunning all offers of marriage and pleasures of the flesh. Such accounts attribute his survival to his possession and use of a breviary, which enabled him to keep track of and celebrate the Christian feast days. Others assert the friar's assimilation

Gerónimo de Aguilar (1489–1531). Spanish Franciscan monk who came to America with Valdivia and, after suffering a shipwreck, was taken prisoner by a Mayan chief on the Yucatán Peninsula where he learned their language. Hernán Cortés rescued him in 1519, and used him as an interpreter. "Geronimo de Aguilar is presented to Cortés after eight years of slavery among the Indians." Drawing by J. Altarriba and engraved by J. Carrafa (1825). (Album/Art Resource, NY)

into Mayan culture included marrying into the local Mayan society. Despite this minor controversy, Aguilar's escape in 1519, at the time of Hernán Cortés's coastal landing on the Yucatán, is without dispute.

Cortés heard of European refugees held by the local Indians. He sent a message to the refugees, offering to include them on his expedition. The message was delayed and Aguilar arrived after the fleet departed. However, he obtained a canoe and rowed to Cozumel where, due to a leak, Cortés's ship had returned for repairs. Aguilar joined the expedition, serving the role of an interpreter for Cortés. Aguilar's first duty as the interpreter was to interpret Cortés's preaching to

the local population, demanding adoration of the cross, and banning the presence of all idols in the temples. Gonzalo Guerrero, Aguilar's fellow shipwrecked survivor, was less cooperative and had no interest in rejoining the Spanish. Instead, he eventually was killed while siding with the Maya against Cortés and his men.

The first test of Aguilar's skills in interpreting Mayan occurred when Cortés's force encountered the Tabascans. Though these natives had previously welcomed the Spanish explorer Juan de Grijalva, the Tabascans assaulted Cortés's expedition with bows and arrows. Efforts by Aguilar to facilitate a ceasefire failed. Only after the awesome noise and deadly fire of Spanish crossbows and guns did the intimidated Tabascans surrender. According to Aguilar's interpretation, the Tabascans friendly to Grijalva were punished by neighboring tribes and forced to promise they would fiercely resist future Spanish expeditions.

An interesting importance associated with Aguilar's service to Cortés involves the perpetuation of native stories connecting Cortés with the god Quetzalcoatl. This association, later claimed by Cortés, is not originally sustained in Cortés's second letter to the Spanish king. Additionally, early postcontact and precontact Aztec documents do not support prophesies of a returning ruler or deity. These perceptions were associated with the Mayan people and were likely communicated to Cortés by Aguilar while the Spanish still resided among the Maya.

Unfortunately for Cortés, his newfound translator's translation skills were restricted to the Mayan language. However, the defeat of the Tabascans provided a solution. One of the Tabascan slaves included a Nahua (Aztec) woman who also spoke Mayan. Through a series of interpretations, Marina (the Christian name for the Nahua slave) provided the interpretation of Nahuatl into Mayan, leaving Aguilar to translate Mayan into Spanish for Cortés. This complex arrangement continued until Marina simplified the process by becoming proficient in Spanish as well.

With the rise of Marina as the primary linguist for Cortés, Aguilar's importance and influence declined. Documents indicate his continued presence in the Spanish forces. He was one of the lucky few that survived the disastrous Spanish defeat at the hands of the Aztec in La Noche Triste in 1520. Friar Gerónimo Aguilar also appears in the eventual triumph by the Spanish as Cortés finally conquered Tenochtitlán in 1521. Little else is known of the friar. He remained in the Valley of Mexico, presumably continuing to serve as a religious leader among the newly conquered Aztec population. Documents intimate that he eventually took an Indian wife and had two daughters. He was awarded a grant of land in Mexico in 1526, which reverted to the Crown upon his death due to his ecclesiastical status.

Rebecca M. Seaman

See also: Hernán Cortés; Cozumel; Juan de Grijalva; La Noche Triste; La Malinche, "Doña Marina"; Quetzalcoatl.

Resources

Eakin, Marshall C. *The History of Latin America: Collision of Cultures.* New York: Palgrave Macmillan, 2007.

Gillesie, Susan D. *The Aztec Kings: The Construction of Rulership in Mexica History.* Tucson: University of Arizona Press, 1989.

Graulich, Michel. *Myths of Ancient Mexico.* Translated by Bernard R. Ortiz de Montellano and Thelma Ortiz de Montellano. Norman: University of Oklahoma Press, 1997.

Landa, Diego de. *Yucatan: Before and After the Conquest.* Translated with notes by William Gates. New York: Dover Publications, 1978.

Prescott, William H. *History of the Conquest of Mexico.* New York: Radom House, 1998.

Sánchez, Carlos Serrano. "Mestizaje y Características Físicas de la Población Mexicana." *Arqueologia Mexicana* 11, no. 65 (February 2004): 64–67.

Ahuitzotl

Ahuitzotl was the eighth emperor of the Aztec Empire. He succeeded his elder brother Tizoc. Despite misgivings of other Aztec leaders because of his age, Ahuitzotl proved to be one of the most successful emperors of the Aztecs. During his reign, the empire was expanded to its greatest extent. Ahuitzotl is also remembered for the massive human sacrifices he ordered during the dedication of the Great Temple at Tenochtitlán.

The exact year of Ahuitzotl's birth is unknown. He was the grandson of the emperor Itzcoatl, the fourth Aztec emperor and founder of the Triple Alliance between Tenochtitlán, Texcoco, and Tlacopan that laid the foundation for the Aztec Empire. Both of Ahuitzotl's elder brothers, Axayacatl and Tizoc, served as emperors before Ahuitzotl. While Axayacatl, as a ruler, was successful in war and left many impressive building projects, his brother Tizoc was a failure. The wealth and power of the Aztec Empire was measured by the tribute and prisoners sent to it by neighboring cities and tribes. During Tizoc's rule, both declined so that many allies and enemies of the Aztecs lost respect and considered war. Tizoc died after only five years on the throne, and it was suspected that he was poisoned.

The office of emperor was not hereditary among the Aztecs. Four days after Tizoc's death in 1486, the leaders of the people met to elect a new emperor, or *tlatoani*. Some opposed Ahuitzotl because they felt only an older ruler would regain respect for the Aztecs. Still, Ahuitzotl was selected. He soon proved that he was an aggressive military leader. His first campaign was to the northwest, against former vassals. The city of Chiapa was taken, along with many prisoners. The prisoners were taken to Tenochtitlán and sacrificed during Ahuiztotl's coronation. Allied and enemy leaders were invited to celebrate with the new emperor so that all might know the degree of respect with which the Aztecs were held. Those who did not attend were considered to be rebels and became the targets of future conquests. Ahuitzotl displayed the extremes of his personality at the coronation. Generous toward his friends, he spent the equivalent of a year's worth of tribute on gifts and celebrations. Immediately after the ritual was completed, he began the serious business of conquest.

Ahuitzotl was a dynamic leader. When the province of Huaxtec rebelled, he quickly mobilized his army and demanded support from allied and subject cities. He used a combination of forced marches, ambushes, and surprise attacks to quickly overwhelm the rebels. During the campaign, Ahuitzotl turned down the offer of quarters in an ally's palace, stating that the place for a king was with his soldiers. Close proximity kept the emperor informed regarding the performance of his armies. Those who fought well were rewarded; those who did not were punished.

In 1487, work on the Great Temple in Tenochtitlán, ordered by Tizoc, was completed. To dedicate the temple, Ahuitzotl arranged for large numbers of captives. Surrounding rulers were again invited. Those who were enemies of the Aztecs arrived in secret to avoid questions from the common people. On the appointed day, lines of prisoners radiated from the temple in the four compass points. Contemporary accounts indicate that one line was more than three miles long. Ahuitzotl and leading nobles stood at the top of the Great Temple. Using sacrificial knives, they cut open the captives' chests and removed their still-beating hearts. The human sacrifice went on for four days. Estimates of the number of victims range from 20,000 to 80,000 people. Accounts described the rivers of blood that ran down the sides of the temple.

During the remainder of his reign, Ahuitzotl conquered the Isthmus of Tehuantepec and Chiapas. He also established control over the Mayas in the jungles of Peten. He conquered the Oaxaca Valley and the Pacific Coast down to Guatemala. The sole opponents whom Ahuitzotl could not conquer were the Tarascans in Michoacan. By his death, he had expanded the borders of the Aztec Empire as far as 700 miles from Tenochtitlán, a huge distance for a people without beasts of burden or wheeled vehicles. Ahuitzotl's other accomplishments included ordering another aqueduct to be constructed to bring more freshwater to the capital.

Ahuitzotl reportedly died in 1502, when his garden was flooded after a dike broke. His sandal apparently slipped on a wet rock, and he hit his head on a stone lintel. Doctors removed parts of his skull, but he apparently died of a subdural hematoma.

Tim J. Watts

See also: Human Sacrifice; Texcoco, Alliance with Tenochtitlán.

Resources

Berdan, Frances F. *The Aztecs of Central Mexico: An Imperial Society.* Florence, KY: Wadsworth, 2004.

Gillespie, Susan D. *The Aztec Kings: The Construction of Rulership in Mexica History.* Tucson: University of Arizona Press, 1992.

Hassig, Ross. *Aztec Warfare: Imperial Expansion and Political Control.* Oklahoma City: University of Oklahoma Press, 1995.

Albornoz, Cristóbal

Cristóbal Albornoz, a Spanish secular priest, arrived in Peru in 1567. He was assigned the role of *visitador,* inspecting the timely payment of tythes by the encomenderos. In 1569 he headed to the region of Huamanga, a center of the rising nativist movement of the Taki Onqoy. New to the area and lacking any connections, he was tasked with investigating and punishing responsible parties for any violations of Spanish colonial policy.

It was in this role that Albornoz encountered news of the rapidly expanding nativist anticolonial movement. The Taki Onqoy revival was a pan-Andean alliance of deities (huacas) and natives from various classes and community backgrounds. The movement emerged in 1560 in the Huamanga region. Spread by *taquiongos* like Juan Chono, human spokespersons or prophets for the huacas, the complex nativist movement combined the increasing opposition to Spanish colonial leadership with growing opposition of native leaders. The *kurakas'* awareness that they might benefit from a void created by the revival, and recognition by the somewhat alienated *yanaconas* that colonial abuse of laborers in the mines undermined their status and authority, helped pull all ranks of Andean society toward the new revival movement.

Albornoz set about investigating the movement and attempting to root out the "heresy." In a region with only about 150,000 natives, Albornoz asserted he found over 8,000 followers of the sect. It was through the investigation of the Taki Onqoy sect that Albornoz achieved his place in Spanish colonial history. The secular priest, sincere in his faith and personally ambitious, sought to capitalize on the discovery of the heresy to propel him into higher office. His series of *Informaciones* reports were in essence documents submitted to justify his promotion to various higher posts in colonial Peru. However, until the 1584 *Informaciones,* Albornoz failed in his quest for promotions.

A study of Albornoz's various reports reveals carefully couched questions that led most witnesses to give short, affirmative responses. Additionally, evidence indicates that Albornoz either carefully handpicked the witnesses he questioned, or the only people willing to submit to his questioning were those who supported him in his promotion attempts, or a combination of both. Despite the limits and silence on certain aspects regarding the Taki Onqoy in the *Informaciones,* it is evident that Albornoz provided details regarding the sect that were unreported in other documents of the era. Specifically, data regarding the location of certain sect leaders, the identification of the structure of some of the leadership, and spread of the sect come out through his reports. However, it is important to note that Albornoz was not attempting to write a thorough analysis of the emerging sect, but to simply highlight the threat posed by the sect and how he was instrumental in the discovery and suppression of this threat.

The result of Cristóbal Albornoz's campaign against the Taki Onqoy and its adherents was in part the identification of a broad spectrum of native heretics to the Catholic faith. Additionally, he distinguished between the different levels of the sect's participants and assigned varying punishments according to the level of importance to the movement. While varying punishments were assigned based on the perceived threat to Spanish control, the majority of the adherents to the new sect were required to undergo instruction in the Catholic faith to facilitate their rejection of the nativist deities. All natives identified by Albornoz's campaign experienced increased demands on their labor and obligations to the Church. The same could not be said about Spanish leaders implicated by his reports.

Cristóbal Albornoz was compelled to play a strategic balancing act in his efforts to root out the heresy and use the success against the heresy in his efforts for promotion. According to practice, once the *visitas* revealed a religious heresy, the *visitador* was not only responsible for investigating and punishing the participant heretics, but also to reprimand and expose the colonial Spanish leaders who allowed the movement to emerge and grow without reporting such a movement to the Crown and Church authorities. In the end, Albornoz was compelled to downplay the Spanish accountability in reporting the incident—and thereby acknowledge that the movement did not rise to the level to necessitate reprimands, while he simultaneously highlighted the importance of the heresy's threat to Catholicism and Spanish authority in Peru. His success in this balancing act is apparent in the continued support by Spanish witnesses willing to testify to his efforts and success over the years in the *Informaciones,* even as his periodic reports and supplications for promotion revised the role and importance of the Taki Onqoy movement in Huamanga. This balancing act was furthered in Albornoz's later work of the *Instrucción,* where he downplays the Taki Onqoy, without even naming the movement. Instead, in this later work, Albornoz provides a step-by-step account of how to extirpate a religious heresy, underlining his competence in this area while de-emphasizing the threat of the nativist movement to Spanish authority.

Historians attempting to understand the early emergence of the Taki Onqoy sect, and those studying the motives of Albornoz arrive at different but related conclusions. His *Informaciones* are invaluable to gleaning facts and piecing together the period and events. However, Albornoz's lack of a deep analysis of the Taki Onqoy movement itself and the absence of opposing witnesses to Albornoz's promotion supplications are indicative of the limited scope of the *Informaciones.* Instead, they provide a picture of an ambitious, politically astute, Spanish religious administrator of 16th-century Peru.

Rebecca M. Seaman

See also: Huacas; Huamanga; *Kuraka;* Taki Onqoy; *Visitas; Yanaconas.*

Resources

Heilman, Jaymie. "A Movement Miscontrued: A Response to Gabriela Ramos's Interpretation of Taki Onqoy." *Colonial Latin American Review.* 11, no. 1 (2002): 123–138.

Millones, Luis. "The Time of the Inca: the Colonial Indians' Quest." *Antiquity.* 66, no. 250 (March 1, 1992): 204–216.

Mumford, Jeremy. "The Taki Onqoy and the Andean Nation: Sources and Interpretations." *Latin American Research Review* 33, no. 1 (1998): 150–165.

Stern, Steve J. *Peru's Indian Peoples and the Challenge of Spanish Conquest: Huamanga to 1640.* 2nd ed. Madison: University of Wisconsin Press, 1993.

Alderete, Julián de

Former *camarero* (steward) to Juan Rodriguez de Fonseca, the Bishop of Burgos, Julián de Alderete was designated the official treasurer, sent from Hispaniola to oversee the royal fifth of treasures gained in Hernán Cortés's expedition against the Mexica. He arrived in Texcoco in the spring of 1521 along with a number of other important additions to Cortés's forces on an expedition lead by Rodrigo de Bastida, an experienced conquistador and merchant. The arrival of Alderete followed the conflict between Cortés and Narváez and the subsequent La Noche Triste disaster that expelled the Spanish from the capital city of Tenochtitlán. At that point in time Cortés was reorganizing his Spanish forces and native allies, as well as building brigantines for the eventual siege against the Aztec emperor Cuahtémoc's forces.

The treasurer brought news to Cortés from Spain that the *caudillo*'s messengers to the Spanish court, and the gold he had sent back, finally arrived and were eventually received by the Crown. As a result, the Bishop of Burgos had fallen out of favor and Cortés received support for his expedition from Charles V. Further evidence of this royal support accompanied Alderete in the form of indulgences for acts committed by the conquistadors, bestowed by the Pope and carried by a Franciscan friar, Fr. Pedro Melgarejo de Urrea.

Alderete, like many other Spanish sent out from Hispaniola, was quickly impressed with the potential for Spanish power and personal wealth to be obtained from a victory over the Aztec Empire. Offering his services as an expert crossbowman, the Spanish dignitary was assigned to accompany some of the *caudillo*'s forces in the battle of Tlaycapan, at the start of the expedition around the southern portion of the lake that Tenochtitlán resided upon, prior to assaulting the capital city. Having demonstrated his skill as a crossbowman, Alderete eventually served as one of Cortés's captains in the extended battle for control of Tenochtitlán.

The eventual violent conquest of the capital produced many casualties on both sides, but limited quantities of the gold so eagerly sought by the Spanish. Alderete is said to have coerced Cortés into approving torture of some of the Aztec caciques, including the emperor, Cuauhtémoc. Alderete's position as the official treasurer, as well as his service to the *caudillo* in the conquest of the capital, convinced Cortés of the need to produce more wealth that could be divided between the emperor's share, his captains, as well as the men in his forces. Little remaining gold was discovered at the time, with only 3,000 pesos worth going to Alderete.

In December of 1521, Cristóbal de Tapia, inspector of Hispaniola, arrived with instructions from the Bishop of Burgos to take control of New Spain from Cortés. Alderete and other conquistadors who had fallen out with the *caudillo* over the poor rewards for their contributions to the expedition welcomed Tapia. Historian Hubert Howe Bancroft asserted that Alderete plotted an attempt on the *caudillo*'s life. While Cortés publicly forgave this indiscretion, he viewed this breach of trust as a betrayal. In 1522, when more wealth was sent back to Spain for the king and others in the Castilian government, a disgruntled Alderete accompanied the shipment, vowing to report to King Charles V his increasingly negative views of Cortés. The report was never submitted. Juan de Alderete fell ill on the initial leg of his journey back to Spain. He died soon after leaving Villa Rica de la Vera Cruz.

Rebecca M. Seaman

See also: Charles V (HRE) or Carlos I of Spain; Cortés, Hernán; Cuauhtémoc; Rodriguez de Fonseca, Juan; La Noche Triste; Narváez, Pánfilo de; Tenochtitlán, City of; Tenochtitlán, Siege of.

Resources

Bancroft, Hubert Howe. *The Worlds of Hubert Howe Bancroft: History of Mexico.* Vol. 2. San Francisco: The History Company, Publishers, 1883.

Diaz, Bernal. *The Conquest of New Spain*. London: Penguin Books, 1963.

Levy, Buddy. *Conquistador: Hernán Cortés, King Montezuma, and the Last Stand of the Aztecs*. New York: Bantam Books/Random House, 2009.

Thomas, Hugh. *Conquest: Montezuma, Cortés, and the Fall of Old Mexico*. New York: Simon & Schuster, 1993.

Almagro, Diego de

Diego de Almagro was the illegitimate son of Elvira Gutierrez and (purportedly) Juan de Montenegro, who abandoned Almagro's mother. After Elvira gave birth to Diego (ca. 1475), her family kept him to preserve her image. Though she later married, Almagro was placed with a maternal uncle, Hernán Gutierrez, who raised him. Almagro fled his uncle's mistreatment and the impoverished region of Extremadura, and worked briefly as a servant in Seville. There, young Diego stabbed a fellow servant in a fight and fled. The timely news of the American discoveries led Almagro to join Pedro Arias Dávila's expedition in 1514, headed for Panama.

In Panama Almagro participated in expeditions under Gaspar de Espinosa, where he served alongside Francisco Pizarro and Hernando de Luque. In one such expedition he lost an eye in combat. In 1525, Pizarro, Luque, and Almagro received permission from the Crown to form the Company of the Levant to mount expeditions to the south. Though a partner, Almagro served as Pizarro's lieutenant and proved especially capable in managing finances and logistics. Almagro arranged Pizarro's 1529 journey back to Spain, to secure support from the monarchy after encountering the Inca. Pizarro secured the title of governor of Peru, while Almagro became the commandant of the coastal city of Tumbez. When the Spanish returned to Tumbez to launch their expedition into Peru, the city proved to be ravaged by a combination of disease and the war of succession between Atahualpa and Huáscar.

Almagro proved instrumental in the conquest of Peru when he reinforced Pizarro in 1533 with 153 men and 50 horses. While the number of Spanish remained vastly inferior to the Incas, these reinforcements shifted the balance of military capabilities in Pizarro's favor after his capture of Atahualpa. Almagro advocated for Atahualpa's execution, arguing that he had outlived his usefulness and posed a danger to the Inca militaries trying to rescue their emperor. Atahualpa's death also advanced Almagro's own interest,

Diego de Almagro fled Spain after killing a fellow servant in a fight and ended up serving alongside Francisco Pizarro in America. Initially a partner with Pizarro, jealousy between Almagro and Pizarro's brothers led to conflict and ultimately resulted in his death at the hands of the Pizarro brothers in 1538. (Bettmann/Corbis)

since he and his men held no stake in Atahualpa's ransom.

After the capture of Cuzco, Almagro journeyed north to secure Sebastian de Benalcazar's conquest of Quito. Almagro prevented one of Cortés's former captains, Pedro de Alvarado, from mounting another conquest of the Inca Empire by purchasing Alvarado's ships and supplies. In exchange, Alvarado agreed to return to Guatemala while his men could remain with Almagro. Using these additional reinforcements, Almagro engaged and defeated the Inca general Quizquiz's force. Quizquiz survived the battle, but shortly thereafter was killed in a mutiny.

In 1534 the Spanish monarchy split Peru into two jurisdictions: a northern province, Nueva Castilla, under Pizarro, and a southern province, Nuevo Toledo, under Almagro. Cuzco putatively fell under Almagro's supervision, but Pizarro's brothers Juan and Gonzalo remained within the city to help oversee the Spanish-designated puppet Sapa Inca. Almagro's faction supported Manco Inca Yupanqui in his quest for recognition, while Juan and Gonzalo Pizarro supported another claimant closer to the Pizarro family, Atoc-Sopa. At Almagro's behest, Atoc-Sopa was murdered. Nonetheless, the abusive treatment of Manco Inca by Juan and Gonzalo Pizarro caused the new Sapa Inca to hide in Almagro's bedroom at one point.

Francisco Pizarro resolved the conflict temporarily by sending Almagro on an expedition to the south in Chile. Hernando de Soto lobbied to be the force's second-in-command, but Almagro appointed Rodrigo Orgonez. Manco Inca sent an auxiliary force, led by his brother Paullu, to aid the expedition. The two-year expedition failed to find great riches and endured severe losses due to conditions in the Andes and attacks from local tribes. Failing to locate vast riches and

smarting from repeated assaults, Almagro's captains urged a return to Peru.

The removal of so many Spaniards during the expedition, and the absence of his benefactor, likely contributed to Manco's decision to rebel against the younger Pizarro brothers. Almagro's force returned to Cuzco in 1537 during the uprising. He opened negotiations with Manco, offering a pardon, but his emissaries failed to secure an agreement. The ensuing armed clashes between Spanish forces under the Pizarro brothers and Almagro forced Manco Inca to terminate his siege of Cuzco. Almagro seized the city, imprisoned Hernando and Gonzalo Pizzaro, and took the remaining Spaniards into his service. Paullu proved a willing collaborator, and Almagro crowned him emperor. Aware of the division within Spanish ranks, and the imprisonment of his brothers, Francisco Pizarro sent Alonso de Alvarado to recapture Cuzco. Rodrigo Orgonez led Almagro's forces, including a native contingent, to successfully defeat Alvarado's army. For a brief time, the Spanish were precariously perched on the brink of their own civil war while surrounded by enemy Inca forces.

Negotiations between Almagro and Francisco Pizarro began through the offices of Gaspar de Espinoza, with the basis for an agreement being, among others, recognition of Almagro's claim to Cuzco, release of Pizarro's brothers, and establishment of a boundary between the two men's jurisdictions. During the negotiations, Gonzalo Pizarro escaped and Almagro agreed to release Hernando under the promise that Francisco Pizarro would hold to the peace. He did not. In 1538 an army under Hernando Pizarro defeated Almagro's forces, again led by Orgonez, at the Battle of Las Salinas. Almagro fled to the stone fortress Saqsaywaman, but shortly thereafter surrendered. Hernando began judicial proceedings against Almagro, and ordered him garroted in July 1538. Almagro's body was then beheaded and put on display in Cuzco.

The execution of Almagro led to significant criticism of the Pizarro family in Peru and at court in Spain. The Almagristas rallied to Almagro's son, Diego (el Mozo). Diego Almagro led a revolt in 1542 that resulted in Francisco Pizarro's death, whereupon the rebels proclaimed the younger Almagro governor. Following the Battle of Chupas, Almagro's son was captured and executed in 1542, effectively ending Almagro's influence in Peru.

Michael Beauchamp

See also: Alvarado, Pedro de; Atahualpa; Huáscar; Las Salinas, Battle of; Luque, Hernando de; Manco Inca Yupanqui; Paullu Inca; Pizarro, Francisco; Pizarro, Gonzalo; Pizarro, Hernando; Quizquiz; Sapa Inca; Soto, Hernando de, in Peru.

Resources

Hemming, John. *The Conquest of the Incas.* New York: Harcourt, Brace, Jovanovich, 1970.

MacQuarrie, Kim. *The Last Days of the Incas.* New York: Simon & Schuster, 2007.

Restall, Matthew. *Seven Myths of the Spanish Conquest.* Oxford: Oxford University Press, 2004.

Thomas, Hugh. *The Golden Empire: Spain, Charles V, and the Creation of America.* New York: Random House, 2010.

Almagro, Diego de (el Mozo)

Diego de Almagro el Mozo (the younger) was the son of Diego de Almagro and an Indian woman from Panamá. Born in 1520, shortly before his father began his partnership with Francisco Pizarro, he became a loyal supporter of his father in the struggles for authority in Peru between the Pizarro brothers and Almagro the elder. Following the 1538 execution of the elder Almagro by Hernando Pizarro, Almagristas plotted revenge. This was fulfilled in June 1541, as armored followers of the deceased Almagro the elder stormed the unprotected residence of Francisco Pizarro and a half-brother of the conquistador.

After nearly 10 years of domination under the Pizarro brothers, the crowds of Lima welcomed the news. Diego "el Mozo" de Almagro was only 21 years of age, yet as the bearer of his father's name, the younger Almagro was carried throughout the city, pronounced the captain general of Peru and governor. The glory lasted but only for a short time. King Charles V already had dispatched Cristóbal Vaca de Castro to undertake the reform and rule of Peru thanks to the upheaval within the colony. Within months of Pizarro's death, Vaca de Castro arrived in northern Peru, where he was joined by old allies of Pizarro. Gathering the support of Pizarrists as they descended toward the south, Vaca de Castro's forces confronted Diego "el Mozo" near Huamanga in the battle of Chupas, in the fall of 1542.

The upheaval of civil war between the Spanish forces coincided with the Neo-Inca movement of Manco Inca. Living in exile at Vilcabamba, the Sapa Inca observed with interest the clashes between the Pizarrists and Almagristas. Willing to support the latter, the Neo-Inca movement benefited from the capture of Diego de Almagro el Mozo in September 1542. Had the young rebel reached the Inca's capital in exile, the civil war would likely have been redirected toward the Inca population. As it turned out, Diego de Almagro the younger was arrested in Cuzco and executed as a rebel, at 22 years of age.

Rebecca M. Seaman

See also: Almagro, Diego de; Pizarro, Francisco; Pizarro, Hernandez; Vilcabamba.

Resources

Hemming, John. *The Conquest of the Incas.* New York: Harcourt, Brace, Jovanovich, Inc., 1970.

MacQuarrie, Kim. *The Last Days of the Incas.* New York: Simon & Schuster, 2007.

Alvarado, Pedro de

Pedro de Alvarado (ca. 1485–1541) was a Spanish conquistador who played a central role in many of Spain's early conquests in the New World. Alvarado participated in the conquest of the Aztecs in Mexico under Hernán Cortés, and later led an expedition against the various Maya kingdoms in the Guatemalan highlands. He is remembered today not only for his prominent role in these early conquests, but also for his particular cruelty toward the native populations he encountered.

Alvarado was born into the family of a minor Spanish noble in the city of Badajoz, in the impoverished region of Extramadura— the home of some many Spanish conquistadors. Typical of younger sons from this region, he could not expect much in the way of an inheritance. Instead, as a young man he headed to the New World to make his own fortune, arriving in Hispanola with some of his brothers in 1510. Alvarado immediately began participating in Spanish military expeditions in the Caribbean. He took part in the violent conquest of Cuba (1511) and later served as a captain in Juan de Grijalva's expedition against the Yucatán (1518). Meanwhile, Alvarado became friends with Hernán Cortés and accompanied the famous conquistador on his conquest of the Aztec Empire. Alvarado served as Cortés's second-in-command for much of the campaign.

The Mexican campaign proceeded easily as the first one. Cortés enlisted as allies various nearby Indian groups resentful of the Aztecs' brutal reign over the area. He also moved quickly to take advantage of the confusion and uncertainty the Spanish arrival caused. Soon, Cortés established his headquarters in the Aztec capital of Tenochtitlán, and took the Aztec emperor, Montezuma II, hostage. When Cortés learned that Diego Velázquez, the governor of Cuba, had sent a second Spanish expedition to arrest him (Cortés, a political rival of Velázquez, had undertaken his expedition despite demands of the governor to return to Cuba), Cortés returned to the coast with a portion of his expedition's forces to confront this new expedition, leaving Alvarado in charge of Tenochtitlán.

Montezuma asked Alvarado to allow the city to celebrate the festival of Toxcatl, a request to which Alvarado consented. During the festival, Alvarado entered the main temple and slaughtered a large group of unarmed Aztec nobles celebrating inside. Alvarado's motivations are not clear. Certainly the Spanish suspected that the Aztecs were planning an armed resistance to drive them out of the city, and Alvarado may have believed that the festival itself served as a cover for organizing such resistance. Surviving Aztecs claimed that Alvarado saw an easy opportunity to gain further treasure for himself and attacked the nobles for their gold. Whatever the reasons for the slaughter, the results were clear. The Aztecs, already growing resentful of the presence of the Spanish and their Indian allies, engaged in open warfare within the city against their enemies.

Cortés returned to Tenochtitlán to find Alvarado and his men besieged within.

Pedro de Alvarado came from minor Spanish nobility in Badajoz, Spain, but served as Cortés's second-in-command in the campaign in Mexico. Noted for his cruelty toward the native populations in America, Alvarado's actions precipitated the violence that led to the infamous La Noche Triste. (Blue Lantern Studio/Corbis)

However, the Aztecs allowed Cortés to reenter the city and reunite his forces with Alvarado's, hoping to trap and kill all the Spaniards at once. After several unsuccessful attempts, the Spanish forces managed to break out of the city one night in a bloody action that cost them dearly in men, horses, and supplies. Alvarado commanded the rear guard during the action and was badly wounded during the escape. The night became known as La Noche Triste (the Sad Night). Despite this setback, Cortés eventually succeeded in conquering Tenochtitlán and bringing the Aztec Empire to an end in 1520.

Following the disastrous La Noche Triste, in 1524 Cortés eventually sent Alvarado to what is now Guatemala for further conquests. With the help of Spanish soldiers and Indian allies from Mexico, Alvarado conquered each of the highland area Maya kingdoms in turn, taking advantage of preexisting hostilities between the kingdoms. Like his previous expeditions, Alvarado's Guatemala campaign produced excessive slaughter and cruelties. At one point in the campaign, in an episode eerily similar to the Toxcatl massacre, Alvarado received an invitation to visit the city of Q'umarkaj (also known as Utlatlan), the capital of a Maya kingdom whose armies he had just soundly defeated. Sensing a trap, Alvarado invited the city's remaining nobles to visit him in his encampment outside the city. He then took the nobles as prisoners when they arrived at the encampment. When the nearby Maya warriors attacked in response, he ordered the captured nobles burned to death and the entire city burned, as well. Alvarado later served as governor of the Spanish territory of Guatemala for 17 years.

Alvarado's exploits in the New World did not end in Guatemala. For seven years he jointly served as the governor of Honduras, which was the result of his clever political maneuvering after leading forces against an indigenous rebellion within the territory. He also spearheaded the conquest of what is now El Salvador, though he was wounded during the expedition and left the completion of the campaign to others. Having heard of the riches of the Inca Empire further south in Peru, Alvarado journeyed to the region, only to find the conquest of the Incas by Francisco Pizarro well underway. Rather than fight against the Pizarro expedition, Alvarado traded the majority of his expedition's manpower and resources to Pizarro in exchange for a lump sum of money and returned to Guatemala. Alvarado's last campaign took place against the Mixton in northern Mexico. He died during the expedition due to injuries received after being trampled by a horse.

Like many Spanish conquistadors of this era, Alvarado had a Spanish wife (two in succession), but also a native mistress, Doña Luisa, a gift from Cortés. Despite his legal marriages, he had no legitimate heirs, though he did have a number of illegitimate offspring in New Spain.

John Gram

See also: Cortés, Hernán; Cuba; Grijalva, Juan de; Hispaniola; La Noche Triste; Montezuma II; Pizarro, Francisco; Tenochtitlán, City of; Toxcatl Massacre; Velázquez, Diego (de Cuéllar).

Resources

Bakewell, Peter. *A History of Latin America.* 2nd ed. Malden, MA: Blackwell, 2004.

Diaz del Castillo, Bernal. *The Conquest of New Spain.* Translated by J. M. Cohen. Baltimore: Penguin Books, 1963.

Foster, Lynn V. *A Brief History of Central America.* New York: Facts on File, 2000.

Thomas, Hugh. *Conquest: Montezuma, Cortés, and the Fall of Old Mexico.* New York: Simon & Schuster, 1993.

Alvarez Chico, Francisco

A Spanish businessman, Francisco Alvarez Chico also served as an official who acted as general spokesman (*procurador-general*) within the newly created imperial holdings in Mexico during the early 16th century. Francisco Alvarez Chico and his brother Rodrigo were born in Oliva, near Medellin, Spain. When the opportunity came to serve under Hernán Cortés as conquistadors in Mexico, the ambitious Extremeños set about helping to establish settlements and to become the leaders of New Spain.

When Cortés was elected *Justicia Mayor* and captain general in the territories of Mexico in 1519, he agreed to found a city to be called Villa Rica de la Vera Cruz. Cortés was to lead an expedition, which included the population of the settlement, consisting of the magistrates, councilors, and other bureaucrats who would run the town, including Francisco Alvarez Chico. All of the councilors were to act together as a *regimiento*, a deliberative institution, in Villa Rica de la Vera Cruz, similar to the practices in Castile.

In July 1519, Cortés set out on his expedition to Tenochtitlán, the capital of the Aztec Empire. Cortés left behind Francisco Alvarez Chico at Vera Cruz to act as the new *procurador*. Alvarez Chico negotiated with Cortés that those left behind to guard the town should have a share in the profits of the expedition. Since the monarchy was to receive a fifth of the booty, and Cortés also demanded a fifth, this left substantially less to divide amongst the rest of the Spaniards.

Alverez Chico's negotiated portion was of little consequence.

By 1520, Cortés initially attempted to seize Tenochtitlán and held the Aztec king Montezuma as a prisoner in the capital city. When he left the city of Tenochtitlán in May 1520 to defeat the forces under Pánfilo de Narvaez who was sent to arrest Cortés, he left Pedro de Alvarado in charge as deputy governor. Alvarez Chico was among those Castilians stationed at Tenochtitlán when the Toxcatl massacre occurred under Alvarado's governance. During the celebration of an Aztec religious festival called Toxcatl, Alvarado abruptly halted the celebration fearing an Indian uprising. Francisco Alvarez Chico insisted to Alvarado that the Spaniards should launch a preemptive assault before the Mexicans could strike. The massacre of the Mexican nobility destroyed mostly members of the Aztec upper classes, and ruined the Aztec people's faith in Montezuma's decisive and effective leadership. News of the massacre drew Cortés back to the capital city where the ensuing uprising resulted in the devastating defeat of the Spanish and their ignoble withdrawal from the city in June 1520.

Following Cortés's retreat from Tenochtitlán, the Spaniards consolidated their gains and regrouped in order to mount a counterattack. Cortés sent two expeditions to purchase new equipment, the first of these consisting of four vessels under the command of Francisco Alvarez Chico and Alonso de Avila. The task of this expedition was to travel to Hispaniola to buy more horses, crossbows, guns, and powder, and to secure more men if possible. In addition to this mission, Alvarez Chico also managed to secure help from Rodrigo de Bastidas at Santo Domingo, an experienced conquistador who brought with him supplies and reinforcements to aid in the military campaign.

Following the destruction of Tenochtitlán by the combined Spanish forces in 1521, in December of that year the inspector of Hispaniola, Cristobal de Tapia, arrived with instructions from Castile to assume control over New Spain. Tapia's instructions required a redistribution of power in the region, which resulted in the conquistadors filing an appeal with the monarchy. Francisco Alvarez Chico, still serving as lieutenant governor of Villa Rica, gave Tapia an order to leave that town and depart for Hispaniola until the appeal with the king had been processed. Alvarez Chico's efforts resulted in Tapia's departure.

Francisco Alvarez Chico participated in one of the most brutal and daring military conquests in all history. Though his misbegotten advise to preemptively attack the Aztec in the Toxcatl massacre almost resulted in the complete annihilation of the Spanish, Cortés nonetheless accomplished the conquest of the Aztec Empire in less than three months, allowing the Spanish to establish a vast landed empire in Central America. Alvarez Chico continued to serve Cortés throughout the 1520s, exploring the coast between Zacatula and Acapulco in 1522. He later died on the island of Santo Domingo.

Justin Pfeifer

See also: Alvarado, Pedro de; Cortés, Hernán; Tenochtitlán; Toxcatl Massacre; Villa Rica de la Vera Cruz.

Resources

Bancroft, Hubert Howe. *History of the North Mexican States, Vol. I., 1531–1800.* San Francisco: A.L. Bancroft & Company, 1884.

Di´az del Castillo, Bernal. *The Conquest of New Spain.* Nendeln: Kraus Reprint Limited, 1967. Works issued by the Hakluyt Society.

Thomas, Hugh. *Conquest: Montezuma, Cortés, and the Fall of Old Mexico.* New York: Simon & Schuster, 1993.

Andagoya, Pascual de

Pascual de Andagoya was a Spanish explorer in the early 16th century. In 1522, he conducted the first expedition southward from Panama under the orders of Governor Pedrarias Dávila. Skirting along the Pacific coast of Colombia, he traveled as far south as Puerto Piñas by the river Biru. There he became the first Spaniard to explore the coastal area and refer to the people and land as "Peru," though the terminology was later applied to the lands further south. Upon return to Panama, Andagoya suffered from an illness that incapacitated him for years, preventing him from further explorations of the region. As a result, the explorer sold his ships to another group of explorers interested in following Andagoya's lead southward: Francisco Pizarro, Diego de Almagro, and Hernando de Luque.

The huge success of Pizarro on his third expedition to Peru resulted in the discovery of great wealth for the Spanish explorer. This must have exasperated Andagoya, a fact evident in his critique of Pizarro in the 1540s. Citing reports of the trial and execution of the Inca emperor, Atahualpa, Andagoya asserted that Pizarro chose to use the reports of enemies of the emperor to justify his execution. He additionally contended that Hernando de Soto sought to substantiate Atahualpa's defense to no avail, since Pizarro plotted to kill the emperor before Soto's return.

Pascual de Andagoya continued to hold resentment toward the conquistador. However, when the city of Cuzco was under siege by Manco Inca Yupanqui, the former explorer reported the situation to the Spanish Crown, assuring the king that needed support would be sent to Peru to assist Pizarro in reclaiming control. A few years later, in another missive sent in 1539, Andagoya presented the continued disarray in Peru, the looting of indigenous grain reserves, slaughtering herds of llama, and abuse of the native population as the policies of Pizarro run amok. These reports not only played a role in undermining support for the Pizarro brothers and their continued control over Peru, they also helped support the assertions of the Dominican "protector" of the indigenous populations of America, Bartolomé de Las Casas. Consequently, the timing and substance of Andagoya's reports contributed to the shaping of the king's changing policies in the Leyes Nuevas of 1542.

Rebecca M. Seaman

See also: Almagro, Diego de; Atahualpa; Charles V (HRE) or Carlos I of Spain; Dávila, Pedro Arias; Las Casas, Bartolomé de; Leyes Nuevas 1542–1543; Luque, Hernando de; Manco Inca Yupanqui; Pizarro, Francisco.

Resources

Gabai, Rafael Varón. *Francisco Pizarro and His Brothers: The Illusion of Power in Sixteenth-Century Peru.* Norman: University of Oklahoma Press, 1997.

Hemming, John. *The Conquest of the Incas.* New York: Harcourt Brace Jovanovich, 1970.

MacQuarrie, Kim. *The Last Days of the Incas.* New York: Simon & Schuster, 2007.

Antisuyu

Antisuyu is one of four major quadrants or administrative regions (suyus) of the Inca Empire, or Tahuantinsuyu. The Inca Empire was divided into quadrants by four lines with the capital, Cuzco, falling at the junction of the four regions. Four royal roads led out of the ancient capital to each section: Chinchaysuyu (NW), Antisuyu (NE), Cuntisuyu (SW), and Collasuyu (SE). The complex system, associated with the Inca religion, astronomy, and calendar, assigned radiating lines (ceques) to each suyu, with nine ceques each assigned to the NW, NE, and the SE (Cuntisuyu reportedly contained 14 ceques).

The region of Antisuyu, greatly expanded in the 1400s under Pachacutin and again in the early 1500s under Huayna Capac, included the high Andean ranges as well as the descent into the Amazon jungle. The region gained its name from the reference to the Antis, the various tribes that inhabited the region. The ruling Inca considered their Antis subjects as "savage." Indeed, the Inca apparently feared the jungle dwellers as much as they detested the hot and humid jungle climate. Nonetheless, the remote region and its native population provided valued trade in goods as well as exceptional warriors and archers for the Inca army.

Following the initial Spanish conquest of the Inca, the Spanish-designated puppet Sapa Inca, Manco Inca Yupanqui, attempted to return power to the Inca. The effort, conducted over almost three decades, was made by Manco Inca Yupanqui (Manco Capac II) and later Titu Cusi Yupanqui and Tupac Amaru (brothers of Manco Inca). These last emperors reigned from the secluded, independent regional city of Vilcabamba, in the upper end of the Amazon. Part of the secluded Antisuyu region, Vilcabamba was used by the last emperors as their government in exile, and as a base to raid Spanish supply lines. The Spanish finally defeated the last emperor in 1572, at his seat of power in the remote Antisuyu.

Rebecca M. Seaman

See also: Chinchaysuyu; Huayna Cápac; Manco Inca Yupanqui; Pachacutin; Titu Cusi Yupanqui; Túpac Amaru; Vilcabamba.

Resources

Davies, Nigel. *The Incas.* Niwot: University Press of Colorado, 1995.

Hemming, John. *The Conquest of the Incas.* New York: Harcourt, Brace, Jovanovich, 1970.

Artisans, Inca

The rapid rise of the Inca Empire resulted in a new level of artistic uniformity throughout the Andes. Inca art was practical, used to create functional or ritual items for daily use. Artistic styles were inherited from earlier cultures inhabiting the region for thousands of years. Skilled craftsmen adapted and modified earlier styles to suit the new empire. Representations of humans in art objects almost entirely vanished with the Inca. Geometric designs and squares of symbolic patterns dominated the visual arts. This created a uniformity that was immediately recognizable throughout the extensive empire, creating cohesiveness among a greatly diverse population.

While a large portion of everyday items were made at home by the workers themselves, luxury goods—fine cloth, jewelry, and ceramics for the nobility—were the work of craftsmen. The very best worked directly for the court, while others worked in centrally located workshops in regional locales. Readily available raw materials were used to create a wide variety of objects for household or ritual purposes. Stone, wood, clay, metal, cloth, and bone were fashioned into decorative, but useful, items.

Inca pottery is the most widely surviving artistic form seen today. Pottery created during the Imperial Period was highly durable and technically advanced. There were two basic types of pottery: mass-produced, standardized imperial ware found throughout the Andes, and much rarer individual pieces that are unique works of art. Scholars have identified 14 different vessel shapes for specific purposes, and a limited number of recurring motifs used to decorate them.

Wood was used as an architectural element in building homes and was also used to create utilitarian objects. Cups and spoons for meals, handles for agricultural tools and weapons, and musical instruments were made from wood. Prestige items were elaborately carved and often inlaid—staffs for officials to be used in office, cups used for rituals, and stools used by leaders were intricately decorated.

The Inca were skilled metallurgists, though they never developed techniques for working hard metals such as iron or steel. They did work extensively with gold, silver, bronze, and copper. The emperor owned all mines and metals, and workers mined them as part of the labor tax. Gold and silver were used exclusively for making items for royalty and ceremonial objects. Bronze, a harder alloy, was used for tools and weapons.

Ornaments, jewelry, and sacrificial offerings were also fashioned from shell or bone. These materials were additionally used as inlays in jewelry, figurines, or wooden objects. Moreover, bone was used to manufacture weaving tools, blanket pins, and musical instruments.

Cloth was especially prized by the Incas and represents their greatest artistic achievement. The importance of cloth was due to the vast amount and types of labor needed to produce it. Almost everyone in the empire was involved with some aspect of cloth production to ensure society's needs were met. Cotton was raised, harvested, washed, combed, dyed, and spun. Llamas and alpacas were herded and sheared. The wool was then washed, carded, dyed, and spun into spools. Then the weavers went to work, designing the pattern and setting up the loom. Weaving was a painstaking, time-consuming task.

The Inca created three types of cloth. The coarsest type was called chusi and was used for rugs, blankets, or storage sacks. A better grade of cloth, ahuasca, was still relatively coarse wool worn by the lower classes. The finest cloth used for the emperor and the nobility was called cumpi. Made from blends of alpaca or vicuña wool and cotton, or sometimes more exotic materials such as bat hair or hummingbird down, this cloth was woven with complex multicolored designs. Cloistered, chosen women and skilled craftsmen produced cumpi cloth in state-supported workshops. A cumpi garment could only be worn by a nonroyal if received as a gift from the emperor in recognition for service to the state—a mark of great prestige.

Stone working was another art form in which the Inca excelled. Monumental stonework reflected in sculpted landscapes, building and wall architecture, and a vast road system are easily recognizable symbols of Inca conquest. Portable stone objects were also created for both everyday and ceremonial use. Hammer and mace heads, grinding stones, and other utilitarian objects were fashioned plainly for daily use, but elaborately carved mortars and pestles, plates and bowls were used during sacrifices, and figurines were created for formal rituals.

The Inca were an artistic people who used available materials to create stylish, utilitarian objects. Despite the constant struggle to survive in a harsh environment, their distinctive style communicated the imperial values of unity and cohesiveness through a variety of media.

Jill M. Church

See also: Inca Elite; Mines, Role of in Peru.

Resources

D'Altroy, Terence N. *The Incas*. Malden, MA: Blackwell, 2002.

McEwan, Gordon. *The Incas: New Perspectives*. New York: W.W. Norton and Company. 2006.

Stone-Miller, Rebecca. *Art of the Andes from Chavín to Inca*. New York: Thames & Hudson, Ltd. 2002.

Suarez, Ananda Cohen and George, Jeremy James. *Handbook to Life in the Inca World*. New York: Facts on File, 2011.

Artisans, Maya

Artisans were the social group in Maya society responsible for making both utilitarian and luxury goods. The activities of this social/economic group were highly specialized. The artisans who produced items for worship were especially recognized, as all aspects of society were strongly linked to sacred practices and rituals. Activities of all the various artisans were sponsored by different gods, and dedicated ceremonies helped promote the correct running of these activities.

Some artisans were able to work full time producing goods. These more specialized craftsmen typically worked in the service of rulers and priests. Their work was important because it linked directly to the trade activity of the society. The Maya stood out among Central American cultures because of their organized trade relations between the various city-states of the area. For this reason, Mayan artisans enjoyed an intermediate status between the highly placed rulers and authorities and lower status of peasants.

Some Mayan artisans were sculptors. They worked mainly limestone with which they produced stelae, monoliths, and sculptures. They also modeled the stucco that covered public buildings. These craftsmen worked in specific stylistic patterns and were considered among the literate people of Mayan culture because they engraved and carved inscriptions in glyphic writing.

Producers of feather mosaics also worked for the elite, making decorations for rulers and warriors, priests' headdresses, fans, and other luxury items. The feather artisans obtained raw materials by hunting tropical birds in their environment with slings and blowpipes, or by breeding certain species in captivity in aviaries. The most prized feathers were the quetzal, also used as currency by the elites.

Painting was an art cultivated by the specialized Mayan artisans. Before the arrival of the Spanish, painting reached a high degree of excellence. It was used to decorate walls of temples, tombs and palaces, ceramics and *codices* or painted books. Painters used a rich palette of pigments of both vegetal and mineral origin. Codices and ethnohistorical information demonstrates that the painters were people who enjoyed great prestige and respect in the community.

Other artisans of luxury goods were the lapidaries, specialists in the manufacture of jade figurines used in ritual contexts. The goldsmiths, who modeled gold and copper, used techniques similar to those used in Central America to make dishes and cups, bracelets, masks, earrings, rings, earflaps and rattles. All of these articles were produced for the Mayan elites.

Another type of artisans combined the production of utilitarian goods with farming activities, which was the main economic activity and means of subsistence of Mayan society. The work of these utilitarian craftsmen was linked to the tribute system. A portion of the tax to be paid was given in the form of labor for the construction, fitting-out, and maintenance of cities, including houses of the rulers (*halach uinic*) and temples. These utilitarian artisans also had to give gifts to the lords and make offerings to the gods through the priests. The gifts took the form of artisan products such as cotton cloth (*patí*) and strings of beads of jade, coral, and shells.

A very common handcraft produced by artisans was cotton cloth. The goddess Ix Azal Uoh, wife of the Sun god, was the sponsor of the weavers. The dyeing, spinning, and weaving of fibers was a female activity practiced at home. The products were for domestic consumption, for sale in local markets, and for the paying of tribute. Even after the Spanish conquest, cloth production remained a common item of production and taxation.

Pottery was also a craft made by women in a domestic environment—specifically pottery made for utilitarian use. It was made collectively, as each group of people was responsible for a part of the process, from the manufacture of molds through the process to the firing of pottery. It is also thought that there were more specialized workshops that made high-quality painted pieces targeted for luxury use, such as the ceramics from the island of Jaina (Campeche).

The manufacture of baskets, ropes, and mats also constituted important artisan activities. The mat (*pop*) was associated with authority when serving as a seat in public places. Mats also saw common usage in households, covering floors and being used as plates and mattresses. They were made by men and women as a complement to their daily activities of farming. The fibers of the plant called *henequen* (*ki*) were used for rope-making, and its importance lasted to the 19th century as the main industry of Yucatán.

The common utilitarian products of artisans were woven into the activities of the people. The products from these activities bridged the periods from pre-conquest Mayan society well into the colonial period under Spanish rule. Likewise, certain specialty artisans carried their crafts over into the colonial era. However, some crafts, namely the working of feathers and painting with the Mayan glyphs, fell out of use with the rise of Spanish authority in the Yucatán.

Marta Martín Gabaldón

See also: Artisans, Mexica; Maya; Yucatán, State of prior to Spanish Conquest; Yucatán, State of prior after Spanish Conquest.

Resources

Miller, Mary E. *Maya Art and Architecture.* London: Thames and Hudson, 1999.

Schele, Linda and David Freidel. *A Forest of Kings: The Untold Story of the Ancient Maya.* New York: William Morrow and Company, 1990.

Sharer, Robert. J. *The Ancient Maya.* Stanford, CA: Stanford University Press, 2006.

Webster, David. "Surplus, Labor, and Stress in Late Classic Maya Society." *Journal of Anthropological Research* 41 (4) (1985): 375–399.

Artisans, Mexica

Artisans were members of a Mexican social class who were in charge of producing goods, both utilitarian and luxury crafts. Artisans' activities were highly specialized. Although they constituted a relatively small group, they produced most of the objects that the inhabitants of the Aztec Empire consumed in homes, palaces, temples, and other public and private buildings. The nature and organization of work for each kind of products—utilitarian and luxury—had different implications for the lives of the producers and consumers.

Bernardino de Sahagun's *General History of the Things of New Spain* and the *Florentine Codex* are the main ethnohistorical sources for the knowledge of craftsmanship.

According to these records, those who produced utilitarian crafts included the following artisans: obsidian or flint-knappers, potters, rope-makers, paper-workers, wood-carvers, sandal-makers, mat-makers, basket-makers, weavers, dyers, tailors, arrow and shield-makers, carpenters, masons, stonecutters, and tanners.

Although there were full-time producers of utilitarian goods, most of these artisans, especially in rural areas, performed their craft as a supplement to daily farming activities. They sold their crafts in the local markets where their production was at the mercy of sales. Nonetheless, some full-time producers worked in Aztec cities in specialized areas where enough market demand sustained the craftsmen. For example, the obsidian knappers from Otumba (settlement near Teotihuacan) were highly sought after for their specialized products.

Pottery was the most abundant craft. All households had a great variety of vessels, and pottery was also used to make religious utensils (figurines and incense burners) and multiple tools. Within this guild, the production was diversified: there was a general "clay worker" who made different types of vessels and a "griddle-maker" who specialized in tortilla griddles.

Obsidian objects were the second craft in abundance. They made knives, razors, scrapers, and arrow points, among other objects. They were used both within and outside the home, for religious ceremonies and military purposes. The artisans were located in areas of the Valley of Mexico where obsidian was found. Despite the high degree of precision, obsidian artisans were part-time specialists and sold their blades directly in the markets.

A particular industry of importance was that of cotton textiles. Besides being used for nobles' clothing, it adorned statues of the gods, was used as shrouds for the dead, and provided padded battle armor, much desired by the warrior class and eventually by the Spanish. It was also used as an item for exchange in markets and for tribute payment, in the form of *quachtli* (a long cloth folded). Women from all social levels were responsible for their production at home, and cloth production was an activity associated with female gender identity.

Some other industries were adopted from other Mesoamerican peoples following the expansion of the Aztec Empire. This was the case of copper and bronze metallurgy, practiced by the Tarascans, enemies of the Aztecs. When the Aztecs conquered territory next to the Tarascan kingdoms, some towns with metalsmiths and copper deposits were assimilated. Locally produced objects were reworked in the Valley of Mexico to give them new shape and hardness, building upon the crafts of their former enemies.

Luxury crafts played an important role in society, as they helped inform others about the status and wealth of the nobles who used the products. Luxury craft items were given as gifts to other nobles in ceremonies to establish political alliances, used by priests in rituals, and included in burials as offerings. The expense restricted demands for these luxury objects.

Luxury craftsmen were known as toltecs. The origin of the term is accredited to the source of their skilled methods and techniques, which were believed to come from the Toltec civilization. The original Toltecs, who predated the Aztecs in the region, lived near the capital city of Tula and were said to be ruled by the god Quetzalcoatl. Their artisan techniques, passed down through the ages, were called *toltecayotl* ("belonging to the Toltecs").

The artisans who produced luxury items were full-time specialists, working in many cases directly for a noble patron. They also sold their products in the market, where major customers were from the nobility. Luxury craft artisans belonged to a sort of "middle class," living in private quarters with members of their own institutions. Although their status was lower than the one of the pochteca (traders), the artisans were tied to merchants through the demand for and trade in many of the raw materials necessary for the luxury crafts. These raw materials came from distant areas, through trade or tribute. Unlike the pochteca, whose class was dynamic and had access to people in power, the craftsmen's class was static. The luxury craft artisans paid taxes, but were exempt from personal service and agricultural work.

The feather mosaics produced by luxury artisans were the most original craft of the Aztecs. With this technique they made fans, shields, warrior's costumes, and decorative hangings. There was division of labor within the households of featherworkers: the master artisan prepared the stencils and backing, and applied the feathers; women dyed and organized the feathers, and children prepared the glue. They lived in special *calpolli* (neighborhoods) in major cities. Within the *calpolli* they had their own school and temple, where they performed public rituals to their tutelary god *Coyotlinahual.* The organization was similar to that of the European guilds, where the office was hereditary and their leaders represented them in front of the central power and justice system.

The goldsmiths, called *teocuitlahuaque,* operated similarly. It is very likely that they learned their techniques of the Mixtecs of Oaxaca, and that many artisans in Tenochtitlán were Mixtec. The tutelary god of the goldsmiths was *Xipe Totec.* In addition to Mixtec influences upon goldsmithing out of Oaxaca, the Aztecs also had lapidaries from other regions that settled in Xochimilco, in southern Tenochtitlán. Each native

community contributed its own techniques and gave obeisance to *Xipe Totec.*

Despite the wide variety of skilled artisans found in the Aztec Empire, certain commonalities occurred in the luxury and utilitarian artisan groups. The importance of maintaining the craft, similar to the European guilds, as well as the importance of religious obeisance to the tutelary gods, pervaded both groups. Status and location of the artisans was determined in part by the raw materials and artistry involved, the demand for the goods, and the ability to practice the craft as a full-time occupation.

Marta Martín Gabaldón

See also: Artisans, Maya; Aztec, or Mexica; Mexico, State of prior to Spanish Conquest; Pochtecas; Tenochtitlán, City of; Tribute, Paid to Mexica.

Resources

Sahagún, Bernardino de. *Florentine Codex: General History of the Things of New Spain.* 12 books. Translated and edited by Arthur J. O. Anderson and Charles E. Dibble. Santa Fe, NM, and Salt Lake City, UT: School of American Research and the University of Utah Press, 1950–1982.

Smith, Michael E. *The Aztecs.* Oxford: Blackwell, 1996.

Soustelle, Jacques. *Daily Life of the Aztecs on the Eve of the Spanish Conquest.* Stanford, CA: Stanford University Press, 1961.

Atahualpa

Atahualpa was the 13th and last major emperor of the Inca Empire, ruling from 1532 to 1533. He was involved in a civil war with his brother Huáscar Inca when the Spanish conquistador, Francisco Pizarro, conquered the Inca. Atahualpa was captured, and although he paid a tremendous ransom of gold and silver, Pizarro still executed him.

Nineteenth-century engraving of Atahualpa, Sapa Inca (emperor) at the time of the Spanish invasion, whose struggle for power with his brother following the devastating epidemics weakened their defenses. (Library of Congress)

Atahualpa was born around 1500 in Cuzco, the capital city of the Inca Empire in Peru. He was the son of Emperor Huayna Cápac. Unlike previous Inca emperors, Atahualpa's mother was not also his father's sister, as was the Inca royal custom to ensure purity in the royal line. According to legend, his mother was a beautiful princess with whom Huayna Cápac had fallen in love as a teenager when he was a soldier subduing her people near Quito, Ecuador. Inca restrictions that an emperor must marry a sister did not prevent relations with numerous concubines. Neither did it restrict eligibility for ascendency to power of legitimate offspring. Additionally, monarchical succession did not automatically descend to the eldest male heir of the previous ruler. However, eligibility of an heir without pure ethnic Inca bloodlines was unlikely.

Though illegitimate, Atahualpa was Huayna Cápac's favored son. He was raised in the capital city, surrounded by wealth. He would have been educated to understand how to interpret the *quipu*, knotted strings the Incas used instead of writing, for accounting and to record stories. He enjoyed a semi-godlike status, as the Inca religion revered the emperor and worshipped the sun.

As the son of the emperor, Atahualpa was trained to command the army. When he was about 13 years old, he went through his rite-of-passage ceremony. After several days of testing of his endurance and military skill, his initiation into adulthood was celebrated with a feast and the giving of his name Atahualpa, which may mean "fortunate warrior." For the next seven years or so, Atahualpa was on a military campaign with his father in Ecuador, near his mother's home area, to suppress a tribal rebellion.

As this rebellion was finally being contained, a new and far more serious threat appeared. In 1526, the emperor and Atahualpa received messages that white men came from the ocean in wooden houses and rode strange beasts. According to the reports, they looted the gold and silver of the Inca palace and temples without fear. These "white men" were the conquistador Pizarro and his soldiers. The most devastating effect of the Spanish upon the culture Pizarro and his men encountered, however, was the transmission of smallpox to the local populace. The disease preceded the Pizarro expedition. Without any prior immunity to the illness, thousands of Incas died within months. In 1527, Emperor Huayna Cápac died of the new illness. His preferred successor as Sapa Inca (unique emperor), Ninan Cuyochi, soon joined him in death from the same illness. The deaths of the emperor and his eldest son led to contests for power among the *panaqa* or royal lineage of wives, children, and other retainers over the course of the next two years. The secondary choice of Huayna Cápac was Huáscar, eldest son of a secondary wife. Though he was crowned, support for another illegitimate brother, Atahualpa, was strong among the nobles and generals.

Pizarro's second unsuccessful arrival on the coast of Peru in the late 1520s coincided with the royal family's struggle for ascendancy to the throne. Additionally, attention was forced elsewhere on the devastating epidemics wracking the region. Before he died, Huayna Cápac designated his son, Huáscar, to be his secondary choice for emperor. Instead of preventing a succession crisis, the belated decision regarding an heir served to exacerbate the internal struggle for authority.

Huáscar was five years younger than his illegitimate brother Atahualpa, and his own legitimacy was suspect. While Huáscar was supported by the nobles in the capital city of Cuzco, his half-brother Atahualpa had been commanding the army for years in the northern territory of Ecuador. Of the two sons, Atahualpa was considered the serious, best prepared heir. Meanwhile, Huáscar was considered poorly prepared, had little interest in the everyday management of the empire, and yet was the declared successor. Both sons were ruthless if their will was thwarted. Atahualpa wanted power and the title of emperor. He expressed his displeasure by not attending his father's funeral in the capital city. Huáscar sent his brother's messengers back to Ecuador, reportedly in women's clothes and without their noses. Atahualpa retaliated by declaring Quito an independent territory with himself as ruler. In 1530, civil war broke out in the empire. Huáscar marched an army 30,000 strong to Ecuador against Atahualpa's 10,000 troops. During the continued conflicts, 15,000 men were lost on both sides. Following one particular battle

in 1532, Huáscar encamped to celebrate his victory. Atahualpa's forces ambushed the camp, capturing Huáscar. Atahualpa then marched on the capital city, Cuzco, which he ransacked, and declared himself emperor. The army of approximately 40,000 already favored the warrior leader and declared loyalty to Atahualpa.

While this civil war was raging, Pizarro, lured by his earlier acquisition of easy gold, returned to Peru on his third attempt with 180 men and some horses. Marching his men into the heart of the mountainous kingdom, he arrived at the valley of Cajamarca, where Atahualpa was encamping with one of his armies. Seeing thousands of Inca soldiers that vastly outnumbered his small contingent, Pizarro invited the emperor to meet him. Believing that this tiny band of men could hardly pose a threat, Atahualpa met Pizarro in November 1532, escorted by 6,000 unarmed men. The emperor was further convinced of the absence of danger by the offering of gifts on the part of the Spanish. With the emperor distracted, Pizarro and his men, using guns and cannon, massacred the entire party, except for Atahualpa.

Pizarro's strategy was to hold the emperor as a hostage and rule through Atahualpa, as Hernán Cortés had ruled through the Aztec emperor in Mexico. However, Atahualpa had his own strategy. He offered a ransom of rooms full of gold and silver. The Incas filled the storerooms with beautifully crafted gold and silver ornaments, chairs, statues, and foundations worth millions of dollars. Pizarro had the gold and silver melted down into blocks. Meanwhile, Pizarro invited Huáscar to meet with him. Fearing that the Spanish might attempt to strike a deal with his brother, Atahualpa sent instructions to have his supporters assassinate Huáscar, ending the continued struggle for power between the two siblings.

Pizarro countered by collecting the ransom and then charging Atahualpa with murder, the worship of idols, and plotting against the government. Not all the Spanish viewed Atahualpa with the same enmity of their superior. The emperor's affection for his young children, his charm, bravery, and intelligence won him the admiration and support of some among the Spanish conquerors. Pizarro and his priest wanted to have Atahualpa burned at the stake, but their advisers convinced them strangulation was a better option. Fear of a rumored attack by armies still loyal to the hostage emperor convinced Pizarro to dispatch his hostage. Atahualpa was killed on August 29, 1533. The anticipated attack never materialized, but Pizarro nonetheless quickly appointed Atahualpa's younger brother as the Inca's successor. A series of puppet emperors, with varying degrees of cooperation for Spanish dominance ensued, culminating with the collapse of the Inca Empire soon after.

José Valente

See also: Cajamarca, Battle of; Huáscar; Huayna Cápac; Pizarro, Francisco.

Resources

Bernand, Carmen. *The Incas: Empire of Blood and Gold.* London: Thames & Hudson, 1994.

Hemming, John. *The Conquest of the Incas.* London: Pan Macmillan, 1970.

Lamar, Curt. "Hernando de Soto before Florida: A Narrative." *The Hernando de Soto Expedition: History, Historiography, and "Discovery" in the Southeast.* Lincoln: University of Nebraska Press, 2005.

MacQuarrie, Kim. *The Last Days of the Incas.* New York: Simon & Schuster, 2007.

Means, Philip A. *The Fall of the Inca Empire and the Spanish Rule in Peru, 1530–1780.* New York: Gordian Press, 1971.

Sancho, Pedro. *An Account of the Conquest of Peru.* With preface and translation by Philip A. Means. New York: Cortes Society, 1917.

Audiencia

The term *audiencia* refers to both a colonial jurisdiction and the judicial body attached to it, which was the highest court in the Spanish colonies. In the first half of the 16th century, Spanish monarch Charles I began organizing the newly conquered American lands into administrative units. The *audiencia* of Santo Domingo, created in 1511, was the first such body in the New World. In the following decades, the Crown further developed the organizational system in the colonies. The largest units established were viceroyalties, of which there were only two until the 18th century. These administrative entities were further divided into around 10 to 14 *audiencias,* which themselves were further divided into smaller units, such as municipalities. To hasten the transition from native to colonial control, the Spanish *organized* the new colonies in a similar manner to the previous rulers. The two viceroyalties occupied roughly the same territory as the fallen Aztec and Inca Empires, and the *audiencias* often were created on the ruins of the former Aztec and Inca provinces.

A judicial position in an *audiencia* was prestigious, and usually given to European-born Spaniards who had attained a law degree. The path of advancement to an *audiencia* judicial office, the *ascenso,* typically started with service in minor tribunals. By working his way up, an official could advance to a position in an important *audiencia.* If he was fortunate, the advancing official could become a judge in one of the *audiencias* that contained a viceroyalty capital in its jurisdiction. Unlike some of the other colonial appointments that had set terms, *audiencia* judges usually held their positions for life, unless they advanced to another *audiencia.* As a political administrative unit, an *audiencia* also had nonjudicial leadership roles, usually either in the form of a president or a captain general.

The majority of *audiencia* judges' time was spent handling criminal and civil cases, particularly appeals, but they had other responsibilities as well. For example, many judges audited different groups and oversaw colonial public works. Since the Crown set up the colonies in such a way that multiple bureaucratic hierarchies purposefully existed side by side, judges' responsibilities often overlapped with those of other officials. *Audiencia* judges typically worked with the political viceroys, the Church, and fiscal bureaucrats. This setup caused tensions between the different groups, with each keeping an eye on the others and reporting to Spain if necessary. Since judges usually held permanent positions, they did have the advantage of time and knowledge of the area. However, the resulting rivalries led to conflicting reports the caused confusion for the Spanish government, as well as for historians in later years.

Audiencia judges were also responsible for publicizing Spanish laws and ensuring these laws were obeyed. One of the most important issues they encountered was native labor. Spaniards turned to the indigenous populations as a source of labor early in the colonial period. To aid in the establishment of Spanish settlements, the crown awarded *encomiendas,* rights of labor, to certain Spaniards, which granted them the labor of a specific amount of natives. In response to the abuse of indigenous peoples, Charles I issued the *New Laws of the Indies* in 1542, which countered some of the mistreatment.

In these new laws, the king also affirmed the responsibility of the *audiencias* to oversee the treatment and conditions of natives. Unfortunately, the caveats included in the new laws created inequitable applications and enforcement of the laws, with the indigenous population usually bearing the burden. Additionally, the distance of the colonies from Spain, the realities of local politics, and the perceived need for labor often resulted in *audiencias* condoning grants of labor far beyond those awarded by the Spanish kings.

As with other bureaucratic positions in Spain's American colonies, the rising financial troubles of the Spanish Empire affected the appointment of *audiencia* judges. Beginning around the mid-17th century, the Crown turned to the sale of offices in the colonies in order to raise more funds. This development had important implications, particularly for *audiencia* offices. Through the purchase of these positions, American-born Spaniards were able to control many of the *audiencias* for the first time. Since these were typically permanent positions, the nature of local politics dramatically changed as a result.

Audiencias were the highest court in Spain's American colonies, and in that position they held an enormous amount of power, particularly in issues of native labor. In their judicial, legislative, and administrative roles, they also served as an important counterbalance to the viceroys and other imperial bureaucrats in the colonies.

John Laaman

See also: Government, Pre-Conquest Aztec; Government, Pre-Conquest Inca; Leyes Nuevas 1542–1543; Slavery, Role of; Spain, Imperial Goals of; Viceroyalty System.

Resources

Burkholder, Mark A., and Lyman L. Johnson. *Colonial Latin America.* 7th ed. Oxford: Oxford University Press, 2009.

McCreery, David J. *The Sweat of Their Brow: A History of Work in Latin America.* Armonk, NY: M.E. Sharpe, 2000.

Phelan, John Leddy. "Authority and Flexibility in the Spanish Imperial Bureaucracy." *Administrative Science Quarterly* 5(1) (June 1960): 47–65.

Ávila, Alonso de

The Ávila family has a complicated story of coincidental names and different last names for brothers, as it was usual in the 16th century. There is a first Alonso de Ávila, conqueror, and a second Alonso de Ávila, involved in the Martín Cortés's conspiracy. They were uncle and nephew.

The first Alonso de Ávila (Ciudad Real, Spain, 1486?—Nueva Galicia, New Spain, 1542) was one of the 10 captains that Cortés took with him from Cuba to the main land in 1518. After the expulsion of the Spaniards from Tenochtitlán, and maybe because Cortés saw Ávila as a potential enemy, he sent him to Hispaniola. His orders were to get help to pursue the conquest of the Aztec Empire. When Ávila returned, the conquest of the Aztec capital was complete. He obtained from Cortés the title of alcalde mayor, major, of the city of Mexico and a privileged location in the Main Square to build his house. Immediately afterward, in 1522, he set sail to Spain, as his subsequent mission was delivering the quinto real to the emperor. The quinto real, or the royal fifth of all the riches obtained, was a right that the emperor had over almost any military conquest. On his journey to Spain, French pirates captured the boat he was travelling in and also the riches it was carrying. Alonso was imprisoned for two years and returned to Spain only after the payment of a ransom.

While in Spain, he met Francisco de Montejo, an old friend of his, who had recently obtained from the emperor the right to conquer the Yucatán Peninsula, a direct result of the Treaty of Tordesillas and Pope Alexander IV's four bulls of 1493. Alonso de Ávila spent a decade in Yucatán and, after that, rejoined Cortés on an expedition to Las Hibueras. None of these expeditions was as successful as the conquest of Tenochtitlán had been. Alonso de Ávila died in Nueva Galicia, north of Mexico, in 1542. His brother Gil González inherited all his possessions, as Alonso died without an heir.

Gil González Benavides was not a conqueror of the first wave: he arrived in Mexico City after the conquest, received lands, and also acted as an administrator of his brother's estate while he was absent. Gil joined some expeditions in the thirties and forties, including that to Las Hibueras. He married Leonor de Alvarado, daughter of a conqueror, Juan de Alvarado. The possession of Cuautitlán, a village that had belonged to his brother Alonso de Ávila, was his main source of income. He and Leonor had three sons and two daughters and, according to Juan Suárez de Peralta, the first Alonso de Ávila cursed them after Gil took control of Alonso's lands during his period in Yucatán. The youngest boy drowned in a latrine and one of the girls committed suicide before professing as a nun. The two elder boys, Alonso and Gil, had an unfortunate end, too.

Benavides's sons, Alonso de Ávila Alvarado and Gil González Dávila Benavides, were criollos: born in America, but from Spanish families. They were rich enough to be considered among the most influential in the Viceroyalty and, although Alonso was richer and more interested in social gatherings than his brother, both were well known. With the arrival of the Marquis of the Valley to New Spain in 1563, Alonso and Martin became close friends and the idea of a conspiracy to enthrone the Marquis began to form in their minds. All the criollos from their close circle—mainly the Quesada brothers and the Cortés brothers—joined the alleged conspiracy.

When the Marquis's wife gave birth to twins, in 1565, Alonso de Ávila organized a fabulous party to celebrate the baptism of the children. During the celebration, the officers from the emperor took notes and collected evidence about the conspiracy. One of the most important of them all was a jar, made of clay from Cuautitlán, with a particular design: a crown. According to Dorantes de Carranz, Alonso de Ávila, dressed as Montezuma II, handed it to Martín Cortés.

Alonso de Ávila and his brother Gil González Dávila were formally accused of treason, incarcerated, and lost all their possessions immediately after that party. The same happened to their friends, with the exception of the Marquis, who received special treatment. The accusation was that of high treason: conspiring against the Emperor. Although they never confessed, their sentence was a death penalty because the officers considered them the instigators of the uprising. They were beheaded.

Covadonga Lamar Prieto

See also: Cortés, Hernán; El Mestizo; Tenochtitlán, Siege of; Viceroyalty System.

Resources

Díaz del Castillo, Bernal. *The True History of the Conquest of New Spain*. Translated with an Introduction and Notes by Janet Burke and Ted Humphrey. Indianapolis, IN: Hackett Publishing, 2012.

Levy, Buddy. *Conquistador: Hernán Cortés, King Montezuma, and the Last Stand of the Aztecs*. New York: Random House, 2008; Reprint, New York: Bantam Books, 2009.

Thomas, Hugh. *Conquest: Montezuma, Cortés, and the Fall of Old Mexico*. New York: Simon & Schuster, 1993.

Ayllón, Lucas Vázquez de

Originally a reluctant Spanish explorer, Lucas Vázquez de Ayllón ultimately became a wealthy planter and founder of San Miguel de Gualdape, the first European settlement in the present-day United States. Born in Toledo, Spain, about 1480, Lucas Vázquez de Ayllón led an obscure early life studying law and serving as a protégé of Bishop Fonseca. In 1502 he was sent to Santa Domingo, Hispaniola. There he made his living as a judge and a sugar planter, among the leading encomenderos. In 1504, his role as judge, responsible for supervising divisions of the island natives and enforcement of encomiendas on Santo Domingo, set the stage for harsh application of Spanish laws concerning the Indians for years to come. By 1517 his interpretation of Spanish policies affirmed that the natives of Hispaniola were incapable of living on their own and were unable to assimilate the Spanish culture. Through his influence, the Heronomite friars reported that the natives of Hispaniola were incapable of living freely among the Spanish. This legal and religious interpretation was used to justify the enslavement of the Indians in the Spanish colonies.

In 1519, the *audiencia* in Santo Domingo was alerted by Juan Carrillo, the public prosecutor, of Governor Diego Velázquez's plan to send Pánfilo de Narváez to arrest and possibly kill Hernán Cortés. The *audiencia* specifically tasked Ayllón with the legal responsibility of thwarting the divisions among the Spanish. In 1520, Ayllón was comfortably situated as a judge. As a supporter of Bishop Juan Rodríguez Fonseca, Ayllón's disapproval of Cortés was well known. News of a rising conflict between Cortés and Narváez prompted the interim governor of Hispaniola, Rodrigo de Figueroa, to order Ayllón to sail to Cuba and stop Narváez from launching an expedition against Cortés. Despite misgivings regarding his mission, the loyal licentiate was determined to implement his orders. Ayllón traveled to Trinidad in Cuba, where he unsuccessfully attempted to prevent the expedition from sailing to Mexico.

Initially sympathetic to Narváez, Ayllón's treatment at the hands of the expedition leader soured him. Though the two Spaniards shared similar opinions of the natives in America, Narváez intentionally displayed patience and friendly relations toward the Totonacs of San Juan de Ulúa in an effort to turn the Indians against any remaining loyalty to Cortés. Ayllón believed that Narváez's refusal to stay in Hispaniola as Ayllón's instructions demanded weakened the Spanish seat of power. Ayllón also disagreed with treating the natives as equals, and his perception of the natives as inferior contributed to his increased bitterness toward Narváez. Repeatedly ignored, Ayllón went so far as to write a letter to Cortés, making his opposition to Narváez and his expedition clear. Blaming the judge for growing divisions within his own expedition, Narváez arrested Ayllón and his clerk, and attempted to ship them back to Cuba. Ayllón managed to convince the sailors to let him off in Hispaniola, where he eventually made his way on foot back to Santo Domingo.

Humiliated and livid, Ayllón channeled his hostility into a series of acrimonious letters back to Spain. These letters condemned the actions of Narváez, going so far as to assert that the affront was to King Carlos I (Charles V HRE). Eventually, Ayllón's correspondence contributed to the defense of Cortés and resulted in the conquistador's eventual appointment as *adelantado*, *repartidor*, captain-general, and governor of New Spain in 1522.

Meanwhile, back in Hispaniola, Ayllón employed Francisco Gordillo in 1521 to travel to the Florida mainland for exploratory purposes. Gordillo's reports indicated that the land of Chicora (along the coast of South Carolina and Georgia) had abundant natural resources and a mild climate resembling that of Spain. This information led Ayllón to believe that a European settlement in the area could thrive, both as a trading center and as a missionary town to convert and control the natives. In mid-July 1526, Ayllón set sail to the north and west with six ships and about 600 people, including several women and slaves, to establish the first European settlement in the present-day United States: San Miguel de Gualdape.

The group spent some time exploring before settling on the site for the new colony in September 1526, most likely on the 29th, the day when feast of Archangels is held to venerate St. Michael. The exact location of the colony is unknown, with various theories suggesting Cape Fear, North Carolina; Winyah Bay, South Carolina; and Sapelo Sound, Georgia. More recent information supports the southernmost location of Georgia, but concrete archeological evidence has yet to be found.

The fledgling colony faced serious hardships almost immediately, including problems with supplies, abandonment by their native interpreters, starvation, disease, and hostility from the natives. Many of the colonists succumbed to the environment, including Ayllón himself, who died on October 18, 1526. During the winter, the colonists bore more hardships and faced a mutiny. In the spring, the remaining 150 survivors abandoned the colony and returned to Hispaniola.

Lisa L. Crutchfield and
Rebecca M. Seaman

See also: *Audiencia*; Charles V (HRE) or Carlos I of Spain; Cortés, Hernán; Encomienda; Narváez, Pánfilo de.

Resources

Cook, Jeannine, ed. *Columbus and the Land of Ayllon: The Exploration and Settlement of the Southeast.* Darien, GA: Lower Altamaha Historical Society, 1992.

Hoffman, Paul E. *A New Andalucia and a Way to the Orient: The American Southeast during the Sixteenth Century.* Baton Rouge: Louisiana State University Press, 2004.

Levy, Buddy. *Conquistador: Hernán Cortés, King Montezuma, and the Last Stand of the Aztecs.* New York: Random House, 2008; Reprint, New York: Bantam Books, 2009.

Thomas, Hugh. *Conquest: Montezuma, Cortés, and the Fall of Old Mexico.* New York: Simon & Schuster, 1993.

Ayllus

The Inca term *ayllus* refers to basic kinship groups found in the Andean kingdom. The Inca people accounted for only a minority of the population in the Inca Empire. Nonetheless, this complex organization of ethnic groups dominated every aspect of the Inca people and their society. The society was held together by kin groups, or *ayllus.* The *ayllus* were responsible for regulating all aspects of life, from spiritual and familial, to social, economic and political. The base Inca society contained approximately 10 main *ayllus,* from which all ethnic Incas could theoretically trace their lineage. As the kingdom conquered different people, the *ayllus* were used to help control newly conquered territories and people. Either newly accepted elites were incorporated into the Inca *ayllus,* or trusted members of varying *ayllus* were placed over recalcitrant populations.

Formally, the *ayllu* was an endogamous group that claimed the same ancestor. In reality, the Inca practiced a more relaxed kinship order, which commonly involved exogamous relations. In the case of the Inca rulers, endogamy continued to be practiced, even following Spanish conquest and conversion into the Catholic Church. This cultural trait so dominated the culture that the Catholic Church granted special dispensation to Sapa Incas who converted so that their marriages to their sisters received approval and recognition.

In practice, the Inca had two versions of the *ayllu,* almost an *ayllu* within an *ayllu.* The intimate form referred to the close kinship of brothers and sisters. In this form, the household *ayllus* included close relatives up to third cousins. However, the more common usage throughout the empire was the community form of *ayllus,* which typically included extended families whose households lived in the same community. Larger communities often boasted more than one *ayllus* within the society.

Leaders of the communities, or *kurakas,* were responsible for organizing the varying *ayllus* for purposes of land distribution, farming, public works, and other communal purposes. In this manner, family kinship groups labored, celebrated, worshipped, and paid tribute together as unit. However, it was the combined contributions of the varying *ayllus* that helped sustain the greater community.

Rebecca M. Seaman

See also: Class, Impact of Spanish on the Inca; Inca Elite; *Kuraka;* Sapa Inca.

Resources

Henson, Sändra Lee Allen. "Dead Bones Dancing: The Taki Onqoy, Archaism, and Crisis in Sixteenth Century Peru." MA Thesis, East Tennessee State University, 2002.

Stern, Steve J. *Peru's Indian Peoples and the Challenge of Spanish Conquest: Huamanga to 1640.* Madison: University of Wisconsin Press, 1993.

Ayni

Commonly defined as reciprocal aid or the sharing of work, the term *ayni* can be applied to any action motivated by the Andean belief in the interdependence relationship within the human community and between that community and its physical and spiritual environment. Thus, *ayni* is frequently used to refer to an action such as helping a neighbor construct a house or work in the field. Andeans practice *ayni* with the understanding that the assistance will be returned when needed, but it is not merely an attempt to gain the help of one's neighbors. Rather, actions characterized as *ayni* express the bond between community members, and thereby reinforce the community. These reciprocal relationships existed not only between Andeans of equal status, but also between the community and its leaders. While leaders could mobilize community members for work on common projects, they were also responsible for reciprocating the favor by providing food and access to resources for the community members who served on these projects.

The emphasis on reciprocal exchange as a unifying force in Andean societies predates both the Spanish and the Inca. In fact, many scholars recognize that these ideas facilitated the rapid expansion of the Inca Empire. The Inca were able to integrate local leaders and their communities into the empire through the use of reciprocity on a grand scale. The classic example of this reciprocal relationship on an imperial scale was the Inca *mita,* a rotational labor system in which laborers from subject communities worked on projects throughout the empire for a set period of time. In return, the Inca provided for the workers and their families and their communities received access to land and resources.

Mark Dries

See also: *Mita.*

Resources

Allen, Catherine J. *The Hold Life Has: Coca and Cultural Identity in an Andean Community.* 2nd ed. Washington, DC: Smithsonian Institution Press, 2002.

Apffel-Marglin, Frédérique, and Proyecto Andino de Tecnologías Campesinas (Peru). *The Spirit of Regeneration: Andean Culture Confronting Western Notions of Development.* London/New York: Zed Books, 1998.

McEwan, Gordon Francis. *The Incas: New Perspectives.* Santa Barbara, CA: ABC-CLIO, 2006.

Aztec, or Mexica

The Aztec Empire is the name commonly used to refer to a group known as the Nahuatl-speaking Mexica and their allies, who came to dominate central Mexico by the 15th century. That empire, however, was short-lived, as Spanish conquerors defeated the Aztecs in the early 16th century.

The Mexica rose quickly from humble origins to a position of great power. They were one of a series of nomadic groups that entered the Valley of Mexico. They had their origins in a region known as Aztlán in the north. After leaving that home, the Mexica wandered for many decades. Much of their early history is fragmentary and unreliable.

The Mexica arrived in the region of Lake Texcoco in the Valley of Mexico in around

1250. The valley was already home to a number of such competing cities as Texcoco and Atzcapotzalco. The existing residents of the valley did not welcome the Mexica, warrior-based society whom they viewed as barbarians. In a very short time, the Mexica developed a reputation as excellent combatants, and other groups utilized them as mercenaries. Nevertheless, they lived a precarious existence and were often driven off their lands to more marginal areas, like the barren territory of Tizapan. Eventually, in the first half of the 1300s, they occupied an island in the lake, where legend has it they saw an eagle on a cactus eating a snake. That sign, today immortalized on the Mexican flag, was an indication from the gods that the Mexica had reached their final destination. On that island, they created the beginnings of what eventually became the great capital city of Tenochtitlán.

In 1376, the Mexica chose Acamapichtli as their first king, or *tlatoani*. Under that first monarch, who claimed descent from the Toltec dynasty, the Mexica consolidated their position and began to expand. Under the *tlatoani* Itzcóatl (1426–1440), the Mexica allied themselves with the Texcoco and Tlacopan. That Triple Alliance conquered Atzcapotzalco in 1428 and established the basis of what became the Aztec Empire.

The Mexica dominated their allies during the reign of Montezuma I (1440–1469), expanded beyond the Valley of Mexico, and took control of much of central Mexico. They carried out even further expansion under a later descendent, Ahuitzotl (1486–1502) and reached as far as Oaxaca, the Gulf Coast, and Guatemala. Thus, when Montezuma II, the Aztec ruler at the time of the arrival of the Spaniards, took power in 1502, he ruled over a vast region. By that time, the Mexica dominated the cultural, political, and economic base of society. Their trade system spanned the entire Mesoamerican region, with the seat of political and economic power centered in Tenochtitlán.

Mexican society was organized around the *altepetl* and *calpulli*. *Altepetl* were regional ethnic states that had hereditary rulers, markets, and temples to the patron deity. *Altepetl* were made up of a number of *calpulli* ("big houses"), which included local rulers and temples. Deeply divided by internal clan rivalries, the stronger Mexica centers used alliances and military might to unify the clans under a single *tlatoani*.

Before the election of their first *tlatoani*, Mexica society had been relatively egalitarian. Soon, the distinction between noble and commoner became greater. The nobility, known as *pipiltin*, received the majority of the land and tribute from conquered areas. They also controlled the government, military, and religious positions. Most commoners, known as *macehualtin*, were agricultural workers, while others served as soldiers. The commoners had little chance for social mobility.

While the Mexica succeeded in conquering much territory, some groups remained independent and hostile. Prominent among these independent groups were the Tarascans and the Tlaxcalans. The Tlaxcalans, in particular, allied themselves with the invading Spaniards and helped defeat the Mexica.

In 1519, the Spanish conqueror Hernán Cortés reached the shores of Mexico. Spaniards based in the Caribbean had already visited the coast of Mexico and begun to hear rumors of a great civilization. When Cortés arrived with just over 500 men, he had several advantages that allowed him to defeat the Mexica: horses gave the Spaniards a military advantage; the Mexica believed that Cortés might be the god Quetzalcoatl, so they responded cautiously rather than fighting Cortés from the start; and disease, particularly smallpox, devastated the indigenous population of Mexico. By 1521, the Spaniards had conquered the once mighty Aztec Empire.

Ronald E. Young

See also: Cortés, Hernán; Montezuma II; Nahuatl Language; Texcoco, Alliance with Tenochtitlán.

Resources

Barghusen, Joan D. *The Aztecs: End of a Civilization*. San Diego, CA: Lucent Books, 2000.

Berdan, Frances F. *The Aztecs of Central Mexico: An Imperial Society*. Florence, KY: Wadsworth, 2004.

Henderson, Keith, and Jane Stevenson Day. *The Fall of the Aztec Empire*. Denver, CO: Roberts Rhinehart, 1993.

Mann, Charles C. *Ancient Americans: Rewriting the History of the New World*. London: Granta Books, 2005.

Smith, Michael Ernest. *The Aztecs*. Malden, MA: Blackwell, 2002.

Aztec-Spanish War

Following the establishment of Spanish control in the Caribbean, expeditions went forth searching for gold, slaves, and advanced, wealthy civilizations. Eventually, Spanish invaders conquered the native peoples of the region now called Mexico. This conquest led to the development of the present-day culture and people of Mexico.

On February 10, 1519, Hernán Cortés departed Cuba for the mainland, stopping along the Yucatán coast where he encountered Gerónimo de Aguilar. Shipwrecked in 1511, Aguilar knew the local Mayan dialect. Near Veracruz, local tribesmen gave the expedition several women. One was fluent in the Aztec language of Nahuatl. The Spanish christened her Doña Marina, better known today as La Malinche. Through Aguilar and Malinche the Spanish could converse with the Aztecs.

Reports filtered back to Tenochtitlán, the Aztec capital, of strangers in the land. The appearance of the light-skinned, bearded Spaniards from the east, in the year of the god Quetzalcoatl, prompted rumors that these invaders represented his prophesied return. Some historians have used this explanation to explain the Aztecs' initial hesitancy to attack the Spanish. However, it is more likely that unwilling subjects of the Aztecs spread the rumors.

As the explorers moved inland, Cortés noticed a pattern: the people they encountered repeatedly expressed discontent with their Aztec rulers. Internal divisions within the Aztec Empire served Cortés well as he attracted disgruntled allies into his forces. The numerous recruits from these divisions made the difference in the Spanish victory. The conquest must be understood as being as much an "Indian conquest" as a Spanish conquest.

Noting the Spanish success in forming alliances with other native peoples, Aztec emperor Montezuma II invited the Spanish to Cholula, where he planned to meet with Cortés. The Cholulans were to take care of the Spanish until Montezuma arrived. The Spanish were suspicious about this arrangement and the accompanying native allies echoed their concerns. When Malinche informed Cortés of a plot to seize the explorers, he called the Cholulan leaders to the central square in front of a religious temple, where the Spanish and their allies attacked, killing as many as 6,000 Cholulans.

From Cholula, Cortés marched toward Tenochtitlán to meet with Montezuma. On November 8, 1519, Cortés and Montezuma met on one of the causeways linking the mainland to Tenochtitlán. Reportedly,

Montezuma gave a short speech, laboriously translated through Malinche and Aguilar. It is not certain how much either man understood the other, but each replied in friendly terms. The Spanish informed the Aztecs that they were arriving as friends, and Montezuma presented the Spaniards with gold necklaces and prostrated himself before the visitors before he gave his address.

Following more speeches, the Spaniards marched into Tenochtitlán, where the Aztecs treated them to food, clothing, and lodging. The explorers then demanded that gold be brought to them. The Aztecs presented beautiful pieces of Aztec gold art and jewelry. Not appreciating the intrinsic value of the indigenous artwork, the Spaniards melted the gold into bars for easier transport.

The Spaniards remained in Tenochtitlán for at least four days before taking Montezuma prisoner, arguing that the Aztecs had attacked Spanish forces at Veracruz. The Aztec society was so complex that the empire did not fall with his arrest. The Aztec account reveals that the other principal chiefs were angry with Montezuma for capitulating to the Spanish arrest. They adjusted to his capture but soon disagreed over how they should act. In the end, resistance evolved over the continued demands by the Spanish for more gold and an end to the practice of human sacrifice.

Effective control of Tenochtitlán by Cortés was complicated when, in April 1520, Cuban governor Diego Velázquez sent a large force under Pánfilo de Narváez to arrest Cortés. Ambassadors from Narváez met with Cortés. The *caudillo* sent the emissaries back to Narváez, giving them gold with the implicit promise that more was forthcoming. These bribes tempted men with dreams of future wealth and resulted in their shift of loyalty to Cortés. Nonetheless, the presence of Narváez's forces revealed to the Aztecs the divisions among the Spanish.

Leaving a contingent of men at Tenochtitlán under his chief officer Pedro de Alvarado, Cortés moved toward Zempoala to confront Narváez. Cortés's forces attacked the Narváez camp and easily defeated the troops. In negotiations with Narváez's men, Cortés convinced them of the great opportunities that awaited them if they were to join the actions against Tenochtitlán. The potential crisis for Cortés turned into an advantage, increasing the men, horses, and supplies for his conquest of Mexico.

Back in Tenochtitlán, Cortés's departure to respond to the Narváez threat encouraged the Aztecs to reassert their control. Aztec nobles held a ceremony to honor the war god Huitzilopochtli, approved by Cortés before his departure. As preparations for the feast continued, Alvarado grew nervous about the Aztecs' behavior. Fearing the threat posed to the Spanish by the massing of native peoples, Alvarado ordered an attack against the ceremony participants, brutally cutting them down and precipitating a battle between the Aztecs and the Spanish forces.

Cortés returned to Tenochtitlán, where he quickly surmised the difficulty of the situation. Recognizing the danger to the Spanish, Cortés decided to leave the city. He persuaded a reluctant Montezuma to speak to the crowds and convince them that the Spanish should be allowed to leave. However, before Montezuma could finish addressing the crowd, some began throwing stones at him, which struck the Aztec king, fatally wounding him. With his death, the Spanish lost any bargaining chip they had with the Aztecs.

Realizing the futility of their situation, the Spanish planned to leave the city at night. Aztec sentinels discovered their attempted escape and sounded an alert. A bloody battle followed as the Spanish fought their way out of the city. Almost 600 Spaniards died

Spanish forces under Hernán Cortés confronting Aztecs in the defense of Tenochtitlán. (Wildside Press)

or were captured that night in the attempted escape, in addition to 1,000 native allies. The Spanish have since referred to this event as La Noche Triste, or "the Sad Night."

Cortés fled to Tlaxcala with his remaining 400 men. They remained there from July 1520 until April 1521 recovering from the devastation of La Noche Triste and making preparations to attack Tenochtitlán. Their Tlaxcalan allies provided additional supplies and men, and more Spaniards from the Caribbean joined the effort when word of the Aztec wealth reached them. By the end of 1520, Cortés had more than 900 Spanish soldiers and more than 100 horses. Moreover, the Spanish native allies numbered in the thousands. The Spanish began to construct ships for deployment on the lake surrounding Tenochtitlán, against the canoes used by the Aztecs.

The Spanish eventual conquest was assisted by an outbreak of smallpox that devastated the native population in September 1520. Even the new Aztec emperor Cuitláhuac died from this epidemic. While the disease affected Spanish foes and allies alike, in the end, it created physical weakness and undermined the leadership in Tenochtitlán. The Spanish apparent immunity to the disease added to their allies' continued support. Cuautéhmoc, the last surviving Aztec ruler who replaced Cuitláhuac, attempted to rally the city against the Spanish but failed to achieve this goal, as many former members of the Aztec alliance abandoned them and turned to support the Spanish.

The Spanish completed building their ships and began the assault against Tenochtitlán in May 1521. Using their brigantines, the Spanish quickly controlled the lake and imposed a blockade to starve the city into surrender. Cortés hoped to seize the city without destroying it, but the nature of the battle soon made that idea impossible. Despite the technological advantage of the Spanish, the people at Tenochtitlán fought bravely and suffered serious casualties as a result. Recognizing that the fighting was not going to be easy, the Spaniards repeatedly urged the Aztecs and their allies to surrender. Rather than risk the lives of his troops through more house-to-house fighting, Cortés deployed siege warfare against Tenochtitlán. The Spanish cut the aqueduct leading into the city, forcing the inhabitants to rely on the unhealthy water from Lake Texcoco. Thereafter, the city's inhabitants became increasingly sick from drinking the unclean water.

In June 1521, while the Spanish attempted a massive frontal attack, the Aztecs counterattacked and captured more than 50 Spaniards. To the horror of their compatriots, the Aztecs sacrificed them in view of the Spanish. The fighting continued for the next two months. By August, much of the once beautiful city was reduced to rubble and the stench of decaying bodies hung in the air. On August 12, 1521, many residents of Tenochtitlán began to flee the city. On August 13, 1521, the 80th day of the siege, the Spanish entered the city and captured Cuautéhmoc.

After the fall of the Aztec Empire, the tribute-paying tribes also fell under the control of the Spanish. The Spanish controlled the Mexico region until the 19th century. Although the great Aztec civilization was destroyed, many of the survivors, Aztec as well as other native peoples of the area, lived among the Spanish, giving rise to a syncretic culture that developed into the Mexican culture of today.

Burton Kirkwood

See also: Aguilar, Gerónimo; Alvarado, Pedro de; Brigantines, Use by Cortés; Cortés, Hernán; Cuauhtémoc; Cuitláhuac; La Malinche, "Doña Marina"; La Noche Triste; Montezuma II; Narváez, Pánfilo de; Tenochtitlán, City of; Tenochtitlán, Siege of; Velázquez, Diego (de Cuéllar); Villa Rica de la Vera Cruz; Zempoala.

Resources

Díaz del Castillo, Bernal. *The Discovery and Conquest of Mexico.* New York: Noonday, 1956.

Elliot, J.H. *The Spanish Conquest in Colonial Spanish America.* Edited by Leslie Bethell. Cambridge: Cambridge University Press, 1987.

Grunberg, Bernard. "The Origins of the Conquistadors of Mexico City." *Hispanic American Historical Review* 74, no. 2 (1994): 263–264.

Leon-Portilla, Miguel. *The Broken Spears: The Aztec Account of the Conquest of Mexico.* Boston, MA: Beacon Press, 1992.

MacLachlan, Colin M., and Jaime E. Rodriguez. *The Forgings of the Cosmic Race: A Reinterpretation of Colonial Mexico.* Berkeley: University of California Press, 1980.

Thomas, Hugh. *Conquest: Montezuma, Cortés, and the Fall of Old Mexico.* New York: Touchstone, 1993.

Aztec-Spanish War, Causes of

The Aztec-Spanish War (1519–1521) occurred in central Mexico. The conflict was fought between the Spanish (and their Mesoamerican allies) and the Aztecs (actually a Triple Alliance of the Mexica of Tenochtitlán, the Acolhua of Texcoco, and the Tepanec of Tlacopan). The causes of the war include rationales from both sides. The native causes for conflict ranged from the resentment toward the Mexica by their subjugated neighbors, the miscalculations of the strengths and weaknesses of the Spanish invaders, and the hesitance on the part of the Aztec leader (*tlatoani*) Montezuma to decisively attack Hernán Cortés's forces. Spanish causes ranged from the personal reasons of individuals to the political agendas of heads of state. The ambition, glory, religious zeal, and greed of individuals in the invading forces often conflicted with the ambitions and power struggles of others, specifically between Cortés and the governor of Cuba, Diego Velázquez. This power struggle was exacerbated by the immediate agenda of King Charles I of Spain (newly elected Holy Roman Emperor Charles V) to acquire wealth from the New World to sustain his Old World Empire.

Native rationales for the war are rooted in Aztec history. The Aztecs arrived in the Valley of Mexico around the 13th century and settled on the swampy southwest border of the valley's lake, where they lived as poor farmers. They created floating fields and established a strong trade in agricultural goods. By 1325, internal rivalry among various Aztec clans resulted in the eventual formation of a league or alliance between the city-states of Tenochtitlán, Texcoco, and Tlacopan. For a century, the Triple Alliance held strong under the leadership of the *tlatoani.*

By the late 15th and early 16th centuries, the cultural, economic, and political base of the Aztecs was firmly established. The Aztec dominated trade relations across the region of Mesoamerica. Their seat of power in Tenochtitlán displayed the wealth of the alliance. A warrior society that thrived on the conquest and capture of neighboring enemies, their capital city also displayed evidence of atrocities, including depictions of enslavement and the skulls of human sacrifices. It was the wealth of Tenochtitlán that attracted the Spanish to the Valley of Mexico. It was the human sacrifice that justified conquest and subjugation of the Aztecs in the minds of the conquistadores. Although the difference between the public slaughter by the Aztecs and public executions by the Spanish is measured more in quantity rather than methodology and practice, the Spanish interpreted the human sacrifice of the Aztecs as evidence of the devil's presence. According to the Spanish, colonization of the region was necessary to exorcise demons from the land.

The Spanish instigation of war with the Aztecs was far more complex than just seeking to "civilize" the native populace or spread the Catholic faith. The realities of Spanish colonial politics and economics dominated the movement toward war. Cortés, descended from a poor family of lesser aristocracy in Medillín, Spain, sought wealth and royal recognition. Under the pretext of conquest and settlement of new territories for the king, Cortés contradicted the authority of Velázquez. Blinded by his own ambitions, Cortés regarded the restrictions of Velázquez as selfish, personal ambitions that conflicted with the goals of the Crown. To circumvent this obstacle, Cortés sought permission for the right of conquest directly from Emperor Charles. However, to ensure the success of his petition, Cortés needed immediate victory and gifts of gold to prove the importance of his conquests. Cortés commanded an expedition to Central America under the instructions of Velázquez to explore and trade, landing at Veracruz in April 1519. Once landed, Cortés disobeyed his instructions and used the expedition to settle and conquer territories in the Yucatán.

Montezuma was aware of Cortes's expedition and sent out messengers to request a meeting, replete with gifts of gold. Spanish historians later asserted that the emperor believed Cortés to be the god Quetzalcoatl. The Aztecs did refer to the Spanish as *teteoh,* a word describing them as gods and as powerful, privileged people. Cortés did not question the gifts, and sent the gold back to Spain, along with his petition for the right of conquest. Meanwhile, he proceeded toward Tenochtitlán. The route to the capital took the Spaniards across the independent territories of the Tlaxcalans, who repeatedly lost to Cortés's forces, but at great cost in Spanish lives. Seeking to capitalize on the internal divisions and hatred the tributary clans felt toward the Aztecs, Cortés made an alliance with the Tlaxcalans.

The Tlaxcalans contributed 20,000 men to Cortés's forces. By November 1519, Cortés entered Tenochtitlán, capturing Montezuma as a hostage. Fearing the execution of their emperor, the Aztecs delayed in attacking the Spanish invaders for seven months. At this point, Aztec and Spanish stories differ greatly. The Aztecs claimed that the Spanish killed Montezuma, while the Spaniards claimed his own people killed him. Certainly, Cortés's need for immediate victory and evidence of access to great wealth in gold was blocked by the stalemate and aided by the removal of Montezuma from power. Following Montezuma's death, the new emperor, Cuitláhuac, immediately attacked Cortés's forces, using the narrow alleys to counter the effectiveness of Spanish horses and weapons and chasing the invaders from the city. Viewing the Spanish retreat as a victory for the Aztecs, however, Cuitláhuac failed to destroy Cortés's fleeing forces. Determined to triumph still, Cortés secured alliances with other vassal states and returned to lay siege to the capital city. Decimated by an outbreak of smallpox, the defending Aztecs fought valiantly, but eventually lost to the superior numbers of Spanish and native invaders.

The final Spanish success was the result of several combined factors that related to the original causes of the war. The internal strife within the Aztec Empire created ready allies and informants for the Spanish. Individual conquistadores' greed for land, wealth, and power combined with a religious zeal to purge the region of demons and establish the Catholic faith. The struggle for the right of conquest between Cortés and Velázquez added to the urgency of the conflict and was fed by royal demands for colonial wealth to support the ambitions of Charles I.

Rebecca M. Seaman

See also: Cortés, Hernán; Cuitláhuac; Montezuma II; Quetzalcoatl; Tenochtitlán, City of; Texcoco, Alliance with Tenochtitlán; Velázquez, Diego.

Resources

Beezley, William, and Colin MacLachlean. *Latin America: The Peoples and Their History.* 2nd ed. Belmont, CA: Thompson Wadsworth Publishers, 2007.

Canizares-Esguerra, Jorge, and Erik R. Seeman. *The Atlantic in Global History, 1500–2000.* Upper Saddle River, NJ: Pearson Education, 2007.

Kelton, Paul. *Enslavement & Epidemics: Biological Catastrophe in the Native Southeast 1492–1715.* Lincoln: University of Nebraska Press, 2007.

Mann, Charles C. *Ancient Americans: Rewriting the History of the New World.* London: Granta Books, 2005.

Pagden, Anthony, ed., trans. *Hernan Cortes: Letters from Mexico.* Introductory Essay by J. H. Elliott. New Haven, CT: Yale University Press, 1986.

Aztec-Spanish War, Consequences of

The consequences of the Aztec-Spanish War can be organized into social, political, and economic categories. Socially, the Aztecs underwent severe traumas following their defeat at the hands of the Spanish. Devastated by repeated outbreaks of disease (smallpox and suspected outbreaks of hanta virus, measles, and typhus), the urban centers of the Aztecs were especially hard hit with human losses. Exact numbers of native populations prior to the Spanish conquest are not available. However, studies indicate the possibility of 15 to 25 million people living in Central Mexico by 1518. Following repeated outbreaks of European diseases, the population declined to around 17 million in 1532, 4 to 6 million by 1545, only 3 million by 1568, and 2 million following the typhus epidemic of 1576. This represents a loss of 87 percent of the population in only 60 years.

The spread of disease was not solely the result of a lack of immunity. The existence of densely populated urban areas contributed heavily to these high mortality rates. The beautiful, clean, well-managed cities of the Aztecs fell into disrepair following Spanish conquest. The massive numbers of dead overwhelmed the ability of the people to dispose of bodies and to maintain the previous standards for disposal of sewage and other waste. Additionally, the devastation wrought by Hernán Cortés's destruction of large sections of the city demolished the aqueduct system that brought necessary freshwater to the city. Additionally, the Spanish had brought pigs with them to the continent well before Cortés's expedition. Rapidly reproducing, the pigs provided a great source of protein but also contributed to the spread and mutation of diseases. The combination of new diseases, dense population, filth, and lack of water and food all served to undermine the previous system of urbanization.

Related to the societal impacts of disease and death were the impositions of the new Spanish order, including the missions. Aztec culture was centered on their religion, with all activities dependent in some fashion upon the leadership and dictates of their beliefs. In an effort to convert the Aztecs from their perceived pagan ways, Spanish missionaries sought to destroy all aspects of the Aztec beliefs, a process that had a ripple effect across native society. Agricultural activities of sowing and harvesting were affected by the destruction of the traditional religious calendars. History, sciences, and mathematics were impacted by the destruction of hieroglyphs by the Spaniards, who feared them as signs of pagan treachery. The educational system, responsible for teaching and training each generation in the skills and arts of each trade, was thrown into complete disarray. The Aztec educational structure was controlled by each clan and fell under the control of priests. The Spanish friars continued the concept of religious control of education, but did not focus on training in crafts and skills that supported the economy. Instead, the focus was on conversion, control, and assimilation into the Spanish culture.

Economic consequences of the Aztec-Spanish War are closely related to the social impacts. The Spanish sought great wealth in the form of gold, silver, and gems from the New World. Tenochtitlán (present-day Mexico City) became a mining center. Additionally, it was necessary to produce food products that could sustain the Aztecs and the Spanish in the region. Prior to Spanish conquest, beautiful botanical gardens existed in the city, and most citizens were farmers. With the advent of Spanish control, the Spanish redistributed land, assigning it to the colonists. While the practice of planting maize and other food products continued for local usage, the planting of sugarcane dominated in regions where this new cash crop could thrive. These labors, both in mining and planting, were conducted by the distribution of natives among the colonial plantations.

Historians dispute the labor practices of the Spanish. While abuses were employed in the colonies, in Spain, Isabella and later Charles V (Carlos I) attempted to suppress the usage of native slave labor. However, even the more definitive New Laws of

Charles V made provisions for the continued practice of *repartimiento* and *encomienda,* both of which provided for limited usage of native laborers. The restricted authorization of such practices made it difficult to regulate labor. Conflicting Spanish systems of governance added to the problem of unenforceability. While the *adelantados* and governors held military, political, and economic power in their assigned regions, the religious oversight of bishops (centered in Havana, Cuba) often came in conflict with secular rule. The contested authority from divergent locations led to the practice of ignoring royal policies. As governors and *adelantados* contested elements of the New Laws, royal officials delayed enforcement of the laws in question.

The conflicting oversight of the Mesoamerican region was further affected by corruption and jealousies between the secular and religious authorities. One-fifth of all wealth earned was demanded by the Crown, followed by the required donations to Catholic bishops. These figures were determined by *audiencias* (royal representatives) out of Cuba, and infrequently adjusted to reflect the realities of acquired wealth. Short of funds, authorities increased demands on native labor and decreased remunerations paid to clan and tribal leaders who provided laborers. By 1545, responding to opposition from the colonies, Charles revoked the most contested portions of his laws regulating native labor, and by 1570 the Crown withdrew interest in the *encomienda* and *repartimiento* systems.

Denied their traditional religion, stripped of much of their culture, and devastated by deadly epidemics, the Aztecs were incapable of organizing effective resistance to the Spanish in the 16th century. Increased local control of the native populace by secular administrators, enforcement of Spanish policies by military personnel, and the assimilation practices of the Spanish missions further reduced the Aztecs from the powerful, dominant society of the 15th century. Encomienda and repartimiento requirements further impacted the populace and contributed to the formation of social castes, with the Aztecs among the lowest ranks of society. Today, the dominant faith of the region is Catholicism, and the traditional Nahuatl language is no longer classified as a "living" language. A series of revolutions in the 19th century toppled Spanish rule, but by this time the Aztecs as a distinct people had all but disappeared.

Rebecca M. Seaman

See also: *Adelantado; Audiencia;* Charles V (HRE) or Carlos I of Spain; Leyes Nuevas Cortés, Hernán; Encomienda; European Diseases, Role of; Mines, Role of in Mexico; Nahuatl Language; Repartimiento; Silver; Slavery, Role of.

Resources

Hanke, Lewis. "Indians and Spaniards in the New World: A Personal View." In *Attitudes of Colonial Powers toward the American Indian,* edited by Howard Peckham and Charles Gibson. Salt Lake City: University of Utah Press, 1969.

Jones, Oakah L., Jr. "Rescue and Ransom of Spanish Captives from the indios barbaros on the Northern Frontier of New Spain." *Colonial Latin American Historical Review* 4, no. 2 (Spring 1995): 128–148.

Kelton, Paul. *Enslavement & Epidemics: Biological Catastrophe in the Native Southeast 1492–1715.* Indians of the Southeast Series. Lincoln: University of Nebraska Press, 2007.

Prescott, William H. *The History of the Conquest of Mexico.* Reprint with Introduction by James Lockhart. New York: Modern Library, 2001.

Villamarin, Juan A., and Judith E. Villamarin. *Indian Labor in Mainland Colonial Spanish America.* Newark, NJ: University of Delaware, 1975.

B

Balboa, Vasco Núñez de

Vasco Núñez de Balboa was the first European to see the eastern coast of the Pacific Ocean, which he called the South Sea. In late September 1513, he claimed the entire ocean for Spain. He pacified the natives of Panama and was the first white man to establish a permanent settlement in the New World.

Balboa was born in 1475 in Jerez de los Caballeros, Estremadura, Spain. His father, Don Nuño Aria de Balboa, was not rich but of royal lineage. His mother was a lady from Badajoz. The youngest of three brothers, Balboa became a page in the household of Don Pedro Puertocarrero in the southwestern Spanish port of Moguer. Balboa grew to be a handsome man with an extraordinary reputation as a swordsman.

In 1500, Balboa sailed on an expedition under Cmdr. Rodrigo de Bastidas and chief pilot Juan de la Cosa. They sailed in the Gulf of Urabá and along the northern coast of present-day Colombia to search for gold and pearls. Bad planning ended the unsuccessful venture. The leaky ship had to be abandoned in Hispaniola (present-day Haiti).

Penniless, Balboa accumulated heavy debts. Then, in 1510, Balboa stowed away on a ship bound for Colombia. That expedition, under the command of Martín Fernández de Enciso, carried supplies to a new settlement at San Sebastian. Upon arrival, they found the settlement abandoned due to lack of food and danger from Indians. Balboa convinced those with him to proceed southwest to Darién on the Isthmus of Panama, a place he had seen on his previous journey. There, they founded the town of Santa María de la Antigua (present-day Acandi), the first permanent settlement in the New World.

A power struggle ensued between Enciso and Diego de Nicuesa, who had been ordered to Darién by King Ferdinand V. Balboa was instrumental in charging Enciso with usurpation. Enciso was banished and returned to Spain, where he sought redress with the king. In the meantime, Ferdinand appointed Balboa as interim governor in 1511; he became supreme commander of the colony in 1513. Upon his arrival in Europe, Enciso brought the same charges of usurpation against Balboa. While governor, Balboa led expeditions from Darién into present-day Panama. He conquered some Indians and made agreements with others nearby. The colony thrived under his leadership.

As early as 1511, Indians told Balboa about a great sea on the western side of the isthmus and a wealthy empire (the Inca Empire) that lay further south. In early September 1513, Balboa led a huge expedition of Spaniards, some 1,000 Indian slaves, and a large pack of dogs to find the sea. The 25-day journey across the Isthmus of Panama proved difficult. Swamps, violent natives, dense jungles, and mountain terrain all contributed to a horrendous experience. Balboa befriended some Indians. Others were enslaved or tortured. Extensive looting gave Balboa substantial treasure.

On September 25, Indian guides informed Balboa that he could see the big sea by climbing a mountain. He climbed the mountain on his own and then asked others to join

Balboa, in artistic rendition depicting him discovering the Pacific Ocean. (Library of Congress)

him. They erected a cross and christened the great sea Mar del Sur, or "South Sea," because it lay on the south side of the isthmus. On September 29, 1513, Balboa waded into the water in full armor and claimed the South Sea and all of its shores for God and King Ferdinand. Approximately seven years later, Ferdinand Magellan, sailing for Portugal, renamed the sea the Pacifica, of peaceful ocean.

The expedition's return trip proved to be rewarding. Balboa captured Indian chief Tubanama and received a huge ransom for him. They fought and defeated numerous other tribes, capturing slaves without losing any of their own members. The group found huge hoards of gold and pearls. Hunger was a problem, however. Instead of carrying adequate provisions, they preferred carrying loot. Consequently, members of the group suffered from starvation.

On January 18, 1514, Balboa was back in Darién, where he sent the treasures to King Ferdinand. While he was away, Balboa's enemies denounced him to King Ferdinand who appointed a new governor, elderly nobleman Pedro Arias Dávila, later known as "Pedrarias the Cruel." Once Ferdinand learned about the discovery of the South Sea, he directed Balboa to serve under Dávila as governor of Panama. Balboa commenced on a new venture, building ships on the South Sea coast. He only made one expedition, to the Pearl Islands, but was unsuccessful due to unfavorable winds.

Balboa's service under Dávila was turbulent. Jealous of the extremely popular Balboa, Dávila grew to fear Balboa's influence over the colony. In an effort to ensure his trust, Dávila betrothed his daughter Maria to Balboa in 1516. Nonetheless, tension between the two men mounted. In December 1518, Dávila and some others framed Balboa on false charges of disobedience and treason. Francisco Pizarro, who accompanied Balboa on his discovery of the South Sea, arrested Balboa. Dávila ordered a speedy trial wherein Balboa was found guilty and sentenced to death. Along with four others, Balboa was decapitated in January 1519 in the Spanish settlement of Acla.

Annette E. Richardson

See also: Dávila, Pedro Arias.

Resources

Anderson, Charles L. *Life and Letters of Vasco Núñez de Balboa: Including the Conquest and Settlement of Darien and Panama, The Odyssey of the Discovery of the South Sea, A Description of the Splendid Armada to Castilla Del Oro, and the Execution of the Adelantado At Acla; A History of the First Years of the Introduction of Christian Civilization on the Continent of America.* Introduction by Ricardo J. Alfaro. New York: Fleming H. Revell Company, 1941.

Bohlander, Richard E., ed. *World Explorers and Discoverers.* Chicago, IL: Maxwell Macmillan International, 1992.

Crone, G. R. *The Voyages of Discovery.* London: Wayland Publishers, 1970.

Owen, Roderic. *Great Explorers.* New York: Mayflower Books, 1979.

Romoli, Kathleen. *Balboa of Darien: Discoverer of the Pacific.* New York: Doubleday, 1953.

Betanzos's Narrative of the Incas

Narrative of the Incas (Summa y narración de los Incas) was written by the Spanish soldier and interpreter Juan de Betanzos based on the testimony of his wife, an Inca princess, and her aristocratic family. Betanzos came to Peru in the 1530s and became an expert on the Inca language, Quechua, serving as a translator for Francisco Pizarro. Based on oral traditions and the personal experiences of its informants, most of who lived through the conquest, Betanzos's *Narrative* is one of the most important accounts of the Inca before and during the conquest of Peru.

Betanzos's wife, Doña Angelina Yupanqui or Cuxirimay Ocllo (d. 1561), was a daughter of the Sapa Inca Huayna Capac. She was betrothed and possibly married to the last powerful Sapa Inca, her brother Atahualpa. Scholars remain unsure if Doña Angelina was "given" to Pizarro as a concubine or if the conquistador forcibly captured her (Pizarro already had two children to an Inca woman named Doña Inez Muñoz). After Pizarro's death, his half-brother Gonzalo arranged for Doña Angelina to marry Betanzos. The couple had one child, a daughter named Doña Maria de Betanzos.

Betanzos wrote the *Narrative* between 1551 and 1557 at the request of the Viceroy of Peru, Antonio de Mendoza. While the degree to which scholars might understand and use Inca *khipu* (*quipu* in Spanish) to understand the past, the knotted cords used to record information assisted the people of Peru in maintaining oral histories of their communities and Inca rule. Using the women of his wife's family, in particular, as informants, Betanzos constructed a narrative of the Inca past organized around the reigns of the Sapa Incas and written in the style of an indigenous song or ballad. Copies of his manuscript were sent to Spain, though modern scholars were unaware of a complete version of it until 1986 when scholar Carmen Martin Rubo discovered an additional 64 chapters in the Palma manuscript at the Fundación Bartolomé March in Palma de Mallorca, Spain. Before this date, only 18 chapters of the *Narrative* were known to still exist (the Escorial manuscript).

The book is divided into two parts, dedicated to pre-conquest history and the Spanish occupation of Peru respectively. The first six chapters focus on the origins of the universe and the reign of Manco Cápac, the first Sapa Inca of Cusco. The remaining chapters of the first part are dedicated to Pachacuti, the ninth Sapa Inca and founder of the Inca Empire from whom Doña Angelina claimed her *panaca* or lineage (20 chapters), and his successors Topa Inca and Huayna Capac (24 chapters). The second part of Betanzos's *Narrative* focuses on the civil war between Doña Angelina's brother Atahualpa and his half-brother Huáscar after the death of their father Huayna Cápac from what many scholars presume to be smallpox. It also tells the tale of Spanish conquest and occupation from the perspective of Doña Angelina's family. As a product of Doña Angelina and her family, the work praises the actions of Atahualpa while condemning those of Huáscar.

Juan de Betanzos's *Narrative of the Incas* represents one the most authentic indigenous accounts of Peru before and during the Spanish occupation. Betanzos claimed to record his relatives' testimonies faithfully, adding his own explanations only when necessary. Nonetheless, the chronological focus on political authorities betrays Betanzos's European influence. While the account certainly reflects the biases of Doña Angelina's lineage and status, and the role of its Spanish author, it offers profound insights on the history of the Inca Empire told through an intermediary with unparalleled access to indigenous society and culture.

Charles V. Reed

See also: Atahualpa; Huáscar; Huayna Cápac; Inca Civil War; Manco Cápac; Pachacutin; Pizarro, Francisco; *Quipu*.

Resources

Betanzos, Juan de. *Narrative of the Incas.* Edited by Roland Hamilton and Dana Buchanan. Austin: University of Texas Press, 1996.

Graubart, Karen. "Indecent Living: Indigenous Women and the Politics of Representation in Early Colonial Peru." *Colonial Latin American Review* 9 (2) (2000): 213–235.

Julien, Catherine. *Reading Inca History.* Iowa City: University of Iowa Press, 2009.

Rostworowski de Diez Canseco, Maria. *History of the Inca Realm.* Translated by Harry B. Iceland. New York: Cambridge University Press, 1999.

Bono de Quejo, Juan

A shipmaster, Juan Bono de Quejo was born in San Sebasitán in Basque territories on the coast of the Bay of Biscay on the northern fringes of Spain. He later relocated to another port city, Palos, Andalucia, in southernmost Spain. He was among those who accompanied Christopher Columbus on his calamitous fourth voyage. Later, he captained one of Ponce de León's ships in the initial exploration of Florida in 1513. That same year, Bono de Quejo testified against Diego Colón, earning him the support of the Bishop of Burgos, Juan Rodríguez de Fonseca, and placing him in the camp of those eventually in opposition to the conquistador Hernán Cortés.

Bono de Quejo's attention turned from merely captaining ships to investing in trade ventures, specifically in the trade of indigenous slaves and pearls. He was supported by Genoese traders such as the Grimaldi brothers, whose Bank of St. George—one of the first incorporated world banks—financed Columbus and Charles V. With such stable financial support, Bono de Quejo made expeditions along the Venezuelan coast, transporting the indigenous slaves he captured back to Cuba. His expedition with Juan de Grijalva to capture slaves on Trinidad in 1516–1517 was particularly infamous.

When Cortés sailed for Mexico to explore and acquire wealth, initially having been supported by Governor Diego Velázquez de Cuéllar of Cuba who then rescinded his support of the expedition, Bono de Quejo was closely aligned to the governor and already critical of Cortés. Velázquez ordered another ally, Pánfilo de Narváez, to organize about 18 brigantines and *naos* to locate and arrest the *caudillo*. Bono de Quejo was selected to accompany Narváez on this punitive mission in 1520. Serving as one of the more important captains on the expedition, he was present at the initial landing on the Yucatán and during the interchanges between the indigenous leaders who initially opposed Narváez's party. Bono de Quejo later communicated much of what he observed, to include the messages between the *caudillo* and Pánfilo de Narváez. He was privy to the gifts of gold sent by Cortés through messengers, meant to divide the loyalties of the Spanish serving under Narváez.

Bono de Quejo's reports of conflicts with and actions by Cortés were typically negative. The disorder among the Spanish, assertions of the *caudillo*'s abuse of the indigenous populations, accusations of Spanish complicity with native cannibalism, and depictions of Cortés as the instigator of internal conflict among the Spanish conquering forces are replete throughout his communications. While Bono de Quejo's depiction of Cortés is that of an inferior, using the diminutive "Cortesillo" to reference the *caudillo,* his support for Narváez is unquestioned, asserting that the leader of the punitive expedition was God-fearing and never intended to fight his fellow Spaniard. Despite the obvious lack of support for Cortés by Narváez's captains, Bono de Quejo and others were initially integrated in the *caudillo*'s forces, largely to assist in supporting the Spanish in holding the Aztec capital, Tenochtitlán. However, following the Spanish defeat during the La Noche Triste, the threat of certain leading "Narvaecistas" convinced the conquistador to send Bono de Quejo and others back to Cuba in December 1520, ironically on Bono de Quejo's own ship.

The Basque shipmaster returned to Mexico in January 1522, with letters of instruction directly from his benefactor Bishop Fonseca. Participant to a last ditched and failed attempt by Fonseca and Velázquez to unseat Cortés from his position of authority in Mexico, Bono de Quejo seemed to realize the futility of this last mission and even regularly visited with the *caudillo* as a dinner guest.

Rebecca M. Seaman

See also: Colón, Diego; Cortés, Hernán; Grijalva, Juan de; La Noche Triste; Narváez, Pánfilo de; Tenochtitlán, City of; Velázquez, Diego (de Cuéllar).

Resources

Bancroft, Hubert Howe. *The Works of Hubert Howe Bancroft: History of Mexico.* Vol. 2. San Francisco: The History Company, Publishers, 1886.

Díaz del Castillo, Bernal. *The Conquest of New Spain.* London: Penguin Books, 1963.

Levy, Buddy. *Conquistador: Hernán Cortés, King Montezuma, and the Last Stand of the Aztecs.* New York: Bantam Books, 2008.

Thomas, Hugh. *Conquest: Montezuma, Cortés, and the Fall of Old Mexico.* New York: Simon & Schuster Press, 1993.

Brigantines, Use by Cortés

The Spanish flat-bottomed boats, brigantines, were instrumental in their eventual conquest of the city of Tenochtitlán. However, the advantage gained was not what Cortés initially envisioned.

The Spanish under Cortés were well armed and possessed some horses, yet the arms and steeds proved to be of little advantage when attacking the Mexica capital of Tenochtitlán. The construction of the main city on an island, with drawbridges and canals fashioned for ease of transportation or for use in defending the city, made the use of a traditional Spanish attack or siege ineffective. Instead, Cortés opted to take advantage of the canals and lake to facilitate an attack by water. Though Cortés destroyed the ships his forces had arrived upon landing along the Yucatán coast, it is quite likely all the valuable equipment, ropes, and sails were recovered for future use. This might well have included the necessary materials to construct coastal vessels of the day, Spanish brigantines.

Hernán Cortés overseeing construction of brigantines. (Album/Art Resource, NY)

With the Tlaxcala as allies, the Spanish began to build 13 brigantines for use in an attack on the Aztec capital city. These fast vessels, 40 feet long, with flat bottoms, shallow drafts and the use of sails and oars to propel them forward, were able to carry the Spanish soldiers, as well as the few cannon and horses under Cortés's control. The brigantines were transported in pieces over land by the Tlaxcala allies of the Spanish and then were assembled on site. Cortés also addressed the problem of launching the ships without the knowledge and interference of the Mexica. To accomplish this, he secretly had an enclosed canal built that flowed into the lake surrounding Tenochtitlán.

On the day the attack began, Cortés sent the alguacil mayor or high constable, Gonzalo de Sandoval, with approximately 35,000 allies, to launch a diversionary attack upon the city of Iztapalapa. Using the brigantines, Cortés and his men sailed onto the lake where they encountered a fleet of canoes. After an initial hesitation on the part of both forces, a wind caught the brigantine sails and the Spanish mowed down the opposing canoes. The initial advance of the Spanish was successful, but the resistance they met from the rooftops made securing the captured causeways impossible.

As the siege dragged on for months, Cortés eventually ordered the aqueducts that supplied water to the city be destroyed. He then used the brigantines to clear the lake of Mexica, thereby assaulting the city from land and water. With freshwater supplies cut and food stores gone, desperation set in for the city and its residents. The spread of Spanish diseases from earlier contact furthered the impact of the siege. Eventually, after almost four months of devastating losses on both sides, the Spanish siege proved successful and resulted in the Aztec emperor, Cuauhtémoc, surrendering Tenochtitlán to the Spanish under Cortés.

Rebecca M. Seaman

See also: Cuauhtémoc; Sandoval, Gonzalo de; Tenochtitlán, Siege of.

Resources

Cortés, Hernando. *Five Letters of Cortés to the Emperor: The Spanish Invasion of Mexico and the Conquest of Montezuma's Empire, as Seen through the Eyes of the Spanish Conqueror.* Translated and with an Introduction by J. Bayard Morris. New York: W.W. Norton, 1991.

Eakin, Marshall C. *The History of Latin America: Collision of Cultures.* Basingstoke: Palgrave Macmillan, 2007.

Sahagún, Bernardino de. *The Florentine Codex: A General History of the Things of New Spain: Book 12: The Conquest of Mexico.* Translated by Arthur J. O. Anderson and Charles E. Dibble. Salt Lake: University of Utah Press, 1975.

C

Cabildo

A traditional form of local governmental structure, the cabildo was a Spanish town council or independent town corporation. European encomendero elite in the American colonies controlled these municipal councils. The Spanish intended the cabildos to endear the local native societies to European governance and thereby prevent abuses that might give rise to uprisings that threatened Spanish settlements and authority.

The establishment of traditional cabildos occurred rapidly as the Spanish allotted lands and labor assignments to the conquerors. In Middle America, this European dominance remained for years. On the frontiers of Mexico, where fewer Spanish civilians settled, the cabildos quickly fell into disuse and were replaced by the establishment of military officers, serving as governors, magistrates, and councils.

In Lima, Peru, as early as the 1550s, encomenderos dominated the cabildo and used it to establish rules and guidelines for society—both native and Spanish. This colonial council oversaw the enforcement of local justice, set limits on the price of corn, regulated weights and measurements, and controlled other sales and contracts for items such as bread and coca leaf. The municipal organization also regulated abuses of the ecology, like deforestation, that affected local societies and their landscapes. Even city planning, such as the assignment of lots for town and granting acreage for farming, fell under the purview of the cabildos.

The Spanish in Peru additionally set up native cabildos as a means of controlling the scattered communities of Indians. Juan de Matienzo advocated this integration of the European cabildo into native societies. Matienzo was a distinguished jurist of the 16th century who also believed the Inca held the advantage over the Spanish in the exchange of religious indoctrination and acculturation for simple silver and gold (which he failed to note was mined by native slave labor). Accordingly, he proposed an inspection and resettlement program to reduce the scattered Indian communities, based on kin relations, into towns. This same inspection provided valuable information for the assignment of tributes and forced labor or *mita*, redistribution of land, and the reorganization of community structures.

The end result of Matienzo's plan was the enhanced control by the Spanish over a group of appointed Indian functionaries who served as the native cabildos. These Indian municipal structures were to work in league with the local *kurakas* (native nobles) who increasingly gained authority through land assignments and marriage relations with Spanish encomenderos. Don Francisco de Toledo implemented Matienzo's plan to reorganize native societies into Indian cabildos. During his 12-year reign as viceroy, Toledo spent five years traveling throughout the Andes on inspections designed to force the reorganization of the region. The result was a Spanish-dominated cabildo in Lima, with Indian cabildos serving the Spanish along the frontiers.

By 1600, local governance of the Spanish colonies was directly in the hands of the encomenderos, military leaders, or native cabildos. Whatever form the municipal organizations took, they culminated in the continued acculturation of native peoples into Spanish religious, social, economic, and political structures.

Rebecca M. Seaman

See also: Encomenderos; *Kurakas*; *Mita*; Toledo, Francisco de.

Resources

Clendinnen, Inga. *Ambivalent Conquests: Maya and Spaniard in Yucatan, 1517–1570.* 2nd ed. New York: Cambridge University Press, 2003.

Stern, Steve J. *Peru's Indian Peoples and the Challenge of Spanish Conquest: Huamanga to 1640.* 2nd ed. Madison: University of Wisconsin Press, 1993.

Weber, David J. *The Spanish Frontier in North America.* New Haven, CT: Yale University Press, 1992.

Cacama

Born circa 1468, Cacama (Cacamatzin) was one of several sons born to the Texcoco *tlatoani* Nezahualpilli. Cacama's father, while the leader of Texcoco, a city in alliance with Tenochtitlán and the Mexica Empire, was nonetheless in bad standing with the Aztec emperor, Montezuma II. Having executed his wife in public (sister of Montezuma), for adultery, Nezahualpilli further aggravated relations with the Mexica by giving safe haven to Montezuma's elder brother who was passed over for leadership of the Aztec Empire. In the midst of a contrived war designed to unseat the Texcoco *tlatoani,* Nezahualpilli died.

The void created by the death of his only legitimate son created a succession crisis. To resolve the dilemma, Texcoco lords and the Mexica emperor were designated electors. Montezuma's animosity toward the deceased *tlatoani* swayed the election in favor of the emperor's nephew by his late sister—Cacama. The decision was not without opposition, as Cacama's younger brother contested the election and a civil war ensued. At the conclusion of the hostilities, Cacama remained the *tlatoani* of the southern portion of Texcoco, while Ixtlilxochitl held the northern section.

Cacama's reign proved rather short. Coming into power in 1516 (dates vary between 1515 and 1517), the young *tlatoani* was a strong supporter of his maternal uncle and benefactor, Montezuma. With the arrival of Cortés, and the Spanish welcome by enemies of the Mexica, Cacama aligned his portion of Texcoco with the Aztec, and served as a close advisor to the emperor, serving on Montezuma's supreme council. Reportedly, Cacama's advice, which contradicted the more militantly defensive advice of Cuitláhuac, Montezuma's brother and presumed heir, was to welcome the Spanish as official dignitaries, relying upon the military to defend the emperor, should such defense be needed.

Following this meeting, in the summer of 1519, Cacama sent emissaries, nephews of Montezuma, to continue negotiations and report back on the Spanish. These emissaries returned with the helmet sent by Cortés, filled with gold dust, as a means of fulfilling the Spanish craving for the metal. Instead of quenching their thirst for gold, the gift wetted the appetite of the invading foreigners. As the Spanish continued their advance toward Tenochtitlán, they were welcomed by Ixtlilxochitl, *tlatoani* of the northern portion of Texcoco. Cacama's advice to the emperor now shifted to coincide with that of Cuitláhuac, urging Montezuma to block admission of the Spanish to the capital and to make war on the invaders.

Montezuma finally determined to welcome the Spanish, and even sent his nephew, Cacama, as an emissary to help ensure peaceful relations. Despite Cacama's distrust of Cortés, he followed his emperor's wishes, treating the conquistador with the Mexican cordiality accorded to all ambassadors of foreign monarchs.

In November 1519, Cortés's forces finally entered Tenochtitlán, where they were greeted by Montezuma and his nobles, including Cacama. Good relations prevailed for almost a week, at which point Cortés, fearful of his precarious position, took the emperor hostage. Before the end of the year, Cacama fled the city, disgusted with the lack of resistance of the Mexica and determined to free his uncle from the Spanish. Returning to Texcoco, Cacama vainly hoped to align with his previously alienated brother, Ixtlilxochitl. Instead, he was himself captured and returned to Tenochtitlán, where he was imprisoned with Montezuma.

In an effort to win his freedom, Cacama convinced Cortés to send men to Texcoco to retrieve gold for the Spanish. The delegation returned to Tenochtitlán with a large quantity of gold and other items of value. Not content, Cortés sent Cacama back to the city with Pedro de Alvarado. Tortured by the Spanish to reveal more of the Texcoco wealth, Cacama produced more valuables. After returning to Tenochtitlán, the *tlatoani* was held in chains with other lords of the Mexica Empire.

Cortés's nemesis Pánfilo de Narváez landed on the coast of Mexico in April 1520. Splitting his forces, Cortés left to engage Narváez, leaving Alvarado to hold the capital city. Vastly outnumbered and led by one of the more reactionary of the conquistadors, events soon got out of control for the Spanish.

Interpreting the preparations for one of the Aztec feasts to be a cover for an uprising, Alvarado ordered his forces to attack the celebrating Mexica on the final day of the feast. The massacre of the unarmed dancers was accompanied by the Spanish killing most of the chained and imprisoned lords. Cacama, still numbered among the Spanish prisoners, died during the butchery known as the Toxcatl massacre, on May 16, 1520.

Rebecca M. Seaman

See also: Cortés, Hernán; Cuitláhuac; Ixtlilxochitl II; Montezuma II; Narváez, Pánfilo de; Texcoco, Alliance with Tenochtitlán; Toxcatl Massacre.

Resources

Allen, Heather. "Literacy, Text, and Performance in the Histories of the Conquest of Mexico." PhD diss., University of Chicago, 2011.

Gillespie, Susan D. *The Aztec Kings: The Construction of Rulership in Mexica History.* Tucson: University of Arizona Press, 1989.

León-Portilla, Miguel. *The Broken Spears: The Aztec Account of the Conquest of Mexico.* Foreword by J. Jorge Klor de Alva. Boston: Beacon Press, 2006.

Thomas, Hugh. *Conquest: Montezuma, Cortés, and the Fall of Old Mexico.* New York: Simon & Schuster, 1993.

Cáceres, Joan de

A conquistador under Hernán Cortés during the conquest of the Aztecs, Joan de Cáceres served as the *caudillo*'s majordomo, or steward, responsible for overseeing all of his household. One of the many from Extremadura who came from the same region in Spain as Cortés, Cáceres was a loyal and trusted associate. According to Bernal Díaz, who accompanied the Cortés expedition and later recorded a brief history of the Spanish conquest, the *caudillo* began to affect the mannerisms and status of a Lord while still at Havana in Cuba, which included structuring a full household with a chamberlain and majordomo—Cáceres.

Cáceres's constant presence at all official and most unofficial encounters between the *caudillo* and other native or Spanish dignitaries during the entire expedition made the majordomo an invaluable source of information regarding the events that lead to the Spanish conquest of the region. To this end, Cáceres was questioned regarding Cortés's actions and policies during an enquiry against the conquistador years later. The wealth of information that Cáceres may have provided historians was limited to the records from the enquiry, however, due to the majordomo's illiteracy. Despite this limitation, his service to the *caudillo* proved profitable for the majordomo, who was quite wealthy by the end of the conquest of Mexico.

Rebecca M. Seaman

See also: Cortés, Hernán; Díaz del Castillo, Bernal.

Resources

Díaz, Bernal. *The Conquest of New Spain.* Translated by J.M. Cohen. London: Penguin Books, 1963.

Thomas, Hugh. *Conquest: Montzuma, Cortés, and the Fall of Old Mexico.* New York: Simon & Schuster, 1993.

Cajamarca, Battle of

The Battle of Cajamarca on November 16, 1532, was perhaps the most definitive battle of the Inca-Spanish War and led to the eventual execution of Inca emperor Atahualpa.

After initial probes along the coast of South America, Spanish conquistador Francisco Pizarro put together a small expeditionary force, including his four brothers. The purpose of Pizarro's expedition was to further explore the interior of the continent, rumored to possess vast amounts of gold. The men arrived in Panama in December 1531. Consisting of 180 men and 30 horses, this force sailed down the west coast of South America, landing at Tumbes on the Peruvian coast in spring 1532 where Pizarro established the coastal settlement of San Miguel. Hernando de Soto joined them there with additional 100 men and 50 horses.

Pizarro's force departed San Miguel in September 1532 and began the ascent of the Andes. The Inca leader Atahualpa, aware of the Spanish progress and in the midst of a civil war with his brother for control of the Inca Empire, sent several deputations bearing gifts of welcome. The presents, some in gold, only heightened Pizarro's hopes. On November 15, Pizarro's men descended a pass that overlooked the Inca city of Cajamarca. The Spanish found the city deserted but were impressed with its massive stone buildings that included several forts. Atahualpa was camped, with some 6,000 warriors and royal attendants (some sources give a figure as great as 30,000–40,000 warriors), in tents near Cajamarca as Pizarro and his men occupied the city.

Pizarro sent 45 horsemen under his brother Hernando Pizarro and Hernando de Soto to ride into the Inca camp and meet with Atahualpa. Horses were unknown to the Incas and may have induced them to believe (as the Aztecs had) that the men mounted on them were emissaries from the gods. Despite this seeming disadvantage, Atahualpa revealed no anxiety.

Spanish emissaries invited Atahualpa to meet with Pizarro in Cajamarca. Atahualpa informed the Spaniards through an aide that they were fasting but would visit the next day. Pizarro planned to duplicate Hernán

Cortés's tactic of seizing the native people's ruler. Pizarro's men were concerned, for they were cut off from additional support with only 100 infantry, 67 cavalry, and were outnumbered at least 35 to 1.

Pizarro deployed his men in the large halls fronting the central square of the city. Atahualpa appeared in the afternoon of November 16, borne on a palanquin with 6,000 warriors and attendants (some sources say 10,000) marching the four miles from their camp. Atahualpa and the procession halted about half a mile from the city, where he sent word to Pizarro that he would not visit that day. Knowing the wait would severely test his men, Pizarro sent word that food and entertainments had been prepared. Perhaps

other inducements were offered as well, for the procession began again, passing between rows of warriors lining the road on either side.

On Atahualpa's arrival in the plaza, Father Vicente de Valverde met him. The Catholic priest told the emperor about Christ and of the Spanish king, Charles V (Carlos I). Growing impatient, Atahualpa took the Bible from Valverde, opened it to look inside, and then threw it to the ground. Valverde snatched up the Bible and ran from the plaza.

As soon as Valverde cleared off the area, Pizarro signaled to open fire on the square with two small cannons. At the same time, Spanish cavalry issued from the buildings flanking the square. The Incas had come

Seizure of Atahualpa, Sapa Inca, as prisoner of Spanish under Francisco Pizarro. (Library of Congress)

as emissaries and were either not armed or armed only with slings and javelins under their clothing and therefore could not resist the Spaniards' heavy cavalry, firearms, and swords. Atahualpa was the only Inca taken alive. Pizarro, mistakenly cut by one of his own men, was the only Spanish casualty according to most sources. Surprisingly, the thousands of warriors outside the city made no effort to come to the rescue of the emperor.

Atahualpa's army began to melt away, especially those men conscripted into it from the newly conquered territories. Atahualpa bargained with Pizarro for his release, offering to fill a room 17-by-22 feet and roughly seven feet high with gold and a second, smaller room twice over with silver. Pizarro agreed, but at the same time he sent Soto to Cuzco to meet with rival emperor Huáscar Inca. On being informed of the Spanish victory at Cajamarca, Huáscar said he would meet with Pizarro and supply even more gold from his father's secret storehouses. Pizarro informed Atahualpa of this, who sent word through an attendant for his generals in the capital to kill Huáscar, which they did.

Although the gold and silver were delivered as promised, Pizarro refused to release Atahualpa for fear of reprisals by loyal Inca military forces. Instead, Atahualpa was charged with the murder of his brother, convicted, and sentenced to be burned at the stake as a heathen. Atahualpa agreed to convert to Christianity and was rewarded by having his execution commuted to strangulation. Control of the area then passed to Pizarro, who spent the next several years quelling rebellions throughout the region.

Spencer C. Tucker

See also: Atahualpa; Charles V (HRE), or Carlos I of Spain; Huáscar; Pizarro, Francisco; Pizarro, Hernando; Soto, Hernando de, in Peru.

Resources

Means, Philip A. *The Fall of the Inca Empire and the Spanish Rule in Peru, 1530–1780.* New York: Gordian Press, 1971.

Prescott, William H. *The History of the Conquest of Peru.* New York: New American Library, 1961.

Richman, Irving Berdine. *Adventures of New Spain: The Spanish Conquerors.* New Haven, CT: Yale University Press, 1929.

Calendar System of Aztec

The Aztec's calendar system provided a way to count time that governed all aspects of life in central Mexico before the Spanish arrived. This system was also known as the Calendar Round. It had its origins in the first millennium BC in the Olmec culture that developed in the Gulf of Mexico, to which belongs a stone inscribed with numerals accompanied by other signs. It was later passed down to all Mesoamerican cultures, which introduced small regional variables.

Basically, the calendar system consisted of two cycles, called *tonalpohualli* and *xiuhpohualli*. *Tonalpohualli* can be translated as "count of the days" or "count of the fates," due to the double meaning of the word *tonalli* (for the Maya, who developed a very similar calendar system much earlier, it is called *tzolk'in*). It consisted of 260 days, as a result of combining the numbers from 1 to 13 with 20 names of days. The names were arranged in this order: *Cipactli* (crocodile), *Ehecatl* (wind), *Calli* (house), *Cuetzpallin* (lizard), *Coatl* (snake), *Miquiztli* (death), *Mazatl* (deer), *Tochtli* (rabbit), *Atl* (water), *Itzcuintli* (dog), *Ozomatli* (monkey), *Malinalli* (grass), *Acatl* (cane), *Ocelotl* (jaguar), *Cuauhtli* (eagle), *Cozcacuauhtli* (buzzard), *Ollin* (movement), *Tecpatl* (flint knife), *Quiahuitl* (rain), and *Xochitl* (flower). This

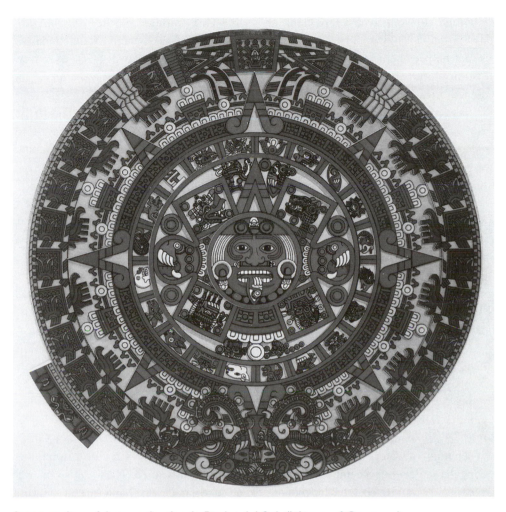

Stone replica of Aztec calendar, la Piedra del Sol. (Library of Congress)

complex system of 20 day-names combined with 13 numerals each used a continuous account. The sequence was: 1 Cipactli, 2 Ehecatl, 3 Calli, 4 Cuetzpallin, and so forth. Each of the sequences progressed one position per day, and at the end, the combination started again. That is, the number 13 was always followed by 1—repeating the cycle; and the figures were accompanied by the consecutive name of the day. Thus, the first day of the cycle of 260 days was *1 Cipactli* and the last one was *13 Xochitl.*

This calendar was also known as the "foreteller calendar," but it was actually a ritual calendar that marked the celebration of different religious ceremonies. The peculiarity was that each numeral and each day sign were related with gods and were associated with some special characteristics. The result was multiple combinations that sometimes were considered favorable, sometimes indifferent, and at other times fateful. Because of this complexity, the Aztec had priests who were experts in the interpretation of the days. This was a very important issue when people wanted to start a business, to arrange a marriage, or to name a newborn, among another matters. The priests were known as *tonalpouhqui* (the one who keeps track of the days or fates). They made use of painted books that helped them make their calculations. Some of these books are among the ritual calendar group of pre-Hispanic codex, as well as one section of *Codex Borbonicus* and the *Aubin Tonalamatl.* They were organized in *trecenas* (groups of 13 elements) that were named with each one of the signs of the days. The number of the day that was at the top conferred part of the features of the *trecena,* such as increasing or decreasing the level of good or bad influences of the different days. The total number of them was 20.

The second cycle, the *xiuhpohualli* or "count of the year," is known as the ritual or sun cycle (the Mayan version is called *Haab*). It consisted of 365 days, in 18 months of 20 days named *metztli* (month, moon; in Maya language, *uinal*), plus a short cycle of 5 days that completed the account. The year began on the day *1 Izcalli* (growth, the name of the first month), followed by *2 Izcalli,* and so on up to *20 Izcalli.* After that, came *1 Atlacahualo* (detention of water, the second month), following the same sequence until the last day of the year, *20 Tititl* (stretch, the 22nd month). After these 360 days came five days called *Nemontemi* (*Wayeb* in Maya language), and after them, the cycle started again. The *Nemontemi* days were believed to be vain and tragic. During these days, the Aztecs tried not to do anything more than daily life necessities. Those born in during the *Nemontemi* days were considered unfortunate.

Both calendar cycles combined to name each day and year, and to establish longer cycles. The combination received the name of Calendar Round. Thus, one date of the Round consisted of four elements:

- One number of the *tonalpohualli* series of 13.
- One name of the *tonalpohualli* list of 20.

- One number of the *xiuhpohualli* series of 20, which changed daily and was repeated every 20, except when it accompanied the *Nemontemi* month (numbering only 1–5).
- One name of the *xiuhpohualli* list of 19 months, which changed every 19 days, except during *Nemontemi* (changing after 5 days).

The presence of the month of five days conferred peculiarity to the system and made it difficult to establish equivalence with the Gregorian calendar. Due to the particular sequence of 20 days and five positions advancing each year, it took four years for the calendar system to coincide. This circumstance led to the existence of four types of years, characterized by the position the *tonalpohualli* days occupied within the *xiuhpohualli* months. They were named by the day of *tonalpohualli* associated with the last day of the year, *20 Tititl.* Thus, the names of the years were *Acatl, Tecpatl, Calli,* and *Tochtli,* each one with a corresponding numeral, from 1 to 13. These days were known as "carriers of year" and served to designate it. Since there were 13 numbers and 4 days, the sequence repeated every 52 years of 365 days. This time period was called *xiuhmolpilli* (binding of the years), and included 52 *xiuhpohualli* and 73 *tonalpohualli.*

At the end of each cycle in a year *2 Acatl,* as it appears in most annals, the great feast known as the New Fire was commemorated. This was a delicate moment, because at sunset, Aztecs did not know if the sun would rise again. To bring about this event and to begin a new cycle, all fires were extinguished and the priests lit a new one in a temple at the top of *Citlaltepetl* (the hill of the star), while they conducted one human sacrifice.

In addition, there were other cycles of different durations, such as the series of the

9 Lords of the Night or the synodic revolution of Venus, which is estimated in 584 days. The latter was an important cycle called *Huehuetiliztli* (old age), equivalent to two Calendar Rounds.

The calculation of the dates through both forms served to organize the religious life of the Aztecs. According to the two main cycles, there were two types of feasts: the "fixed," associated with the 365-day calendar and the "movable," identified by the one of 260-day calendar.

Marta Martín Gabaldón

See also: Aztec, or Mexica; Mexico, State of prior to Spanish Conquest.

Resources

Boone, Elisabeth H. *Cycles of Time and Meaning in the Mexican Books of Fate.* Austin: University of Texas Press, 2007.

Leon Portilla, Miguel. *Aztec Thought and Culture: A Study of the Ancient Nahuatl Mind.* Translated by Jack Emory Davis. Norman: University of Oklahoma Press, 1963.

Nicholson, Henri B. "Religion in Pre-Hispanic Central Mexico." *Handbook of Middle American Indians,* vol. 10. Edited by Robert Wauchope. Austin: University of Texas Press, 1971: 395–446.

Read, Kay A. *Time and Sacrifice in the Aztec Cosmos.* Bloomington: Indiana University Press, 1998.

Smith, Michael E. *The Aztecs.* Oxford: Blackwell, 1996.

Calendar System of Inca

The Inca employed two calendars, one based on solar cycles and the other on lunar cycles. The daytime calendar, based on the movements of the sun, was approximately 365 days long and was used for economic activities such as agriculture, construction, and warfare. The lunar calendar consisted of 41 eight-day weeks and was used to schedule rituals and religious celebrations. How the Inca dealt with the 37-day discrepancy between the two is unknown. There are few physical artifacts relating to the calendars. In part, studies are complicated by the lack of a written language. The Inca retained important information on *quipus*—a system of intricately knotted and colored strings used to record data, which are not well understood. The almost total destruction of the Inca culture by the invading Spanish in the 16th century, which included the eventual banning of *quipus*, also contributed to the lack of information and physical artifacts.

The Incas kept a close eye on the sky, but were primarily concerned with the movements of the sun, moon, and certain constellations. Most astronomical bodies were considered to be deities; therefore they were simply venerated. The Pleiades were a particular focus, because their appearance and disappearance aligned with the planting and harvesting of maize, a crucial crop. It was also believed that the brightness of that star cluster determined the crop yield.

As sun worshippers, the Incas became experts of horizon astronomy—tracking celestial events as they occur on the horizon of the hills around Cuzco, the capital of the empire. Pillars on the hills tracked the positions of celestial objects to determine the timing for crop planting and harvest, and dates for important rituals and ceremonies. Temples and observatories were also built for that purpose in outlying administrative and religious centers.

The Incas had a very complex ceremonial calendar, filled with rituals corresponding to the agricultural year. Additional ceremonies for special occasions were huge, theatrical events, taking place in large plazas of cities and administrative centers that could accommodate the masses. The lunar calendar began in December—the onset of the rainy season and the summer solstice. The first month, Capac Raymi, means "principal festival," and was the most important event of the year. Coca, potatoes, and quinoa were planted. Puberty rituals were held for boys and girls; feasts, festivities, and sacrifices were offered; and taxes and gifts for the Sapa Inca arrived in Cuzco.

January (Camay Quilla) found farmers preparing their fields for more crops. A continuation of the previous months' puberty ceremonies included a mock battle among the boys raised to adult status. Later in the summer, during February (Hatun Puquy) and March (Pacha Puquy), potatoes and other root vegetables were harvested. Llamas and guinea pigs were sacrificed nightly in rituals to improve grain and corn yields. April (Ariguaquiz) had farmers chasing away animals and birds from the newly sprouted corn plants. Additional ceremonies encouraged crops to ripen for harvest. The sixth month (Hatun Cuzqui) was the month of great cultivation, much like our present-day Thanksgiving. The maize harvest was celebrated and ceremonies honoring the Sapa Inca took place. In June (Aucay Cuzqui), the winter solstice festival of Inti Raymi was celebrated. Called the warriors cultivation, Inti Raymi was only attended by male Incas with royal blood. During the ceremony, 100 brown llamas were sacrificed to the sun on a hill near Cuzco. July (Chahua Harquiz) was the heart of the Inca winter. Foods were freeze-dried for storage, and men served their required labor to the state by repairing roads, bridges, canals, and irrigation systems. Additional sacrifices were offered to the gods for blessings on the systems that carried needed water to their fields.

A spring-like season slowly arrived in the ninth month of August (Yapaquiz), and September (Coya Raymi) began another planting season. Additional grain and vegetable crops were planted only after corn and potato crops were secure. The solemn festival of Citua was celebrated to prevent illness, and marked the beginning of the rainy season, when many people were likely to get sick. Rites were performed to cleanse and purify Cuzco and its residents. Days of dancing and feasting followed. October (K'antaray) was dedicated to promoting ample crops. The primary concern was to have sufficient water for the maturing crops—but not too much water. The usual sacrifice of 100 llamas took place, but if there was drought, additional sacrifices were made to coerce the gods to provide rain. The final month of the ritual calendar, Ayamarca, corresponded to November on the modern calendar. This season was for honoring the dead and for preparing the young men who would be initiated as adults in the next month.

Some rituals were held on special occasions not tied to the ceremonial calendar. The most important, Itu Raymi, was used to get the attention of the gods during dire circumstances. When there was a severe crisis, such as a plague, severe drought, natural disaster, or a war, visitors from the provinces were expelled from Cuzco. Citizens would fast, perform rituals, and make sacrifices of llamas or children, depending on the severity of the crisis. A two daylong feast followed, with dancing and drinking.

Funerals, especially of the Inca ruler, required extremely elaborate rituals. Family members of the deceased wore black for up to one year after the death. For the funeral of the ruler, ceremonies lasted about a month and thousands of llamas and children were sacrificed in his name. The coronation of a new emperor similarly involved lavish ritual and sacrifice.

While work consumed the daily lives of the Inca via the solar calendar, religion dominated the nocturnal calendar. Every month contained at least one major religious celebration and three or more lesser rituals, totaling 120 days of religious ceremony throughout the year. The Inca believed that nothing happened spontaneously—everything was caused by a supernatural force. These ceremonies had to be performed at specific times to encourage the gods to look with favor on the Incas.

Jill M. Church

See also: *Quipu*; Sapa Inca.

Resources

Aveni, Anthony F. *Stairways to the Stars: Sky-watching in Three Great Ancient Cultures*. New York: Wiley, 1997.

Bauer, Brian S. *Astronomy and Empire in the Ancient Andes: The Cultural Origins of Inca Sky Watching*. Austin, TX: University of Texas Press, 1995.

D'Altroy, Terence N. *The Incas*. Malden, MA: Blackwell, 2002.

McEwan, Gordon. *The Incas: New Perspectives*. New York: W.W. Norton and Company. 2006.

Calendar System of Maya

The Maya of Middle America developed a calendar system that was more precise than the systems found in Europe at the same time. Though still uncertain how such precision was accomplished, it is apparent the Maya developed this system over 1,000 years before the Gregorian modifications were made to the European Julian Calendar. In reality, the Maya constructed three different calendar systems: the 260-day sacred year, or tzolkin, based on counts of 13 days; the 360-day year (tun) involving lunar months, based on 18 months of 20 days; and the "perfect year" calendar of 365 days, or haab, which added five days and 6 hours to form a precise solar year.

The calendar system traditionally used (haab) was based on the Maya's numerical system. The Maya used a counting system that was based on fives and twenties. In a like fashion, the calendar system commonly employed months (uinals) of 20 days (kins). Eighteen months completed a year of 360 days (tun), with an additional five days and six hours incorporated to account for the 365.242 days earth took to rotate around the sun. The extra six hours were incorporated every four years as an extra day. The result is a virtually perfect year. To account for the minimal error, and to align dates involving religious ceremonies with the more secular haab calendar, a more complex, extended "Calendar Round" was developed.

The Calendar Round attempted to synchronize the tzolkin and haab calendars to weave the religious ceremonies so integral to the Mayan society and calendric systems, with the more secular aspects of governing and business. Combining the 20-day cycles with the religious cycles based on the numbers 1 through 13, the Maya created a vast number of combinations. The result was the "Calendar Round" of 52 years—the precise number of years before any particular date returned to the original position it held at a calendar sequence.

The tun calendric system separated the 20-day cycles from the additional five plus days of the solar year. This calendar was involved in the Long Count calendric records: containing 20 days in a cycle; 18 cycles in a tun (360 day year); 20 tuns in a katun (7,200 days); 20 katuns in a baktun (144,000 days); 20 baktuns in a pictun (2,880,000 days); 20 pictuns in a calabtun (57,600,000 days); 20 calabtuns in a kinchiltun (1,152,000,000 days); and

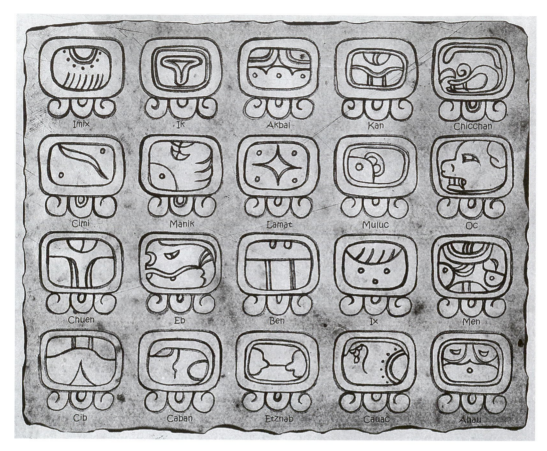

Maya calendar's glyphs of 20-day cycle. (Airi Pung/Dreamstime)

20 kinchiltuns in an alautun (23,040,000, 000 days). The purpose of this complex system was an extremely accurate calendar that enabled the Maya to monitor vast spans of time with relative ease. Before the arrival of the Spanish, the Long Count calendar was replaced with a shorter version. The Short Count employed the 20-day month, an 18-month year, 20 tuns of 360 days comprising each katun, and then 13 katuns completing a short count cycle of approximately 256-1/4 of Gregorian calendar years.

The 18 months in the traditional Mayan calendar, starting at their New Year (mid-July), were as follows: Pop, Uo, Sip, Sotz, Tzec, Xul, Yazkin, Mol, Ch'en, Yax, Sac, Ceh, Mac, Kankin, Muan, Pax, Kayab, and Cumhu. These were followed by the five "unlucky" days of Wayeb. These months were associated with specific activities, such as sowing crops, harvests, and hunts. Additionally, each month typically had specific feast days and ceremonies to help protect the society from associated evils for that period within the year.

Each 20-day cycle was assigned 20 characters, aligned in the traditional groups of five days per cycle, with four cycles for the month. The start of each of the four cycles within the month was known as Kan, Muluc, Ix, and Cauac. Each year of the four-year cycle had one of these four numbered days associated with it—for a year of Kan, a year of Muluc, and so forth. Each of the four designated years had its own augury that was appeased in the celebrations during the extra five days prior to the start of the year associated with the augury. The four designations were also associated with the four cardinal directions of south, east, north and west, as well as the colors red, white, black, and yellow, respectively. In each respective year, a set of ceremonies was held, using the city gate corresponding with the cardinal direction of the year.

The five remaining days of each year were never named, as such a practice was considered unlucky. The five days were used as ceremonies and rites that guaranteed success in the impending New Year by appeasing the gods. In the year designated Kan, the augury was Hobnil, and the demon appeased through the celebrations was Kan-uvayeyab. An additional demon, Bolon-tz'acab, was represented by a statue erected in a public location within the town, typically the house of the community leader in charge of the festivities. Additional sacrifices, often of blood, were made to the demon Kanal-acantun. These ensured an escape from illness in the following year. Special incense and drinks were also incorporated into the celebrations, typically based in part on maize, likely in an effort to protect the local crops. As a final portion of the celebrations for the year Kan, a sacrifice of a dog or human, was made to the idol Itzamná-kauil, presenting the heart of the dog or human along with a variety of food.

The year assigned the character Muluc was associated with the augury of Cansicnal. For preparation of this year's cycle, the demon to be appeased was Chac-uvayeyab, along with the additional demon Kinchahau. This latter demon's statue as placed in the house of a leading figure, where similar ceremonies involved incense and maize. Following gifts of food and other offerings, sacrifices of human blood were taken forcibly from young boys. Special sacrifices of squirrels and unembroidered cloth completed the celebration of the unlucky five days prior to the start of the year Muluc, designed to protect against drought and blights on the maize crop.

Similarly, the year Ix was associated with the augury Sac-sini, and the demon Sac-uvayeyab. The leader of the unlucky-day festivities had a statue of the god Itzamná placed outside his residence. Following the traditional sacrifices of incense and maize and dances, special offerings of turkey and quail, as well as offerings of blood were presented to prevent feared evils such as various physical ailments, drought, hunger, thefts, and conflicts.

The New Year represented by the character Cauac had the following attributes. The augury was Hosan-ek and the demon was represented by a statute outside the western gate of the town was Ek-uvayeyab. An additional statue of the demon Vacmitun-ahau was located in front of the house of the principal leader of the festivities. In addition to the traditional sacrifices of incense- and maize-based drinks, blood sacrifices and dances were offered to the demon Ekel-acantun. These sacrifices ensured an escape from the possibility of death, failed crops, devastation by ants and birds, and ensuing hunger.

In addition to accounting for four-year cycles to accommodate the additional six hours in the solar year, the Maya also broke down their Katun (20-year periods) into two 10-year periods; each was associated with separate idols or spirits. The first 10 years were devoted to a series of sacrifices and ceremonies designed to protect the region from serious harm, all devoted to the first idol. The later 10 years of any 20-year cycle was marked by the burning of incense to the second idol as a means of sustaining the same protections for the community.

It is no surprise, with the extreme complexity involved, that the Spanish did not embrace this system. The integration of the calendar system into the faith of the Mayas, considered idolatrous by the Spanish friars and conquistadors, provided further justification for the rejection. Despite the detailed and exact science behind the system of accounting for the days of the year and cycles of years, the Mayan calendar fell victim to the spread of Spanish culture and Catholicism in the Yucatán region.

Rebecca M. Seaman

See also: Calendar System of Aztec; Calendar System of Inca; Maya.

Resources

Clendinnen, Inga. *Ambivalent Conquests: Maya and Spaniard in Yucatan, 1517–1570.* 2nd ed. Cambridge: Cambridge University Press, 2003.

Gallenkamp, Charles. *Maya: The Riddle and Rediscovery of a Lost Civilization.* 3rd rev. ed. New York: Viking Penguin, 1985.

Landa, Friar Diego de. *Yucatan: Before and After the Conquest.* Translated with Notes by William Gates. New York: Dover Publications, 1978.

Schwartz, Stuart B., ed. *Victors and Vanquished: Spanish and Nahua Views of the Conquest of Mexico.* Boston: Bedford/St. Martin's, 2000.

Camargo, Diego Múñoz

Born ca. 1525, Diego Múñoz Camargo was the son of the Spanish conquistador Diego Múñoz and a noblewoman of the Tlaxcala. As a mestizo growing up in the early colonial days of New Spain, Camargo was immersed in the culture and language of both parents. At a young age, he was tasked with providing instruction regarding the Catholic faith to Indians who had arrived in Mexico with Cabeza de Vaca. Camargo later served as governor of Tlaxcala, holding the position repeatedly over the years. He additionally used his family connections to retain strong ties to leading Spanish authorities in New Spain for the first century of its existence.

According to Hubert Howe Bancroft, in 1579, Diego Camargo was commissioned by the Spanish Crown to write a report of the Tlaxcala. Much of the information from that report appears in the massive collection known as the *Relaciones Geográficas* (Geographic Relationships). Between 1576 and 1595, Camargo also compiled a history of the Tlaxcala entitled *Historia de la Cuidad y República de Tlaxcala* (History of the City and Republic of Tlaxcala). The completed work contained three books. Book one covered the history of pre-conquest Tlaxcala from the indigenous perspective. In this volume, Camargo related how these enemies of the Aztec migrated into the region north of Tenochtitlán and managed to remain independent of the Mexica Empire. Book two focused upon the actual Spanish conquest of the region and the immediate post-conquest history of the Tlaxcala. It is through this book that much information emerged regarding the Tlaxcalan alliance with the Spanish during the conquest of the Mexica. Book three was a brief coverage of the region's natural history. Though the books were used by a number of significant researchers over the years, they were not published until 1870.

Through Camargo's efforts the first history, blending insights and traditions of the Tlaxcala with those of the Spanish, was compiled. His own knowledge of the Tlaxcala and his wife's connections as a noblewoman of Tlaxcalan and Texcocan lineage combined to create the most thorough coverage of the regional history to that date. Like other early historical accounts of the first century after Spanish conquest, a strong bias favoring one cultural group was evident. In Camargo's *Historia de la Cuidad y República de Tlaxcala,* that bias is clearly in favor of the Tlaxcalan historical account.

Rebecca M. Seaman

See also: Aztec, or Mexica; Tlaxcala, Battle of.

Resources

Bancroft, Hubert Howe. *The Works of Hubert Howe Bancroft: History of Mexico. Vol. II—1521–1600.* San Francisco: A.L. Bancroft & Company, 1883.

Cline, Howard F., ed. *Handbook of Middle American Indians Volume 13: Part Two. Guide to Ethnohistorical Sources.* San Antonio: University of Texas Press, 1973.

Pardo, Oxvaldo F. *The Origins of Mexican Catholicism: Nahua Rituals and Christian Sacraments in Sixteenth-Century Mexico.* Ann Arbor: University of Michigan Press, 2009.

Schwarz, Stuart B., ed. *Implicit Understandings: Observing, Reporting and Reflecting on the Encounters between Europeans and Other People in the Early Modern Era.* Cambridge: Cambridge University Press, 1996.

Camayos

A specialized group of male Inca workers, *camayos* performed sole tasks for nobility or for the state. Within the highly stratified social hierarchy of the Inca Empire, *camayos* represented an entirely male group of workers who performed a singular job for the entirety of their adult lives. This differed from the *mitimaes* who farmed or performed other specialized tasks for set periods of time. The assigned jobs of *camayos* ranged vastly in both the type of work and level of expertise, including agricultural, industrial, and academic positions. Many *camayos* fulfilled basic labor positions within the agricultural sector, serving as both llama and coco farmers on large estates. Inca society also required numerous skilled workers. In addition to trade metalsmiths and engineers, many *camayos* were tasked as miners of fine minerals and other dangerous hard labor positions.

While the majority of *camayos* performed manual labor, an exclusive minority of specialists was selected as *quipo camayos.* The *quipo camayos* acted as the record keepers, historians, and accountants for the Inca society. *Quipo camayos* kept detailed accounts, using a collection of multicolored strings and knots to record what had been consumed and received and then transferring or assisting in the transfer of the data into ledgers.

Camayos were assigned to a singular noble, and in turn these workers were required to relocate with those respective nobles. As a result, *camayos* often lived away from their family groups, or *ayllus,* in large groups referred to as pueblos by the Spanish, which consisted of men who performed the same job. While living apart from their *ayllus,* close connections were maintained, in part to determine if representative numbers from set households were sustained. Despite a communal yet dislocated lifestyle, *camayos* experienced some benefits from serving a single noble, outside of the purview of the local lord. One notable benefit was the policy that *camayos* were exempt from all taxes placed upon the Inca people.

Camayos, like all Inca people, did not choose their professions or the nobles they served. Forced resettlement and specialization, which originated under the Inca Empire and continued under the Spanish, disrupted the communal self-sustaining lifestyles common in Inca society. Additionally, many *camayos* were initially relocated across the empire and were ill equipped for the climate or the positions into which they were placed.

For the Spanish, the Inca resettlement practice assisted the Spanish in conquering the empire. However, for the Inca population, the continued use of relocated *camayos* resulted in a large number of illnesses, injuries, and premature death.

Justin Pfeifer

See also: *Ayllus*; *Quipu*.

Resources

Cobo, Bernabe. *History of the Inca Empire: An Account of the Indians' Customs and Their Origin, Together with a Treatise on Inca Legends, History, and Social Institutions.* Austin: University of Texas Press, 1979.

Collier, George Allen, Renato Rosaldo, and John Wirth. *The Inca and Aztec States, 1400–1800: Anthropology and History.* New York: Academic Press, 1982.

Walker, William. *Drugs in the Western Hemisphere: An Odyssey of Cultures in Conflict.* Wilmington, DE: Scholarly Resources, 1996.

Cañari

An indigenous group in southern Ecuador, the Cañari were most commonly known for their fierce fighting abilities. Their fighting skill was originally recognized during the Inca conquest of Ecuador, during which the Cañari put up a determined resistance. Once the tribe was defeated, the Inca relocated the Cañari soldiers under the mitmaq program in order for them to work as personal Inca guards.

During the civil war that occurred at the time of the Spaniards' arrival in South America, between rival Inca claimants Atahualpa and Huáscar, Cañari soldiers were present on both sides of the conflict. The Cañari faired poorly no matter which side of the struggle they chose to aid. Siding with Huáscar led to the death of many Cañari, the razing of their buildings, and the general attempts to wipe out several towns in Cañari territory by Atahualpa as he gained an upper hand in the struggle. Those that sided with the victor, Atahualpa, were similarly unfortunate as the capture of Atahualpa by Spaniards at Cajamarca resulted in the slaughter of many unarmed Cañari guards.

However, during the conquest of Peru, Cañari soldiers who decided to align their efforts with the Spanish played a crucial role in Francisco Pizarro's divide-and-conquer tactics that had proven to be successful in Mexico. Local Andean leaders—such as Rumiñahui—had been able to gather large, multicultural militias in order to resist Spanish intrusions. After the initial Spanish conquest of Peru, the Cañari were pivotal in their assistance of the Spaniards during Manco Inca Yupanqui's rebellion and in the siege of Cuzco in 1536–1537. During this nearly yearlong battle, less than 200 Spaniards were pitted against 100,000–400,000 indigenous combatants. Consequently, it was extremely necessary for them to acquire help from indigenous auxiliaries such as the Cañari.

This ethnic group continued to assist the Spanish in suppressing armed Indian rebellion after the siege of Cuzco ended in 1537, with the creation of the neo-Inca resistance state of Vilcabamba. During Spain's negotiations with the third Inca of Vilcabamba, Titu Cusi Yupanqui, Don Diego Rodriguez de Figueroa was accompanied by as many as 150 Christian Cañari, in an attempt to persuade the Inca to convert to Catholicism. This strategy ultimately proved successful, as Titu Cusi Yupanqui eventually was baptized under the name Diego de Castro.

Ryan Gillen

See also: Atahualpa; Cajamarca, Battle of; Castro, Diego de; Cuzco; Huáscar; Inca Civil War; Manco Inca Yupanqui; Pizarro, Francisco; Rumiñahui; Titu Cusi Yupanqui; Vilcabamba.

Resources

Bauer, Ralph. *Introduction to an Inca Account of the Conquest of Peru.* Boulder: University of Colorado Press, 2005.

Means, Philip Ainsworth. *Fall of the Inca Empire and the Spanish Rule in Peru: 1530–1780.* New York: Gordian Press, 1964.

Phelan, John Leddy. *The Kingdom of Quito in the Seventeenth Century: Bureaucratic Politics in the Spanish Empire.* Madison: The University of Wisconsin Press, 1967.

Prescott, William. *History of the Conquest of Mexico and History of the Conquest of Peru.* New York: Random House, 1966.

Capitulacion de Toledo

This official agreement between Empress Isabella, wife of Carlos I of Spain (Charles V of the Holy Roman Empire), and Francisco Pizarro, was signed July 26, 1529. The *Capitulacion de Toledo* authorized the Spanish exploration and conquest of the Inca Empire. Prior to the 1529 agreement between Pizarro and Empress Isabella, Pizarro was a wealthy conquistador within the army of Vasco Núñez de Balboa. After agreeing to join fellow soldiers, Diego de Almagro and priest Hernando de Luque, the trio assembled a military force tasked with determining the existence and location of the Inca Empire in Peru. Pizarro arrived on the west coast of South America, documenting the boundaries of the Inca Empire with the help of reconnaissance work conducted by explorer and navigator Bartolomé Ruíz about the land and peoples encountered.

Following confirmation of the Inca Empire's existence from information gathered at the coast of Tumbes on Peruvian soil, Pizarro returned to Panama to seek authorization from the governor of Panama to undertake another expedition to the south. However, when the governor of Castilla de Oro (Panama), Pedro de los Rios, refused to authorize another such venture after Pizarro's first two attempts to seize the Inca holdings ended in failure. Determined to succeed and control the wealth of the Inca, Pizarro left for Spain to negotiate the terms of exploration with the imperial monarchy. Pizarro departed Panama for Spain in the spring of 1528, reaching Seville in the early summer of that year.

Emperor Charles V met with Pizarro and promised to support his plan for the conquest of Peru. However, Charles V was forced to leave for Italy, prompting his wife Isabella to act in his stead. Under the authority of Empress Isabella in the *Capitulacion de Toledo,* Pizarro was given orders to explore and conquer new territories extending up to 600 miles south of the Santiago River, separating modern Columbia and Ecuador. In addition, Pizarro was permitted to conquer territory 200 leagues along the coastal regions. By 1534, Pizarro's territory had expanded to 275 leagues in an area known as the Kingdom of New Castile.

In addition to vast spans of territory, under the *Capitulacion* each of the original triumvirate was awarded titles of distinction. Pizarro was knighted under the Order of Santiago and also was named governor and captain general of New Castile. Almagro was awarded the title of mayor of the fortress of Tumbes, and made governor and captain general of New Toledo. However, for Almagro, the territory granted to him was insufficient in comparison to the lands received by Pizarro. Additionally, Luque was given the title of bishop of Tumbes and the title of Protector of the Indians.

The *Capitulacion* instructed that Pizarro should raise a military force of 250 men within six months, of whom a 100 could be drawn from overseas colonies. Pizarro used this opportunity to convince his half-brother

Hernando at Trujillo, along with other close family and friends, to join him on the expedition, including the already noted military leader Hernando de Soto. When the expedition was ready and left in 1530, it included three ships, 180 men, and 27 cavalry horses. Pizarro's third, and final, expedition left Panama for Peru on December 27, 1530. By 1533, Pizarro's forces had effectively decimated the central leadership of the Inca Empire under the Sapa Inca Atahualpa, and spent the next few decades trying to gain a firm control over the people and property of the region. In the process, the initial structure of the new Spanish colony, laid out in the *Capitulacion de Toledo,* fell into disarray. The original three ringleaders and other ambitious conquistadores competed for power and wealth in New Castile as the riches of the former Inca rulers fed their avarice.

Justin Pfeifer

See also: Almagro, Diego de; Balboa, Vasco Núñez de; Charles V (HRE) or Carlos I of Spain; Luque, Hernando de; Pizarro, Francisco; Pizarro, Hernando; Ruíz, Bartolomé; Soto, Hernando de, in Peru.

Resources

Gabai, Rafael Varon. *Francisco Pizarro and His Brothers: The Illusion of Power in Sixteenth Century Peru.* Oklahoma: University of Oklahoma Press, 1997.

Marley, David. *Wars of the Americas: A Chronology of Armed Conflict in the Western Hemisphere.* Santa Barbara, CA: ABC-CLIO, 2008.

Ramirez, Susan E. *To Feed and be Fed: The Cosmological Bases of Authority and Identity in the Andes.* Stanford: Stanford University Press, 2005.

Caribs

The word Carib refers to a language group that distinguishes natives living in the Caribbean region on the Lesser Antilles. The Caribs were an indigenous population that settled throughout the islands of the western Caribbean Sea. The Europeans who began to arrive in the late 15th century considered the Caribs the most aggressive indigenous group in the Caribbean islands. Although the Caribs put up substantial resistance to European conquest, they eventually succumbed to European weapons and diseases.

The Caribs are thought to have originated in the Orinoco jungles of Venezuela in South America. They began to settle the islands of the Caribbean Sea a few hundred years before the Europeans arrived. The previous inhabitants of the islands, the Arawaks, gradually gave way to the Caribs, who tried to seize more territory in the region when the Spanish conquistadores arrived. As a result, the Spanish began immediately to seize the islands from them in order to plunder the land for gold. Eventually, the Spanish and other Europeans, including the Dutch and Portuguese, established sugarcane plantations with the Caribs working as slaves.

The Caribs fought to preserve their land and freedom, but their wood and stone weapons were no match for the steel weapons of the Europeans. The native population fell victim to one of three typical fates under Spanish rule: abusive treatment and overwork as labors washing for gold; captives of slave raids for work in sugar fields or for sale to other Spanish-controlled islands; or death due to a variety of deadly epidemics introduced by the Spanish. The Caribs could not withstand the deleterious effects of smallpox, typhus, and measles brought over by the Europeans. Quickly, the Europeans spread stories that the Caribs were cannibals, although those stories may have been fabricated in order to satisfy the legal statutes that only cannibalistic people could be enslaved. In fact, the Europeans circulated the erroneous belief that "Carib" meant cannibalistic.

Living among the islands, the Caribs developed seafaring and boat-making skills. Unlike the Mayas on the continent, the Caribs developed vessels that could accommodate 150 people. The trunks of ceiba trees were hollowed out to create boats. These vessels enabled the Caribs to travel between the islands and even the American continent.

The Caribs managed to retain control of the islands of Dominica and St. Vincent into the 17th century, but their communities eventually either died out or assimilated into European or slave communities. The last speaker of the Carib language died in the 1920s.

Although the Caribs essentially died out as a distinct population group, a number of people of Carib descent still live in the Caribbean area. Many of the African slaves who were brought to the West Indies intermarried with the Caribs. A group of interracial peoples of African and Carib descent left St. Vincent in 1796 and resettled in Central America, where their descendants are known today as the Garífuna.

Ryan Hackney

See also: Columbus, Christopher; European Diseases, Role of.

Resources

Kirby, I. E, and C. I. Martin. *The Rise and Fall of the Black Caribs.* Kingstown: St. Vincent & the Grenadines National Trust, 1998.

Thomas, Hugh. *Conquest: Montezuma, Cortés, and the Fall of Old Mexico.* New York: Simon & Schuster, 1993.

Wilson, Samuel M. *The Indigenous People of the Caribbean.* Gainesville: University Press of Florida, 1997.

Castro, Diego de

Born the second son of the Sapa Inca, Manco Inca Yupanqui, and given the Inca name of Titu Cusi Yupanqui, the eventual Inca emperor took the name of Diego de Castro upon his baptism in 1568. The choice of name was meant to flatter the Spanish authorities: Viceroy Diego López de Zúñiga y Velasco who died suddenly in 1564, as well as Lope García de Castro who soon thereafter succeeded him in the role of governor and captain general. At the time, Titu Cusi was governing in exile from Vilcabamba, using diplomacy and delay tactics to avoid submitting to Spanish authority.

Rebecca M. Seaman

See also: Manco Inca Yupanqui; Sapa Inca; Titu Cusi Yupanqui; Vilcabamba.

Resources

Hemming, John. *The Conquest of the Incas.* London: Pan Macmillan, 1970.

Titu Cusi Yupanqui. *An Inca Account of the Conquest of Peru.* Introduced, Translated, and Annotated by Ralph Bauer. Boulder: University of Colorado Press, 2003.

Castrovirreina

In 1591, Viceroy García Hurtado de Mendoza ordered Pedro de Cordoba y Mexía to found a Spanish settlement high in the central Andes following the discovery of silver deposits in the area the previous year. Named for the Viceroy's wife, Teresa de Castro, the mining town thrived initially due to its fortunate location. Despite its altitude and cold climate, the town enjoyed easy access to water from Lakes Choclococha and Orcococha. The mercury necessary to refine silver was also readily available from the nearby mines of Huancavelica. In light of these favorable conditions and in order to ensure royal revenue, Viceroy Mendoza assigned a quota of 2,100,000 conscripted indigenous laborers (*mitayos*) from the surrounding region to the mines of Castrovirreina, although the number was later reduced.

Scholars continue to debate whether forced labor or wage labor was more common in the mines. In 1600, the Crown established a royal treasury to register silver production. Despite its initial success, the mines' output peaked in the 1620s before decreasing steadily. Registered production ceased in 1662 when local miners were unable to drain the flooded mines and the royal treasury closed. The Spanish authorities also reassigned the indigenous laborers, ending Castrovirreina's golden age. Small-scale mining likely preceded the founding of the city and continued after the major production ended in 1662. Today Castrovirreina is the capital of the province and district of the same name in the Department of Huancavelica, Peru. Pastoralism, particularly of alpaca, is the main economic activity.

Mark Dries

See also: Mercury; *Mita*; Silver; Slavery, Role of.

Resources

Brown, Kendall W. *A History of Mining in Latin America: From the Colonial Era to the Present.* Diálogos Series. Albuquerque: University of New Mexico Press, 2012.

Cook, Noble. *Demographic Collapse, Indian Peru, 1520–1620.* Cambridge/New York: Cambridge University Press, 1981.

TePaske, John Jay, and Kendall W Brown. *A New World of Gold and Silver.* Leiden, Netherlands; Boston: Brill, 2010.

Chalco

The city of Chalco, under the Aztec Empire, was located on the southeastern arm of the large Lake Texcoco that dominated the Valley of Mexico. On a backwater branch of the lake, designated Lake Chalco, the city had a population of approximately 6,000 at the time of Hernán Cortés's initial advance toward the capital city of Tenochtitlán. The arrival of the conquistador in early November of 1519 created a great deal of concern among the Mexica council of leaders, for the city was known for its history of rebellions against the Aztec Empire. Evidence of this concern is found in the message conveyed to Cortés by four Aztec emissaries, asking the Spanish to return home, indicating that Montezuma was ill, the road to the capital was bad, and the there was no food available to feed the Castilians.

Despite the reception of the Spanish by the people of Chalco, and their history of poor relations with the Mexica, the town and its leaders were not spared when smallpox descended upon the city in September 1520. The devastation to indigenous population from so many native deaths was increased by the failure of the Spanish to contract the illness in large numbers. When the king of Chalco and others died, successors were suggested by Cortés, leaving him the dominant political influence in the southeastern region of Lake Texcoco. By December of 1520, the Chalco fears of Mexica reprisals were overcome by hopes of an alliance with the Spanish. With the Tlaxcala and the people of Chalco joining his forces, Cortés was able to win over more cities to the Spanish, helping to shift the balance of power from the dominant Aztec Empire gradually to that of the conquistadors.

The significance of Chalco's realignment was evident through repeated attempts by the new Aztec emperor, Cuauhtémoc, to reclaim control of the city. Understanding that significant position of his new ally, Cortés sent his most loyal and dependable captain, Gonzalo de Sandoval, to protect and hold the city, thereby securing the continued loyalty and support of neighboring cities he had brought under his authority. The loss of Chalco was devastating to the Mexica. Not only did it trigger a domino effect of other cities succumbing to Spanish dominance; it signaled

Spanish entering Chalco in 1519, from Lienzo de Tlaxcala manuscript. (*Lienzo de Tlaxcala,* facsimile, ca. 1890)

the collapse of the perimeter defense of the capital city. The Aztec capital was located on an island in the middle of Lake Texcoco, and the lake surrounded by allied cities that were kept under close control by the empire. As Chalco and other cities along the lakeshores abandoned the Mexica in favor of the Spanish, the only defenses left to the Aztec was the control of the causeways and the protection the water provided. Even that was lost as Cortés revealed his brigantines and the natives of Tlaxcala, Texcoco, Chalco and others joined in repairing the causeways for access by the invading Spanish.

Chalco, a consistent irritant to the Aztec Empire, became an important ally to Cortés during his siege of Tenochtitlán. The loyalty and significant support, despite small numbers, was honored by Cortés when, at the end of the conquest, he retained the city as part of his own personal encomienda.

Rebecca M. Seaman

See also: Cortés, Hernán; Cuauhtémoc; Sandoval, Gonzalo de; Tenochtitlán, Siege of; Texcoco, Alliance with Tenochtitlán.

Resources

Diaz del Castillo, Bernal. *The Conquest of New Spain.* Translated with Introduction by J. M. Cohen. London: Penguin Books, 1963.

Levy, Buddy. *Conquistador: Hernán Cortés, King Montezuma, and the Last Stand of the Aztecs.* New York: Bantam Books, 2009.

Thomas, Hugh. *Conquest: Montezuma, Cortés, and the Fall of Old Mexico.* New York: Simon & Schuster, 1993.

Chanca

The Chanca polity was a Late Intermediate culture (ca. 1000–1400 CE) that emerged following the decline of Huari influence (600–1000 CE) in the southern Andes, and remained powerful until their eventual defeat by the Incas ca. 1450. Subsequent Inca settlements and cultural influences were far-reaching, especially evident in the major site of Sondor, as well as in many smaller Inca and non-Inca sites in the region, according to a major archaeological survey by Brian S. Bauer, Lucas C. Kellett, and Miriam Aráoz Silva (2010).

According to legend, the genesis of the Inca Empire dated from the Inca defeat of the Chanca army, under Anccu Huayco, by a smaller Cuzco force in the mid-15th century. The battle took place at Yahuarpampa near Limatambo, northeast of Cuzco, on the edge of the Inca heartland. This watershed moment is often dated to 1438, but this is highly speculative. Nor is it clear which king was the ruling Capac Inca at the time. There exist several variant and conflicting accounts of the same event. However, most scholars agree that a young Inca prince, either Hatun Tupa or Cusi Yupanqui, rescued an embattled Inca army; these later became the emperors Viracocha and Pachacutec (Pachacutin), respectively. Juan de Santa Cruz Pachacuti Yamqui Salcamaygua, an early colonial native chronicler, also recorded a legend that the tide of battle was turned only after stones were magically turned into Inca warriors.

There is some dispute as to the exact identity of the Chanca peoples, the extent of their power and settlement area, and the wider territories over which they may have exercised hegemony. It is clear that the Chanca heartland was the resource-rich Andahuaylas region of the southeastern highlands of Peru. However, the term "Chanca" is often used loosely (and erroneously) to embrace ethnicities and chiefdoms further afield, such as the Huanca, Huari, and Yauyos. Mention of a Chanca confederation also seems open to doubt, though early colonial documents studied by Catherine Julien (2002) indicate that the Andahuaylas region was settled by a myriad of small ethnicities, partly located in 32 towns. One source records that the battle of Yahuarpampa was fought between the Incas and the Chancas, Huantas, and Soras. The Chanca sphere of influence extended perhaps as far north as the erstwhile Huari (Wari) homeland in the Ayacucho region, in which the Inca sun temple of Vilcashuaman is located. Social organization of the Chanca was organized around two moieties, Hanan and Hurin, which in turn contained multiple lineages (*ayllus*). These moieties were founded by two mythical brothers, Uscovilca and Ancovilca, which were also the names of the two principal Chanca idols (*huacas*). The Incas retained both—moieties and the *ayllus* cultural elements—following their conquest of the Chanca. Another fundamental division found in the Chanca society was that between agriculturalists (*huari*) and pastoralists (*llacuaz*), as elsewhere in the central sierra.

Despite the lack of clarity as to identity and the extent of the Chanca polity, the present state of research suggests that use of the identifier Chanca should be restricted to the ethnic groups settled in the Andahuaylas region, and that the diverse Chanca peoples and ethnicities were perhaps less integrated than previously thought.

David Cahill

See also: *Ayllu*; Hanan; Huacas; Hurin; Pachacutin.

Resources

Bauer, Brian S. Bauer, Lucas C. Kellett, and Miriam Aráoz Silva, with contributions from Sabine Hyland and Carlo Socualaya Dávila. *The Chanka: Archaeological Research in Andahuaylas (Apurimac), Peru.* Los Angeles: Cotsxen Institute, 2010.

Bruhns, Karen Olsen. *Ancient South America.* Cambridge: Cambridge University Press, 1994.

D'Altroy, Terence N. *The Incas.* Oxford: Blackwell, 2002.

Morris, Craig, and Adriana Van Hagan. *The Incas: Lords of the Four Quarters.* London: Thames & Hudson, 2011.

Prem, Hans J. *The Ancient Americas: A Brief History and Guide to Research.* Translated by Kornelia Kurbjuhn. Salt Lake City: University of Utah Press, 1997 [1989].

Charles V (HRE) or Carlos I of Spain

Holy Roman Emperor Charles V, who also was known as Carlos I in Spain, was one of the most powerful European kings who reigned from 1519 to 1558. He inherited Spain, the Netherlands, Germany and central Europe, parts of Italy, and territory in Latin America. A teenager when he assumed the monarchy, he nonetheless held it all together through astute military and political strategy. One of the greatest threats to the unity of this Catholic kingdom was Martin Luther and the emergence of Protestantism.

Charles was born on February 24, 1500, in Ghent, Belgium, into one of Europe's most powerful royal families, the Habsburgs. He was the son of Philip the Handsome and Joanna, the crown princess of Spain. When Charles was six years old, he lost both of his parents. His father died, and his mother was declared insane by her father, Ferdinand, and confined to a convent in Spain. His aunt, Margaret of Austria, raised Charles; in what is now Belgium and the Netherlands. Margaret ruled the Netherlands until her nephew came of age in 1515. There were three primary influences in Charles's life: his aunt Margaret; his chamberlain, Sieur de Chievres, with whom he often disagreed; and his priest, Adrian of Utrecht, who later became Pope Adrian VI. Charles learned to negotiate between these mentors and to be loyal to the Catholic Church.

Charles began his 40-year reign when he was 15 years old, when his aunt presented him with the crown of the Netherlands. Then a year later, his maternal grandfather died, and he became king of the powerful and extensive kingdom of Spain, parts of Italy, and the rich territories in Latin America. Crowned as King Carlos I of Spain, Charles arrived in that country at the age of 16, unable to speak Spanish. He appointed his old tutor and priest, Adrian, to important posts in his government. Then three years later, in 1519, he received the crown of the Habsburg Empire, Germany, and central Europe when his paternal grandfather, Maximilian I, died. At 19 years old, Charles ruled over the most extensive empire in Europe. Gold and silver poured into his kingdom from Latin America, where Hernán Cortés defeated the Aztec Empire in 1521 and Francisco Pizarro took control of the Inca Empire a decade later. The massive infusion of wealth from Latin America financed Charles's many wars.

Charles's foreign policy set the stage for Spain's colonial relations for the next century. Charles V, in league with Henry VIII of England, fought Francis I of France for control of Italy. When Charles backed out of his promise to marry Henry's daughter Mary and rejected Henry's call to break up the French kingdom, Henry VIII changed sides, and the battle began again. The sheer size and complexity of the Holy Roman Empire prompted repeated shifts in international alliances. However, the wealth of Spain's New World colonies—and the need to protect that wealth—along with the intertwining of religious and political struggles throughout the HRE dominated his 40 years of rule.

Charles's reign was defined by the great schism in the Catholic Church known as the Reformation. The Church rejected the views put forth by Luther in 1521. Charles, young and newly crowned emperor of the HRE, issued a formal condemnation of Luther's ideas in hopes of securing unity of his vast, complex empire through the support of the Church. This confrontation formally began the Reformation and the emergence of Protestantism as a permanent fixture in the Western world. Over the next decades, princes in Charles's German kingdom began to ally themselves with Luther in the Schmalkaldic League.

Charles's response was to attempt to unify the kingdom through war. While he destroyed the armies of the German Protestant princes in 1547, religious and political rebellion continued. Charles was defeated at Saxony in early 1551 when his ally suddenly switched sides. Out of this defeat, Charles signed the Treaty of Passau in 1552, which legally recognized Protestantism. Europe remained the focus of religious and political struggles during Charles V's reign, but even while he attempted to defend Catholic hegemony and retain dominance over the continent, his opponents began exploring and laying claim to territories in the New World of America.

In the Spanish colonies, political, military, and religious servants of the king vied for wealth, authority, and the king's ear. One particular issue that divided the various groups was the status and rights of the diverse indigenous populations of the Caribbean, Mexico, and South America. Swayed by Bartolomé de Las Casas, a former colonist and encomendero who became a Dominican friar and campaigned for native rights, Charles V issued the New Laws of 1542, which limited encomienda service. Eight years later, the continued abuse of Indians prompted the 1550 Vallodolid debate between Las Casas and Juan Ginés de Sepúlveda, who argued that Native Americans were less than human and needed Spanish masters to acquire salvation and civilization. Again, Charles supported Las Casas who had lived among the Indians in America.

By the 1850s, in his fifties, Charles suffered from gout and fatigue. In an unusual move, he abdicated the throne of the Holy Roman Empire and awarded the title to his younger brother, Ferdinand I, who had been governor of the Habsburg lands for many years. His son, Philip II, became king of the Netherlands and Spain. Charles spent the last three years of his life in retirement at the monastery in San Jeronimo de Yuste in Spain, from which he advised his son on matters of state. Charles died on September 21, 1558. In the Spanish colonies, while official Spanish policy perpetuated Charles's rulings, little effort was made to enforce such edicts as the New Laws, devastating the indigenous populace of the New World.

Jose Valente

See also: Cortés, Hernán; Encomienda; Las Casas, Bartolomé de; Leyes Nuevas 1542–1543; Philip II of Spain; Pizarro, Francisco; Sepúlveda's *De Orbe Novo (Historia del Nuevo Mundo)*.

Resources

Chamberlin, Russell. "Charles V: Europe's Last Emperor?" *History Today* 50, no. 2 (2000): 2–3.

Hanke, Lewis. "Indians and Spaniards in the New World: A Personal View." In *Attitudes of Colonial Powers toward the American*

Indian, edited by Howard Peckham and Charles Gibson. Salt Lake City: University of Utah Press, 1969.

Headley, John. *The Emperor and His Chancellor: A Study of the Imperial Chancellery under Gattinara.* Cambridge: Cambridge University Press, 1983.

Richardson, Glenn. "Charles V 'Universal Soldier.'" *History Review* 38 (2000): 42–47.

Thomas, Hugh. *Conquest: Montezuma, Cortés, and the Fall of Old Mexico.* New York: Simon & Schuster, 1993.

Chasquis

Plural for *chasqui,* the term refers to runners used by the imperial Inca for purposes of conveying goods and messages along their extensive road systems. The Inca imperial road system was in place only about 100 years by the time of the Spanish conquest.

Throughout the empire, the Inca designated stopping points—or tampos— stationed at approximately three-kilometer distances. These "rest stops" provided more than just rest for the runners who plied the roads of the empire, but also for travelers and even military units. The tampos housed well-trained runners who were used in a relay type system designed to transport news and goods at an average rate of 150 miles per day.

To accomplish the task set out for the *chasquis,* physical training was crucial. The road systems throughout the empire were diverse, ranging from small, dirt footpaths, to extended rope bridges, to well-worn trade routes. Physical speed, agility, and endurance were necessary for the runners to safely traverse the routes at the speed required.

While physical abilities and agility were a must, an even more important attribute of the *chasquis* was their training and skills in remembering verbatim the communications related to them by other runners. From childhood, these messengers were trained to memorize messages in specific detail. This was especially important due to the Inca lack of a traditional written language. Their method of recording through knotted cords, or *quipu,* was a skill known to the *quipu* masters. For specific details and complex messages, oral communications were relied upon, necessitating the use of *chasquis.*

A *chasqui* would run at a fast pace from one tampo to the next. Upon arriving, he would communicate the urgent message, or pass on the package for deliverance, to the next *chasqui.* The process, repeated along the extensive road network, allowed for the communication of messages and goods from the northern capital of Quito to the southern original capital of Cuzco, a distance of approximately 1,000 miles, in less than one week's time.

Though the Inca system of relaying messages was crude in comparison to Spanish standards, the speed with which the Inca messages traveled across the rugged terrain far exceeded Spanish abilities, even with horses. Limits on the amount of goods to be transported through such a system hindered the use of the system as a means of effective trade. Additionally, confining the *chasquis* to only those possessing the physical and mental training from childhood proved problematic as the indigenous population was reduced by wars and disease. Yet, for over 100 years, the Inca use of *chasquis* succeeded in maintaining communications and competing with other means of communication employed by the Inca enemies and allies in the region.

Rebecca M. Seaman

See also: *Quipu.*

Resources

Crandall, John. "The Inca and Their Roads." *Latin American History.* http://suite101 .com/article/the-inca-and-their-roads-a8761 (accessed, Oct. 23, 2012).

Hyslop, John. *The Inka Road System.* Orlando, FL: Academic press, 1984.

Malpass, Michael A. *Daily Life in the Inca Empire.* Westport, CT: Greenwood Press, 1996.

Salomon, Frank. *The Cord Keepers: Khipus and Cultural Life in a Peruvian Village.* Durham, NC: Duke University Press, 2004.

Chichen Itza

The city of Chichen Itza was the major religious, political, and economic capital of the Mayan people within the Yucatán until the 1200s. At that time, the city was abandoned and its origin and demise remained a mystery for the next several centuries. In recent years, archaeologists and historians have pieced together elements of the past to try to understand the origins and fall of the city.

According to archaeological evidence, several ruins found at Chichen Itza are out of character with the base Mayan culture. The use of colonnades, interior courts, exterior platforms displaying human skulls, art depicting non-Mayan dress, and art forms all confirm this interpretation. Oral traditions of the Yucatán Maya related stories of an invasion from the west by the Itza, a Nahua-speaking people. These traditions correspond to evidence of structural and artistic renovations to the capital city around the 10th century.

Further archaeological digs and historical research eventually linked some of the architectural designs employed in Chichen Itza to ruins of the Toltecs from Mexico. Additionally, similar art forms were shared by both cultures. According to historical records of the Aztec, Quetzalcoatl, a god in human form, was driven from Mexico toward the east. This reference to Quetzalcoatl

Chichen Itza historic site, located in northern Mexico's Yucatán Peninsula, included an observatory used to track the movement of Venus in relation to the serpent god, Quetzalcoatl. (Corel)

is mirrored in the Yucatán oral traditions, indicating that a similar being came from the west and ruled in Chichen Itza in the 10th century. While the threads of oral traditions and archaeological finds support a Mexican-Toltec conquest and temporary dominion over the former capital, conclusive evidence remains yet to be found.

Another mystery surrounding Chichen Itza is the cause of its decline and fall. While exact details are missing, evidence does exist supporting conclusion of military conflict in the region, resulting in repeated attacks on the once acknowledged center of Yucatán societies. Rising out of the conflicts, the Cocom dynasty emerged and came to power. This family located their seat of power in Mayapán. Using forced alliances with other Mayans as well as employing mercenaries from neighboring Mexican societies of the Yucatán, the Cocom dynasty established their authority over the northern Yucatán. As Mayapán rose in importance, Chichen Itza declined and was eventually abandoned. By the time of Spanish conquest in the early 1500s, Chichen Itza had been long abandoned and in ruins. The Maya of the region had little knowledge of the origins or eventual location of the former rulers of this once great city.

Rebecca M. Seaman

See also: Aztec, or Mexica; Maya; Nahuatl Language; Quetzalcoatl; Yucatán, State of prior to Spanish conquest.

Resources

Clendinnen, Inga. *Ambivalent Conquests: Maya and Spaniard in Yucatan, 1517–1570.* 2nd ed. Cambridge: Cambridge University Press, 2003.

Gallenkamp, Charles. *Maya: The Riddle and Rediscovery of a Lost Civilization.* 3rd rev. ed. New York: Viking Penguin, 1985.

Landa, Friar Diego de. *Yucatan: Before and After the Conquest.* Translated with Notes by William Gates. New York: Dover Publications, 1978.

Schwartz, Stuart B., ed. *Victors and Vanquished: Spanish and Nahua Views of the Conquest of Mexico.* Boston: Bedford/St. Martin's, 2000.

Chimborazo, Battle of

The Battle of Chimborazo refers to two separate conflicts that occurred near Chimborazo. The original use of the name referenced an early conflict in the Inca Civil War (1529–1532) between the forces of the half-brothers and co-claimants to the Inca throne, Huáscar and Atahualpa. The battle was a decisive victory for the forces of Atahualpa. The second use of the name, often including the name, Mount Chimborazo, references the final defeat of the Incas as the empire fell to the forces of Francisco Pizarro.

In the later 1520s, the Inca emperor (known by the title Sapa Inca) Huayna Cápac died of smallpox while on campaign. His initial appointed successor, Ninan Cuyochi, died shortly thereafter of the same disease. Huayna Cápac also supported his son, Huáscar, as an alternative successor. Huáscar was Huayna Cápac's son of pure royal blood from a marriage to his full sister. Nonetheless, Huayna Cápac had also given much power and prestige to Atahualpa, his son from a nonroyal marriage. When Cápac and Ninan Cuyochi both died, Atahualpa claimed that the governing authority that his father had given him over a small northern portion of the empire was akin to independent sovereignty from the rule of his brother, Huáscar. Because he was not of pure royal blood, Atahualpa was considered ineligible to succeed his father as Sapa Inca. However, while the prominent nobles and religious leaders supported Huáscar's claim, a large portion of the army, including many of the best generals, declared their loyalty to Atahualpa. It was

Atahualpa who had accompanied his father on campaigns, making a name for himself for his military exploits, while Huáscar remained in the capital of Cuzco to rule in his father's absence.

Intent upon securing his rightful claim to the entire empire, Huáscar invaded the northern province controlled by Atahualpa. Though Huáscar's forces outnumbered his half-brother's, Atahualpa had better-trained warriors led by more capable generals. Supported by Quizquiz and Chalicuchima, both excellent generals who had served his father, Atahualpa countered Huáscar's invasion near Chimborazo. The defeat cost Huáscar one of his best generals, Atoc, who was captured after the battle, then tortured and killed. More importantly, however, the defeat put Huáscar permanently on the defensive. After Chimborazo, Huáscar would continue to fight a losing war against Atahualpa's superior forces, eventually falling into the hands of his half-brother, who had him killed. Later, Spanish forces under Francisco Pizarro arrived in the empire as Atahualpa was still consolidating his power. Taking advantage of the chaos of the ongoing civil war, Pizarro captured and executed Atahualpa, and then conquered the Inca Empire himself.

In 1532, Francisco Pizarro's forces descended upon the Inca Empire. Over the next several years, contesting captains under Pizarro vied for notoriety and rewards through their military exploits. One such leader, Sebastián de Benalcázar, led a small force north toward Ecuador, intent upon capturing the Inca leader Rumiñahui and securing the city of Quito and the gold within—said to have been diverted by Rumiñahui when he heard of the death of Atahualpa at Pizarro's hands. The Spanish and Inca forces met near Mount Chimborazo. There, the superior numbers of the Incas threatened to defeat the forces of Benalcázar, despite the presence of horses and canon. According to legend, as Benalcázar prepared to retreat, a volcanic explosion occurred in the nearby mountains. The Inca interpreted this event as a sign that they should withdraw, while the Spanish saw it a sign from God of their right to control the region. The withdrawal of the Inca from Chimborazo signaled the end of the major resistance to the Spanish conquest. Though Rumiñahui burnt the northern capital city of Quito and none of the sought after gold was discovered, the unexpected victory of Mount Chimborazo saw the rapid decline of the power of the Sapa Inca and rapid increase in Spanish colonial power in Peru.

Both battles fought in the northern province held special significance for Inca history. The first Battle of Chimborazo began the internal rift between the royal Inca family, leading to Pizarro's ability to successfully defeat numerically superior forces. The final Battle of Mount Chimborazo solidified Spanish control over much of the Inca Empire, while it also symbolized the ascendancy of the Spanish and breakdown of Inca imperial authority. The once great Inca Empire collapsed under the weight of civil war and foreign invasion within the span of just over five years.

John Gram and Rebecca Seaman

See also: Atahualpa; Cuzco; Huáscar; Huayna Cápac; Ninan Cuyochi; Pizarro, Francisco; Quizquiz; Rumiñahui; Sapa Inca.

Resources

Brundage, Burr Cartwright. *Empire of the Inca.* Norman: University of Oklahoma Press, 1985.

Brundage, Burr Cartwright. *Lords of Cuzco: A History and Description of the Inca People in Their Final Days.* Norman: University of Oklahoma Press, 1985.

Conrad, Geofrey W. and Arthur A Demarest. *Religion and Empire: The Dynamics of Aztec and Inca Expansionism.* Cambridge: Cambridge University Press, 1984.

Chinchaysuyu

Tahuantinsuyu (the four parts united) was the name given to the Inca Empire when it was created through the conquests and alliances of Pachacutin and his son, Túpac Inca Yupanqui. From these conquests, Pachacutin created four territories or *suyus*. The point where the four *suyus* met was in the city of Cuzco, the governmental capital of the newly structured empire.

Chinchaysuyu was the northernmost territory of the Inca Empire under Pachacuti. It was also the largest of the four *suyus*. Extending as far north as modern-day Colombia, it included such original indigenous cities as Cajamarca and Quito. The Inca royal road ran from Quito in the far north to Cuzco at the base of the territory, providing for efficient communications not only within the region, but also from one region to another. This accomplishment was notable, especially in the Andean mountains, where rope bridges were used to span from one steep mountainous slope to another.

The name Chinchaysuyu was derived from one of the ethnic groups in the region, that of the Chincha. However, Chinchaysuyu was very diverse. Geographically, the region included the desert and coastal terrain along the Pacific Ocean, the Andes Mountains, and even elements of the inland jungles and rainforests. To govern such ethnically diverse regions, the conquering Inca surveyed the properties and people of Chinchaysuyu, determining their value and use to the empire. Then they selected individuals and families from the region and removed them to the distant region of Antisuyu. In this manner, the conquered people were divided and resettled to prevent further rebellion against the empire. The Inca then instituted *kuraka* or local lords approved by the Inca leadership. Intermarriage between Inca and the local *kuraka* helped strengthen loyalties and guarantee more centralized control.

Rebecca M. Seaman

See also: Antisuyu; *Kuraka*; Pachacutin; Tahuantinsuyu; Túpac Inca Yupanqui.

Resources
Gamboa, Pedro Sarmiento de. *History of the Incas.* Translated and Edited by Sir Clements Markham. Cambridge, UK: Hakluyt Society, 1907.

MacQuarrie, Kim. *The Last Days of the Incas.* New York: Simon & Schuster, 2007.

Cholula Massacre

The city of Cholula, about 25 miles from Tlaxcala, was part of the Aztec Empire. By the time Cortés approached the city, it had been inhabited for a thousand years and boasted approximately 50,000 houses, 25,000 soldiers, and a population of well over 100,000. Cholula was the largest city encountered by the early Spanish conquistadors prior to arriving at Tenochtitlán. Cholula also held great religious significance and was sometimes referred to as the Rome of Middle of America. The city hosted the temple of Quetzalcoatl. This historical/mythological figure's long beard, exhortations against human sacrifice, and other purported similarities to the Spanish heighted fears by Montezuma that Cortés might represent the return of the long-exiled deity.

In October 1519, Cortés set out from the Totonac territory to Tlaxcala, where he met initial armed resistance. After initial setbacks, Cortés convinced the Tlaxcala to ally with his forces against their long-term enemy, the Aztec. From Tlaxcala, the Spanish intended to pass through Cholula en route Tenochtitlán. Cortés was warned previously by the Totonacs and later by the Tlaxcaltec leaders to avoid Cholula for fear of an ambush. He was informed that the route through Cholula was longer, the city heavily fortified, and the people there not to be trusted. Cortés nonetheless shrugged off the warnings of his new allies, and chose to follow the advice of Montezuma's emissary, Olintetl. Surrounded by potential enemies and smarting from the earlier conflicts with the Tlaxcala, Cortés opted to appease both groups. He acquiesced to the Aztec advice to travel through Cholula. Simultaneously, he welcomed the presence and assistance of Tlaxcala warriors and carriers. He also took with him the unsettling Tlaxcala advice to kill all Mexica he encountered.

Upon arriving in the territory of Cholula, Cortés was met by a large contingency of Cholulan leaders bearing maize cakes and turkey. Following elaborate ceremonies, Cortés proclaimed his usual discourse against human sacrifice and exhorted the Mexica to worship the Christian God. The records indicate that the Spanish were welcomed in the city, while the Tlaxcala were turned away. However, records from both the Spanish and the Aztec admit a small presence of Tlaxcala was allowed among those admitted to the city. The Spanish received housing and sustenance, though quantities of food lessened each day. Despite the seemingly peaceful relations during the visit, tensions rose. Rumors circulated about Cholulan plots to kill the Spanish upon their exodus from the city. These rumors were reinforced when Doña Marina (Cortés's native interpreter) relayed that she was encouraged to stay behind when the Spanish left to avoid being killed by a planned ambush.

While at Cholula, Cortés received conflicting advice from Montezuma's emissaries. First he was dissuaded from continuing on to Tenochtitlán. Emissaries cited such reasons as the impassability of the road, lack of provisions along the way, that the emperor's fierce animals would tear the Spanish apart, and even that Montezuma would die of fear from a visit by the Spanish. Unconvinced, Cortés indicated his intention to advance to Tenochtitlán, at which point the emissaries extended invitations from Montezuma.

By the third day in Cholula, the only provisions extended to the Spanish and their allies were wood and water. Alerted to possible violence, Cortés demanded to meet with the leaders, to no avail. Word spread that the streets of the city were barricaded and stones piled on the roofs. When confronted by Cortés, Tlaquiach, the temporal ruler of Cholula, said Montezuma indicated the Spanish should not be assisted in any manner. Further questioning of two priests from the city revealed that Montezuma's instructions to his subjects concerning the Spanish constantly vacillated from day to day. The priests also confirmed Doña Marina's assertion that thousands of warriors awaited the Spanish on the road to Tenochtitlán.

The Spanish and Aztec accounts differ greatly as to the start of the violence. Aztec accounts indicate Cortés's attack was completely unprovoked. This is highly unlikely, as Cortés consistently employed diplomacy in his other initial encounters, except for Cholula. According to Spanish accounts, violence resulted from reported plots of the Aztec to ambush their forces, reports confirmed through the interrogation of two Cholulan priests. Cortés decided upon a preemptive strike against the city as a message to all potential enemies in the region. On the premise of a formal farewell, he asked the city leadership and the intended Cholulan

Slaughter of Mexicans by the Spaniards at Cholula, October 1519. (Ridpath, John Clark, *Ridpath's History of the World,* 1901)

escorts to meet in a central courtyard. Cortés then used his combined Spanish and native forces to close off the area and massacre the entrapped people. The allied Tlaxcaltec warriors, still outside the city, entered and wreaked their vengeance.

After two days of horror and violence, at least 5,000 lay dead. Cortés ordered the streets cleared of the bodies. He ordered surviving priests and nobles to recall escaped citizens, ensuring that they would be safe. He discovered the Aztec emissaries from Montezuma, safely hidden in the city. Blaming the Cholulan leadership and asserting that he knew Montezuma had no hand in the attempt on the lives of the Spanish, Cortés informed the emissaries of his intent to advance toward Tenochtitlán. Prior to leaving the city, he admonished them to deny their false gods and charged them with abandoning their practice of human sacrifice. It is ironic that the conquistador who was sometimes associated with Quetzalcoatl, the god who abhorred human sacrifice, succeeded in suppressing a likely ambush by killing such a large numbers of the local populace. Yet the controversial massacre resulted in the pacification of further resistance against the small band of Spaniards and their Tlaxcaltec allies.

Rebecca M. Seaman

See also: Cortés, Hernán; La Malinche, "Doña Marina"; Quetzalcoatl; Tenochtitlán, City of; Alliance with Spanish.

Resources

Leon-Portilla, Miguel, ed. *The Broken Spears: The Aztec Account of the Conquest of Mexico.* With Foreword by J. Jorge Klor de Alva. Boston: Beacon Press, 2006.

Levy, Buddy. *Conquistador: Hernán Cortés, King Montezuma, and the Last Stand of the Aztecs.* New York: Bantam Books, Random House, 2009.

Schwartz, Stuart B., ed. *Victors and Vanquished: Spanish and Nahua Views of the Conquest of Mexico.* Boston: Bedford/St. Martin's, 2000.

Thomas, Hugh. *Conquest: Montezuma, Cortés, and the Fall of Old Mexico.* New York: Simon & Schuster, 1993.

Christianity, Impact of on the Aztec

In 1524, a group of Franciscans generally referred to as "The Twelve" arrived in New Spain under the leadership of their superior, Martin de Valencia. Many, including their leader, belonged to strict groups of the Order of St. Francis that followed the Observant tradition. These were men willing to suffer for their beliefs, men filled with missionary fervor. They landed in a world imagined as the soil for the new church. This was the land that God had chosen because it was pure from the corruption of the church in Europe. It was their mission, indeed their divine calling, to prepare the indigenous population, in the eleventh hour of the world, for the second coming of Christ and the establishment of his Kingdom. They carried with them a copy of the mandate that Francisco de Los Angeles, their minister general, had given them immediately before boarding ship in Spain, telling them that they were called to prepare the way for Jesus Christ.

Only five years later, Fr. Bernardino de Sahagún followed in their footsteps. Sahagún was part of the same mendicant order as the Twelve and bearer of the same dream. He had volunteered, as was the custom, to make the journey obligated under the minister general's mandate to preach to and convert those indigenous people of New Spain living under the "yoke of the satanic thrall." It did not take long for Sahagún to come to the conclusion that the first friars had been misled and their early claims of baptisms in the thousands were wide exaggerations. The numbers had been there, but the conversions were untrue and/or incomplete. The old gods held sway.

The indigenous people of the Americas conceptualized the universe in absolutely different modes from those of the Spanish. Serge Gruzinski, professor of Latin American Studies, has explained that since the pre-Hispanic "conceptions of the divine was not governed by the principles of exclusive monotheism, [. . .] the Christian image was integrated into the native field." It seemed natural for the Nahua to simply adopt the new God, or Gods into their already busy pantheon. It can be argued that the claims of Catholic monotheism might have not appeared as clear-cut for people who had just begun to conceptualize Christian mythology. The tripartite Christian God, Father, Son, and Holy Ghost, plus the Virgin Mary and the host of saints created an impression of a more plural cosmology. Plurality would then appear familiar to the multicultural people of New Spain. It was within Nahua tradition to incorporate the Gods of the victor. According to prominent scholar James Lockhart, victory was clear evidence of the power of the victor's god. "One expected a conqueror to impose his god in some fashion, without fully displacing one's own; the new god in any case always proved to be an agglomeration of attributes familiar from the local pantheon and hence easy to assimilate." To add to this, the perception of Christian polytheism, the different approaches to evangelization, and even the differences between the Franciscan and Dominican philosophical traditions, created the illusion of a shared multiplicity familiar to the Nahua.

In 1539, Don Carlos Ometochtzin, Cacique of Tezcoco, demonstrated that a plural worldview was still alive. His exposition eventually resulted in his trial and execution by an Inquisition. However, in speeches in his town, Ometochtzin explained Nahua acceptance of plurality and their use of Christianity's internal differences to validate the continuation of their own. Sahagún noted how the indigenous people, after having received the sacrament of baptism, would declare that they believed in the Catholic tripartite God: God the Father, the Son, and the Holy Ghost, while inside they continued respecting their gods as gods, serving them, and making offerings and celebrations to them. Although the Franciscan was limited to an either-or proposition, where the Nahua either converted truthfully or lied, for the indigenous people the adoption of these new Gods was part of their tradition. It was a strategy for survival, and a way to access the potency of the new Gods. The attempt to integrate Christianity, and to establish a proper relation with the new aspects of the Supernatural, did not imply an abandonment of the old ways. The familiar gods still maintained their places and purposes. Their significance was braided with the people's identities and histories.

In *Totecuyoane,* the Nahuatl document that records the answers given by indigenous leaders to the first Twelve in 1524, the elders made a polite yet passionate defense of their beliefs:

> You say
> that we don't know
> the Omneity of heaven and earth.
> You say that our gods are not original.
> That's news to us
> and it drives us crazy.
> It's a shock and it's a scandal,
> for our ancestors came to earth
> and they spoke quite differently.

The Nahua, even as they integrated Christianity, did not forsake their gods. The image is compelling: Franciscans stood on one side, convinced of the superiority and rightfulness of their vision, and with self-absorbed eloquence condemned the Nahua belief system, even mocking it at times. In their corner, they lectured the Nahua about the fallacy of their gods, demoting them all to mere demons and preaching of their damnation and the damnation of all who continued to worship them. On the other side, the Nahua elders, with delicate subtlety, presented and defended their gods. The conflict is evident, even within the context of the highly contaminated Spanish version of events. The elders lectured the friars, defending their attachment to those they held as *Teotl* (Divinities): "The god called *Huitzilopochtli* [. . .] was very robust, of great strength, and war-like [. . .]. He was like a live fire and was feared by his enemies [. . .] because of his strength and dexterity in war, the Mexicans held him in great esteem." Again, "The god *Tezcatlipoca* was held as true god, invisible, who was everywhere, and they said that only he understood the rules of the world." One after another the Nahua explained their gods and their significance, giving ample details of their natures, stories, and celebrations. Indigenous attachment to their Sacred did not and could not have ceased. It was imbedded in Nahua identity. The friars' perception of deceit was simplistic, as is any idea of clear conversions. A "double-mistaken-identity" logic, theorized by James Lockhart, allowed each side to perceive the other as functioning within familiar parameters. In many ways the Christianity that entered the new world was reformulated by its people into something new, a hybrid, for a lack of a better term, belief system, a Nahuatlized Christianity.

SilverMoon

See also: Franciscans, Role of; Sahagún, Bernardino de.

Resources

Brotherson, Gordon. *Book of the Fourth World: Reading the Native Americas Through Their Literature.* Cambridge: Cambridge University Press, 1992.

Clendinnen, Inga. *The Aztec: An Interpretation.* Cambridge and New York: Cambridge University Press, 1991.

Dibble, Charles E. "The Nahuatlization of Christianity." In *Sixteenth Century Mexico: The Work of Sahagún,* edited by Munro S. Edmondson, 225–233. Albuquerque: University of New Mexico Press, 1974.

Gruzinski, Serge. *The Conquest of Mexico: The Incorporation of Indian Societies into the Western World, 16th–18th Centuries.* Cambridge: Polity Press, 1993.

Lockhart, James. *The Nahuas after the Conquest: A Social and Cultural History of the Indians of Central Mexico, Sixteenth through Eighteenth Centuries.* Stanford, CA: Stanford University Press, 1992.

Rabasa, José. *Franciscans and Dominicans under the Gaze of Tlacuilo: Plural-World Dwelling in an Indian Pictorial Codex.* Morrison Library Inaugural Address Series 14. Berkeley: Doe Library, University of California at Berkeley, 1998.

Rivera, Luis N. *A Violent Evangelism: The Political and Religious Conquest of the Americas.* Louisville, KY: Westminster/John Knox Press, 1992.

Sahagún, Bernardino de. "Arte Adivinatoria." In *Joaquín García Icazbalceta's Bibliografía Mexicana del Siglo XVI: Catálogo Razonado de Libros Impresos en México de 1539 a 1600,* edited by Agustín Millares Carlo, 327–387. México: Fondo de Cultura Económica, 1954.

Sahagún, Bernardino de. "El Libro perdido de las Pláticas o Coloquios de los Doce Primeros Misioneros de México." Selection published under the title *The Lords and Holy Men of Tenochtitlan Reply to the Franciscans, 1524.* Edited by Kenneth Mills and William B. Taylor. Colonial Latin America: A Documentary History. Wilmington, DE: A Scholarly Resources, Inc. Imprint, 1998.

Sahagún, Bernardino de. *Historia General de las Cosas de Nueva España: Y Fundada en la Documentacion en Lengua Mexicana Recogida por los Mismos Naturales.* Edited by Angel María Garibay. Book I. México City: Editorial Porrua, 1956.

Christianity, Impact of on the Inca

The Incas had a polytheistic faith, each with a specific purpose that determined their position in the spiritual hierarchy. An anthropomorphic faith, the Inca imbued their gods with human behavior and emotions—a trait that served the Spanish well when introducing the Christian God. However, the Incas believed their gods caused natural phenomena and it was essential to keep them happy so these natural disasters could be avoided. This desired outcome was achieved through the use of ceremonies and sacrifices.

A somewhat confusing aspect of the pre-conquest Inca faith includes the concept of Huacas, sacred elements that included holy places or temples and natural physical features where the Incas made their offerings to their gods in an effort to please or appease them. The pre-conquest Inca performed a variety of sacred ceremonies to appease their deities, which included occasional human sacrifices. However, these sacrifices were only performed during important events in the life of the Inca emperor, such as his illness, death, or the succession of a new emperor to the throne. As the Spanish later attempted to introduce Catholicism, the religious authorities attacked and destroyed many of the Inca Huacas, thereby undermining their influence and destroying them as ceremonial sites for indigenous rituals.

Christianity was introduced to the Inca in 1532 with the arrival of Francisco Pizarro and his Spanish army. Atahualpa, the Inca emperor or Sapa Inca, agreed to meet Pizarro at the plaza of Cajamarca. The emperor was accompanied by 5,000 to 6,000 armed men, and an additional portion of his army of 35,000 was nearby, the result of having just defeated his half-brother and contender to the throne of the Inca. Pizarro sent his second in command, Hernando de Soto, as well as friar Vicente de Valverde and native interpreter Felipillo to speak with Atahualpa about the Spanish presence. Despite the use of an interpreter, communications broke down at this meeting. The friar made a speech and presented Atahualpa with a Bible. Not knowing the significance of this unfamiliar item, the emperor looked at it and presumably tossed it aside, setting off a series of events that quickly led to his capture and the fall of the empire.

From the beginning, the conflicting ideals of faith played a role in relations between the two societies. Pizarro's chaplain greeted the king with the announcement that King Charles V of Spain was the only true king and that the Christian god was the only true god. This double affront to the position of the Inca Emperor and the Inca gods was a serious breach in protocol. Through the interpreter, Fr. Valverde delivered the "Requirement," indicating that Atahualpa and his people must convert to Christianity, and if he refused, he would be considered an enemy of the Church and of Spain. With far superior numbers, Spanish demands for the Incas to reject their traditional faith were deemed offensive.

Atahualpa's initial refusal to accept this new religion and god, and his act of disrespecting the sacred text presented by friar Valverde, led Pizarro to attack the Inca army in what became known as the Battle of Cajamarca. The Spanish advantage of surprise, plus their use of guns, horses, and other novelties, enabled them to capture Atahualpa and kill much of his remaining army. Once Atahualpa understood the Spaniards' intentions, he offered them a ransom of 13,420 pounds of gold and 26,000 pounds of silver in exchange for his release. Pizarro accepted the offer and promised to release Atahualpa once the ransom was received; however, Pizarro's partners suggested that Atahualpa be executed in the event that the Inca leader wanted retaliation. Pizarro wished to find reason for executing Atahualpa without angering the people he wished to control. Despite the Sapa Inca fulfilling the ransom request, the Spanish convicted him of killing his brother Huáscar and plotting against Pizarro and his forces.

Typical of the Spanish treatment of the indigenous Inca populace, Atahualpa was encouraged to embrace the Christian faith before his execution. Typical of the indigenous beliefs, the Spanish victory in battle indicated the failure or weakness of their own deities in relation to the Spanish deity. It is not surprising that Atahualpa agreed to this last minute conversion prior to his execution. Conversion to the Christian faith did not result in the Spanish forgiving the Sapa Inca for his perceived faults, nor convince them to stay his execution, though they did agree to use garroting as a more honorable means of execution.

The initial victory over Atahualpa's forces was due to Spanish surprise, effective use of ambush, technology, and fear of the loud guns, and use of dogs and horses. However, the continued victories of the Spanish against the extensive Inca Empire were in part due to the religious perceptions of the people. Pizarro effectively portrayed the Spanish God as one who sought justice for the death of the Sapa Inca's brother, thereby winning the support of the brother's, Huáscar's, armies and supporters. Nonetheless the forces of Atahualpa continue to fight in opposition under the able generals of Quizquiz and Rumiñahui.

Pizarro filled the void in Inca leadership and helped defeat those loyal to the deceased Sapa Inca by designating brothers of Atahualpa and Huáscar as the new leaders of the empire. After the first failed attempt of selecting a replacement Sapa Inca, another brother—Manco Inca—was presented the "royal fringe." The new Sapa Inca, while initially cooperative with the Spanish, eventually fled and led his empire from seclusion. There is no evidence of him embracing Christianity; however, just before his death at the hand of Spaniards, he reputedly asserted that the Christian God was more powerful than the Inca Sun god—represented by the person of the Sapa Inca. Each of his sons in turn became Sapa Incas, ruling for years before adopting the Christian faith for themselves, and at times, for their children. In each instance, the Sapa Inca took Christian saint's names and welcomed missionaries at their courts. In the case of Titu Cusi, second son of Manco Inca, a Franciscan monk not only was sent to serve the emperor, but to educate his children. Indeed, Titu Cusi dictated his history of the Inca Empire to an Augustinian monk, Fray Marcos García, resulting in a mixture of Inca views and Spanish interpretations of a presumably indigenous history of the Inca. Martin Pando, the Spanish-educated mestizo secretary to the emperor, later transcribed the history.

The final Sapa Inca, Tupac Amaru, reigned briefly from 1571 to 1572 and was a confirmed opponent to the Spanish and their Christian faith. Yet, after a short period of rule, he was captured and brought before the Spanish at Cuzco. Following brief instruction in the Christian faith, he, too, was baptized

and publicly professed the Christian faith. Tupac Amaru went further, however, instructing the Inca people that their own faith was false, and that the priests and Sapa Inca had spoken for the gods because their gods were just lifeless statues. Despite this profession being followed by the execution of the emperor, the Inca population abandoned their traditional faith in large numbers from this point forward.

The cessation of Inca hostilities against the Spanish and their Christian faith, and the large numbers of professed converts to Catholicism, did not imply true conversion in a sense understood today. Instead, the Incas were typical of many indigenous populations as they embraced the new monotheism of Christianity. The native people of Peru incorporated old pagan practices, including ceremonies and even worship of idols, into the practice of Catholicism. The Spanish and the Church were complicit in this mixture of indigenous practices and Christian tenets, providing dispensation for the marriage of noble Incas to their own siblings as a means of ensuring continued support for Spanish rule and Christian dominance in the former empire.

The new faith became the framework of the Incas' religious practices, with converts adopting Christian names for themselves and their communities, baptizing their children, and even having their children educated by the Christian friars. It was the later practice that prompted the greatest reforms to indigenous religious beliefs and cultural norms. Within a single generation, the noble families of the Inca were educated in Spanish language, belief systems, and other cultural traits; intermarried with the local encomenderos, political authorities and military leaders; and provided models for Inca submission to and adoption of Christianity. While old practices continued to exist, the greatest persistence in indigenous faith practices became relegated to rural communities.

Monae S. Merck and Rebecca M. Seaman

See also: Atahualpa; Cajamarca, Battle of; Huacas; Huáscar; Manco Inca Yupanqui; Pizarro, Francisco; Quizquiz; Rumiñahui; Sapa Inca; Titu Cusi Yupanqui; Túpac Amaru.

Resources

Bauer, Ralph, ed., trans., and intro. *An Inca Account of the Conquest of Peru.* Boulder: University of Colorado Press, 2003.

Cobo, Bernabé. *History of the Inca Empire: An Account of the Indians' Customs and Their Origin, Together with a Treatise on Inca Legens, History, and Social Institutions.* Translated and edited by Roland Hamilton. Austin: University of Texas Press, 1979.

Julien, Catherine. *Reading Inca History.* Iowa City: University of Iowa Press, 1999.

Legnani, Nicole Delia. "Introduction." In *Titu Cusi: A 16th Century Account of the Conquest.* Cambridge: Harvard University Press, 2005.

Niles, Susan. *The Shape of Inca History. Narrative and Architecture in an Andean Empire.* Iowa City: University of Iowa Press, 1999.

Class, Impact of Spanish on the Inca

Pre-conquest Inca society, while attempting to structure a system devoid of strict class structures, was nonetheless a dual class society. The *kurakas* (local leaders or lords), the Sapa Inca and his extended family and noble supporters, and the nobility of subjected people who were loyal to the Inca ("Inca by privilege") made up the upper class or nobility in the empire. The vast majority of the society was comprised of commoners, whether they were members of the local *ayllus* (clans) serving as farmers, or members of the *yanas* or *yanaconas* (full-time servants who often worked far from their home communities and outside of their own *ayllus*). This was not a system of haves and have-nots, though, as the Inca society practiced a form of reciprocity, where the nobility gathered *mita* or tribute for storage and use in times of need, and were tasked with serving as the caretakers of the common classes under their authority.

With the arrival of the Spanish under Francisco Pizarro, several shifts began to take place in the Inca society. The first obvious impact was the transfer of authority from the Inca nobility to the Spanish. In an effort to convert the indigenous population and extract labor for the purposes of mining or agricultural purposes, the Spanish conquistadors were granted encomiendas that placed entire Indian communities under their authority. This shifting of local authority, from the relatively benevolent or at least well-intended authority of the Inca to the self-motivated, profit-oriented authority of the Spanish foreign, was the second stage of major class upheaval.

The Inca nobility undertook direct action to stanch the loss of their authority. To a certain extent they proved successful. The family members of the Sapa Inca, at least those who embraced the Catholic faith, were granted encomienda and bound in marriage to the Spanish conquistadors. By the end of the first generation, the Inca Empire existed more in name than in reality. Within it, the class structure had shifted. The Spanish encomenderos and government officials (*visitadors*, viceroys, governors, military leaders, *audiencias*, etc.) were clearly at the helm of power. Ruling beside them, though with little power, were the Inca nobility, now professing the Catholic faith and Spanish names. The third rung in the class ladder was comprised of those elements of the Spanish colonizing forces that served the Crown but held little authority for themselves. At the bottom of this class structure were the masses of Inca and non-Inca peoples. Instead of independent farmers or servants who worked directly for a noble person (*yanaconas*), these lower class Indians were reduced to serving in encomienda or repartimiento. Still required to pay tribute, but at an accelerating rate, the Indians were quickly reduced to the equivalent of serfdom. Within a few generations, even the nobility of the Inca were reduced to peonage, leaving the indigenous populace at the lower rungs of society and the Spanish (as well as some lower placed mestizos) firmly in power.

Rebecca M. Seaman

See also: *Audiencia*; *Ayllus*; Encomenderos; Encomienda; *Kuraka*; *Mita*; Pizarro, Francisco; Repartimiento; Sapa Inca; Viceroyalty System; *Visitas*; *Yanaconas*.

Resources

Hemming, John. *The Conquest of the Incas.* London: Pan Macmillan, 1970.

MacQuarrie, Kim. *The Last Days of the Incas.* New York: Simon & Schuster, 2007.

Means, Philip A. *The Fall of the Inca Empire and the Spanish Rule in Peru, 1530–1780.* New York: Gordian Press, 1971.

Sancho, Pedro. *An Account of the Conquest of Peru.* With Preface and translation by Philip Ainsworth Means. New York: Cortes Society, 1917.

Stern, Steve J. *Peru's Indian Peoples and the Challenge of Spanish Conquest: Huamanga to 1640.* 2nd ed. Madison: University of Wisconsin Press, 1993.

Class, Impact of Spanish on the Mexica

Transformation in the social stratification of the Mexica, including cultural and social changes, followed the Spanish conquest of the Mexica people. It was originated from the transformation of the independent indigenous kingdoms into communities subordinate to the Spanish.

Aztec society can be characterized as a system of classes, determined by the position occupied by the different groups in the systems of production and of social economy. More rigorously, it can also be categorized as a stratified or estate society, where nobility differs from the rest of the people by virtue of their lineage or birth.

In pre-Hispanic times, the main division was between nobles (*pipiltin*) and commoners (*macehualtin*). The basis of the economic power of the nobility rested on its power over the land and labor of the commoner groups associated with it. The *pipiltin* obtained their authority by inheritance and conquest. After every victory, the ruler (*tlatoani*) effected a distribution of part of the dominated lands between the most distinguished principals and warriors of the nobility. Commoners were obliged to give periodically a tribute in labor and goods to their lords, while the nobles controlled the main forms of economic production: agriculture, tribute, and trade.

At the same time, the dominant estate of nobles included three basic levels: the king or *tlatoani,* who was the ruler of a city or lordship; the lord or *teuctli,* who was the head of a manor house, and the noble or *pilli,* the authority. The primary way to acquire the status of a noble was to be born within a noble family. Nonetheless, some mobility was provided through accrued merits in the military, commercial, craftwork, and priestly classes, thus allowing for some commoners to ascend to the rank of nobility.

The commoners were organized into territorial units called *calpules,* which were neighborhoods that held the land in common. There was also some social differentiation between commoners, based on their various occupations. Merchants and artisans held higher positions in society and paid tribute differently. Furthermore, the *terrazgueros* or laborers (*mayeque*) occupied a lower status since they worked the land of a noble. These *mayeques* provided domestic service to nobles and paid part of their harvest as tribute. There were also kind of slaves (*tlacotin*), who preserved their personal freedom but were forced to be in service to the nobility.

The first major change introduced with the arrival of the Spanish was the sociopolitical separation between the "Republic of Indians" and the "Republic of Spanish," as separate societies or political communities integrated respectively by Indians and Spanish. Thus, the entire indigenous population became part of a group legally different from the rest of the people. While the old nobles formed a subgroup with well-defined privileges—and so they remained until the end of the colonial era—most of the population was composed of commoners. Within this group, it continued being *terrazgueros* at the service of the noble. Nominally, Indian slavery ended in 1550.

During this early colonial period two ranks of nobility were recognized: the caciques (*chiefs*), who were the successors of the pre-Hispanic kings or lords, and the *principales* (local rulers), relatives of the *caciques* or descendants of the *pipiltin*. The Spanish ruled through these noble Indians, who were granted important privileges in turn, including the conservation of their titles, lands, and *terrazgueros,* in addition to the hispanization of their lifestyle. Their noble houses (*teccalli*) were compared with the *mayorazgos* (primogenitures) of Castile.

A third social group developed from the importation of black slaves from Africa to work on plantations, ranches, or mining areas. In 1639 Indian slavery was legally prohibited in America, but the slavery of black Africans continued until Independence. These imported slaves were at the bottom of the social scale, even when they escaped and achieved their freedom, becoming *cimarrones* (runaways).

The second major impact caused by the arrival of the Spanish was the phenomenon of *mestizaje* (mixed "races"). It was originated when the European population mixed with the indigenous and African peoples. The word *mestizo* (one progenitor of "white race" and one of "indigenous race") was used to name one of the "castes" or "mixtures" that integrated the social stratification of New Spain, as well as *mulatto* (one progenitor of "white race" and one of "black race"). This miscegenation of races generated a whole system of nomenclature to classify people based on the purity of their blood. The social status of *mestizos* and *mulattos* was considered very low, which prevented them from gaining access to education, property, and command positions.

Over a period of time, the Spanish administration modified the indigenous stratification system. It minimized the old noble power and equalized all social classes to the same level. This process, known as *macehualización,* received a major boost in the eighteenth century.

Marta Martín Gabaldón

See also: Aztec, or Mexica; *Macehualtin*; *Mayeques*; Mexico, State of after Spanish Conquest; Mexico, State of prior to Spanish Conquest; *Pipiltin*; Tribute, Paid to Spain.

Resources

Carrasco, Pedro. "Cultura y sociedad en el México Antiguo." In *Historia General de México,* 153–233. México D.F.: El Colegio de México, 2000.

Carrasco, Pedro. "La transformación de la cultura indígena durante la colonia." *Historia Mexicana* 25, no. 2 (1975): 175–203.

Deans-Smith, Susan. "Culture, Power and Society in Colonial Mexico." *Latin American Research Review*. 33, no. 1 (1998): 257–277.

Douglas Cope, Robert. *The Limits of Racial Domination: Plebeian Society in Colonial Mexico City, 1660–1720*. Madison: University of Wisconsin Press, 1994.

Coatzacoalcos

Coatzacoalcos is the name given to a large coastal government that resisted Aztec political and military control. Today, this designation includes a large portion of southern Veracruz as well as sections of the other federal states of Tabasco, Chiapas, and Oaxaca. A river bearing the name also runs through the region. The peoples of the region were culturally diverse, but are thought to have strong ancestral ties to the Olmecs. One estimate places the population at the time of Hernán Cortés's arrival and conquest at 50,000 individuals. This population was spread across roughly 75 villages or settlements. Caciques, or village leaders, answered to a central authority at the settlement of Coatzacoalcos. Women and men both served in political offices.

Coatzacoalcos remained independent from the Aztecs, through force of arms. No tributes were paid to Tenochtitlán. However, some political unity did exist between the two societies. Coatzacoalcos did agree to the establishment of a trading network with the Aztec Empire. Tlapallan, homeland of the deity Quetzalcoatl, was thought by some Aztecs to be within the boundaries of Coatzacoalcos.

In May 1522, after the fall of the Aztec Empire, Cortés sent Gonzalo de Sandoval, one of his lieutenant conquistadors, to found a town at Coatzacoalcos, which was named Villa del Espiritu Santo Coatzacoalcos. He then distributed encomiendas among the Spanish inhabitants, establishing a tributary labor system used by the Spanish in occupied areas in the New World. By 1531, the Coatzacoalcos designation was reduced in scope; its population and territory were reassigned to Veracruz, the Marquesado del Valle, Chiapas, and Tabasco. Today, Coatzacoalcos is a thriving port on the Mexican coast in the federal state of Veracruz.

Michael D. Coker

See also: Cortés, Hernán; Encomienda; Sandoval, Gonzalo de.

Resources

Bricker, Victoria Reifler. *The Indian Christ, the Indian King: The Historical Substrate of Maya Myth*. Austin: University of Texas Press, 2009.

Himmerich y Valencia, Robert. *The Encomenderos of New Spain, 1521–1555*. Austin: University of Texas Press, 1996.

Collasuyu

The largest and southernmost quarter of Tahuantinsuyu, the Inca name for their combined empire, covering an area that ranged from the Pacific shores of the Atacama Desert over the mountains to the eastern tropical forest that descend into the Amazon River Basin. The region was named after the Aymara-speaking people, the Colla, in the Lake Titicaca basin. The Collasuyu quadrant, comprised mainly of high plains and mountains, falls within the region known as the altiplano (the high plain). In this region, seasonal rainfall ranged from 50 cm or more. Despite the close proximity of the region to the equator, the high altitude kept temperatures cool and tolerable. In the Lake Titicaca basin, Aymara-speaking kingdoms were densely settled. The large population and valuable minerals in nearby mines made the people targets for the first conquests by the Cuzco Inca. The land along Lake Titicaca was responsible for the region being known as the breadbasket, and therefore the power base of highland Tahuantinsuyu.

On the altiplano, agriculture was possible despite the obstacles the region presented for farming: altitude, frost, hail, erratic rainfall, and poor soils that required frequent fallowing all made the development of highly specialized crops extremely necessary. Grains were grown in this region, such as quiñoa and cañihuas. The Inca also grew tuber crops, including more than 60 types of potatoes. Above 3,900 meters in elevation, vast expanses of dry puna grasslands provided grazing for herds of llama and alpaca. Its rich agropastoralism, plus the symbiotic connection between farming and herding, turned Collasuyu into the most populated region of the Andes during the reign of the Incas and later Spanish. Famous cities from the region included Tiwanaku and Pukara.

The region also contained the Atacama Desert. The desert had few oases and small coastal valleys for agriculture. However, the nearby coast was home to rich marine life and fishermen were able to catch mollusks, fish, sea mammals, and marine birds. Anchovies could be caught in nets year-round. The desert benefited from the proximity of these resources and managed to remain self-sufficient from the high-valley agriculture.

Ryan Gillen

See also: Antisuyu; Chinchaysuyu; Contisuyu; Tahuantinsuyu.

Resources

Bushnell, G. H. S. *Ancient Peoples and Places: Peru.* New York: Praeger, 1966.

Moseley, Moseley. *The Incas and Their Ancestors: The Archaeology of Peru.* New York: Thames and Hudson, 1993.

Colón, Diego

Son of Christopher Columbus, Diego Colón raised at court, where he held the position of page at the time of his father's voyage of initial discovery. Colón came to Hispaniola in 1509 to replace the former governor, Fr. Nicolás de Ovando. Colón served under the title of Second Admiral of the Indies and governor of the Indies. Married to María de Toledo y Rojas, Colón's connections at court assisted in positioning him in America. His appointment as governor was in part a reaction of the Crown to the harsh implementation of Queen Isabella's Real Cedula of 1503 that resulted in the extermination of many of the Tainos Indians on the islands.

Colón's treatment of the indigenous population was an improvement over his

Diego Colón (Columbus), eldest son of Christopher Columbus. (Look and Learn/The Bridgeman Art Library)

predecessor, a fact made necessary by the constant protests of the Dominicans at court. However, his relations with the increasing Spanish settlers were strained. In 1511 he sought the title of viceroy of the Indies, hoping to hold authority over all islands and Spanish possessions in the New World at that time.

Diego Colón's new arrival in the islands, with his father's titles and privileges in hand, immediately put him at odds with the established Spanish settlers. With growing encomiendas and large plantations, these well-heeled colonists had the power of feudal lords and wielded that power to restrict Colón. The zeal with which these encomenderos sought to further their own wealth led the Dominicans, specifically Bartolomé de Las Casas, to oppose the treatment and policies meted out on the indigenous Tainos population. One of the strained relations Colón had with the Spanish colonists was with his subordinate, Diego Velázquez de Cuéllar. Initially the chief accountant to Ovando, Velázquez was simultaneously indebted to Colón and jealous of the power the son of Christopher Columbus held. As the settlements spread from one island to another, Velázquez sought to rise in recognition by the Crown, from that of lieutenant governor of Cuba to governor and even *Adelantado*.

Colón's own ambitions, evidenced by his insistence on being called "the Admiral" and his trips back to Spain to seek the title of viceroy, opened the door for others to grasp power for themselves. At the time of the second decade of the 16th century, numerous explorations of Caribbean islands were conducted, spreading the authority and based of Spanish power. Explorations and trade with the coastal rimland of Middle and South America supplemented these island expeditions. Initially conducting raids and trade for slaves to work in the island plantations and mines, explorers discovered evidence of greater wealth and advanced societies. These previously undiscovered territories became the object of ambitious conquistadors who sought to use the Spanish legal system to claim new lands and wealth for Spain while also gaining new titles of authority for themselves. The void created by Colón's absence from the Caribbean furthered these quests for power and added to the unchecked aggression of the Spanish toward the indigenous population.

Diego Colón's tenure as governor of the Indies came to an end in 1518. In 1521, the Christmas day revolt on Colón's sugar plantation was the first major slave revolt in the colonies. The incident prompted the establishment of slave ordinances designed by Colón and intended to prevent future slave revolts on the islands. Four years later, Diego Colón died in Spain in 1526.

Rebecca M. Seaman

See also: *Adelantado*; Columbus, Christopher; Encomenderos; Encomienda; Hispaniola; Las Casas, Bartolomé de; Ovando, Fr. Nicolás de; Velázquez, Diego (de Cuéllar).

Resources

Guitar, Lynne. "Boiling It Down: Slavery on the First Commercial Sugarcan Ingenios in the Americas (Hispaniola, 1530–45)." In *Slaves, Subjects, and Subversives: Blacks in Colonial Latin America,* edited by Jane G. Landers and Barry M. Robinson. Albequerque: University of New Mexico, 2006.

Prescott, William H. *The History of the Conquest of Mexico.* London: Continuum International Publishing Group, 2009.

Thomas, Hugh. *Conquest: Montezuma, Cortés, and the Fall of Old Mexico.* New York: Simon & Schuster, 1993.

Columbus, Christopher

Italian-born navigator and explorer Cristoforo Columbo [Columbus] was born in the

Italian city-state of Genoa, in 1451. Columbus received little or no formal education in his youth. Indeed, he never wrote in Italian, although he did learn to read and write in both Spanish and Portuguese. Columbus spent much of his youth working as an apprentice to his father, who was a master weaver and part-time wineshop owner, but by his own account, Columbus took to the sea at a "tender age."

At the age of 19, Columbus made his first trading voyage in the Aegean Sea. In his early twenties, he began to make longer voyages to Marseilles, Tunis, and the Greek isles. In 1476, Columbus set out for Flanders and England, but French privateers sunk his vessel. He landed penniless in Portugal and was taken in by one of many Genoese living in Lisbon. There, Columbus acquired most of his knowledge of navigation.

Although the Portuguese were in the process of developing a trade route to India by sailing around Africa, Columbus advocated sailing west to reach the Indies. Inspired by the writings of Florentine cosmographer Paolo Toscanelli, Cardinal Pierre d'Ailly's *Image of the World,* and Marco Polo's account of the Far East, Columbus asserted that the Earth's circumference was much smaller than it actually was and that a western route would be shorter. When the king of Portugal rejected Columbus's proposal to finance the voyage, he turned to King Ferdinand V and Queen Isabella I of Spain. In April 1492, Isabella I of Castile agreed to make Columbus governor of any new lands he acquired and offered him 10 percent of all wealth he recovered for Spain. Commanding the *Santa Maria,* the *Pinta,* and the *Niña,* Columbus departed Spain on August 3, 1492, and after a trying two-month voyage reached the island of San Salvador in the Bahamas on October 12. After landing on Cuba and Española (later called Hispaniola), where he left a garrison of 40 men, Columbus returned to Spain in 1493.

He did not return to Spain empty handed, though the riches of gold and spices evaded Columbus. The Spanish gathered and shipped 500 of the local Taino Indians as gifts for the court of Queen Isabella and King Ferdinand. Of the 500 hostages, 300 survived the voyage and were sold. Likewise, Arawaks and eventually Caribs in the islands claimed by the Spanish explorers were soon enslaved, providing labor in the fruitless search for gold, and eventually in farming such cash crops as sugarcane.

Upon his return, Isabella commanded Columbus to sail again immediately. He embarked on a second expedition with 17 ships and 1,000 colonists in September 1493. On returning to Española, he discovered that the natives had killed garrison he left behind. Columbus established the colony of Isabella near modern Cape Isabella in the Dominican Republic. He also landed on Dominica, Guadeloupe, and Antigua and explored the coast of Cuba. Before returning to Spain in 1496, Columbus founded Santo Dominigo as the capital of Española. This second voyage was dedicated in part to the search for gold and the capture of further slaves from the native population.

In the wake of further enslavement, forced labor, and Spanish demands for food, the local Taino abandoned their timid relations with the Europeans. Bartolomé Colon, a brother of Columbus, served as the leader of the Española settlement in the absence of his elder sibling. His natural leadership abilities proved invaluable in quelling a potentially devastating uprising, leaving the Spanish still dominating the island and the Columbus family still tenuously governing the settlement.

In May 1498, Columbus, who still asserted he had reached Asia, set out on his third expedition. He landed on the island of Trinidad and sighted what is now Venezuela, discovering the continent of South America. When

Artistic rendition of Christopher Columbus and crew first sighting the New World on the Santa Maria in 1492. (Library of Congress)

he arrived in Santo Domingo, Columbus found the colony of Española in revolt. Spanish demands of labor and food and the impact of disease on the native Taino combined with the frustration of the colonists' failure to find wealth expected with the Far East; the result was explosive. Across the Atlantic in Spain, discontented colonists successfully persuaded Ferdinand and Isabella to remove Columbus as governor of Española in May 1499 and appoint Francisco de Bobadilla to establish order in the colony. Columbus was subsequently arrested and sent back to Spain in chains. On his return, Isabella pardoned Columbus but refused to restore him to office as governor of Española.

In May 1502, Columbus ventured on his fourth and final expedition. Hampered by a hurricane, he managed to reach Honduras and searched in vain along the Central American coast for a passage across the continent to Asia. In January 1503, Columbus landed at Panama and established a colony there. By June that same year, his fleet was marooned near Jamaica. After returning to Spain in 1504, Columbus found he had lost not only his title as governor of the Indies but his chief support in the person of Isabella, who died earlier that year. Suffering from arthritis, humiliated, and frustrated by the elusive fame and wealth he so fiercely sought, Columbus died in Valladolid, Spain, on May 20, 1506.

Columbus did not live to see the great wealth resulting from his Spanish claims in the New World. His discovery of the

Americas eventually presented undreamed of opportunities for Europeans while it simultaneously brought drastic changes to the diets, economies, and political structures throughout the continent. Unfortunately, Columbus's successful contact with the New World also marked the beginning of several centuries of famine, disease, enslavement, dislocation, and violence for the Native American peoples already living in the Western Hemisphere.

Paul G. Pierpaoli Jr.

See also: Caribs; Cuba; Hispaniola; Slavery, Role of.

Resources

Davidson, Miles H. *Columbus Then and Now: A Life Reexamined.* Norman: University of Oklahoma Press, 1997.

Di Giovanni, Mario. *Christopher Columbus: His Life and Discoveries.* San Gabriel, CA: Columbus Explorers, 1991.

Wilson, Samuel M. "Columbus, My Enemy." *Natural History* 99, no. 12 (December 1990): 44–49.

Conquistadores

Meaning literally "the conquerors," the term conquistadores referred to the kinship these Spanish explorers felt with those who had accomplished the Reconquista (reconquest) of Spain from Muslim Moorish control in 1492. Many conquistadors were initially poor, as tradition prohibited Spanish noblemen from engaging in manual work; others sought to escape religious prosecution of the Spanish Inquisition. The New World offered these conquistadors opportunities to seek new fortunes in South and Central America, Mexico, parts of the Caribbean, and portions of the present-day United States.

The Spanish fought for control over these new colonies with the Portuguese, their chief imperial rival. This rivalry was finally settled under papal arbitration in the Treaty of Tordesillas of 1494. This treaty divided the territory conquered outside of Europe between the Spanish Crown and the Portuguese along a north-south meridian running 1,100 miles west of the Cape Verde Islands off the west coast of Africa. The territory to the east belonged to Portugal and the land to the west to Spain. In 1506, Pope Julius II officially sanctioned this division. This opened the way for Spanish exploration and colonization in the New World.

The Spanish conquest of the Americas began in 1492 with the arrival of Christopher Columbus. The Caribbean regions were conquered first but these did not provide sufficient treasure to make the conquerors rich. Juan Ponce de León secured the island of Puerto Rico, while Diego Velázquez took Cuba. Hernán Cortés became the first significantly successful conquistador. He overpowered the Aztecs during 1520–1521 and brought Mexico under Spanish rule. A decade later, Francisco Pizarro was responsible for conquering the Incas in South America.

The conquistadores brought with them European diseases, such as smallpox, influenza, measles, and typhus, which were disastrous to the Native American populations who had no immunity to them. European diseases, in many cases, wiped out between 30 and 90 percent of the native populations. In respect to the Aztecs and the Incas, the diseases significantly weakened their populations—which had initially outnumbered the Spanish—and thereby the trauma of disease aided the Spanish conquistadores in their effort to colonize the Americas.

The legends of immeasurable wealth located in golden cities such as El Dorado enticed many Spanish adventurers to leave for the Americas. Oftentimes they came back empty-handed; however, those who did manage to bring precious metals back to Spain propagated the impression of seemingly endless sources of gold and silver in the New World. Over time, the Spanish rulers relied too heavily on these imports, thereby overstretching the Crown's budget to the point of bankruptcy. This undermined the Spanish and European economies and led to rampant inflation in Spain.

Native American populations suffered greatly at the hands of the conquistadores. Wanton killings, enslavement, rape, torture, and other abuses perpetuated the stereotype of Spanish cruelty that came to be known as the "black legend." This term referred to the infamous Spanish Inquisition and later to the behavior of the Spanish conquistadores in the colonies. Early Protestant historians, describing the period of Spanish colonization, often depicted the Spanish conquistadores as being fanatical, cruel, intolerant, and greedy, thus perpetuating the black legend.

Contemporary Spanish accounts of native mistreatment by the conquistadores contributed to the passage of the Spanish colonial laws, known as the New Laws, in 1542. These laws were designed to protect the rights of Indians and to prevent the exploitation of indigenous peoples by the conquistadores. The enslavement of the natives in the New World colonies came under further scrutiny in the Valladolid Debate of 1550–1551. This debate sought to determine whether Native Americans had souls, as white Europeans were believed to possess. Bartolomé de Las Casas, a Dominican friar, argued that the full humanity of the natives was evident because they indeed did possess souls. The Jesuit priest Juan Ginés de Sepúlveda, however, maintained that the indigenous peoples in the New World did not have souls and, therefore, could be enslaved. Spanish king Carlos I (Charles V—HRE) confronted with this debate, ordered an end to the aggression against the natives, and ordered a jury of eminent scholars to hold a hearing on the subject. The jury ruled in favor of treating the natives as human beings, who were presumed to have immortal souls.

Before attacking indigenous populations, Spanish policies demanded the conquistadores read to the native peoples a document known as the *Requerimiento*. It provided an overview of world history, with the focus on Christianity. It demanded that the indigenous peoples accept the king of Spain as their supreme ruler on behalf of the pope and allow missionaries to introduce them to Christianity. This document came into being after the Catholic Church in Spain asserted that the wars against Native American peoples were unjust and immoral. For the conquistadores, the *Requerimiento* served as a loophole to put the native populations in a position in which they would reject Christianity and could, therefore, be attacked without facing the wrath of the Catholic Church or the king.

Often by force, the Indians were gradually converted to Christianity. Missions, established to convert the natives, were typically associated with Presidios for the purpose of controlling any resistance to Spanish dominance. In combining these two structures, the conquistadores played an important role in purging most native cultural practices. Nonetheless, the natives often blended their traditional customs and beliefs with Catholic traditions.

The desire of individual conquistadors to seek their fortunes combined with the Crown's determination to spread the Catholic faith and Spanish Empire throughout the New World. While some regions of the Americas boasted extreme riches that captivated the Spanish and led to long-term settlements, other regions proved devoid of obvious mineral wealth. The constant push of conquistadors, to claim for Spain new lands with plentiful resources, succeeded in spreading Spanish culture, authority, the Catholic faith and diseases. In the end, Spanish culture outlasted imperial authority; and the Catholic faith and deadly diseases both influenced the indigenous population for centuries to come.

Anna Rulska

See also: Charles V (HRE) or Carlos I of Spain; Columbus, Christopher; Cortés, Hernán; European Diseases, Role of; Las Casas, Bartolomé de; Leyes Nuevas Pizarro, Francisco; Ponce de León, Juan; *Requerimiento*; Sepúlveda's *De Orbe Novo (Historia del Nuevo Mundo)*; Velázquez, Diego (de Cuéllar).

Resources

Barghusen, Joan D. *The Aztecs: End of a Civilization.* San Diego, CA: Lucent Books, 2000.

Baudez, Claude F., and Sydney Picasso. *Lost Cities of the Maya.* New York: Harry N. Abrams, 1992.

Hakim, Joy. *The First Americans.* New York: Oxford University Press, 1993.

Jones, Mary Ellen. *Christopher Columbus and his Legacy: Opposing Viewpoints.* San Diego, CA: Greenhaven, 1992.

Wood, Michael. *Conquistadors.* Berkeley: University of California Press, 2000.

Contisuyu

Contisuyu (or Cuntisuyu) was the indigenous name for the small, southwestern quarter of Tahuantinsuyu (the collective four regions of the Inca Empire) that stretched north from Cuzco to the Pacific coast near the Ica Valley and south to the Moquegua Valley. The dry western slopes of the Andes and the coastal desert characterize the region. Historically there is usually no annual rainfall below elevations of 1,800 meters, making much of the region barren. However, the mountain slopes consist of a variety of ecological zones, which were utilized under the Inca in a system presently known as vertical archipelagos. This localized trade in such a geographically diverse region allowed *ayllus* (kinship groups) to supply all of their items of need, as well as luxury items such as copper. Despite innovative processes developed in order to meet the region's need, the aridity of the Contisuyu made this quarter of Tahuantinsuyu relatively poor in comparison to the other three regions.

Such infertile land in the desert required the indigenous residents to make intensive use of marine assets and animal hunting through a resource known as *lomas,* coastlands that were covered by sea fog in winter months, which led to the development of flora during these months. Pre-Columbian herders used *lomas* to provide fodder for large herds of camelids such as alpacas and llamas. However, during El Niño years, the region was wet enough to support some specialized crops. Higher up on the Andean slopes, above 1,800 meters, 15 rivers crossed the desert. These rivers supported terrace farming but the mouth of the rivers near the ocean contained decreasing amounts of water, reducing the number of people that the rivers were able to support.

Ryan Gillen

See also: *Ayllus*; Antisuyu; Chinchaysuyu; Collasuyu; Tahuantinsuyu.

Resources

Andrien, Kenneth. *Andean Worlds: Indigenous History, Culture, and Consciousness under Spanish Rule, 1532–1825.* Albuquerque: University of New Mexico Press, 2001.

Moseley, Michael. *The Incas and Their Ancestors: The Archaeology of Peru.* New York: Thames and Hudson, 1993.

Corregidores

Spanish government employees, in charge of several aspects of justice and administration in local spheres, were called *corregidores*. These *corregidores* protected the royal interests in America; ruling over a jurisdiction designated a *corregimiento*. The administrative positions had their origin in the kingdom of Castile in the 14th century, where they were created to represent the monarchy in towns and cities. They also were known as *alcaldes mayores* (main mayors), to differentiate between the royal administrative role of *corregidores* and the ordinary mayors of the town councils. They were additionally referred to as *justicias mayores* (main judges), according to one of their numerous functions. In these cases, the etymologies are enlightening about the responsibilities of *corregidores*: a *regidor* was a town councilor or mayor, and then, the *co-regidor* co-governed with the councilors elect. Due to the fact that these officials represented the kings, the adjective *mayor* (main) accompanied the noun *alcalde* (mayor).

Corregidores were introduced in America just after the Spanish conquest. During the 18th century, in 1786, through the Bourbon Reforms, *corregidores* were substituted by *intendentes* (intendants). This same period saw the *corregimientos* turned into *partidos* or *subdelegaciones* (names for another sort of administrative area).

The imposition of *corregidores* on the American colonies constituted the first effective measure by the Spanish to establish royal authority at a local level, putting them in those indigenous villages that had not been assigned an encomienda. In lieu of such grants that gave control over land and Indians to an encomendero, and the accompanying royal right to receive the tributes that indigenous people as vassals paid to the Crown in exchange for encomenderos insuring their well-being, protection and indoctrination of native persons, *corregidores* provided similar functions over the local populace. In this context, *corregidores* were also known as *corregidores de indios*. Between 1531 and 1535, the *Real Audiencia* (supreme court of justice in each Spanish American viceroyalty and district) appointed more than 100 *corregidores* in villages and towns under direct control of the Crown.

The *corregidores* functions consisted of the administration of indigenous subjects while also serving as magistrates, tax collectors, and bailiffs. Consequently, the three attributes of the civilian branches of government were concentrated in the office of the *corregidores:* administration, justice, and estate. These colonial administrators often received assistance in legal matters from lawyers called *asesores* (consultants) or *consejeros* (advisers). If their districts were too vast, *corregidores* also received assistance from subordinate delegates known as *tenientes* (deputies).

The authority of *corregidores* was above the internal administration of the *pueblo de indios* (village of Indians) or cabildo, which was composed by indigenous people occupying the posts of *gobernador* (governor), *alcaldes, regidores,* and other lesser officials. From this position, *corregidores* could also interfere in the affairs of the encomiendas, which raised the opposition of the encomenderos. An example of *corregidores* supremacy over the encomenderos occurred in the decade of 1550, when a royal decree ordered that all encomiendas were allocated to a *corregimiento*. From then on, Spanish American territory was divided into many contiguous civil jurisdictions under the control of an officer of the Crown. This organizational process was long and full of problems. It was achieved in the decade of

1570, in the Viceroyalty of New Spain under the command of Viceroy Martin Enriquez de Almansa and in Peru under Francisco de Toledo (1569–1581).

On a hierarchical scale in the colonies, above the *corregidores* were located the *alcaldes mayores,* who ruled over territorial units called *provincias* (provinces) or *alcaldías mayores* (great mayoralties). For example, in the decade of 1570 when major territorial divisions were reassigned, New Spain was divided into about 70 provinces controlling more than 200 *corregimientos.* With the serious decline in population that occurred during the 16th century, some townships were annexed to neighboring jurisdictions by 1600, and by mid-17th century there were no differences between the functions of *alcalde mayor* and *corregidores.* Both terms became synonymous.

With the royally decreed reforms of the 1540s and 1550s, real efforts were made by Spain to protect the indigenous populations of the colonies from oppressive administration. According to the law, the magistrates should not reside in the districts ruled by them in order to maintain the impartiality of their decisions. The instructions given to the *corregidores* stressed good Christian practices, as well as watching the obligation to treat the Indians well, ensuring that elected public offices in the villages were occupied by good Christians, and in general, guaranteeing that Spanish-Indian relations remained without any problem. In sum, legally they were tasked with protecting indigenous people from any damaging interference of Spanish colonists, including by the *corregidores* themselves.

In practice, many *corregidores* resided in their jurisdictions. Although indigenous villages governed themselves with relative autonomy in administrative and religious affairs, and had contact with *corregidores* regularly to settle matters of justice, *corregidores* became increasingly embedded in local societies. They even opened up beneficial economic relations associated with productive and commercial activities, such as the monopolistic institution called *reparto de comercio* (trade distribution). Despite legal restrictions stating otherwise, the physical distance separating colonial *corregidores* from the viceroyal power allowed the former to act with great independence. Consequently, *corregidores* accumulated significant power and, in the name of that authority, committed many abuses.

Marta Martín Gabaldón

See also: Cabildo; Encomienda; Encomenderos; Peru, State of after Spanish Conquest; Toledo, Francisco de; Tribute, Paid to Spain; Yucatán, State of after Spanish Conquest.

Resources

Gibson, Charles. *The Aztecs under Spanish Rule. A History of the Indians of the Valley of Mexico. 1519–1810.* Stanford, CA: Stanford University Press, 1964.

Lockhart, James. *The Nahuas after the Conquest: a Social and Cultural History of the Indians of Central Mexico, Sixteenth trough Eighteenth Centuries.* Stanford, CA: Stanford University Press, 1992.

Lockhart, James. *Spanish Peru, 1532–1560: a Colonial Society.* Madison: The University of Wisconsin, 1968.

Martin, Cheryl E. "Institutions and society in colonial Mexico." *Latin American Research Review* 25, no. 3 (1990): 188–198.

Cortés, Hernán

As conqueror of the Aztec Empire in Mexico, explorer of Guatemala and Honduras, and leader of the first expeditions to California, Spanish conquistador Hernán Cortés contributed significantly to the establishment of

European domination in America. His conquests helped shape the history of the southwestern United States and Mexico.

Cortés was born in 1485 to a poor, noble family in Medellin, in the dry area of Extremadura, in Castile—now Spain. He was the son of Martín Cortés de Monroy, a poor military captain who fought in many wars, and Catalina Pizarro Altamirano. The family history of participation in regional wars almost exclusively includes private internal struggles fought within Extremadura. A sickly and only child in a region known to produce soldiers, Cortés's parents placed him initially as an acolyte in a local church and then sought to give him a quality education. Cortés studied Latin and grammar at the age of 12 in Salamanca, and probably attended the University of Salamanca, where he studied to become a lawyer. He did not complete his studies, but instead returned home to Medellín in 1501 when he was 17. In addition to his love of Latin and literary works, picked up from his time in Salamanca, Cortés increasingly dedicated himself to the martial arts, and to gambling, both of which played a role in his decision to leave school to go to the New World and make his fortune.

Cortés journeyed to Seville to join the expedition under Fr. Nicolás de Ovando, a distant relative and also from Extremadura. Injured while climbing through a girl's window in the capital city, he did not travel to America with Ovando in 1504, fortunately, as two-fifths of the expedition died shortly after arriving in Hispaniola and another fifth suffered from severe illness. Instead, Cortés delayed further, first in Seville and then in Valladolid, where he briefly served as a notary. This experience played a significant role in his later knowledge of policy and Castilian law in the Indies. He finally left for Santo Domingo on a fleet of merchant ships in 1506. For six years, Cortés lived as a landowner in Santo Domingo. Governor Ovando sent Cortés on an expedition to Xaragua, the western region of Hispaniola where the recent massacre by Diego Velázquez was still well remembered and served as a brutal introduction to the practices of conquest in the New World.

By 1509 Cortés's observations of the economic and demographic decline in Hispaniola, along with observations of the growing wealth of those seeking wealth on the mainland, prompted him to move to Darien in Central America (south of the Yucatán). Again, a medical ailment prevented his travels, saving him from a failed venture that ended in shipwreck. In 1511, he joined Diego Velázquez's expedition to Cuba. For his participation, the new governor rewarded Cortés with the position as his secretary and gave him an encomienda land grant in Cuba where he lived until 1518. He supplemented his income as notary with raising cattle and panning for gold in the river at Cuvanacan. With this new wealth, Cortés built a hacienda and fathered a daughter by an Indian girl. In the next seven years in Cuba, Cortés had a series of disagreements with his benefactor, Velázquez. In 1514, local settlers, desirous of larger apportionments of Indians, selected Cortés to represent them to petition the governor. Velázquez responded by dismissing and arresting his assistant, though he later pardoned him and extended the grants of Indians. Another conflict arose when Cortés courted, seduced, and then rejected Catalina, one of the sisters of his fellow encomendero, Juan Suárez, and sister to the new romantic interest of the newly widowed Velázquez. The governor again arrested Cortés, who escaped but eventually was reconciled when he eventually married Catalina.

In 1518, Velázquez appointed Cortés to lead a mission to the unexplored lands to the west, the area now known as Mexico.

Despite several altercations with the governor, Cortés had proved himself a capable leader and administrator. Yet his military skills had rarely been employed. Nonetheless, Velázquez perceived him to be clever and cool under pressure. While observant of Cortés's qualities, the governor obviously underestimated the ambition and subservience of the adventurer. The governor tasked Cortés with sailing to help the Grijalva expedition, which was experiencing difficulties. Velázquez provided a couple of ships and asked Cortés to provide the rest, owing to the new wealth acquired by him from his gold mines.

Several Spanish ships had landed in Mexico before Cortés's expedition. The reports of wealth and gold tempted Cortés and his followers, although they also wished to conquer new lands for their king and find new civilizations that they hoped to convert to Christianity. For all of those reasons, Cortés accepted the governor's commission and funded a mission to Mexico with his own personal fortune and arrived in Cozumel, off the coast of Mexico, on March 12, 1519. Again, the governor's vision of the expedition differed greatly from Cortés's. The instructions maintained that service of God was the primary mission, with discovery of lands to be claimed for the Crown as secondary. All Indians encountered were therefore to be read the *Requerimiento* that placed them under the king's authority in return for protection and conversion. These same Indians were to be treated well. No native women were to be seduced or raped. Even gambling and cards were prohibited. Unaware that Grijalva had returned, Cortés was to inquire regarding any news of Grijalva as well as Cristóbal de Olid, who had already been sent to find the conquistador and his troubled expedition. Intended as an exploratory and rescue mission, the ideals outlined in the governor's instructions were circumvented easily by way of the loopholes in the contract signed by Velázquez and Cortés.

In preparation for his expedition in 1518, Cortés sought out Pedro de Alvarado, who had recently returned from Middle America. Alvarado willingly agreed to finance his own ship, as well as men and horses for the voyage. Cortés's traditional caution was tossed aside in his collaboration with Alvarado. Large-scale preparations alarmed Velázquez, who eventually attempted to revoke Cortés's commission. Sensing the impending loss of his greatest opportunity, Cortés decided to leave Santiago immediately.

Rushed out of port to avoid the loss of his commission, Cortés was compelled to make a series of stops to acquire food for the expedition, where he obtained provisions and further recruits. Velázquez sent messages to many ports and officials, including letters to two captains of ships in the fleet, seeking to delay or block the provisioning of the venture. Despite these efforts, Cortés was able to convince the recipients of the letters to cooperate with his undertaking, and even to enlist in his expeditionary fleet. Cortés went so far as to order Diego de Ordaz (one of Velázquez's appointees who threw his support behind Cortés) to seize a Spanish ship carrying food provisions, a ship that was added to the invading fleet when the ship's captain decided to join in the venture.

By the time Cortés arrived on the Mexican coast, the private expedition became virtually a public affair, with many settlers from Cuba and others joining in through loans, cooperation, or active participation. According to a muster in 1519, he now commanded 11 ships, not counting Alvarado's, who was absent at the time. He additionally had about 530 Europeans under his authority. Weaponry in his expedition included crossbows, 12 arquebuses (guns), 14 pieces of artillery, as well as breech-loading cannon. His personnel included about one-third from Andalusia, a quarter from Old Castile, and one-sixth from Extremadura. Two Franciscan friars accompanied the expedition, as did a few Spanish women. Craftsmen, professionals, and slaves also traveled with the fleet, including hundreds of Indians, despite Velázquez's instructions. Sixteen horses made the journey, along with several "war" dogs—probably Irish wolfhounds or mastiffs. Of the captains and commanders within the expedition, several had close ties to Velázquez, some had long disliked Cortés, but most were loyal friends from Extremadura.

Cortés cruised the Yucatán Peninsula in February 1519. His first landfall was Cozumel, where he found Alvarado and his missing ship. The Indians of the local village had fled inland, probably from the depredations of Alvarado. Cortés reached out to the native Maya, giving gifts, promising good treatment, and encouraging their return. While still at Cozumel, the expedition encountered two Spanish captives who had escaped captivity, Gerónimo Aguilar and Gonzalo Guerrero. His next encounter with Mayans, at Potonchan, was less friendly, ending in a battle and Spanish victory due to the use of artillery and the native method of fighting. It was at Potonchan, at the battle of Centla, that the Spanish first used horses in military conflict to great effect in the Americas.

From encounters with the Mayan people living in that area of Mexico, Cortés heard of an empire based in central Mexico, confirming what Alvarado had already conveyed to him in Cuba. He also acquired a native Nahua woman, Malinalli (baptized Marina—also known as La Malinche), who spoke both Mayan and Nahuatl, the language of the Mexica. She served as interpreter, in conjunction with Aguilar, and later as Cortés's mistress. By April 1519, using his interpreters, Cortés

encountered and solidified friendly relations with the Totonacs. This society sought allies for assistance in their struggle with the warlike Mexica further inland. The Spanish and Totonacs exchanged gifts and friendship. The next day, Easter, the emperor, Montezuma II, sent emissaries to observe the Spaniards. Discovering that their main concern was gold, the Mexica emissaries, festooned in feathers, gave the Spanish many valuable gold gifts, jewels, and highly valued Mexica featherwork. Convinced of great wealth to be obtained from the Mexica, Cortés decided to ally with the Totonacs to conquer the prosperous and populous Mexica civilization in the name of the king of Spain for its great wealth and to spread Christianity in a new country.

That civilization, known today as the Aztec Empire, was centered in the city of Tenochtitlán on Lake Texcoco. From about the year 1000, the indigenous populations of central Mexico attained an advanced level of knowledge in such areas as astronomy, architecture, painting, agricultural methods, literature, and philosophy. The Aztecs were originally a nomadic, warlike culture from northern Mexico. Starting in the 14th century, they adapted the civilization of central Mexico and gained power through alliances with the kingdoms already established around Lake Texcoco. In the middle of the 15th century, the Aztec emperors sought tribute and captives from other areas of Mexico. They also sent out colonists to spread their culture. Living off their tribute and their very productive system of agriculture, the Aztecs built the enormous, well-planned metropolis of Tenochtitlán (present-day Mexico City). Several great Aztec emperors succeeded in conquering much of central Mexico before a weaker ruler, Montezuma II, came to power.

Aware of the military success of the few Spanish against the numerous Mayan people,

Montezuma sent extravagant gifts that would demonstrate to Cortés the might of the Triple Alliance of the Mexica. A quick and decisive action by Montezuma could have crushed the Spanish force of 400 men. Instead, Cortés failed to understand the importance of gifts like peacock feathers, while the gold and gems convinced him of the glory and wealth to be acquired through the conquest of the Aztec. Consequently, the Spanish refused to withdraw and the Aztec, wary of the Spanish military abilities and concerned of Cortés and the Spaniards, with their horses, beards, and white skin, fulfilled omens predicting the return of the god Quetzalcoatl from exile, delayed in reacting. Meanwhile, Cortés discovered the deep divisions within the Aztec Empire, which were the result of oppressive tributes and the practice of capturing and sacrificing neighboring peoples.

With the encouragement of the Totonacs, Cortés sought an alliance with the Tlaxcalans, rebels against their Aztec overlords. Initially the Tlaxcalans resisted the approaches of the Spanish. The Tlaxcalans viewed the Totonacs accompanying the Spanish as nominal vassals of the Mexica. After several small costly skirmishes and repeated peace offerings by Cortés, an alliance was formed when the Tlaxcalan confederation fractured, threatening to open them to conquest by the Aztec. Xicoténcatl the Elder allied with Cortés against the Aztecs. Collaboration of the Spanish with enemies of the Aztec still went unopposed by Montezuma II, in part due to the concurrent harvest season, which depleted the agricultural society of its military resources. Cortés misinterpreted this lack of resistance in 1519 as a sign of weakness, an impression further supported by his earlier easy conquests of the Maya. Meanwhile, the Tlaxcalans and Totonacs brought Cortés information and troops that would help him defeat the Aztecs.

Hernán Cortés's conquest of Mexico. (Library of Congress)

On November 18, 1519, the Spaniards entered Tenochtitlán through an eight-mile-long causeway that led across Lake Texcoco to the island city. Montezuma greeted them wearing sandals with golden soles and jewel-encrusted uppers. Cortés committed grave errors against the Aztec culture by looking at that godlike ruler directly and attempting to embrace him. Despite the diplomatic blunder, the Spanish and Aztec leaders exchanged gifts: Cortés gave glass beads, and the Aztec emperor presented his Spanish guest with a necklace containing eight solid gold pendants in the shape of large crustaceans. Instead of imprisoning or confining the Spanish as suggested by Cuitláhuac (the emperor's brother), Montezuma spared no expense in hosting them, though he questioned Cortés in hopes of determining the purpose and threat posed by the strangers. Foremost of the possibilities considered by Montezuma was that the Spanish represented the return of Quetzalcoatl, a traditionally humane ruler/deity who, while demonstrating typical human excesses, opposed the practice of human sacrifice. Cortés's repeated protestations to the Maya, Totonac, and Tlaxcalans against human sacrifice and cannibalism help explain this misinterpretation by the Aztec leader.

After such an easy entrance into the well-fortified city, Cortés repaid his host by imprisoning Montezuma in his own palace. Surrounded by enemies, Cortés demanded the emperor serve as a negotiator between the Spanish and Aztec. The captured but wily emperor insisted he had lost all authority and suggested the release of his brother, Cuitláhuac, who immediately rallied the populace against the encircled Spanish.

Between the fall of 1519 and spring of 1520 several events impacted Cortés and his expedition. Back in Cuba, Velázquez heard of the potential wealth discovered by his former assistant. Realizing that Cortés intended to circumvent Velázquez's new authority as *adelantado* by sending the king's one-fifth of all gold directly to Spain, the decision was made to send an old friend and fellow conquistador, Pánfilo de Narváez, to arrest and hang Cortés. In May 1520, Narváez's arrival in the Yucatán forced Cortés to leave Pedro de Alvarado in control of the situation in Tenochtitlán, while he dealt with the threat to his authority.

With Cortés temporarily absent and Cuitláhuac released, for organizing the Aztec successfully against Alvarado's forces, desperate measures were undertaken. Montezuma was compelled to address the people to calm them. Instead, unknown assailants of his own people, perhaps even his nephew, Cuauhtéoc, killed the ruler. Violence dominated the valley city. The empire lost more leaders, as many Aztec nobles were murdered by Spaniards led by Pedro de Alvarado, trapped as they danced at a religious celebration in an enclosed plaza. A smallpox epidemic also decimated the Aztecs, killing Montezuma's brother Cuitláhuac, who was the successor to Aztec Empire.

By 1521, the Spaniards under Cortés returned to destroy Tenochtitlán and imprison the last emperor, Cuauhtémoc. Cortés and his followers tortured Cuauhtémoc for information on the lost treasure of the Aztec emperors but could not extract the knowledge they sought. Cortés dragged Cuauhtémoc along on a failed attempt to conquer more societies south to Honduras, finally hanging the successor to the Aztec Empire in 1524.

Cortés' violent and self-aggrandizing approach to conquering the Aztec Empire and his circumvention of his superiors resulted in numerous attempts to undermine him before the Crown. Through Charles V's reorganization of the Council of the Indies, it was learned that Bishop Fonseca had withheld information and requests regarding Cortés's testimony by a series of former allies of Velázquez, who went on to join Cortés's expedition. The previous negative reports earned Cortés a bad reputation with king, who appointed Antonio de Mendoza, not Cortés, the first viceroy of New Spain, as Mexico was then called. Cortés did hold the office of *adelantado* and governor temporarily, but only retained the land and title of the marquis of the Valley of Oaxaca. The final investigation of the Council favored Cortés, and though he was encouraged to repay Velázquez for money spent on the fleet of 1518, all other disputes were relegated to a court of justice and Velázquez was ordered to refrain from meddling in Cortés's affairs. In the end, Cortés remained an incredibly wealthy man.

Mendoza and Cortés also competed for exploration of the Pacific coast of Mexico. Cortés built ships in Acapulco and sent five expeditions north in search of pearls and gold. Cortés' ships discovered La Paz, at the south end of Baja California, in 1533, although at that time, Baja was thought to be an island. Cortés led another expedition, convincing 400 settlers and 300 slaves to join him. Most of the hopeful colonists died of starvation, attacks from the indigenous people living in the region, and shipwrecks. A fifth expedition led by Francisco de Ulloa navigated the Sea of Cortés in 1539 and explored the peninsula of Baja California, finally moving up the coast of the Pacific against foul winds and currents. That final expedition disappeared, leaving Juan Rodríguez Cabrillo, who was supported by Cortés's rival Mendoza, to discover what is now the state of California, in 1542.

After those humiliations, Cortés returned to Spain where he was hailed as the grand conquistador. His desire for adventure prevailed and he led additional expeditions, including his last, a luckless voyage to Algiers in 1541. The failures were many but were counterbalanced by the enormity of his success over the Aztecs and the wealth and power that conquest brought Spain. Nonetheless, the last five years of Cortés's life was spent in obscurity. Though offered a knighthood, he declined the honor. His determination to return to Mexico was thwarted by illness. In 1547, his drafted his final will, made his final confession, and died in Seville at age 62 on December 2, 1547.

Nicole von Germeten and
Rebecca M. Seaman

See also: Aguilar, Fr. Gerónimo de; Alvarado, Pedro de; Cuauhtémoc; Cuitláhuac; Encomienda; Guns, Impact of; La Malinche, "Doña Marina"; Ordaz, Diego de; Ovando, Fr. Nicolás de; Potonchan, Battle of; Tenochtitlán, Siege of; Totonacs, Alliance with Spanish; Velázquez, Diego (de Cuéllar).

Resources

Almazán, Marco. "Hernán Cortés: Virtù vs. Fortuna." *Journal of American Culture* (June 1, 1997): 131–137.

Hassig, Ross. "How Cortés Won by Losing." *Military History* 24, no. 3 (May 2007): 60–69.

Innes, Hammond. *The Conquistadors*. London: Collins, 1969.

Ober, Frederick. *Hernando Cortés: Conqueror of Mexico*. New York: Harper & Row, 1905.

Rosen, Harry, and Irwin Blacker, eds. *The Golden Conquistadores*. Indianapolis, IN: Bobbs-Merrill, 1960.

Thomas, Hugh. *Conquest: Montezuma, Cortés, and the Fall of Old Mexico*. New York: Simon & Schuster, 1993.

Weber, David J. *The Spanish Frontier in North America*. New Haven, CT: Yale University Press, 1992.

Cortés, Martín El Criollo

Martín Cortés de Zúñiga was born in Cuernavaca, Mexico, in 1531. He was the first legitimate male heir of Hernán Cortés, conqueror of the Aztec Empire, and Luisa de Zúñiga, a Spanish noblewoman. By the time of his birth, his father already had two other sons and three daughters. The oldest of these previous offspring had been also named Martín Cortés. To avoid confusion, the older Martín received the nickname of El Mestizo, as his mother was Doña Marina/Malintzin/La Malinche, Cortés's cultural mediator and translator during the conquest of the Aztec Empire. The youngest was El Criollo. Martín Cortés de Zúñiga, as the first-born from his father's legal marriage, inherited the title and benefits of the marquisate of the Valley of Oaxaca, granted by the Emperor Charles V (HRE—Carlos I of Spain) to Hernán Cortés in 1529.

Martín Cortés El Criollo travelled to Spain with his father and his brothers Martín and Luis in 1540. It was the first voyage for the young Martín, probably eight years of age. They stayed there until 1563, at which time El Criollo obtained from the emperor an agreement regarding the family dispute over possessions of land in New Spain. During the two decades in Spain, Martín El Criollo joined the military and participated in the battle of Saint Quintin (1557) and some others, alongside his two brothers. He also married one of his cousins, Ana de Arellano.

The Spanish inhabitants of New Spain received Martín with the highest of honors upon his return to the land in 1563. However, as historians of this time agree, Martín was the richest man in the Spanish territory and showed an excessive pride and lack of respect to the older conquerors and their heirs. Some of the younger Spanish colonists, however, enjoyed the new ways he brought from the metropolis and sided with him. Among the most prominent of these supporters were the Ávila brothers, Alonso de Ávila and Gil González de Ávila.

During the Easter of 1568, the officials from the government discovered that El Criollo, his brothers, and a group of young criollos were plotting against the emperor, planning to crown the marquis as king. Some of the accused were tortured, as El Mestizo and Luis Cortés, the Ávila brothers were beheaded, and the majority of criollo supporters of the marquis, Martín, were sent into exile without the possibility of returning to New Spain. The three Cortés brothers were sent away from their land of origin and, although pardoned in 1574, only Luis Cortés ever returned.

El Criollo was the second marquis of the Valley of Oaxaca in Mexico, and his son Fernando inherited the title as third marquis of the Valley. Interestingly enough, El Mestizo also named his first-born Fernando, so the cousins had also the same name, as it had happened with their respective fathers. After the death of the third marquis, Fernando, the fourth marquis was also a son of El Criollo, Pedro. Both of them died without a legitimate heir, and a niece, Estefanía, eventually inherited the marquisate, thereby retaining the lands granted originally to Cortés within the family.

Covadonga Lamar Prieto

See also: Ávila, Alonso de; Charles V (HRE) or Carlos I of Spain; Cortés, Hernán; La Malinche, "Doña Marina".

Resources

Díaz del Castillo, Bernal. *The Conquest of New Spain.* Edited by Janet Burke and Ted Humphrey. Indianapolis, IN: Hackett, 2012.

Lanyon, Anna. *The New World of Martín Cortés.* Sydney: Allyn & Unwin Press, 2003;

Reprint, Cambridge, MA: De Capo Press, 2004.

Prescott, William. *History of the Conquest of Mexico.* London: Continuum, 2009.

Suarez Peralta, Juan. *Noticias Historicas de la Nueva España.* Madrid: Justo Saragoza, 1878.

Thomas, Hugh. *Conquest: Montezuma, Cortés, and the Fall of Old Mexico.* New York: Simon & Schuster, 1993.

Coyoacán

In the 15th century, Coyoacán was a Tepanec village located on the southern shore of Lake Texcoco in central Mexico. The village was originally named Coyohuacán, which in the Nahuatl language means "the place of coyotes."

The Tepanecas had originally settled the western shores of Lake Texcoco and were primarily farmers and stoneworkers. They were related to the Aztecs and both groups of Mesoamericans spoke Nahuatl.

Coyoacán is thought to have been established during the 11th century. Located on the shore of the lake that dominated central Mexico, the city served as a busy center of trade for the Tepanec people (Tepanecas). During the time of the Spanish conquest, Hernán Cortés established Coyoacán as the first capital of New Spain. Today it is one of the 16 boroughs of Mexico City.

The Tepanecas ran Coyoacán as a completely independent city-state, or *altepetl,* under the ruler of their own kings. The Tepanec people were at the height of their power in the early 15th century, during the rule of Tezozomoc, a power that lasted until his death in 1426.

In 1428, the Aztec Triple Alliance brought the Tepanecas and their cities, including Coyoacán, under the rule of the Aztecs. The Tepanecas chafed under Aztec domination. When conquistador Hernán Cortés arrived in the region, the Tepanecas welcomed him and allowed him the use of Coyoacán as a base of operations.

Hernán Cortés landed on the east coast of Mexico in February 1519 and immediately claimed the land for the Spanish crown. Allying himself with enemies of the Aztecs, Cortés invaded the Aztec Empire. After a brief period of authority over the city, using the emperor Montezuma as a hostage, the Spanish fled Tenochtitlán during the disastrous La Noche Triste in June 1520. By mid-August of the following year, the *caudillo* had managed to destroy the Aztec capital of Tenochtitlán and conquer the Aztecs. While Tenochtitlán was being restored, Cortés used Coyoacán as his headquarters, making it the first capital of New Spain from 1521 to 1523.

Coyoacán remained a separate city until the middle of the 19th century, when it was incorporated into the federal district of Mexico City. In 1928, it became one of the 16 boroughs of Mexico City.

Karen S. Garvin

See also: Cortés, Hernán; La Noche Triste; Tenochtitlán, City of.

Resources
Díaz del Castillo, Bernal. *The History of the Conquest of New Spain.* Edited by David Carrasco. Albuquerque: University of New Mexico Press, 2008.

Prescott, William H. *History of the Conquest of Mexico.* New York: Continuum, 2009.

Cozumel

The island of Cozumel (Quintana Roo, Mexico) lies approximately 17 kilometers off the east coast of the Yucatán peninsula in the Caribbean Sea. Cozumel is formed of limestone over bedrock, has an area of 647 km², and rises no higher than 13 meters above sea level at its highest natural point. The name derives from the Yucatec Maya term *cuzamil,* or "land of the swallows."

Evidence dates to the third century BCE of seminomadic hunters and gatherers living on the island. Slow, steady population growth occurred during the Pre-Classic and Classic eras as successive waves of Maya migrated to Cozumel. The rise of Chichén Itzá on the Yucatán during the Post-Classic period strengthened Cozumel's position within a centuries-old trade network. During that time, the Maya settled in offshore islands to supply cities with marine resources and other commodities. By 1200 CE a great city center and dozens of minor dependent communities, including divided fields and house lots, filled the island. The thousands of inhabitants may have provided the infrastructure to support pilgrimages to its shrines, the most important being the shrine of the goddess Ixchel, patroness of childbirth, pregnancy, and fertility.

In 1518, Juan de Grijalva, captain of an expedition out of Cuba, landed and celebrated the first Catholic mass in Mexico. He took possession for the Kingdom of Castile, naming the island "Santa Cruz de la Puerta Latina." In 1519 Hernán Cortés landed on Cozumel. He reported seeing "fine buildings of stone for the idols, and a fine town." The inhabitants had fled to the woods upon the earlier arrival of Pedro de Alvarado, one of the *caudillo*'s captains. Alvarado had already looted the city for turkey and women—as well as stripped the temples of valuable ornaments. With Cortés's arrival, the Spanish set up camp at the town and set about repairing relations.

Despite the earlier abuses of Alvarado, Cortés experienced the same welcome from the indigenous population as Grijalva. Like his predecessor, the *caudillo* observed the apparent lack of human sacrifices, as well as the superior building technology and political structure. Comparing these newly encountered natives to those of the Caribbean islands who practiced human sacrifice and were reputed to be cannibals, Cortés perceived the people of Cozumel to be "truly humans" who could be won over to the Catholic faith from their practice of worshipping idols.

After a brief, and initially futile attempt to rescue two shipwrecked Spaniards reported to be held captive in the Yucatán, Cortés put into motion the events leading to the conquest of Mexico. While some experts believe that the island of Cozumel was thickly settled at the time of the *caudillo*'s encounter, others argue that since much of the area was unfit for cultivation, the island was probably uninhabited. Nevertheless, disease and warfare so ravaged Cozumel following this early contact that, in the 16th century, not even the parish priest was required to live on the island. Cozumel remained almost completely abandoned until the 20th century.

Charles Heath

See also: Alvarado, Pedro de; Cortés, Hernán; Grijalva, Juan de.

Resources

Chamberlain, Robert S. *The Conquest and Colonization of Yucatan, 1517–1550.* New York: Octagon Books, 1966.

Gerhard, Peter. *The Southeast Frontier of New Spain.* Princeton, NJ: Princeton University Press, 1979.

Gómara, Francisco López de. *Historia de la Conquista de México, Tomo I.* México. D.F.: Editorial Pedro Robredo, 1943.

Landa, Friar Diego de. *Yucatan Before and After the Conquest.* Translated by William Gates. New York: Dover Publications, 1978.

Miller, Mary Ellen and Karl Taube. *The Gods and Symbols of Ancient Mexico and the Maya: An Illustrated Dictionary of Mesoamerican Religion.* New York: Thames and Hudson, 1993.

Rathje, William L. "The Origin and Development of Lowland Classic Maya Civilization." *American Antiquity* 36, no. 3 (July 1971): 275–285.

Rathje, William L. and Jeremy A. Sabloff. "Ancient Maya Commercial Systems: A Research Design for the Island of Cozumel, Mexico." *World Archaeology* 5, no. 2, Trade (October 1973): 221–231.

Sabloff, Jeremy A. "It Depends on How We Look at Things: New Perspectives on the Postclassic Period in the Northern Maya Lowlands." *Proceedings of the American Philosophical Society* 151, no. 1 (March 2007): 11–26.

Secretaría de Turismo. "Quinto Informe de Labores." SECTUR, México.

Thomas, Hugh. *Conquest: Montezuma, Cortés, and the Fall of Old Mexico.* New York: Simon & Schuster, 1993.

Cuauhtémoc

Cuauhtémoc, the last emperor of the Aztec Empire, reigned from 1520 until his capture by the Spanish. He resisted the Spanish conquistadores from their first appearance, led Aztec warriors in their final battle, and endured tortured at the hands of Spaniards seeking treasure after his defeat. Fearing Cuauhtémoc's ability to lead an uprising, Hernán Cortés executed the captive emperor in 1522.

Cuauhtémoc was born around 1494 into a distinguished family of Aztec nobles. Nephew to Emperor Montezuma II, he became Montezuma's son-in-law after marrying Princess Tecuichpo. By the time of the Spaniards' arrival in the early 1500s, Cuauhtémoc had become a leader of Aztec troops under his uncle and distinguished himself as a military commander in numerous battles.

Unlike many other members of the Aztec nobility, Cuauhtémoc distrusted and disliked the Spaniards from their first encounter. When the Spaniards seized the royal palace and held Montezuma hostage in 1519, it was Cuauhtémoc who organized Aztec resistance. When Cortés left Tenochtitlán to confront a rival expedition under Pánfilo de Narváez, Cuauhtémoc rallied the Aztecs against the foreigners who had taken their emperor prisoner. Captain Pedro de Alvarado, left in charge during Cortés's absence, actively repressed Aztec religion, massacring a large number of Aztec noblemen as they

Cuauhtémoc, last Aztec emperor, 1522. (North Wind Picture Archives)

celebrated one of their ritual festivals. Enraged, Cuauhtémoc mobilized his troops as the triumphant Cortés returned to the city with reinforcements.

Cuauhtémoc then led the attack against the Spaniards, who barricaded themselves inside the emperor's palace. When Montezuma was forced to go to the rooftop to tell his Aztec subjects to end resistance, Cuauhtémoc brandished a spear in defiance and mocked Montezuma, allegedly so inciting the gathered crowd that they killed the emperor with a hail of stones. After the death of Montezuma, a council of Aztec nobles elected his brother Cuitláhuac as the *Huey Tlatoani* (emperor) of the Aztecs in 1520. Cuitláhuac had also distrusted the Spaniards and helped lead the armed resistance against the Spanish invaders. His reign proved short-lived, however, as he died in October 1520 in the great smallpox epidemic that decimated the city. Before his death, the Aztecs drove the Spaniards out of Tenochtitlán on June 30, 1520, a defeat that came to be known as La Noche Triste (The Sad Night).

With Cuitláhuac's death, Cuauhtémoc was selected as his replacement. Cuauhtémoc mobilized Tenochtitlán for a long struggle against the Spaniards and their indigenous allies. He fortified the central plaza and brought tons of food and provisions to the island city in preparation for a long siege. He then destroyed all bridges and causeways leading to the city, turning it into a fortified island defended by between 200,000 and 500,000 warriors from the Aztecs and their neighboring allies. Cortés, in turn, successfully regrouped his forces to retake Tenochtitlán. Assisted by his Tlaxcalan allies, Cortés built 13 ships to assault the city by water as well as land. Before starting his offensive, Cortés urged Cuauhtémoc to surrender the city. Cuauhtémoc refused,

threatening to sacrifice Christian converts to the Aztec gods.

The Spanish attack began in March 1521 with assaults on the nearby towns and cities. Cuauhtémoc launched several successful counterattacks but had to withdraw whenever faced with Spanish reinforcements with heavy cavalry and cannon. After defeating the surrounding cities, the Spaniards launched their fleet of small ships. Realizing that the Aztecs could not win in open combat with the mounted Spaniards and their heavily armed ships, Cuauhtémoc resorted to urban guerrilla warfare, ambushing the Spaniards and their allies from rooftops and alleyways in bloody house-to-house fighting. The Spanish responded by systematically leveling every building, throwing the debris into the lake. This forced the defenders back into what became a smaller and smaller piece of territory.

Cuauhtémoc and his Aztec army were eventually defeated as much by famine and disease as by force of arms. On August 13, 1521, the emperor was captured as he attempted to leave to find reinforcements for the starving city. Cortés initially treated Cuauhtémoc with respect, even promising to allow him to continue as emperor as long as he accepted the supremacy of Spanish rule.

That initial civility ended after the city of Tenochtitlán yielded no gold or jewels to the Spanish conquerors. The Spaniards tortured Cuauhtémoc to find where the treasure was hidden. Cuauhtémoc stubbornly refused to reveal the treasure's location, and secretly planned further Aztec resistance against the Spanish invaders from his position in captivity.

In 1522, Cortés traveled to Honduras to punish a rebellious Spanish captain. He brought Cuauhtémoc along rather than risk an uprising in his absence. A Christian convert supposedly revealed in the course of the journey that Cuauhtémoc planned to kill Cortés and lead a rebellion against all Spaniards in Mexico. Accused and found guilty of treason, Cuauhtémoc and other noblemen were hung on February 26, 1522. The uncompromising resistance and bravery of Cuauhtémoc in his struggle with foreign invaders made him a legendary figure in Mexican culture.

Thomas Edsall

See also: Alvarado, Pedro de; Brigantines, Use by Cortés; Cortés, Hernán; Cuitláhuac; Guns, Impact of; Horses, Impact of; La Noche Triste; Montezuma II; Narváez, Pánfilo de; Tenochtitlán, Siege of.

Resources

Berdan, Frances F. *The Aztecs of Central Mexico: An Imperial Society.* Florence, KY: Wadsworth, 2004.

Gillespie, Susan D. *The Aztec Kings: The Construction of Rulership in Mexica History.* Tucson: University of Arizona Press, 1992.

Townsend, Richard F. *The Aztecs.* London: Thames and Hudson, 1992.

Cuba

The largest of the Caribbean islands, Cuba was populated by the Tainos at the time of Christopher Columbus's discovery. Columbus sailed along the coast of Cuba in his first voyage, and claimed the island was Japan, confirming his assertion that he had discovered a western route to the Far East. He additionally recorded in his diary his perceptions of the people of Cuba, asserting that one community at the Rio de Mares did not know evil, had no weapons, and were timid, while others were portrayed by him as shrewd and more civilized.

The island was covered in forests at the time of first contact with Europeans and produced mahogany and cedar, along with a wide variety of birds. The native Tainos grew a root crop, cassava. Extensive agriculture was limited, in part by the lack of adequate farming tools and the presence of extensive root systems in the wooded environment.

Circumnavigated by Sebastián de Ocampo in 1509–1510, the island of Cuba was invaded by Diego Velázquez de Cuellar in 1511. Velázquez went on to serve as the governor of Cuba for several years, overseeing the conquest and settlement of the island. Though considered benevolent in comparison to other Spanish colonial governors at the time, his policies precipitated the demise of the indigenous Tainos people. Part of the policies that precipitated declining native populations were rooted in Spanish perceptions of the Cuban populace as cannibals, which were first voiced by Columbus. Those perceptions, though likely incorrect, were connected by the conquistadors and encomenderos with the refusal of the Tainos to abandon their polytheistic beliefs, providing the Spanish the necessary justification for violent raids against the native population. Further violence was rationalized with the discovery of the presence of one chief, Hatuey, who had escaped the massacre of Xaragua on Santo Domingo. Hatuey again resisted the Spanish authority and imposition of the Catholic faith on Cuba. His rejection of Catholicism and Spanish dominance resulted in an agonizing death.

A large island, Cuba's conquest was accomplished through the coordinated efforts of a number of famous conquistadors. Pánfilo de Narváez accompanied Velázquez in his invasion and conquest of Cuba. Narváez had already assisted in the violent subjugation of Jamaica. Hernán Cortés, who later meted out similar punishments and subjugation upon the Aztec people of Mexico, also participated in the subjugation of the Cuban populace and was rewarded for his efforts with an encomienda grant.

Following its conquest, the Cuban island was initially renamed "Juana" after Queen Joanna of Spain. With the queen in seclusion, the name became unpopular and was replaced temporarily with Fernandina, in honor of King Ferdinand. This name, too, proved unpopular and the island was returned to the original native designation of Cuba, though few if any of the native population remained alive to enjoy the irony.

In the first decades of Spanish settlement, gold was discovered on Cuba. The potential for great wealth drew increasing numbers of settlers who proceeded to enslave the Tainos population. Overworked, underfed, exposed to disease, and often executed, the Tainos numbers dropped rapidly. The precipitous drop in the native population was accompanied by the rapid increase in swine brought by the Spanish that in turn negatively affected the health of the indigenous population and had a ripple effect upon the ecological environment.

As mining declined and deforestation occurred, agriculture dominated the island economy. In the absence of an indigenous labor force, the Spanish imported increasing numbers of African slaves. The first arrival of African slaves occurred in the first decade after conquest, but by the end of the colonial period, approximately 50 percent of the island's population was comprised of Africans. This rapid shift in racial demographics grew out of the Spanish drive to obtain mineral and then agricultural profits. The indigenous population, soon made extinct, was unable to prevent their own demise, much less the drastic changes in the island's landscape.

Rebecca M. Seaman

See also: Columbus, Christopher; Cortés, Hernán; Narváez, Pánfilo de; Velázquez, Diego (de Cuéllar); Xaragua Massacre.

Resources

Clendinnen, Inga. *Ambivalent Conquests: Maya and Spaniard in Yucatan, 1517–1570.* 2nd ed. Cambridge: Cambridge University Press, 2003.

Gibson, Charles. *Spain in American.* New York: Harper & Row, 1966.

Palencia-Roth, Michael. "The Cannibal Law of 1503." In *Early Images of the Americas: Transfer and Invention,* edited by Jerry M. Williams and Robert E. Lewis. Tucson: University of Arizona Press, 1993.

Thomas, Hugh. *Conquest: Montezuma, Cortés, and the Fall of Old Mexico.* New York: Simon & Schuster Press, 1993.

Cuitláhuac

Cuitláhuac was the 10th emperor of the Aztec Empire. A council of noblemen chose him to be emperor in 1520 after an angry crowd of Aztecs killed the previous emperor, Montezuma II, for apparent collaboration with the Spaniards. His reign lasted less than a year before he died in a smallpox epidemic. Cuitláhuac has the distinction of being the only Aztec emperor to defeat the Spaniards in battle, as his successor Cuauhtémoc suffered total defeat at the hands of the invaders.

Cuitláhuac was born in 1476 and came from a noble lineage. He was the son of the sixth Aztec emperor, Axayacatl, and the brother of the ninth Aztec emperor, Montezuma II. As such, Cuitláhuac played an important role in governing and administering the tribute and alliance system of the Aztec Empire. His brother Montezuma entrusted him with diplomatic missions and sensitive negotiations after becoming emperor. Montezuma also appointed him lord of the important city of Ixtalpalapan before the Spaniards arrived in Aztec territory.

Cuitláhuac consistently advised resistance to the Spanish advances. He forcibly argued that Montezuma should use any means to prevent the entry of the Spaniards into the Aztec island capital. He became one of the main proponents of fighting the Spaniards, including a failed assault at the town of Cholula in 1519, which resulted in a Spanish massacre of the townspeople.

In November 1519, Spanish conquistador Hernán Cortés entered the Valley of Mexico and arrived at Tenochtitlán. Montezuma arranged a meeting with Cortés. Cuitláhuac attended the meeting as one of the representatives of the Aztec nobility. He and his brother strongly disagreed on the nature of the Spanish leader. Montezuma believed that Cortés was the incarnation of the Aztec god Quetzalcoatl. The Aztec religion believed that Quetzalcoatl, described as having hair of gold, would return to Tenochtitlán after traveling across the seas. The blonde-haired Cortés matched that description. Cuitláhuac and many other Aztec nobles, however, did not share Montezuma's belief in the Spaniard's divinity and remained suspicious of the heavily armed strangers.

Their suspicions proved valid when Cortés took Montezuma, Cuitláhuac, and a large number of important nobles captive a short time after entering the city. Cortés kept them prisoners in the palace of Axayacatl. In May 1520, Cortés returned to the coast to fight rival Spaniard Pánfilo de Narváez, who had been sent to arrest him. In his absence, his designated commander, Captain Pedro de Alvarado, slaughtered a large number of Aztec nobles celebrating a ritual festival in a manner that he found offensive.

Cortés returned to find his forces under serious attack. The Aztecs besieged the Spanish headquarters. At Montezuma's request, Cortés set Cuitláhuac free in order to appease the enraged Aztecs. This possibly represented Montezuma's last-minute plan to right his mistakes and ensure strong leadership for his people. As soon as he was freed, Cuitláhuac directed the military assault against the Spaniards.

A council of noblemen named Cuitláhuac as great speaker of the Aztecs after the ensuing death of Montezuma. Cuitláhuac had never trusted the Spaniards, and he began to organize for war with the help of his nephew Cuauhtémoc. Cuitláhuac moved to enlist more troops and maintain allies in an effort to defeat the Spaniards. The Aztecs' greatest victory came on June 30, 1520, when Cuitláhuac directed the battle that forced the Spaniards from Tenochtitlán. A powerful force of 100,000 Aztec warriors routed the Spaniards and decimated Cortés's army, forcing them to retreat from the city into the lands of their Tlaxcalan allies. That night became known as La Noche Triste, or The Sad Night, in which the Spaniards suffered many casualties and lost control of Tenochtitlán.

Cuitláhuac's immediate task as the new emperor involved building and maintaining alliances with the cities and towns around the island city of Tenochtitlán. He also had to ensure the loyalty of tribute-paying regions and prevent defections to the Spaniards. Aztec rulers, appointed by Montezuma and Cortés as puppets, had to be replaced with loyal officials. A series of tributary rebellions forced Cuitláhuac to divide his forces in order to consolidate his power. This weakened his army and prevented him from launching an offensive when the Spanish were at their weakest. His greatest failure came from his inability to convince the powerful city of Tlaxcala to break its alliance with the Spaniards.

Though successful in repelling the Spanish invasion of Tenochtitlán, Cuitláhuac's reign lasted only 80 days before he died in a smallpox epidemic that raged throughout the capital city. The Aztecs had captured a number of Spaniards and Tlaxcalans during battle, and according to several sources, one of the prisoners carried the smallpox virus, which quickly spread after the Aztecs consumed him in a cannibalistic ritual. Cuitláhuac, as emperor, was one of the first to consume the flesh of his enemies in a religious ceremony. In October 1520, Cuitláhuac died, leaving his nephew Cuauhtémoc to lead the final battle against the Spanish as the last of the Aztec emperors.

Thomas Edsall

See also: Alvarado, Pedro de; Cortés, Hernán; Cuauhtémoc; European Diseases, Role of; La Noche Triste; Montezuma II; Narváez, Pánfilo de; Quetzalcoatl; Tribute, Paid to Mexica.

Resources

Berdan, Frances F. *The Aztecs of Central Mexico: An Imperial Society.* Florence, KY: Wadsworth, 2004.

Díaz del Castillo, Bernal. *True History of the Conquest of Mexico.* London: Penguin Books, 1966.

Gillespie, Susan D. *The Aztec Kings: The Construction of Rulership in Mexica History.* Tucson: University of Arizona Press, 1992.

Hassig, Ross. *Aztec Warfare: Imperial Expansion and Political Control.* Oklahoma City: University of Oklahoma Press, 1995.

Cuzco

Cuzco of modern Peru was once the ancient holy city that served as the capital of the Inca Empire. It lies 12,000 feet up in the Andes Mountains and is one of the oldest continuously inhabited cities in the Western Hemisphere.

The Inca, who were among the great empires to fall to Spanish conquest in the 16th century, established themselves in the Cuzco Valley, in what is now Peru, around 1200 CE. According to oral tradition, the Sun god, Inti,

identified Cuzco as the Inca's promised land and the legendary first king, Manco Cápac, founded his kingdom there. In 1438, Emperor Pachacutin Inca Yupanqui began a process of conquest that resulted in an empire that stretched 2,500 miles down the cordillera of the Andes, with Cuzco as its capital. Pachacutin built an imperial system of government at Cuzco and forced regional tribes to become vassals to the Inca lords. Cuzco, with a population of 20,000 at its height, remained under Inca rule until 1533, when the Spaniards under Francisco Pizarro conquered it.

Cuzco was laid out on a grid plan in the shape of a puma, a sacred animal. The Inca fortress of Sacsahuamán, on a plateau on the northern edge of the city, forms the head of the sacred puma. Two sacred rivers were channeled through the city, which was laid

Artistic rendition of the Inca capital of Cuzco, with the main square, Inca palace and temple, as well as the four main roads leading out toward the extreme reaches of the Inca Empire. (Jay I. Kislak Collection, Rare Book and Special Collections Division, Library of Congress)

out in quadrants that radiated out through the kingdom. The angles of the quadrants are uneven and seem to have been based on astrological lines in the Milky Way. Any visitor to the city was required to stay in the quadrant assigned to his home village.

The center of the scheme was the Corycancha or golden enclosure (renamed Temple of the Sun by the Spanish), founded in legend when the first Inca was sent to earth by the sun. He struck the ground with a gold rod until the rod was drawn into the earth at the proper spot for the building of the temple. The temple was oriented to the summer solstice, and the niche where the first solstice rays fell each year still remains. The Inca would sit in the niche at the solstice to receive the rays of the sun as it rose. Then a priest would light a sacred fire from the first solstice rays by reflecting them from a gold mirror. Corycancha was the "pivot of heaven," where the lines of sky and earth came together near the crossing of the sacred rivers. Cuzco means "navel of the world" in Quechua, the Inca language, which is still spoken there. It is from this historic and religious center that the Inca Empire, or Tahuantinsuyu—meaning four regions or quadrants—governed over its many component parts and peoples.

The Spaniards had little respect for the Inca monuments and stripped them of their extensive gold. The Temple of the Sun, for example, had 700 panels, each weighing five pounds—all of pure gold—which were removed and melted into ingots by the Spanish. The temple walls remained, although some have been incorporated into colonial Christian churches. Three chambers dedicated to the moon, the rainbow, and thunder can be visited in the Church of Santo Domingo, and other elements of the temple are still visible though no longer complete. During the Inca period, the temple was surrounded by an ornamental garden of corn, potatoes, and other local foods, each plant made of gold and jewels—all of which were also confiscated by the invading Spanish.

Cuzco's ecological environment changed rapidly under the Spanish as well. Tuber crops and native grains such as quinoa dominated during the Inca rule. The valley was also home to large forests. Within less than a century, the Spanish introduced wheat and stripped the forests for use in braziers. Today, even the salt flats that collected on the floor of the basins have become victims of modern urban growth.

Norbert Brockman

See also: Manco Cápac; Pachacutin; Pizarro, Francisco; Religion, of Pre-Conquest Inca.

Resources

Bauer, Brian S. *Ancient Cuzco: Heartland of the Inca.* Austin: University of Texas Press, 2004.

Brockman, Norbert C. *Encyclopedia of Sacred Places.* Santa Barbara, CA: ABC-CLIO, 1997.

Reinhard, John. "Sacred Peaks of the Andes." *National Geographic* (March 1992): 84–111.

Sallnow, Michael. *Pilgrims of the Andes: Regional Cults in Cuzco.* Washington, DC: Smithsonian Institute Press, 1987.

Von Hagen, Victor Wolfgang. *Highway of the Sun.* Boston: Duell Sloan & Pearce, Little and Brown, 1955.

D

Dávila, Pedro Arias

During his life of over 80 years, Pedro Arias Dávila aided the Castillian monarchy's hegemonic expansion throughout the Iberian Peninsula and the newly colonized Americas. His role in this expansion included fighting during the wars of the Spanish Reconquista, administrating the Spanish-American colony of Castilla del Oro, and founding the city of Panama.

Born (in 1440s) into one of the most influential, aristocratic families of crypto-Jews in Segovia, Pedro Arias Dávila y Ortiz de Cota (also known as Pedrarias Dávila, or Pedro Arias de Ávila) maintained close ties with the Spanish monarchy throughout his life. His grandfather, Diego Arias de Ávila, served as advisor to King Enrique IV and as the *Contador General* (general accountant). Enrique IV and Isabela la Católica dubbed Dávila's father, Pedro Arias Dávila, "el Valiente" ("the brave") in recognition of his military exploits. Similar to the previous generations of patriarchs, Pedro Arias Dávila strengthened his relationship with the monarchy, and in 1485, married Isabel de Bobadilla y Peñalosa, an intimate friend of Isabela I, and daughter of Francisco de Bobadilla, the conquistador of Granada.

Like his father before him, Dávila distinguished himself as a soldier earning the nicknames "El Galán" and "El Gran Justador" ("the gentleman" and "the great jouster," respectively) for his equestrian prowess and his skill with a lance. During his various campaigns of *La Reconquista* and the Spanish Crown's other wars in Europe and North Africa, Dávila fought against Moorish forces in Granada. He also participated in military tours in what is now Algeria, including the conquest of the city of Oran under the leadership Pedro Navarro, in addition to serving in Portugal and France.

This military experience and loyalty to the Spanish monarchy gained the attention and confidence of King Ferdinand II of Aragon. In 1514, the monarch appointed Dávila, despite his age of 70, as the commander of the largest expedition to the Americas. Dávila arrived at the city of Santa Marta in Colombia. He then traveled on to Darién, the capital of the Spanish colony of Castilla de Oro—comprised of what is modern-day Nicaragua, Costa Rica, Panama, and northern Colombia. There, he was assigned to oversee court proceedings against the colonial governor of Darién and first European to reach the Pacific Ocean, Vasco Núñez de Balboa. Dávila tried and executed the governor on January 15, 1519.

After the execution, Dávila assumed the role of governor and captain general of Castilla de Oro. Soon after, he abandoned the capital of Durién and founded Panama City on August 15, 1519. Five years after the city's founding, he began to concentrate regional governance there, installing Panama City as the new colonial capital. Despite the inhospitable climate of the Central American Isthmus, replete with undesirable conditions for early colonizers, Panama City quickly became the first major capital and point of commerce on the American mainland.

As governor, Pedro Arias Dávila licensed many of the early conquistadors in the region, such as Francisco Hernández de Córdoba who lead expeditions in what is now modern-day Nicaragua and founded the cities Granada and León. Though Hernández de Córdoba was an officer of Dávila, the 80-five-year-old governor soon viewed his subordinate as a traitor and sentenced him to death in 1526. In the same year, Dávila sponsored the expedition agreement with Francisco Pizarro and Diego de Almagro, which resulted in the conquest of Peru. Close to the end of his life, Dávila retired from his position as governor of Panama and moved to León in Nicaragua. There he was installed as the new governor on July 1, 1527, until his death on March 6, 1531 at approximately 90 years of age.

Though an administrator under the same Spanish colonial apparatus as conquistadores such as Hernán Cortés and Francisco Pizarro, Pedro Arias Dávila is set apart from his contemporaries as the most cruel and ambitious representation of colonial authority. During his office as governor of Panama, indigenous and Spanish people alike called Dávila "Furor Domini" ("wrath of God" in Latin) because of his severe and relentless mistreatment of both. His quick execution of colonial administrators Vasco Núñez Balboa and Francisco Hernández Córdoba gave further credence to Dávila's epithet. And unlike other contemporary conquistadors, Pedro Arias Dávila was never romanticized as a leader because of his age, his military experience, and his position as a wealthy member of the aristocratic elite. Instead, Bartolomé de las Casas, in his *Brevísima relación de la destruición de las Indias* (*A Brief History of the Destruction of the Indies*), cites Dávila as the orchestrator of numerous massacres and injustices against the native men, women, and children of the region, and names him one of the worst tyrants of the Spanish colonial system.

Christopher Alex Chablé

See also: Almagro, Diego de; Balboa, Vasco Núñez de; Las Casas, Bartolomé de; Pizarro, Francisco; Reconquista, Impact of on Spanish Policy in America.

Resources

Cantera Burgos, Francisco. *Pedrarias Dávila y Cota, capitán general y gobernador de Castilla del Oro y Nicaragua: sus antecedentes judíos.* Madrid: Universidad de Madrid, 1971.

Gitlitz, David M. *Los Arias Dávila de Segovia: entre la sinagoga y la iglesia.* San Francisco, CA: International Scholars Publications, 1996.

Mena García, Carmen. *Pedrarias Dávila o "La ira de Dios": una historia olvidada.* Sevilla: Universidad de Sevilla, 1992.

Rubiano, Pablo Alvarez. *Pedroarias Dávila: contribución al estudio de la figura del "Gran Justador," gobernador de Castilla del Oro y Nicaragua.* Madrid: Instituto Gonzalo Fernandez de Oviedo, 1944.

Díaz del Castillo, Bernal

Born in Medina del Campo, Valladolid, the Spanish soldier and conquistador died in Guatemala sometime between 1584 and 1586. Díaz is known today for his literary account of the conquest of Mexico and the Aztec Empire by Hernán Cortés in which he took part personally. Some 60 years later, Díaz wrote down his experience of the conquest of Mexico as a soldier. Since that time, Díaz's account has served as the most often quoted and most reliable reference of the Spanish conquest of the Aztec Empire.

Bernal Díaz was born in Medina del Campo in the 1490s, though the exact year is unknown. Of a poor family and having a very minimal education, he began service in the military at a young age as a common soldier. Hoping for greater opportunity in life, he embarked for the New World in 1514 on an expedition under the command of Pedro Arias Dávila. Three years later he took part in the ill-fated expedition of Francisco Hernandez de Córdoba to the Yucatán in 1517. This expedition provided the first detailed information about advanced societies on the mainland, written by Díaz. Still unlucky in his search for wealth, Díaz returned to the mainland a year later in 1518 under the command of Juan de Grijalva. This later expedition also met resistance and came under attack by the native Indians. As a member of these two attempts to establish Spanish posts in the Yucatán, Díaz probably took part in the battle of Potonchan and entered the Indian cities of Cingapancuga as well as Texcoco. Yet the biggest adventure of his life took place one year later.

In 1519, in his mid-twenties, Díaz set out on an expedition lead by Hernán Cortés against the then unknown Aztec Empire. It was yet another undertaking that sought to establish Spanish rule on the Mexican mainland. According to his later memoirs, Díaz took part in the whole expedition, from the embarkation from Cuba, to landing on the Mexican shore through the conquest of Tenochtitlán. He was present at most of the 119 battles against various Indians of the region, and was wounded in the battle of La Noche Triste when Cortés and his soldiers barely avoided annihilation in the Mexican capital. During the campaign, Díaz met and talked to the Aztec emperor, Montezuma II. Bernal Díaz was respected by Cortés and was entrusted with important tasks.

Following the conquest of Mexico, Díaz was granted several encomiendas in the New World. These encomiendas included a grant as early as September 22, 1522, at Potonchan, as well as later grants at Teapa, Tecomaxtlhuaca, and Mechoacan. Driven by his quest for wealth and economic security, Díaz continued to look for new possibilities and, presumably, more profitable encomiendas. Soon after the victory over the Aztecs at Tenochtitlán, he joined an expedition of an old friend of Cortés and himself, Gonzala de Sondovala. Cortés sent the expedition south to the province of Coatzacoalcos. There, after several skirmishes with Indians, Díaz again received property in the form of an encomienda, yet still did not settle in the area. Instead, he continued fighting against Indian uprisings. He took part in Luis Marín's expedition to Chiapas and Rodrigo Rangel's struggles in Copilco and Amatan. After several smaller campaigns and encounters with the indigenous population of Middle America, Díaz finally decided to settle on his encomienda at Chamula in Espritu Santo.

In 1524 Cortés once more summoned Díaz from his estate, to set out on an expedition to conquer Honduras. This time the Spaniards failed and did not manage to colonize that territory until years later.

In 1539 Díaz went back to Spain for the first time since he originally left in 1514. After only two years he returned to New Spain, whereupon he decided to move from Mexico to Guatemala, where he resided for the rest of his life. In 1550, Díaz once again traveled to Spain, this time as a representative of the cabildo of Guatemala. There he pled the case of the perpetuity of the encomiendas in the New World before the Council of the Indies. The result was not positive and he returned to Guatemala with nothing to show for his efforts.

Bernal Díaz spent the rest of his life in Guatemala, dividing his time between running his property, writing, and some public activity. He died in there most probably in 1564, but dates four years later can also be found in his biographies.

In the early 1550s Díaz started to write the first chapters of his famous work. The writing itself was continued in the years 1564–1568, at which time it was doubtlessly inspired by and reacting against the publication in Spain of the work *Cronica de la Conquista de Nueva España* by Francisco Lopez de Gómara. In his work, Gómara gives most if not all the credit for the conquest of Mexico to Hernán Cortés, omitting all or most of the other participants. Díaz composed his own description of the conquest of Mexico, likely utilizing Gómara's published work, though his own version gave credit to the other conquistadors along with Cortés. Some historians suggest that he might have also read the accounts of Paolo Giovio and Gonzalo de Illescas. This does not seem likely, as they were published in Latin, and came out relatively late for him to be able to use them (1564–1565).

The result of his endeavors, a broad, four-volume account of Hernán Cortés's campaign and conquest of Mexico, was written in a lively Catalan language. It was available in 1568 as *Historia verdadera de la conquista de la Nueva Espana*. The account was finally published in 1632 in a Spanish edition.

Díaz's account of the campaign is a dynamic story told by a simple soldier. His work contains many references to the everyday life during the campaign, as well as a myriad of observations referring to the conquered territory and its indigenous inhabitants. Díaz tried to give justice to all participants of the expedition and discussed all of the 119 battles and encounters between the Spanish and their allies against the Aztecs and their supplementary troops. Today his account remains the most often published and translated account of the conquest of Mexico.

Jakub Basista

See also: Cortés, Hernán; Dávila, Pedro Arias; Encomienda; La Noche Trista.

Resources

Brooks, Francis J. "Motecuzoma Xocoyotl, Hernán Cortés, and Bernal Díaz del Castillo: The Construction of an Arrest." *Hispanic American Historical Review.* 75 (May 1995): 149–183.

Díaz del Castillo, Bernal. *The True History of The Conquest of New Spain.* Translated with an Introduction and Notes by Janet Burke and Ted Humphrey. Indianapolis, IN: Hackett Publishing, 2012.

Thomas, Hugh. *Conquest: Montezuma, Cortés and the Fall of Old Mexico.* New York: Simon & Schuster, 1993.

Thomas, Hugh. *The Conquest of Mexico.* London: Pimlico Press, 2004.

Thomas, Hugh. *Who's Who of the Conquistadors.* London: Cassell & Company, 2007.

Díaz, Fr. Juan

A secular priest from Sevillano, Spain, Fr. Juan Díaz was a chaplain on Juan de Grijalva's 1518 exploration of coastal Yucatán. From his reports, historians learned that the indigenous towns on the island of Cozumel were much more complex in their architectural structures, urban infrastructures, and agricultural advancements. Fr. Díaz climbed the temple built to the chief goddess, Ix Chel, where he noted the presence of bones and idols, obviously the result of sacrifices by the local population. It was at one of these towns that the priest celebrated mass, the first noted by the expedition in the newly explored territory.

As the Grijalva expedition continued on to explore the coast of the Yucatán, Díaz continued to record his perceptions of the buildings and cities as equal to the Spanish city of Seville. As the explorers extended their stay in the Mayan town of the Campeche region, the initially friendly welcome turned to requests and then demands for the Spanish to leave. Though more restrained than Hernández de Córdoba in an earlier expedition, Grijalva continued to turn down traditional offerings of gifts and to demand gold. As relations soured, Fr. Díaz recorded the use of cannon to frighten the native population, as well as the use of fire and crossbows to kill some of the Maya.

While Fr. Juan Díaz's assessments provided valuable information of native culture and society at the time of early contact, they also provided misinformation. One such example was the assertion that the Totonac people of the region of Veracruz were circumcised, and therefore Jewish or Muslim. Reflecting the biases of the Spanish against not just the Jews and Muslims but also the Mayas, Díaz's remarks belied a lack of understanding that the priests drew blood for their sacrifices and personal offerings that caused the "deformation."

Following the return of Grijalva's expedition to Cuba, another expedition, also ordered by Governor Diego Velázquez, set sail for the Yucatán. The secular priest Juan Díaz again accompanied the expedition, this time under the guidance of Hernán Cortés. One of the two priests on the voyage, Juan Díaz helped offer masses on a daily basis. Nonetheless, he soon earned the displeasure of the *caudillo,* Cortés, when he participated in a mutiny attempt perpetuated by supporters of Governor Velázquez and those desiring to return to Cuba. Arrested and threatened with a hanging, Cortés ultimately released Díaz after a brief imprisonment.

It is not certain if the relations between the conquistador and the priest were permanently affected by this brief incident. However, soon thereafter, Cortés requested the Crown to send Dominican or Franciscan friars, but not secular priests (like Díaz). When the conquistador left Tenochtitlán to confront the forces of Pánfilo Narváez, he left Díaz in the capital with Pedro de Alvarado, choosing to take Fr. Bartolomé de Olmedo instead. In the late 1520s, when the *caudillo* was being investigated for the handling of the gold and gems intended for the king's fifth in the disastrous La Noche Triste, Díaz's testimony indicated the gold was entrusted to persons other than the assigned treasurer. Certainly, the priest's origins from Sevillano, instead of the Extremadura region where Cortés originated from, played a role in their relations.

Fr. Juan Díaz remained in New Spain following the conquest of the Aztec. It was there that he was killed by Indians, presumably while breaking up idols used for native worship.

Rebecca M. Seaman

See also: Alvarado, Pedro de; Cortés, Hernán; Grijalva, Juan de; La Noche Triste; Narváez, Pánfilo; Olmedo, Fr. Bartolomé de; Velázquez, Diego (de Cuéllar).

Resources

Engelhardt, Zephyrin. *The Missions and Missionaries of California,* Vol. 1. San Francisco: The James H. Barry Company, 1908.

Levy, Buddy. *Conquistador: Hernán Cortés, King Montezuma, and the Last Stand of the Aztecs.* New York: Bantam Books, 2009.

Thomas, Hugh. *Conquest: Montezuma, Cortés, and the Fall of Old Mexico.* New York: Simon & Schuster, 1993.

Duero, Andrés de

Small in stature, Andrés de Duero hailed from Tudela del Duero near Vallodolid. He traveled to Cuba, where he served as Governor Diego Velázquez's secretary in the second decade of the 16th century. It was in this role that he became a close friend and ally of Hernán Cortés, then a magistrate of a town on the island. Duero and the king's accountant to the colony, Andrés de Lares, convinced Velázquez to appoint Cortés as commander of the expedition to explore Yucatán further for possible wealth from the Mexica Empire. Indeed, the governor's instructions to Cortés, naming him the *caudillo* and setting forth the mission and restrictions of the expedition, were drafted by Duero.

Unlike many of Cortés's other friends and allies, Duero was not the adventurous type, instead being content to serve in administrative roles and delve into business ventures. Because of his role as an investor the secretary hosted a secret meeting with Cortés and some of his trusted captains. There, not only did the group agree to make the *caudillo* captain general of the expedition, but Duero and Lares committed secretly to partner with Cortés, helping to finance his expedition.

Financing from Duero was a significant part of Cortés's eventual success. Velázquez's increased concerns about the *caudillo*'s ambitions led to the governor threatening to remove Cortés as the commander. Duero not only helped finance the expedition quickly, but he also secretly advised the *caudillo* about the threat posed by Velázquez, encouraging the quick organization and embarkation of the expedition.

Following the sailing of the expedition, Duero continued to play a supportive role for the venture back in Cuba. Cortés instructed Duero to use monies from the conquistador's mines on the island to send back to his father in Spain. These monies were used in part to curry favor for Cortés and his request for authority over the regions he planned to conquer.

The following year, Velázquez commissioned another expedition under Pánfilo Narváez to arrest or kill Cortés. It was at this time that the unlikely adventurer Duero joined the excursion. Whether Duero accompanied Narváez out of concern for his previous investment or to ensure moderate action toward Cortés is unknown—it could possibly be both. Duero and Narváez arrived in the Yucatán in the spring of 1520. At that time Cortés was ensconced in the Aztec capital of Tenochtitlán where he held the Emperor Montezuma II and his family as hostages. Duero played a moderating influence on Narváez during a flurry of exchanges between the two conquistadors. Narváez, who seemed intent on arresting or killing Cortés, was convinced by Velázquez's secretary to treat Cortés's messengers with courtesy—even welcoming them to dine with him. Duero was well aware of, and seemingly complicit in, the distribution of gold among Narváez's men by these same messengers as means of swaying them in favor of Cortés.

Following Cortés's eventual defeat and integration of Narváez's forces into his own, Duero joined the *caudillo* as he returned to Tenochtitlán to view the great wealth of the city. Instead of the Spanish being firmly in control, the secretary observed the disastrous La Noche Triste (Sad Night) where the invaders were violently expelled from the city, losing the king's gold in the process. It was following this devastating loss that Duero joined Narvaecistas in calling for a return to Cuba. The business-minded secretary interpreted the events of late June 1520 as indicative of the Spanish failure in the region and demonstrative of an increasingly bad investment. Additionally, Duero placed no trust in the Tlaxcala that Cortés used as allies.

Dismayed at his old friend and partner's questioning of his decisions, Cortés proposed to demonstrate the loyalty and ability of the Tlaxcala, as well as the ability of the Spanish to successfully prosecute the conquest of the Mexica Empire. He offered to conduct a campaign in conjunction with the Tlaxcala against the well-fortified Aztec stronghold at Tepeaca. Cortés asserted that this would be proof of the Spanish ability to conduct the campaign and the Tlaxcala abilities and trustworthiness. The campaign was as successful as it was barbarous.

Following the defeat of Tepeaca, Cortés turned his attention back to the Narvaecistas. Those still wishing to return to Cuba were allowed to travel back. He sent Duero back with this group. However, evidence seems to indicate that he and Duero had repaired their relationship following the defeat of the Tepeaca. Cortés sent his friend and partner back to Cuba with gold and gems for purpose of sending the wealth back to the *caudillo*'s father, again for the purpose of sponsoring efforts to promote the conquistador as "captain-general" and *adelantado* of New Spain. Duero was also entrusted with a letter from the *caudillo* to his wife. Andrés de Duero returned to Cuba in 1520, were he continued to serve as a liaison between Cortés and his father in Spain.

Rebecca M. Seaman

See also: Cortés, Hernán; La Noche Triste; Narváez, Pánfilo.

Resources

Díaz del Castillo, Bernal. *The History of the Conquest of New Spain.* Edited by David Carrasco. Albuquerque: University of New Mexico Press, 2008.

León-Portilla, Miguel. *The Broken Spears: The Aztec Account of the Conquest of Mexico.* Foreword by J. Jorge Klor de Alva. Boston: Beacon Press, 2006.

Levy, Buddy. *Conquistador.* New York: Bantam Dell, 2008.

Schwartz, Stuart B., ed. *Victors and Vanquished: Spanish and Nahua Views of the Conquest of Mexico.* Boston: Bedford/St. Martin's, 2000.

Thomas, Hugh. *Conquest: Montezuma, Cortés, and the Fall of Old Mexico.* New York: Simon & Schuster, 1993.

Durán, Fr. Diego (1537–1588)

Diego Durán was born in Seville, Spain, around the year 1537. Durán later studied to be a Dominican friar and penned three important works on the religion and customs of the natives in Mexico: *Book of the Gods and Rites* (ca. 1576–1579), *The Ancient Calendar* (1579), and *The History of the Indies of New Spain* (1580–1581).

Little is known of Durán's birth and early life. It is known that he was born in Seville though the exact date is unknown; 1537 is considered to be the year in which he was born. Early in his life, perhaps between the ages of two and five, Durán moved with his family to live in Texcoco (Tetzcoco) in the Spanish colony of New Spain (Mexico). His family was not wealthy and his father was likely a low government official for the colony of New Spain. Living in Texcoco until around the age of 12, Durán was able to learn the language of the Aztecs: Nahuatl.

Around the age of 12, Durán and his family relocated to Mexico City, the capital of New Spain. It was here that he began to receive a more formal education. Diego Durán grew up at a time when two cultures were clashing together. The Aztecs, though already conquered, continued subtle resistance by continuing to display pieces of their culture. Simultaneously, Catholic Spain was implementing policies intended to assist in governing their New World colony. Temples began to go into disrepair while churches were built to take their place physically and culturally. The two cultures clashed with regard to language, religion, politics, and ethnic background, thereby creating a difficult atmosphere for Mexico City. Spaniards and natives alike remembered the conquest and the roles played by people like Hernán Cortés and Moctezuma II (Montezuma). It was in this atmosphere that Diego Durán grew up and was thus influenced.

By the age of 19, on May 8, 1556, Durán entered the Monastery of Santo Domingo (St. Dominic) to study as a Dominican novice. Later, as a friar, Durán traveled around to convert the natives. As a young missionary, the many different people with whom he regularly came into contact influenced Durán for the remainder of his life. He became learned in the culture of the natives and began to see flaws in the Spanish approach to converting the indigenous population. The clergy did not minister to the true needs of the natives, thereby allowing their pagan cultures and practice to continue unchecked.

The primary important consequences of Durán's life were the works he produced.

The three books he wrote emerged out of his life experiences as a man of both the Old World of Europe and the New World of the natives. Durán felt he could correct several wrongs by educating those around him with the knowledge he was able to acquire through his travels as a friar and his extended stay in New Spain. Friar Durán used various written sources he had access to, as well as listened to the stories of many natives who were young at the time of the Spanish conquest. These individuals were indispensable sources of knowledge about Aztec life before the influence of Spain and Roman Catholicism, and gave Durán a comprehensive oral history of the Aztec people and their religion.

The Book of the Gods and Rites was Durán's first book, which was written between 1576 and 1579. This guidebook was an account of the customs and culture of the Aztec. The second book, *The Ancient Calendar,* was written around the year 1579 and was a description of the intricate way the Aztecs counted time. The last book, *The History of the Indies of New Spain,* was written

Doña Marina given to Cortés as a Spoil of War by Diego Durán. (The Gallery Collection/Corbis)

between 1580 and 1581 and served as an important history of the Aztec people from their beginnings in the ninth century to the present day of Durán's times; the writing was based on legends and the common beliefs of the natives he interviewed.

A fourth work has never been found and was possibly never written; however, Durán mentions *The Treatise on Things Past* as being a continuation of his earlier works. All of these written books are collectively known as the Durán Codex and were written with the purpose of exposing the pagan traditions the natives had mingled with their new Catholic faith. Legendary heroes were being blended with biblical characters and Spanish religious leaders did not notice. His writing went largely unnoticed and fell into obscurity. By the 1580s Durán's health was deteriorating and he had strong misgivings about his fellow members of the Catholic clergy. Friar Diego Durán died in Mexico in 1588, leaving his works for others to learn from and build upon in the years to come.

Matthew Blake Strickland

See also: Cortés, Hernán; Montezuma II; Nahuatl Language.

Further Reading

Durán, Diego. *Book of the Gods and Rites and the Ancient Calendar.* Translated and edited by Fernando Horcasitas and Doris Heyden. Norman: University of Oklahoma Press, 1971.

Durán, Diego. *The History of the Indies of New Spain.* Translated and edited by Doris Heyden. Norman: University of Oklahoma Press, 1994.

Schwartz, Stuart B., ed. *Victors and Vanquished: Spanish and Nahua Views of the Conquest of Mexico.* Boston: Bedford/St. Martin's, 2000.

Villela, Khristaan D., and Mary Ellen Miller, eds. *The Aztec Calendar Stone.* Los Angeles: The Getty Research Institute, 2010.

E

Education, Pre-Columbian Mexico

At a time when European formal education was only available to a chosen few, accessed only across the ocean, the Mexica developed educational institutions that functioned efficiently and included everyone, regardless of gender or social status. Pre-conquest education for children was compulsory for the Mexica. At birth, parents offered their children to one of two institutions (if we do not separate the pre-Hispanic school for music), the *calmecac*—most often attended by the sons of the noble class or *pipiltin*—and the *telpochcalli*—most often attended by the children of the commoners or *macehuales.* The parents took up education in the early years aided by the handing down of *huehuetlatolli,* or words of the elders. These were discourses that taught the Mexica how to be a Mexica. They instructed them in proper behavior at any given time in life: birth, marriage, parenting, health, work, death, etc. Fathers took on the job of teaching their sons and mothers taught their daughters. Parents were supported, and perhaps kept to the rules, by the *calpulli* (or calpolli), a term that means "big house" and which refers to a kin subunit of the basic social structure of the empire, the *altepetl.* Severe punishments were part of the upbringing of Mexica children at all levels of their formation. The records describe such punishments as being hit with maguey thorns or sticks, being left to lay on wet floors with hands and feet bound, making them breathe chili smoke, etc. Obedience and compliance appear to have been paramount.

The *calmecac* were built adjacent to or within temples. There is not enough information from existing sources to tell how many of these schools existed, but it is evident that it was a privilege for a *calpulli* to have one such school, and that not all of the *calpulli* had one. These schools were more easily found in capital cities. There, the young received an education both sophisticated and intensive at the hands of the wisest of men, the *tlamacazque* (priest-teachers), also called *tlamatimine* (teachers). These were the schools that prepared those who would eventually rule. In these upper level institutions, which functioned under the protection of the god Quetzalcoatl, the young nobles (and at times some *macehuales* who had distinguished themselves), under strict discipline, grew to become stoic and measured men who were to approach rule with unequivocal self-control in adulthood. These schools were part of the imperial framework of the Mexica, and hence tight regulations and censorship were in place in their running. This highly controlled style mirrored the very qualities most sought after in good leaders and admirable men in the Mexica world.

Once the children of the *pipiltin* were of proper age, around five according to some sources, or 10 according to others, their parents would leave them under the care of the high priests and teachers so that the *tlamatimine* would raise them according to the customs of the *calmecac.* The *calmecac* focused on turning out leaders (*tlatoque*), priests, scholars/teachers (*tlatimini*), healers (*tizitl*), and codex painters (*tlacuilos*). Students learned the rituals of their religion, theology, the art of rhetoric, divine songs, astrology, the interpretation of dreams, and all other forms of sacred knowledge. They studied ancient and contemporary history, pictographic literacy, the use and meaning of the Mexica calendar system, geometry, and astronomy. The *calmecac* shared with the *telpochcalli* the training in military arts, history, and religion. Sources note that boys trained at the *calmecac* started their military training at 15 and at 20 they would be considered as fit for battle. The aim of this upper level school was, after all, to produce the leadership of the Mexica society. Although scholars separate the curriculum into distinct subjects for ease of expression, these subjects should be understood in a more organic way: as interrelated and inseparable areas of study for the Mexica.

Life at the *calmecac* was rigorous. Boys would get up before sunrise and stopped work before sunset to prepare for bloodletting rituals. The students of the *calmecac* ate and slept at their school and had intense work and ritual schedules. At midnight they rose to offer prayers to the gods (and would be punished with maguey thorns if they failed to rise). When students grew to become priests they had to adhere to a vow of chastity. However, most boys left to marry around the age of 20.

The *telpochcalli,* translated often as the house of the youth, was dedicated to the god Tezcatlipoca. The lack of dedication to Huitzilopochtli, the god of war of the Aztec, is, according to renowned scholar José María Kobayashi, a sign of the antiquity of the schools, which must have predated the period of Aztec ascendance in the valley of Mexico and hence their tutelary god. The *telpochcalli* trained in history, religion, trade, and the military arts. To create camaraderie and loyalty to one's *telpochcalli,* students were allowed to eat in their own homes, but had to sleep and spend the rest of their days at the school with their teachers and cohorts. Exceptions could be made to allow students a few days off to attend to their families' farming obligations. Their duties meant to develop discipline as well as physical and mental toughness. Life was somewhat less strict in the *telpochcalli* than at the *calmecac.* For example, chastity was not mandatory, however, drunkenness could be punishable by death. Each *calpulli* had its own *telpochcalli.*

Girls were also expected to be educated in Mexica society. Although much of the teaching of women was left to their mothers, the state also ran centers aimed at this task, the *calmecac* and the *ichpochcalli.* If a girl was promised to the *calmecac,* her mother had to bring offerings to the school every 20 days until the child was able to do it herself. Once she entered the school she would live, according to Kobayashi, as *cihuatlamacazque,* priestess, guarded by older women or *cuacuacuiltin* until she was ready for marriage. The *ichpochcalli* was more service-centered. Women could also enter a life of religious service inside temples and could receive training in the medical arts as *tizitl,* providing obstetric service to other women.

What is most unusual with regard to pre-conquest Aztec education, when comparing it to the European norm, is the pervasiveness of education throughout society, for upper and common classes, males and females. The trend of focusing upon religious, military, and basic education is found in both cultures, as were strict curricula and stern punishment. Despite this notable Aztecan advantage, the Spanish conquest brought compulsory missionary structures and education that conveyed the Spanish perception of superiority over the indigenous society with regard to education.

SilverMoon

See also: *Macehualtin; Pipiltin; Tlamatimine.*

Resources

Gruzinski, Serge. *The Conquest of Mexico: The Incorporation of Indian Societies into the Western World, 16th–18th Centuries.* Translated by Eileen Corrigan. Cambridge, MA: Polity Press, 1993.

Kobayashi, José María. *La Educación Como Conquista: Empresa Franciscana En México.* 2nd ed. México: El Colegio de México, 2002.

Lockhart, James. *The Nahuas after the Conquest: A Social and Cultural History of the Indians of Central Mexico, Sixteenth through Eighteenth Centuries.* Stanford, CA: Stanford University Press, 1992.

Sahagún, Bernardino de, Alfredo López Austin, and Josefina García Quintana. *Historia General De Las Cosas De Nueva España.* 3 vols. México: CONACULTA, 1988.

Education, Pre-Columbian Peru

The education of pre-contact Inca was determined in part by the element of the society—or class—that existed within. The Inca society attempted to structure an existence at the local level that contained at least a semblance of no class divisions. However, the reality remained that the *kurakas,* no matter how benevolent in their intentions, still collected and distributed goods according to the needs of their *ayllus* or clans. As a result, there existed a true class system of sorts: the commoners accounting for the majority of Inca and paid tributes, while the nobility, those who owned great estates, were exempt from the *mita.*

Class structure played a role in Inca education. Again, the attempt was made to have a classless society where all received an education. However, the reality existed that the common Inca, or common subjects of the Incas, received a rudimentary education. The basic education taught to commoners was designed to ensure basic knowledge that, in turn, would assist in the continuation of the society and the economy. Meanwhile, those Inca classified as nobility received a deeper education.

The sons of Inca lords, whether they were the local *kurakas* or relatives of the Sapa Inca, were sent to the capital of Cuzco for their education. There they were steeped in far more than just how to read the unique Inca recording system of *quipu.* Instructions were given regarding their faith, as well as exercises in the proper use of diplomacy. Included in the nobility were the families of subject rulers. By providing some education to all people of Inca lineage, the state was able to set the Inca apart from dominated foreign societies. However, some subjected societies were closely aligned to the Inca royalty. In these cases, such highly placed allegiance was rewarded with the title of "Inca by privilege." Families of subject rulers, who were deemed Inca by privilege, also received an advanced education for their sons, as well.

Far outnumbered by the diverse societies they ruled, the Inca relied on structure and charisma to hold sway over the largest empire in the Western Hemisphere. With some education provided to all Incas, this required the ruling *kurakas* and Sapa Incas to have a strong education and ability to use information to lead effectively. Knowledge of the various societies, the resources within the empire, and the geographic features of the empire were imperative to maintaining control and the respect of their own people. Another area of knowledge that was important to the ability of the Inca to govern effectively was a broad understanding of the Inca religion.

According to the pre-conquest Inca faith, multiple deities were worshipped, but two remained dominant. Inti, the Sun god, was directly related to the Sapa Incas who ruled the empire. Knowledge of this god, and the ability to interpret messages from the deity as they related to good governance, was a means of maintaining authority and control. The second deity, Viracocha, the creator god, had a blurry connection to the Sapa Incas. Nonetheless, it was Viracocha who created all, and from whom all bounty came. Closely related to this creator god was the power of yet another crucial deity. Illapa, or the thunder god, was the deity who provided rain. Inca leaders, whether local *kurakas* or Sapa Incas, were required to understand the key deities and how to appeal to them in such a fashion that disasters and calamities were avoided. Failure to understand these key roles could lead to the upheaval in the tenuous Inca Empire.

With charisma, and knowledge of the empire or local province providing the source of authority for the Incas, a proper education was essential. However, even with a good education and accompanying skills in diplomacy, there was no guarantee of success. With the advance of smallpox in the vanguard of the Spanish exploration, the Sapa Inca Huayna Cápac and his designated heir both died suddenly. Left to rule were two competing half-brothers, Huáscar and Atahualpa. While both had been educated in the proper fashion of noble sons and possible heirs, Atahualpa received additional training from his father in the area of military skills. This gave him the advantage when the two brothers went to war in the late 1520s. By 1532, Atahualpa defeated and captured Huáscar. No sooner had he accomplished this feat than the Spanish forces of Francisco Pizarro arrived, ambushing the young Sapa Inca and taking him hostage. Those wily and determined to manipulate the Spanish into releasing him for a huge ransom, Atahualpa did not reckon the greed and yearning for power of the conquistadors. After receiving their demanded ransom, Pizarro still had Atahualpa executed.

The combined impact of disease, rapid loss of four emperors in five years, undermined the faith of the people in their own rulers and even their deities. Instead, the Inca and their subjects interpreted the series of events to mean that their own gods had abandoned them in favor of the Christian god of the Spanish. The relatively young and naive successors to the Inca throne were incapable of using their own traditions and beliefs to counter the authority of the Spanish and convince their own people of their legitimacy to rule. Indeed, two of the last three Sapa Incas (Sayri and Titu Cusi) spent time living under Spanish control, which affected their perceptions of governance. Attempts made to recover Inca authority and apply the knowledge and education of their ancestors, through the Neo-Inca movement under Manco Inca Yupanqui, and the Taki Onqoy movement under Titu Cusi and Túpac Amaru, were too little and came too late to preserve Inca authority in Peru.

Rebecca M. Seaman

See also: Atahualpa; *Ayllus;* Huáscar; Huayna Cápac; *Kuraka;* Manco Inca Yupanqui; *Mita;* Neo-Incas; Pizarro, Francisco; *Quipu*; Sapa Inca; Sayri Túpac Taki Onqoy; Titu Cusi Yupanqui; Túpac Amaru.

Resources

Bernand, Carmen. *The Incas: Empire of Blood and Gold.* London: Thames & Hudson, 1994.

Hemming, John. *The Conquest of the Incas.* London: Pan Macmillan, 1970.

MacQuarrie, Kim. *The Last Days of the Incas.* New York: Simon & Schuster, 2007.

Mann, Charles C. *Ancient Americans: Rewriting the History of the New World.* London: Granta Books, 2005.

Means, Philip A. *The Fall of the Inca Empire and the Spanish Rule in Peru, 1530–1780.* New York: Gordian Press, 1971.

Sancho, Pedro. *An Account of the Conquest of Peru.* With Preface and translation by Philip Ainsworth Means. New York: Cortes Society, 1917.

El Mestizo

Martín Cortés, or "El Mestizo," was born in 1522. He was the son of Hernán Cortés and Malintzin (also called Doña Marina or Malinche), who had acted as Cortés's cultural mediator and interpreter during the Spanish conquest of the Aztec Empire. By the time El Mestizo was born, Cortés's first wife, Catalina Suárez "La Marcayda," had rejoined her husband in Coyoacán after the fall of Tenochtitlán. She died at the end of 1522.

Before the birth of El Mestizo, Cortés had fathered Catalina Pizarro out of wedlock. After him, Luis (1525), Leonor (1527), and María were born to different mothers. When his father married Luisa de Arellano, a noblewoman from Spain, in 1528, Martín was not yet known as El Mestizo. He became so in 1531 when his half-brother Martín El Criollo was born from this legitimate marriage. This meant that, although El Mestizo was older, the second Martín was the heir to their father's possessions. However, Pope Clemente VII legitimized El Mestizo—and his siblings Luis Cortés and Catalina Pizarro—by virtue of a papal bull in 1529.

When he was still a young boy in 1529, El Mestizo moved with his father's household members to Spain. There, Emperor Charles V (HRE, Carlos I of Spain) gave Hernán Cortés the title of marquis of the Valley of Oaxaca. When Cortés returned to Spain in 1540, he took with him his three sons: Martín El Mestizo, who was travelling to Spain for the second time; Luis Cortés; and Martín El Criollo, who was around eight years of age then. The three were raised together and joined his father in his military pursuits: they were present in the battle of Saint Quintin (1557). They served Emperor Charles and also Emperor Philip II. In fact, during his first travel to Spain, El Mestizo was even page of Philip while he was still the prince. Little is known about his years in Spain. It is said, but not easy to proved through documents, that he was a member of the army of Don Juan de Austria, the emperor's illegitimate son who commanded the Spanish troops in many famous battles.

The three brothers returned to New Spain in 1563. There they remained until 1568. Their father had died in 1547 and they all had been litigating for two decades for the properties in New Spain. When they actually returned, the criollo population, of Spanish parents—or at least fathers—and born in New Spain, received the sons of Cortés with the highest honors. However, El Criollo despised many of these criollos and consequently lost their support. That is very likely how the viceroyalty officers discovered the uprising the brothers were plotting with the help of the Ávila brothers and some other young criollos.

In 1568, El Mestizo was tortured in search of a confession about the uprising and charged with burdening fines. After that, the brothers were exiled from New Spain for life, although the Emperor pardoned them and authorized their return in 1574. There are not enough documents to demonstrate if El Mestizo returned, but apparently he did not. He died in Spain at the end of the century, very likely in 1595.

Covadonga Lamar Prieto

See also: Ávila, Alonso de; Charles V (HRE) or Carlos I of Spain; Cortés, Hernán; Cortés, Martín El Criollo; La Malinche, "Doña Marina."

Resources

Díaz del Castillo, Bernal. *The Conquest of New Spain.* Edited by Janet Burke and Ted Humphrey. Indianapolis, IN: Hackett, 2012.

Lanyon, Anna. *The New World of Martín Cortés.* Sydney: Allyn & Unwin Press, 2003; Reprint, Cambridge, MA: De Capo Press, 2004.

Prescott, William. *History of the Conquest of Mexico.* London: Continuum, 2009.

Suarez Peralta, Juan. *Noticias Historicas de la Nueva España.* Madrid: Justo Saragoza, 1878.

Thomas, Hugh. *Conquest: Montezuma, Cortés, and the Fall of Old Mexico.* New York: Simon & Schuster, 1993.

Encomenderos

Based on the root word, *encomendar*—meaning "to entrust"—the word originated in feudal Spain. The encomendero was typically a citizen of great status or a soldier whose significant service was rewarded. The Crown of Spain entrusted these encomenderos with the right or duty to collect tribute from a specified number of assigned laborers. As the Spanish contested for control of the Iberian peninsula from the Moors, Spaniards were offered awards of lands freed from Moorish control.

With Columbus's arrival in the West Indies, he extended similar grants of lands and the services of native laborers to his men in an unplanned manner. Within a decade, the new administrator of Hispaniola, Fr. Nicolás de Ovando, used a very structured method of assigning lands, setting specific numbers of conquered Indians to landowners designated as encomenderos. In Middle America, encomenderos specifically collected tributes from one or more pueblos or communities of Native Americans.

Originally, the privilege of tribute collection was given for a lifetime, and often this privilege could be passed on to designated heirs for up to two generations.

In addition to the collection of tributes from indigenous populations, the encomenderos did take on the burden of certain responsibilities. Encomenderos provided military service to the Crown along frontiers. With regard to the natives, encomenderos were tasked with defending indigenous subjects, as well as to provide for their spiritual well-being. In reality, the first several decades of American conquest saw a virtually one-sided practice, with encomenderos collecting tribute in the form of food and other goods, using their authority over the people to enrich themselves and the ability to use natives as laborers (presumably paid labor). Unfortunately, this imbalanced system allowed for the physical abuse of the Indians, resulting in death from disease, overwork, malnutrition, and even outright massacres.

Carlos I of Spain (Charles V, Holy Roman Emperor) established the Leyes Nuevas (New Laws) of 1542 to curb the worst abuses of the encomenderos. Limits on numbers of assigned native laborers, and assurances of paid labor, were established to prevent the practice of collecting tribute in the form of labor. Instead, tribute was to be paid in the form of goods collected, such as maize, other foods, or even precious metals. Encomenderos were required to convert the natives. Carlos's reforms also prohibited generational assignments of encomiendas. Regrettably, the logistics of the colonies, Carlos's preoccupation with European affairs, and his eventual retirement from the role of king and emperor, allowed the powerful colonial encomenderos to circumvent, challenge, and even ignore the legislated reforms. Carlos's heirs to the Spanish throne continued to allow the creation and extension of new titles of encomendero as a means of controlling and governing their Spanish colonies.

Examples of typical abuses that continued to be employed by encomenderos well into the 1600s include the use of personal service or direct labor as form of tribute demanded. This particular practice provided the encomenderos with virtually indigenous slave labor. The status of encomenderos in America did not include the assignment of lands, and actually forbid the settlement upon Indian lands. However, in the southwest, this restriction was often ignored as reality of the distances involved in frontier life. Indeed, the responsibilities of defending and converting the encomendado (natives entrusted to the Spanish) along the extensive frontiers seemed to make the settlement upon indigenous lands a necessity.

The extensive use and abuses by the encomenderos came to a rather abrupt halt with the Pueblo Revolt of 1680. Locally, the practice of privileged Spaniards living among the natives appeared dangerous. However, the real collapse of the system was due to the disinterest of the Crown in continuing to collect the tribute from distant, scattered pueblos, and villages along extensive frontiers.

Rebecca M. Seaman

See also: Charles V (HRE) or Carlos I of Spain; Ovando, Fr. Nicolás de; Leyes Nuevas 1542–1543; Slavery, Role of.

Resources

Charles I, King of Spain. "De La Libertad De Los Indios." *Recopilacion De Leyes de Los Reynos de Las Indias,* 2nd ed. Madrid: Por Antonio Balbas, 1756.

Stern, Steve J. *Peru's Indian Peoples and the Challenge of Spanish Conquest: Huamanga to 1640.* 2nd ed. Madison: University of Wisconsin Press, 1993.

Thomas, Hugh. *Conquest: Montezuma, Cortés, and the Fall of Old Mexico.* New York: Simon & Schuster, 1993.

Weber, David J. *The Spanish Frontier in North America.* New Haven, CT: Yale University Press, 1992.

Encomienda

The word "encomienda" comes from the Spanish word *encomendar,* meaning to entrust. Spanish conquistadors employed the encomienda throughout the Spanish Empire in return for services to the Crown. The encomendero, or holder of the encomienda, received a revocable grant from the Crown that included the native peoples occupying the land. The encomendero did not actually possess native lands, although his absolute power made him the de facto local ruler.

First used in Spain against the Moors, then established by the Castilian Crown for the empire in May 1493, the encomienda system was designed to spread Catholicism and Spanish civilization to the natives as well as to protect Spanish settlements and their native workers against outside attack. For such services, natives were bound to provide labor to the encomendero. By the Law of Burgos, any encomendero with 50 people or more under his care was required to instruct a young male who could teach the others the tenets of Catholicism and other "civilizing" lessons. The Crown also encouraged intermarriage as a means of civilizing the natives.

The Spanish employed two common labor systems in their American colonies: the encomienda and repartimiento. Encomiendas were the preferred practice in Middle and South America. The Crown awarded grants, or encomienda, to conquistadors or other prominent settlers through the local viceroys or *audiencias.* Initially granted in the form of a specific number of an expressly designated group of Indians, the encomiendas were intended for use of native labor for one generation. However, Spanish recipients of encomienda easily obtained extensions to their original grants, and control of local native groups even occasionally passed on to the heirs of some encomenderos.

The encomienda was not designed to be inheritable, and the natives theoretically retained ownership of their lands as well as independence from encomendero legal or political control. However, in practice they were often subjected to significant and arbitrary exploitation at the hands of the encomienda holder. Far from official oversight and control, the conquistadors indulged their voracious appetites for wealth. Unwilling to perform manual labor themselves, ambitious encomenderos acquired lands of their own and established a plantation-like economy based upon free labor performed by the natives. The encomenderos eventually became landed gentry, living off the backs of indigenous peoples, many of whom became virtual slaves. Empowered to set the amounts of tribute (tax) that could be collected from the natives, encomenderos used that power to exact huge concessions from the indigenous population.

The encomienda system suffered from other problems in the Caribbean region. Use of the native labor centered initially on the mining for gold and later on the intensive labor in sugarcane fields. Combined with the unintentional introduction of devastating diseases such as smallpox, typhus, malaria, and yellow fever, the close proximity of native workers and Spanish masters enforced by the system took its toll. Very soon, abuses of the system in the Caribbean led to major population losses. The Caribbean encomienda was all but defunct within a generation. The larger populations and expansive territories of the continents of Middle and South America extended the use of encomienda throughout the early colonial empire of the Spanish.

The New Laws issued by Charles V (Carlos I of Spain) in 1542, and the establishment of the Council of the Indies, set limits on the amount of tribute and established local government in the form of the *audiencia*. These laws prohibited slave raids, enslavement due to war, and a variety of other means used to enforce labor. However, the language of the laws included special caveats that allowed exceptions to all natives—even those yet to be discovered—and established special licenses by the king for the purpose of perpetuating the use of native labor. While ostensibly designed to improve treatment of Native Americans and abolish encomienda and repartimiento within the span of a generation, within 20 years of the passage of Charles V's New Laws, documents demonstrate the increase in special licenses that permitted control of entire Indian towns for multiple generations. The encomenderos quickly took control of local governments and the encomienda continued, although it evolved ultimately into the repartimiento, and eventually became debt peonage.

The intended acquisition of temporary laborers and legislation of humane restrictions quickly failed in the Caribbean, and eventually was circumvented on the continents of Spanish America. However, the impact of the religious dictates, and goals of acculturating the natives in the name of civilization, proved effective during the colonial era and beyond.

John H. Barnhill and
Rebecca M. Seaman

See also: *Audiencia*; Charles V (HRE) or Carlos I of Spain; Encomendero; Leyes Nuevas 1542–1543; Repartimiento; Slavery, Role of.

Resources

Charles I of Spain. "De La Libertad De Los Indios." *Recopilacion De Leyes de Los Reynos de Las Indias.* 2nd ed. Madrid: Por Antonio Balbas, 1756.

Elliott, J. H. *Imperial Spain: 1469–1716.* 2nd ed. New York: Penguin, 2002.

John, Elizabeth Ann Harper. *Storms Brewed in Other Men's Worlds: The Confrontation of Indians, Spanish, and French in the Southwest, 1540–1795.* 2nd ed. Norman: University of Oklahoma Press, 1996.

Priestly, Herbert Ingram, ed. and trans. "Don Luis De Velasco to Don Tristan de Luna y Arellano, Mexico, October 25, 1559." *The Luna Papers: Documents Relating to the Expedition of Don Tristan de Luna y Arellano for the Conquest of La Florida in 1559–1561.* Vol. 1. Deland: Florida State Historical Society, 1928.

Villamarin, Juan A. and Judith E. *Indian Labor in Mainland Colonial Spanish America.* Newark: University of Delaware, 1975.

Escobar, Alonso de

Alonso de Escobar was a page to Hernán Cortés during the Spanish conquest of the Aztec Empire. Before the expedition he had been an early settler and land holder on the island of Hispaniola. While little is known of his origins, most speculate that he was from Salamanca. Sources indicate that he was a member of the coterie surrounding Diego Velázquez, governor of Cuba, serving originally as the governor's page. As a result he was encouraged to join the Cortés expedition, and eventually became the *caudillo*'s page. He served as the captain of one of the 11 ships that sailed in the expedition from Cuba in 1518, and was the sole ship that failed to meet with the rest of Cortés's fleet at Cozumel, presumably because the ship was lost at sea.

Escobar's vessel and crew were found at Puerto Deseado, the harbor previously discovered by the explorer Juan de Grijalva in 1517.

Escobar, like a number of other loyal adherents to the Cuban governor, declared his opposition to breaking ties with Velázquez, which the members of the expedition did shortly after landing on the Yucatán peninsula at the future site of Villa Rica de la Vera Cruz. This conspiracy against the *caudillo*'s leadership seems to have been spurred by Cortés's intentions of proceeding inland to encounter and possible conquer the Aztec emperor, Montezuma II. After a brief period as prisoner and a few difficult encounters with Cortés, Escobar decided to remain in the *caudillo*'s retinue.

The one thing on which most historical sources agree is that Cortés appointed Escobar as the treasurer of the portion of the booty that belong to the king, the royal fifth. The *caudillo* made this appointment as he readied to return to the coast to encounter the Narváez expedition, sent by Governor Velázquez to arrest Cortés. Probably due to the earlier conflict with Escobar, Cortés decided to leave his page and other former Velázquez advocates in Tenochtitlán under the leadership of his strong ally and second in command, Diego de Almagro. The *caudillo* entrusted some 132,000 pesos of gold to Escobar, worth at least 100,000 ducats. Following Cortés's victory against Velázquez and his return to the Aztec capital, the Spanish were forced to retreat from Tenochtitlán during the La Noche Triste (the Sad Night), when the Aztecs rose up to expel the Spanish in June 1520. The royal fifth was loaded into the saddlebags of a mare, and Escobar set out with the expedition to flee the city. He was killed during that action, and the gold intended for the king was lost.

John Schwaller

See also: Almagro, Diego de; Cortés, Hernán; Cuba; Grijalva, Juan de; Hispaniola; La Noche Triste; Montezuma II; Narváez, Pánfilo de; Tenochtitlán, City of; Velázquez, Diego (de Cuéllar) ; Villa Rica de la Vera Cruz.

Resources

Díaz del Castillo, Bernal. *The History of the Conquest of New Spain.* Edited by David Carrasco. Albuquerque: University of New Mexico Press, 2008.

Grunberg, Bernard. *Dictionnaire des conquistadores de Mexico.* Paris: L'Harmattan, 2001.

Thomas, Hugh. *Conquest: Montezuma, Cortés, and the Fall of Old Mexico.* New York: Simon & Schuster, 1993.

Thomas, Hugh. *Who's Who of the Conquistadores.* London: Cassell & Company, 2000.

Estancia

The colonial estancias, or cattle and sheep ranches, were largely rural ranches that often originally specialized in a particular livestock. An example existed in specialized hog ranches in the West Indies. These specialized ranches eventually evolved into highland haciendas that were more economically diversified in order to maintain self-sufficiency. The Spanish Crown viewed the establishment of livestock ranches as not only an economic necessity—to provide for local needs and for purposes of export, but as a movement toward civilizing indigenous natives that still employed nomadic hunting practices.

The granting of lands for the purpose of creating an estancia was usually undertaken at the local level. The municipal town councils, or cabildos, had the authority to assign lots for homes, shops, small farms, and large estates of grazing lands. These *mercedes,* or land grants, were sometimes in the form of common lands for the purpose of open grazing. In Mexico as well as in South America,

the large unused grassy plains gave way to cattle ranching on large estancias. This resulted in valuable exports of beef and leather. However, the expansion of the cattle industry quickly overran Indian crops, displaced entire villages, and eventually overgrazed grasslands.

The meat for local consumption from the estancias was usually in the form of pigs and chickens. However, estancias also provisioned the expeditions of conquistadors. Cortés depleted the livestock population on Cuba for his initial expedition to Mexico in 1519. While pigs were intentionally included in the conquest practices of New Spain for their rapid reproduction and acclimation, cattle eventually replaced the pig in value for Spanish colonists owning estancias. In Peru, the estancias initially raised cattle. However, the grazing habits of cattle damaged the Inca crops. Cattle provided the Spanish with much desired beef, as well as milk, cheese, and valuable leather. Nonetheless, the highland estancias gradually converted to raising sheep, whose grazing patterns made use of lands damaged by cattle overgrazing.

Rebecca M. Seaman

See also: Cabildo; Cortés, Hernán; *Mercedes.*

Resources

Stern, Steve J. *Peru's Indian Peoples and the Challenge of Spanish Conquest: Huamanga to 1640.* Madison: University of Wisconsin Press, 1993.

Zadik, Benjamin Joseph. "The Iberian Pig in Spain and the Americas at the Time of Columbus." MA Thesis, University of California, 2000.

European Diseases, Role of

The Spanish introduced a host of European diseases into the New World that certainly facilitated Spain's conquest of the Americas. Old World diseases such as smallpox, typhus, mumps, measles, plague, and influenza, among others, caused the rapid decline of native populations. When European diseases first afflicted New World populations, they caused "virgin soil" epidemics, which meant that the peoples had no prior exposure to the microorganisms that caused these diseases thus had not developed any natural immunity and consequently suffered very high mortality.

Because of their isolation from the Old World for thousands of years, and because they domesticated few animals (most Old World human epidemic diseases were shared with, spread by, or related to diseases in their domesticated animals), Native Americans suffered fewer virulent epidemic diseases than did the peoples of the Old World. However, the New World was not a disease-free environment. Human skeletal and mummified remains, as well as codices, sculptures, wall paintings, and other artistic representations, show some of the ailments that they suffered including cleft palate, clubfoot, leishmaniasis (an insect-born fungus that destroys facial tissue), Chagas disease (also caused by a tropical insect that introduces a protozoa, *Trypanosomiasis cruzi*, into the body), other parasites, respiratory and dysenteric diseases, skin disease, blindness, dental problems, wounds and fractures, heart problems, tuberculosis, pneumonia, and probably yaws and syphilis (both treponemal diseases).

The first serious epidemic outbreaks of diseases with European origins occurred within two decades of Columbus's 1492 encounter with natives in the Caribbean. Although not conclusively identified, described symptoms indicate that influenza may have been the culprit. Regardless of the causes of these epidemic episodes, the consequences were clear: the virtual demise of Caribbean native populations.

The most deadly of European epidemic diseases to afflict Native Americans was smallpox. Smallpox probably arrived by ship directly from Spain. Abundant eyewitness accounts indicate an outbreak began in 1518 in the West Indian islands of Hispanola, Puerto Rico, and Cuba. These accounts indicate 30 percent or more of the natives died from the disease, as well as significant numbers of Spaniards. Thus, when Hernán Cortés began his adventure to conquer the land now called Mexico in February 1519, smallpox was already in the vicinity.

Cortés organized his expedition in Cuba, sailed to the mainland with over 500 men, and used a combination of diplomacy and fighting to make his way to the interior. He reached the center of the Aztec Empire and its capital, Tenochtitlan, by November 1519, picking up native allies along the way. Although the first encounter between the Spanish and the Aztec emperor Montezuma II was peaceful, relations soon soured. Montezuma was eventually killed in the ensuing conflicts. In the meantime, Cuban governor Diego Velázquez sent a force of 600 men against Cortés because the conquistador had left Cuba without official sanction. Cortés defeated this contingent and forced the survivors to join him. Among this group of survivors was a young man just recovering from smallpox he contracted during the outbreak on the islands. Likely still contagious, this encounter occurred in 1520 during the rainy season when it was generally cool and wet. The climatic conditions provided the perfect environment for the disease vectors responsible for the spread of smallpox. With the capital city under siege, epidemic conditions amenable to the spread of smallpox, and overcrowding and hunger impacting the besieged city, the disease indeed spread rapidly among

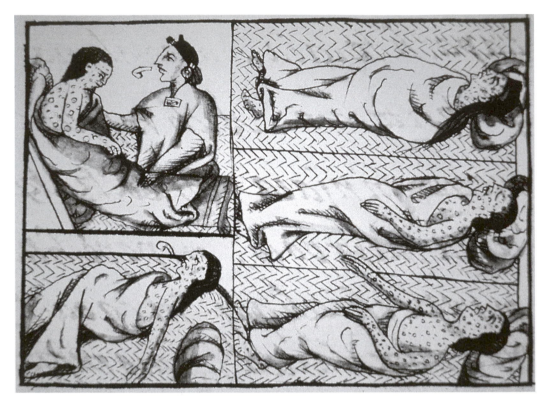

Aztec people of Mexico dying of smallpox introduced by the Spanish, copied from the *Florentine Codex,* ca. 1540. (Peter Newark American Pictures)

the completely vulnerable native population. The epidemic killed and sickened many, including the new young emperor selected to take Montezuma's place, his brother Cuitláhuac. A descendant of one Aztec royal family, Fernando de Alva Ixtlilxochitl, wrote in the latter part of the century in his *Horribles crueldades* that Cuitláhuac ruled no more than 40 days, for he died during this terrible outbreak of smallpox.

Furthermore, the Aztec accounts found in the *Florentine Codex* described the horror: "There was much perishing. Like a covering, covering-like, were the pustules. Indeed many people died of them, and many just died of hunger. There was death from hunger; there was no one to take care of another; there was no one to attend to another."

Smallpox killed so many in some villages that there were no adults left to provide food or care for the sick.

Cortés regrouped and returned to Tenochtitlán in late 1520. There he encountered fierce fighting for months, but from a weakened people. Decimated by disease and rapidly changing leadership, the Aztec Empire fell to the Spanish in August 1521 after a long siege.

In addition to the epidemic that afflicted the Aztec peoples, a report in the late 1560s indicated a plague among the Yucatec Maya had occurred about 50 years previously. This reported occurrence coincided precisely with the first documented outbreak of smallpox on the Caribbean islands. The plague struck not far from the Yucatec mainland near where the Spanish were making a coastal recon-naissance, although Spain delayed attempts to conquer the Yucatec Maya until the 1540s. Diego de Landa's *Relacion de las cosas de Yucatan* said: "After that there came again a pestilence, with great pustules that rotted the body, fetid in odor, and so that the members fell in pieces within four or five days." Though not directly the cause of the Yucatec Mayan fall over a decade later, the plague disrupted indigenous societies, economies, and cultures, weakening them at inopportune times in their history.

In the late 1520s and early 1530s, small-pox or another European disease likewise played a role in the demise of the Inca Empire in South America. During the recon-naissance of the Peruvian coast, south from Panama, in the years before an expedition led by Francisco Pizarro marched inland, a scourge hit the Inca Empire. Descriptions by locals indicate that this scourge might have been smallpox. It killed the reigning Inca emperor Huayna Capac, as well as his designated heir apparent to the throne. From the *History of the Inca Empire* by Father Bernabe Cobo, written in the late 16th and early 17th centuries, description of this epidemic is available based on evidence that Cobo had collected while in Peru: "Shortly after the first arrival of the Spaniards in this land, while the Inca was in the province of Quito, smallpox broke out among his subjects, and many of them died. . . . And later he got smallpox." Cobo goes on to say that a healer told the Inca's aides to take him out into the sun (this request seemed reasonable since the Inca represented the sun, who was said to be his father), but he died. The death of the Sapa Inca and his heir apparent threw the empire into a dynastic war between two half-brothers. Though oral tradition indicated Huayna Capac desired his sons Atahualpa and Huáscar to co-rule the empire

if Ninan Cuyochi (heir apparent) could not serve as Sapa Inca, the brothers soon went to war. So when Pizarro entered the empire in 1532, the Inca society was suffering from the impacts of the ravaging plague and civil war. Taking advantage of the scenario, Pizarro captured the victorious brother, Atahualpa, enriched himself, and conquered the Inca Empire.

Over the course of the 16th century, native populations declined precipitously wherever the Spanish traveled and settled. According to historians Alfred Crosby and Paul Kelton, the smallpox pandemic that began in around the 1520s was the most devastating disease episode in world history. Additionally, four to five epidemic crises occurred in Mexico from 1520 to 1625 involving small-pox, measles, typhus, mumps, and other diseases—some called *zahuatl* or *matlaza-huatl,* Nahuatl words that referred to diseases with a rash. These epidemics caused an 80 to 95 percent reduction in the native population in central Mexico in just a century.

The 17th century in New Spain (Mexico and Central America) experienced fewer countrywide epidemics precisely because the native population had declined to just under a million, and the white and mixed population was comparatively small, under 200,000, too small to sustain widespread epidemics until the end of the century.

South America, conquered much later than most of New Spain, likewise experienced widespread epidemics in the 16th century and periodic regional epidemics in the 17th century. Diseases involved were the same as those that afflicted New Spain, but also included diphtheria, scarlet fever, and the plague. The plague affected peoples living in the Andes, where their domesticated llamas and alpacas harbored the fleas that caused plague in both humans and animals. The infected fleas were probably introduced to New World animals by flea-infested rats that arrived by ship from Spain.

European diseases contributed to Spain's conquest of indigenous empires by adversely affecting Native American populations. Yet, as those colonial empires began to fall apart in the late 18th and early 19th centuries, the Spanish Empire embarked on an ambitious effort to control smallpox, the most terrifying of those diseases, by organizing expeditions to introduce the new smallpox vaccination to its vast empire from Spain to the Americas to the Philippines.

Angela T. Thompson

See also: Atahualpa; Cortés, Hernán; Cuitláhuac; Huayna Capac; Huáscar; Inca Civil War; Montezuma II; Ninan Cuyochi; Tenochtitlán, Siege of.

Resources

Cobo, Bernabé. *History of the Inca Empire.* Translated and edited by Roland Hamilton. Foreword by John H. Rowe. Austin: University of Texas Press, 1979.

Cook, Noble David. *Born to Die Disease and New World Conquest, 1492–1650.* Cambridge and New York: Cambridge University Press, 1998.

Cook, Noble David and W. George Lovell, eds. *"Secret Judgments of God": Old World Disease in Colonial Spanish America.* Norman: University of Oklahoma Press, 1991.

Cook, Sherburne F. and Woodrow Borah. *The Indian Population of Central Mexico, 1531–1610.* Berkeley: University of California Press, 1960.

Cortés, Hernán. *Letters from Mexico.* Translated and edited by A. R. Pagden. Introduction by J. H. Elliott. New York: Orion Press, 1971.

Crosby, Alfred. *Columbian Exchange: Biological and Cultural Consequences of 1492.* Foreword by Jr. R. McNeill. Westport, CT: Praeger Publishers, 2003.

Crosby, Alfred. *Ecological Imperialism: The Biological Expansion of Europe, 900–1900.* Studies in Environment and History Series. Cambridge, UK: Cambridge University Press, 2004.

Díaz del Castillo, Bernal. *The Conquest of New Spain.* Translated by J. M. Cohen. Baltimore: Penguin Classics, 1963.

Garcilaso de la Vega, El Inca. *Royal Commentaries of the Incas and General History of Peru.* Translated with an introduction by Harold V. Livermore. Foreword by Arnold J. Toynbee. Austin: University of Texas Press, 1965.

Ixtlilxochitl, Fernando de Alva. *Horribles crueldades de los conquistadores de Mexico, y de los indios que los auxiliaron para subyugarlo a la corona de Castilla.* Suplemento a la historia del Padre Sahagún. Redactado por Carlos Maria Bustamante. Mexico: Imprenta de Alejandro Valdes, 1829.

Kelton, Paul. *Epidemics & Enslavement: Biological Catastrophe in the Native Southeast, 1492–1715.* Lincoln: University of Nebraska Press, 2007.

Landa, Diego de. *Landa's Relación de las cosas de Yucatán A Translation.* Edited with notes by Alfred M. Tozzer. New York: Kraus Reprint, 1968.

Sahagún, Bernardino de. *Florentine Codex. General History of the Things of New Spain.* Book 12. *The Conquest of Mexico.* Translated from the Aztec into English, with notes and illustrations, by Arthur J.O. Anderson and Charles E. Dibble. Part 13. Santa Fe, NM: School of American Research and University of Utah, 1955.

Viola, Herman J. and Carolyn Margolis, eds. *Seeds of Change: A Quincentennial Commemoration.* Washington: Smithsonian Institution Press, 1991.

Extirpadores

Plural for *extirpador,* the term refers to the Spanish priests and friars who took part in the campaign of the Catholic Church against idolatry. In 1571, King Philip II announced his decision to remove the indigenous population of the New World from the authority of the Spanish Inquisition, on the basis of their lack of comprehension about the Catholic faith and its prohibitions. In its place, the Church instigated a new campaign, which also targeted the same intolerance for divergent beliefs and similar harsh punishments against elements of the native populations. The targets of this new campaign were the natives who most resisted conversion and cooperation with the Spanish Catholic authorities.

The anti-idolatry campaign was significantly employed as an answer to the millenarian religious revival among the Inca of Huamanga, known as the Taki Onqoy (dancing sickness). The movement attempted to reverse the influences of the Spanish on Inca culture, society, and religion by banning any cooperation or participation in Spanish societal practices. The sect blamed all disease and upheavals in recent Inca history upon the discarding of the traditional Inca beliefs and practices. Converts often experienced convulsions that the Catholic priests interpreted as signs of possession by evil spirits. Participants were publicly shamed, compelled to reject their indigenous beliefs, and confess the errors of their ways.

Occasionally large groups of natives joined in this form of religious rebellion. In those cases, the *extirpadores* publicly shamed the native practitioners with whippings, shaving of their heads, and even with destruction by burning of their *huacas* or religious totems. In response, the most extreme Inca priests poisoned themselves. The Taki Onqoy outbreak of nativism reached a peak in 1613. While extirpation continued to be employed for years, the extreme campaign against native idolatry waned from this point forward.

Rebecca M. Seaman

See also: Huacas; Huamanga; Phillip II of Spain; Taki Onqoy.

Resources

Becker, Marc. "Extirpation." *New Dictionary of the History of Ideas.* http://www.yachana.org/research/extirpation.pdf (cited August 1, 2011).

Henson, Sändra Lee Allen. "Dead Bones Dancing: The Taki Onqoy, Archaism, and Crisis in Sixteenth Century Peru." MA Thesis, East Tennessee State University, 2002.

Hudson, Rex A., ed. *Peru: A Country Study.* Washington: GPO for the Library of Congress, 1992. http://countrystudies.us/peru/5.htm (cited on July 22, 2011).

Stern, Steve J. *Peru's Indian Peoples and the Challenge of Spanish Conquest: Huamanga to 1640.* Madison: University of Wisconsin Press, 1993.

F

Fernández de Oviedo, Gonzalo

A historian writing shortly after the Spanish conquest of New Spain, Gonzalo Fernández de Oviedo followed in the pattern of other authors of the era, glorifying Spain's conquests and overlooking the means by which that conquest was achieved. Nonetheless, the official court historian of Charles V condemned the reading of the *Requerimiento* in the early years of conquest. Oviedo admitted that the document was read in a tongue that was not understood by the natives, and used to justify enslaving them.

This blend of adulation for Spanish conquest and critical evaluation of specific actions and incidents provides more balance to the recording of history regarding the Spanish colonization of the Americas. Oviendo's own background as a former conquistador helps explain some of the bias, especially his refusal to decry the devastation of the indigenous population on the island of Hispaniola, a series of events he was involved in as one of the conquerors.

Rebecca M. Seaman

See also: Charles V (HRE) or Carlos I of Spain; *Requerimiento*.

Resources

Restall, Matthew. *Seven Myths of the Spanish Conquest.* Oxford: Oxford University Press, 2003.

Thomas, Hugh. *Conquest: Montezuma, Cortés, and the Fall of Old Mexico.* New York: Simon & Schuster, 1993.

Florentine Codex

The *Florentine Codex*, or *La Historia General de las Cosas de Nueva España* (*The General History of the Things of New Spain*), is a 12-book encyclopedia. The codex represents the oral history and beliefs of the Mexica or Aztec people as recorded, compiled, and edited by the Franciscan friar Bernardino de Sahagún between 1547 and 1590. While the work's text was written through a European intermediary, Sahagún, it contains some 2,000 illustrations drawn by Aztec *tlacuilos* (artists or scribes) and is regarded by scholars as one of the most important native accounts of the Mexica life and the Spanish conquest of Mexico. Unlike precontact codices, which consisted of symbolic and pictorial representations rather than written texts, the codex directed by Sahagún recorded the traditions of the Aztec people in both Nahuatl and Spanish (he imposed the Latin alphabet on the former while the latter was heavily censored).

Sahagún also sought to preserve and demonstrate Nahuatl vocabulary, "to write about it in the Mexican language, not so much in order to extract some truths from the very Indians who took part in the conquest as in order to set down the language of the things of war and of the weapons that the natives use in it, so that from there one can take appropriate words and expressions for speaking in the Mexican language on this topic." The codex, produced in both Nahuatl and Spanish ca. 1578–79, is commonly known as the *Florentine Codex* because the Biblioteca

Aztec priest holding a beating heart is an example of the oral history and beliefs of the Mexica or Aztec people, as recorded through images and in Spanish by the Franciscan friar, Bernardino de Sahagún. In this image, the victim was held by priests while his chest was opened with a flint knife and his still throbbing heart ripped out and offered to the sun. (Bettmann/Corbis)

Medicea Laurenziana in Florence, Italy, possesses one of the most pristine and complete versions of it.

Long before the arrival of Europeans, the people of central Mexico recorded the past and their traditions in pictorial and symbolic codices as well as oral histories. Native codices (somewhat of a misnomer) were painted on animal hide or paper and sewn, glued, or folded into accordion-like screen-fold manuscripts. Building on indigenous historical methods, Sahagún's codex communicated information about the gods and their origins, ceremonies, soothsayers, omens, rhetoric and moral philosophy, the universe, kings and nobles, merchants, people, "earthly things," and the conquest through images and text. The Florentine manuscript, one of several versions of the history, is formatted into two columns with a Nahuatl narrative on the left side of each page and a Spanish summary on the right.

Spanish officials sought to destroy preconquest records, leaving few for historians to use and making the *Florentine Codex* even more significant (the fourth Aztec emperor, Itzcoatl, similarly had all records that pre-dated 1427 and the rise of the Mexica in the Valley of Mexico destroyed). However, Sahagún and other Spanish missionaries believed that gathering information about and understanding indigenous beliefs was crucial to the process of converting indigenous people to Christianity. Sahagún believed that "these people [the indigenous people of central Mexico] are our brothers, descendants from the trunk of Adam like ourselves, they are our fellowmen whom we are obliged to love as ourselves." Many missionaries and colonial officials did not share Sahagún's sympathy for local cultures, and his manuscripts were taken from him in 1875 (only to be returned). On many occasions, the Spanish Crown ordered him to stop his work based on the reports of these contemporary missionaries and officials.

Historians debate the degree to which the codex represents an indigenous "voice" on the Aztec experience before and during the conquest and that to which it represents the views of the colonizers. The production of the codex was undoubtedly informed by the role of Spanish intermediaries, the aftermath of conquest, and Renaissance art. At the same time, it appears that Sahagún, an early ethnographer of sorts, genuinely sought to understand and represent the peoples and cultures of central Mexico. Missionary-educated *tlacuilos* were educated in Spanish, Latin, and their own indigenous languages, providing them with access to and knowledge of both cultures. Through converted *pipiltin* who had received education in the *calmecac,* specifically the *tlatoque* noble-born students of the priesthood, Sahagún provided questionnaires to his native informants and sought information from the Mexica, their allies, and their enemies (the Tlaxcala, the Texcoco, and the Chalco in Tepepulco, Tlatelolco, and Tenochtitlán). While a useful and reliable indigenous source in many respects, the codex might be best understood as the product of the encounter, made through the intersection of Nahua and Spanish cultures and worldviews.

The *Florentine Codex* is the most expansive and detailed indigenous account of the conquest (Book Twelve). Native informants, who later converted to Christianity some 30 years after the events, described the events. According to historian Stuart Schwartz, the sample of informants disproportionately represented Spanish allies, the Tlatelolca, who criticized Tenochtitlán and its leader, Montezuma II, and highlighted Tlatelolca bravery. The role of Christian conversion also informed indigenous recollections of conquest. For instance, according to Schwartz, Sahagún's converted informants identified local gods as "devils." At the same time, the treachery and unprovoked violence of the Spanish conquerors and their indigenous allies, especially during events such as the massacre at Toxcatl, are described in specific and graphic detail in the Nahuatl account. Many of the codex's illustrations offer vivid depictions of the violence of conquest.

While the Spanish account glosses over these excesses, it is at other times faithful to the Nahuatl language narrative. In sum, the *Florentine Codex* is a product of the colonial encounter, influenced by both Spanish and indigenous historical methods, worldviews, and cultures. While it cannot be understood as a representation of pre-conquest culture, it is the most expansive and authentic indigenous account of life in the Valley of Mexico before and during the Spanish conquest.

Charles V. Reed

See also: Montezuma II; Nahuatl Language; *Pipiltin*; Toxcatl Massacre.

Resources

Anderson, Arthur J. O., and Charles E. Dibble. *The Florentine Codex: General History of the Things of New Spain.* Vol. 1, Introductions and Indices. Salt Lake City: University of Utah Press, 1982.

Lockhart, James, ed. *We People Here: Náhuatl Accounts of the Conquest of Mexico.* Berkeley: University of California Press, 1993.

McKeever-Furst, Jill Leslie. "Codices." *Encyclopedia of Latin American History and Culture.* 2nd ed. Vol. 2. Edited by Jay Kinsbruner and Erick D. Langer. Detroit: Charles Scribner's Sons, 2008.

Schwartz, Stuart B. *Victors and Vanquished: Spanish and Nahua Views of the Conquest of Mexico.* New York: Bedford/St. Martin's, 2000.

Terraciano, Kevin. "Three Texts in One: Book XII of the Florentine Codex." *Ethnohistory* 57, no. 1 (Winter 2010): 51–72.

Franciscans, Role of

A religious order of the Roman Catholic Church, the Franciscan Order is know formally as the Order of Friars Minor (OFM). St. Francis of Assisi is credited with founding the Friars Minor in 1209. The order played a prominent role in Spanish colonial history and the spreading of Christianity in the Americas.

Spain's colonial ventures were based on two main precepts. Such enterprises were to facilitate the search for riches to fill the coffers of the Crown and enrich individuals, and in return they were to convert nonbelievers to Roman Catholicism. The Franciscans, along with the Jesuits, were the prime agents of Spain's missionary aim to convert and civilize the natives of New Spain. These orders were prominent actors throughout Spain's rule in the New World. The Franciscans arrived in the New World as early as Christopher Columbus's second voyage in 1493.

The Franciscans were most prominent in what is now Mexico, New Mexico, Arizona, Texas, and California. Less is known of the early Franciscan presence in South America. Though historical evidence indicates a Franciscan presence among the early Spanish expedition by Pizarro against the Inca, these Franciscans friars kept few if any records. If the appointed leader of the Franciscans to Peru, Fray Marcos de Niza, is an example, their presence was not welcomed by Pizarro and was short-lived. The first successful Franciscan missions to Peru took hold in the later part of the 1500s.

To assist in their evangelistic efforts in the colonies, the Franciscans founded six missionary colleges in Mexico to train friars to reach out to the natives. Franciscans ingrained themselves so deeply into the Spanish Empire that many priests became colonial administrators. Friars accompanied virtually every conquistador foray in the New World. Hernán Cortés appealed to the Crown for Franciscans to evangelize the natives of Mexico in 1522, immediately following his conquest of the Aztec.

Spanish New World conquests were brutal affairs. The Franciscans were appalled by the acts of the Spanish conquistadors and thus asked the Crown to allow them to govern the natives. Because of their concerns, the Franciscans made tremendous inroads in converting the natives of Mexico to Roman Catholicism. The order opened universities, hospitals, churches, missions, schools, and other vital social institutions throughout the colony. In addition, friars served as administrators in the colonial government and as advisers to military and civilian officials throughout Mexico. The Franciscans also worked outside the "civilized" core of Mexico.

Friars accompanied Francisco Vásquez de Coronado on his trek into the southwest of the present-day United States. Though unsuccessful in checking Coronado's greed and abuses, the Franciscans sent large numbers of missionaries into the recently explored lands, founding missions in New Mexico, Arizona, and Texas. The missionaries, alone or in pairs, ventured to lands outside of Spain's control without weapons or the protection of troops. The first missionaries lived with the natives, learning their language and, at every opportunity, seeking converts.

Franciscan missionaries in New Mexico won many converts and built large missions. Missionaries generally used moral suasion but could be as harsh as the conquistadors, for the Inquisition was brought to bear on natives who refused to convert or reverted to their former beliefs. The Franciscans successfully controlled Spanish New Mexico, ruling the colony in the name of the Spanish government through missions that dotted the hinterlands and converted their native charges. These missions were based on agriculture, with friars and "mission Indians" raising crops and livestock.

The Franciscans' heyday in the region came to a bloody halt with the Pueblo Revolt of 1680. The revolt caught the Spanish completely by surprise; after bitter fighting and the slaughter of many friars and their native adherents, the Spanish Franciscans were expelled from the region for 12 years.

Though the Franciscans eventually returned to New Mexico to evangelize the natives, the order never again held so much power in the region. The Franciscan push into the southwest, specifically California, did manage to help ward off Russian settlement there. The Franciscans also worked to evangelize the Apache tribes in Mexico and New Mexico.

The Franciscans additionally established missions in Florida (La Florida), which at that point encompassed the southeastern coast from present-day South Carolina into southern Florida. As in Mexico, the Franciscans faced great obstacles there, including a series of deadly uprisings. The Franciscans were considerably less successful in converting Native Americans in the southeast, partly due to the presence of competition for alliances with the British and French in the region. Overall, while the Franciscans accompanied Spanish conquest and settlement throughout the New World, they were most successful in converting and assimilating indigenous populations into the Catholic, Spanish culture in the North American southwest, Middle America, and South America.

Rick Dyson

See also: Christianity, Impact of on the Aztec; Christianity, Impact of on the Inca; Cortés, Hernán; Pizarro, Francisco; Santa Cruz of Tlatelolco, College of.

Resources

Lippy, Charles, Robert Choquette, and Stafford Poole. *Christianity Comes to the Americas: 1492–1776.* New York: Paragon House, 1992.

Norris, Jim. *After the "Year Eighty": The Demise of Franciscan Power in Spanish New Mexico.* Albuquerque: University of New Mexico Press, 2000.

Phelan, John Leddy. *The Millenial Kingdom of the Franciscans in the New World.* 2nd ed. Berkeley and Los Angeles: University of California Press, 1970.

Richard, Robert. *The Spiritual Conquest of Mexico.* Translated by Leslie Byrd Simpson. Berkeley and Los Angeles: University of California Press, 1966.

Stockel, H. Henrietta. *On the Bloody Road to Jesus: Christianity and the Chiricahua Apaches.* Albuquerque: University of New Mexico Press, 2004.

G

Garay, Francisco de

From the Basque region of Spain, Francisco de Garay traveled to the New World on Columbus's second voyage of 1593. Serving as a notary for the expedition, Garay eventually strengthened his ties to the "admiral" by marrying his sister-in-law. He later participated in the settlement of Hispaniola, where he acquired an encomienda that produced great wealth from the discovery of gold. He used this wealth over the years in his other regional ambitions.

Garay consistently displayed a restless personality, and sought greater fame and authority in the Caribbean. He was repulsed in his attempt to subjugate Guadalupe by the Carib warriors of the island. After trading pearls for a short time, he was appointed governor of the island of Jamaica. While praised as a capable leader, he nonetheless failed to turn around the deteriorating economy of the colony, largely due to the irreparable damage wrought by Spaniards losing their stock on the environment.

Following Cuban governor Diego de Velázquez's sponsored explorations of the Yucatán, revealing the presence of great wealth, Garay sent a petition to the king of Spain, seeking the right to discover lands north of the river St. Peter and Paul—referred to as Pánuco. Approved for this quest, Garay was given the rank of *adelantado* and vice-regent of the lands northward from the river. He immediately outfitted three ships with 270 men, horses, provisions, and arms. The expedition set sail under Alonso Alvarez Pineda in 1520.

Garay's Pánuco expeditions resulted in dismal failures. The first attempt, under Pineda, approached the coast near Cortés's settlement of Villa Rica de la Vera Cruz. Aware of Cortés and his men's demeanors, Pineda refused to allow his crew to be lured to shore, as others had done. Though a small boat did land to "rescue" stranded Spaniards, only two of Pineda's men were captured by Cortés's forces. Nonetheless, the 1520 expedition failed in its attempt to claim and settle the lands prior to other Spanish claims. Indeed, alerted of Garay's interest, Cortés sent requests back to Spain to prevent other captains of New Spain from competing for the same territory, presumably in an effort to prevent division within the Spanish colonies.

Despite Cortés's efforts to block competition, in 1521 Garay again requested approval, this time to settle Pánuco for Spain. Juan Rodriguez de Fonseca, Bishop of Badajoz, Palencia and Burgos, and opponent of Hernán Cortés, granted Garay's request for a settlement. By 1523, Garay mounted an expedition, boasting 9 naos (merchant/passenger ships), 3 brigantines, 145 horses, 850 Castilians, and additional indigenous foot soldiers. The fleet arrived at Rio de Palmas, north of Pánuco, in July 1523. After establishing a town, named Gayana in the founder's honor, Garay marched his forces to Villa Rica de la Vera Cruz, supposedly to arrest Cortés. The Spanish floundered on their route southward, with numerous soldiers dying or abandoning the effort.

By the time Garay's expedition confronted Cortés's forces, news had reached Mexico of the royally approved titles and honors for Hernán Cortés—with accompanying orders for Garay to discontinue his expedition. Cortés confiscated the former's ships and incorporated the remaining soldiers still accompanying Garay into his own forces. Garay was taken back to Mexico where he was treated well, but died of a stomach ailment on the day of Christmas in 1523. His forces that had remained at Gayana fell to native uprisings of the local Huaxtecs, the result of poor treatment at the hands of the Spanish colonial administrators.

Rebecca M. Seaman

See also: *Adelantado*; Brigantines, Use by Cortés; Caribs; Columbus, Christopher; Cortés, Hernán; Rodriguez de Fonseca, Juan; Velázquez, Diego (de Cuéllar).

Resources

Diaz del Castillo, Bernal. *The Memoirs of the Conquistador Bernal Diaz Del Castillo, Written by Himself, Containing a True and Full Account of the Discovery and Conquest of Mexico and New Spain.* Translated by John Ingram Lockhart. Vol. 1. London: J. Hatchard & Son, 1844.

Levy, Buddy. *Conquistador: Hernán Cortés, King Montezuma, and the Last Stand of the Aztecs.* New York: Bantam Books, 2009.

Thomas, Hugh. *Conquest: Montezuma, Cortés, and the Fall of Old Mexico.* New York: Simon & Schuster, 1993.

Gifting, Practice of

The practice of gifting, explained by historians, anthropologists, and sociologists with the closely related concept of reciprocity was an important part of the societies and cultures of both pre-Columbian and post-conquest Latin American cultures and has been an important topic of study for scholars. While scholars have traditionally identified gift exchange, or reciprocal, economies with premonetary and precapitalist societies in Latin America and elsewhere, such economies have remained important to communities and groups that often exist on the fringes of or outside of the "modern" capitalist system. The exchange of gifts established and symbolized relationships between and within social groups, between patrons and clients, between rulers and subjects, and between Europeans and indigenous Americans. When Europeans and indigenous people met each other in colonial encounter, the practice of gifting established relationships commenced the project of cultural and commercial exchange and symbolized the status and power of the "giver." In cultures and encounters across Latin American history, gifts have served as symbolic capital that bound people together in power relationships and interdependence.

The meaning of exchanges is disputed by scholars, though most would agree that they vary by situation, culture, and social context. In *The Gift* (1925, published in English in 1954), the French sociologist Marcel Mauss argued that the exchange of gifts in "archaic societies" represented "total prestation" (*préstation totale*), meaning that gifts are always given under the precondition of reciprocity. While his work did not specifically examine Latin American societies, it does identify the ways in which the practice of gifting served multivalent functions (political, religious, economic, social, etc.) and the need to understand gifts as more than commodities. In his 1972 book *Stone Age Economics*, Marshall Sahlins theorized three types of reciprocity: generalized (altruistic exchange with no immediate expectation of return), balanced (equal exchange), and negative (nonreciprocal). This brief article by no means offers a complete exploration of gifting practices and scenarios in Latin America but does offer an example of the diversity of those practices.

In the southern Andes, pre-Inca and Inca *ayllus* communities participated in exchange of crops based on a system of specialization, and commoners exchanged their labor in the form of *mita* (tributary services) with *kurakas* (lords) for land as well as physical and spiritual security. Reciprocity within *ayllus* could reflect social equality (between equals or near equals, such as was the case with *ayni* or reciprocal labor) or inequality (between commoners and their lord, in the most severe cases). During the expansion of the Inca Empire, the emperors at Cusco expanded their rule through gifts of land, food, women, and manufactured goods to potential and current *kurakas,* military chiefs, and priests, in exchange for obedience and, if this method failed, they resorted to conquest. Because of the generosity that this system required, the Sapa Inca maintained massive storehouses of food and other items, requiring the employment of agricultural laborers and artisans in mandatory state service. Spanish administrators and colonial-era *kurakas* sought to exploit this system by using reciprocal bonds to extract more and more labor, sometimes inspiring commoners to challenge or rebel against the relationship of reciprocation through violence or colonial courts.

Across Mesoamerica, the practices of gifting and reciprocity served diverse political, social, religious, and economic purposes. In Mayan societies, pottery was exchanged between elite families in order to solidify alliances and to enrich the status and prestige of the gifting family. Less ritualized and more spontaneous forms of giving or reciprocity often involved the exchange of labor. In the Nahua, Mixtec, and Tlaxcalan societies of Mexico, gifting between families at marriages, funerals, birthdays, and other ritual occasions enforced links between families.

In the *mayordomía* or *fiesta* system, the civil-religious hierarchy of Mesoamerican societies was put on display through feasts and ritual gifting. Cultural anthropologists have argued that ritual displays such as the fiesta served to increase the prestige and status of the *mayordomo* who sponsored them. Gifting was also part of a Mesoamerican system of borrowing and credit, with food and gifts granted with the expectation of future reciprocity.

The exchange of gifts between the Aztec emperor Montezuma II and Cortés demonstrated how the practice of gifting possessed complex and competing meanings. After the massacre at Cholula, for instance, Cortés demanded a ransom of gold to prevent further destruction. In the mind of Cortés, gifts from the emperor symbolized submission and bribery. For Montezuma, however, they represented his dominance and imperial power, as he gave gifts to his allies and rulers who had become subordinate to him.

As the example of Montezuma and the work of historians, sociologists, and anthropologists suggests, the practice of gifting and reciprocity were woven through the political, social, religious, and economic fabric of Latin American societies. They also demonstrated that the traditional dichotomy between commodity and gift, precapitalist and capitalist economies, do not aptly explain this constellation of practices that continues to thrive in contemporary Latin American societies.

Charles V. Reed

See also: *Ayllus; Ayni*; Cortés, Hernán; *Kuraka; Mita;* Montezuma II.

Resources

Abercrombie, Thomas. *Pathways of Memory and Power: Ethnography and History among and Andean People.* Madison: The University of Wisconsin Press, 1998.

Hastorf, Christine Ann. *Agriculture and the Onset of Political Inequality before the Inka.* New York: Cambridge University Press, 1993.

Mauss, Marcel. *The Gift: The Form and Reason for Exchange in Archaic Societies.* New York: W.W. Norton, 2000 reprint.

Wells, E. Christian. "Recent Trends in Theorizing Prehispanic Mesoamerican Economies." *Journal of Archaeological Research* 14, no. 4 (December 2006): 265–312.

Zulawski, Ann. *They Eat from Their Labor: Work and Social Change in Colonial Bolivia.* Pittsburgh: University of Pittsburgh, 1994.

Gold, Role of in Spanish Expeditions

Spanish colonization efforts from their inception were aimed at two objectives: gold and proselytizing the Catholic faith. Christopher Columbus's first expedition to the New World was actually an attempt to reach China and open up trade with that fabled empire. Make no mistake about it; Columbus's primary motivation for his voyages was to enrich himself and the coffers of the Spanish Crown. Once Columbus accidentally rediscovered the Americas, Spanish explorers turned their attention to searching these new lands for riches.

While gold was not found in great quantities on the islands of Hispaniola, Cuba, and Puerto Rico, tales of riches made their way to the ears of Spanish explorers. Gold was of prime importance to the Spanish as the nation sought to oust its Muslim conquerors of Spain and later in its quest to be the dominant power across the globe. All of these endeavors cost money and Spanish desire for gold to fund its geopolitical ambitions knew no bounds. Virtually every Spanish explorer focused on history sought gold and would go to any length to acquire it.

The desire for gold was fueled by the nature of Spanish exploration. The conquistadors funded their own expeditions: by monies from their families and private investors along with funds from the Spanish Crown. However, the amount given by the Crown to these explorers was minimal; the lion's share of funding the expedition fell upon the explorer and his backers. The Spanish Crown gave the conquistadors its blessing and gained a share of the profits from the expeditions. Hence these explorers undertook a great deal of the risk and gained a large share of the profit from whatever treasures they recovered. Conquistadors gained land grants from the Crown in the New World, from the lands explored by them in their expeditions. Conquistadors' profits had to garner them enough money to pay their backers and pay their men who accompanied them on their expeditions. Additionally, 20 percent (royal fifth) of mineral wealth must be remitted back to the Spanish Crown to assist in supporting the imperial goals of Spain.

The prime motivators of these early conquistadors was to discover treasure to enrich themselves, fame to insure their place in society, land to settle or sell, and conversion of the natives from their pagan religion to Catholicism. The conquistadors were a vainglorious lot, showing their prowess on the field of battle, and the resulting acclaim from these successes led to more personal wealth. Early encounters with native populations were dominated by the Spanish desire for gold, and often led to impatience when dealing with these polities. Gold was always demanded from native leaders and often times, in the beginning of Spain/native interactions, gold was given freely as the natives sought peaceful interaction with the strange newcomers. Montezuma II is said to have acquiesced to Cortés's request through messengers that a helmet be filled with gold dust, presumably in hopes that the Spanish thirst for the mineral would be quenched and they would leave his territory. As the interactions between the Spaniards and natives became more contentious, the conquistadors became more ruthless and insistent in their demands for gold.

The stampede for gold was fueled by the reports of explorer Vasco Núñez de Balboa. His trek across the Isthmus of Panama in 1513, which lead to the "discovery" of the Pacific Ocean, further incited the Spanish lust for gold. Balboa's feat was an extraordinary accomplishment as the expedition fought through dense jungle. Balboa reported finding an abundance of natural resources, exotic food, wildlife, and rivers of gold. While it is true that Balboa did indeed find gold on his journey, his exaggerated claims led to a rush of expeditions to discover more riches.

In 1519 conquistador Hernán Cortés left Cuba for what is present-day Mexico. Cortés had two goals in mind: converting whatever natives he encountered to Catholicism and the pursuit of gold. He landed in March that year. Any pretense of peaceful contact was belied by the makeup of the Cortés expedition, which included 32 crossbowmen, 12 men with muzzle-loaded handguns, 14 pieces of small artillery, some cannons, 16 war horses, and a slew of vicious war dogs. Cortes's encounter with the vast Aztec Empire set the tone for all subsequent encounters with natives in the Americas. Despite his use of diplomacy and occasionally charm to manipulate the Aztecs and others into accommodating his desires, plunder, rape, torture, and forced conversion to Catholicism are the legacy most often left by Spain's ruthless conquest of the peoples they encountered. The desire for wealth, fame, and power even resulted in the Spanish turning on each other, as evidenced by the conflict between Cortés and Pánfilo Narváez at Zempoala in 1520.

Cortés's foray into the Aztec Empire eventually led to the destruction of that empire. The Aztecs, initially far outnumbering the Spanish, were eventually decimated by disease, paralyzed by fear, intimidated by the Spaniards on their horses, and no match for the thunderous new weapons and novel strategies. In combination with the numerous indigenous allies Cortés assembled, the Aztecs were subdued in a relatively brief span of two years. The sacking of the Aztec capital of Tenochtitlán in 1521 yielded troves of gold and silver for Cortés. Once news of the conquest of the Aztec Empire and its riches made their way back to Madrid, the rush of other conquistadors into the Americas commenced.

The Inca Empire located in the present-day countries of Peru, Ecuador, Argentina, Chile, and Bolivia was a rich and powerful empire. The Incas, from their mountain valley in Peru in 1400, conquered their neighbors and had reached their zenith by 1531. The Inca Empire spanned 2,500 miles, ruled by a small number of Incas over what some estimate to be 12 million subjects who spoke 20 languages. The Inca Empire was incredibly rich in gold and silver. Francisco Pizarro, one of the most experienced explorers in the Caribbean, heard rumors of the wealth of the Inca. His expeditions in 1524 and 1526 ended in failure in that neither one of these forays netted any treasure. Finally in 1527, a third expedition reached the outskirts on the Inca realm and discovered gold objects. With the support of his partners, Diego de Almagro and Hernando de Luque, Pizarro returned to Spain with news of his discovery. In Spain, Pizarro recruited troops, gathered financial backers, and secured complete control of the expedition from Spanish authorities. By the time Pizarro left for Peru, his expedition included such infamous conquistadors as his partner Almagro and Hernando de Soto.

Pizarro's final expedition left Panama at the end of 1530, and in early 1532 it reached the Inca city of Tumbes. Pizarro pushed on, finally encountering the Inca ruler Atahualpa in the city of Cajamarca. At this meeting Pizarro insisted the Incas submit to the authority of the Spanish Crown. Atahualpa rejected the invader's demand. Matters took a bloody turn when Pizarro's priest presented the emperor with a Bible, which was discarded by the Inca ruler. Enraged, the Spaniards massacred the Inca retinue and took the emperor hostage. In order to spare his own life, Atahualpa offered to pay a ransom in gold and silver. Hence an order was sent throughout the Inca Empire for treasures to be sent from all reaches of the empire to fill a room in Cajamarca. This vast booty was dispersed amongst the Spaniards in the city, along with a sizable amount (royal fifth) sent back to Spain. This was done not once but twice; despite his demands being met, Pizarro eventually executed Atahualpa on July 26, 1533. With Atahualpa removed, Pizarro appointed a puppet emperor, who would allow his men to push onward to the Inca capital of Cuzco, which was captured in November 1533. The Spanish took the remaining treasure from the capital city of Cuzco. Despite the puppet Sapa Inca Manco Inca Yupanqui's eventual resistance, the Incas were virtually subdued after a revolt in 1537.

The conquests of the two main empires in the Americas did not slacken Spanish thirst for gold. Mines in the America's disgorged prodigious quantities of gold and other precious metals, but still tales of gold reached the ears of Spanish authorities and men of fortune. The most persistent rumor that reached Spanish ears, from natives and a few Spanish souls who ventured into unexplored lands, was the fabled city of Cibola supposedly one of the seven cities of gold said to exist north of Mexico. However, rumors of wealth in Central America, and even in the upper reaches of the Amazon, continued to pull old and new conquistadors alike into the frontiers of the New World. Again the thirst for individual fame and riches, along with the Spanish government's need for gold to support its rivalry with other European nations, propelled the exploration and claiming of new lands.

Rick Dyson

See also: Almagro, Diego de; Atahualpa; Cajamarca, Battle of; Cortés, Hernán; Luque, Hernando de; Manco Inca Yupanqui; Narváez, Pánfilo; Soto, Hernando de, in Peru; Tenochtitlán, Siege of; Velázquez, Diego (de Cuéllar); Zempoala.

Resources

Diaz, Bernal. *The Conquest of New Spain.* Translated with Introduction by J. M. Cohen. London: Penguin Books, 1963.

Means, Philip A. *The Fall of the Inca Empire and the Spanish Rule in Peru, 1530–1780.* New York: Gordian Press, 1971.

Pagden, Anthony, trans. & ed. *Hernan Cortes: Letters from Mexico.* New Haven, CT: Yale University Press, 1986.

Prescott, William H. *The History of the Conquest of Peru.* New York: New American Library, 1961.

Richman, Irving Berdine. *Adventures of New Spain: The Spanish Conquerors.* New Haven, CT: Yale University Press, 1929.

Thomas, Hugh. *Conquest: Montezuma, Cortés, and the Fall of Old Mexico.* New York: Simon & Schuster, 1993.

Thomas, Hugh. *Rivers of Gold: The Rise of the Spanish Empire from Columbus to Magellan.* New York: Random House, 2003.

Vilches, Elvira. *New World Gold: Cultural Anxiety and Monetary Disorder in Early Modern Spain.* Chicago: University of Chicago Press, 2010.

Government, Pre-Conquest Aztec

The government structures of the Aztec prior to conquest and contact with the Spanish are divided into two areas. The local level of government was formed around large city structures, incorporating the needs of provisioning and protecting the city and its population. These cities and their surroundings formed the basis of larger regional structures, or states. The highest level of government structures focused on the functions of managing the Aztec Empire. In all areas of the Aztec government, the positions of power were held by the nobility, or the *pipiltin*. Like their European cousins, the Aztec nobility controlled most of the valuable lands, laid claim to the tributary payments, and dominated the government, military, and religious hierarchies of the empire.

At the foundation of the Aztec government was the *calpulli*, present in all Aztec communities. The *calpulli* was a collective unit of individuals, usually consisting of several families, but not always. The *calpulli* owned land communally, and the leadership of the *calpulli* saw to the education of the *calpulli*'s children, as well as the collection of the *calpulli*'s taxes. Historians sometimes view the structure of the early *calpulli* as evidence of an egalitarian past. However, in the later Aztec Empire, the leaders of the *calpulli*, while theoretically elected, were typically inherited positions. The leaders of the various *calpulli* in a city formed the city council. Drawn from the members of the city council was yet another council that consisted of only four members. The leader of this inner council was called the *tlatoani* (*tlatcani*) who served as the true leader for the city, as well as the surrounding areas.

The regional level of government comprised the *altepetl*. Formed of many *calpulli*, these regional ethnic states boasted of hereditary rulers with their own set of deities and temples. The internal divisions between the member clans required strong rulers with capable militaries to maintain control. Often this was achieved through the securing of local and regional alliances under the control of the governing *tlatoani* for each particular state.

At the national level, the Aztec Empire was actually an alliance between three Mesoamerican city-states: Tenochtitlán, Texcoco, and Tlacopan. This alliance was initiated by the *tlatoani* Itzcóatl who reigned from 1426 to 1440. However, the inhabitants of Tenochtitlán, known as the Mexica, were the dominant partners in the alliance. Tenochtitlán was originally comprised of seven founding *calpulli*. Over time, voluntary and forced migratory groups increased that number of *calpulli* to 20. In addition to providing the political base for the city, these 20 *calpulli* also were connected ritually to the 20 daynames in the Aztec calendar system.

Tenochtitlán served as the capital of the empire, and the *tlatoani* of Tenochtitlán (known as the *huey tlatoani*) served as the emperor. The *huey tlatoani* was responsible for external matters of empire while another individual, the *cihuacoatl*, governed Tenochtitlán itself and served as an advisor to the emperor. The *cihuacoatl* was always a close relative of the *huey tlatoani*. Through the power of their alliance, and bolstered by the military might of the Mexica, the Aztecs soon conquered an empire of impressive size.

However, the Aztecs did not rule an empire in the traditional sense. Instead, it is sometimes called an informal empire because it did not exert direct rule over conquered territories. When the Aztecs conquered surrounding city-states, they often allowed friendly local rulers to remain in power, but replaced the leaders of particularly resistant cities with Aztec officials. They also allowed conquered cities to maintain a great deal of freedom. In exchange, the Aztecs demanded sizeable tributes from those they conquered.

At its height, the Aztec Empire consisted of 38 tributary provinces. In addition to securing favorable local rule, the Aztecs also built roads and other infrastructure in conquered territories in order to increase the flow of trade, as well as tribute. To secure an efficient trade and tributary system, the Aztecs depended on a vast network of tribute officials overseen by an official in Tenochtitlán, called the petlacalcatl. They also depended on a hereditary class of merchants, known as pochteca, who received certain exemptions and privileges within the empire for their service as diplomats, spies, and even judges in some instances.

Besides the obvious benefits of tribute, there was an ideological drive behind the expansion of the Aztec Empire. The Aztecs especially venerated the sun god, Huitzilopochtli, and believed they lived in the final age of humanity, after which the world would be destroyed. To stave off this destruction, Huitzilopochtli needed constant blood sacrifices. To obtain these sacrifices, Aztec warriors waged war throughout Mesoamerica. It was the constant drive for the offer of human sacrifices to their insatiable deities, in conjunction with the benefits of trade and tributes, that pushed the empire to expand and that sustained the Aztec rule over their vast Mesoamerican empire. However, this same set of priorities, combined with the internal clan divisions and animosities held by the subjected ethnic states and even allies toward the conquering Aztecs, undermined the cohesiveness of the empire. With the arrival of Cortés and his conquering armies, it was the divisions within the imperial structure that enabled the outnumbered Spanish

forces to win an unforeseeable victory over the seemingly undefeatable Aztecs.

John Gram

See also: Aztec, or Mexica; Calendar System of Aztec; Huitzilopochtli; *Pipiltin;* Tenochtitlán, City of.

Resources

Clendinnen, Inga. *Aztecs: an Interpretation.* Cambridge: Cambridge University Press, 1995.

Smith, Michael. *The Aztecs.* 3rd ed. Hoboken, NJ: Wiley-Blackwell, 2012.

Townsend, Richard F. *The Aztecs.* 3rd ed. London: Thames & Hudson, 2009.

Government, Pre-Conquest Inca

Inca history is based in large part on genealogies and legends connected back to what was understood as primordial time. According to the Incas, their imperial origins can be traced back to the deified Manco Cápac (Manqo Qhapaq), who was said to have come to power somewhere around 1000 CE. Consistent with the mythologies of other Andean peoples, the Incas believed that their ancestors emerged from earthly, sacred places. In ancient times, Inca legend tells us a cave called *Tampu T'oqo* (House of Windows) existed at *Pacariq-tambo* (Inn of Dawn). The Creator God called forth from a central cave named *Qhapaq T'oqo* (Rich Window) the four brothers and four sisters who became the Inca ancestors. From two adjoining caves, called *Maras T'oqo* and *Sutiq T'oqo,* he also summoned the Maras and Tambos peoples. At some point, the eight Inca peoples were paired off, finally becoming husband and wife. Almost immediately the Inca couples decided to seek fertile lands by which they could enrich themselves. The principal couple, named Manqo Qhapaq and Mama Oqllu, allied themselves with the Tambos and formed two sets of five *ayllu*, or "descent groups."

This newly formed clan set off in search of abundant lands, although they initially found no suitable locale at which to settle. At one point during their wandering, Mama Oqllu gave birth to a son named Zinchi Roq'a, who would become the second Inca ruler. The members of the group eventually found themselves on top of a mountain, from which they could see an abundant valley over which arched a beautiful rainbow—clearly an obvious sign of their long-sought homeland. Before they descended the mountain, Mama Waqo cast two golden rods into the valley below. The first did not stick, indicating that the soil was not fertile. The second "plunged deep into the earth at Wanaypata," revealing to the group that they finally had found their home. Upon entering the area that came to be known as Cuzco, the group members marked their claim to the site; but they were forced to displace the peoples of the valley in order to take firm control of their new homeland. Although they suffered occasional setbacks, the Inca finally established themselves at Cuzco. Having accomplished this, they divided the world into four parts and built the first house of the sun at Indicancha.

It is clear from this legend how thoroughly Inca mythology is woven through the history of the people. As in the legend, the Inca literally divided their world into four parts (*suyu*), with the political and social center at Cuzco. Indeed, the Inca name for their realm, Tahuantinsuyu (Tawantinsuyu), means the "four parts." The upper level of the Inca political structure was comprised of four "lords" who ruled over the respective divisions of the empire and who acted as advisors to the emperor in Cuzco. The most populous of the four parts of the Inca realm was Chinchaysuyu, which was named after the highly respected Chincha

etnía, or ethnic group, of the south-central region of Peru, an area that stretched across the Peruvian coast, the adjacent highlands, and the north Andes. Antisuyu, which was named for the forests of the montaña—and identified in the Hispanic form as the Andes, was located to the northeast of Cuzco. Collasuyu, which extended from Peru's southern highlands down through central Chile in a north-south direction paralleling the border with Argentina, represented the largest geographical part of the empire. The smallest part of the realm was Contisuyu, which claimed only a small stretch of land extending from Cuzco to the Pacific.

Beyond the basic political units of the monarch and his lords, the Inca world was defined by a complex hierarchical system that melded together notions of kinship and ancestor worship with ethnicity and a rigidly defined class structure. Significantly, in the Inca realm, both mummies of kings and queens who had long been dead as well as the community's oracular icons participated in communal activities by way of cults or *panaqas* (royal lineages) comprised of their descendants. Although the Spanish pointed to this practice as a clear example of the "handiwork of the Devil," the Incas understood it as perfectly natural, as in their minds the world was certainly populated not only be the living but also by the dead, spirits, and the gods. The king, along with his royal family, was granted a position at the apex of the Inca social order, known as the Sapa Inca. Although two classes of Inca aristocrats and an honorary group of Inca nobility existed alongside the royal leader, the king was considered not only to be the absolute ruler of the Inca state, but also to be a divine being that possessed a heavenly mandate to govern the world. Notably, even though they were accorded this special status, each of the all-too-human Inca rulers, in order to maintain control of his realm, was forced to rely heavily on his advisors and to work closely with the members of what proved to be an extremely powerful aristocracy.

The Incas drew no distinction among positions of power, and thus the king generally represented a mix of political, social, military, and sacred leadership. For the Incas, the ideal ruler passed through three stages during his lifetime. Initially he would prove himself to be a brave warrior, earning the respect and support of the Cuzco nobility. Once he had been anointed the "Sun who rules the land," he would be revered as a god, one that had been blessed with powers greater than those of any other beings who tread upon the earth. Finally, in death, he would be exalted as a being with "great vitality," one who "feasted and conversed with the quick and the dead by day and retired to his quarters for repose at night." Despite these linkages between the Sapa Incas and their deities, the line of political descent was not compelled to go through the eldest born male heir, nor even the eldest male born to the "principal wife" (typically eldest sister of the emperor). However, since most successions followed the tradition of bestowing power on the eldest son, the Inca Empire occasionally experienced upheaval in its government and society when that succession principle was not followed. Such was the case at the time of the Spanish arrival into Peru, with two brothers, their armies, and their allied *panaqas* engaging in civil war for nearly five years. This breach in the Inca governmental structure allowed for internal struggles to affect the relations between the Incas and the Spanish intruders, resulting in the eventual collapse of the empire.

Philip C. DiMare

See also: Chinchaysuyu; Collasuyu; Contisuyu; Inca Civil War: Inca Elite; Manco Cápac; Sapa Inca; Tahuantinsuyu

Resources

D'Altroy, Terence N. *The Incas*. Malden, MA: Blackwell, 2003.

DiMare, Philip C. "The Amerindian World." In *Cliffs World History,* edited by Fred N. Grayson. Hoboken, NJ: Wiley, 2006.

Fagan, Brian M. *Kingdoms of Gold, Kingdoms of Jade: The Americas before Columbus.* New York: Thames and Hudson, 1991.

Hemming, John. *The Conquest of the Incas.* London: Pan Macmillan, 1970.

MacQuarrie, Kim. *The Last Days of the Incas.* New York: Simon & Schuster, 2007.

Grado, Alonso del

Alonso del Grado was one of the more famous members of the Cortés expedition into the Aztec Empire. He was a member of the petty nobility, perhaps from Alcántara near Cáceres, in the Extremadura region of Spain. He sailed to the Indies, probably before 1515. He was a minor encomendero at La Concepción on the island of Hispaniola before joining the Cortés expedition in 1518. Bernal Díaz described him as a very prudent man, well presented, and a great writer, though not much of a soldier. After the expedition landed in Mexico, he was elected one of the *regidores* (alderman or councilor) of the town of Villa Rica de la Vera Cruz and became one of the treasury officials, the *veedor* (overseer). In his role as *regidor,* Grado was one of the Spaniards who participated in the charade of announcing Cortés's role in fulfilling Velázquez's instructions for the expedition. Upon the *caudillo*'s resignation, the council immediately elected Cortés as the chief justice of Vera Cruz (*Justicia Mayor*) and general of His Majesty's armies.

As the expedition moved inland and began to suffer increased losses from injuries and sickness, Grado began to press for a return to the relative safety of Vera Cruz. He feared tempting God's protection and patience, and strongly opposed some of the more rash and cruel actions of another captain, Pedro de Alvarado. Once the expedition entered Tenochtitlán, Cortés finally sent Grado to Vera Cruz as a chief constable, *alguacil mayor,* reducing the dissention within his ranks. Grado caused some problems in Vera Cruz, seeking to enrich himself, exploiting the natives and forcing them to provide him with food, jewels, and native servers. He was arrested by one of Cortés's lieutenants, Gonzalo de Sandoval, who sent him in chains to Cortés in Tenochtitlán, probably for having been more loyal to Velázquez, governor of Cuba, than to Cortés. Cortés imprisoned Grado and subjected him to public humiliation in the stocks. Ultimately Cortés had him released and withdrew all the charges. Later, Grado resumed his duties as a treasury official, as *contador* (accountant). He was obviously a close adviser to Cortés because he was one of the co-signers of the third letter to the Crown written by Cortés, dated May 15, 1522. As the total conquest of Mexico proceeded, he suggested the possibility of rebelling from royal control. Nevertheless, he was chosen by Cortés to accompany the payment of royal taxes back to Spain, in 1522–23.

Grado was known more as a businessman than as a valiant fighter. After the fall of Tenochtitlán, he led a force into the Isthmus of Tehuantepec. In these expeditions, he frequently accompanied another captain, Luis Marín. After the conquest, he was appointed as an inspector of the Indians. With the encouragement of Cortés, Grado married Tecuichpo or Doña Isabel in 1526, one of the daughters of Montezuma II, the last Aztec emperor. Unfortunately he died a year after the wedding. By virtue of his marriage, he received the town of Chiautla in encomienda.

He and Doña Isabel had no children and upon his death the encomienda was reassigned. Grado did have one natural child, a daughter.

John Schwaller

See also: Alvarado, Pedro de; Cortés, Hernán: Encomenderos; Encomienda; Montezuma II; Tecuichpo ("Doña Isabel").

Resources

Díaz del Castillo, Bernal. *The History of the Conquest of New Spain.* Edited by David Carrasco. Albuquerque: University of New Mexico Press, 2008.

Grunberg, Bernard. *Dictionnaire des conquistadores de Mexico.* Paris: L'Harmattan, 2001.

Kalyuta, Anastasia. "The Household and Estate of a Mexica Lord: 'Información de doña isabel de Moctezuma,' México." *FAMSI,* 2007. http://www.famsi.org/reports/06045/06045Kalyuta01.pdf (accessed November 14, 2012).

Thomas, Hugh. *Conquest: Montezuma, Cortés, and the Fall of Old Mexico.* New York: Simon & Schuster, 1993.

Thomas, Hugh. *Who's Who of the Conquistadores.* London: Cassell & Company, 2000.

Grijalva, Juan de

Juan de Grijalva de Cuellar was an early Spanish explorer and conqueror in the Americas. As a young man he participated in the conquest of Cuba and served as a minor official. He is best known for leading a major expedition that explored the coastal territories of Mexico and came into contact with the advanced civilization of the Mayas in 1518. This expedition directly laid the groundwork for the conquest of Mexico as Grijalva mapped the region, received reports about a rich kingdom in the interior, and made contact with the Aztecs.

Explorer, Juan de Grijalva, who explored coastal Yucatán for Governor Diego Velázquez. (Corbis)

Born in the Spanish town of Cuéllar around 1480, Grijalva arrived in the Americas before reaching his 20th birthday. He served alongside his uncle, Diego de Velázquez, in the conquest and subjugation of the island of Cuba during 1510–1511. Grijalva then served in minor posts under his uncle in the new colony. Little else is known about his early life in the Indies.

In 1517, the Spaniards in Cuba received reports that led to Grijalva's discoveries along Mexico's Gulf Coast. A small slave raiding expedition to capture Caribs, led by Captain Francisco Hernández de Córdoba, was blown into uncharted territory. The Spaniards landed on the Yucatán Peninsula, and for the first time they encountered an advanced civilization in the New World. The expedition returned to Cuba filled with exciting tales and, more importantly, gold artifacts.

Velázquez prepared a stronger second expedition to explore the new lands. He chose Grijalva as captain general of a fleet of four ships. Grijalva and Velázquez selected Pedro de Alvarado, Francisco de Montejo, and Alonso de Avila to serve as captains. More than 240 soldiers and sailors signed on for the Grijalva expedition, including many veterans from the Córdoba voyage. Grijalva also brought along two captive Mayas, named Melchior and Julian, as translators. By the time the expedition left Havana on April 8, 1518, it had swelled into one of the largest seen in the Indies.

The Grijalva expedition sailed hundreds of miles up the Gulf Coast as far north as the Río Panuco (near present-day Tampico, Mexico) before returning to Cuba. The expedition first encountered the island of Cozumel and then crossed to the mainland, where they found what Spanish soldier and author Bernal Díaz del Castillo later described as three large towns with stone houses and large towers. The explorers saw many other towns, which Grijalva avoided anchoring near for fear of attack. They finally landed near Campeche in the hope of finding water and friendly natives. They found neither and instead fought a battle that left a single Spaniard dead and 40 wounded.

Eventually the Spaniards encountered Mayas who sought trade and not battle. After presenting the Mayas with a few trinkets and glass beads, Grijalva had his Maya translators explain that they wanted gold. The next day, the leader of the Mayas presented a golden crown, breastplate, and bracelets to Grijalva. In return, the Spaniards offered the Mayas European clothing and a velvet cap. According to Díaz, the Maya chieftain informed Grijalva that there was plenty more gold farther up the coast to the west in a land called "Mexica."

Encouraged by these reports of gold, the fleet continued along the coast. North of San Juan de Ulúa, the Spaniards explored a large gulf with three islands. Grijalva sent Montejo to greet a group of finely dressed natives who had gathered on the mainland. These were the first Aztecs encountered by the Spaniards. After Grijalva explained that they were only interested in gold gifts, the Aztecs presented him with golden bars, masks, idols, and a crown of gold and jewels.

Grijalva's fleet continued as far northwest as Tampico before turning back toward Cuba. When the expedition stopped to make repairs, Grijalva decided to send Alvarado ahead to Cuba with the golden ornaments and treasure. Alvarado gave a detailed report to Velázquez after presenting 4,000 pesos worth of treasure. The governor immediately planned another expedition to be led by Hernán Cortés instead of waiting for his nephew's return. Although many argued that Grijalva should lead the expedition, Velázquez stood by a decision he would later regret, as Cortés turned against him after landing on the mainland.

Although eclipsed by Cortés and robbed of his glory in the conquest and colonization of Mexico, Grijalva's expedition played a pivotal role in the exploration and later conquest and colonization of Mexico and Central America. Significantly, most of his captains and crew took part in subsequent conquests: Alvarado conquered Guatemala during 1522–1524, Montejo conquered the Yucatán during 1527–1537, and Ávila conquered the Yucatán and Honduras during 1533–1537. Grijalva went on to command several smaller expeditions that explored and traded along the Central American coast before he died from wounds suffered during a battle with Central American natives in 1527.

Thomas Edsall

See also: Alvarado, Pedro de; Ávila, Alonso de; Díaz, del Castillo, Bernal; Hernández de Córdoba, Francisco; Montejo, Francisco de; Velázquez, Diego de; Yucatán Peninsula.

Resources

Díaz del Castillo, Bernal. *The True History of the Conquest of New Spain.* Translated with an Introduction and Notes by Janet Burke and Ted Humphrey. Indianapolis, IN: Hackett Publishing, 2012.

Grijalva, Juan de. *The Discovery of New Spain in 1518.* Edited by Henry R. Wagner. Germantown, NY: Cortes Society, 1969.

Innes, Hammond. *The Conquistadors.* London: Collins, 1969.

Guns, Impact of

The small band of military mercenaries, explorers, and adventurers that were responsible for most of the military success of the Spanish during their conquest of the Americas carried with them some of the highest military technologies known to exist during the 16th century. Of particular notice was their use of gunpowder-driven artillery in the form of ballistic cannonry, pistols, and the precursor of the smooth bore musket and later rifles, the notorious harquebus. Eyewitness chronicles estimate that the conquistadors carried with them a small complement of guns, which consisted of small cannons known as falconets, infantry shotguns such as the harquebus, hand pistols, and bronze cannons with enough gunpowder to power their thrust. By the time of the arrival of the conquistadors on the shores of Central and South America during the first waves of the American conquest, cannons and guns had sufficiently improved to become somewhat portable and useful on the battlefield. This constituted a technological edge on the part of the European armies capable of inflicting casualties, psychological terror, and physical damage, but not substantial enough a benefit to tilt the fate of battles.

The American civilizations during the time of the European conquest were technologically in a Neolithic stage, and thus were unaware of and had not experienced, developed, or come into contact with gunpowder. In this battle between Stone and Iron Age cultures, it becomes apparent that Europeans had a clear technological advantage, and perhaps no other weapon during this time made this as dramatically clear as artillery. Nevertheless, the guns brought by the conquistadors still suffered from technological deficiencies, which limited their impact, in particular their weight, accuracy, slow and cumbersome firing, loading rates, reliability of firing as well as the susceptibility of gunpowder to weather conditions. These factors, juxtaposed to the rapid firing and accuracy of native archery and the lethal blows by obsidian clubs, saw the advantages of the European technology effectively countered by the native's lesser technology.

Cortés used artillery, despite its mechanical shortcomings, highly effectively as a siege weapon and in more limited ways as cavalry and infantry support. However, its most cunning use was as a tool of psychological intimidation and terror, which, when combined with the terrifying noise of the weaponry, exploited the unfamiliarity of these types of armaments to native groups. The conquistadors effectively utilized this unfamiliarity, by engaging in shows of force and demonstrations in which the theatrical effects of artillery were showcased. This strategy was often employed in conjunction with the reading of the *Requerimiento* as a means of intimidating the indigenous populace into surrendering to Spanish control.

Perhaps the most effective strategic use of guns during the conquest of the Americas was witnessed during the Siege of Tenochtitlán where cannons and harquebusiers, emplaced on makeshift boats constructed by Cortés and his men for the purpose of crossing the lakes that surrounded the city of Tenochtitlán, proved pivotal in crushing the defenses of the Aztec capital. It is during this battle that the military advantages of European artillery were dramatically demonstrated, as these weapons aided in the capture and destruction of the city.

In the case of the conquest of the Inca Empire, during the 1530s, cannons were of limited worth, beyond the previously discussed psychological use. In Peru, the technological inefficiencies of 16th-century gunnery were greatly exacerbated by the geographical features of the rugged, mountainous Andean landscape where the battles of the Inca conquest were waged. In Spanish conquest of the Inca, the use of the harquebus was more widespread than during the Mexican conquest, as more of the conquistadors had access to them. However, their use was not sufficient to subdue several of the Inca rebellions, which took place in the years after the fall of Cuzco. Indeed, an effective method of resistance by the Inca rebels included incorporating the use of captured Spanish horses and harquebuses in skirmishes against the Spanish invaders.

Despite their obvious technological advantage, artillery cannot be thought to have played a decisive role in the conquest of the Americas, providing instead just an additional element in the superior military arsenal of the European armies. The technological limitations of 16th-century guns made their technological value high, but their military impact minimal. In the end, it is clear that no single technology was responsible for the demise and conquest of Native American empires.

Jesús E. Sanabria

See also: Aztec-Spanish War, Causes of; Aztec-Spanish War, Consequences of; Inca Civil War; Inca-Spanish War, Causes of; Inca-Spanish War, Consequences of; Tenochtitlán, Siege of.

Resources

Cortés, Hernán. *Letters from Mexico.* Translated and edited by Anthony Pagden with Introductory essay by John Huxtable Elliott. New Haven/London: Yale University Press, 2001.

Diamond, Jared M. *Guns, Germs, and Steel: The Fates of Human Societies.* New York: W.W. Norton, 2005.

Koch, Peter O. *The Spanish Conquest of the Inca Empire.* Jefferson, NC: McFarland, 2008.

Levy, Buddy. *Conquistador: Hernán Cortés, King Montezuma, and the Last Stand of the Aztecs.* New York: Bantam Books, 2008.

Parker, Geoffrey, ed. *The Cambridge Illustrated History of Warfare: The Triumph of the West.* Cambridge /New York: Cambridge University Press, 1995.

Raudzens, George. *Technology, Disease, and Colonial Conquests, Sixteenth to Eighteenth Centuries: Essays Reappraising the Guns and Germs Theories.* History of Warfare Series, Vol. 2. Leiden, Netherlands/ Boston: Koninklijke Brill NV, 2001.

Wood, Michael. *Conquistadors.* Berkeley: University of California Press, 2000.

H

Hanan

Hanan Cuzco refers to the upper portion of the city of Cuzco, the location of the ruling elite of the Inca Empire. Divided in the mid-14th century by the sixth emperor, Inca Roca, the ruling family governed from Hanan Cuzco for over 150 years. Historians often reference this ruling branch as the Hanan dynasty. By the early 16th century, the spreading empire saw leaders like Huayna Cápac relocate much of governing authority and family to the more northerly region near Quito. They still based their authority around Quito at the time of the Spanish arrival in the 1530s.

The Hanan dynasty, while still centered in upper Cuzco, built a series of palaces, many around the great square of Aucaypata. As each emperor rose to power, they built their own personal palaces. Though later destroyed by the Spanish, these palaces were reported and used by Pizarro and his brothers, who were awed by the Inca's precise stone construction.

The Hanan dynasty was the dominant leadership of the Inca Empire beginning with the rule of Inca Roca. Prior to that time, evidence indicates ruling elite came from the Hurin dynasty. From Inca Roca in the 14th century until the rule of Pachacutin Inca in the 15th century, evidence indicates the ruling Inca was of the Hanan dynasty, but some authority was shared with a corresponding member of the Hurin dynasty. Pachacuti simplified the chain of authority, but the relationship between Hanan and Hurin remained quite complex.

In addition to referencing the divisions between upper and lower Cuzco, and denoting the ruling dynasty, the two names also refer to the two moieties that dominated the ruling elite. The Hanan, the stronger, more dominant moiety, identified closely with the military, while the Hurin moiety primarily identified with the priests. It was the association with the military that enabled the Hanan dynasty to expand the empire. This expansion of territory brought the Inca, Huayna Cápac, to the region around Quito. This same expansion of the empire also led to the civil war that existed at the point of the Spanish arrival under Francisco Pizarro. Huayna Cápac favored his sons, by different mothers, who accompanied him in his military campaigns. When the emperor was struck down with smallpox, his son, Ninan Cuyochi, was briefly designated as his successor. Unfortunately for the Hanan dynasty, Ninan Cuyochi also died of the disease, leaving the leading priests and generals to determine the next successor. With the priests supporting a legitimate descendant, Huáscar, of the Hurin dynastic line still centered in Cuzco, and the military leaders of the northern provinces around Quito supporting Atahualpa, a civil war broke out in the empire.

The divisions within the imperial leadership were inflamed by Spanish manipulation. Following the capture and execution of Atahualpa, and the death of his half-brother Huáscar, Pizzaro supported one son after another of the diseased Inca, Huayna Cápac. In each case, the designated Sapa Inca was required to govern under Spanish oversight from the occupied upper city of Cuzco. Abusive treatment of the ruling elite by the younger brothers of Pizarro repeatedly prompted the Inca to flee the city. There they governed in exile, leading native military forces and priests in opposition to the Spanish rule. United through Spanish oppression, the Hanan dynasty and their Hurin cousins were permanently removed from ruling status with the execution of Túpac Amaru in 1572.

Rebecca M. Seaman

See also: Atahualpa; Huáscar; Huayna Cápac; Hurin; Ninan Cuyochi; Pachacutin; Pizarro, Francisco; Sapa Inca; Túpac Amaru.

Resources

Davies, Nigel. *The Incas.* Niwot: University of Colorado Press, 1995.

MacQuarrie, Kim. *Last Days of the Inca.* New York: Simon & Schuster, 2007.

Zuidema, R. T. "Hierarchy and Space in Incaic Social Organization." *Ethnohistory* 30, no. 2 (Spring 1983): 49–75.

Hernández de Córdoba, Francisco

Francisco Hernández de Córdoba was a Spanish conquistador who led the first major expedition that attempted to conquer the Mayas in the Yucatán Peninsula of Mexico. Born in Spain in 1475, he arrived on the island of Cuba in 1511. He soon became one of the leading Spanish citizens on the island, enjoying life as a wealthy planter. A group of Spaniards on the island approached Hernández de Córdoba about the possibility of leading an expedition to the west in search of wealth and indigenous slaves. Córdoba agreed to lead the group, and he and two other men financed the voyage. More than 100 people joined the expedition, each of whom would

share in any trade or plunder. Among those who accompanied Córdoba was Bernal Díaz del Castillo, the famous chronicler of the Spanish conquest of Mexico.

In February 1517, three ships under Hernández de Córdoba's command headed west from Cuba. After several days of sailing, he and his men encountered a large town unlike anything the Spaniards had seen in the Caribbean. They had arrived on the Yucatán Peninsula where they came in contact with northern lowland Maya civilization. The Mayas were well dressed in cotton cloth, in contrast to the naked inhabitants the Spaniards had encountered on the Caribbean islands. There were houses, magnificent temples, streets, squares, and marketplaces. The structures were skillfully built of stone and brick. There were also signs of an advanced religion. So impressive was this settlement that the Spaniards named it Great Cairo.

The Mayas met the Spaniards in 10 large canoes that carried 40 or 50 people each.

Francisco Hernández de Córdoba, Spanish explorer. (Tarker/The Bridgeman Art Library)

Some of the natives boarded the Spanish ships, and the two groups exchanged gifts. They later returned with their leader, who led Hernández de Córdoba and a number of Spaniards to shore and took them to their town. When a group of Mayas ambushed Córdoba and his men, the Spaniards were able to fend off the attack and escape. They also took two prisoners, who were later baptized and named Julian and Melchior. These two would serve as interpreters between the Spanish and the Mayas of the Yucatán. The Spaniards also found enough gold objects to encourage further exploration.

Hernández de Córdoba and his crew made another stop at Campeche. Sensing that the Mayas might again attack, the Spaniards quickly left. They did stay long enough to see evidence of human sacrifice. Hernández de Córdoba then had his ships stop again along the coast of the Yucatán Peninsula in order to fill their casks with drinking water. Greatly outnumbered by the Mayas, the ensuing encounter was a disaster for the Spaniards. The Mayas killed more than 50 Spaniards, and almost all the remaining survivors, including Hernández de Córdoba, were wounded. Some of the Spaniards made their way back to the ships in order to return to Cuba.

The trip home was a difficult one for Hernández de Córdoba and his men. Having abandoned their water casks during the last battle, the group was compelled to stop repeatedly for water where hostile encounters took their toll. One ship became unseaworthy, and since there were not enough men to sail it, they burned it. The expedition also stopped in Florida on the way back to Cuba, where again Hernández de Córdoba's group fought with the indigenous people they found.

Upon arriving in Cuba, the wounded Hernández de Córdoba returned to his home. Within 10 days he died from the injuries he suffered at the hands of the Mayas in the Yucatán.

Despite the ultimate failure of the expedition, the tantalizing tales of riches led Governor Diego Velázquez to send larger and better-equipped expeditions to Mexico. In fact, Velázquez seems to have argued that the lands were claimed in his own name. After Hernández de Córdoba died, Velázquez continued the explorations of mainland Mexico in his own name. In 1518, he sent a group of some 200 Spaniards headed by his nephew Juan de Grijalva. Then in 1519, the famous expedition of Hernán Cortés set sail for Mexico.

Ronald E. Young

See also: Cortés, Hernán; Díaz, del Castillo, Bernal; Grijalva, Juan de; Julián, Mayan Interpreter; Velázquez, Diego (de Cuéllar).

Resources

Díaz del Castillo, Bernal. *The True History of the Conquest of New Spain.* Translated with an Introduction and Notes by Janet Burke and Ted Humphrey. Indianapolis, IN: Hackett Publishing, 2012.

Hernández de Córdoba, Francisco. *The Discovery of Yucatán.* Edited by Henry R. Wagner. New York: Kraus Reprint Co., 1969.

McAlister, Lyle N. *Spain and Portugal in the New World, 1492–1700.* Minneapolis: University of Minnesota Press, 1984.

Hernández Portocarrero, Alonso

One of the young officers under Hernán Cortés in his expedition of conquest in Mexico, Alonso Hernández Portocarrero was originally from the region around Seville in Spain. In addition to serving as a conquistador on this historical invasion of Mesoamerica, Hernández Portocarrero was briefly honored by his captain general by being presented with La Malinche, also known as Doña Marina, the former Aztec slave of the

Maya. The gift was soon reclaimed when Cortés realized that Malinche could translate the Nahuatl language of the Aztecs into Mayan and vice versa, assisting the Spanish in communication with the indigenous population of the region.

Rebecca M. Seaman

See also: Cortés, Hernán; La Malinche, "Doña Marina"; Nahuatl Language

Resources

Díaz del Castillo, Bernal. *The True History of The Conquest of New Spain.* Translated with an Introduction and Notes by Janet Burke and Ted Humphrey. Indianapolis, IN: ackett Publishing Co., Inc., 2012.

Thomas, Hugh. *Conquest: Montezuma, Cortés, and the Fall of Old Mexico.* New York: Simon & Schuster, 1993.

Hispaniola

Prior to the arrival of Christopher Columbus, the Tainos Indians inhabited the island of Hispaniola. These people, who made up the primary population of the Greater Antilles islands, formed peaceful societies that practiced limited agriculture as well as fishing and gathering. Called Haiti by the natives on the island, the Tainos population was divided into five small kingdoms. Each kingdom was governed by a cacique. The arrival of Columbus, and his establishment of Fort La Navidad, brought drastic changes to the island and its people.

With Columbus's second voyage, nearly 1,500 men accompanied him to establish a colony on La Isla Española or Hispaniola. The Spanish included about 200 gentlemen and craftsmen, a number of adventurers seeking quick wealth, soldiers, sailors, and 20 knights. Divided internally, and preying upon the native population, relations quickly broke down. Native women were seduced or raped, men were enslaved, and those who resisted were punished or killed. By 1500, the lack of promised wealth and reports of corruption caused the Crown to end the leadership of Columbus and his brothers, replacing them with a series of royal appointees.

One of the royal appointees, Fr. Nicolás de Ovando, created a structured society, divided the island into 17 districts, each with its own municipal council that was responsible for governing locally. Ovando also instituted the encomienda, a system of assigning the indigenous population as laborers and potential converts to designated landowners. These policies introduced a pattern of dealing with the Tainos that created virtual enslavement. Even rumored native resistance to the new policies was met with extreme oppression, like the massacre of Xaragua in 1503.

Within very few years, the once dense population of Hispaniola was decimated. No census was taken upon first contact, so initial numbers of the Tainos are unknown. Evidence shows the first major epidemic, probably European in origin, occurred within a year of first contact, with a devastating influenza outbreak. After severe losses due to influenza, small pox and other diseases, abuse by the Spanish, transportation off the island and massacres, there were only 60,000 Tainos left on the island in 1507. Within 40 years of initial contact, only 600 remained. Disease was a major factor, but other practices played important roles in this rapid depopulation.

The conquering Spanish were permitted to collect tribute from the Tainos. Acceptable tribute was demanded in the form of gold, 25 pounds of cotton, or through service as laborers for the Spanish. Increasingly, the normal tribute became the labor assignments. Men were detailed to work in mines, assigned heavy labor in fields, or transported abroad.

Women were sometimes assigned to fields, compelled to serve in the households, or reduced to the role of mistresses for the Spanish. In addition to the tributary demands, the Tainos were also compelled to provide food for the Spanish, reducing their own stores and leading to malnutrition. Children died in increasing numbers, as did men working in the mines. Women, separated from their husbands and overworked, bore fewer children and died in greater numbers. These policies and practices, though touted as a means of reducing the natives to Christianity and civilizing them, resulted in the genocide of the local Tainos Indians.

The island of Hispaniola continued to serve as a base for the Spanish. With the depopulation of the Indians, increased changes in the traditional agriculture also occurred. Pigs were the first invading animal species, but cattle, horses, dogs, and aggressive, invasive plants destroyed the natural habitat, causing extensive deforestation. With the demise of the Tainos, the resulting loss of native cultures and the devastation to the local ecology, Hispaniola of the late 16th century bore little resemblance to the pre-Columbian island of Haiti encountered by Columbus in 1492.

Rebecca M. Seaman

See also: Columbus, Christopher; Encomienda; Ovando, Fr. Nicolás de; Xaragua Massacre.

Resources

Corbett, Bob. "Pre-Columbian Hispaniola—Arawak/Taino Indians." *The History of Haiti.* http://www.hartford-hwp.com/archives/43a/100.html (accessed July 22, 2011).

Gibson, Charles. *Spain in America.* New York: Harper & Row, 1967.

Lovell, W. George. "'Heavy Shadows and Black Night': Disease and Depopulation in Colonial Spanish America." *Annals of the Association of American Geographers* (September 1992): 426–443.

Thomas, Hugh. *Conquest: Montezuma, Cortés, and the Fall of Old Mexico.* New York: Simon & Schuster, 1993.

Horses, Impact of

The impact of horses in the Spanish conquest of the Aztec, Maya, and Incas was tremendous. For the Maya and Aztec natives of Central America, the horse was a novel creature, and one that was initially viewed as mystical, powerful, and eventually spiritual in nature. To the Inca of the South American Andes, who already used the llama for beasts of burden, the horse was nonetheless awe-inspiring, especially when used in military campaigns.

Hernán Cortés, whose father has served the monarchy as a cavalry officer, quickly understood the fear and awe inspired by the presence of his horses. This fear and awe were rooted in the novelty of horses, as well as their strategic use by the Spanish military in the cavalry and artillery. Before his siege of the Aztec capital of Tenochtitlán, Cortés employed horses in his defeat of and eventual alliance with the Tlaxcala. The use of cavalry techniques helped repulse the vastly superior numbers of Tlaxcalans, though at great cost in numbers of horses killed, including several horses ridden by Cortés. Nonetheless, it is the use of the Spanish arms (more for the smoke and noise produced than their accuracy), ships, and military strategy, combined with the use of horses, that produced the awe in the Tlaxcala kingdom. This awe helped the Spanish negotiate an alliance with Tlaxcala and other ethnic groups in opposition to the Aztecs.

While Cortés's few horses assisted disproportionately the Spanish success against the Aztec Empire, they were of little use in jungles of the Yucatán and Nicaragua.

Despite this fact, the Spanish forces under Francisco Pizarro and Hernando de Soto disembarked from the isthmus in 1532 for Peru with over 60 horses in tow. This decision greatly assisted the conquistadors in their invasion of the Inca Empire. As Pizarro's forces approached Cajamarca where the Inca emperor Atahualpa was encamped with his army several thousand strong, the decision was made to employ horses to intimidate the Inca, much as Cortés had done with the Aztec. To this end, Hernando de Soto approached the seated emperor on his steed. Surprisingly, Spanish accounts indicate that Atahualpa displayed no angst or surprise. While the Spanish were able to traverse the route to Cajamarca more rapidly due to their cavalry, it did not have the initial intended impact as desired by Pizarro.

The region of Peru under the Incas was a combination of coastal plains and rugged mountains. Great on the flat lands, the Spanish horses were of little help on the steep hills and mountains of the Andes. Indeed, the Inca use of rope bridges to span rivers and gorges made for rapid movement of the Inca forces while the Spanish were forced to travel extensive distances to accommodate their horses. Nonetheless, the horses and Spanish cavalry proved indispensible in battle as the two sides collided in the 1530s. Pizarro's forces used stampedes of horses to scatter, trample and frighten the Inca infantry. Less disciplined in displaying stoic indifference than their emperor, or perhaps disheartened by the Spanish capture and execution of Atahualpa, this tactic of equestrian routs was very effective in the conquest of the Inca Empire.

Eventually the Inca adapted to the Spanish military tactics. During the Neo-Inca resistance movement under Manco Inca Yupanqui, the Inca captured and used Spanish horses as their own mounts. The Inca assimilation of horses into their armies, and alteration of military strategies to accommodate their use of Spanish horses and arms, was similar to the later North American Plains tribes of the 19th century. As a result, the Spanish advantage of horses was effectively countered. The Neo-Incas managed to retain a government in exile in the Vilcabamba region for decades after the initial Spanish conquest of the Inca Empire.

The Spanish need of native labor presented a dilemma with regard to controlling access to horses. As labors through repartimiento or encomiendas, the various nations of Native Americas were introduced to the care and breeding of horses. To prevent these same natives from developing their own herds, the Council of the Indies prohibited the native populations in their empire from owning or riding horses. Despite such attempts to regulate native access to horses, eventually horses were owned bred and used by Indians, much in the same manner as their Spanish conquerors. Nonetheless, access and assimilation of horses by native cultures in Middle and South America came too late to neutralize the Spanish advantages at the time of conquest.

Rebecca M. Seaman

See also: Atahualpa; Cortés, Hernán; Neo-Incas; Pizarro, Francisco; Soto, Hernando de, in Peru; Tlaxcala, Battle of.

Resources

Díaz del Castillo, Bernal. *The True History of The Conquest of New Spain.* Translated with an Introduction and Notes by Janet Burke and Ted Humphrey. Indianapolis, IN: Hackett Publishing, 2012.

Hemming, John. *The Conquest of the Incas.* New York: Harcourt Brace Jovanovich, 1970.

Walkolak, Steve. "Cortés's Inland Expedition." *Military History* 24, no. 3 (May 2007): 64–65.

Welton, Jerry. "The Policies of Hernan Cortes, as Described in his Letters." PhD diss., University of Illinois at Urbana-Champaign, 1954.

Huacas

Huacas refers to a sacred element within Inca religion. One use of the term Huacas is a generic identifier for a person, place, or item imbued with a holy or mystic nature. Curiosities or oddities such as mortal remains, fetishes, and totems may bear the title. Man-made items placed at sites considered holy could also be categorized as a Huacas.

Oddly formed rocks or natural items may be broadly classified as Huacas. Geological features of unusual appearance or of mundane appearance, but holding historic or religious significance may be classified as a Huacas, such as mountains, battlefields, ruins, or streams. Spiritual forces tied to a natural site, such as a river or valley, were also defined as Huacas. The supernatural force or entity residing in the water or earth was responsible for the sanctity of the site.

This sweeping definition makes the sheer number of Huacas associated with Inca culture rather vast. Worship of Huacas was seen as complimentary to the worship of established gods. Historian and priest Father Bernabé Cobo cataloged roughly 330 in the Cuzco region alone (the area around the Inca capital in Peru). These temple Huacas radiated outward, along sightlines toward the horizon called ceques, from a central Sun temple. Each of these Huacas corresponded with a calendar day, which signaled the time that particular site would be of increased spiritual importance.

Hierarchy did exist within the Huacas rank. Father Cobo's list only reflects the Huacas deemed important by the Inca state, and not those of more local importance in Cuzco, which is far more numerous and inclusive group. Scale did factor into the importance of some Huacas, a towering mountain was seen as a more powerful Huacas than a boulder; the Huacas of a lake was more powerful than the Huacas of a pond.

A thread common to Huacas is the presence of some form of ancestral reverence. Common Inca Huacas were family tombs. Some Huacas were distant ancestors, now responsible for guiding descendents of their bloodline through the future ages. Maintenance of Huacas generally fell to extended kinship groups, but in some cases the Inca government appointed the caregivers.

Huaques were also powerful Huacas. Translated, the term means "brother" or refers to an older family ancestry. While rooted in a familial term, the Huaques were often statues of former Inca leaders or rulers, which may not follow a genealogical path.

One example of a Huacas is the hill of Huanacauri. A creation myth places four deities at this site in the dawn of Inca history. One account has one of the brothers being killed by the others, only for him to reappear on a ridge of this mountain later in the brothers' travels. Other stories have one or more of their number turning into stone at Huanacauri or the nearby ranges, rendering the locales and their contents divine by association.

Sacrifices were frequent at Huacas. Human sacrifices were practiced at the larger Huacas in conjunction with important ceremonial festivals or holidays. Livestock might be slaughtered at another such site. Material articles such as coca leaves, or the most common offering recorded, seashells, may serve sufficiently at another site. These offerings were either burnt, buried, or in the cases of Huacas waterways, cast in.

Numerous Huacas were believed to possess power of divination. Possessors of the reliquary artifacts, pilgrims in the sacred presence, or those who were themselves considered Huacas could foretell the future. To achieve the needed altered perspective, alcohol or drugs were sometimes taken. Some of the more potable items were transported from place to place; Huacas thought to lend strength or courage on the battlefield might be taken to war.

With the conversion of the Inca population to Christianity, many Huacas were destroyed and the *taquiongos,* human spokespersons for the Huacas, were executed. A few notable Huacas still remain, and of course the geological features could not be effaced. Machu Picchu remains a popular travel destination and Huacas. Sacrifices, of a sort, are still offered to mountain Huacas. Modern travelers still carry stone to difficult summits where they are deposited in exchange for a blessing of strength to finish their journey. This act of almost passive novelty may capture some of the essence regarding how Huacas operated, but does not accurately portray the religious and cultural importance played in the everyday life of the Incas.

Michael D. Coker

See also: Christianity, Impact of on the Inca; Human Sacrifice; Peru, State of Prior to Spanish Conquest.

Resources

Bauer, Brian S. *The Sacred Landscape of the Inca: The Cusco Ceque System.* Austin: University of Texas Press, 2011.

McEwan, Gordon F. *The Incas: New Perspectives.* New York: W. W. Norton, 2008.

Niles, Susan. *The Shape of Inca History: Narrative and Architecture in an Andean Empire.* Iowa City: University Of Iowa Press, 1995.

Huamanga

The region of Huamanga lies in the southwestern portion of modern Peru, slightly south and inland from the capital city of Lima. The dominant city of the region, also known originally as Huamanga, was founded in 1539, shortly after the arrival and conquest by of the Spanish over the native Inca Empire. The region and its cities lay outside of the governmental centers of power in early colonial times. Yet the presence of a strong agricultural base and valuable mines made this rural district of great economic value to the new Spanish colony.

The Inca acquired the region of Huamanga through their 15th-century conquest over the Chanca, during the reign of Pachacutin Inca Yupanqui. The rapid expansion throughout the entire region ensued, with the population reduced to a peasantry status of agricultural workers. Additionally, the indigenous population was infused with foreign ethnic groups, including those considered "Incas by privilege" as a means of controlling the region.

With the Spanish conquest of the Inca in the 1530s, the puppet emperor Manco Inca eventually fled to northwest of Cuzco to the general region. Loyal supporters of the Inca created a "Neo-Inca" resistance movement that threatened Spanish control and the transport of shipments of goods and gold between the inland capital and the coastal ports. Pizzaro's lieutenant, Vasco de Guervara, was sent to the region to provide needed support to the small contingent of harried Spaniards under siege by the Neo-Inca movement. Under Guervara, an outpost was established, which latter was officially proclaimed the "City of San Juan de la Frontera de Huamanga" and served as a center of Spanish authority in the midst of the neo-Incas territory.

The divisions between the various ethnic groups, established early on by the Incas to control the local population, continued in use by the new Spanish conquerors. The local peasantry served in the role of agricultural laborers, as well as labor for the mines that eventually dotted the Huamanga region, theoretically protected from abuses by a cabildo of encomendero elites. The failure of this cabildo to adequately protect the rights and possessions of the local Indians became apparent within two decades with the emergence of the reactionary Taki Onqoy sect that developed in Huamanga. Yet, despite the underlying differences and conflicts between the native populations and the Spanish, the region and city of Huamanga became an economic center, with gold, silver, and mercury mines, as well as developing coca plantations. The Indian-white cooperation in the quest for commercial profit moved Huamanga from a rural, sparsely populated frontier region to a major economic focal point of Spanish-controlled Peru.

Rebecca M. Seaman

See also: Cabildo; Chanca; Encomenderos; Manco Inca Yupanqui; Neo-Inca; Pachacutin; Taki Onqoy.

Resources

Davies, Nigel. *The Incas.* Niwot: University of Colorado Press, 1995.

Stern, Steve J. *Peru's Indian Peoples and the Challenge of Spanish Conquest: Huamanga to 1640.* 2nd ed. Madison: University of Wisconsin Press, 1993.

Huancavelica

The region of Huancavelica is a low, mountainous region on the western portion of the Andes, lying immediately east of Lima, Peru. The city of Huancavelica lies in the eastern portion of the region, in the more rugged mountain terrain. The mercury mine for which the town was founded is located immediately south of the city of Huancavelica.

Mercury was discovered in the mountains of Huancavelica in 1563, shortly after the Spanish embraced the cheap and effective practice of using amalgamation to separate silver from raw ore in the colonies. To facilitate the effective mining of this valuable element in the production of silver, the then viceroy Francisco de Toledo ordered the founding of the town of Huancavelica. Populated mainly by indigenous people who were tasked with the mining of mercury, Huancavelica grew in size, importance, and wealth for the next few decades.

In 1572, Toledo imposed a resettlement policy on the Inca population, mainly as an answer to resistance posed by the Neo-Inca movement and the Taki Onqoy movement. It was through the resettlement procedure that he was able to create the city of Huancavelica. To maintain the population, due to the unfortunately deadly toll of mining mercury, the viceroy also employed the use of the *mita,* a native form of corvée labor or repartimiento system in Peru. By demanding all males to serve six months of labor every seven years, Toledo was able to initially man the mine outside of town. However, the high mortality rates resulted in the viceroy manipulating the *mita* system, thereby requiring families to replace workers who died while working in the mines with other family members.

By the 17th century the silver mining and colonial administrators, who sought personal financial gain from their positions, began to realize that royal scrutiny prevented them from reaping extreme profits from mining silver. The use of mercury for separating the silver ore enabled the Spanish officials to discern how much silver was actually mined, and compare that quantity to the amount shipped and paid in tythes and taxes. The only means to escape such oversight was to return to the more primitive practice of using smelting to separate the ore.

With the gradual return of silver processing to smelting, demand for mercury declined. The accompanying scrutiny of followers of Las Casas, who firmly believed the use of indigenous laborers was unethical, especially in the deadly mercury mines of Huancavelica, also placed pressure on the abandonment of mercury as the primary method of extricating silver from the raw ore. By the late 17th century, mercury production was in decline. It was not until the 18th century and the end of the Spanish colonial control of Peru that mines like Huancavelica fell into disuse. The location of the town and mine created a city based solely on the profits from mining mercury. With the decline and abandonment of the mining, the town had little to support its population. The resulting widespread poverty of the largely indigenous populace of Huancavelica remains a dominant feature to this day.

Rebecca M. Seaman

See also: Las Casas, Bartolomé de; Mercury; *Mita;* Neo-Incas; Repartimiento; Silver; Taki Onqoy; Toledo, Francisco de.

Resources

Keen, Benjamin and Keith Haynes. *A History of Latin America.* 8th ed. Boston: Houghton Mifflin Harcourt, 2009.

Lowry, Lyn Brandon. "Forging an Indian Nation: Urban Indians under Spanish Colonial Control." PhD diss., University of California, Berkeley, 1991.

Pearce, Adrian J. "Huancavelica 1700–1759: Administrative Reform of the Mercury Industry in Early Bourbon Peru." *Hispanic American Historical Review* 79, no. 4 (November 1999): 669–702.

Huanta

Located in the south central Andes of Peru, Huanta is the northernmost province in the Ayacucho Region, north of the Huanmanga province. The montaña of the Huanta was especially productive for coca farming. Following the Inca conquest of non-Inca regions in the 1460s, foreign ethnic groups were relocated to the Huanta province, ensuring the division of the population into opposing groups that prevented the formation of successful political opposition to the Inca Empire.

The Inca Empire further extended their control over non-Inca populations in places like Huanta by establishing *mitmaq* or "Incas by privilege" settlements. These pro-Inca, privileged ethnic groups were granted access to valuable holdings such as the best coca fields of Huanta. In return, they were expected to serve as loyal supporters of the Inca government. This rather unique method of controlling subservient communities enable the Inca to reap substantial harvests from profitable regions like Huanta, and use the excess produce to fill stockpiles for distribution throughout the empire. The means to supply stores of goods was through the force migration of divergent groups and the designation of privileged ethnic minorities, all at the expense of local unity.

The impact of Inca settlements of divergent ethnic groups was the extension of ethnic rivalries into the colonial era. Instead of focusing resistance and unifying *ayllus* against the invading Spanish, the competing ethnic groups depended upon the Spanish authorities to settle economic and political disputes at a local level. The previous practice of using war to resolve local disputes between rival peoples was replaced by the structured Spanish legal system. Rather than resolving the issues, the availability of legal solutions, especially for groups too weak to have pursued self-interests without intervention, extended and intensified ethnic rivalries in the region. This rivalry continued past the colonial era, to the period of independence and beyond.

Rebecca M. Seaman

See also: *Ayllus;* Huamanga; Peru, State of prior to Spanish Conquest.

Resources

Méndez, Cecilia. *The Plebian Republic: The Huanta Rebellion and the Making of the Peruvian State, 1820–1850.* Durham, NC: Duke University Press, 2005.

Steve J. Stern. *Peru's Indian Peoples and the Challenge of Spanish Conquest: Huamanga to 1640.* 2nd ed. Madison: University of Wisconsin Press, 1993.

Huáscar

Huáscar Inca was the 12th emperor of the Inca Empire, reigning from 1527 to 1532. The death of his father, Emperor Huayna Cápac, resulted in the priests selecting the emperor's original deathbed choice for successor, Ninan Cuyochi, to wear the royal fringe. However, Ninan Cuyochi soon after died of the same smallpox epidemic. With the emperor and his selected heir both dead, the decision was made to honor the recent political decisions of Huayna Cápac and divide the empire into two parts, one ruled solely by Huáscar and the other coruled by Huáscar and his younger brother Atahualpa. Instead of resolving the dilemma of governance, the decision plunged the Inca world into civil war. The divided and weakened Incas became easy prey for the Spanish in 1532.

Born around 1495 in the capital city of Cuzco, Huáscar was one of the oldest of Huayna Cápac's reported 500 sons. He was named heir at an early age because he descended from the union between the Sapa Inca and the Inca's first sister. Officially designated heir, Huáscar's father groomed him for the role of emperor. Huayna Cápac left Huáscar behind to administer Cuzco when he went to the northern provinces, near present-day Quito, Ecuador, to continue his conquest and expansion of the Inca Empire. Atahualpa, the emperor's favorite son through a non-Inca wife and Huáscar's half-brother, along with Ninan Cuyochi, his eldest son from a lesser wife, accompanied Huayna Cápac on these northern campaigns. As the conquests expanded the Inca territories, Huayna Cápac began to feel that the empire had grown too large to be ruled by a single emperor from Cuzco. Before becoming ill and dying in 1527, he made a fateful decision to divide the empire administratively into two parts. On his deathbed, the emperor seemed to provide for the continued unity of the empire's governance by designating his eldest son, Ninan Cuyochi, to hold the position of Sapa Inca. He also provided instructions for the division of rule, should Ninan Cuyochi die soon after. With the ensuing deaths of father and son, Huáscar was accordingly designated to rule one half of the empire from Cuzco while Atahualpa jointly ruled the second half of the empire from Quito in the north.

The decision to divide the empire between Huáscar and Atahualpa was exacerbated by the impact of diseases introduced by the advancing Spanish explorations. It was smallpox, introduced from distant contact with the Spanish, which was responsible for the death of Huayna Cápac and Ninan Cuyochi.

With the sudden death of the accepted Inca, and the spread of a deadly and mysterious epidemic across the empire, the introduction of a split government further divided the increasingly fragile realm.

This proved to be an error, as old rivalries and jealousies grew into open conflict between the two half-brothers. The Inca armies and administrators had already begun to divide into factions supporting either Huáscar or Atahualpa years before Huayna Cápac's death. A majority of the powerful Inca bureaucrats and nobility in Cuzco aligned themselves with Huáscar, whose lineage honored the traditional lines of descent. Atahualpa, in contrast, had the support of the powerful northern army. The death of Huayna Cápac eventually moved the empire into a prolonged and bloody civil war that only ended after the arrival of Spanish invaders under the command of Pizarro in 1532.

Despite old rivalries, Atahualpa did not rebel against his brother for five years after his father's death. The two appeared to be coexisting peacefully with little interference into the other's half of the empire. Atahualpa, however, used this time to assure himself of his army's loyalty and win support from some of the nobility. In 1532, he openly rebelled against his brother, quickly gaining a reputation for ruthlessness. He slaughtered all the men, women, and children of several towns that supported his brother as a warning to all those who opposed his bid to take over the empire. Atahualpa then moved south with his armies, camping near the town of Cajamarca. The two brothers then waged a brutal war that cost the lives of thousands of Incas and seriously eroded the wealth and food supplies of the empire.

In a chance event, the Spaniards landed at Tumbes on the northern coast of Peru in 1532. Aware of the civil war, Pizarro sent emissaries to request a meeting with Atahualpa.

As the Spaniards traveled to Cajamarca for the meeting, Atahualpa sent them a message announcing that he was now the sole ruler of the empire. Atahualpa had received news that his armies had taken Cuzco and captured Huáscar. The Spaniards, in turn, promised him support against his enemies. At the meeting to discuss these matters on November 16, 1532, in Cajamarca, Pizarro and his soldiers revealed their true intentions by kidnapping Atahualpa and making him a hostage.

After the Battle of Cajamarca, Pizarro initially allowed Atahualpa to meet with his advisers from captivity. Atahualpa used one of these meetings to give the order to execute Huáscar. However, Huáscar's death in 1532 at the hands of his half-brother's militaries did not end the civil war, as his supporters continued to fight against Atahualpa. Pizarro, in a Machiavellian twist, used Huáscar's execution as an excuse to find Atahualpa guilty of treason and to order the Inca's death by strangulation. Pizarro naively hoped that the death of this powerful ruler, and the recent division of the empire in a civil war between Huáscar and Atahualpa, would produce a weak, decapitated yet wealthy empire, ripe for Spanish conquest. Instead, the divisions threatened to turn the armies of the dead Incas against the far outnumbered Spanish invaders.

Realizing his error, Pizarro named Túpac Huallpa, another son of Huayna Cápac, as the new emperor in order to fill a dangerous power vacuum in the Andean empire. Túpac Huallpa, however, allied himself with Huáscar's faction. As a result, Atahualpa's supporters continued to fight against Túpac Huallpa and the Spaniards, believing that only Atahualpa's son was the legitimate heir to the empire. After Túpac Huallpa's death, possibly from smallpox, the Spaniards continued to ally themselves with Huáscar's faction by placing his brother Manco Inca Yupanqui on the throne. Manco helped the Spanish destroy the remnants of Atahualpa's support, ensuring the Spanish conquest of central Peru in 1536.

Huáscar thus became one of the last of the great Incas who ruled one of history's largest empires. His inability to address the divisions in the empire led to civil war and his death. His reign can be seen as a transition between the once all-powerful Inca Empire and the destruction and integration of his possessions into a vast new Spanish Empire in the Americas.

Thomas Edsall

See also: Atahualpa; Cajamarca, Battle of; European Diseases, Role of; Huáscar; Huayna Cápac; Inca Civil War; Manco Inca Yupanqui; Pizarro, Francisco; Túpac Huallpa.

Resources

Bernand, Carmen. *The Incas: Empire of Blood and Gold.* London: Thames & Hudson, 1994.

Hemming, John. *The Conquest of the Incas.* London: Pan Macmillan, 1970.

Means, Philip A. *The Fall of the Inca Empire and the Spanish Rule in Peru, 1530–1780.* New York: Gordian Press, 1971.

Huayna Cápac

One of the great Inca emperors responsible for significantly expanding the empire, Huayna Cápac ruled from 1493 until his untimely death in 1527. He was particularly noted for wars of expansion in the northern region, as well as construction of key roads and other public works that assisted communications within the empire. Upon his death and the immediate death of his presumed heir, two sons claimed the throne of Sapa Inca. The resulting civil war between the brothers and their supporters helped set the empire up for conquest by the Spanish in 1532.

Huayna Cápac, born ca. 1464, became the Sapa Inca following the death of his father, Túpac Inca Yupanqui, in 1493. Both his father and grandfather, Pachacuti, took the Inca people from a small cluster of villages around Cuzco to an empire that stretched along the Andes Mountains. Huayna Cápac reigned for 34 years. During that time period, he continued wars and alliances that increased the empire to the height of its expansion. Huayna Cápac's expansion significantly extended Inca holdings into the north, while he also worked to connect the distant territories by an intricate road system, with highways covering 25,000 miles. He additionally annexed and built up the city of Tumbes, on the coast, the city from which Pizarro launched his inland invasion of Peru in 1531.

For years, Huayna Cápac fought wars in the northern Andes, not just to acquire new territories, but to secure a location for

Huayna Cápac, 12th Inca Emperor, ca. 1493–1527. (Brooklyn Museum of Art/The Bridgeman Art Library)

governance. That location proved to be the city of Quito. While Cuzco continued to be the primary capital of the empire, centered on the four original territories of Tahuantinsuyu, Quito was the favorite city of the Sapa Inca. He set the city up to be a secondary capital and governed from that location for much of his reign. His favorite concubine was the daughter of the former king of Quito, and she gave birth to who is often cited as Huayna Cápac's favorite son, Atahualpa. It is his relationship with his numerous sons, and the lack of a son through his primary wife (the line of traditional succession), that contributed to the disruption of the Inca Empire in the 1520s.

Huayna Cápac had a serious dilemma of numerous sons, though none through primary wife. His eldest son and obvious choice for successor, Huáscar, was not considered a capable leader by Huayna Cápac's generals. In addition to Huáscar's focus on pleasures instead of the daily drudge of governing, he had little experience in military matters at a time when the empire struggled with internal resistance by dozens of ethnic minorities. Huáscar remained primarily in Cuzco, far removed from wars of expansion and from a close rapport with his father. The second son, the presumed heir by those close to Huayna Cápac, was Ninan Cuyochi. He was also born of an Inca mother and royal sister, though not the primary wife. Along with his younger brother, Atahualpa, Ninan Cuyochi continually collaborated with his father, Huayna Cápac, fighting wars of rebellion in the north and establishing Quito as a second capital for the empire.

Huayna Cápac fell ill in 1527, probably with smallpox. He conferred with his nobles, and informed them he wished Ninan Cuyochi to succeed him; he urged them to consult the priests or oracles. He indicated that if that choice should not be acceptable, then to consult the same priests on the succession of Huáscar. Obviously, as the father of both, Huayna Cápac preferred an heir who professed strong leadership and military command. Unfortunately, the priests found both choices to be filled with grave omens. The nobles decided to opt for the younger but more experienced brother, Ninan Cuyochi. When they approached Huayna Cápac to inform him, they discovered he had died. Nobles traveled to bestow the royal fringe on Ninan Cuyochi, where they found the emperor's first choice had also succumbed to the same illness. This left Huáscar as the other alternative.

Some historical records refer to a decision by Huayna Cápac to put Atahualpa on the throne. In reality, such a decision violated the practice of the Inca rulers—to select heirs from the pure Inca line. The preference was to select heirs whose lineage descended from the primary wife, a pure Inca sister to the current Sapa Inca. However, it was also possible for an heir to be selected from offspring of other sisters to the Sapa Inca, or even other Inca wives or concubines. In the case of Atahualpa, his mother was not ethnically an Inca, removing him from legitimacy by pure bloodlines, thereby making his selection as Sapa Inca unlikely.

Another version regarding the succession crisis often repeated in historical texts indicates Huayna Cápac divided the empire between his two sons. This version bears out Huayna Cápac's practice of governing from Quito while maintaining Cuzco as the official capital. Nonetheless, this violated the very meaning of the role, Sapa Inca (unique emperor) as well as the practice of having a sole ruler of the empire. While precedent existed for an heir to be selected outside of the eldest, selecting an heir outside of the ethnic Inca lineage was far less likely. Precedent did exist for brothers or cousins to contest for power, with the successful victor taking the royal fringe. The complexity and outcome of this particular succession crisis indicates that Huayna Cápac followed precedent in selecting the more capable son over the eldest son, in lieu of any male offspring from his primary wife. Yet he simultaneously avoided declaring an even younger son as his heir, though possibly his favorite, Atahualpa, due to mixed ethnic heritage.

Nonetheless, the younger, experienced brother, Atahualpa, with the support of nobles and generals, challenged the authority of Huáscar. The succession crisis following Huayna Cápac's death is often interpreted as the Sapa Inca having unwittingly destroyed the empire by setting up a contest for power between his sons. Historians also view the extreme expanse of the empire, reached under Huayna Cápac, as the underlying cause of the destruction of the Inca Empire. The conquered minorities provided willing allies for the Spanish invaders. They also provided the initial contacts with the Spanish, whose presence in the early 1520s helped spread the very disease, through trade and communication with the Inca, that eventually claimed Huayna Cápac's life.

Rebecca M. Seaman

See also: Atahualpa; Huáscar; Ninan Cuyochi; Sapa Inca; Tahuantinsuyu.

Resources

Hemming, John. *The Conquest of the Incas.* San Diego, CA: Harcourt, 1970.

MacQuarrie, Kim. *The Last Days of the Incas.* New York: Simon & Schuster, 2007.

Sancho, Pedro. *An Account of the Conquest of Peru.* Translated by Philip Ainsworth Means. New York: Cortes Society, 1917.

Titu Cusi Yupanqui. *An Inca Account of the Conquest of Peru.* Translated, Introduced and Annotated by Ralph Bauer. Boulder: University Press of Colorado, 2005.

Huexotzinco

Huexotzinco was a powerful Nahua ethnic state located in central New Spain's Upper Atoyac River Basin, to the east of the volcano Iztaccihuatl. The polity achieved regional military and political prominence by the mid-14th century, extending control over the region to the south known as Huehuequauhquechollan or Acapetlahuacan (today's Atlixco Valley). During the reign of the Aztec lord Tizoc (1481–1486), the Triple Alliance began to wage imperialist war on Huexotzinco. A formidable opponent, Huexotzinco maintained its independence from Aztec rule through its prowess in warfare and tenuous alliances with the neighboring polities of Tlaxcallan (Tlaxcala) and Chollolan (Cholula). Internal struggles between Huexotzinco's political elite and priests of the region's primary deity, Mixcoatl-Camaxtle, weakened the polity beginning around 1498. By around 1515, Huexotzinco owed allegiance to Tlaxcala, a one-time ally, demonstrating the state's relative decline over the second half of the 15th century.

In 1520 Huexotzinco allied with Hernán Cortés and the Spaniards, contributing warriors and supplies to the 1521 conquest of the Aztecs at Tenochtitlán. After the Spanish victory, Cortés claimed Huexotzinco for himself in encomienda, raising pigs there between 1521 and 1524. The area also became an important early site of Franciscan evangelization and home to the impressive 16th-century Franciscan friary of San Miguel. During Cortés's 1529 absence from New Spain, Spaniard Nuño de Guzmán infringed upon Cortés's holdings in Huexotzinco. He recruited the support of the region's indigenous elite and donations of warriors and provisions for a conquest expedition into western New Spain. In addition to bolts of cloth, arrows, and other mundane items, the polity supplied a colorful and unique feather standard bearing the earliest known image of the Virgin Mary and the Christ child produced in the indigenous Americas. Despite Huexotzinco's contributions to Spanish conquest and various petitions to Spanish authorities over the course of the 16th century, Huexotzinco never received recognition or privileges equal to those afforded to Tlaxcallan.

Erika R. Hosselkus

See also: Cholula Massacre; Cortés, Hernán; Encomienda; Franciscans, Role of; Tlaxcala, Battle of; Tenochtitlán, City of; Tenochtitlán, Spanish Rule of.

Resources

Congress, Library of. *Codice de Huexotzinco.* Mexico City: Library of Congress, Coca-Cola Export Corporation, Ediciones Multi-arte, 1995.

Córdova Tello, Mario. *El convento de San Miguel de Huejotzingo, Puebla.* Mexico City: INAH, 1992.

Dyckerhoff, Ursula. "Grupos étnicos y estratificación socio-política. Téntativa de interpretación histórica." *Indiana* 19/20 (2002/2003): 155–196.

García Icazbalceta, Joaquín. *Don fray Juan de Zumárraga, primer obispo y arzobispo de México, estudio biográfico y bibliográfico.* Mexico City: Andrade y Morales, 1881.

Lockhart, James, ed. *We People Here: Nahuatl Accounts of the Conquest of Mexico.* Berkeley: University of California Press, 1993.

Muñoz Camargo, Diego, Luis Reyes García, and Javier Lira Toledo. *Historia de Tlaxcala: Ms. 210 de la Biblioteca Nacional de París.* Tlaxcala, México: Gobierno del Estado de Tlaxcala; Centro de Investigaciones y Estudios Superiores en Antropología Social; Universidad Autónoma de Tlaxcala, 1998.

Pilar, García del. "Relación de la entrada de Nuño de Guzmán." In *Nueva colección de documentos para la historia de México,* edited by Joaquín García Icazbalceta. Mexico City: Andrade y Morales, 1886–1892.

Prem, Hanns J. *Matrícula de Huexotzinco.* Graz, Austria: Akademische Druck- u. Verlagsanstalt, 1974.

Prem, Hanns J. *Milpa y hacienda: Tenencia de la tierra indígena y española en la cuenca del Alto Atoyac, Puebla, México (1520–1650).* Mexico City and Puebla: CIESAS, Estado de Puebla, Fondo de Cultura Económica, 1988.

Salas Cuesta, Marcela. *La iglesia y el convento de Huejotzingo.* Mexico City: Universidad Autónoma de México, Instituto de Investigaciones Estéticas, 1982.

Huitzilopochtli

Huitzilopochtli is the name of a premier deity worshipped by the Mexicas, the dominant native people of northern Mexico at the time of Spanish conquest. Scholars have translated the name to mean "Hummingbird on the left," "The Hummingbird from the left," "The Hummingbird's left," or "Hummingbird from the South." The direction left had been associated with the south, hence the multiple translations.

The genesis of the deity Huitzilopochtli also has an array of variations. One version has his mother, the earth goddess Coatlicue, becoming impregnated by a ball of feathers. These feathers were gathered by Coatlicue and placed in a sash around her body or fell upon her when she was asleep. The resulting pregnancy was a matter of disgrace for another member of the Mexica pantheon: Coyolxauhqui, Coatlicue's daughter and sister to the unborn Huitzilopochtli. Coyolxauhqui rallied her 400 other brothers and led them in an attack against their mother.

Huitzilopochtli spoke to his mother from the womb, bracing her for the attack. The most common thread in this story asserts that

Huitzilopochtli, Aztec god of war, sun, and patron deity of Tenochtitlan. (Julioaldana/Dreams time.com)

Huitzilopochtli was birthed fully grown, arrayed for battle, and slayed his sister, Coyolxauhqui. After he cut off Coyolxauhqui's head, he then attacked his 400 half-brothers in turn. Decapitated by her newborn brother, Coyolxauhqui's headless body was rolled down a hill, coming apart in the process. Elements of this battle have led scholars to believe this is to represent the daily "death" and "rebirth" of celestial objects such as the sun, stars, and moon. Human sacrifices made at the base of the Temple of Huitzilopochtli on a stone designated with the likeness of Coyolxauhqui may also be tied to this creation myth.

Huitzilopochtli was associated with militaristic warrior qualities, whose divine exploits were looked to with reverence. The beginnings of Tenochtitlán are also rooted in the mythology of Huitzilopochtli. According to one tradition, the Mexica were led from their homeland of Aztlán, also referred to as the "seven caves," through a place of wilderness by following Huitzilopochtli's totem and the direction of his priests. These holy men were thought to communicate directly with their god in times of crisis, via his fast-twittering voice. This journey splintered the pilgrimage; one group left after an ill-omen; the other faction continued on, comprising the Mexica. The Mexica were told to settle on a land between lakes, and they would know it was the correct spot by a sign.

This arduous journey continued for hundreds of years, with Mexica settlements trailing in its wake. At one point Malinalxochitl, a sister of Huitzilopochtli, caused trouble for the wanderers. Huitzilopochtli rescued his people from this plight by banishing Malinalxochitl. This conflict further soured the relationship between siblings.

The Mexica arrived at Chapultepec, looking for their promised land. Besides dealing with the settlers already established in the region, they also faced a divine threat. Copil was born of Malinalxochitl and was determined to kill Huitzilopochtli. As the Mexica moved into the already settled lands, they had a range of enemies to mobilize against them. Copil, trained in sorcery by his mother, prepared to destroy his uncle and called upon the local population to turn back these Mexica invaders.

Huitzilopochtli ordered that his followers slay Copil, remove his heart, and bring it to him. The faithful successfully defeated Copil's designs, killed him as ordered, and brought his heart as instructed to their god. Huitzilopochtli ordered a priest to hurl the heart into a lake. The place where it landed was called Tlacomolco. The heart landed upon a stone that sprouted a cactus, which in turn attracted a feeding eagle. Feathers, from this predator's kills, circled the base of the cactus. This was the sign that inspired the searchers to found Tenochtitlán. Through his earthly intermediaries, Huitzilopochtli is said to have ordered the building of four quarters in the city, with a temple to him at the center.

The origin of this god, like the building of Tenochtitlán, may be much more mundane. His identity and campaigns may be based on a distant cultural hero later credited with divine attributes. Nonetheless, worship of Huitzilopochtli greatly impacted centuries of Aztec culture and remained embedded in Aztec life during the time of Spanish contact.

Michael D. Coker

See also: Aztec, or Mexica; Tenochtitlán, City of.

Resources

Clendinnen, Inga. *Aztecs: An Interpretation.* Cambridge: Cambridge University Press, 1995.

Manuel, Aguilar-Moreno. *Handbook to Life in the Aztec World.* 2nd ed. New York: Oxford University Press, 2007.

Read, Kay A., and Jason J. González. *Mesoamerican Mythology: A Guide to the Gods, Heroes, Rituals, and Beliefs of Mexico and Central America.* New York: Oxford University Press, 2002.

Human Sacrifice

Human sacrifice is the offering up of a human life, usually in honor of a deity or to appease the anger of a deity. The sacrifice of the human is often part of an attempt to commune with a deity and share in the deity's divinity. Alternatively a human life, viewed as the most valuable commodity possessed by an individual or society, may be offered to a god as an act of appeasement or expiation. There

are two main types of human sacrifice: the offering of a human to a god and the burying or killing of a human to accompany a recently deceased individual into the afterlife.

Human sacrifice was practiced by many Mesoamerican cultures. For instance, the Inca practiced human sacrifice for the accession of a new ruler to the position of Sapa Inca. As representatives of the Sun god, the Sapa Inca's death or coronation warranted extreme symbols of honor. Sometimes the ceremonies included the burying of selected children alive in honor of the Inca Sun god. As in other regions of Latin America conquered by the Spanish, the Inca practice of human sacrifice gave added justification to the invading conquerors for seizing the region, its power, and controlling the population, presumably as a means to convert them from existing pagan practices.

Human sacrifice is most closely associated with Aztec society, for thousands of people were sacrificed each year in Aztec rituals. Aztec mythology tells that the creator-gods sacrificed themselves in order to create the world and life on Earth, including humans. For this reason, the Aztec believed that they needed to offer the gods human lives in order to show their gratitude to the Sun gods and earth deities who had brought forth life.

Three myths in particular explain the Aztec need for sacrifice. One myth tells that in order to create the current race of humans the god Quetzalcoatl retrieved the bones of the dead from the underworld and transported them to the land of origin, Tamoanchan. There the bones were ground into a powder, which was then mixed with the blood of the gods to create new human life. Thus the Aztec believed that they owed their existence to the self-sacrifice of the gods. Another creation myth tells that when Quetzalcoatl joined forces with another god,

Aztec human sacrifice on Templo Mayor, Tenochtitlán, depicting waiting victims as well as skulls of past sacrificial victims. (De Agostini Picture Library/The Bridgeman Art Library)

Tezcatlipoca, to create the current world, they tore apart the goddess Tlaltecuhtli in order to form the universe. The goddess was distressed at her treatment and needed to receive human blood and hearts in return for sustaining human life. A third myth tells that after the creation of the Earth, its people, and their food and drink, all the gods gathered in Teotihuacan, the place of darkness, in order to discuss who was to become the new sun. The god Nanahuatl was elected and after a period of penance he leapt into divine flames and was reborn as a sun in the east. However, the sun would not travel across the skies and would only follow a path across the heavens once all the other gods had sacrificed themselves, too. Only this self-sacrifice by the gods could revive the sun and set it in

motion. Thus, the Aztec believed that they had to feed the sun with a never-ending supply of sacrificial victims in order to prevent the sun from losing the energy it required to keep in motion.

The Aztec conducted human sacrifice for purely ritualistic and spiritual reasons and not as a bloody form of entertainment. Indeed the Aztec did not use the term human sacrifice but rather *nextlaualli,* meaning the sacred debt payment to the gods. As the most precious commodity, human life was chosen as the means of repayment.

Aztec human sacrifice was carried out by various methods. The most frequent methods of sacrifice included excision of the heart followed by decapitation, decapitation followed by heart excision, slitting the throat, flaying, immolation followed by heart excision, scratching followed by heart excision, shooting with arrows followed by heart excision, dropping a victim from a height, drowning, and burying alive. Other less popular means of sacrifice included impaling, stoning, bludgeoning, ripping out entrails, crushing victims in a falling house, and squeezing them in a net. In order to ensure a fresh supply of humans to sacrifice, the Aztecs waged war on neighboring peoples to capture new victims. Thousands of prisoners were sacrificed at single events, with the victims of sacrifice chosen for their outstanding attributes. For instance, victims were often warriors invested with great bravery. It was considered a great honor to be chosen as a sacrificial victim, for as a sacrificial offering, the victim was assured a place in paradise.

Human sacrifices corresponded to festival days, usually to honor a particular deity, and each had its own name in Nahuatl. One example of a sacrificial event was the yearly festival of Toxcatl held in Tlacochcalco, dedicated to the god Tezcatlipoca. Each year a handsome young man was chosen to impersonate Tezcatlipoca on the day of the sacrifice, and for the year running up to the sacrificial day the youth would be afforded a life of luxury and presented with the best of everything, including four mistresses. The chosen victim was treated with great respect; he was seen as the living embodiment of the god. On the day of the sacrifice, various rites and rituals were performed, then the youth was placed on his back on a stone slab and, using a ceremonial knife, a priest would stab him in the chest, remove his heart and show the still-pulsating organ to the assembled audience. Another sacrificial feast day was Tlacaxipehualiztli, held in honor of Xipe Totec, Huitzilopochtli and Tequizin-Mayahuel at the Temple of Yopico. During this festival, captured warriors and slaves would impersonate the gods and the sacrifice would consist of the removal of the victim's heart and the flaying of their skin. The skin would then be draped over a youth chosen to represent a deity.

The Aztec extreme practices of human sacrifice shocked the invading Spanish. Hernán Cortés specifically targeted this practice in his communications with the Aztec leaders. As in the later case of Pizarro's forces in Peru, the Spanish in Mexico and even the Caribbean used the indigenous practices of sacrificing humans to their pantheon of gods as justification for conquering, enslaving, and culturally assimilating the native population.

Victoria Williams

See also: Cortés, Hernán; Nahuatl Language; Pizarro, Francisco; Quetzalcoatl; Sapa Inca.

Resources

Aguilar-Moreno. *Manuel Handbook to Life in the Aztec World.* Oxford: Oxford University Press, 2006.

Berghaus, Günter. "Ritual and Crisis: Survival Techniques of Humans and Other Animals," in *Performance Research: On Ritual*, edited by Ric Allsopp and Günter Berghaus. Center for Performance Research 3, no. 3 (Winter 1998): 65–73.

Bremmer, Jan ed. *Studies in the History and Anthropology of Religion 1: The Strange World of Human Sacrifice.* Leuven: Peeters, 2007.

Scott Littleton, C. ed. *Gods, Goddesses, and Mythology.* Vol. 11. New York: Marshall Cavendish Corporation, 2005.

Hurin

The term Hurin is typically a reference to the lower region of the city of Cuzco. Hurin Cuzco was the original seat of authority for the Inca dynasty that governed the city, and was also referred to as Coricancha. Though some discrepancy exists, most resources attribute the division of the city into two parts, an upper (Hanan) and lower (Hurin) section, to the reign of Inca Roca in the middle of the 14th century.

The term also refers to one of two ruling moieties in the Inca society. The Hurin moiety represented the lower dynastic branch of power. This reference to moieties is not unique to the Inca, but was common to several native societies throughout the region, long before the Inca came to power in the region of Cuzco.

Rebecca M. Seaman

See also: Cuzco; Hanan.

Resources

Davies, Nigel. *The Incas*. Niwot: University of Colorado Press, 1995.

Zuidema, R. T. "Hierarchy and Space in Incaic Social Organization." *Ethnohistory* 30, no. 2 (Spring 1983): 49–75.

Inca Civil War

The internal conflict in the Inca Empire, between descendants of the Sapa Inca Huayna Cápac, was fought for nearly five years over who should hold ultimate authority. The Sapa Inca, a hereditary position, was supreme head of the government, military, and all spiritual matters within the Inca Empire. When the 10th Sapa Inca, Topa Inca Yupanqui, died in the latter part of the 15th century, his first-born son, Sapa Inca Huayna Cápac, became the ruler of the Tahuantinsuyu kingdom, an empire spanning the Andes for nearly 3,000 miles. Huayna Cápac's principle wife (first sister) lived in Cuzco with their sons, Ninan Cuyochi and Huáscar. Huayna Cápac had a third son, Manco Cápac, with another of his sisters. The Sapa Inca spent his last years in Quito, Ecuador, with his Ecuadorian wife (daughter of the last Shyri ruler of Quito whose kingdom Huayna Cápac had conquered) and their son Atahualpa. It was Atahualpa and his half-brother Ninan Cuyochi, who accompanied Huayna Cápac on military campaigns and were his constant companions. Huayna Cápac died circa 1526, possibly from smallpox, and first-born Ninan Cuyochi became Sapa Inca. Ninan Cuyochi was Sapa Inca only briefly before he too succumbed to smallpox in 1527. Huayna Cápac possibly suspected that Ninan Cuyochi's reign would be short. Subverting the fundamental laws of the empire, Huayna Cápac decreed Huáscar and Atahualpa should share power in the event of Ninan

Cuyochi's death. Atahualpa would inherit the ancient kingdom of Quito, leaving Huáscar to rule of the rest of the kingdom, centered out of Cuzco. Along with the northern kingdom, Atahualpa inherited a large, experienced and loyal army with two capable commanders: Quizquiz and Chullcuchima, Atahualpa's maternal uncle.

The two brothers effectively shared power for a while, but within five years, civil war broke out. Huáscar's troops captured and imprisoned Atahualpa near Tumebamba, in the district of Cañaris, within Quito territory. Managing to escape, Atahualpa marched his army 60 miles south of Quito, defeating Huáscar's forces at Ambato. At Tumebamba, Atahualpa slaughtered the Cañaris people, who were loyal to Huáscar, and razed the city. He then created a base camp at Cajamarca, remaining there rather than entering enemy territory. As Atahualpa's troops neared Cuzco, Huáscar followed the poor advice of his priests, which was waiting until Atahualpa's troops were near the city before meeting for battle on the plains of Quipaipan, contrary to common military logic. Atahualpa's army was more experienced, well led, and disciplined; Huáscar's army had been hastily assembled. Nonetheless, both forces fought ferociously over an entire day for control of all of Tahuantinsuyu. Atahualpa finally captured and imprisoned Huáscar in a mountain stronghold at Xuaxa. Victorious, he then invited all Incas to Cuzco to partition the kingdom between Atahualpa and Huáscar. Once the leading Inca leaders of the empire were gathered, Atahualpa's men slaughtered them to ensure no one held a higher claim to the throne than their leader. Atahualpa became Sapa Inca, but only briefly, for these events happened in the spring of 1532, a few months before the arrival of the Spanish.

Francisco Pizarro, who had arrived in Peru about a year earlier, learned that part of Atahualpa's army was encamped about 10 or 12 days away, near Cajamarca. Pizarro had only 177 men and 67 horses by the time he arrived at the city where the Sapa Inca's forces were camped. He entered the city on November 15, 1532, and used deception to capture Atahualpa. Captured, the newly recognized ruler of the Inca Empire was held for ransom.

Meanwhile, Huáscar remained a heavily guarded prisoner of the Sapa Inca at Andamarca. When Atahualpa learned Pizarro was considering which brother to recognize as Sapa Inca, Atahualpa ordered that Huáscar be murdered. Pizarro, not satisfied with the sizeable ransom paid for the release of the Inca emperor, found Atahualpa to be an increased liability. He charged the Inca with the murder of Huáscar and sentenced him to be burned alive in the plaza at Cajamarca on August 29, 1533. When Atahualpa agreed to convert to Roman Catholicism, Pizarro garroted him instead. The execution of the emperor, on the heels of the recent struggle for power, resulted in the kingdom falling into chaos. Pizarro thought the Spanish appointment of an heir to the Inca throne might restore social order and secure the region under Spanish control. The plethora of immediate descendants presented the conquistador with a dilemma. Huáscar's younger brother, Manco, still lived in Cuzco, but Atahualpa's younger brother, Toparca (Túpac Hualpa), was nearby in Cajamarca. Pizarro approved the appointment of Toparca, who briefly became Sapa Inca. When Toparca suddenly died, rumor spread that he was poisoned.

Manco claimed the throne, and Pizarro supported the claim, using it as an opportunity to guarantee the placement of Spanish officials in important positions within the Inca imperial structure, and to replace the Inca Sun god with Roman Catholicism.

With Manco Inca on the throne in the traditional capital of Cuzco in 1535, and with Atahualpa's general, Challcuchina, executed, it appeared the Spanish had firm control over the empire in and around the capital. General Quizquiz tried to stop the Spanish takeover, but his own men killed him. Assured of Spanish hegemony, Pizarro left his younger brothers to rule Cuzco as the advisors to the figurehead Inca ruler, Manco. This period also saw the rise of Catholic influence in the city, removing much of the indigenous religious practices and inserting Catholicism instead. In the midst of pious attempts by religious orders to gain control, and the abusive treatment of Manco Inca by the Pizarro brothers, the military broke into factions. The rupture left an opening for the puppet Sapa Inca to flee from Cuzco and revive a government in exile.

The deaths of Huáscar and Atahualpa brought disarray to Tahuantinsuyu, and the confederation began to crumble. The resulting extension of the original civil war was the pivotal event that allowed the Spanish to achieve their goal of conquest, for without the revolution dividing the Tahuantinsuyu, a handful of Spanish soldiers could never have prevailed over the military might of the largest civilization of the pre-Columbian Americas. The corruption of the Pizarro brother's in their ruling of the Inca almost resulted in the reunification of the empire. Yet, the division between the *panaqas* seeking control of the empire for the various branches of the ruling elite, the bitterness from almost 10 years of political and military struggles, combined with suspicions of Inca collaboration with the Spanish in poisoning legitimate heirs to the throne, proved too hard to overcome. Manco Inca did escape and began a decades-long struggle against the Spanish. However, the previous Inca Civil War prevented his authority from ever extending throughout the entire empire.

Debra J. Sheffer

See also: Atahualpa; Cajamarca, Battle of; Cañari; Huayna Cápac; Huáscar; Manco Inca Yupanqui; Quizquiz; Tahuantinsuyu.

Resources

D'Altroy, Terrence N. *The Incas.* Hoboken, NJ: Wiley-Blackwell, 2003.

Davies, Nigel. *The Incas.* Boulder: University Press of Colorado, 2007.

Gabai, Rafael Varón. *Francisco Pizarro and His Brothers: The Illusion of Power in Sixteenth-Century Peru.* Translated by Javier Flores Espinoza. Norman: University of Oklahoma Press, 1997.

Gamboa, Pedro Sarmiento de. *History of the Incas.* Translated and Edited by Sir Clements Markham. Cambridge, UK: Hakluyt Society, 1907.

Hemming, John. *The Conquest of the Incas.* Tequesta, FL: Mariner Press, 2003.

MacQuarrie, Kim. *The Last Days of the Incas.* New York, New York: Simon & Schuster, 2007.

Inca Elite

The peoples of the Andes developed a class system based on inherited status long before the Inca Empire. The state of constant warfare within Peru consolidated power in the warrior class and gradually within several families. Inca elites resembled elites of other kingdoms in Peru, with a royal family claiming descent from the sun. Success in war allowed the Inca to secure more goods and productive territory for elite use and exploitation, which allowed for further conquests.

Though ruled by an emperor, Inca elites exercised considerable influence. The royal family's utilization of multiple wives and the absence of primogenitor allowed the nobility to regularly intervene during succession crises. Below the royal family were 10 elite familial groups, the *panaqa*, which emerged through a system of split inheritance, whereby a royal successor inherited the position of emperor while other descendents inherited property in order to continue their ancestor's legacy, including looking after his mummy. These 10 groups were split between upper and lower Cuzco (Hurin), with upper Cuzco families (Hanan) as the more prestigious. The *panaqa* advised the emperor and served in the highest state offices. Another 10 familial groups, more distant relatives of the royal family, existed in status below the *panaqa*. The *panaqa* maintained residences in the center of Cuzco and the other kin groups further out. A third group of elite was "Inca by privilege," ethnic Quechua groups who lived near Cuzco early on during the Inca conquests, and then others granted the privilege for meritorious service.

The class system was readily apparent in dress, homes, and other signs. Spaniards, upon their arrival, immediately picked up on this and called the elite "orejones" (large ears) given the gold disks that elite members wore in their ears. Local elites were expected to live four months of the year in Cuzco and have one male child there year round to be acculturated into Inca ways. Elite members were exempt from taxation, could own their own estates, could not be tried by officials of lesser status than themselves, and generally received more lenient punishments if they did commit a crime. Especially honored members of the nobility could ride upon a litter. The emperor regularly granted gifts to members of his family, the court, and the nobility, using the produce of the state, and they in turn made gifts to others such that it had a trickle-down effect. Gift giving helped create relationships of reciprocity and assured local loyalty across ethnic lines. During times of war, elite orejones served as the guard force that surrounded the emperor. Nobles were rewarded for valorous battlefield conduct with offices or lands.

The emperor Pachacutin (Pachucuti) in 1438, and his son Tupac Inca after their conquest of Cuzco's neighbors and the creation of an Inca Empire, needed elites to administer it. Pachucuti divided the empire into four quarters, each headed by an *apu.* Below them were 88 regional governors who carried out executive and judicial functions; in almost all cases these men were ethnically Inca. The Inca used a decimal system of government with officials overseeing households of 10, 50, 100, 500, 1,000, 5,000, and 10,000. Inca officials supervised a local bureaucracy coopted into the empire. Each decimal unit was led by a *kuraka* who generally was part of a local elite, and who inherited his position, though confirmation of his office needed to come from the Inca. Traditional chiefs thus continued to exercise influence much as they had before the Inca conquest. Local elites' male children were educated in Cuzco, partially as hostages for good behavior, but also to assimilate the future elite into Inca culture. If an official proved particularly capable, he might be named an Inca by privilege. At the same time, Cuzco exercised due diligence on local conditions by utilizing inspectors who reported to an inspector general, who in turn was generally a member of the royal family.

Spaniards effectively replaced the Inca elite. With the Spanish system of governance,

which initially recognized the rule of Manco Inca, the system persevered in areas near the capital. However, in more distant areas, the bureaucracy transitioned back to a system of local leadership and regional elites increased their prerogatives. Under the Spanish, Inca servants who were free of tribute, *yanaconas,* began to play some of the essential facilitator roles in dealing with indigenous peoples, effectively replacing much of the bureaucratic Inca elite.

Michael Beauchamp

See also: Cuzco; Gifting, Practice of; Hanan; Hurin; Pachacutin; Quechua Language; Túpac Inca Yupanqui; *Yanaconas.*

Resources

D'Altroy, Terence N. *The Incas.* Malden, MA: Wiley-Blackwell, 2003.

Hemming, John. *The Conquest of the Incas.* New York: Harcourt, Brace, Jovanovich, 1970.

MacQuarrie, Kim. *The Last Days of the Incas.* New York: Simon & Schuster, 2007.

Inca Roads

The Inca road system, or *capac ñan,* was a huge, complex symbol of the authority and power of the Inca Empire. This network of highways reached across mountains, deserts, and jungles, and included over 25,000 miles of roads serviced and maintained by the people as part of their obligation to the state. The roads were vital for transporting goods and people rapidly throughout the vast empire. The core of the highway system, and a well-engineered canal system, were already in place in areas heavily occupied by earlier empires. This gave the Incas an advantage as they came to power, enabling them to move their armies quickly from place to place. The highway system was an administrative and communication tool, and could only be used by authorized individuals on imperial business. Commoners could not use the highways without obtaining special permission.

The backbone of the imperial highway system consisted of two main north-south roads. The coastal highway began in Tumbez on Peru's northern border with Ecuador, and followed the coastline south, eventually meandering inland to Chile's rich central valley. The highland route passed through the Andes Mountains, extending from Quito, Ecuador, to Mendoza in modern Argentina. Shorter, lateral highways connected the main highways at towns and administrative centers. Incrementally smaller roads and trails connected the tiniest towns and villages to the larger network.

Inca roads varied greatly in width and construction, adapting to local environmental challenges. The wheel did not exist in Inca culture, so roads were designed for foot traffic and pack animals like the llama. Therefore, unlike traditional modern highways, Inca roads could ascend steep slopes with stone steps or sharp switchbacks, and be as little as three feet wide. In easier terrain, roads were a more typically 13 to 16 feet across, expanding to 33 feet or more as one approached a city or administrative center. Road surfaces ranged from smooth paving stones on well-traveled routes to dirt footpaths in inhospitable regions. Where the ground was marshy, raised causeways were constructed. Culverts and gutters diverted the water from the road surface, making them passable in any weather. Low walls were often constructed on the margins to keep them clear of windborne debris. Tunnels and retaining walls were frequently seen features in higher altitudes.

Bridges were a critical part of the highway system. The Andes are extremely rugged, with steep canyons and fast moving rivers. Simple stone bridges were constructed over the narrowest bodies of water. Wider rivers required wood superstructures, often several trees laid side by side, with the surface smoothed and filled in with dirt. The most remarkable invention of the Inca culture though was the woven fiber suspension bridges spanning deep gorges in the central Andes. The materials used to weave the ropes varied by location, and these bridges required nearly continual maintenance. Citizens paid a tax to the government in the form of labor, and the maintenance of the roads and bridges was a large part of this service.

The road system facilitated rapid communication and the transportation of goods throughout the empire. Delivery of messages and packages was done by trained runners, or *chasquis,* and operated in a relay system. *Chasquis* could pass messages over 150 miles per day, surpassing even carriers on horseback. Tambos, or rest stops, provided food and shelter for travelers and traders. They varied in size and services provided depending on their location, but over 2,000 tambos were established across the empire at intervals of a day's walk.

The Inca highway system with its tambos, storage centers, and post houses with *chasquis,* linked the Inca Empire into a single communication, transportation, and administration network spanning thousands of miles of rugged terrain. It enabled government officials, military troops, and caravans of goods and products to travel swiftly and safely to their destinations. Citizens were never beyond either the protection or supervision of the state. Inca roads served as both the means and the symbol of the power of the Inca Empire.

Jill M. Church

See also: *Chasquis.*

Resources

Hyslop, John. *The Inka Road System.* Orlando, FL: Academic Press, 1984.

Johnson, Robert W. "The Irony of the Capac Nan." *The Social Studies* 83 (1992): 21–24.

Malpass, Michael A. *Daily Life in the Inca Empire.* Westport, CT: Greenwood Press, 1996.

McEwan, Gordon. *The Incas: New Perspectives.* New York: W. W. Norton, 2006.

Suarez, Ananda Cohen and Jeremy James George. *Handbook to Life in the Inca World.* New York: Facts on File, 2011.

Incas

At the time of the Spanish conquest of Peru in the 16th century, the Inca Empire stretched over a region that encompassed the Andes Mountains in South America. Named for the ethnic group that dominated one of the New World's greatest indigenous empires, the Inca Empire ruled over a domain that implemented massive public work projects and imposed a system of government, the power of which was unrivaled in South America.

According to Inca legends, the first group of Incas migrated to the Cuzco Valley in the 13th century. They soon dominated the surrounding region and achieved victory over the Chanca tribes in the mid-15th century. The leader of the Incas at that time, Pachacutin, built an imperial system of government at Cuzco and forced regional tribes to become vassals to the Inca lords. By 1500, the Inca Empire included most of present-day Peru and parts of Ecuador, Chile, Argentina, and Bolivia.

Much of what is considered Inca culture was assimilated from the people already populating the region. The Quechua language was a common form of language spoken by numerous indigenous peoples in the central Andes region. Commonly spoken prior to the rise of the Incas, it was used by them to help unite their growing empire. The class structure and local religious/political structure also merged into the Inca society from commonly held traits found in a wide variety of pre-Inca Andean cultures. The local lords or *kurakas* were responsible for overseeing the religious rituals as well as the acquisition and distribution of provisions for the general populace and for any religious ceremonies.

Inca culture also was divided into kinship groups known as *ayllus,* both the basic close family kinship groups and the large community kinship groups. Again, this was a practice utilized by neighboring cultures and used by the Incas as a unifying factor for their growing empire. A unique aspect introduced into the kinship concept by the Incas, probably by the emperor Pachacutin, was the imperial kinship group, or *panaqa*. This structure included not only the immediate family of the emperor or Sapa Inca, but also incorporated future descendants and the servants of the family. The *panaqa* of the Sapa Inca supported the emperor during life, and continued to serve by caring for his mummy long after death. As a new emperor was chosen, he developed a new *panaqa* structure from out of the old one he had himself belonged to prior to ascending to the throne. In this fashion, with each subsequent ruling Inca, the old *panaqa* structure would fracture and compete for attention and economic support in the form of lands and positions that helped sustain the family and servants of the *panaqa*.

Other features that predated the Inca included the presence of dual moieties representing military and priestly duties. Embraced by the Incas, these moieties became known as the Hanan and Hurin dynasties. It was the Hanan dynasty with its military focus that was responsible for the 15th-century rapid spread of the empire, which reached its greatest extent through northern expansion under the emperor, Huayna Cápac.

In 1527, Huayna Cápac died of smallpox. The disease had been transmitted across the Andean region by natives in contact with members of the Spanish expeditions across Central and South America. The deaths of Huayna Cápac and his appointed heir (who died soon after the emperor) set off an internal civil war for control of the Inca Empire. Emperor Huáscar became the ruler in 1527 but was challenged by his brother, Atahualpa, who controlled a large part of the Inca Army. By 1532, Atahualpa captured Huáscar, imprisoned him, and took control of the empire as Emperor Atahualpa, just as the Spanish were entering his territory.

The rise of the Spanish in the Andes brought forth those elements already present in the Inca culture that contributed to internal rifts among the Incas and enabled the invaders to turn competing groups of indigenous peoples against each other. In particular, the rapid succession of one Sapa Inca after another—with five serving as emperors in a period of seven years—fractured the royal kinship units into competing *panaqas*. Additionally, with the strain of five years of internal civil war between Huáscar and Atahualpa, followed by the demands and ravages of the invading Spanish, the local *kurakas* found it increasingly difficult to sustain adequate stores of goods for hard times ahead.

Spanish forces under Francisco Pizarro attacked and captured Atahualpa near the town of Cajamarca. In a surprise attack, the Spanish, with far superior weapons and the benefit of surprise, slaughtered the Inca entourage, captured Atahualpa, and held the Inca ruler hostage. The Incas paid a huge ransom in gold and silver for the release of Atahualpa, but the Spanish killed him anyway in the summer of 1533.

The Spanish used their new-found authority in the region to appoint a series of puppet Incas that helped them maintain control. When they appointed Emperor Manco Inca Yupanqui, in Cuzco, the Spanish were initially firmly in control, until their abuses forced him into a government in exile and years of armed rebellion. From their remote capital of Vilcabamba, the Inca continued to resist, using Spanish arms and even their horses to wage war against the foreigners. Though the Inca continued to exist in the small enclave in the Amazonia region for several years, the Spanish had definitively conquered the former Inca Empire, and the last Inca ruler, Túpac Amaru, was captured and executed in 1572.

ABC-CLIO

See also: Atahualpa; *Ayllus*; Cajamarca, Battle of; Chanca; European Diseases, Role of; Huáscar; Huayna Cápac; *Kuraka*; Manco Inca Yupanqui; Pachacutin; Pizarro, Francisco; Quechua; Sapa Inca; Túpac Amaru; Vilcabamba.

Resources

Adelaar, William F. H. *The Languages of the Andes (Cambridge Language Surveys).* Cambridge: Cambridge University Press, 2007.

Cobo, Bernabe, *History of the Inca Empire: An Account of the Indians' Customs and Their Origin, Together with a Treatise on Inca Legends, History, and Social Institutions.* Translated and edited by Rowland Hamilton, Texas Pan American Series. Austin: University of Texas Press, 1979.

Davies, Nigel. *The Incas.* Niwot: University of Colorado Press, 1995.

MacQuarrie, Kim. *Last Days of the Inca.* New York: Simon & Schuster, 2007.

Williams, Brian. *The Kingfisher Reference Atlas: An A-Z Guide to Countries of the World.* New York: Kingfisher Books, 1993.

Zuidema, R. T. "Hierarchy and Space in Incaic Social Organization." *Ethnohistory* 30, no. 2 (Spring 1983): 49–75.

Inca-Spanish War

The Spanish conquest of the Inca Empire of Peru was even more of an amazing feat than the conquest of the Aztec Empire in Mexico. The Inca Empire was highly centralized and was able to field many thousands of soldiers. Unlike those who conquered the Aztecs, the Spanish in Peru were unable to rely extensively on rival groups of natives as allies. The destruction of Inca society and the looting of the empire are one of the great tragedies of Latin American history.

By 1532, the Spanish were well established in Mexico. The fabulous wealth of the Aztec Empire encouraged adventurers to seek their fortunes among the other native groups, of which they became aware. Many of the natives of Central America were soon attacked by groups of Spaniards. As they expanded into the region of modern day Panama, the Spanish learned of another great empire to their south.

The Inca Empire, centered in modern-day Peru, included parts of Bolivia, Chile, Colombia, and Ecuador. It was a prosperous political entity, based on the exchange of goods from one climatic area with those of differing climatic areas. The empire was tied together with roads, designed for foot traffic, but equivalent in quality and extent to those of imperial Rome. The Inca Empire was highly centralized with a bureaucracy of provincial and local authorities, or *kurakas*. The ultimate power rested with the emperor, or Sapa Inca.

Militarily, a total of 90,000 men could be mobilized, based on universal conscription. The conscription was limited by the need for the farmer-soldiers to return to their homes to plant and harvest the crops that sustained their communities and the empire. The army was supported by strategically placed storehouses of food and weapons. The lack of horses for use in transportation and cavalry style attacks presented a weakness, though it was countered by the inability of the Spanish horses to cross the numerous suspended rope bridges. The greatest weakness of the Incas was their failure to use metal for weapons or to develop effective slashing weapons.

In 1531, an expedition headed by Francisco Pizarro sailed south from Darien, on Panama's west coast. It consisted of 180 men, 37 horses, and 2 cannons. The small army

Artistic rendition of the Inca-Spanish military conflict, pitting the Spanish guns and horses against the Inca armed with bows and arrows in the jungles of the Inca Empire. (Library of Congress)

landed at Tumbes on the Peruvian coast. In 1532, Pizarro led his men inland, and they climbed up into the Andes until they reached Cajamarca, a relatively small city on a plateau on the eastern slopes of the Andes. On November 16, 1532, Pizarro met with Atahualpa, emperor of the Incas who was encamped outside of Cajamarca, recently having defeated his half-brother, Huáscar, in a five-year civil war for power over the empire. Atahualpa was accompanied by 30,000 warriors (exaggerated figures of 80,000 were reported by Pizarro). Proclaiming his friendship, Pizarro lured Atahualpa and 3,500 mostly unarmed followers into a meeting in the great square at Cajamarca. Pizarro exhorted the emperor and his followers to accept Christianity, but Atahualpa, unfamiliar with the concept of books, threw the Bible that Pizarro's priest presented him to the ground. The Spaniards interpreted the act as the signal to attack. From hidden positions around the square, the conquistadors opened fire on the Incas and cut them down from all sides. Pizarro himself seized Atahualpa and took him prisoner. The steel armor and weapons of the Spanish were nearly impervious to the few weapons present among the diplomatic delegation of Incas.

After the Battle of Cajamarca, Pizarro demanded and received a huge ransom of gold and silver for Atahualpa. The Inca, desperate to protect their Sapa Inca, representative of their Sun god, Inti, scattered to various sectors of the empire to gather wealth in the form of gold plates, idols, and other items of silver and gems. While the process of collecting and presenting the ransom was underway, Atahualpa, still treated as an imperial hostage, sent his own messengers out to order the execution of his half-brother to prevent Huáscar from aligning with the Spanish. With the successful collection of the ransom, Pizarro reneged on his original conditions. Instead of releasing Atahualpa, Pizarro declared the Sapa Inca guilty of murdering his own brother and had him executed for conspiracy and heresy.

Pizarro was joined by additional Spaniards under his partner in the Inca expedition, Diego de Almagro. Accompanied by the newly appointed Sapa Inca, Túpac Huallpa (selected by Pizarro and approved by Inca priests), the two conquistadors moved against the Inca capital city of Cuzco. En route to the capital, the new emperor fell ill and died. The Incas were virtually paralyzed by the repeated loss of their emperors, as well as the continued division within the empire caused by the recent civil war. The city fell virtually without bloodshed in November 1533, which gave the Spanish a huge bounty of gold and silver. The Spanish were able to assume control over the Inca Empire and crowned Manco Inca Yupanqui as a puppet emperor.

The conquest of Cuzco and Spanish appointment of Manco Inca is typically viewed as the culmination of the Spanish conquest and end of the Inca-Spanish war. However, Pizarro's scattering of his forces to locate and collect even more wealth, combined with his brothers' abuse of the new Sapa Inca, brought about unexpected resistance. The Incas revolted under Manco Inca and laid siege to Cuzco in 1536. When they were unable to take the city, many of the conscripted Inca soldiers gave up and returned to their homes and crops. The continued resistance under Manco Inca, known as the Neo-Inca movement, continued until his death in the 1544.

Tim J. Watts

See also: Almagro, Diego de; Atahualpa; Cajamarca, Battle of; Horses, Impact of; Huáscar; *Kuraka*; Manco Inca Yupanqui; Pizarro, Francisco; Sapa Inca; Túpac Huallpa.

Resources

Bernand, Carmen. *The Incas: Empire of Blood and Gold.* London: Thames & Hudson, 1994.

Heath, Ian. *Armies of the Sixteenth Century: The Armies of the Aztec and Inca Empires.* Vol. 2. Guernsey, UK: Foundry Books, 1999.

Hemming, John. *The Conquest of the Incas.* New York: Harvest Books, 1970.

Kessell, John L., ed. *Remote beyond Compare.* Albuquerque: University of New Mexico Press, 1989.

Means, Philip A. *The Fall of the Inca Empire and the Spanish Rule in Peru, 1530–1780.* New York: Gordian Press, 1971.

Ulrich, Laurel Thatcher. *Good Wives: Image and Reality in the Lives of Women of Northern New England, 1650–1750.* New York: Alfred A. Knopf, 1982.

Varón Gabai, Rafael. *Francisco Pizarro and His Brothers: The Illusion of Power in Sixteenth-Century Peru.* Oklahoma City: University of Oklahoma Press, 1997.

Inca-Spanish War, Causes of

The causes of the Inca-Spanish War of 1531–1533 can be traced to the conditions of Spanish society in the 16th century, the frail structure of Inca society in the 1530s, and Hernán Cortés's recent conquest of the Aztecs of Mexico. For the Incas, the recent death of Emperor Huayna Cápac left two competing sons vying for authority. Recent outbreaks of disease also played a role in the Spanish conquest. For the Spanish, the oft-cited rationales of "God, Gold, and Glory" driving conquistadores proves inadequate. In reality, conquistadores such as Francisco Pizarro were driven almost exclusively by glory, or a desire for status.

Of illegitimate birth, Pizarro sailed to Hispaniola in 1502, where he served in the military forces of the governor there. He accompanied Vasco Núñez de Balboa to Panama in 1513, where he remained as a colonizer. Upon hearing of great wealth obtained by Cortés in Mexico, Pizarro undertook a series of voyages, seeking wealth and thereby an increase in his social rank. His first voyage, in 1524, proved unsuccessful and costly. His second, in 1526–1527, threatened to repeat the failures of the first until his second-in-command encountered an Inca raft containing gold, silver, gems, and beautiful woven cloth. Unconvinced of the potential for wealth and conquest to the south, Panama's governor refused Pizarro's request for another voyage. Returning to Spain, Pizarro sought support from the king for an expedition to discover the source of the valuable metals. There he encountered Cortés, whose personal success inspired the ambitions of Pizarro. The increased wars of empire under Carlos I of Spain (Charles V of the Holy Roman Empire) necessitated not only increased wealth from the New World, but also securing large territories as a means of preventing competing European powers from obtaining their own American colonial empires. The Spanish hopes for further acquisitions of wealth in America resulted in the king granting Pizarro the title of governor over all South American territories he could claim and bring under Spanish control. With 180 men and a small fleet, Pizarro left Spain in 1530.

The Inca territory Pizarro set out to conquer was large and diverse. This extremely hierarchical kingdom, stretching 32 latitudinal degrees from Ecuador to southern Chile, was the largest empire on earth at the time. To Pizarro, the rumors of great wealth held a strong attraction, as did news of a civil war within the Inca Empire. After costly struggles along a rugged coastline, Pizarro headed inland, where he encountered the forces of the new Inca emperor, Atahualpa, at Cajamarca. The emperor had recently achieved victory in the ongoing conflict with his brother Huáscar. Pizarro's encounter with Atahualpa and his extensive army of men gathered in the valley at Cajamarca placed the small Spanish contingent at an extreme disadvantage. After a brief, tense meeting, the conquistador requested a meeting with the emperor the next day. The Spanish concealed their artillery and cavalry in the stone arcades surrounding the square of the city. Fearing an ambush by the Incas, the Spanish sent out the expedition's priest to meet Atahualpa, with a prearranged signal for attack if needed. The priest offered the emperor a gift, in the form of a worn Bible, as he informed the Inca leader of the need to repent and confess the Christian faith. When Atahualpa tossed the seemingly valueless gift aside, the sign for attack was given, catching the Incas off guard and resulting in thousands of natives massacred without a single Spanish loss during the Battle of Cajamarca.

Well aware of the success of Cortés in the use of a royal hostage, Pizarro captured Atahualpa for the purpose of ransom and control. The ransom offered was a room filled with gold and silver. In accordance with ransom provisions, Pizarro, who melted the precious metals into bars and sent it for shipment back to Spain, received the wealth. However, increasing tensions in the region revealed the somewhat delayed organization of Inca forces to lay ambush to the Spanish expeditionary force. Far outnumbered, Pizarro decided to count on the divisions within the empire and executed Atahualpa.

Pizarro's strategy was to divide and conquer, seeking alliances with local subjugated villages. The strategy benefited from the extremely hierarchical structure of the Incas

and from the recent outbreak of disease in the Inca Empire. Smallpox began spreading through the empire in 1524–1525, killing Huayna Cápac, one of his possible heirs, and many other close relatives of authority in 1526–1527. Military leadership of the empire was decimated by the epidemic. The long incubation period and high numbers of fatalities, combined with the superb network of roads connecting the otherwise isolated Inca villages, all contributed to devastating losses throughout the empire. With designated regents dead, the two younger sons of the emperor each sought control, leading to a civil war.

Pizarro's decision to execute the successful brother, Atahualpa, gave the conquistador the opportunity to dictate the successor to the throne. Pizarro met with the military and political leaders of the Incas and designated Túpac Huallpa, brother of Atahualpa and Huáscar, as the ruler. The new emperor swore allegiance to Spain, understanding this to be the means of reacquiring power over the empire. Unfortunately for the new emperor and Pizarro, Túpac Huallpa suddenly died, leaving further disarray in the empire and diverse claimants to the throne. Pizarro's limited forces were spread even thinner by his efforts to hold strategic towns and provide escorts for shipments of gold back to Spain. Taking advantage of military plans shared by disgruntled subjects of the Incas, Pizarro secured alliances with several native towns, leaving the divided Inca forces increasingly isolated and rudderless.

Despite the continued unrest within the empire, the decision of Pizarro to send off gold bars to Spain and the dissolution of the highest echelons of Inca power helped solidify Spain's control of the vast Inca territories. Despite divisions within Pizarro's own ranks, and his eventual death, the Spanish were determined to hold and control the wealth of this distant realm.

Rebecca M. Seaman

See also: Atahualpa; Cajamarca, Battle of; Cortés, Hernán; Huáscar; Huayna Cápac; Inca Civil War; Pizarro, Francisco; Spain, Imperial Goals of.

Resources

Kelton, Paul. *Enslavement & Epidemics: Biological Catastrophe in the Native Southeast 1492–1715.* Lincoln: University of Nebraska Press, 2007.

MacQuarrie, Kim. *The Last Days of the Incas.* New York: Simon & Schuster, 2007.

Mann, Charles C. *Ancient Americans: Rewriting the History of the New World.* London: Granta Books, 2005.

Sancho, Pedro. *An Account of the Conquest of Peru.* With Preface and Translation by Philip Ainsworth Means. New York: Cortes Society, 1917.

Inca-Spanish War, Consequences of

The consequences of the Inca-Spanish War are intertwined with the relationship between disease, societal structure, and geography. Epidemics on the "virgin soil" of the Inca Empire wreaked havoc on the population, culture, and economics of the realm. These same epidemics brought about the demise of the Inca hierarchy. Despite conquest at the hands of the Spanish, the isolated location of the empire allowed for the survival of certain native cultural traits.

The political and social hierarchy of the Incas is central to understanding the outcome of the wars of conquest. The Incas gained control of a geographically and culturally fragmented empire by way of conquest, marriage, and religious precepts. Rulers of the various kingdoms and villages held vassalage relationships, often solidified through marital relations with the ruling emperor and his *panaqa,* or royal lineage (ruler, wives, children, retainers).

Further complicating this structure, the Incas believed Inca rulers created a new *panaqa* upon ascending to the throne. The old *panaqa* of dead emperors continued to exist and assert power, especially economically, retaining all previous wealth and lands. In times of stable population and leadership, these old *panaqa* wielded less power, as the members were woven into the lineage of the new ruling *panaqa.* However, with the arrival of smallpox and the resulting death of Emperor Huayna Cápac in 1527, a series of rulers reigned in rapid succession, leading to competing "undead" *panaqa* whose wealth and authority contested that of the reigning emperors. The litany of dead emperors retaining earthly wealth joined an increasing list of living claimants to the Inca throne in the 1530s. The practice of emperors solidifying power by marrying sisters and having offspring through a multitude of wives resulted in numerous contenders to royal power. As smallpox decimated the ruling elite, tracing the lineage of the next emperor became quite complex.

The minimal number of Spanish invaders helped drive the struggle for power among royal contenders. The primary "weapon" that assisted the Spanish was the horse. However, the extremely steep mountains, stepped paths, and suspended bridges, as well as the Incas' use of the bola, effectively countered the advantage of having horses. The superior numbers of the Incas during and following the war encouraged attempts by numerous leaders to regain control from the Spanish.

The disruption of the hierarchical structure, and therefore the destruction of the cultural base and the economic and political system, prevented a successful Inca revolution. That disruption was largely the result of disease. Some understanding of the numbers impacted by fatal epidemics is necessary. Epidemiology studies indicate that initial epidemics in areas with no native immunity typically result in a fatality rate of approximately 40 percent. Due to the intricate system of roads and urban structures within the Inca Empire, however, estimates indicate that the first epidemic (1524–1525) claimed close to 48 percent of the population. Smallpox struck twice again during the 1530s, once in 1558 and again in 1565. Other epidemics of typhus, measles, influenza, and diphtheria took additional tolls on the devastated population. Within 80 years of the Spanish conquest, nine out of every 10 inhabitants of the Inca Empire died from disease.

As in Europe following the devastating bubonic plague, the huge death toll in the Andes and surrounding territories completely disrupted the economy of the Incas, left cities abandoned, and farms and herds unattended. Politically, the Incas failed to recover from the devastation.

The unique leadership structure, with its continued practice of dead emperors and living and "undead" *panaqas* claiming large tracts of land, was part of the problem as the death toll increased. The Inca policy of discouraging innovation and initiative on the part of lower-level subjects, placing all responsibility and authority in the highest echelons of the Inca chain of command, left the politically fractured empire in ruins. The result was not only a rather unexpected victory on the part of a handful of Spanish conquerors, but rule by minority for years to come.

The minority Spanish rulers immediately set about assimilating the Incas and eradicating the Inca religious practices and replacing them with the Catholic faith. The Spanish particularly focused on the Inca worship of the creator god Viracocha and worship of the Sun god Inti. The lack of a formal writing system (outside of the complex knotted cords of the *quipu*) and disruption of the Inca hierarchy contributed to the relatively quick demise of the indigenous faith. Other Spanish customs, such as control of the land by the elite, were easily imposed on the population, due to a close resemblance to the practices of the old Inca ruling class. The Spanish distributed land for farming among the native populace. These farms were worked by using a labor system of repartimiento and encomienda. This same native populace provided labor for the mining of ores for shipment back to the Spanish Crown and the Catholic bishops.

With repeated episodes of ravaging epidemics, the Spanish continued to control the region with relatively small numbers. Consequently, much of the physical presence and daily cultural practices of the old Inca Empire survived. The use of aqueducts and irrigation continued, with some well-designed structures surviving to this day. Remnants of stone buildings survived. Yet the remote religious centers like Machu Pichu fell into disrepair from lack of use. The continued presence of a majority native population helped maintain everyday cultural practices, from the types of food eaten to the intricate weaving and dyeing of cloths. Yet little attention was given to perpetuating the metallurgical arts of the Incas. The minimal Spanish presence also helps explain the lasting presence of native languages, especially in the higher elevations of the Andes. Spanish remains the language of business and politics.

Far removed from other Spanish outposts by geographic obstacles and distance, the Incas and their subjects experienced mixed consequences as a result of the Inca-Spanish War. Disease proved the greatest impact on society, devastating the political structure and affecting the economy and culture. Yet, despite major changes in language, religion, and politics, the native populace of the region retained more of its cultural heritage than most colonized people. The small number of Spanish colonists and the isolated location of the region are largely responsible for this cultural continuity.

Rebecca M. Seaman

See also: Encomienda; European Diseases, Role of; Huayna Cápac; Religion, of Pre-Conquest Inca; Repartimiento.

Resources

Kelton, Paul. *Enslavement & Epidemics: Biological Catastrophe in the Native Southeast 1492–1715.* Lincoln: University of Nebraska Press, 2007.

MacQuarrie, Kim. *The Last Days of the Incas.* New York: Simon & Schuster, 2007.

Mann, Charles C. *Ancient Americans: Rewriting the History of the New World.* London: Granta Books, 2005.

Sancho, Pedro. *An Account of the Conquest of Peru.* Preface and Translation by Philip Ainsworth Means. New York: Cortes Society, 1917.

Ircio, Pedro de

Pedro de Ircio, also known as Pedro Dircio, and his brother, Martín de Ircio, were well-known members of the Cortés expedition. Both were from the village of Briones in Logroño. Before joining Cortés, Pedro de Ircio sailed first on the Grijalva expedition. Bernal Díaz del Castillo described Pedro as being of medium height, a passionate man, full of talk about what he would accomplish. He had some sort of problem with one of his legs. While he might have been a blowhard,

he became one of the leading captains of the Cortés expedition. Díaz compared Ircio in a negative manner to Agrajes, a character from the novels of chivalry that were popular at the time. Agrajes was supposedly a king of Scotland, famous for being an expert swordsman. The reference implied that Díaz felt Ircio did not live up to his own reputation, though records of his actions seem to indicate abilities typical of other leading officers on the expedition.

Ircio became a captain after the expedition landed at Veracruz, and the village council was established. He possibly also joined Francisco de Montejo on the expedition to Pánuco, which occurred after the landing at Veracruz but before the expedition moved inland. Ircio occupied an important place in the encounters with the Tlaxcalans, and later as the expedition entered Tenochtitlán. When Cortés left Tenochtitlán to march part of his forces to the coast to confront Pánfilo de Narváez, a captain sent by Diego Velázquez, governor of Cuba, to capture Cortés and regain control of the expedition, Ircio was second in command to Gonzalo de Sandoval. Following the defeat of Narváez, Cortés incorporated the defeated forces into his own ranks. The now larger Spanish force, augmented by the men formerly under Narváez, returned to Tenochtitlán. There the population was in rebellion against the Spanish, whom they eventually expelled. The incident, known as the La Noche Triste (Sad Night) was a low point for Cortés's expedition. Following this defeat, Pedro de Ircio and several others, both supporters of Narváez and some of those typically loyal to Cortés, signed the 1520 letter from Segura de la Frontera, also known as Tepeaca. This letter, expressing a defeatist attitude and demanding to return to Cuba, exasperated Cortés, especially since even close friends like Andrés de Duero signed it.

Despite Ircio's participation in questioning Cortés's decisions following the La Noche Triste, he seems to have returned to good standing in the eyes of Cortés. He was elected as one of the two municipal justices (*alcaldes*) at Tepeaca. In the final assault on Tenochtitlán, he distinguished himself in capturing several of the bridges that pierced the causeways linking the city to the shore. Immediately after the fall of Tenochtitlán, Cortés sent him to help govern Veracruz. He served as a captain with Sandoval in later engagements. Some of the later fighting in which he participated included the ones to the Zapotec region, Coatzacoalcos, and to Honduras. He was granted the encomienda of Maxcalzingo.

In 1527, Pedro de Ircio was denounced as a blasphemer to the Bishop of Mexico who was acting as Inquisitor. He died shortly thereafter in Mexico.

John Schwaller

See also: Cortés, Hernán; Díaz del Castillo, Bernal; Duero, Andrés de; Grijalva, Juan de; La Noche Triste; Montejo, Francisco de; Narváez, Pánfilo; Sandoval, Gonzalo de; Tenochtitlán, Siege of; Velázquez, Diego (de Cuéllar).

Resources

Díaz del Castillo, Bernal. *The History of the Conquest of New Spain.* Edited by David Carrasco. Albuquerque: University of New Mexico Press, 2008.

Grunberg, Bernard. *Dictionnaire des conquistadores de Mexico.* Paris: L'Harmattan, 2001.

Thomas, Hugh. *Who's Who of the Conquistadores.* London: Cassell & Company, 2000.

Ixtlilxochitl II

Ixtlilxochitl II was the grandson of Ixtlilxochitl I, Texcoco *tlatoani* who unsuccessfully defied the Mexica in the early 1400s. Upon the death of his father, Ixtlilxochitl II and his brother competed for control of Texcoco. Neither son was considered legitimate and the selection of the next *tlatoani* was left to the lords of Texcocan towns and the Aztec emperor, Montezuma II.

Ixtlilxochitl's brother, Cacamatzin (Cacama), was the son of Nezahualpilli and the sister of Montezuma—who was executed by her husband. Cacama received support from his maternal uncle, the Aztec emperor Montezuma II, while Ixtlilxochitl II opposed his brother's ascendency to power (and alliance to Montezuma). The election of Cacama prompted Ixtlilxochitl to raise a rebellion, on the grounds that Cacama had betrayed the Texcoco people in an effort to gain more power. The end result of the internecine conflict was the division of the Texcoco kingdom into two parts, with Ixtlilxochitl II gaining the northern half of Texcoco.

In the summer of 1519, Hernán Cortés approached Zempoala (Cempoallan) where he carried on a dialogue with leading men from the area, specifically the *tlatoani* known as the "fat cacique." It was from this source that Cortés received encouragement to approach Ixtlilxochitl and the Texcoco, to create an alliance that might defeat the great Aztec emperor Montezuma.

As Cortés approached Texcoco the *tlatoani* came out to greet the Spanish, fed them, and communicated their desire to form a friendship. In turn, Cortés used the opportunity to try to convert the leading men of Texcoco, succeeding in not only the willing acceptance of the population to the new faith, but their acceptance of King Charles V (HRE) as their emperor and the sacrament of baptism for the leading princes. Ixtlilxochitl, whose godfather was Cortés, was baptized as Hernando.

With the strong support of Texcoco, Cortés continued on to Tenochtitlán, where Montezuma also welcomed them. Following the Spanish seizing of Montezuma as their hostage, and the continued cooperation of the emperor, the Texcoco *tlatoani* Cacama withdrew his allegiance to his uncle, choosing to rebel against the Spanish instead. Returning to his homeland, Cacama was seized and turned over to the Spanish. The stories of his arrest vary, some asserting that Ixtlilxochitl captured and presented Cacama to Cortés, while other simply indicate he was kidnapped by allies of the Spanish for his plots against Cortés.

In the spring of 1520, Cortés left Tenochtitlán to confront Pánfilo de Narváez, under order by the governor of Cuba to arrest Cortés. When he returned to the Aztec capital, conditions had broken down and the Spanish were repulsed during La Noche Trista (Sad Night). With large losses, Cortés turned to the friendly Texcoco under Ixtlilxochitl. The *tlatoani*'s eagerness to ally with Cortés caused some concern, but provided the opportunity for the Spanish to not only recover from their losses, but to take advantage of the lake at Texcoco to build and launch boats for use in the siege of Tenochtitlán. Thousands of Texcoco dug a channel, over a mile long and 12 feet deep, to connect the city of Texcoco with the lake surrounding Tenochtitlán. As a result, Cortés was able to sail 12 flat-bottomed brigantines to help lay siege to the Aztec capital from land and water.

Following the successful alliance of the Texcoco and Spanish, the positive relations between Cortés and Ixtlilxochitl continued. In the midst of upheaval, after the death of Montezuma and the eventual defeat of Tenochtitlán, it was Ixtlilxochitl II who provided a restoration of order. The *tlatoani*'s usefulness to Cortés went beyond military and civil administration. It was Ixtlilxochitl who first embraced Catholicism and encouraged his people to do the same. In the wake of the Spanish conquest of the Aztec, it was Ixtlilxochitl who welcomed friars to the Texcoco, helped spread Christianity, and even built the first Catholic Church in Mexico.

Interestingly, while Cortés promised to reveal to the Spanish king the important assistance of Ixtlilxochitl and other native allies to the Spanish conquest and conversion of Mexico, no mention of the *tlatoani* is made in the letters the conquistador sent back to Spain. Instead, it was left to Ixtlilxochitl's grandson, the Mestizo historian Fernando de Alva Ixtlilxochitl, to relate the role of the Texcoco leader. While in many ways, Fernando de Alva provides clarity regarding lineage and certain events, there is also an obvious attempt on his part to present the history of his family and the Texcoco people in a favorable light. However, while other primary records do acknowledge the role of the *tlatoani* of Texcoco, they often do so without specific references to Ixtlilxochitl II.

Rebecca M. Seaman

See also: Cacama; Cortés, Hernán; La Noche Triste; Montezuma II; Narváez, Pánfilo de; Texcoco, Alliance with Tenochtitlán; Tenochtitlán, Siege of; Zempoala.

Resources

Allen, Heather. "Literacy, Text, and Performance in the Histories of the Conquest of Mexico." PhD diss., University of Chicago, 2011.

Gillespie, Susan D. *The Aztec Kings: The Construction of Rulership in Mexica History.* Tucson: University of Arizona Press, 1989.

León-Portilla, Miguel. *The Broken Spears: The Aztec Account of the Conquest of Mexico.* Foreword by J. Jorge Klor de Alva. Boston: Beacon Press, 2006.

Thomas, Hugh. Conquest: Montezuma, Cortés, and the Fall of Old Mexico. New York: Simon & Schuster, 1993.

J

Jesuit Order, Role of

The Society of Jesus, or Jesuits, came into existence as a new religious order of priests in Spain in 1534. Headed by the Spanish soldier-priest, Father Ignacio Loyola, they were a religious order that functioned under a strict quasimilitary regimen and whose original founding members were soldiers. Part of the Spanish tradition of militant religious orders, the zeal with which the Jesuits strove to combat the Protestant Reformation gave impetus to the Catholic Church's efforts to rejuvenate itself from within—an initiative which came to be known as the Counterreformation. That same zeal was apparent in the way the Jesuits pursued their goals of missionary work and education in the New World.

The Jesuits reached Peru in 1568, over three decades after Francisco Pizarro arrived with his men. Their arrival in New Spain or Mexico is dated to 1571, a half-century after Hernán Cortés's conquest of the Aztecs. Along with the Franciscans, the Society of Jesus established and maintained missions that ministered to indigenous people in remote rural villages throughout Mesoamerica and the Andes. From central South America to present-day Arizona, the missions were one component of an elaborate network of Jesuit endeavors. Across Latin America, Jesuits amassed property in the form of plantations, haciendas, and rudimentary workshop-factories known as *obrajes,* and used the profits to support the missions and the *colegios,* which trained young men to become priests, lawyers, teachers, administrators, and entrepreneurs.

In the first few years, the Jesuits conducted mass baptisms of the conquered Nahua, Maya, Inca, and other Andean people. Yet as time passed, they began to recognize how superficial the natives' conversions had been. Old beliefs survived and became inextricably intertwined with Christian teachings. The Jesuits looked upon such behavior as a corruption of Catholic doctrine and the foundation for potential heresies. In the 1570s, their correspondence with church authorities in Europe revealed considerable disappointment. Realizing the difficulty if not the outright futility of trying to convert adults, the Jesuits turned more and more to the task of supervising and educating young indigenous males. As some of these novices began to criticize their elders for persisting in their pre-Columbian beliefs and customs, the Jesuit missionaries expressed satisfaction.

To meet the challenge of converting the natives to Christianity, the Jesuits were dedicated and determined to succeed through a variety of approaches, to include learning the local languages. Sometimes these efforts met with rejection, but more often, their linguistic strategy bore fruit. Their efforts to train an elite cadre of young native men in Spanish and Catholic doctrine enabled the early church to publish confessional instructions and other religious works in Nahuatl, the language of the Aztecs; several Maya dialects; and Quechua, the pre-conquest lingua franca of the Andes. Native nobles also manned the positions that worked for the clergy. Yet a large number of Indians clung tenaciously to their old creeds and rites. The eradication of "idolatry" took generations, but syncretism was the overarching result of the collision between Jesuit teachings and native ways.

In the 16th and 17th centuries, Europeans on both sides of the Atlantic became obsessed with witch-hunts. As the principal movers and shakers of the Counterreformation, the Jesuits guided and directed many of the trials aimed at rooting out "witches," whom they regarded as heretics and enemies of the Roman Catholic Church. Hence, the Jesuits led the effort to eradicate idolatry in Peru. They applied their European witch-hunting experience in the Andes. Like in Europe, the proceedings to rid the Andean world of idolaters tore the region's social fabric. The Jesuits and their Franciscan brethren conducted these trials as part of the Holy Office of the Inquisition.

The Jesuits amassed extensive landholdings in America over the years. Throughout western South America, they claimed lands that had once hosted the various Andean cults. As landowners, the Jesuits became astute businessmen, and they used their managerial skills in supporting and operating their missions. Agricultural produce as well as arts and crafts from Indian missions reached markets from Chile to northern Mexico. Through the employment of African slave labor, Jesuit plantations produced the lion's share of wine and sugar in coastal Peru and parts of Ecuador.

The real legacy of the Jesuits is one of compassion and empathy. Though their religious beliefs and practices gave them a reputation for rigidity, the altruistic manner in which they approached their duties as priests and teachers was both impressive and unmatched. They were determined to protect the Andean, Mayan, and Nahua people from the harshness of colonial law and exploitation at the hands of Spanish laypersons. This posture ultimately incurred the wrath of the Spanish Crown—a reality that led to the Jesuit's expulsion from all of Spain's American colonies in the second half of the 18th century. Today, while showing little regard for the conquistadores, South American and Mesoamerican historians continue to hold the Jesuits in high esteem for their loyalty to indigenous people and their unyielding determination to carry Christian teachings to those same Indians.

Jeffrey Kent Lucas

See also: Cortés, Hernán; Franciscans, Role of; Nahuatl Language; Pizarro, Francisco; Quechua Language.

Resources

Burkhart, Louise. *The Slippery Earth: Nahua-Christian Moral Dialogue in Sixteenth-Century Mexico.* Tucson: University of Arizona Press, 1989.

Lane, Kris, and Matthew Restall. *The Riddle of Latin America.* Boston, MA: Wadsworth, 2012.

León-Portilla, Miguel. *The Broken Spears: The Aztec Account of the Conquest of Mexico,* revised edition. Boston, MA: Beacon Press, 1992.

Martin, Cheryl, and Mark Wasserman. *Latin America and Its People.* 3rd ed. Boston, MA: Prentice Hall, 2012.

Restall, Matthew. *Seven Mythos of the Spanish Conquest.* New York: Oxford University Press, 2003.

Silverblatt, Irene. *Moon, Sun, and Witches: Gender Ideologies and Class in Inca and Colonial Peru.* Princeton, NJ: Princeton University Press, 1987.

Woodrow, Alain. *The Jesuits, a Story of Power.* New York: G. Chapman, 1995.

Juicio de Residencia

From the earliest decades of Spanish occupation of American territories, sons defended fathers, the oppressed implicated governors, and officials jockeyed for power in detailed written accounts submitted to royal officials at regular intervals. One class of documentary procedure that served this purpose is the *juicio de residencia,* or an official account of tenure in office. Most regional and local authorities that served at the behest of the Spanish monarchy were required to participate in a review of their time in office before moving on to the next step in their careers or lives. For example, the regional governors known as viceroys were closely scrutinized in regular *juicio de residencia* inquiries.

The *juicio de residencia* was a judicial process that was stipulated in the laws of Castile and the Indies. When an official reached the end of his time in office, a *juicio de residencia* provided a mechanism for the review of his performance in an official capacity. It was customary for the departing official's successor to act as the judge in the *juicio de residencia,* leading the evaluation process. The Spanish Crown ordered the start of most *residencias* by official decree and outlined instructions for the institution or individual overseeing the process. The instructions often identified certain individuals to be questioned in evaluating the subject of the inquiry; however, it was customary for military and government subordinates to be questioned regarding the official's diligent pursuit of justice in Spain's American colonies.

In the 1540s, Cristóbal Vaca de Castro was sent by the Spanish Crown to Peru to broker peace between warring Spanish officials. Despite his successes and loyalty to the Crown, Vaca de Castro was imprisoned on false charges and sent back to Spain. Through the course of compiling his *juicio de residencia,* evidence emerged that helped lawyers exonerate Vaca de Castro. Like many *juicio de residencia* dossiers, Vaca de Castro's includes sworn testimonies, letters, royal decrees, copies of correspondence, and other related documentation. As in the case of Vaca de Castro, the *juicio de residencia* focused on the administration of justice and how the official had exhibited proper respect for royal authority.

Hernán Cortés provides a famous example of the *residencia* process. The testimonies gathered in his review are valuable for information gleaned from oral testimonies of illiterate members of his expedition. Yet these and other testimonies add to the confusion about Cortés, his expedition, and his leadership following the conquest. Those members of his forces who never shared his confidence used this opportunity to seek revenge. Those who felt slighted by limited rewards, but who held Cortés in great esteem, provided conflicting testimonies, leaving later historians to wonder about their loyalties and/or the truth of their testimonies. As to be expected, those Extremeños who were consistently part of his inner circle contributed supportive testimony, some consistent with other given testimonies and some obviously biased in favor of the *caudillo.* In Cortés's case, the questionnaires, hearings, and defense against accusations continued on for years. In the end, he was exonerated of most charges, and retained his titles and lands, though he was charged with repaying Governor Velázquez for monies invested in the initial expedition.

The central focus of many *residencias* encompassed issues regarding the indigenous American populations and the finances of the territory managed by the official under review. Cristóbal Vaca de Castro's *residencia,* like many others, resulted in discovering abuses of power and facilitating useful governmental reforms. While the *juicio de residencia* served as a vehicle for the Crown to control its distant officials, it also summarized the life's work of colonial officials. It is through such reviews that historians find a wealth of information, some biased and contradictory, for use in reconstructing the past.

Emily A. Engel

See also: Cortés, Hernán; Velázquez, Diego (de Cuéllar).

Resources

Burkholder, Mark, and Lyman Johnson. *Colonial Latin America.* Oxford: Oxford University Press, 2000.

Mills, Kenneth, William B. Taylor, and Sandra Lauderdale Graham. *Colonial Latin America: A Documentary History.* Wilmington, DE: Scholarly Resources, 2002.

Restall, Matthew, and Kris Lane. *Latin America in Colonial Times.* Cambridge: Cambridge University Press, 2011.

Thomas, Hugh. *Conquest: Montezuma, Cortés, and the Fall of Old Mexico.* New York: Simon & Schuster, 1993.

Julián, Maya Interpreter

Captured, baptized, and renamed by the Spanish (there is no available record of his original name), Julián or Julianillo was probably the first indigenous person to serve as interpreter for the Spanish in Tierra firme or the continental Americas, in New Spain or present-day Mexico. From Cape Catoche (Ecab) in the northern tip of Yucatán, Julián was also among the first continental indigenous peoples to experience close encounters with Spanish forces, albeit to their detriment, in the form of the first expedition of the region launched by the governor of Cuba, Diego Velázquez, and led by Francisco Hernández de Córdoba in February 1517. Julián "the sad" was one of two Yucatec Mayas captured by Hernández de Córdoba during a skirmish with Maya warriors

in March 1517. Julián and a Maya fisherman christened "Melchor" were forced to accompany the expedition for the duration of the journey and on its return to Cuba two months later.

Velázquez interrogated Julián and Melchor in Havana following the expedition; Hernández de Córdoba died of his wounds shortly after his arrival. Reports of riches were reinforced by the testimony of Julián. He was probably the principal source of information, considering the Spaniards' characterization of Melchor as "the silent one." Arguably, Julián played a significant role in influencing or reinforcing the governor's decision to send another expedition back to Yucatán, though likely in hopes of facilitating his own escape. According to his testimony, there were substantial deposits of gold in Yucatán as well as several Christians in captivity in Yucatán communities on the peninsula. Both assertions later proved false.

Julián spent the next year in Cuba, learned Spanish, and was trained as an interpreter. When the second expedition sailed under the governor's nephew, Juan de Grijalva, in April 1518 and made way for the "island" of Yucatán (later renamed Santa Maria de los Remedios), Julián accompanied the crew as an interpreter. Upon their initial landing at Cozumel (Ah-Cuzamil-Peten), Julián served as the voice for Mayas and Spaniards in the first encounter on the island. Julián further served as the medium through which Grijalva and the Spanish first learned of the various facets of Maya culture, including ritual sacrifice.

There is some dispute about the proficiency of his Spanish; Gonzalo Fernández de Oviedo reported it as limited while Peter Martyr suggests a certain level of fluency. Julián appears nevertheless to have played a central role as interpreter and mediator during the Grijalva expedition, most effectively among the Yucatec Maya. In one such instance, near Champoton just south of Campeche, Julián acted as mediator and negotiator between Grijalva's men, desperately seeking to resupply their ship with freshwater, and Yucatec Maya warriors anxious to expel the foreigners. A Maya leader had set a torch of incense between his men and the Spanish, warning them to leave before its extinguishment. Julián, though unable to prevent the eventual assault, played a crucial role in alerting the Spanish, delaying the attack, and enabling the Spanish to prepare their defenses and escape.

Whether independently or via some triangulation through another Maya captive (christened Pedro Barba), Julián remained the primary interpreter for the Spanish among the Yucatecan and other Mayas like the Chontal. Mentioned most prominently in the Grijalva expedition as chronicled by Fernández de Oviedo, Julián played the same enabling role for the Spanish among the Mayas as La Malinche (Malinali/Marina/Malintzin) later played among the Mexica-Aztecs. Escaping in July 1518, he is reported to have died sometime just prior to the more famous expedition of Hernán Cortés.

Julián provided the model for the classical "go-between," as interpreter, liaison, negotiator, guide, and perhaps even as advisor to the Spanish. Before the rescued Spaniard Gerónimo de Aguilar or the Aztec La Malinche, Julián conveyed both Spanish and indigenous interests, and facilitated the expansion of Spanish knowledge regarding the continental Americas.

Jason Yaremko

See also: Aguilar, Fr. Gerónimo de; Cortés, Hernán; Cozumel; Grijalva, Juan de; La Malinche, "Doña Marina"; Velázquez, Diego (de Cuéllar); Yucatán, State of prior to Spanish Conquest.

Resources

Díaz del Castillo, Bernal. *The Discovery and Conquest of Mexico.* Translated by Irving A. Leonard. New York: Farrar, Straus, and Cudahy, 1956.

Fernández de Oviedo, Gonzalo. *Historia general y natural de las Indias,* Part I. Edited by José Amador de los Rios. Madrid: Imprenta de la real academia de la historia, 1851.

Grijalva, Juan de. *The Discovery of New Spain in 1518.* Translated and Edited by Henry Wagner. New York: The Cortes Society, Kraus Reprint Co., 1942.

Las Casas, Bartolomé de. *Historia de las Indias.* Edited by Y. D. José Sancho Rayon. Madrid: Imprenta de Miguel Ginesta, 1876.

Martyr D'Anghera, Peter. *De Orbo Novo: The Eight Decades of Peter Martyr D'Anghera, Vol. II.* Translated by Francis Augustus MacNutt. New York: Burt Franklin, 1970.

Thomas, Hugh. *The Conquest of Mexico.* London: Hutchinson, 1993.

Townsend, Camilla. *Malintzin's Choices: An Indian Woman in the Conquest of Mexico.* Albuquerque: University of New Mexico Press, 2006.

K

Kuraka

In pre-conquest Peru, a *kuraka* was an Inca lord who acquired his position of authority over the community by virtue of his close kin relationship to the previous *kuraka*. The lowest of the three elite ranks in Inca society, they were the native leaders of outlying areas conquered by the Inca as the empire spread through the Andes. The position was in part that of the local community's representative, tasked with dealing with other communities within the Inca Empire. Other political responsibilities included the enforcement of claims by community members to resources and the redistribution of land rights within the community. Economically, the *kuraka* lord bore responsibility for the acquisition, storage and distribution of necessary supplies for the immediate community and its outlying territories.

Related to the political and economic elements of authority were the *kurakas'* religious responsibilities. Local lords bore responsibility for the complex rituals that were an integral part of Inca society. This included the organizing of the rituals and provisioning of supplies necessary for the same. It also included the need to provide for gifts that were part of religious and political expectations.

Military duties dominated a large portion of the lord's time. The *kuraka* defended the households and community against possible invasions. He also protected community property and upheld societal norms. If the lord proved successful in his duties, the community would provide labor for his personal economic interests. That labor might include herding his animals or weaving cloth, to such mundane tasks as fetching food and water.

With the arrival and conquest of the Inca by the Spanish under Francisco Pizarro, *kurakas* were divided in their loyalties. Sensing the shifting power, some transferred their allegiance to the Spanish to protect their local communities from annihilation. Others, with close relations to the Sapa Inca (unique emperor), remained loyal to the Inca in hopes of preserving their traditional communities and cultures. Those who sided with the Spanish still boasted they could trace their lineage back to the first great Sapa Inca, Manco Cápac, thus guaranteeing continued privileged status under the Spanish for themselves and their descendents.

Rebecca M. Seaman

See also: Class, Impact of Spanish on the Inca; Government, Pre-Conquest Inca; Manco Cápac; Pizarro, Francisco; Sapa Inca.

Resources

Stern, Steve J. *Peru's Indian Peoples and the Challenge of Spanish Conquest: Huamanga to 1640.* Madison: University of Wisconsin Press, 1993.

Szilagyi, Anca. "The Inka Ruling Class and its Mythic Foundations." http://www.anca-szilagyi.com/inka.html (accessed July 25, 2011).

L

La Malinche, "Doña Marina"

Born into a noble Nahua family on the eastern perimeter of the Aztec Empire, La Malinche was sold or traded into slavery as a child, following her father's death and her mother's remarriage. She ended up among the coastal Chontal Mayas where she was discovered and came into the possession of Hernán Cortés in 1519, following the successful conquest of Potonchan. Baptized as Doña Marina, she soon became invaluable to the Spanish expedition as an interpreter.

Malinche was not the only interpreter among Cortés's expedition. Prior to landing and founding the city of Villa Rica de la Vera Cruz, Cortés rescued a stranded Spanish friar, Gerónimo de Aguilar. Fluent in Mayan, Aguilar served as one of the *caudillo*'s primary interpreters among the coastal Maya. However, as the expedition encountered emissaries from Tenochtitlán, Aguilar was unable to translate the Aztec language of Nahuatl into Spanish. Cortés quickly realized the potential in Malinche, who he had already gifted to one of his lieutenants (Alonso Hernández de Puertocarrero), and reclaimed her for his own use. In this manner, La Malinche translated Nahuatl into Mayan and Aguilar translated the Mayan into Spanish. This cumbersome process was fraught with potential for misinterpretation, especially since the Nahuatl spoken by Doña Marina was common in the southern regions of the empire and had distinct differences from that spoken in Tenochtitlán, the Aztec capital. Nonetheless, this dual translation process continued until the gifted linguistic ability of Malinche enabled her to learn Spanish—thereby making Aguilar's services less crucial.

Cortés's dependence upon Malinche as his interpreter is evidenced by her consistent presence with him during his conquest of Mexico. According to the history recorded by the conquistador Bernal Díaz, Doña Marina was indispensible to Cortés and the expedition. Spanish documents and artistic portrayals, as well as Aztec written and artistic records, place Malinche at the *caudillo*'s side, typically using glyphs to indicate her role in communicating between the Aztec and Spanish. In addition to translating the dialogue between the Aztec and conquistadors, she was likely able to convey the meaning and importance behind Aztec cultural norms to the Spanish who would have had little to no understanding of the indigenous society.

Historians have portrayed Doña Marina in various ways: some highlight her importance to the Spanish expedition while others depict her as a traitor to her own people. Spanish efforts to communicate not only their aims to subjugate the indigenous population, but also to convert them to the Christian faith were assisted through her apparently willing involvement and translations. In the shifting allegiances of the time, it is safe to assert that Malinche provided valuable services to the Spanish and even to the emperor, Montezuma II, by communicating the desires and demands of both sides. Her experience of having been traded by her own family into slavery at a fairly young age and coming to maturity in a different native society—one typically at odds with the Aztec—would have influenced her perceptions of "national"

La Malinche, or Doña Marina, in a scene from the Lienzo Tlaxcala, demonstrating her constant service as interpreter for Cortés. (*Lienzo Tlaxcala*)

loyalty. It is impossible to determine whether that personal experience alienated her from her native culture or increased her loyalty to the Aztecs. With her freedom provided by the invading Spanish who elevated her to the role of chief interpreter, La Malinche's service and loyalty to Cortés and his expedition was not surprising.

Historians also give attention to La Malinche's personal relationship with Cortés. During the initial conquest of Mexico, the relationship—while close—was one of conquistador and interpreter. However, following Cortés's successful dominance of Tenochtitlán, Doña Marina became one of the *caudillo*'s mistresses. Malinche gave birth to Cortés's first son, named Martín after Cortés's father and later known as Martín El Mestizo, who was born out of wedlock. In this role as lover or concubine, La Malinche was not alone. Cortés had at least three illegitimate children, some while being married to Spanish noble women, and some in between his two official marriages. Despite his personal relationship with Doña Marina, or maybe because of it, the *caudillo* helped arrange a marriage between his interpreter and Juan de Jaraillo, a Spaniard of moderately high rank. He additionally contributed an encomienda as a dowry. Historians differ on her death. According to some, La Malinche died a few years later in 1527 or 1528. Others record her surviving until 1551.

Rebecca M. Seaman

See also: Aguilar, Fr. Gerónimo de; Cortés, Hernán; Díaz, del Castillo, Bernal; Encomienda; Montezuma II; Nahuatl Language; Tenochtitlán.

Resources

Díaz, Bernal. *The Conquest of New Spain.* Translated by J. M. Cohen. London: Penguin Press, 1963.

Diel, Lori Boornazian. "Manuscrito del aperreamiento (Manuscript of the Dogging): A "Dogging" and Its Implications for Early Colonial Cholula." *Ethnohistory* 58, no. 4 (Fall 2011): 585–611.

Restall, Matthew. *Seventh Myths of the Spanish Conquest.* Oxford: Oxford University Press, 2004.

Thomas, Hugh. *Montezuma, Cortés, and the Fall of Old Mexico.* New York: Simon & Schuster, 1993.

La Noche Triste

"La Noche Triste" (June 30, 1520) is the name given to the costly nighttime retreat of Spanish forces from the city of Tenochtitlán during the conquest of Mexico. In the disastrous chaos of the night's events, perhaps 600 Spaniards and over a 1,000 Indian allies died or were captured.

In 1519, Hernán Cortés began his conquest of the Aztec Empire in what is now Mexico. Because of uncertainty regarding the true identity and motivations of the Spaniards, as well as the Spanish capture of the Aztec emperor, Montezuma II, Cortés was able to quarter his small army in the Aztec capital of Tenochtitlán that winter. Cortés occupied the city with no violence, and the Aztecs provided the Spanish and their Indian allies with food and water, while they lived in one of the city's palaces. Hearing that one of his political rivals, Governor Diego Velázquez of Cuba, had sent a second Spanish expedition to Mexico to arrest Cortés (who had undertaken his conquest illegally), Cortés left Tenochtitlán and journeyed to the coast to confront this new expedition. He left Pedro de Alvarado in charge of the Spanish forces still left in the Aztec capital.

Alvarado feared an imminent uprising by the Aztec warriors in the city following the departure of Cortés. When the Aztecs (with the permission of both Cortés and Alvarado) began to celebrate the festival of Toxcatl, Alvarado became convinced that the festivities were a prelude to an Aztec attack upon the Spanish. Therefore, Alvarado ordered a preemptive strike upon the celebrants, massacring several hundred unarmed Aztec nobles, and provoking open armed conflict between the Aztec and Spanish forces. Alvarado and his men retreated to their palace headquarters, where they were besieged.

Cortés returned from the coast not only having dealt with the threat of the second expedition under Pánfilo de Narváez, but actually supplementing his forces with some of its members. When he arrived again at Tenochtitlán, it was clear to Cortés that something was wrong. The Aztecs allowed Cortés and his forces to reenter the city and reunite with the forces under Alvarado, hoping to trap and finish off the Spanish and their allies once and for all.

An eight-day battle commenced between Cortés's forces and the city's warriors. Things went from bad to worse for the Spanish, who daily suffered losses from their already limited numbers. In a desperate bid for peace, Cortés even forced the kidnapped Emperor

Montezuma II to command the Aztecs to stop fighting, which the hostage emperor did from the roof of the palace stronghold. Montezuma was met with a shower of rocks and projectiles from his own people and was gravely wounded. He died a few days later, though the circumstances of his death are not entirely clear.

With supplies running out and Montezuma dead, the Spanish knew they had to escape from the city. After several unsuccessful attempts, they decided to try a midnight escape on June 30. Having packed what stolen treasure they could carry, the Spanish and their Indian allies began quietly making their way out of the city, crossing its many canals with makeshift bridges they had formed out of ceiling beams from their palace headquarters.

Unfortunately for the Spanish and their allies, an Aztec woman drawing water from one of the canals spotted them. She sounded the alarm, and soon Aztec warriors swooped down upon the Spanish from all sides. The result was utter chaos. Many Spanish and their Indian allies drowned trying to cross the collapsing makeshift bridges. Others died in combat with the Aztec warriors. Still others were captured and later sacrificed in the celebrations that followed. All in all, Cortés lost perhaps 600 Spaniards and over 1,000 Indian allies, almost all of his horses, all of his artillery, and a great deal of the treasure he had acquired thus far. Though Cortés eventually returned to conquer the city of Tenochtitlán and indeed the entire Aztec Empire, the Spanish referred to the night's events as "La Noche Triste" (the Sad Night) because of the great losses incurred during the disastrous retreat.

John Gram

See also: Alvarado, Pedro de; Cortés, Hernán; Montezuma II; Narváez, Pánfilo de; Tenoch-titlán, Siege of; Toxcatl Massacre; Velázquez, Diego (de Cuéllar).

Resources

Bakewell, Peter. *A History of Latin America.* 2nd ed. Malden, MA: Blackwell, 2004.

Diaz del Castillo, Bernal. *The Conquest of New Spain.* Translated by J. M. Cohen. Baltimore: Penguin Books, 1963.

Thomas, Hugh. *Conquest: Montezuma, Cortes, and the Fall of Old Mexico.* New York: Simon & Schuster, 1993.

Las Casas, Bartolomé de

Bartolomé de Las Casas was the earliest crusader for human rights in the New World. Much information about the one-time adventurer, encomendero, friar, and bishop, including his birth year is debated, with some asserting his birth occurred in 1474 and other in 1484. All agree that he arrived in the Americas as an adventurer in 1502. There, he witnessed the exploitation and slavery of the native populations. Returning to Latin America as a priest, he called on the church and the state to practice true Christianity and support the rights and dignity of the Indians. Though his contemporaries spurned many of his ideas, his powerful writings influenced Latin American revolutionaries of the 19th century.

Las Casas was born in Seville, Spain. He was the son of Pedro de Las Casas, a merchant. As a child, he was part of the crowds that welcomed Christopher Columbus back from his voyage to the Americas, and his father sailed on Columbus's second voyage to the New World. Las Casas studied Latin and theology in Seville. When he was 20, he fought with the local militia to suppress a Moorish uprising in the neighboring city of Granada.

In 1502, Las Casas made his first voyage to the Americas with Nicolás de Ovando, the governor of the island of Española (Hispaniola). Already in possession of family holdings on the island, he was granted additional land by royal charter for his role in subduing an Indian rebellion. The grant included the forced servitude of Indians to work the land, a system called encomienda. Las Casas began farming his lands and even at this early stage began preaching to his Indians to convert them to Christianity. Four years later, he returned to Europe to take vows with the Dominican order in Rome. When he returned to Española in either 1510 or 1512, he was ordained as a priest and probably celebrated his first mass in America. At this point in his life there was no indication of his eventual fervor for defending the indigenous populace from Spanish abuses. Fray Bartolomé de Las Casas became chaplain to Diego Velázquez de Cuéllar's troops during their conquest of Cuba. He received more land and the accompanying encomienda as a reward. Yet, as his later writings indicate, the Dominican friar already began to question the abusive treatment of the local natives at the hands of the Spanish due to his observations in the Cuban conquest.

That campaign seemed to be a turning point in Las Casas's awareness. He became conscious of the moral implications of the enslavement of Indians, the miserable and humiliating working conditions on the farms and in the mines, and the hypocrisy of forced evangelization. At the approximate age of 40, he gave up his claim to his land and became an outspoken advocate for the rights of the native people. He began to lobby for an end to the encomienda system, initially appealing to King Ferdinand, then later through the Regent, Francisco Jiménez de Cisneros, and eventually to Charles V (Carlos I of Spain). Pointing out that the encomienda was a form of slavery, he based his crusade on the messages of Jesus Christ in the Bible.

Returning to Spain in 1515, Las Casas gained the support of the cardinal archbishop of Toledo, Francisco Jiménez de Cisneros. Fray Las Casas was appointed priest-procurator of the Indians. He developed a plan for colonization that would enable farmers and native populations to live together peacefully. Charles V, the Holy Roman emperor and the king of Spain, granted land and permission for an experimental colony. Cisneros selected the Jeronymite order to serve as commissioners in the experience, and Fray Las Casas was tasked with choosing the friars who would recruit farmers to Curmána, Venezuela. As part of the plan, Las Casas recommended that Indians be paid wages and be gathered in villages where they should be provided with hospitals and churches. Las Casas additionally sought administrative oversight of the proposed colony—trading with the Indians and preventing further slave raiding expeditions into the interior of South America. To prevent continued abuse to the natives already under Spanish authority, he also recommended that African slaves be shipped to the colony. With a great sense of shame, he renounced this suggestion some years later when he realized that Africans should have as many rights as the American natives he was trying to protect. After the colony in Venezuela failed, Las Casas entered a Dominican monastery in Santo Domingo, where, over the course of 10 years, he wrote *Historia de las Indias (History of the Indies)*.

In the 1530s, Las Casas worked to protect the rights of Indians in Mexico, Nicaragua, Peru, and Puerto Rico, with the most success in Guatemala. In 1537, Pope Paul III officially recognized that Indians were rational and should receive instruction in the Bible and acceptance in the church. After this, Las Casas began writing *Brevísima relación de las destuyción de las Indias occidentales (Brief Report on the Destruction of the Indians)*. In it, he asserted: "Now Christ wanted his gospel to be preached with enticements, gentleness, and all meekness, and pagans to be led to the truth not by armed forces but by holy examples, Christian conduct, and the word of God, so that no opportunity would be offered for blaspheming the sacred name or hating the true religion because of the conduct of the preachers. For this is nothing else than making the coming and passion of Christ useless, as long as the truth of the gospel is hated before it is either understood or heard, or as long as innumerable human beings are slaughtered in a war waged on the pretext of preaching the gospel and spreading religion."

Las Casas plainly accused the Europeans of subverting fair laws, and in fact enacting unjust laws, to support their own power and greed in the New World. He used his treatises as a campaign for the 1542 New Laws, which restricted the oppression and exploitation of native populations, with the intention of eliminating the use of encomienda and repartimiento within 20 years. However, as Las Casas expected, the New Laws were ignored and even revoked in the Americas, resulting in the actual increase of encomienda grants over the next two decades. He was determined to enforce the New Laws himself and returned to Guatemala in 1545. European colonists stridently protested until they forced Las Casas to return to Spain in 1547.

Exhausted from his unsuccessful efforts to enforce the New Laws in America, upon his return to Spain Las Casas was thrust into another stressful situation. He was challenged to a series of debates by the noted secular scholar, Juan Ginés de Sepúlveda concerning the spiritual status of the souls of Native Americans. At the Valladolid debates, Sepúlveda asserted that Indians did not possess souls like white Christians, and it was the moral duty of the Spanish to control these inferior beings in the form of slavery as a means of civilizing and Christianizing them. Las Casas was able to clearly present his ideas, defending the rights of the Indians, gaining continued support from Charles V.

The various indigenous people of New Spain recognized fray Las Casas's efforts on behalf of the natives. Some, like the principal leaders of the Nahua (Aztec) in Mexico, wrote letters directly to Charles V, begging him to appoint Las Casas as a bishop and their defender. Should he not be able, due to Las Casas's health or possible death, these leaders implored the Spanish monarch to send a similar Christian of goodwill from Charles's own royal court to protect the Nahua from the plentiful wrongs and abuses of the local Spanish in America.

From the age of 75 until his nineties, Las Casas continued to tirelessly lobby from Spain for the protection of Indians of the New World through writing and public debate. He reiterated that the Indians were equal and not inferior to Europeans. He spoke in defense of Indians suing for freedom in court. He advised the Spanish court and the Council of the Indies. Recognizing the power of Las Casas's ideas, the king of Spain ordered that all of Las Casas's published and unpublished writings be preserved when he died in Madrid on July 31, 1566. To this day, Nicaragua and Cuba regard Las Casas as a national hero, the true "defender of the Indians." Bartolomé de Las Casas and his works greatly impacted the Spanish policies regarding Native Americans through much of the 17th century. Declared the protector of the Indians, his penchant for exaggeration both strengthened the Crown's determination to reform colonial regulations concerning indigenous people of New Spain, while encomenderos also used it to justify circumventing the same regulations. Without a doubt, Las Casas brought attention to the treatment of subjugated peoples during the early Spanish colonial era. The debate he raised over the status of the souls, abilities, and rights of Native Americans was a forerunner of similar debates that continued through the centuries.

José Valente

See also: Charles V (HRE) or Carlos I of Spain; Encomienda; Leyes Nuevas 1542–1543; Ovando, Fr. Nicolás de; Slavery, Role of; Velázquez, Diego (de Cuéllar).

Resources

Adorno, Rolena. "Discourses on Colonialism: Bernal Diaz, Las Casas, and the Twentieth Century reader," *MLN* 103, no. 2 (March 1988): 239–258.

Brown, Robert McAfee. "Review: *Witness: Writings of Bartolome de las Casas.*" *Christian Century,* 109 (July 1, 1992): 655–656.

Hanke, Lewis. *Bartolomé de Las Casas: An Interpretation of his Life and Writings.* Hague: Martinus Nijhoff, 1951

Hugh, Thomas. *Conquest: Montezuma, Cortés, and the Fall of Old Mexico.* New York: Simon & Schuster, 1993.

Kicza, John E. "Indian Freedom: The Cause of Bartolome de Las Casas, 1484–1566, A Reader." *Hispanic American Historical Review* 76 (November 1996): 774.

León-Portilla, Miguel, ed. *The Broken Spears: The Aztec Account of the Conquest of Mexico.* Translated by Angel Maria Garibay K. with Foreword by J. Jorge Klor de Alva. Boston: Beacon Press, 2006.

Wagner, Henry, and Helen Rand Parish. *The Life and Writings of Bartolomé de Las Casas.* Albuquerque: University of New Mexico Press, 1967.

Las Salinas, Battle of

The Battle of Las Salinas, a brief skirmish between the Spanish armies of Francisco Pizzaro and Diego de Almagro, took place on April 6, 1538, at the salt leaches near Cuzco, Peru. It was not the first time Spaniards faced off against each other in the New World, but it was the first major conflict between Spanish forces in Peru. The Pizzarists' victory ensured their rule over Peru and Chile until the Spanish Crown took administrative control.

The battle was the culmination of Pizzaro's and Almagro's ambition to control the Inca capital of Cuzco, which at the time represented the wealth of Peru. Pizarro, whom Charles V (Holy Roman Emperor, Carlos I of Spain) had appointed governor of Peru, established Lima as the Spanish Peruvian capital in January 1535. Pizarro sent his old colleague and rival, Diego de Almagro, to both command Cuzco and to undertake the conquest of Chile. Unable to fulfill both roles simultaneously, Almagro was forced to concede the oversight of Cuzco to Pizarro's younger brothers, Hernando and Gonzalo, during his exploratory expedition to Chile.

Meanwhile, the Spanish Crown awarded Pizarro and Almagro territories with the desirable Cuzco on the disputed borderland. After Almagro left Cuzco for Chile, the Pizarro brothers' poor treatment of the acknowledged Sapa Inca, Manco Inca Yupanqui, resulted in the Inca fleeing to set up an opposition government. Under his leadership, the Incas besieged the city of Cuzco. When Almagro returned, he used his military forces of Spanish and Inca allies to not only lift the siege but also imprison Hernando Pizarro for his role in turning the once cooperative Sapa Inca against the Spanish. Francisco Pizarro and Almagro negotiated a peace settlement that left Almagro in charge of Cuzco pending notification from Spain. In keeping with the agreement, Almagro released Hernando Pizarro.

As soon as Hernando had reached safety, Francisco Pizarro terminated the treaty and warned Almagro to leave Cuzco. The elder Pizzaro had previously called upon governors in other Spanish territories to assist him in quelling the Inca rebellion. Now Pizarro convinced the arriving troops that Almagro was a traitor. Pizarro started the march to Cuzco but age caught up with both the rival conquistadors. Pizarro informed his troops that his brother Hernando would lead the assault while he returned to Lima. Almagro, enfeebled to the point of being carried by litter, turned over his troops to Rodrigo Orgóñez. Morale ebbed amongst the Almagrists. On the eve of battle, nearly 20 percent of Orgóñez's 500 soldiers had to be forced to the battlefield. They retreated once the actual fighting began.

Orgóñez decided not to meet Hernando Pizzaro on the open field, despite his cavalry superiority. Instead he planned a defensive position in the salt leaches five kilometers south of Cuzco, where an arroyo and a marsh provided protection. He put allied Indians on his left flank, guarding the incoming Inca highway, and his infantry in the center guarded by cavalry on both flanks. His infantry was deficient in both manpower and the number and quality of firearms compared to the enemy Spanish forces they confronted. When Hernando Pizzaro's scouts found the road to Cuzco blocked by Indians, Pizzaro had his own Indians do battle against them. Then Pizzaro sent a group of arquebusiers and crossbowmen across the marsh. These soldiers established a line of fire from behind a hill and covered the subsequent infantry and cavalry crossing. Orgóñez ordered his infantry forward; but the pikers wilted under the enemy's chain-shot and retreated into Orgóñez's cavalry position. His horsemen were forced to regroup while Pizzaro led his cavalry across the marsh and formed a line of battle. The two cavalries charged tournament style with both Pizzaro and Orgóñez

jousting, though not against each other. Orgóñez's forces were routed. Pizarro's horsemen and infantry inflicted most of the battle's fatalities on the retreating or already surrendered enemy. Around 200 Almagrists and 50 Pizarrists died, including Orgóñez (murdered) and Almagro (later executed by Hernando Pizzaro for treason).

The carnage from the Battle of Las Salinas, the subsequent execution of Almagro, and the increasingly defiant attitude of the Pizarro brothers turned the Spanish Crown against the conquistadors. Hernando Pizarro, upon his return to Spain, was held in prison for 20 years. Because of the brutality amongst Spanish factions displayed at Las Salinas, Spain eventually established the viceroyalty in Peru.

Jeff Ewen

See also: Almagro, Diego de; Charles V (HRE) or Carlos I of Spain; Manco Inca Yupanqui; Pizarro, Francisco; Pizarro, Hernando.

Resources

Prescott, William. *History of the Conquest of Peru.* Vol. 1. London: Richard Bentley, 1850.

Stewart, Paul. "The Battle of Las Salinas, Peru, and Its Historians." *The Sixteenth Century Journal* 19, no. 3 (Autumn 1988): 407–434.

Laws of Burgos

The Law of Burgos, enacted in 1512, was Spain's first attempt to regulate the treatment of native populations in the New World. The laws, pushed for primarily by the Dominican Order, were concerned with mistreatment of native populations. The Law of Burgos was meant to pertain to all of Spain's colonies. After first contact, Spanish conquistadors had no qualms with torturing, killing, and raping natives in their quest for treasure.

Spanish practices of brutality even extended to many missionaries sent to convert the native population to Catholicism. In such cases, overzealous missionaries resorted to torture and other coercive measures to ensure conversion and cooperation among their neophytes.

Spanish treatment of the native population did not improve once conquest was complete. Native populations, those not decimated by war, soon fell victim to disease. Those natives not killed by war or pestilences were forced to work on plantations or in mines. Natives entered into the state of encomienda, the Spanish method of land ownership and control of the native populations. This method of controlling lower segments of the population was already in place in Spain and brought to the New World. Encomienda gave Spanish lords the right to collect tribute from native villages and to force the natives to give their labor to the encomenderos. Native laborers were not compensated. In return, the encomenderos promised to provide housing for native population, protect the natives, and to facilitate their conversion to Christianity. This system was not designed to give Spanish overseers control of native lands; nor did it provide a means of preventing the exploitation of the natives. In practice, the system quickly devolved into slavery. The encomienda was given as a reward by the Spanish Crown to the same individuals who explored the lands and subdued the natives.

Ideally, the natives were allowed to retain ownership of their lands, raise crops and livestock to feed themselves, and work only a small portion of their time on the projects of their encomenderos. In practice however, the natives were overworked and exploited by the very Spaniards assigned to protect them. Disease and malnutrition ran rampant throughout the villages, further decimating

the population. The Spanish preoccupation with acquiring gold and silver also caused the neglect of the efforts to convert the natives to Christianity.

The condition of the native population caused consternation amongst the Dominican monks in the Caribbean. The order was concerned with the spiritual condition of the tribes, but these monks were also dismayed by the natives' living conditions and the amount of work forced upon the potential converts. In a sermon on Christmas Day in 1511, Friar Antonio de Montesinos denounced treatment of the native population by the encomenderos. Even the encomendero Bartolome de Las Casas in Hispaniola joined the chorus urging reforms in the way natives were treated, a call he carried with him back to Spain where he underwent ordination in the Dominican Order. These individuals, along with their brethren, pushed for more humane treatment of the natives. A papal bull or decree that obligated Spain to treat the peoples they encountered with a degree of humanity gave their arguments added weight. King Ferdinand responded to this tumult by calling for a meeting of leading theologians and officials in Burgos, Spain, in 1512. On December 27, 1512, the Laws of Burgos were announced.

The Laws of Burgos called for more humane treatment of natives, prohibiting beating, whipping, and decreeing that they were to be provided clothing, housing, food, and a more rigorous religious instruction. The law did not prohibit exploitation but sought to humanize the treatment of the exploited natives. Unfortunately, this attempt to ameliorate the treatment of the native population was unsuccessful. The native Tainos of Hispaniola continued to suffer and eventually became extinct as a people. This loss of the indigenous labor pool did not extinguish Spanish growth in the New World, nor did it soon humanize their treatment of forced labor. The abusive treatment bestowed by the Spanish upon the Tainos was extended to the Caribs and eventually mainland populations of the Maya, Mexica, and Incas. With the obvious failure of the Laws of Burgos and the continual decline of indigenous populations, the Spanish turned to the importation of African slaves to supply their labor needs.

Rick Dyson

See also: Encomienda; Encomenderos; Las Casas, Bartolomé de; Slavery, Role of.

Resources

Clayton, Thomas. *Bartolomé de las Casas and the Conquest of the Americas.* Malden, MA: Wiley-Blackwell, 2011.

Simpson, Lesley Byrd. *The Laws of Burgos of 1512–1513: Royal Ordinances for the Good Government and Treatment of the Indians.* San Francisco: J. Howell, 1960.

Leyes Nuevas 1542–1543

The Leyes Nuevas, or New Laws of 1542–1543, were the culmination of a series of debates and policy decisions that occurred during the reign of Charles V (Holy Roman Empire). The intent of the laws was to improve the treatment of the indigenous population by virtue of eradicating the practices of encomienda and repartimiento in New Spain. Typical of many well-intended policies, the Leyes Nuevas had limited results.

The Spanish colonial policies grew out of medieval practices that were also employed during the Reconquista. The explorers and conquistadors employed similar societal hierarchies and labor systems in the Caribbean and other New World colonies. Viewing the natives of the Americas as inferior for their polytheistic religious beliefs, unfamiliar political systems, and unusual cultures, the Spanish justified the reduction and enslavement of the Indians.

One such method of controlling native labor was through the state of encomienda. Used historically by the Spanish as a means of regulating the lower segments of the Spanish population, the encomienda not only provided much needed labor but also afforded a source of tribute for the encomenderos. The indigenous population of the Americas soon came under similar labor systems.

The need for laborers to support the small Spanish populations of the West Indies resulted in the extreme abuse of the native populations in the Caribbean. To remedy these abuses and presumably to provide an environment conducive to converting the indigenous population, Queen Isabella's Real Cedula of 1503 was implemented. Instead of winning converts, this early colonial policy established virtual enslavement and allowed for the extreme quest for gold to justify working the natives to their deaths.

By 1510 the arrival of the Dominicans to the islands brought a counter proposal to Spanish policies. The 1512 law of Burgos was the first attempt of Spain to regulate the use and treatment of indigenous populations. The system employed was the encomienda. Again, the intentions of the system were to provide much needed labor, but also to task the encomenderos with the responsibility of carry for and converting the native laborers. Ideally, this law prohibited the beating and execution of the Native Americans. It also permitted the Indians to own their own lands, raise their own food, and only work a portion of their time on projects for the encomenderos. The reality of disease, overwork, and Spanish greed for mineral wealth negated the best of intentions.

The exploration of new lands in Middle and South America, and the subsequent discovery of great wealth for the conquistadors and Spanish Empire, increased the atrocities wrought upon the indigenous populations. Whether the Tainos or Caribs of the West Indies, the Mayas of the Yucatán, the Aztecs of Mexico, or the Incas of Peru, Spanish practices continued virtually unchecked. To justify the treatment, conquistadors read the *Requerimiento,* elaborating upon the history of the Christian world, the foundation of the Catholic Church, and the sovereignty of the Spanish Crown overseas. Often read in Latin, the indigenous people were informed of their vassal status and encouraged to accept this state or risk a "just war" and enslavement.

In the 1520s, the former colonist Friar Bartolomé de Las Casas vociferously argued against the encomienda system, the *Requerimiento,* and the use of forced conversions. He was challenged by the leading Spanish humanist Juan Ginés de Sepúlveda. Sepúlveda asserted the superiority of the Spanish culture and Catholic faith and the inferiority of the pagan natives of the New World.

Charles V was swayed by Las Casas and embraced a legalistic version of the Dominican friar's arguments. As a result, he issued the Leyes Nuevas of 1542–1543. These New Laws forbade the abusive systems of encomiendas and repartimientos. Nonetheless, the Crown was aware of the shortage of labor in the colonies, and the inability of Spain to enforce the humane edicts. Consequently, while forbidding the existing labor systems, Charles also provided caveats that permitted the continued use of encomiendas. In this fashion, Spanish interests were protected. Special grants were provided that enacted special licenses the perpetuated encomiendas and repartimientos. Indeed, instead of eliminating the enslavement and abuse of native peoples, the New Laws initially increased

complete control by the Spanish over entire native cities.

Though the initial impact of the Leyes Nuevas was detrimental to the indigenous societies, the new policies nonetheless redefined and modified the system of labor used to control the Indians. Within three generations the practice of multigeneration obligations of labor through repartimientos and encomiendas ceased. The demands for tribute continued, as did the need for labor in mines and on plantations. The Leyes Nuevas of 1542–1543 ambitiously sought to redefine the system of indigenous labor in a more humane fashion. In the end, it did improve conditions, but the special caveats that attempted to protect the colonial economic system perpetuated the old abuses well into the 17th century.

Rebecca M. Seaman

See also: Charles V (HRE) or Carlos I of Spain; Encomenderos; Encomienda; Las Casas, Bartolomé de; Laws of Burgos; Repartimiento; *Requerimiento*; Sepúlveda's *De Orbe Novo* (*Historia del Nuevo Mundo*).

Resources

Chamberlain, Robert S. "Castilian Backgrounds of the Repartimiento-Encomienda." *Contributions to American Anthropology and History* 5, no. 25 (June 1939), in Carnegie Institute of Washington, Publication 509. Washington, DC: Carnegie Institute of Washington, 1939.

Charles I of Spain. "De La Libertad De Los Indios." *Recopilacion De Leyes de Los Reynos de Las Indias.* 2nd ed. Madrid: Por Antonio Balbas, 1756.

Charles I of Spain. *The New Laws for the Government of the Indies and for the Preservation of the Indians, 1542–1543.* Introduction by Henry Stevens and Fred Lucas. London: Chiswick Press, 1893; reprint, Amsterdam: N. Israel, 1968.

Hanke, Lewis. *All Mankind is One: A Study of the Disputation Between Bartolomé de Las*

Casas and Juan Ginés de Sepúlveda on the Religious and Intellectual Capacity of the American Indian. DeKalb: Northern Illinois University Press, 1995.

Hanke, Lewis. *Bartolomé de Las Casas: An Interpretation of his Life and Writings.* Hague: Martinus Nijhoff, 1951

Hanke, Lewis. *The Spanish Struggle for Justice in the Conquest of America.* Dallas, TX: Southern Methodist University Press, 2002.

Hoffer, Peter C. *Law and People in Colonial America.* Baltimore, MD: Johns Hopkins University Press, 1998.

Villamarin, Juan A. and Judith E. Villamarin. *Indian Labor in Mainland Colonial Spanish America.* Newark: University of Delaware, 1975.

Lienzo de Tlaxcala

Lienzo de Tlaxcala, also known by the title of "Historia de Tlaxcala," is a pictorial history created in 1550 to depict Tlaxcala's role in the Spanish conquest on the Aztec Empire. "Lienzo" may refer to the medium of the piece: linen or other cloth. However, it is possible that the images were placed on bark paper. Three originals were commissioned; the first was to be sent to Charles V (HRE), the second to Viceroy Luis de Velasco in Mexico, and the third to hang in the town hall or archives of Tlaxcala. In 1787 don Nicolás Faustino Mazihcatzin y Calmecahua provided what remains the primary source for information on the Lienzo de Tlaxcala. He described the Lienzo de Tlaxcala that had remained in Tlaxcala. Shortly after Calmecahua wrote of it, it was sent to the archives in Mexico City to be copied. Tlaxcala requested the return of the item in 1867, when it was determined it had been lost. The other two originals have also been lost. Several copies have survived into the modern age.

The Lienzo de Tlaxcala was commissioned by Viceroy Luis de Velasco, and administered by a local Spanish administrative unit called the cabildo. The names of the actual artists who painted the images remain unknown. Although intended to be artwork that would highlight Tlaxcala's role in the Spanish dominance of the Aztec Empire, the artists drew upon the long-established existing Aztec native tradition of using images to record historical events. The actual style is a partial melding of indigenous tradition and the influence of more European styles.

Forty-two color plates with roughly 80 color scenes were painted, glossed with Nahuatl, the primary Aztec language. These images were drawn to depict specific historical scenes, chosen to highlight Tlaxcala's cooperation with Spanish authority, and their continued loyalty to the new order. Images to be immortalized were carefully considered for political gain. As such, the historical events showcasing Tlaxcala and Spanish unity were reinterpreted for maximum impact. Included in the scenes are several heroic couplings of Cortés and Tlaxcala on the battlefield, broad overviews of the Spanish campaign, and the baptism of Tlaxcala leaders into the Catholic fold. Another notable element is the depiction of Tlaxcala tameme, porters or bearers of Spanish war material. Later victories of the Spanish and Tlaxcala forces over other regions outside Montezuma's domain are also depicted.

In 1791 Joseph Antonio Alzate y Ramirez, the Mexican cleric, scientist, and journalist, made a statement that aptly captured the mission of what remains one of the most popular pieces of indigenous conquest art. "Let us not say that a few hundred Spaniards conquered New Spain. Let us say, rather, that powerful armies united and inspired by the

Lienzo de Tlaxcala, the illustrated Aztec history from ca. 1550. This image uses symbolism and images of the Spanish and Aztec to portray the Battle of Xallipatlavaya. (Archives Charmet/ The Bridgeman Art Library)

gallant and enterprising Spanish battled against the Aztecs, and then we will not be untrue to history."

Michael D. Coker

See also: Cabildo; Charles V (HRE) or Carlos I of Spain; Montezuma II; Nahuatl Language; Tlaxcala, Battle of.

Resources

Matthew, Laura E., and Michel Oudijk. *Indian Conquistadors: Indigenous Allies in the Conquest of Mesoamerica.* Norman: University of Oklahoma Press, 2007.

Schwartz, Stuart B. *Victors and Vanquished.* Boston: Bedford/St. Martins, 2000.

Lima

The capital of modern-day Peru, Lima was historically an important costal city for the Spanish. Founded by Francisco Pizarro in January 1535 under the name of Cuidad de los Reyes, the conquistador sought to situate the Spanish capital closer to the sea where it could be more easily provisioned with goods from Europe. The city's name soon reverted to a derivation of the native name, Lima. Pizarro's new capital also provided enhanced lines of communication for the Spanish and a better climate and elevation, more conducive to the soldiers' health.

Located close to the coast, Lima became the center of incoming Spanish goods as well as newly arriving conquistadors who hoped to capitalize on the discovery of gold and silver wealth from the Inca Empire. It was those same newly arrived soldiers of fortune that Pizzaro sent inland to relieve the besieged city of Cuzco. Within a year of being established, the new capital served as a launching point of relief expeditions for Cuzco during the continued wars with the Inca.

In 1536, the rebelling Inca ruler, Manco Inca Yupanqui, ordered one of his best generals, Quizo, to attack the Spanish city of Lima, to push the Spanish back into the sea. The reputation of the Spanish cavalry prompted Quizo to delay his attack until he gathered more warriors. When he finally laid siege to the city, it was from the heights of the Cerro de San Cristóbal, just across the Rimac River from Lima, in order to prevent a cavalry assault. After six days of siege, Quizo led a full-scale attack, leaving his position of security. The decision proved fatal, with the flat lands around Lima and the walls of the city providing excellent positions for the Spanish defenders. Quizo was killed along with several other strategic leaders of Manco's forces. Lima withstood the attack and continued to serve as the base of the Spanish military and government.

When Pizarro established Cuidad de los Reyes (Lima), he did so as a *republica de españoles,* or city for Spaniards. The Spanish used a system of localized control of the indigenous populace in America that administered Indian towns separately from Spanish towns. The system was intended to provide administrative structures that worked for both societies, while simultaneously leaving the Spanish in ultimate control. The attempt to restrict Lima's population to only Spanish residents was doomed to fail since the Spanish desired native laborers in the cities where Spaniards lived.

While Lima was established as a city of Spaniards and administrated as such, it was also designed to serve as the capital of the new colony established by Pizarro. As a result, the exceptional autonomy of the city's cabildo was countered by the rule of the colony's viceroy from the city. This dual role was further complicated by the presence of the central religious authority, the center of judicial authority, and eventually the *corregidores* de indios or supervisor over the Indians in the colony. The multiple layers of administration and conflicting interests created a bureaucratic nightmare that allowed for corruption and confusion. Yet despite the complex nature of the urban administrative structure, Lima served the Spanish colonial empire well as the seat of the Viceroyalty of Peru.

Rebecca M. Seaman

See also: Cabildo; *Corregidores*; Manco Inca Yupanqui; Pizarro, Francisco; Viceroyalty System.

Resources

Hemming, John. *The Conquest of the Incas.* New York: Harcourt Brace Jovanovich, 1970.

Keen, Benjamin, and Keith Haynes. *A History of Latin America.* 8th ed. Boston: Houghton Mifflin Harcourt, 2009.

Lowry, Lyn Brandon. "Forging an Indian Nation: Urban Indians under Spanish Colonial Control." PhD diss., University of California, Berkeley, 1991.

López de Gómara, Francisco

Francisco de López de Gómara was the private secretary and official biographer for Hernán Cortés in 1552. In his coverage of the Spanish conquest of the America, Gómara interestingly denies Christopher Columbus credit for discovering the New World, while he simultaneously glorifies Spain's conquest in all its violence and devastating impact on the indigenous population. Specific praise is given to Cortés as the embodiment of all the grandeur associated with Spain's discovery and conquest.

Comparisons of Gómara's works to other contemporaries and later historians provide some useful insights about his views on events. Not surprisingly, he depicts Cortés as honorable and brave, following the laws of Spain in his conquest of the Aztecs. Cortés is also portrayed as wise and able to discern trickery, both on the part of the indigenous population and by his own men. When confronted with resistance and rebellion, Gómara's portrayals of the *caudillo* consistently show a decisive leader who applies the letter of the law, often to the worst offender, and then mercifully allows the other offenders to go free on the premise that they had learned their lesson.

As a biographer and personal secretary, Gómara's glorification of Cortés is understandable. However, the chronicler goes even further in praising his idol than Cortés, who was known for his own self-aggrandizement. Nonetheless, the account does provide further information concerning the Spanish conquest of the New World, albeit information that needs to be read with a grain of salt.

Rebecca M. Seaman

See also: Cortés, Hernán.

Resources

Restall, Matthew. *Seven Myths of the Spanish Conquest.* Oxford: Oxford University Press, 2003.

Thomas, Hugh. *Conquest: Montezuma, Cortés, and the Fall of Old Mexico.* New York: Simon & Schuster, 1993.

Lucanas

Located in the southern portion of Peru, the Lucanas province is the largest found in the Ayacucho region. The region is associated with a tribe of indigenous people, eventually absorbed into the Inca Empire.

The Lucanas and Soras peoples, located in the south of Huamanga, were targets of the expanding Inca Empire. Wealthy and well-organized, the Lucanas were economically independent. Their valuable lands and labor came at a cost, however, as the Inca laid siege to the Lucanas fortress for two years before the well-provisioned community ran out of supplies and fell.

With the arrival of the Spanish in 1533, some of the Lucana communities quickly aligned themselves with the invaders, recognizing the strength of their military. These Spanish Lucana allies also acknowledged the potential of a Spanish conquest of Cuzco. For those Lucana communities who sought escape from Inca dominance, the Spanish provided an opportunity for the breakup of the Inca domination of the region and a return to Lucanas independence.

Despite the early willingness of some Lucana communities to throw their hopes behind the Spanish, others remained firm supporters of the Inca imperial leadership. In the 1530s, when Sapa Inca Manco Inca Yupanqui was fleeing his Spanish oppressors, it was the Lucana that provided necessary assistance. Selecting 20 of the fastest runners from among their number, the Lucana bore Manco Inca and his wife in their arms, as was the tradition for transporting royal Incas. Likely of the *chasquis* messengers, these runners were capable to rotating their efforts to run great distances faster than horses could travel in the Andes Mountains. In this relay fashion, the Lucana managed to secret the Sapa Inca away from Spanish cavalry sent to capture the escaping emperor. Even the use of Rodrigo Orgóñez's forces on horseback was not equal to these gifted runners on the rough and narrow trails of the Inca highlands.

Rebecca M. Seaman

See also: *Chasquis*; Manco Inca Yupanqui; Sapa Inca.

Resources

MacQuarrie, Kim. *The Last Days of the Incas.* New York: Simon & Schuster, 2007.

Steve J. Stern. *Peru's Indian Peoples and the Challenge of Spanish Conquest: Huamanga to 1640.* 2nd ed. Madison: University of Wisconsin Press, 1993.

Lugo, Francisco de

Francisco de Lugo appeared many times in Bernal Díaz del Castillo's history of the conquest. Díaz accompanied multiple expeditions, most notably the voyage of conquest under Hernán Cortés. In his chronicles he described Lugo as a captain of several of the expeditions, who strived hard. Lugo was the illegitimate son of Alvarado de Lugo, the elder, the lord of some towns near Medina del Campo, in the province of Valladolid. He was probably a distant relative of both Diego Velázquez, governor of Cuba, and of Bernal Díaz.

Despite Lugo's connections to Velázquez, who initially selected Cortés to lead the expedition and then later attempted to stop the conquistador, he became a staunch supporter of Cortés. Lugo was one of the few conquistadors who brought a war dog along. These animals greatly terrorized the natives. As owner of a dog, he also collected an additional portion of any booty collected by the expedition. Lugo took part in the May 1520 battle against Pánfilo de Narváez, who was sent by Velázquez to attempt to halt Cortés from conquering Mexico. Lugo was one of the leaders of the fore guard during the La Noche Triste, the flight from Tenochtitlán when the natives threatened to destroy the Spanish army. Following that devastating defeat, Francisco de Lugo is believed to be among those who signed the 1520 letter from Segura de la Frontera (Tepeaca) after the expedition regrouped following the rout from Tenochtitlán. This questioning of Cortés seems to have been temporary, for by late fall of the same year he was again considered in the group of close friends and allies of the *caudillo*.

After the eventual fall of Tenochtitlán, Lugo became one of the lieutenants of an expedition led by Cristóbal de Olid to Honduras, and then later went with Gonzalo de Sandoval to settle Coatzacoalcos, on the Gulf coast of the Isthmus of Tehuantepec. He was named as one of the court agents for New Spain in 1526, at which time he was a legal resident of Veracruz. He probably received an encomienda in the Coatzacoalcos region. Francisco de Lugo died of natural causes sometime around 1532.

John Schwaller

See also: Cortés, Hernsán; Díaz del Castillo, Bernal; Encomienda; La Noche Triste; Narváez, Pánfilo; Sandoval, Gonzalo de; Tenochtitlán, Siege of; Velázquez, Diego (de Cuéllar).

Resources

Díaz del Castillo, Bernal. *The History of the Conquest of New Spain,* edited by David Carrasco. Albuquerque: University of New Mexico Press, 2008.

Grunberg, Bernard. *Dictionnaire des conquistadores de Mexico.* Paris: L'Harmattan, 2001.

Thomas, Hugh. *Conquest: Montezuma, Cortés, and the Fall of Old Mexico.* New York: Simon and Schuster, 1993.

Thomas, Hugh. *Who's Who of the Conquistadores.* London: Cassell & Company, 2000.

Luque, Hernando de

Fray Hernando de Luque was a priest who was serving in Panamá during the 1520s. In that position he befriended Francisco Pizarro and Diego de Almagro. Desirous of wealth from discoveries and conquests, the three partners agreed to join forces and finances to undertake an exploratory venture southward along the Pacific coast of South America.

Luque handled much of the finances, possibly even seeking further silent investors such as Judge Gaspar de Espinosa. When the expedition finally left in 1524 the first attempt proved a failure. Two years later the group again funded a second attempt. This attempt was equally disappointing in wealth brought home, but did discover evidence of great wealth to be had further inland. Luque and Almagro encouraged Pizarro to travel to Spain to seek approval for their mission, and grants from King Charles V.

Pizarro did get permission from the king, but his instructions called for him to receive almost all titles and authority, with Almagro being placed in charge of the coastal city of Tumbes. Once again the three partners worked to build up their expeditionary force. Pizarro recruited individuals like Hernando de Soto. Almagro recruited more ships, horses, and men. Meanwhile Luque continued to handle the finances and sought further investors.

In the early 1530s, the expedition finally set sail. Luque once again remained behind. While the expedition went on to make great discoveries of the Inca Empire in Peru, the partnership was crumbling. Pizarro and Almagro were soon at odds with each other. Meanwhile, Luque died in Panama, never to see the land he had worked so hard to settle.

Rebecca M. Seaman

See also: Almagro, Diego de; Charles V (HRE) or Carlos I of Spain; Pizarro, Francisco; Soto, Hernando de.

Resources

Hemming, John. *The Conquest of the Incas.* London: Pan Macmillan, 1970.

MacQuarrie, Kim. *The Last Days of the Incas.* New York: Simon & Schuster, 2007.

M

Macehualtin

The original clan structure, or *calpultin*, of Aztec society adopted a two-tier social class system when the Mexica moved to the region that became their capital city, Tenochtitlán. The more elite class was known as the *pipiltin* and the more numerous commoners, or peasantry, were called the *macehualtin*. The divisions between the two classes deepened in the 15th century when Montezuma I introduced rules of conduct that would clearly designate status. The ordinary *macehualtin* were prohibited from wearing the more valuable cotton clothing, instead making their simple dress from maguey fiber. Their cloaks stopped at their knees, and they were required to go barefoot in the presence of their superiors.

Macehualtin were not permitted to own land or property in their own names. Instead, traditional clan groups communally farmed lands assigned to them. Their houses were limited to single-story structures. Even eating utensils were dictated in the class rules. Earthenware without paint or glaze was the standard for the lower class. Schooling was available, but traditionally only skilled education was provided for the *macehualtin*. Few commoners received instruction in the standard topics of astrology, reading, writing, or theology.

There were exceptions to the rules of class in the first few decades. Those *macehualtin* who distinguished themselves at war sometimes received grants of land in their own names, were released from the burden of paying tribute, or were even allowed to wear cotton. However, opportunities for such freedoms were limited for commoners. With the rise of Montezuma II, the class distinctions became even further embedded. Thus, the Aztec society the Spanish encountered appeared quite rigid and traditional, with little if any leeway for change. Ironically, a *macehual* (singular) was responsible for bringing Montezuma II the first news of the Spanish ships landing on the coast.

Rebecca M. Seaman

See also: Montezuma II; *Pipiltin*.

Resources

León-Portilla, Miguel, ed. *The Broken Spears: The Aztec Account of the Conquest of Mexico.* With Foreword by J. Jorge Klor de Alva. Boston: Beacon Press, 2006.

Thomas, Hugh. *Conquest: Montezuma, Cortés, and the Fall of Old Mexico.* New York: Simon & Schuster, 1993.

Machu Picchu

Founded by the Inca Empire around 1460, Machu Picchu, which means "old peak" in the Quechua language, was an ancient city in the Andes Mountains in Peru. It is located about 43 miles northwest of Cuzco at an altitude of approximately 8,000 feet. The ancient site encompassed several different components of Inca culture, including agriculture, religion, and urban dwelling.

Machu Picchu is situated on the top of a ridge over the Urabamba River and near Huaynca Picchu. The Inca ruler, Pachacutin Inca Yupanqui, built the city between 1460

Machu Picchu, the remote, ceremonial Inca city of the Sapa Incas. (Ben Ferguson)

and 1470. Machu Picchu served several different functions, although its role as a religious ceremonial site seems to have garnered the greatest attention. It is believed to have been used as a religious retreat for royalty. The highest region of Machu Picchu was probably used for ceremonial purposes, as it is too high in the mountains to have been used for agriculture and as it was probably also impractical for governmental or military purposes. It was in a fairly secret location, and few people knew it existed. The city eventually consisted of about 200 buildings, most of which were homes. It included a few temples and other public buildings and warehouses.

The whole site was carefully planned and executed, and the buildings were designed to fit into the existing landscape. The buildings were constructed of masonry in a polygonal shape that was typical of late Inca architecture. The blocks were carved from granite with stone or bronze tools. The blocks were cut precisely to fit together without mortar so tightly that nothing could fit between them. The houses were gathered in groups of 10 around small courtyards and were connected by narrow alleyways. They had thatched roofs and trapezoid-shaped doors, but most of them had no windows.

The Incas raised livestock and grew crops. Using terraces around the city, the domesticated plants included maize and potatoes. The Incas also employed sophisticated irrigation techniques to maximize their harvests.

At the highest plateau, archaeologists have found an *intihuatana,* a column of stone used by priests to prevent the sun from disappearing after the winter solstice. The *intihuatana* appears to have been akin to a sundial. Few *intihuatanas* remain today because the Spaniards destroyed them. However, the Spaniards never found Machu Picchu.

The Incas were ravaged by smallpox in the early 1500s. By the time Francisco Pizarro conquered the Incas in 1532, Machu Picchu had been mostly abandoned. In 1911, Hiram Bingham, a professor from Yale University in the United States, happened across the site, which had remained nearly untouched since the 16th century.

Amy H. Blackwell

See also: Pachacutin.

Resources

Bernand, Carmen. *The Incas: Empire of Blood and Gold.* London: Thames & Hudson, 1994.

Bingham, Hiram. *Lost City of the Incas: The Story of Machu Picchu and Its Builders.* Westport, CT: Greenwood Press, 1981.

Burger, Richard L., and Lucy C. Salazar. *Machu Picchu: Unveiling the Mystery of the Incas.* New Haven, CT: Yale University Press, 2008.

Maize

A plant of the grass family native to America, maize provided the main food to the Mesoamerican peoples before and after the Spanish arrived. In the 17th century, maize was introduced into Europe and then spread to the rest of the world. It was prepared in many forms for food consumption, and it was also immersed in the field of beliefs and cosmological conceptions.

The Spanish used the Taíno word *maize* to refer to the cereal crop whose scientific name is *Zea mays* (belonging to the family of *Poaceae,* which includes other cereals and to the genus *Zea*). It acquired many names, depending on both the geographic region—*choclo* in the Andean region or *elote* in Mesoamerica—as well as the parts and stages of maturity of the plant—*olote* to refer to the trunk with the kernels separated from it and *jilote* or *xilote* to name baby corn.

Maize comes from a wild species called *teocintle* (teosinte), a short and bushy plant. The process of domestication could have begun 7,500 to 12,500 years ago. In the lowlands of the Balsas River valley (southwestern Mexico) were found milling tools with maize residue, approximately 8,700 years old. It is estimated that 7,000 years ago a primitive type of maize was grown in southern Mexico, Central America, and northern South America. Ancient maize was also found in the Guilá Naquitz cave, Oaxaca (3500 BC), and in Tehuacán, Puebla (3000 BC). Apart from these diverse origins, it is generally recognized that at the time prior to the Pre-Classic period (2500 BC), maize was already domesticated and in the process of becoming one of the main products of Mesoamerican sedentary peoples.

In hunter-gatherer groups, the harvest activity was essentially feminine. Consequently, women were associated with the process of selective manipulation of the plant, which led to its full domestication. This first stage of "incidental domestication" was followed by another of "specialized domestication," in which the relationship between maize and human groups was intensified. Then maize became a human plant, meaning it is not able to reproduce itself but needed the intervention of man. In addition to adapting its growth to very diverse environmental conditions, producing it in both dry and irrigated land, humans developed techniques and tools to process and store maize. Among these tools were *metates* for grinding, pots for cooking and storing, and *comales* (griddles) to heat *tortillas*. Maize was the major staple food (along with squash, potato in Andean region, quinoa, beans, and amaranth) of most pre-Hispanic North American, Mesoamerican, South American, and Caribbean cultures.

The most important technique used to process maize is called *nixtamalización*. It consists of boiling the grains in water with the calcium compound of lime to trigger a chemical process that alters the properties of maize. In this manner, its nutritive potential increases and the digestion is facilitated. *Nixtamalización* could have been done from very early times. Otherwise, maize would not have the importance it gained. Around 1,000 BC, maize became the essential ingredient of the Mesoamerican diet, and in the days before the Spanish conquest, it was the main food. This created a relationship between the population growth and the increasing complexity of political and economic relations on one hand to the high productive capacity and the fact that grains could be stored for a long time on the other hand. With the arrival of the Spanish and the new European products and crops (wheat, mainly), maize underwent changes and adaptations. Today it remains a fundamental part of the Mesoamerican and South American diet.

A negative associated with the same *nixtamalización* process is the resulting iron-deficiency anemia. Maize, already poor in proteins and iron, further depleted iron in Native Americans following the adding of lime to the processing of the kernels. In essence, the excess calcium inhibited the body's ability to absorb iron. Consequently, those societies that became increasingly dependent upon maize as a primary food source also saw an increase in female fertility and population expansion, while they simultaneously saw a shortening of life spans and an increase in infant mortality. In those societies with maize as the dominant food source, anemia occasionally increased to the point of suppressing the immune system. However, throughout most of the Americas, maize typically supplemented diets, except in periods of extreme hardship (drought, wars).

Because of the domestication of maize, there are a wide variety of species—between 220 and 300 in the Americas. The different varieties were used in the preparation of the various dishes. Although people used to eat the corncob or the grains simply boiled and seasoned, most of the dishes were made from the mass obtained in the *nixtamal*. Perhaps the original way in which this mass was consumed was in the form of *tamales* (dough with some stew inside, covered with the maize leaf and cooked). However, the *tortilla* (flat round dough, cooked on the *comal*) in its different versions was—and remains—the quintessential food. Additionally, the maize was used to make beverages, both nonalcoholic, such as *atole,* and alcoholic, as *pozol, chicha,* and *tesguino.*

In the symbolic aspect, maize was very important to Mesoamerican peoples. The different stages of grain development were put on an equal footing with the course of society, and marked the ritual life and social and productive activities, such as war. Maize was used even in certain rites of divination. In the mythical discourse there was a deep association between human being and maize. We can observe it in some Mayan sources of the 16th century: the *Popol Vuh* tells that the gods created man from a mixture of white and yellow maize, and the *Annals of the Cakchiquel* mention the mixture of maize dough with the blood of tapir and snake. With regard to one of the goddesses of maize among the Mexica, Chicomecoatl, it was said to be "the body and the life of men." Maize also played an important role in the arrangement of the Universe, as its plant was located in the center, like *axis mundi*.

Marta Martín Gabaldón

See also: Aztec, or Mexica; Tribute, Paid to Mexica.

Resources

Christenson, Allen J. "Maize Was Their Flesh: Ritual Feasting in the Maya Highlands." In *Pre-Columbian Foodways: Interdisciplinary Approaches to Food, Culture, and Markets in Ancient Mesoamerica,* edited by John E. Staller and Michael Carrasco, 577–600. New York: Springer, 2009.

Kelton, Paul. *Epidemics & Enslavement: Biological Catastrophe in the Native Southeast, 1492–1715.* Lincoln: University of Nebraska Press, 2007.

Staller, John E. *Maize Cobs and Cultures: History of Zea mays L.* New York: Springer, 2010.

Staller, John E., Robert H. Tykot, and Bruce F. Benz. *Histories of Maize in Mesoamerica. Multidisciplinary Approaches.* Walnut Creek, CA: Left Coast Press, 2010.

Warman, Arturo. *La historia de un bastardo: maíz y capitalismo.* México D.F.: Universidad Nacional Autónoma de México-Fondo de Cultura Económica, 1995.

Malquis

In Inca society, the mummies or *malquis* were recognized by members of an *ayllu*— or in case of the Inca nobility, members of a *panaca*—as their ancestors. Worshipped as the creator, the complex practice of ancestral worship became interconnected with worship of Viracocha, the creator god. As the original creator of the goods and properties bequeathed to their descendants, the mummies wielded real power over the real world in the minds of their children. Successful harvests, childbirth, health, abundant rain, and sunshine all reflected the benevolent attention of one's *malquis*.

To ensure that the possessions passed down from one's ancestor would produce plenty and result in health and long life, members of a particular *ayllu* had to fulfill certain obligations. The mummy must be protected and properly cared for. The descendants also were required to make offerings and give obeisance to the appropriate Huacas and even the *malquis* of their ancestors.

Rebecca M. Seaman

See also: *Ayllus;* Huacas.

Resources

Isbell, William. *Mummies and Mortuary Monuments: A Postprocessual Prehistory of Central Andean Social Organization.* Austin: University of Texas Press, 1997.

Stern, Steve J. *Peru's Indian Peoples and the Challenge of Spanish Conquest: Huamanga to 1640.* 2nd ed. Madison: University of Wisconsin Press, 1993.

Manco Cápac

The legendary founder of the Inca dynasty, Manco Cápac, is said to have emerged from an underground journey with his brothers in the 11th century. Different origin stories indicate there were eight original siblings, four brothers and four sisters, all whom emerged out of a cave or underground passage and then were sent out to conquer and rule other people of the Andes. Still another legend holds that the creator god, Viracocha created humans in the image of statues he had already made of stone. This later legend fits with archaeological evidence of stone statutes developed by some of the predecessors of the Inca, the Tiwanaku. All legends bear similarities to other ancient Native American origin stories, most of which have humans created out of the earth (holes in the ground, from the mountains or out of water).

In the case of Manco Cápac, the mythical figure emerged from a cave at Pacaritambo with his brothers and sisters to create the first *ayllu* (kinship group) to which all Sapa Inca could trace their ancestors. The brothers oversaw the other *ayllus* that emerged from two other caves, all in the proximity of Cuzco. Though Manco Cápac was probably also a historical figure, there is no documented evidence that supports his actual existence. Purportedly, he married his sister, and they gave birth to Sinchi Roca, considered by some to be the first historically documented figure among the Sapa Incas. More recent archaeologists and historians attribute the first four Inca (Manco Cápac,

Manco Cápac, legendary founder of the dynasty, in a crude 17th-century depiction. (Author's Collection)

Sinchi Roca, Lloque Yupanque, and Mayta Cápac) to mythological origins.

Another version of the Inca origins and Manco Cápac comes from El Inca, Garcilaso de la Vega. Half Spanish and half Inca, he traveled to Spain at the age of 21 and after a career of military service, wrote about the Inca late in his life. According to Garcilaso, the Sun god, Inti, created Manco Cápac and his sister/wife Mama Occlo, setting them on an island in Lake Titicaca. They traveled north to where Cuzco is today, finding a village where people lived in squalor. Here, the couple trained the people about agriculture, animal husbandry, and about the arts. This version of the Inca sanitizes the Inca image of most objectionable traits, such as human sacrifice.

Additional tenets that originated within the Manco Cápac myth include assertions of divine connections to the Sun god, Inti. This assertion was passed on to each generation. However, according to the relation of Pedro Sarmiento de Gamboa's *History of the Incas,* the final Inca, Túpac Amaru, publicly admitted prior to his execution that the divine connection of the Incas to the Sun god was a lie used to manipulate the people. The first mythological account of such deception appears when Manco Cápac donned armor of gold that reflected the sun's rays, and housed a gold disc in the Sun temple as a means of convincing the people of his connection to the Sun god, Inti.

Whatever the origin of this mythical founder, all Inca traced much of their cultural heritage to Manco Cápac. In addition to being the ancestral figure for all later Incas, he is portrayed as having a violent temper, often credited with killing his own brothers. Practices of incest among the Inca rulers are also traced to Manco, and were justified as a means of keeping the royal and divine bloodlines pure. Woven together with the various narratives of the mythical first Inca and the origins of the empire were a plethora of animistic deities, local tribal huacas (spirits or totems), and a string of shrines and holy places, such as the caves associated with the creation stories. In each instance, Manco Cápac appears as the founding Inca and the founder of Cuzco.

Rebecca M. Seaman

See also: *Ayllus;* Huacas; Sapa Inca; Sarmiento's *History of the Incas*; Túpac Amaru; Vega, Garcilaso de la.

Resources

Covey, R. Alan. "Multiregional Perspectives on the Archaeology of the Andes during the Late Intermediate Period (c. A.D. 1000–1400)." *Journal of Archaeological Research* 16 (September 2008): 287–338.

Gamboa, Pedro Sarmiento de. *History of the Incas.* Translated and edited by Sir Clements Markham. Cambridge: Hakluyt Society.

Hemming, John. *The Conquest of the Incas.* San Diego, CA: Harcourt Brace Jovanovich, 1970.

Henson, Sändra Lee Allen. "Dead Bones Dancing: The Taki Onqoy, Archaism, and Crisis in Sixteenth Century Peru." MA Thesis, East Tennessee State University, 2002.

MacQuarrie, Kim. *The Last Days of the Incas.* New York: Simon & Schuster, 2007.

Manco Inca Yupanqui

Also known as Manco II, he was one of several sons born to Huayna Cápac in 1516. His rise to the position of Sapa Inca (unique emperor) was paved by the deaths of his father and brothers, which were attributed to Spanish-introduced disease, war, and execution. The Spanish crowned him initially as a puppet emperor. Within two years, poor treatment by the Europeans compelled him to flee the capital of Cuzco and begin a guerrilla war against his oppressors that outlasted his own life.

Huayna Cápac, Sapa Inca until his death in 1527, gave birth to hundreds of children. With his untimely death due to smallpox, his son Ninan Cuyochi was designated Inca. However, Ninan died of the same disease before news of his title arrived. Huayna's secondary choice was for his eldest son, Huáscar, to receive the royal fringe of the Sapa Inca. Undisciplined and uninterested in the daily duties of ruling, Huáscar was reluctantly approved by the nobles. His lack of military experience at a time when the empire was experiencing internal upheaval from rebellions and disease resulted in a younger brother, Atahualpa, contesting the authority of Huáscar. Many nobles and military leaders favored the younger brother and the empire erupted in civil war.

The civil war devastated villages and agricultural production, while disease continued to traumatize the population. Into this morass, Francisco Pizarro entered the region. Atahualpa's recent success and capture of his half-brother, Huáscar, left him in control of a huge army of over 40,000 men. However, the Spanish used their horses, weapons, surprise, and the tactics of dividing Inca subjects against their emperor to overwhelm and capture Atahualpa. Pizarro demanded and received a ransom of gold and silver. Nonetheless the Spanish executed Atahualpa. In his place, Pizarro crowned the eldest surviving son of Huayna Cápac, Túpac Huallpa, who reigned only three months before dying of illness.

In 1533, another son of Huayna Cápac approached Pizarro, seeking the title as Sapa Inca. Manco Inca Yupanqui was promised the title and royal fringe designating his status as emperor if he assisted the Spanish in capturing Cuzco. Pizarro viewed Manco much as his predecessor Túpac, a useful puppet to help control the rebellious Inca. Manco Inca represented the Cuzco faction within the empire, and presented Pizarro with the opportunity of appearing the hero who liberated the capital from the northern dominance of Atahualpa's supporters. Initially, the 17-year old Inca complied with his expected role. With the support of Manco, the Europeans captured Cuzco. With the city under Spanish control, Pizarro crowned Manco Inca as Sapa Inca, the fifth Inca in a span of six years.

Pizarro asserted his role was to ensure that the Cuzco faction should hold power. In reality, he sought to control the seat of power, and the mineral and agricultural wealth of the empire. To accomplish his agenda, Pizarro carefully treated Manco with proper respect. Thirty years older than his younger brothers who accompanied him, Pizarro realized that by accommodating the young emperor, the Spanish could easily control the empire. The younger Pizarro brothers were not so shrewd. When Francisco Pizarro was absent from Cuzco, the Pizarro brothers taunted, abused, and humiliated the emperor. Manco so feared for his life that he reportedly fled for protection to the bedchambers of Diego de Almagro, *adelantado* for the southern portion of Peru.

Manco's worst fear became reality by the fall of 1535. Originally partners on the South American expedition, Pizarro and Almagro now competed for control of their new conquest. King Charles I hoped to quell the division by awarding Pizarro the northern part of Peru and Almagro the southern part. Almagro set off to explore his southern kingdom with a small Spanish army and thousands of native warriors and porters to carry supplies. Manco Inca insisted that his younger brother, Paullu, join Almagro on the expedition. Meanwhile, Francisco Pizarro left Cuzco to establish ports along the coastline. Manco Inca was left to face the Pizarro brothers on his own. The youngest brother, Gonzalo Pizarro, sated his lust for power, wealth, and beautiful women by targeting the possessions of Manco Inca, to include the Inca's primary wife, his sister through whom the pure bloodline of the Inca's would descend. Manco's naiveté regarding his Spanish allies melted away, revealing the abuses to his person and household. Additionally, reports from around the various provinces of the empire revealed similar treatment of the native population. In November of the same year, Manco Inca called a secret meeting of the ruling Inca. He laid out a strategy for a rebellion in the form of guerilla warfare against the Spanish and any native people who supported the foreigners.

The rebellion began with a siege of Cuzco in hopes of expelling the Spanish. While successful in isolating the foreigners in a city that was devastated by warfare, Manco was unsuccessful in defeating his enemy. After nine months under siege, Almagro returned from Chile. In an effort to win over the emperor and the besieged Spanish, Almagro immediately sought a conference with the Sapa Inca. No longer a naive teenager, Manco Inca rejected Almagro's advances. Meanwhile, the Pizarros interpreted Almagro's decision to negotiate with the Inca prior to rescuing the city as a betrayal. The Pizarro forces attacked Almagro's armies. Paullu, previously loyal supporter of Manco Inca, initially threw his army behind Almagro but then shifted sides again to support the Pizarros. Eventually Almagro was defeated and killed and the Spanish proclaimed Paullu as the new Sapa Inca. Supporters of Almagro and Pizarro continued to war against each other, enabling Manco Inca to carry on his devastating guerilla war against both sides.

Four years later, loyal supporters of Almagro assassinated Francisco Pizarro. Seven surviving assassins fled to Vilcabamba for protection from Manco Inca. For two years, the emperor cautiously protected the assassins while continuing his campaign against the Spanish. By 1544, political conditions shifted in Spanish-controlled Peru, affording the assassins an opportunity to leave their self-imposed exile. When Manco Inca next visited their exile in Vitcos, they killed their unsuspecting benefactor, in front of his young son. The rebellious Inca emperor was dead, but his resistance movement against the foreign invaders continued for another 25 years.

Rebecca M. Seaman

See also: Almagro, Diego de; Huayna Cápac; Paullu Inca; Pizarro, Francisco; Sapa Inca; Túpac Huallpa; Vilcabamba.

Resources

Gamboa, Pedro Sarmiento de. *History of the Incas.* Translated and Edited by Sir Clements Markham. Cambridge, UK: Hakluyt Society, 1907.

MacQuarrie, Kim. *The Last Days of the Incas.* New York: Simon & Schuster, 2007.

Pedro Sancho. *An Account of the Conquest of Peru.* Translated by Philip Ainsworth Means. New York: The Cortex Society, 1917.

Matienzo, Juan de

Juan de Matienzo was a jurist and an entrepreneur. He traveled to Peru in search of wealth in the mid-16th century. It was there that he became involved in the process of luring the Sapa Inca Titu Cusi Yupanqui from out of his government in exile at Vilcabamba.

Matienzo was typical of so many Spanish colonists and conquistadors at the time, in that he was convinced of the effectiveness and honorability of the encomendero system. He sought not only to organize indigenous labor under Castilian rule, but to guarantee the indoctrination of the Incas in the Catholic faith.

With Matienzo's assistance, the conditions of the Treaty of Acobamba were renegotiated. Titu Cusi sought further guarantees of proper treatment of the Inca at the hands of the Spanish. He additionally sought approval for his son to receive dispensation from the Church to marry his first cousin. Finally, Titu Cusi would himself receive a sizeable repartimiento. In return, the Sapa Inca promised to descend from his refuge in Vilcabamba.

The treaty was finally agreed to and signed in 1566. However, the condition concerning dispensation for his son was not documented until 1569, at which time Titu Cusi complied with the document.

Rebecca M. Seaman

See also: Acobamba, Treaty of; Titu Cusi Yupanqui.

Resources

Jacobs, James. "Tupac Amaru: The Life, Times, and Execution of the Last Inca." *The Andes Web Ring.* http://www.jqjacobs.net/andes/tupac_amaru.html (accessed May 20, 2012).

Stern, Steve J. *Peru's Indian Peoples and the Challenge of Spanish Conquest: Huamanga to 1640.* 2nd ed. Madison: University of Wisconsin Press, 1993.

Titu Cusi Yupanqui. *The Conquest of Peru: An Inca Account of the Conquest of Peru.* Translated, Introduced, and Annotated by Ralph Bauer. Boulder: University Press of Colorado, 2005.

Maya

The exact origins and settlement of Mayan people, in the region now known as the Yucatán, is unknown. However, archeological evidence revealed that permanent settlements, with house platforms, pottery, and grinding stones indicative of agricultural practices, existed in the region as early as 2000 BC. The discovery of these archaeological ruins directly beneath later Classic period structures (250–800 CE) supports theories of these formative societies giving rise to the later Mayan civilization. One of the strongest theories of origins suggests enduring influences from the Olmec society that dominated the Mesoamerican region prior to the Mayas.

Whatever the source of certain Mayan cultural traits, from their hieroglyphic writing to the calendric rounds and agriculture, these inventions achieved their highest form in the middle of the Classic period. This Golden Age of Mayan culture wove the math and science of astronomy and calendar systems with their religious beliefs. The advancement of their math was evident in such unusual early inclusions as the concept of zero—not adopted by the Europeans until the Middle Ages. In the Mayan calendar, the astronomical precision became evident. Additionally their calendar indicates that, unlike their European counterparts, the Maya perceived life and events as cyclical, as opposed to linear. Weaving their religious perceptions into their system of charting the days and years, the Maya calendar involved the various deities of good and sometimes evil taking turns bearing the burdens of life. The success, or lack thereof, of the benevolent deities to shoulder these burdens over the course of their assigned year determined the events that affected the lives of the Mayan people.

Mayan societies were scattered throughout the region of the Yucatán and into the heart of Mesoamerica. At varying periods, these independent communities would experience peace and prosperity and then wars and famines. Despite their independent nature, the Mayan city-states participated in formal, territorial organization, sometimes resembling a loose empire, while most often resembling confederations of related allies. At different points in the past, the center for the more unified sociopolitical eras resided in initially Chichen Itza and then, following a civil war in the 1200s, in Mayapan. When calamities beset the overall Mayan region, fragmentation of these formal organizations occurred, resulting in civil wars. However, even in the midst of these periods of strife, elements of cooperation appear when outside forces invade the Mayan territories.

At the point of Spanish exploration and conquest of the Yucatán, the Mayan people were experiencing the aftermath of one of the civil wars that saw the fall of Mayapan. With scattered independent communities, the authority centered under the individual strong religious/political leaders known initially as *k'uhul ajaw* or holy lords. This concept of political and religious leadership centralized in a singular person appeared throughout the Mayan communities at the time of the Spanish conquest and continued in the early colonial period, though the name shifted to one more of Spanish linguistics, such as rey, or cacique or king.

Much like the invading Spanish, the acknowledged native leaders, or *ajaw,* were supported by an intensively hierarchical system of lesser lords and priests. Indeed, the greater the hierarchical structure, the greater the authority of the holy lord over the city-state. Those lords capable of extending their authority over neighboring cities displayed the strongest authority.

At the time of Cortés's arrival in the Yucatán in 1519, that authority of these caciques was mainly restricted to their own city-state. However, it is evident from the reports of some that collaboration among the caciques occurred as a means of warding off the invasion and influence of the Spanish. The Maya seemed to use this system of collaboration as a means of restricting the authority of the Aztec, whose Triple Alliance had spread into the region, demanding the payment of humans for sacrifice and laborers on a regular basis.

From the reports of Spanish traders in the first two decades of the 16th century, as well as the later reports of stranded individuals such as Fr. Gerónimo de Aguilar and the conquering forces of Cortés, a picture of an advanced society appears. The Spaniards, dismayed at the lack of high civilization and wealth evidenced by the Tainos and Caribs of the Caribbean islands, were impressed with the majestic structures, well-laid out cities, and evidence of gold found in the Yucatán Mayan communities. While impressed with the architecture and social structure, the Spanish were dismayed by the evidence of blood sacrifices, typically small sacrifices made by self-administered cuts on the priests, but also inclusive of occasional human sacrifices.

Believing that the Maya represented a more advanced culture that could support Spanish desires for wealth and land, the Spanish used these practices of idolatry to justify their assertions of supremacy and use of war to conquer the Mayan people. The scattered nature and shifting alliances of the Maya sometimes assisted the Spanish in their object of conquest. Certainly, the Mayan desire to use the Spanish to reject Aztec authority played into the Spanish hands. However, it was almost 40 years before the Spanish firmly controlled the numerous Mayan communities

of Mesoamerica, taking advantage of their growing native allies, the impact of disease on the indigenous populations, and the impression made by the success of the small number of Spanish upon the previously indomitable Aztec Empire.

Rebecca M. Seaman

See also: Aguilar, Fr. Gerónimo de; Calendar System of Maya; Caribs; Chichen Itza; Cortés, Hernán; Yucatán Peninsula; Yucatán, State of after Spanish Conquest; Yucatán, State of prior to Spanish Conquest; Zempoala.

Resources

Clendinnen, Inga. *Ambivalent Conquests: Maya and Spaniard in Yucatán, 1517–1570.* 2nd ed. Cambridge: Cambridge University Press, 2003.

Diaz, Bernal. *The Conquest of New Spain.* London: Penguin Books, 1963.

Gallenkamp, Chares. *Maya: The Riddle and Rediscovery of a Lost Civilization.* New York: Viking Penguin, 1985.

Jackson, Sarah E. "Continuity and Change in Early Colonial Maya Community Governance: A Lexical Perspective." *Ethnohistory* 58, no. 4 (Fall 2011): 683–726.

Landa, Diego de. *Yucatan: Before and After the Conquest.* Translated with Notes by William Gates. New York: Dover Publications, 1978.

Thomas, Hugh. *Conquest: Montezuma, Cortés, and the Fall of Old Mexico.* New York: Simon & Schuster, 1993.

Mayeques

The term refers to a social class, or possibly profession, within the Mexica society. While still technically classified as part of the *macehualtin* class, this group was neither free nor truly enslaved. The closest comparison to European class structures would be serfdom. The *mayeques* worked the land for others, though typically for only a set period of time. Likely this group was descended from captives or slave populations in the Aztec society. Like the other *macehualtin,* the *mayeques* had little if any wealth and were required to serve in the military, pay tributes (taxes), and contribute to public works. Unlike the rest of the *macehualtin,* the *mayeques* could not take part in public festivals.

Often the *mayeques* services were attached to land grants, similar to serfs. Originally, the *calpulli* of the Mexica were clan or kinship groupings. However, as the Aztec society became larger and more complex, the *calpulli* became more complex as well, responsible for land distribution, public labor drafts, and allotments for military service. Eventually, the nobility broke free of the *calpulli* restrictions. Claiming private lands, these nobles also required elements of the populace, the *mayeques,* to serve them by farming their lands. They did not extend the full rights of citizenship to their serf-like laborers. Instead, by prohibiting participation in communal activities and keeping the laborers distinctly separate, the nobility managed to isolate them from the rest of the Mexica society. Yet the *mayeques* status, though slightly lower than the typical *macehualtin,* still managed to remain above the classification of real slaves, or *tlatlacotin.*

Rebecca M. Seaman

See also: Aztec, or Mexica; *Macehualtin.*

Resources

León-Portilla, Miguel, ed. *The Broken Spears: The Aztec Account of the Conquest of Mexico.* With Foreword by J. Jorge Klor de Alva. Boston: Beacon Press, 2006.

Prescott, William H. *History of the Conquest of Mexico.* 1843. New York: Harper & Brothers; reprint, New York: Random House Modern Library Paperback, 2001.

Thomas, Hugh. *Conquest: Montezuma, Cortés, and the Fall of Old Mexico.* New York: Simon & Schuster Press, 1993.

Mercedes

The Spanish term *mercedes* refers to land grants made in New Spain. The *merced* (singular) could be granted simply for use of the land, or for ownership of the land in question. These land grants often were associated with encomiendas. Privileged Spaniards or deserving military officials were either granted lands or purchased lands through a *merced,* and then would also receive additional grants of encomienda, assigned indigenous people, for the purpose converting to Christianity, collecting tribute from, and for use as paid laborers. Unlike the original grants to encomenderos, *Mercedes* were not automatically passed on to one's heirs. A special fee had to be paid to make a *merced* hereditary.

In the initial years, Spanish land grants were not distributed, except in small portions. Instead, early explorers and conquistadors sought wealth through other means. Additionally, Indian agriculture supplied the early Spanish needs. When land was distributed in the first few decades, the governor of the colony distributed the land grants. However, as the cabildos, or town councils, were established, *mercedes* came under their authority. Extensive indigenous depopulation due to disease, migration, and war coincided with the development of Spanish town councils. The initial lack of structure by cabildos in assigning and recording *Mercedes* in New Spain resulted in a hodgepodge of land claims. Not until the establishment of the 1571 *Composición* was a system implemented that provided sufficient structure to clarify landholdings.

In Peru, the small number of Spanish colonists relied upon the Inca for food supplies, either through tribute or military conquests.

This dependence and the tentative hold of the Spanish over the Inca delayed the immediate assignment of land grants. Within a decade, *Mercedes* were granted to not only Spanish encomenderos in Peru, but also to their native *kurakas* (native lord) as a means of establishing large estancias (ranches).

Rebecca M. Seaman

See also: Cabildo; Encomienda; Encomendero; Estancia; *Kuraka.*

Resources

Gibson, Charles. *Spain in America.* New York: Harper & Row, 1967.

Stern, Steve J. *Peru's Indian Peoples and the Challenge of Spanish Conquest: Huamanga to 1640.* Madison: University of Wisconsin Press, 1993.

Mercury

The importance of Mercury in the Spanish colonial empire was rooted in the mining and processing of silver. Originally, the method for processing the silver was a crude but inexpensive series of steps that included breaking up the ore with heavy hammers, followed by smelting the ore. The problem with regard to the colonial silver mines was that the mines were typically found in regions with a shortage of fuel supplies for the smelting process. By 1556 a new procedure of amalgamation was discovered, wherein mercury was used to separate silver from the raw ore.

In 1563, approximately 250 miles southeast of Lima, mercury was discovered on a high mountainous outcrop. Mercury mining immediately proved profitable to the struggling Peruvian colony. By 1572, under the leadership of the new viceroy, Francisco de Toledo, the town of Huancavelica was established for the purpose of developing the mercury at the site. As the only major mercury-producing mine in the Spanish American colonies, and with silver serving as the major metal of preference at that time, Huancavelica gained in wealth and status. Nonetheless, the town's population remained primarily indigenous, a result of the use of native laborers for the mining process.

Over the years, the mining of mercury resulted in high mortality rates. The poor conditions, lack of ventilation, extreme temperatures between the mines and the surface, in addition to handling of the deadly material, all increased the death rates of the miners. To maintain the numbers needed to guarantee the necessary supplies of mercury, Toledo and later administrators used a variety of techniques to acquire indigenous miners. Toledo's *mita* system, which employed a version of the repartimiento, worked initially, but the increased death rates could not be sustained solely by forced labor.

Use of a wage labor system worked to a limited extent, but the workers soon realized that cost of their labor far exceeded the pay received. The incorporation of the repartimiento *mercancias* combined the repartimiento labor system with compulsory purchase of goods from the district administrators. This system often was combined with the practice of extending desired advancements of goods and cash to "help" the natives cover rising tribute payments. Together, the lure of cash advancements that indebted the working populace and wage labor provided a means of compelling the Incas and other indigenous people to continue working in the deathtrap mercury mines.

It was not the death toll of the process that caused a declining support for using the amalgamation process, however. Corrupt colonial officials eventually discovered that the Crown could effectively track the production of silver—and therefore the evasion of paying the royal fifth and other related taxes—by the amount of mercury purchased by the silver mines. With such knowledge, mercury diminished as a preferred method of extracting the silver ore, thus guaranteeing the ability of the colonial officials and mining administrators to divert profits from the mines to their own benefit. Nonetheless, the importance of mercury in conjunction with the mining of silver survived throughout the Spanish colonial period of Peru.

Rebecca M. Seaman

See also: Huancavelica; *Mita;* Repartimiento; Silver; Toledo, Francisco de.

Resources

Keen, Benjamin and Keith Haynes. *A History of Latin America.* 8th ed. Boston: Houghton Mifflin Harcourt, 2009.

Pearce, Adrian J. "Huancavelica 1700–1759: Administrative Reform of the Mercury Industry in Early Bourbon Peru." *Hispanic American Historical Review* 79, no. 4 (November 1999): 669–702.

Mexico, State of after Spanish Conquest

The Spanish conquest of the Aztecs and other Mesoamerican peoples served economic as well as religious purposes. The conquistadores initially sought gold, but early colonists and the Crown employed Indians as silver miners and farm workers. Also, missionary priests accompanied the conquistadores and began immediately to proselytize Roman Catholic Christianity. Hence the two institutions that most greatly impacted native people were the encomienda, a grant of native labor with geographic boundaries to a high-ranking Spaniards, which organized Indian labor for financial profit and the Catholic Church.

After Hernán Cortés's successful conquest of the Aztec Empire in 1521, a steady stream of mostly male Spaniards came to settle in the new colony, known as New Spain. They built the colonial capital, Mexico City, over the ruins of Tenochtitlán. Other Spanish settlements replaced Aztec towns as well. A few of the Nahua or Aztec nobility learned Spanish and took part in the colonial economy. Many Nahua people died from diseases to which they had no immunity. Most of those who survived stayed in their home communities and continued to speak Nahuatl, but adopted Christianity as the religion of their conquerors. Yet in some ways, life remained the same for most indigenous people, who continued to communicate with one another in their native tongues. These new subjects of the Spanish Empire adopted Christianity as the religion of their conquerors.

In the months following the conquest, Hernán Cortés persuaded the reluctant Spanish king, Charles V (HRE—Carlos I of Spain), to permit the establishment of the encomienda system throughout the conquered areas of Mesoamerica. Under this arrangement, Indians living in an area encompassed by an encomienda had to deliver goods and provide services to the encomendero; in return, at the Spanish Crown's insistence, the encomendero was responsible for protecting the Indians and fostering their conversion to Christianity. Most of the Indian labor was dedicated to farming and mining.

While exploiting Indians, the encomienda system also allowed Nahua village government and cultural mores to continue. Most encomienda boundaries corresponded to the previous Aztec *altepetl* or administrative areas, and this precolonial political structure remained in place for at least a century beyond the conquest. The Spaniards used it principally to control land distribution and to collect taxes.

In the religious realm, Spanish and other European Catholic missionaries journeyed into Nahua territory rapidly and energetically. They set out to convert all the Indians to Christianity as quickly as possible and were largely successful. They became popular among the Indians by learning the Nahuatl language and the Aztec religion so as to deliver meaningful homilies and lessons, and by protecting the Indians from excessive exploitation at the hands of encomenderos and Spanish officials.

Employing indigenous manual labor, the missionaries led the way in constructing church buildings. Typically, whether in small villages or in Mexico City, Spanish churches stood atop the ruins of Aztec temples when completed. This practice sent an unmistakable message that the Christian god was superior and must be worshiped in lieu of the Aztec deities. For the Nahuas, these Christian structures meant continuity in the location and importance of a sacred venue. Local churches were a source of pride and identity among indigenous villages.

Throughout the 16th century, epidemics repeatedly devastated Mesoamerica's native people. Measles, smallpox, typhus, mumps, and other unidentified diseases appear to have reduced the Nahua population from 1.2 million in 1521 to less than a quarter million by 1600. As the Nahua population diminished, the Catholic friars promoted a policy of *congregación,* whereby Indians were brought together into new, larger towns, all with churches. This practice helped missionaries protect the Indians from excessive exploitation at the hands of unscrupulous Spaniards while enabling colonial administrators to collect taxes more easily.

The Nahuas quickly became nominal Christians while clinging to some of their old religious ideas. Lacking the concept of "religion" or even "faith" per se, they instead blended Aztec and Christian beliefs into a syncretic amalgam. This meant that most Nahuas accepted Catholic sacraments and worship routines against the backdrop of surviving precolonial traditions. This melding of indigenous and European religions expressed itself through the display of Aztec symbols and artifacts in early colonial churches and convents.

In terms of continuity and change, the Spanish conquest affected Aztec civilization by eliminating human sacrifice along with other Aztec institutions and rites. The Aztec Empire came to an abrupt end in 1521, along with intertribal warfare and external symbols of imperial Nahua religion. On the other hand, conventional cultural practices survived and persist today in practically all Mexican households and communities.

Jeffrey Kent Lucas

See also: Charles V (HRE) or Carlos I of Spain; Cortés, Hernán; Encomienda; Encomenderos; Nahuatl Language; Tenochtitlán, City of.

Resources

Fisher, Andrew B., and Matthew D. O'Hara, eds. *Imperial Subjects: Race and Identity in Colonial Latin America.* Durham, NC: Duke University Press, 2009.

Griffiths, Nicholas, and Fernando Cervantes, eds. *Spiritual Encounters: Interactions between Christianity and Native Religions in Colonial America.* Lincoln: University of Nebraska Press, 1999.

Lockhart, James. *The Nahuas after the Conquest: A Social and Cultural History of the Indians of Central Mexico, Sixteenth through Eighteenth Centuries.* Stanford, CA: Stanford University Press, 1992.

Smith, Michael E. *The Aztecs.* 3rd ed. Malden, MA: Wiley-Blackwell, 2012.

Yannakakis, Yanna. *The Art of Being In-Between: Native Intermediaries, Indian Identity, and Local Rule in Colonial Oaxaca.* Durham, NC: Duke University Press, 2008.

Mexico, State of prior to Spanish Conquest

The Aztec Empire is often referred to as the state that developed in the center of Mexico before conquest by the Spanish. This imperial era fell approximately between 1428 and 1521 AD, from the government of the emperor Itzcoatl (1428–1440) to the one of Cuauhtémoc (1521). Other terms used to identify this period of Aztec rule include the Triple Alliance Empire (in reference to the alliance between the three cities that held the power after defeating Azcapotzalco: Tenochtitlán, Tetzcoco, and Tlacopan), the Mexican Empire (referring to one of the Aztec nations who's pilgrimage took them from the mythological place of Aztlan to the Valley of Mexico), and the Culhua-Mexican Empire (a name the actual inhabitants gave their state, due to the fact that other Mexica belonged to the empire, though they did not govern over it).

The Mexican Empire is often characterized as a unitary system but actually was composed of multiple cultural systems that unified independent Middle American city-states. The Mexican state began to take shape one century before the foundation of the Aztec capital, Tenochtitlán, in 1325 AD, and flourished during the archaeological period known as Late Post-Classic (1350–1520). During the Mid-Post-Classic period (1150–1350), the Aztec people arrived to the center of Mexico and established their city-state with dynastic and market systems. Over time, a series of innovations came along and changed the previous system, converting it into a dense commercial net of exchanges, with the highlands of central Mexico as a center. Finally, during the second part of this period, the center came into contact with the Mexican basin and the Aztec Empire launched itself toward the conquest of large areas of Middle America.

Three imperial characteristics help define the Aztec state. One of the most obvious characteristics was the existence of an imperial capital, consisting of a large and complex urban structure, Tenochtitlán, where the state's ideological display of power took place. Another defining characteristic of the Aztec state involved control of a territory through economical processes, imposing tributes upon subjugated provinces, and political ones, military conquest, reorganization of settlements, and coercion of local elites. A final imperial characteristic included the projection of political and cultural influence upon an area that exceeded the imperial territory, evidenced by the presence of commerce and the worship of Aztec gods and rituals beyond their borders.

The strategies implemented by the Aztec in order to guarantee imperial domain can be divided into four spheres. The economical area underlines the aforementioned imposed tribute and the extension of dense commercial networks inside the Mexico Valley in conjunction with the outer provinces. These economic policies and activities were articulated through a system of market places and by a vast group of professional merchants or pochtecas. At a political level practices aimed at eliminating and seizing local administrative positions to impose specialized political and tributary hierarchies that worked hand in hand. The strategies aimed at borders came to light when conflicts with enemy states resulted in a stalemate; then border city-states were founded, to act like "client states" that did not pay taxes. On an elite level, connections between ruling classes, although politically separated, were joined through matrimonial alliances as well as through the practice of gift giving and participation in important events and ceremonies.

The model of empire employed by the Aztec was the hegemonic model or indirect domination. It was an "incomplete empire," different from a territorial empire or direct domination, which requires a military presence in order to guarantee control. A main characteristic of the Aztec model was the nonexistence of a permanent Imperial army aimed at directly occupying territories. The frequent reconquest campaigns, undertaken from Tenochtitlán, evidence this fact. Parallel to the eventual use of force to guarantee internal control, structures were developed enabling the dominated to collaborate inside the system that dominated them, be it through fear of punishment or be it with a conviction legitimized through a calculated imperial ideology.

Concerning territorial organization, the empire was composed of a coalition: the Mexicas of Tenochtitlán, the Acolhuas of Texcoco [Tezcoco], and the Tepanecas of Tlacopan, all of them neighboring cities known as *huey tlatocayotl* (great kingdoms). The Mexicas exerted leadership over the coalition. The Triple Alliance was composed of three states with their respective capitals, each with its own supreme leaders or *huey tlatoque* and in charge of a vast imperial region. The tributes obtained from the commonly conquered regions were taken to Tenochtitlán, from where they were distributed among the three kingdoms. Each capital had under its domain a vast number of minor seigniories or *tlatocayotl* that were spread out along the territory in an interspersed manner; that is to say, subjugation did not present a spatial continuity. The Triple Alliance also had attached to it cosmological religious aspects. In the nucleus (the three capitals), and in the outskirts (subjugated domains), each of the three sectors had their own idea of the Universe, each of which was clearly distinguishable and associated to one capital city.

Marta Martín Gabaldón

See also: Aztec, or Mexica; Cuauhtémoc; Pochtecas; Tenochtitlán, City of; Texcoco, Alliance with Tenochtitlán; Tribute, Paid to Mexica.

Resources

Berdan, Frances F., Richard E. Blanton, Elisabeth Hill Boone, Mary G. Hodge, Michael E. Smith, and Emily Umberger. *Aztec Imperial Strategies.* Washington, DC: Dumbarton Oaks Research Library and Collections, Trustees for Harvard University, 1996.

Brumfield, Elisabeth M. "Aztec State Making: Ecology, Structure, and the Origin of the State." *American Anthropologist* 85, no. 2 (1983): 261–284.

Carrasco, Pedro. *Estructura político-territorial del Imperio Tenochca. La Triple Alianza de Tenochtitlan, Tetzcoco y Tlacopan.* Mexico D.F.: Fondo de Cultura Económica, 1996.

Smith, Michael E. *The Aztecs.* Oxford: Blackwell Publishers, 1996.

Millenarianism

A faith-based principle held by secular or religious entities or movements, millenarianism asserted the belief in an ultimate transformation of the world within a 1,000-year period. Millenarian religious movements expect imminent and total collective salvation in the conception of bringing about a utopian world. Christianity posits the second coming of the religious figure Jesus Christ within the millenarian paradigm. Native American millenarian movements in the 16th century attempted to provide certain groups among the indigenous population with a hopeful outlook during a time of significant change. This religious ideology provided the impetus to spark a series of native revolts against Spanish colonial forces.

The Spanish conquests in Central and South America did not immediately end native resistance. Native resistance to the conquest took various forms, including insurrection, religious movements, and wars. Millenarian and messianic movements provide extraordinary opportunities to view an entire society shaken with doubts, which allowed for collective protests, choices, and dreams to come to the surface. Such movements occurred not only in America but also in Africa and Asia because of European colonization. The imaginary ideological reconstruction of native society through utopian religious millenarianism attempted to shape conditions in the real world. While they ultimately failed, ensuing native uprisings such as the Mixton War of 1541–42 in Mexico challenged the view of native acquiescence to the Spanish military conquests.

The Mixton War was typical of native millenarian movements in that it combined armed resistance to the Spanish with religious zeal a return to their traditional beliefs. This combination demanded a rejection of all things Spanish, including the Catholic faith. Leaders of the Mixton War, which was fought primarily by the Caxcanes against the Spanish and their native allies, included Don Diego, a Zacatecas Indian, and Francisco Tenamaztle, also of the Zacatecas region. As the Spanish extended their hold over northwestern Mexico, conquering and conducting slave raids under such oppressive leaders as Nuño Beltrán de Guzmán, new converts to Catholicism such as Tenamaztle chose to reject their new faith and the oppressive power behind it. The movement was initially successful, and resulted in the defeat of numerous Spanish forces, to include Governor Oñate's force, and the conquistador Pedro de Alvarado who was killed by the rebels. When the Spanish, under Viceroy Antonio de Mendoza, quelled the rebellion in 1542, the millenarian revolutionaries were severely punished or executed. Though the excessive atrocities used to crush the movement prompted an investigation by the Council of the Indies, they also deterred future millenarian movements in the region for years to come.

In Peru, the millenarian movement Taki Onqoy (Taqui Ongoy or dancing sickness) of the 1560s roused up a section of the Indian masses. The Taki Onqoy was a religious sect in the provinces of central Peru, especially the region of Huamanga. Preachers of the sect announced the end of Spanish rule in the Americas, calling for conscious awakening of the traditional religion and a war against Christianity. Taki Onqoy doctrine blended aspects of Spanish and Indian cultures, with the belief that the native gods would emerge triumphant over the Christian God. Though Pizarro defeated the natives, they prepared for a mass uprising to drive the Spaniards from the country.

As with many millenarian movements, the Taki Onqoy predicted an event of cosmic significance, which in turn would alter the balance of power and return the glory of the Inca Empire. Aspiration toward revolt drew support from a traditional view of the world, reinterpreted to respond to a colonial situation. Only those Indians who were faithful to the cult would be admitted to the new empire. The Taki Onqoy rejected any form of acculturation, including any connections with the Catholic Church. However, despite hostility to Spanish influences, native beliefs had undergone significant ideological and sociocultural changes.

Preachers traveled from village to village, exhorting Indians to revive the old gods and reject Christianity. Yet the Taki Onqoy did not take the form of a military organization, and rather believed that liberation from the Spaniards would be achieved after the native gods defeated the Christian God. The Spaniards quickly quelled any expectation of divine intervention. The Church denounced members of the Taki Onqoy as heretics, and Spanish authorities rounded up the movement's leaders subjected them to corporal punishment. By the late 1570s, the Taki Onqoy was eradicated as a significant religious movement.

Justin Pfeifer

See also: Alvarado, Pedro de; Christianity, Impact of on the Aztec; Christianity, Impact of on the Inca; Huamanga; Taki Onqoy.

Resources

Hunt, Stephen. *Christian Millenarianism: From the Early Church to Waco.* Bloomington: Indiana University Press, 2001.

Pollard, Helen Perlstein. "Tenamaxtli y Guaxicar" (review). *Ethnohistory* 46 (Winter 1999): 192.

Rinehart, James. *Apocalyptic Faith and Political Violence: Prophets of Terror.* New York: Macmillan, 2006.

Wachtel, Nathan. *The Vision of the Vanquished: the Spanish Conquest of Peru through Indian Eyes.* New York: Barnes and Noble, 1977.

Mines, Role of in Mexico

When Hernán Cortés and his men encountered the peoples of the Aztec Empire in 1519, they received as gifts beautiful objects of gold and made clear their desire for more. The Aztecs prized these objects as pieces of art and were horrified when the Spanish melted them down into gold bars destined to be used as money. After conquering the Aztec capital of Tenochtitlán in 1521, Cortés and his lieutenants looted most of the gold objects made by the Aztecs and their neighbors, and within a few decades most of this easily obtainable precious metal made its way into the Spaniards' coffers.

Yet the Spanish wanted more, and to find it they explored beyond the Aztec center for other possible sources of metallic wealth. Copper, precious, and semiprecious stones continued to be mined on a small scale, as they had been by the Aztecs. Additionally, a few silver and gold mines were exploited around the central valley in the 1530s. Nonetheless, within decades of the conquest of Tenochtitlán, the quest for precious metals drew the Spaniards as far north as the present-day southwestern United States, and southward to Honduras and Guatemala. Most often they were disappointed in their quests. However in 1546, in the northwestern spine of the Sierra Madre mountains, a small group of Spanish found, or were shown by local natives, silver-bearing rock. Further examination of the rugged bluffs in the area revealed a rich silver vein. From this tentative start, the Spanish developed a mining camp and, subsequently, the mining city of Zacatecas.

In fact, most of the precious metal the Spaniards discovered in the 16th century was not gold, but silver. Indeed, most of the silver they found was in veins running through the semiarid mountains of the Sierra Madre, particularly in those that ranged both northwest and northeast of the central valley of Mexico, with some in the mountains just south of the central valley. In these same ranges, along the roads from the northern mining camp at Zacatecas south to Mexico City and roads northeast from the central valley, the Spanish later developed the silver mining centers of Guanajuato (1550), Pachuca (1552), Real del Monte (1552), and San Luis Potosi (1592). Further to the northwest of Zacatecas, mines developed at Sombrerete (1558) and Parral (1567). While silver became the most important source of colonial wealth, a few gold mines also were developed west and south of Mexico City and into Honduras. Gold was also found in or near many veins of silver.

At first, silver mining methods were crude and simple, prospectors and a few servants with picks and shovels worked surface veins in pits and then tunneled into the ground to follow the richest veins. To follow those veins deeper, however, required more sophisticated technology and capital. Deeper tunnels were blasted with gunpowder, and pumps run by hand or whims removed water from tunnels below the water table. In some places adits, or drainage canals, were dug. The ore was refined by smelting, a process requiring extensive fuel resources, usually wood. After a few decades, the development of the amalgamation process increased the production of silver in the mines, a process that involved mixing the ore with mercury and salt, in *haciendas de beneficio,* or refining mills. The mercury for Mexican mines came mostly from Spain, assisting the Spanish in estimating the amount of ore produced by comparing the amount of mercury consumed in the process. The Spanish Crown, as the owner of all subsoil rights in its dominions, encouraged the proliferation of mine claims, hoping to earn evermore royalties.

As mines proliferated, demand for labor grew. Furthermore, most mines were located in sparsely populated areas with hostile natives, so the workforce had to be attracted or forced to the mines to work. *Mineros,* or mine owners, attracted some workers with wages and the promise of a share of the ore. These included the *barreteros,* pickmen or cutters, and blast men—who specialized in using gunpowder for blasting. Indian laborers often served as *tenateros,* ore carriers using hide sacks, bags, or buckets to carry ore out of the mines; and patio *azogueros,* mound stampers who mixed mercury, salt, and ore to extract the silver. Indian workers also dug the adits. Tenateros and refinery workers in the larger refineries earned wages and sometimes food rations. A majority of the workforce in the early years of the colony were forced laborers, mostly Indian slaves, Indian servants or *naborias,* and encomienda or repartimiento Indians, as well as some African slaves. In addition to human labor, large numbers of animals, especially mules, worked around mines and refineries and, of course, transported ore and supplies. As the use of mercury impacted the health of miners, and the deep, poorly vented mines increased working hazards, the Spanish found it more and more difficult to recruit workers for the mines without the use of forced labor, labor taxes, as well as the use of credit extended to wage earners through a sort of company store.

Mexican mines produced precious metals that directly enriched both individuals and the imperial government. This same wealth was used to expand the Spanish Empire and its colonial economy, as the mines increased demands for local agricultural products— grains, hides, meat, and other foodstuffs. Additionally, demand increased for mining supplies, and for all kinds of luxury goods from Europe and Asia, creating an imperial economy that virtually spanned the globe in the 16th century. Yet, all did not glitter for the native population, which declined precipitously as the century wore on because of displacement, labor abuse, attrition, and the relentless onslaught of European diseases.

Angela T. Thompson

See also: Encomienda; European Diseases, Role of; Gold, Role of in Spanish Expeditions; Mercury; Repartimiento; Silver; Slavery, Role of.

Resources

Bakewell, Peter, J. ed. *Mines of Silver and Gold in the Americas.* Aldershot, UK: Variorum, 1997.

Bakewell, Peter J. *Silver Mining and Society in Colonial Mexico, Zacatecas, 1546–1700.* Cambridge: Cambridge University Press, 1971.

Brading, David A., and Harry E. Cross. "Colonial Silver Mining: Mexico and Peru." *Hispanic American Historical Review* 52, no. 4 (November 1972): 545–579.

Keen, Benjamin, and Keith Haynes. *A History of Latin America.* 8th ed. Boston: Houghton Mifflin Harcourt, 2009.

Prieto, Carlos. *Mining in the New World.* New York: McGraw-Hill, 1979.

West, Robert C. *The Mining Community in Northern New Spain: The Parral Mining District.* Berkeley: University of California Press, 1949.

Mines, Role of in Peru

The role of mines in Peru can be viewed from different vantage points. The Inca nobility originally saw the mines as resources from their gods, intended for their own use, and as a means of empowerment before their subjects. The Inca subjects have no voice in the early colonial history, but seem to have believed, with their nobility, that gold and mines were gifts of the gods intended to glorify their Sapa Inca. To the Spanish, the gold was theirs for the taking. Like the Inca, the Spanish perceived a divine providence behind their access to so much gold.

Original perceptions regarding the gold and silver had little bearing in the reality of mining the mineral wealth. Mining for the minerals in preconquest Peru was based on the temporary labor of the various *ayllus,* through a labor tax. Demanding about two to six weeks labor per year, the process of mining was still hard but the impact on the indigenous laborers was minimal.

With the arrival of the Spanish and seizure of power from the Incas, the process of acquiring gold, silver, gems, and eventually mercury from the mines changed drastically. The labor used to mine the minerals was compulsory, shifting from the traditional *mita* labor requirement to a system of repartimiento. Laborers were still to be used for a short span of time and compensated with gifts for their service. Unfortunately, the demands for the length of service increased from one month, to two, to a year or more. Meanwhile, compensation for services decreased, until no gifts were exchanged for the tributary labor. The requirement for the encomenderos and other Spanish authorities, in employing proper labor allotments and gifting requirements, was seldom enforced on a consistent basis.

As gold mining declined in productivity, silver mining increased. However, the costly process of separating the ore from rocks and other debris was prohibitive. The employment of an indigenous process, using air, helped, but was too slow. The discovery of amalgamation, using mercury to coat the valuable metal, thus adding to its weight and allowing it to settle while the debris was washed away, increased silver mining productivity and the amount of silver processed for shipment. The detrimental impacts of the amalgamation process, as well as the hazards of mining for mercury, combined with the continued impact of disease on the Inca people of Peru. With rapidly declining population levels, the mine administrators had to pursue other means to get laborers. Offers of rewards and wages lured some indigenous people into the mines, but the impact of the harsh conditions and poisoned environment prevented miners from continuing long-term employment.

By the middle of the 17th century, the profitability of the mines declined to the point where a number of mines were abandoned. The unsafe working conditions were made worse by the lack of adequate pumps to clean water out of the mines. Over the course of approximately 100 years, the Incas

Pack train of llamas carrying silver from Potosi mines in Peru, 1602. (Library of Congress)

experienced a shift from independent, communal farming to tenant farming for encomenderos, to compulsory though temporary labor in mines, to virtual slave labor in mines. The deadly introduction of mercury to simplify the process of separating the silver increased the need for laborers and wage systems were introduced as a means of recruiting the needed workers. However, the combination of unhealthy conditions, exposure to deadly epidemics, and the necessary abandonment of unsafe mines spelled the end to the massive mining boom that dominated the first century of Spanish colonization of Peru.

Rebecca M. Seaman

See also: *Ayllus;* Encomenderos; *Mita;* Repartimiento; Sapa Inca; Silver.

Resources

Arias, Santa. "Empowerment through the Writing of History: Bartolomé de Las Casas." In *Early Images of the Americas: Transfer and Invention,* edited by Jerry M. Williams and Robert E. Lewis. Tucson: University of Arizona Press, 1993.

Bakewell, Peter J., ed. *Mines of Silver and Gold in the Americas. An Expanding World.* Vol. 19. Aldershot, UK: Ashgate Variorum, 1997.

Davies, Nigel. *The Incas.* Niwot: University of Colorado Press, 1995.

Garner, Richard L. "Long-term Silver Mining Trends in Spanish America: A Comparative Analysis of Peru and Mexico." *American Historical Review* 93 (October 1988): 898–936.

Keen, Benjamin, and Keith Haynes. *A History of Latin America.* 8th ed. Boston: Houghton, Mifflin, Harcourt Publishing, 2009.

Means, Philip A. *The Fall of the Inca Empire and the Spanish Rule in Peru, 1530–1780.* New York: Gordian Press, 1971.

Pagden, Anthony, trans. & ed. *Hernan Cortes: Letters from Mexico.* New Haven: Yale University Press, 1986.

Prescott, William H. *The History of the Conquest of Peru.* New York: New American Library, 1961.

Sluiter, Engel. 1998. *The Gold and Silver of Spanish America, c. 1572–1648: Tables Showing Bullion Declared for Taxation in Colonial Royal Treasuries, Remittances to Spain, and Expenditures for Defense of Empire.* Berkeley: University of California, Bancroft Library, 1998.

Mita

A draft Indian labor system was developed and applied in Latin America by the Spanish conquistadores modeled on an earlier Inca system of servitude. The Spanish adopted the system under the instructions of Viceroy Francisco de Toledo in 1573, based on its previous utilization by the Incas in the 15th century and at the time of Spanish conquest. Toledo hoped to solve the problem of insufficient workers for the silver mines in Patosi and Huancavelica. Later, in the 17th century, the *mita* was implemented in other parts of the empire in Peru. The *mita* system, as implemented by the Spanish, was not homogenous within the empire and varied throughout the distant provinces of the country. The system also differed in principle from the ancient Indian system. Some elements of the system were also implemented in the Philippines, which administratively belonged to the same state structure as that used in Peru.

Mita, as a concept of draft labor, existed in the Inca period when the Quechua Indians (Incas) utilized it as a system of services rendered by inhabitants of the empire to the state. The word itself meant a period of service, which every family was obliged to carry out on behalf and for the good of the state. Similar in some aspects to the later French corvée, the *mita* in the Inca Empire functioned as a public service of the empire itself and its aristocracy. It was mostly connected with the imperial and community-oriented projects, such as road building, construction of fortifications, of public buildings, but also palaces and houses of the aristocracy and the emperor. It could also mean working on farmland for the good of all society. Inhabitants of the Inca Empire were all obliged to work a certain amount of time, meaning all heads of households were under the *mita* system. One was drawn into the system as early as 15 years of age and the obligation ended at the age of 50. Participants in the public works did not receive any payment, but the state administration took care of their families during workers' absence, if such was the need. There were special officials, assigned by the state, who were responsible for controlling the flow of the working force.

Mita was connected with life and wealth guarantees for those who worked. One's *mita* was limited to a set number of days, which, on top of the public service, enabled them to cultivate their own fields and feed their families. Soldiers going away to war had their fields taken over and cultivated by those serving local *mita* obligations. This traditionally Inca form of *mita* drastically changed with the Spanish conquest of the native empire.

When Viceroy Francisco de Toledo implemented a Spanish variation of the *mita* into their empire in 1573, the new system employed unqualified workers to work in the revitalized silver mines in Potosi. Seeking to find workers, while bearing in mind the royal prohibition to compel Indians to work in mines, de Toledo introduced a semivoluntary system that included compensation for the laborers. The Spanish initially drafted 13–17 percent of Indians from their villages to work for a year. During that time, the drafted natives worked in cycles: a week of labor followed by two weeks rest without work. While this measure was employed, only one-third of the drafted Indians were effectively working in Toledo's *mita* system at any time. The drafted laborers were paid for their work, although compensation was not high and often returned to the Spaniards. These conditions were soon changed repeatedly by the state and local administration and new rules were imposed. As a result, *mita* was implemented in various areas under a wide variety of structures, and often on specific, localized regulations.

Under the *mita* system the local Indian communities were increasingly obliged to fill certain quotas of workers for a determined period of time in a set branches of the economy.

The initial system of Indian labor for minimal compensation soon became a repressive system. The compensation paid for work was, in most cases, recovered through a system of loans, taxes, fees, and payments for accommodations and food.

In addition to the Spanish embracing of the *mita* system in Peru, the *mita* system was the base for mine production and other forms of labor in central Mexico. In New Spain the *mita* supplied workers for farms. In Quito and Tucuman, textile factory workers were recruited this way. It was utilized in coastal plantations and state infrastructure projects throughout the Spanish Empire in America (e.g., road maintenance).

Over time, Indians had very little chance of leaving the *mita* system and becoming truly independent. Today, many historians regard it as a slave labor system. Most recent research indicates that the *mita* system had very negative impact on the territories where it was developed, implemented, and utilized for a long time. Regions included in the *mita* system in the 17th century are considerably poorer today, as the system had long-lasting negative effects on people's wealth and local economy. The Spanish colonial practice of *mita* was finally abolished in 1812.

Jakub Basista

See also: Mines, Role of in Mexico; Mines, Role of in Peru; Silver; Toledo, Francisco de.

Resources

Cole, Jeffrey A. *The Potosi Mita, 1573–1700.* Stanford, CA: Stanford University Press, 1985.

McCreery, David. *The Sweat of Their Brow: A History of Work in Latin America.* Armonk, NY: M. E. Sharpe, 2000.

Villamarin, Juan A., and Judith E. Villamarin. *Indian Labor in Mainland Colonial Spanish America.* Newark: University of Delaware Press, 1975.

Mixtecs

According to archaeologists, the Mixtec came from Mexico's central plateau region, perhaps as early as the 700s CE. By the end of the first millennium they settled themselves in the mountainous regions of Oaxaca in loose city-states.

Divided into four social classes, Mixtec society emerged around vital city-states, including Tilantongo, the capital; Coixtlahuaca; Mitla; Teozacoalco; Tlaxiaco; and Yagul. Mixtec society was divided into four classes: kings and nobles, who received divine right to rule from the god Qchi, a variant of the Mesoamerican god Quetzalcoatl; free people, who were mainly agriculturists and artisans; tenant farmers and servants; and slaves. Mixtec culture was closely interwoven with the Oaxaca valley's Zapotec culture, with whom they battled and also intermarried. The two groups formed pivotal alliances throughout Mixtec history.

Politically, Mixtec kings each had authority over a small city-state. Kings were polygamous, marrying the daughters of neighboring kings and often taking noble women as concubines. Kingship was passed down through traditional ruling families. Meanwhile, the tenants and servants and the slaves were at the other end of the social spectrum. The former had lost their rights as free persons and had to serve the free classes for a period of time, and the latter were completely devoid of rights and could be sacrificed in religious ceremonies.

The Tilantongo dynasty, begun during the 900s, was the most significant dynasty in Mixtec history. However, the Second Tilantongo dynasty, led by Eight Deer Jaguar Claw, had the greatest impact. Eight Deer Jaguar Claw eventually took over Tula, crowning himself the new Toltec emperor. By the next century, the Mixtec began moving southward into the Oaxaca valley.

In addition to the Zapotec, Mixtec history was interwoven with the powerful Aztec. When the Aztec ruler Montezuma II defeated the Mixtec in the early 1500s, the Mixtec formed a short-lived alliance with the Zapotec. Soon after, the Zapotec joined the Aztec, and when Spanish conquistadores arrived in the beginning of the 16th century, both the Zapotec and the Aztec signed a peace treaty with the invaders.

Meanwhile, the Mixtec formed the last center of resistance to the Spaniards in the region. There, they held out until Spanish conquistador Pedro de Alvarado finally defeated their forces in 1524. Despite that defeat, the Mixtec continued to reside in the Oaxaca valley, where they currently number approximately 500,000.

Thanks to the preservation of several ancient codices (historical records), the Mixtec are the best-known non-Maya Mesoamerican culture. Archaeological evidence suggests that at least four ancient codices detailed historical events, genealogical records, and the pantheon of gods and goddesses. The Mixtec codices, including the well-known Vienna Codex, appeared to be painted pictographs on folded deerskins. Although the Mixtec writing system was crude and primitive, relative to other Mesoamerican societies, it did provide early evidence of the inner workings of the culture.

Mixtec art was renowned among the neighboring tribes. They were most famous for their gold and turquoise jewelry, metalwork, and pottery. Mixtec artists frequently traveled to the Aztec kingdom, serving in the king's court. Additionally, Mixtec-made carvings of the household gods, and they built temples throughout their settlements.

Jessica Sedgewick

See also: Alvarado, Pedro de; Quetzalcoatl.

Resources

Austin, Alfredo López, and Leonardo López Luján, *Mexico's Indigenous Past.* Translated by Bernardo R. Ortiz de Montellano. Norman: University of Oklahoma Press, 2001.

Carmack, Robert, et al. *The Legacy of Mesoamerica: History and Culture of a Native American Civilization.* Upper Saddle River, NJ: Prentice Hall, 1996.

Coe, Michael D. *Mexico: From the Olmecs to the Aztecs.* New York: Thames & Hudson, 1994.

Peterson, Frederick. *Ancient Mexico: An Introduction to the Pre-Hispanic Cultures.* London: George Allen & Unwin. 1959.

Montejo, Francisco de

Three Spanish explorers and conquistadors involved mainly in the exploration and conquest of Yucatán shared this same name. All three of them were relatives and are often mistaken in historical books. The oldest, Francisco de Montejo y Alvarez (*el Adelantado*), was father to Francisco de Montejo y León (el Mozo) and uncle to Francisco de Montejo (el Sobrino, the nephew). All three were involved to varying degrees in the attempts to conquer the Yucatán and Mexico.

Francisco de Montejo y Alvarez (*el Adelantado*) was born in Salamanca in 1479/80 to a noble family. In 1514, he embarked on a trip to the Caribbean and took part in Pedro Arias Dávila's expedition to Darien (Panama), which was disappointing. It was the same expedition in which Bernal Diaz de Castillo took part. Returning with the company from Darien, he reached Cuba with the others, where he entered the service of the governor of the island, Diego Velázquez. In 1518, he joined Juan de Grijalva's expedition to the Gulf of Mexico and in particular to Yucatán as one of its captains. Most probably, during this expedition he met with artifacts and possibly individuals connected with the Aztec civilization for the first time. One year later, in 1519, he joined Hernán Cortés on the expedition to Mexico, took part in the first meetings and clashes with the native Indians, and in the founding of the city La Rica Villa de la Vera Cruz. Upon this achievement, he was sent by Cortés to Spain to report on the undertaking. Thus he did not take part in the conclusive moments of defeat of the Aztecs and the conquest of Tenochtitlán.

In Spain in 1526 he was granted the titles of *adelantado* and capitan general of Yucatán by the king, Carlos I (Charles V—HRE). During this visit home he married Beatriz de Herrera and in 1527 left for the New World with his illegitimate son and a nephew, both of the same name. In the years 1528–1533, he took part in three attempts to conquer Yucatán: from the sea, from the west, and from the east—all attempts brought no long-lasting successes, as the Spanish forces were driven back by the attacks of the Mayas.

In 1533, Montejo was granted a royal decree to conquer territories of Puerto Caballas and Naco in nearby Honduras. What resulted was a conflict with Pedro de Alvarado, who had a parallel privilege dating from 1532. In the end it was Alvarado who immediately prevailed, when he claimed he had conquered Honduras and became its governor till 1540. At that point the office was finally bequeathed upon Montejo.

Montejo realized the governorship and managed to install administration loyal to him in Honduras. His rule was not very successful and in 1550 he was recalled to Spain following a series of complaints from the Spanish settlers. Formal charges eventually resulted in a special commission being set up to investigate them. He died in poverty in Spain either in 1553 or 1554.

Francisco de Montejo y León (el Mozo), born in 1502, was an illegitimate son of Montejo de Alvarez and Ana de Leon. As a young man, he joined his father on the latter's second trip to the New World in 1527. Upon arrival in America, he became engaged in various campaigns on the borders of Yucatán and Mexico.

In 1528, he reached the now lost city of Santa Maria de la Victoria (first Spanish city on the Mexican territory) with the mission to pacify the area. Two years later, he was entrusted with the task of a peacekeeping campaign in the region. Most of these undertakings were executed either on direct orders from his father, or in full accord with the latter's policy and aims. Thus, several years later he was forced to leave Santa Maria de la Victoria when his father was dismissed and replaced by Balthazar Osorio as the Mayor of Tabasco. By this time, he had practically the whole region of Grijalda River under control.

When in 1553 an Indian uprising started in Tabasco, and de Montejo senior was restored to his previous function, his son, "el Mozo," once again undertook the task of pacifying the region, which he accomplished in 1537. For his service, the young de Montejo was awarded the post of captain general and governor of Tabasco in 1539. Nonetheless, after one year he set out on an expedition to conquer Yucatán. This time he was partly successful and gained control of the western part of the province, founding a city of Merida on the site of the former Mayan city of Ichkansihóo (T'Hó). This is where Francisco de Montejo y León (el Mozo) settled, though he moved on to Guatemala a few years later. He died in Guatemala in 1565.

Francisco de Montejo (el Sobrino, the nephew) was the nephew of de Montejo y Alvarez and cousin of el Mozo. Born in 1514, Montejo "el Sobrino" went to America with his uncle and cousin when he was only 13. He took part in the attempts to conquer Yucatán in 1527. He was best known for his participation in the third and last stage of conquest of Yucatán. In 1543, he founded the town of Valladolid (Zaci) in Chouac-Ha.

During the third attempt to conquer Yucatán, Montejo "el Sobrino" fought along with his cousin and took an active part in preventing and clearing Mayan conspiratorial attempts against the invaders. Having secured the controlled territories, el Sobrino, along with el Mozo, progressed eastward along the Yucatán peninsula. This time the Mayan territory came under the Spanish yoke.

El Sobrino, who was one of the leaders of the campaign, settled in Merida. There he was respected leader, and was entrusted with a post on the council. He died there in 1572.

Jakub Basista

See also: Charles V (HRE) or Carlos I of Spain; Cortés, Hernán; Dávila, Pedro Arias; Grijalva, Juan de; Villa Rica de la Vera Cruz.

Resources

Chamberlain, Robert Stoner. *The Conquest and Colonization of Honduras 1502–1550.* New York: Octagon Books 1966.

Chamberlain, Robert Stoner. *The Conquest and Colonization of Yucatán 1517–1550.* New York: Octagon Books 1966.

Rubio Mañe, J. Ignacio. *Monografia de los Montejos.* Merida, Yucatan, Mexico: Liga de Accion Social 1930.

Thomas, Hugh. *Who's Who of the Conquistadors.* London: Cassell & Company, 2000.

Montezuma II

Montezuma II was the ninth emperor of the Aztec Empire, reigning from 1502 to 1520. After earning a reputation for both cruelty and reforms that favored the nobility, he met his match in 1519 when the Spaniard Hernán Cortés used Machiavellian tactics to take Montezuma hostage and begin the destruction of his once seemingly invincible empire.

Montezuma was born in 1466 and came from a distinguished lineage that included his uncle Emperor Axayacatl, who ruled the Aztec Empire from 1468 to 1481. Raised and educated in the island capital of Tenochtitlán, Montezuma proved himself from a young age as a soldier, an important distinction in a militaristic society. He first served as a warrior and then a captain under several emperors following the death of his uncle. He also gained important political experience as a leader and ruler during the early years of his life.

Montezuma was serving as an official in Tolocán, to the west of Tenochtitlán, when Emperor Ahuitzotl died in 1502. Later that year, a council of noblemen chose Montezuma as the next Aztec emperor. He assumed the position at the height of the Aztec Empire's power. Ahuitzotl had greatly expanded the empire in terms of territory and influence following the unsuccessful and militarily weak reign of Emperor Tizoc. Montezuma thus had the fortune of inheriting a vigorous empire that controlled most of central Mexico and whose influence stretched from the present-day southern United States to the middle of Central America.

The geographic extent of the empire made it difficult to control. Almost from the day he was named emperor, Montezuma had to suppress rebellions and revolts throughout his territory. A 1502 rebellion in the provinces of Nopallan and Icpatepec allowed Montezuma to demonstrate his abilities while it also provided a large number of captives to be sacrificed and ritually consumed at his coronation. The bloody suppression of that rebellion earned Montezuma a reputation as a harsh ruler. His army killed large numbers of villagers, took others as captives, and forced the survivors to pay crushing tributes.

Montezuma also earned a reputation as a reformer. The Aztec nobility had grown in numbers during the reign of previous emperors and clamored for offices and positions. In the old system, the nobility received only a limited number of the best jobs in the empire. Montezuma changed this by removing commoners from important posts and replacing them with noblemen. He then removed all royal servants without a title, creating many jobs for the lesser nobility. These changes won Montezuma the gratitude and support of the growing nobility. At the same time, he also cultivated the support of Aztec commoners. By the end of the first 10 years of his reign, Montezuma had consolidated his power, becoming one of the most powerful and autocratic rulers in Aztec history.

Montezuma then engaged in a series of successful military campaigns that increased the size and power of the empire. During 1503–1504, he continued the ancient rivalry of the Aztecs with the Tlaxcalans. Then from 1505 to 1510, Montezuma turned his attention to the south, bringing the Mixtec and Zapotec cultures under the vassalage of the Aztec Empire. After 1510, Montezuma turned inward and faced serious rebellions and revolts throughout his territories. During that period, Montezuma began receiving news from Aztec traders that strangers had been sighted and several captured as slaves by the Mayas of the Yucatán.

In an unfortunate coincidence for Montezuma, the news was accompanied by such ill omens as falling stars that alarmed religious and secular leaders. After consulting auguries and priests, Montezuma was informed that the return of their ancestral god, Quetzalcoatl, could be expected in 1519. That proved to be the year that Cortés and his expedition of Spanish conquerors arrived on the Mexican coast.

Shaken by fear and religious fervor, Montezuma sent the Spaniards gifts of gold and silver. Instead of assuaging gods, however, the gifts instead persuaded the Spaniards to stay and try to conquer a land of obvious riches. On November 8, 1519, Cortés and his men arrived in Tenochtitlán. Montezuma welcomed them warmly, over the objections of his brother, Cuitláhuac. Meanwhile, Cortés took the opportunity to seize the emperor and attempted to use the Aztec capital as headquarters for the conquest of Mexico.

Although imprisoned and living as a captive, Montezuma continued to rule the empire.

Reception of Hernán Cortés by the Emperor Montezuma. (Library of Congress)

responded with a hail of stones that killed him. Aztecs (as well as many later historians) claimed that the Spaniards had killed Montezuma, but there is no evidence for that claim.

Cuitláhuac became emperor after Montezuma's death but died of smallpox after forcing the Spaniards from Tenochtitlán in a great battle, La Noche Triste. His successor Cuauhtémoc then led the final and ultimately futile defense of the Aztec capital against the Spaniards and their Mesoamerican allies. Montezuma's indecisive and wavering reaction to the Spanish invaders has, fairly or unfairly, earned him a reputation of indecisiveness and weakness that vastly overshadows his record as one of the Aztec's most powerful emperors.

Thomas Edsall

See also: Ahuitzotl; Alvarado, Pedro de; Cuauhtémoc; Cuitláhuac; La Noche Triste; Quetzalcoatl; Tenochtitlán, Siege of.

He even managed to plan rebellions and attacks on the men he now recognized as invaders from a foreign land. By April 1520, however, Montezuma had lost power and legitimacy among his Aztec subjects. When Cortés left Tenochtitlán to fight rival Spaniard Pánfilo de Narváez, the Aztecs rose against the Spaniards. After Cortés returned to the city, Montezuma persuaded him to release his younger brother Cuitláhuac to appease the angry Aztecs. This action probably represented a last-minute effort to ensure his brother's succession and guarantee further resistance.

Upon his release, Cuitláhuac assumed control of the armed struggle against the Spaniards. After the Aztecs surrounded Cortés and his men in late June 1520, Montezuma was forced to a rooftop to order his subjects to end all resistance. The Aztecs, disgusted with their once formidable emperor, reportedly

Resources

Berdan, Frances F. *The Aztecs of Central Mexico: An Imperial Society.* Florence, KY: Wadsworth, 2004.

Gillespie, Susan D. *The Aztec Kings: The Construction of Rulership in Mexica History.* Tucson: University of Arizona Press, 1992.

Hassig, Ross. *Aztec Warfare: Imperial Expansion and Political Control.* Oklahoma City: University of Oklahoma Press, 1995.

Motolinia's *Historia de los Indios de la Nueva España*

Born Toribio Paredes in Benavente, Castille-Leon, he took the vows of poverty and became a Franciscan monk, a role that qualified him for assignment to New Spain shortly after Hernán Cortés's conquest of the region. By 1524, Cortés's experience with attempts to remove his authority and newfound wealth prompted requests for the Church to send Franciscans—whose vows of poverty he hoped would remove them from such temptations. Young Fray Toribio de Benavente was one of the first 12 such friars to arrive for the purpose of building churches and converting the *Indios.*

An astute individual, Benavente quickly picked up the Nahuatl language. With this knowledge, he was able to communicate and discern critical elements of the native culture. Fr. Benavente became a detailed observer of minute details, which he recorded and later included in his history of the region. In the *Historia de los Indios de la Nueva España,* the friar—known by the Aztec appellation "Motolinia," meaning "the poor one"—conveyed specific details about many aspects of Aztec society. Descriptions of the intricate work of goldsmiths, indigenous dances, and continued idolatry of the people are covered in his work. His portrayals of the declining population provided some insight into the affects of economic upheaval wrought by the Spanish, as well as major epidemics. Sequential waves of smallpox, measles, plague, influenza, whooping cough, and mumps devastated entire urban centers. Especially hard hit were the traditional upper classes, or *pipiltin,* of the Aztec society. Maybe in response to the high incidence of death from diseases Fray Benavente began baptizing the native population in mass ceremonies, claiming to have baptized 400,000 *Indios.*

It is his mass baptisms that set Fray Benavente apart from some of his contemporaries who voiced similar support of indigenous rights. The Franciscan monk was very close to Las Casas for many years, due to shared perceptions of the native soul and worth. However, Motolinia's practice of mass baptisms alienated the Dominican missionary by the 1550s. Accusations by Las Casas of Cortés's abusive treatment of the indigenous populations was also a topic for discussion in his book—and focused on Benavente's defense of Cortés.

Beyond his missionary work, Fray Benavente's major contribution was his *Historio.* In addition to the descriptions of Aztec society and culture, Motolinia's *Historio* provides a revealing look at Cortés. As the *caudillo*'s priest confessor, Benavente was privy to a side of the conquistador not readily seen by others. In his work, he examines Cortés's faith and sincerity of belief. In part from this reflection, Motolinia provides a strong support of Cortés in his role as conqueror and provider for Spanish prosperity and indigenous salvation.

Rebecca M. Seaman

See also: Cortés, Hernán; Las Casas, Bartolomé de; Nahuatl Language; *Pipiltin.*

Resources

Restall, Matthew. *Seven Myths of the Spanish Conquest.* New York: Oxford University Press, 2004.

Thomas, Hugh. *Conquest: Montezuma, Cortés, and the Fall of Old Mexico.* New York: Simon & Schuster Press, 1993.

N

Nahuatl Language

The traditional language of the Aztec or Mexica people, Nahuatl, has seen use in oral and written form well before the arrival of the Spanish during the period of colonial conquest. In writing, Nahuatl had different forms, with the more common central Mexican form used by literate elites and well-educated artisans and merchants. The elite priestly classes employed a more ritualistic form of Nahuatl that was restricted to only a few. Meanwhile, in the distant provinces of the empire, more parochial versions of Nahuatl existed, combining local cultural and linguistic concepts and phrases into the dominant lingua franca of Nahuatl.

With the conquest of the Spanish, Nahuatl remained the dominant language for business and communication throughout New Spain. It was the dominance of Nahuatl that encouraged Hernán Cortés to employ the services of a native woman, known as La Malinche or "Doña Marina," on a daily basis. Cortés initially rescued and used Fr. Gerónimo de Aguilar to assist in communicating with the coastal Mayas. However, Aguilar's abilities in speaking Mayan served little use past the immediate coastal areas. Indeed, as the Spanish the use of Nahuatl in regions previously independent of the Aztec imperisal controls saw the introduction of Nahuatl as a common form of communication between indigenous local languages, the Nahuatl-speaking mestizos often employed by the Spanish, and Spanish Peninsulars and Creoles.

Spain's determination to convert the indigenous populations of New Spain supported the use of Nahuatl. When Cortés requested the Church to send Franciscan missionaries to help convert the newly conquered population, some of the more zealous friars began to learn Nahuatl as a means of proselytizing more effectively. Fray Toribio Paredes de Benavente (commonly known as Motolinia) was one of these initial Franciscan friars who embraced the Nahuatl language, even translating the Christian texts for usage by the Mexica population. By the 1560s, bishops of Mexico began to track those missionaries who had multilingual skills, employing them to assist the Church in its efforts to preach and to translate religious documents.

With the miscegenation of the Spanish conquerors and the native population, a growing mestizo element played a key role in the changing role and influence of Nahuatl in New Spain. As more than just intermediaries between the Spanish and Aztec parents, or Spanish conquerors and Aztec subjects, these mixed blood offspring served as active participants in negotiating and shaping differing cultural heritages, employing their language and cultural skills to help smooth communications in their homes and societies. It is from these mestizos that the Church and Spanish administration sought able linguists.

The results of this decision included the shifting of cultural norms and the shifting usage of language. Nahuatl, already employing different forms prior to Spanish conquest, increased its usage across the Middle American region, and with the spread of the language to new cultures came changes in the language itself. In the Central American region, the indigenous Pipil impacted the dominant colonial usage of Nahuatl and created a unique written standard for the region. In the Sierre Norte, the dominance of the Zapotec ethnic population resulted in a written form of that language for trade and religious texts; while the minority Mixe population of the same region, without a significant mestizo or other official translator presence, was compelled to use Nahuatl in its oral and written form to communicate with the local Zapotecs, as well as the Spanish.

While the use of oral and written Nahuatl facilitated the Church's mission of proselytizing the indigenous peoples across New Spain, the shifting forms of Nahuatl and the persistent presence of indigenous religious practices and beliefs created their own set of problems. The neophyte mestizos, used to translate religious texts, incorporated elements later deemed as errors and even heresies. With the arrival of the Inquisition to the Americas, these errors, in a written form often unintelligible to the Inquisitors, were considered dangerous. Consequently, shortly after the Church embraced indigenous translators and missionaries with linguistic abilities in the Nahuatl language, a reaction occurred wherein the Church began to expunge the use of written native texts for use in converting and educating native populations. The widespread use and expediency of Nahuatl as the lingua franca of the region delayed this reaction, but eventually the Church's determination to eradicate the use of indigenous forms of literature undermined the dominance of oral and written forms of Nahuatl in New Spain.

Rebecca M. Seaman

See also: Aguilar, Fr. Gerónimo de; Cortés, Hernán; La Malinche, "Doña Marina"; Motolinia's *Historia de los Indios de la Nueva España*.

Resources

Christensen, Mark Z. "The Use of Nahuatl in Evangelization and the Ministry of Sebastian." *Ethnohistory* 59, no. 4 (Fall 2012): 691–711.

Matthew, Laura E., and Sergio F. Romero. "Nahuatl and Pipil in Colonial Guatemala: A Central American Counterpoint." *Ethnohistory* 59, no. 4 (Fall 2012): 765–783.

Nesvig, Martin. "Spanish Men, Indigenous Language, and Informal Interpreters in Postcontact Mexico." *Ethnohistory* 59, no. 4 (Fall 2012): 739–764.

Pizzigoni, Caterina. "Conclusion: A Language across Space, Time, and Ethnicity." *Ethnohistory* 59, no. 4 (Fall 2012): 785–790.

Restall, Matthew. *Seven Myths of the Spanish Conquest*. New York: Oxford University Press, 2003.

Schwaller, John F. "The Expansion of Nahuatl as a Lingua Franca among Priests in Sixteenth-Century Mexico." *Ethnohistory* 59, no. 4 (Fall 2012): 675–690.

Schwaller, Robert C. "The Importance of Mextizos and Mulatos as Bilingual Intermediaries in Sixteenth-Century New Spain." *Ethnohistory* 59, no. 4 (Fall 2012): 713–738.

Thomas, Hugh. *Conquest: Montezuma, Cortés, and the Fall of Old Mexico*. New York: Simon & Schuster, 1993.

Yannakakis, Yanna. "Introduction: How Did They Talk to One Another: Language Use and Communication in Multilingual New Spain." *Ethnohistory* 59, no. 4 (Fall 2012): 667–674.

Narváez Expedition

Named for its commander, the expedition refers to the 1520 undertaking by Pánfilo de Narváez to capture Cortés, under the orders

of the then governor of Cuba, Diego de Velázquez de Cuéllar. Narváez had served
alongside Velázquez in previous conquests,
including the subjugation of Cuba. His cruel
efficiency, while unimaginative, was ideal
for Velázquez's purpose, which was to prevent Cortés from succeeding in invading the
wealthy empire of the Aztecs. The governor
wished to use the conquest of Mexico as leverage to gain the coveted title of *adelantado*. Reports of Cortés's ambitions resulted
in Velázquez rescinding his appointment of
Cortés, but not before the *caudillo* had left
Cuba and sailed for the mainland.

Narváez's role in the governor's plans was
to organize a force capable of apprehending
Cortés and either killing or bringing him back
to Cuba to answer to Velázquez. Assembling
the fleet the governor had already begun to
organize, Narváez managed to pull together
19 ships, 20 cannon, and about 80 harquebusiers. He additionally had 120 crossbowmen
and 80 cavalry. This meant his force was almost twice the size of Cortés's initial expeditionary force.

The punitive expedition had very clear
orders—to follow Cortés, capture him (or
kill him if capture was impossible), and return him to Cuba. However, the expedition
ran into problems from the start, including
division within the ranks of the men recruited,
the presence of smallpox in the expeditionary force, and the unexpected appointment
of a judge to accompany the force—by orders of the *audiencia* of Santo Domingo.
The judge, Lucas Vázquez de Ayllón, was
to serve as an intermediary between the two
Spanish conquistadors in order to prevent
dissention among the Spanish in the presence of the indigenous population.

From the outset, Narváez resented the
presence of Ayllón. When the expedition arrived on the island of Cozumel—after the
earlier arrival of Ayllón—the resentment

grew. Emissaries from Cortés, who secretly
dispersed gold among the least loyal supporters of Narváez, also carried precious gifts
to Ayllón. The judge responded by urging Narváez to settle his differences with
Cortés peacefully. The highly volatile conquistador had Ayllón arrested and ordered
him sent back to Cuba.

Meanwhile, Narváez located his forces in
a more defensive position, in the indigenous
town of Zempoala. Using the religious center, including the pyramid, as the location
for his defensive placements, the conquistador began preparing for a battle with the
forces of Cortés. Aware of the growing dissention among his own forces, and hoping
to carry the battle to Cortés on the plains
outside of Zempoala, he ordered cavalry and
foot soldiers out onto a plain, about a mile
from the city, in the midst of foul weather.
After several hours of waiting in vain, he
finally withdrew all except two sentries.
The rain-soaked forces returned back to
Zempoala, where they retired for the remainder of the night.

Expecting the battle to occur the next
day, and with two sentries posted in the
likely location of Cortés's approach to
the city, Narváez and his men slept. Their
slumber was short-lived, though, as Cortés
was close behind the withdrawing soldiers.
Tired from the difficult march through the
mud and rain, Cortés motivated his men by
reminding them of their own experience in
comparison to Narváez's untested men. The
familiarity of Cortés with the layout of Zempoala from his previous stay there, and the
earlier negotiated alliance with the Totonac
people of the town, added to the attackers'
confidence. Splitting his forces, Cortés sent
his loyal supporter, Gonzalo de Sandoval,
against Narváez and his captains resting in
the thatched shelter at the top of the pyramid. Another force, complete with lances,

was tasked with securing the cavalry on the outskirts of the town, preferably without harming the horses.

Exhausted and convinced any conflict would occur the next day, Narváez and his men were caught off guard. Though the conquistador recovered quickly, and brandished a double-handed broadsword, his efforts had little effect. One of Sandoval's men, wielding a lance, struck Narváez in an eye, blinding him in that eye for life. With the thatched hut burning around them, the defenders surrendered soon thereafter.

With Narváez in custody, his captains quickly yielded, agreeing to join Cortés's forces. Only two men under Cortés died, while Narváez lost approximately 15, and several more were wounded. The horses were captured without harm. Though the expedition began as a sizeable force intended to defeat Cortés and his mission, the result was quite different. Narváez was imprisoned, but most of his men, cannon, horses, and weapons were added to the Spanish military might. This assimilation of Narváez's men included one who was contaminated with the smallpox virus. The Narváez expedition, while a major threat to Spanish control in Mexico as the invading forces turned on each other instead of the Aztecs, eventually led to the conquest of the indigenous population. Not only did Cortés gain reinforcements whose zeal for gold ensured their shifting allegiance, but the presence of smallpox, though hazardous to the Spanish, led to the eventually epidemic that undermined the numerical superiority of the indigenous population.

Rebecca M. Seaman

See also: *Adelantado*; *Audiencia*; Ayllón, Lucas Vázquez de; Cortés, Hernán; Sandoval, Gonzalo de; Tenochtitlán, City of; Totonacs, Alliance with Spanish; Velázquez, Diego (de Cuéllar); Zempoala.

Resources

Diaz, Bernal. *The Conquest of New Spain.* Translated with Introduction by J. M. Cohen. London: Penguin Books, 1963.

Levy, Buddy. *Conquistador: Hernán Cortés, King Montezuma, and the Last Stand of the Aztecs.* New York: Bantam Books, 2009.

Pagden, Anthony, trans. & ed. *Hernan Cortes: Letters from Mexico.* New Haven: Yale University Press, 1986.

Thomas, Hugh. *Conquest: Montezuma, Cortés, and the Fall of Old Mexico.* New York: Simon & Schuster, 1993.

Narváez, Pánfilo de

Born circa 1470 in Spain, Pánfilo de Narváez traveled to the Spanish Caribbean colonies in hopes of gaining lands and wealth. There, he partook in the expedition and conquest of Hispaniola and later Cuba. His cruel efficiency won his numerous grants of land and encomiendas of indigenous labor, as well as the lasting condemnation of Bartolomé de Las Casas, who accompanied Narváez in the subjugation of Cuba. In 1519, following Hernán Cortés's early embarkation upon a voyage to explore and conquer Mexico, Cuba's governor Diego de Velázquez de Cuéllar's suspicions led him to send ships to stop the Mexico venture. When his attempt failed, Velázquez set about organizing an expedition designed to capture and/or kill Cortés. The outbreak of smallpox on the island of Cuba convinced the governor to appoint a subordinate to apprehend Cortés. He selected Pánfilo de Narváez for his brutal efficiency.

Older than most Spanish conquistadors and experienced, the Cuban governor's confidence in Narváez seemed well placed. However, the dogged determination and willingness to use cruelty that helped Narváez accomplish his tasks also contributed to

Pánfilo de Narváez (left, balcony) was a Spanish hidalgo (noble) sent by Governor Velázquez to arrest Hernán Cortés (center) in the midst of Cortés's conquest of the Aztecs of Mexico, 1520. (Library of Congress)

dissention in his ranks. News of the governor's intent to send an expedition to discipline and arrest Cortés reached the *audiencia* of Santo Domingo—at odds with Velázquez for endangering the security of Cuba by depleting its defenses. The result was the assignment of judicial appointee, Lucas Vázquez de Ayllón, to provide oversight and prevent internal conflict among the Spanish forces.

Narváez's arrogant self-esteem chafed at the seeming affront to his abilities. An opponent of Cortés, Ayllón's initial predisposition toward Narváez's mission soon faded under the poor treatment meted out to the judicial dignitary. In the end, the explorer arrested Ayllón and attempted to send him back to Cuba on one of his ships, but not before the expedition landed in Mexico.

The punitive expedition sailed for Mexico with 19 ships and several hundred soldiers—twice as many as Cortés's forces. Narváez boasted 20 cannon, 120 crossbowmen, and almost 100 cavalry horses. His contingent additionally carried an unknown visitor—the smallpox germ. The soldiers in his company were adventurers seeking fortune, as well as escape from the raging epidemic in Cuba. They initially stopped at Cozumel, where the indigenous population was soon decimated by disease.

Following a brief stop at Cozumel, Narváez made slow progress down the western coast of the Yucatán Peninsula, experiencing severe weather. Another ship was lost in the storm, and six other damaged. The expedition arrived in April 1520 at the future site of Veracruz—about 40 miles south of where Cortés previously established Villa Rica de la Vera Cruz, a month after having set sail from Cuba. The ship carrying Ayllón arrived earlier. The judge's advice to sail further so as not to antagonize the local Totonac people was ignored by the proud conquistador. Though Narváez did attempt to maintain peaceful relations with the indigenous population, internal divisions among his own people and the strain of feeding so many of the foreign invaders began to take its toll on relations. Blaming the *audiencia* of Santo Domingo's judge for creating dissention, Narváez had him arrested.

Once he had established the short-lived San Salvador, Pánfilo de Narváez proceeded to establish contact with Montezuma II, emperor of the Aztecs. Montezuma was told that the Spanish with Cortés were bad men and were to be captured and removed. He was also informed that, once this task was complete, the Spanish would leave, desiring no gold or permanent settlements in Mexico. Yet within days, Narváez's message to the emperor shifted, revealing that his king commanded him to colonize the area, as well as to release Montezuma and return that which was stolen from him. The duplicity of the messages revealed to the emperor that this new Spanish leader was also a conquistador, intent upon subjugating the Aztec.

Narváez quickly learned of the fort and community of Villa Rica de la Vera Cruz and sent three emissaries to inform the residents of his orders to arrest Cortés. The notary Alonso de Vergara, the priest Vasco de Guevara, and one of the soldiers Antonio de Amaya were instructed to announced Cortés's treason and give the forces under Captain Gonzalo de Sandoval (Cortés's appointee) an opportunity to join Narváez. Instead, Sandoval seized the messengers and delivered them to Cortés at Tenochtitlán. Amazed by the beauty of the Mexica city, and plied with precious gifts (including some for Ayllón), the three quickly shifted their allegiance to Cortés. Mounting on horses, they returned to the coast, where they reported their initial capture yet good treatment by the *caudillo* Cortés. The gifts they kept secret and used to encourage dissention among Narváez's ranks. Ayllón, impressed by his gifts, again voiced concern over conflict between the two conquistadors. This proved the final straw and the judge was placed on a ship with instructions to take him back to Cuba.

Narváez, outmaneuvered by Cortés, moved his forces to the city of Zempoala. There he compelled the "fat cacique" to allow him to erect defenses in the midst of the religious center. Only when the Spaniard turned his men loose on the citizens of the town did the Zempoalan leader realize his mistake. Narváez took troops and cavalry out to the plains to meet Cortés, but retired all but two entries when the *caudillo* failed to appear and rain made conditions miserable. Instead, he retreated back to Zempoala, where he was awaken by Sandoval's men attacking the fortified pyramid where he had taken residence. Narváez was captured, but only after an injury that cost him his eye. He remained a captive at Vera Cruz for three years, while his men were absorbed into Cortés's forces, which soon returned to Tenochtitlán to deal with an uprising precipitated by Pedro de Alvarado's actions. Finally released from prison, Narváez was welcomed at Tenochtitlán by Cortés before heading back to Spain. In

Spain, news of Governor Velázquez and Narváez's failed attempts to block Cortés's conquest of the Aztec were met with disfavor, as the wealth from the invasion began to arrive in the peninsula. While Pánfilo de Narváez was criticized for his role, he was nonetheless granted permission to undertake an expedition to Florida. The expedition proved disastrous for most involved, and resulted in the death of its leader, in 1528.

Rebecca M. Seaman

See also: Alvarado, Pedro de; Ayllón, Lucas Vázquez de; Cortés, Hernán; Montezuma II; Sandoval, Gonzalo de; Tenochtitlán, City of; Totonacs, Alliance with Spanish; Velázquez, Diego (de Cuéllar); Zempoala.

Resources

Díaz, Bernal. *The Conquest of New Spain.* Translated with Introduction by J.M. Cohen. New York: Penguin Books, 1963.

Levy, Buddy. *Conquistador: Hernán Cortés, King Montezuma, and the Last Stand of the Aztecs.* New York: Bantam Books, 2009.

Pagden, Anthony, trans. & ed. *Hernan Cortes: Letters from Mexico.* New Haven: Yale University Press, 1986.

Thomas, Hugh. *Conquest: Montezuma, Cortés, and the Fall of Old Mexico.* New York: Simon & Schuster, 1993.

Neo-Incas

The Neo-Inca refers to a resistance movement of Incas loyal to the emperor, and intent upon returning authority to the Inca. While some Inca had resisted from the start, the trigger for the movement seems to have occurred under the puppet leadership of Manco Inca in the first years of Francisco Pizarro's control of the empire.

Following the initial military conquest and ensuing search and seizure of vast quantities of gold and silver from the Inca royal and religious treasuries, Pizzaro sought to subjugate the people and control the regions around Cuzco. To accomplish this objective, he distributed encomiendas, granting lands and Indian laborers to his strongest supporters among the Spanish conquistadors. The treatment of those indigenous laborers, including demands for tribute, and service in Spanish military forces, in addition to more traditional labor demands, served to alienate growing numbers of Inca. When combined with these same encomenderos' use of the Inca populace to locate and loot their traditional shrines for gems and gold objects, the result was a growing resistance to the powerful new Spanish government.

The Neo-Incas coalesced around the puppet emperor, Manco Inca, whose continued authority seemed supported by Francisco Pizarro. However, Pizarro's brothers undermined that perception, and the Sapa Inca finally realized the danger his life was in and the threat posed to his rule. Manco Inca's escape from Cuzco to a fortress northwest of the city was quickly followed by a series of raids against the Spanish supply and trade routes, as well as attacks on indigenous supporters of the Spanish.

No one particular incident triggered the rise of the Neo-Incas resistance movement. It was the realization of the common Inca population that their culture and beliefs were under attack, along with the abusive treatment of the Inca elite, from the *kurakas* to the Sapa Inca himself, that helped spread disillusionment. The timing of such events as Hernando Pizarro's forcing former captains of Atahualpa to reveal the location of religious shrines and the subsequent pillaging of those same shrines by Pizarro's forces helped solidify the movement and pulled Inca from a variety of social classes into the Neo-Inca resistance effort.

Manco's Neo-Inca rebellion was initially quite successful. Uniting the ruling Inca from around the empire, Manco Inca established a long siege upon the Spanish-controlled city of Cuzco. Unfortunately, the success did not last long. After nine months of siege, the Sapa Inca was incapable of forcing a Spanish surrender. Instead, returning Spanish forces forced Manco's forces to withdraw to his distant fortress.

The Spanish established various military centers for defense and to launch counterattacks. One such example was Huamanga, which helped secure the trade routes leading from Cuzco to the coast. The seemingly insignificant numbers of the Spanish forces were reinforced by indigenous peoples who were either compelled to join the military ranks by the encomenderos or who willingly aligned with the Spanish as a means of escaping the authority of the Sapa Incas, who had previously compelled tribute and service of the same population.

The Spanish attempt to defeat the Neo-Inca rebellion suffered its own setbacks. Hindered by internal dissention and competition between the Pizzaro brothers and leading military leaders, some Spanish found themselves fighting against other forces from Spain. Division among the Spanish was so deep that Diego de Almagro, *adelantado* for southern Peru, occasionally sided with the Incas and then his own countrymen. His shifting stance resulted in his eventual assassination, and prompted his followers to, in turn, assassinate Francisco Pizzaro and flee to the protection of Manco Inca Yupanqui.

After almost a decade of struggle, the tides shifted in favor of the Spanish forces. Manco Inca was incapable of unseating the Spanish from Cuzco and eventually was himself assassinated in 1544, by the same individuals who killed Pizzaro. While the Neo-Inca resistance movement did not die with Manco Inca, the rebellion had reached its peak and continued to decline over the next three decades.

Rebecca M. Seaman

See also: *Adelantado*; Almagro, Diego de; Atahualpa; Cuzco; Encomenderos; Encomienda; Huamanga; *Kuraka*; Manco Inca Yupanqui; Pizzaro, Francisco; Sapa Inca.

Resources

Gabai, Rafael Varón. *Francisco Pizarro and His Brothers: The Illusion of Power in Sixteenth-Century Peru.* Translated by Javier Flores Espinoza. Norman: University of Oklahoma Press, 1997.

Hemming, John. *The Conquest of the Incas.* New York: Harcourt Brae Jovanovich, 1970.

Stern, Steve J. *Peru's Indian Peoples and the Challenge of Spanish Conquest: Huamanga to 1640.* 2nd ed. Madison: University of Wisconsin Press, 1993.

Nezahualcoyotl (1402–1472)

Nezahualcoyotl was king of Texcoco and one of the founders of the Aztec alliance that conquered most of central Mexico before the arrival of the Spanish conquistadors. He has also been honored as a poet and philosopher king who established a just rule of law for his people. Other accomplishments include great architectural feats and the establishment of a temple to an unknown and unknowable god, a monolithic religion, which rejected the pantheism of the Mesoamericans. However, his descendants may have credited many of these accomplishments to Nezahualcoyotl in hopes of currying favor with the Spanish clergy after the conquest.

Nezahualcoyotl ("fasting coyote") was born on April 28, 1402, in the city of Texcoco, the capital of the Acolhua people, on the eastern shore of the lakes in the Valley of Mexico. He was the son of Ixtlilxochitl I and Matlalcihuatzin, rulers of Texcoco. Ixtlilxochitl came into conflict with the Tepanecs, an invading people who founded the city of Azcapotzalco. In 1418, the Tepanecs conquered Texcoco. Nezahualcoyotl witnessed his father being killed by Tepanec soldiers and was captured before he could flee. According to tradition, Nezahualcoyotl escaped imprisonment when a loyal retainer took his place in prison. Nezahualcoyotl went into exile, first in Huexotzinco, then in Tenochtitlán in 1422. His mother had been a member of the Mexica ruling family in Tenochtitlán, and Nezahualcoyotl was warmly received there. He spent the next eight years in that city, where he was educated and trained as a *tlatoani,* or ruler.

Nezahualcoyotl took advantage of a change in rulers in Atzcapotzalco to present himself as a loyal subject to the Tepanecs. The offer was rejected and Nezahualcoyotl was forced to hurriedly leave for Texcoco. However, before he left he managed to reestablish contacts in the city with his loyal followers. Over the next six years, Nezahualcoyotl was forced to move continually to stay ahead of Tepanec agents.

In 1428, a number of cities in the area united against the Tepanecs. Nezahualcoyotl was one of the leaders and founders of the coalition. The major city-states in the coalition were Tenochtitlán, Tlacopan, and Texcoco. These states were united by language and a common heritage. The alliance became the basis of the Aztec Empire. They were joined by smaller cities and by dissidents inside Atzcapotzalco. The allies destroyed Atzcapotzalco and freed Texcoco. Nezahualcoyotl resumed his rightful role as ruler, installed by the Mexica of Tenochtitlán. His principal wife was a Mexica princess, which helped tie him to Tenochtitlán. Nonetheless,

in most of his policies, Nezahualcoyotl was a junior partner to the rulers of Tenochtitlán. He later had over 40 wives and fathered more than 100 children.

As king, Nezahualcoyotl has been credited with many achievements. He implemented a rational code of laws. Different councils were created, including ones for finance, war, justice, and culture. The last council was known as the council of music. An academy for the arts was created, which was open to talented students from all over Mesoamerica. Nezahualcoyotl also created an extensive library that was later lost in the Spanish conquest. He built an impressive dike, which divided the lake so that salt water could not contaminate the freshwater that Tenochtitlán and other cities needed for their drinking water. Other architectural achievements included impressive temples and public buildings. Nezahualpilli succeeded his father, Nezahualcoyotl, and continued many of his father's policies and achievements.

Native American historians writing after the Spanish conquest credited Nezahualcoyotl with many accomplishments that have been called into question. These writers included some of his descendants, such as Juan Bautista de Pomar and Fernando de Alva Cortes Ixtlilxochitl. These native chroniclers were anxious to prove the worth of their culture, to preserve it from destruction by the Spanish. They wanted to show that Mesoamerican achievements were advanced and lacked only Christianity to be the equal to the Europeans. One example of this is that they credited many poems and songs to Nezahualcoyotl as the sole writer. These works were written down in arrangements similar to those in European works. However, Acolhua poetry from the 15th century normally followed traditional themes and was modified over generations.

Later historians also credited Nezahualcoy-otl with being a peaceful ruler. Contemporary records that survived counter this assertion, indicating that he participated in many wars waged by the Aztec Empire during his kingship.

Perhaps most controversially, the later writers credited Nezahualcoyotl with a form of monotheism. He supposedly came to experience an "unknown, unknowable Lord of Everywhere" and rejected the pantheon of other gods worshipped in the past. Nezahualcoyotl purportedly built a temple to this god and ordered that no blood sacrifices of any kind be offered in the temple. On the other hand, it is recorded that Nezahualcoyotl built temples to the major gods worshipped in Tenochtitlán on the main pyramid in the center of Texcoco, indicating that he continued to worship, or at least supported the worship of these gods.

Although some of Nezahualcoyotl's accomplishments can be questioned, he played an important role in Mesoamerican history in helping to found the Aztec Empire. He died in Texcoco on June 4, 1472.

Tim J. Watts

See also: Aztec, or Mexica; Mexico, State of prior to Spanish Conquest; Tenochtitlán; Texcoco, Alliance with Tenochtitlán.

Resources

Lee, Jongsoo. *The Allure of Nezahualcoyotl: Pre-Hispanic History, Religion and Nahua Poetics.* Albuquerque: University of New Mexico Press, 2008.

Leon-Portilla, Miguel. *Fifteen Poets of the Aztec World.* Norman: University of Oklahoma Press, 2000.

Schwaller, John F. *In the Palace of Nezahualcoyotl: Painting Manuscripts, Writing the Pre-Hispanic Past in Early Colonial Tetzcoco, Mexico.* Berkeley: Academy of American Franciscan History, 2011.

Ninan Cuyochi

One of approximately 500 illegitimate offspring of the Inca emperor, Huayna Cápac, Ninan Cuyochi briefly was assigned the title of Sapa Inca upon his father's death from smallpox. His own death, in 1527, occurred soon after, resulting in a reign that is often excluded from the lineage of the Sapa Incas of Peru, and the eruption of civil war as other sons of Huayna competed for the throne.

Huayna Cápac followed the Inca royal tradition of marrying his sister, Cusi Rimay Coya, as a means of preserving the pure bloodlines of the Sapa Inca. This match produced no male offspring, and Huayna also took other sisters, nonrelated Inca women as wives and concubines. From these relations, he reportedly produced hundreds of children. None of the sons was classified as legitimate by the Inca standards. This posed a dilemma for the powerful Sapa Inca, who wished to pass the central control of the extensive empire on to a capable ruler who could perpetuate his family's reign. Huayna's decision was complicated by news of strange men (Spaniards) who invaded the distant perimeters of the empire. Messengers also brought news of another unwanted visitor—a deadly epidemic of an unknown and frightening disease spread rapidly throughout the empire.

The eldest of Huayna's sons was Túpac Cusi Hualpa, or Huáscar. While not legitimate, as the eldest son, it was understood that he could easily become the logical successor to Huayna Cápac. Regrettably, Huáscar bore only a few traits necessary to govern the far-reaching and diverse Inca holdings. He drank to excess, slept with married women, and was generally uninterested in the military and mundane aspects of governing. In response to this reality, Huayna groomed two other adult sons to succeed him as Sapa Inca: Ninan Cuyochi and Atahualpa. Ninan, elder of the two brothers, served in the wars of northern expansion along with his younger brother, Atahualpa. Both gained good reputations as military leaders, significantly assisting their father in fighting the Pastos in the far north.

While in the northern coastal region of Huancavelica, Huayna Cápac received news of a rampant epidemic devastating the empire. The pestilence already claimed several close relatives of the Sapa Inca, including his brothers and primary wife. In an attempt to establish order, he traveled to his secondary capital of Quito, where he fell ill from the same disease. Huayna sent for nobles to record his wishes for a successor. The first choice presented was for Ninan Cuyochi, loyal son and capable military leader. However, Huayna indicated that the nobles should perform a calpa (kallpa, ritual dissection of a lamb to read the Sun god's wishes). Should the calpa not support Ninan Cuyochi, Huáscar was to be the second choice for Inca.

The ritual was performed for both sons, with negative results in each case. When the nobles returned to Huayna to relate the news, they discovered he had already died. Ninan was selected as the next Sapa Inca. The royal fringe designating authority was taken to Tumipampa to be bestowed upon Ninan Cuyochi. Sadly, the eldest son had already died of the same disease. Desperate, the nobles decided to take the fringe back to Cuzco where Huáscar was officially given the title of Sapa Inca. Huayna's final wishes resulted in the title being contested by Huáscar's younger and more capable brother, Atahualpa. The result was a civil war throughout the empire at the same time that the Spanish invasion under Francisco Pizarro pushed inland to conquer the Inca Empire.

Rebecca M. Seaman

See also: Atahualpa; Huáscar; Huayna Cápac; Pizarro, Francisco; Sapa Inca; Túpac Huallpa.

Resources

Gamboa, Pedro Sarmiento de. *History of the Incas.* Translated and Edited by Sir Clements Markham. Cambridge, UK: Hakluyt Society, 1907.

MacQuarrie, Kim. *Last Days of the Inca.* New York: Simon & Schuster, 2007.

Ojeda (Hojeda), Alonso de

At least two Spanish conquistadors of this same name participated in the initial conquest and settlement of Spain's early American colonies.

The first, much more known and quoted, was born in 1466/68 at Cuenca. Connected with the exploration of Guyana, Trinidad, Tobago, Curacao, Aruba, and Colombia, Ojeda was famous for giving the current name to Venezuela. He also founded Santa Cruz. He died on San Domingo in 1515. The second Alonso de Ojeda, born probably in Moguer or Badajoz, was one of Hernán Cortés's soldiers.

Alonso de Ojeda was born in the second half of 1460s in Cuenca New Castile, to an impoverished noble family in Burgos (authors vary between 1466 and 1470). In his youth, he served as a page for Spanish aristocrats, including the archbishop of Burgos. Participation in the conquest of Grenada was his first military experience, which turned attention to his skills in this field. In 1493 he was commissioned to join Christopher Columbus in his second journey.

During the expedition, Alonso was involved in many struggles against the natives, some of which became legendary. An example of such a conflict was the defeat of the Indians in the battle of Vega Real or Jáquimo. According to tradition, he was extremely harsh, cruel, and unjust to the Indians. During this trip he found a gold mine on the island of Haiti, spurring on further Spanish settlement and conquest of the island of Hispaniola.

After this first experience, Ojeda was sent on an expedition to America in the years 1499–1500, along with Juan de la Cosa and Amerigo Vespucci. The voyage explored and mapped the shores of Venezuela and Guyana. They were among the first Europeans to discover the northern shores of South America. They discovered the delta of Orinoco and Maracaibo. It was on this expedition that Ojeda gave the name to Venezuela, as either Little Venice (in Spanish describing numerous houses on poles in water), or derived from the indigenous population referring to themselves as the *Veneciuela.*

The return of this expedition to Spain was significant, not due to riches found and acquired, but due to their contribution of new geographical information. The exploration and mapping of the northern boundaries of the South American continent by Ojeda and his colleagues greatly impacted European knowledge of Western Hemisphere geography, an importance that cannot be overlooked. Ojeda's expedition searched about 3,000 km of the South American shore.

Some historians claim that during this trip Ojeda's expedition met with an English expedition of John Cabot sailing south from the territory of Newfoundland. Scarce documents, which still need to be enriched and reread, suggest such a meeting, but give no hint as to how the meeting ended: did Ojeda sent Cabot back north, did he imprison the Italian in Henry VII's service, or possibly even kill the Bristol expedition?

In the years 1502–1510, de Ojeda undertook several additional expeditions to the shores of South America seeking gold, pearls, and other riches, as well as engaging in numerous bloody skirmishes with the local Indians. Undertaking his trip in 1502, he received financial backing by Spanish merchants who chartered four ships for him. Ojeda also held a royal patent of the governor of Coquibacoa. He did found a colony of Santa Cruz on the Guajira Peninsula, at Bahia Honda. Unfortunately, the settlement, first Spanish settlement in Colombia, did not survive even three months.

In 1508, Alonso de Ojeda went on one more expedition during which the colony of Nova Andalucía and Uraba was founded, with Ojeda as its governor. In 1510, the first Spanish town (barely a fort in reality) in South America, San Sebastian, was founded by Ojeda.

This was to be his last expedition. He spent the next five years in Santo Domingo, partly in a monastery of St Francis, where he died in poverty in 1515.

Alonso de Ojeda: Much less is known about the second Ojeda, and so far the place and date of his birth has not been determined. He first appears among Cortés's adventurers subduing the Aztec Empire. However, earlier he may also have been involved in the conquest of Cuba in 1511, as well as later, after the defeat of the Aztecs, in the expedition to Honduras in the 1520s. He was definitely a good soldier, at times responsible for provisioning the Spanish troops and responsible for training young soldiers. He was named as one of the first settler of San Alfonso. Having married, he went to have seven children. He shared half ownership in the Titlepec encomienda. He died most probably in poverty in the 1530s.

Jakub Basista

See also: Columbus, Christopher; Cortés, Hernán; Hispaniola.

Resources

Diaz del Castillo, Bernal. *The Conquest of New Spain.* Edited by Janet Burke and Ted Humphrey. Indianapolis, IN: Hackett, 2012.

Helps, Sir Arthur. *The Spanish Conquest in America: and Its Relation to the History of Slavery and to the Government of Colonies.* London/New York: John Lane, 1900–04.

Thomas, Hugh. *The Conquest of Mexico.* London: Pimlico, 2004.

Thomas, Hugh. *Who's Who of the Conquistadors.* London: Cassell & Company, 2007.

Olid, Cristóbal de

One of the conquistadors who served Governor Diego Velázquez de Cuéllar, in relation to the expedition of Juan de Grijalva in 1518, Cristóbal de Olid was sent out to locate the explorer who was believed lost. According to the instructions given to Hernán Cortés by Velázquez the following year, Grijalva and Olid were both still unaccounted for. However, Grijalva had already returned to Cuba and Olid went on to sail with Cortés after linking up with the conquistador in Trinidad. While not one of the inner circle of Extremaduras Cortés surrounded himself with, Olid was nonetheless one of the *caudillo*'s more dependable captains in the foray across Mexico from 1519 to 1521. This was a surprising fact since he had once been loyal to Velázquez who was by that time the nemesis of Cortés.

So much did the *caudillo* trust Olid that, shortly after landing in the Yucatán, Cristóbal de Olid was entrusted with a company command of approximately 50 soldiers. Olid rewarded that trust with a strong demonstration of leadership, time after time over the next two years. By the time the Castilians had established an alliance with the Tlaxcalans, traditional enemies of the Mexica, Olid and the other premiere captains under the *caudillo* received gifts of girls of noble birth from Tlaxcala.

Olid continued to display loyal and capable support to Cortés during the events leading up to and beyond the La Noche Triste (the Sad Night) of June 1520. Having returned to Tenochtitlán after defeating the forces of Pánfilo Narváez, Cortés found the city in rebellion against the Spanish—then under the leadership of his subordinate, Pedro de Alvarado. The *caudillo* determined that the Aztec emperor, Montezuma, should address the Mexica in an effort to quell the uprising. When Montezuma refused, it was Olid who helped convince the emperor to address the crowds. As leading Aztecs responded by hurling stones and spears at their leader, Olid and Fr. Bartolomé de Olmedo tried to shelter the emperor, to no avail. The shower of missiles killed Montezuma, and the violence of the crowd only increased. By the evening of June 30, 1520, the Spanish realized they must flee the city or risk certain death. Again, Olid played a leading role in providing tactical support to the main military force under Cortés as the combined native and Castilian forces fought their way out of the city surrounded by water.

Over the next several months following the La Noche Triste disaster, Cortés used his captains, including Olid, to conduct reconnaissance expeditions around the lakes of central Mexico. They were also responsible for capturing cities and negotiating alliances with native leaders of communities that began to shift from fearful compliance with the Aztecs to hopeful allegiance to the Spanish. By the time the Spanish were ready to launch their spring siege on Tenochtitlán, Olid had risen to be one of three captains Hernán Cortés trusted with leading his four-pronged assault on the capital city.

It is the aftermath of the conquest of the Aztecs that brought out the worst in many of the conquistadors in Mexico. Unhappy with the paucity of profits following such intensive fighting, Olid and others long loyal to Cortés were willing to recognize the newly appointed governor of New Spain, Cristóbal de Tapia. Cortés managed to politically outmaneuver forces led by Governor Velázquez in Cuba and Juan Rodríguez Fonseca in Spain seeking his removal, and received support from the Crown to maintain his position, along with further titles and authority. Those conquistadors who agreed to recognize Tapia as governor were ostracized from the inner circle of the *caudillo*.

By 1522, Olid was encouraged to undertake a mission further south. Disgruntled and seeking fame and fortune much like his previous mentor had done, Olid was eventually branded a rebel. In 1524, Cortés personally traveled to Honduras to punish his former captain. Most records agree that Olid was finally beheaded as a rebel in 1525, an ignoble death for the Spanish conquistador. After the death of Olid, Cortés relented from his anger and referred to Olid in the complimentary terms of "a Hector in single combat."

Rebecca M. Seaman

See also: Alvarado, Pedro de; Cortés, Hernán; Grijalva, Juan de; La Noche Triste; Montezuma II; Narváez, Pánfilo; Olmedo, Fr. Bartolomé de; Tapia, Andrés de; Tenochtitlán, Siege of; Velázquez, Diego (de Cuéllar).

Resources

Díaz del Castillo, Bernal. *The Conquest of New Spain*. Translated by J. M. Cohen. London: Penguin Press, 1963.

León-Portilla, Miguel. *The Broken Spears: The Aztec Account of the Conquest of Mexico*. Foreword by J. Jorge Klor de Alva. Boston: Beacon Press, 2006.

Levy, Buddy.*Conquistador: Hernan Cortes, King Montezuma, and the Last Stand of the Aztecs.* New York: Bantam Books, 2008.

Restall, Matthew. *Seventh Myths of the Spanish Conquest.* Oxford: Oxford University Press, 2004.

Schwartz, Stuart B., ed. *Victors and Vanquished: Spanish and Nahua Views of the Conquest of Mexico.* Boston: Bedford/St. Martin's, 2000.

Thomas, Hugh. *Montezuma, Cortés, and the Fall of Old Mexico.* New York: Simon & Schuster, 1993.

Olmedo, Fr. Bartolomé de (1485–1524)

Fr. Bartolomé de Olmedo was a priest and friar of the Order of the Blessed Virgin Mary of Mercy, also known as the Mercedarian Friars. The missionary was commonly referred to as Fray Bartolomeo in keeping with the practice in Spain at the time. Chaplain, confidante, and advisor of Hernán Cortés, Fr. Bartolomé accompanied the Spanish conquistador on his expedition to Mexico City. Fr. Olmedo is best remembered as a voice of reason and tolerance during the expedition, and for his opposition to the efforts of conquest. He was especially opposed to the Spanish destruction of idols and temples. He advocated using Christian examples of love and spirituality as examples to help win over and convert the native peoples, not violence and destruction.

Fray Bartolomeo was born in 1485, in Olmedo, Spain, the son of a medical doctor. Fr. Olmedo was well educated and likely studied at the University of Valladolid, not far from his family home. He spent time at the monasteries of Segovia and Olmedo prior to leaving to join the expedition to the New World. He arrived in Santo Domingo in 1516, at the age of 31. From Santo Domingo, Olmedo traveled on to Havana. In 1519, he accompanied Cortés on his famous expedition to Mexico, being the first known Franciscan missionary to land in Cozumel and then in Veracruz. On April 24, 1522, Fr. Bartolomé de Olmedo, along with Pedro de Alvarado, arrived at Tehuantepec. The local monarch, Cosijopii, a relative of the Emperor Montezuma, welcomed them. Following interaction with Fr. Olmedo, Cosijopii converted to Catholicism and later even built the convent of San Domingo. By Fray Olmedo's own estimate he baptized over 2,500 natives. Some of his first and most notable baptisms include that of the famous La Malinche, Cortés's interpreter, since she had learned Spanish, giving her the Christian name, Marina. He additionally baptized many of the Aztec nobility who embraced Catholicism in the first few years of Spanish occupation. After Montezuma's capture, Fray Bartolomeo spent time with the captive emperor and attempted to convert him, but Montezuma died before he accepted the Christian faith or was baptized.

An advocate of reason, Fr. Olmedo denounced atrocities and violence. Instead, he chose to show respect and act in ways that demonstrated Christian care for the native people. Olmedo was reported to have a very positive disposition, often singing with a strong and pleasant voice. It was his constant advisory role to Cortés, usually admonishing the great conquistador to be patient, which produced the greatest impact on the Spanish. One example given by the chronicler Bernal Diaz is the relation of Cortés asking Olmedo's advice regarding seeking permission from the emperor, Montezuma, to build a church in the central plaza, near the temple of the greatest Aztec gods.

Fr. Olmedo agreed with the sentiment, but discouraged the timing of the request due to the current temperament of the Aztec emperor. When Cortés persisted, Montezuma and his priests reacted angrily, as predicted by Olmedo's advice.

In his role as the expedition's priest, Fr. Olmedo offered mass to the conquistadors regularly, usually using his strong voice to conduct the services in chants. He also employed his faith in administering the sacraments, including that of Extreme Unction (Last Rites) following the disastrous defeat of the Spanish at the La Noche Triste in late June and early July 1520. Though opposed to the use of violence to conquer the indigenous population, the friar's spiritual service helped keep the religious objectives of the Spanish at the forefront. While Fray Bartolomeo interpreted those objectives as intended to conduct missionary work and convert the Aztecs, others in his company employed harsher religious actions— destroying temples and enslaving the population as a means of controlling the region for Spain. Persistent in his missionary purpose, Fr. Bartolomé de Olmedo is credited not only with numerous conversions, but also with saying the first mass in a converted temple in Tehuantepec.

Fr. Bartolomé de Olmedo's preferred method of winning over converts was through devotion to Mary, the Virgin of Mercy. Early accounts reveal that he would place an image of Mary on the altar and use the Aztec's questions about the image to inform them about Christianity. Whether he was aware of the role of imagery in the Aztec culture is doubtful. However, it is likely that the introduction of this devotion to Mary at an early stage prompted the widespread reception of Christianity following the apparition of the Lady of Guadalupe a few years later.

During the entire initial Spanish expedition into Mexico, Fray Olmedo consistently remained with Cortés as his faithful advisor in areas of religion and in negotiations. Upon his death at 39 in Mexico in November 1524, Alonso Suazo, a lawyer and colonial judge in Mexico, gave the news to Cortés, telling him that "all of Mexico had mourned his death and that the Indians had not eaten from the time of his death until he was buried." The Franciscans celebrated his funeral mass. He was buried in Santiago de Tlatelolco.

Scott R. DiMarco

See also: Cortés, Hernán; Díaz, del Castillo, Bernal; La Malinche, "Doña Marina"; La Noche Triste; Montezuma II.

Resources

Gruzinski, Serge. *The Conquest of Mexico.* London: Polity Press. 1993.

Order of the Blessed Virgin Mary of Mercy. "Until the Tridentine Reform (1492–1574): Inception of Evangelization." http://order ofmercy.org/charism/survey/chapter-3/ (accessed July 5, 2012).

Padden, R. C. *The Hummingbird and the Hawk.* New York: Harper & Row, 1967.

Schwartz, Stuart B., ed. *Victors and Vanquished: Spanish and Nahua Views of the Conquest of Mexico.* Boston: Bedford/St. Martin's Press, 2000.

Thomas, Hugh. *Conquest: Montezuma, Cortés and the Fall of Old Mexico.* New York: Simon & Schuster, 1993.

Ordaz, Diego de

Diego de Ordaz was a very important figure in the conquest of Mexico. Originally from Castroverde de Campos, in the province of León in Spain, he arrived in the New World in about 1510. He was described by Bernal

Díaz del Castillo as a good swordsman, brave and wise, of good height, with a black beard. He spoke with a stammer, which caused him to pronounce certain words very badly.

Ordaz participated in conquests in what is now Colombia, and also in Cuba. In Cuba he became a member of the retinue surrounding the governor of the island, Diego Velázquez de Cuéllar. He joined the expedition of Hernán Cortés at the behest of Velázquez, who feared that Cortés might attempt to set out on his own and conquer the newly discovered territory. Velázquez hoped his recruits would keep the ambitious Cortés in check. Ordaz was one of the captains of the ships that sailed under Cortés from Cuba to Mexico.

When Cortés staged his rebellion against Velázquez, Ordaz was arrested and charged with treason against the new leadership. Nonetheless, he easily switched his affiliations and became a close advisor to Cortés. When Velázquez learned of his treachery, he confiscated all of Ordaz's goods and possessions in Cuba. Ordaz was an eyewitness to many of the astounding events of the conquest, including climbing the snow-capped volcano, Popocatepetl. He eventually gained a coat of arms from the Crown, which was decorated with the image of the volcano.

In the first year of Cortés's invasion, while the *caudillo* returned to the gulf coast to confront the punitive expedition sent by Velázquez under Pánfilo Narváez, Ordaz was sent to pacify some villages near the capital city of Tenochtitlán. He was undertaking this assignment when word arrived that the Spanish forces of Pedro de Alvarado in Tenochtitlán were under siege by the natives. He returned in time to participate in the flight from the city, the La Noche Triste (the Sad Night). In that conflict, he was wounded in three places and lost a finger.

In the fall of 1520, Ordaz was sent to Spain to argue Cortés's case before the Crown,

leaving before the final assault and siege on Tenochtitlán. While in Spain he was made a member of the prestigious military-religious order of Santiago and granted his coat of arms. He was appointed a municipal justice of the Mexican city of Segura de la Frontera (Tepeaca), later becoming a permanent alderman for that city. Both during and following the conquest, Ordaz engaged in trade between the islands and New Spain and continued to petition the crown for preferment and opportunities. In 1530 the Crown engaged him to carry out the conquest of Marañon, a vague region in what is now Venezuela, the Guyanas, and Brazil. He sailed with three very large ships and some 500 men, landing initially in Trinidad, for water and other provisions. From there, he found the Orinoco and sailed up. When his ships could go no further inland, he disembarked and marched on. He was attacked by natives and forced to retrace his steps. After several other attempts, and confrontation with natives, he eventually sailed to Santo Domingo, seeking additional men and provisions. When he was unable to accomplish this, he sailed for Spain, dying en route, possibly poisoned.

John Schwaller

See also: Alvarado, Pedro de; Cortés, Hernán; La Noche Triste; Narváez, Pánfilo; Tenochtitlán, Siege of; Velázquez, Diego (de Cuéllar).

Resources

Díaz del Castillo, Bernal. *The History of the Conquest of New Spain.* Edited by David Carrasco. Albuquerque: University of New Mexico Press, 2008.

Grunberg, Bernard. *Dictionnaire des Conquistadores de Mexico.* Paris: L'Harmattan, 2001.

Hemming, John. *The Search for Eldorado.* London: Joseph, 1978.

Thomas, Hugh. *Who's Who of the Conquistadores.* London: Cassell & Company, 2000.

Orellana, Francisco de (ca. 1511–1546)

Francisco de Orellana, the conquistador credited with consolidating the Spanish settlement in Ecuador, became the first European to successfully navigate the Amazon River for the majority of its course. Possibly related to famous conquistador Francisco Pizarro, Orellana was born in Trujillo, Extremadura, Castile (Spain). His exact birth date is unknown, though estimates range from 1490 to 1511. He went to the Caribbean in the 1520s, saw service in Nicaragua, and subsequently assisted Pizarro in the conquest of Peru in the 1530s. It was on that expedition that he ultimately lost an eye in battle. In return for his services, Orellana was granted land on the Ecuadorean coast. There he founded the city of Guayaquil and served as governor. Several locations in modern-day Ecuador are named after him, including the province of Orellana and its capital.

Around 1541, Orellana joined an expeditionary force under Pizarro's brother, Gonzalo, to explore areas east of Quito (Ecuador) into the South American interior. The expedition was mostly concerned with finding riches like those of the Incan Andes, such as gold and cinnamon (which was in abundance in the Amazon region). The expedition was plagued with difficulties, which included desertion and sickness. Orellana was charged with leading a small group ahead of the main party to secure provisions. Instead of returning to Gonzalo's aid, Orellana and his men continued on an impromptu exploration of the Amazon River system. Historians have debated whether Orellana willingly abandoned Gonzalo or was reacting to forces beyond his control. Through a series of adventures, Orellana and his men made their way down the Napo River (an Amazon tributary), secured provisions, and fought with natives. They reached the mouth of the Napo at the point where it met the Amazon. They eventually reached the Amazon's mouth around 1542. Orellana made his way to the island of Cubagua (Trinidad) and then home to Spain.

Gaspar de Carvajal, a chaplain and one of Orellana's men, wrote a first-hand account of the Amazon expedition. Excerpts were published in books during the 16th century. In 1894, Chilean historian José Toribio Medina included Carvajal's account in his book *The Discovery of the Amazon.*

On his return to Spain, Orellana boasted of New World riches and of encounters with female warriors reminiscent of the Amazons of Greek myth. These tales inspired the name "Amazon" for the South American region; only later was the name applied to the river, which was originally named after Orellana. Although the Treaty of Tordesillas divided the New World between Spain and Portugal, thereby placing the Amazon largely within Spain's jurisdiction but its mouth under Portuguese influence, Orellana secured a grant from the Spanish king to establish New Andalusia in the lands he explored. He departed for South America in 1545. During his ill-fated return, only one of his ships made it to the Amazon's mouth. Orellana and his crew began to explore the area in a small vessel, which capsized. His exact fate remains unknown.

Orellana has become part of contemporary popular culture. In *Indiana Jones and the Kingdom of the Crystal Skull* (2008), the fourth installment of the film franchise about the fictitious adventurer-archeologist Henry "Indiana" Jones Jr., the titular hero allegedly discovers Orellana's lost grave in Peru, which contains a mysterious crystal skull and clues to El Dorado's secrets. Orellana's voyages also inspired the film *Aguirre, the Wrath of God* (1972) and Colombian novelist William Ospina's *The Country of the Cinnamon.*

Eric Martone

See also: Pizarro, Francisco.

Resources

Levy, Buddy. *River of Darkness: Francisco Orellana's Legendary Voyage of Death and Discovery Down the Amazon.* New York: Bantam Books, 2011.

Medina, José Toribio, ed. *The Discovery of the Amazon.* New York: Dover, 1988.

Millar, George Reid. *Orellana Discovers the Amazon.* New York: Heinemann, 1955.

Otomi

Otomi is an indigenous nation that inhabited, since pre-Hispanic times, a discontinuous territory in central Mexico, in the present states of Mexico, Hidalgo, Queretaro, Guanajuato, Michoacan, Tlaxcala, Puebla, and Veracruz. The largest volume of Otomi population currently resides in Mexico, Hidalgo, and Queretaro. The ethnic population speaks the Otomi language, from the Otopamean branch, belonging to the Otomanguean linguistic family. They refer to themselves with different names like *ñätho, hñähñu, ñäñho,* and *ñ'yühü,* due to the enormous dialectal diversification. "Otomi" is an ethnonym in Nahuatl language derived from *otómitl,* which means "one who walks with arrows."

Historians believe groups of oto-pame (within which are the Otomi) migrated from the Tehuacán Valley and reached the Basin of Mexico around the fourth millennium BCE. They occupied their current Otomi ethnic territories and their language was clearly differentiated from the rest of Otopamean

ones in the Classic Period (300–900 CE). Thus, they are believed to have participated heavily in the flowering of the first cities in Mesoamerica, as Cuicuilco, Ticoman, Tlatilco Tlapacoya, and especially Teotihuacan. Recognizing that the population of the Valley of Mexico during the height of Teotihuacan was mainly Otomi, it is no coincidence that the ruling elite of the city was also of that ethnic origin.

The twilight of Teotihuacan (900 CE) marked the end of the Classic Period and the beginning of the Post-Classic (900–1521 CE). At this time Nahuatl-speaking groups came to central Mexico, including those who later were called Mexica and dominated the empire when the Spanish arrived. The Nahuas displaced the Otomi groups eastward to the region of Puebla-Tlaxcala, while in the rest of the territory they developed some important states.

One of these states was Xicocotitlan Tollan (Tula, Hidalgo), developed between the 10th and 12th centuries, called Mähñem'ì in Otomi. It was ruled by the group Nahua "Toltec," with broad participation of the Otomi. Later, the Otomi kept a center of power in Xaltocan that dominated a large area to the north. Meanwhile, other Otomi groups came under the aegis of the Tepanec state of Azcapotzalco, led from the Basin of Mexico by one Nahua group. Xaltocan ended up succumbing to them in the decade of 1390.

After the defeat of Azcapotzalco and the erection of the Triple Alliance (a coalition between the states of Tenochtitlán, Texcoco, and Tlacopan) in 1428, the domains of the Tepaneca, in the western part of the present state of Estado de Mexico, were assigned to Tlacopan. The Otomi participated as military auxiliaries in the wars carried out by the Mexica, as they shared with them one ritual aspect of the war inspired by Teotihuacan.

This aspect consisted in maintaining the sun with blood and human hearts. In addition, the Nahua people absorbed much of the culture of the Otopamean. In this sense, the god of storms and hunting, Mixcoatl, seemed to have an Otomi origin. Thus, the Otomi peoples were an integral part of the political, military, economic, and social scene of central Mexico before the Spanish arrived.

During the Spanish conquest the Otomi played an important role. After an initial confrontation between Hernán Cortés and the Otomi of Tlaxcala in 1519, in the La Noche Triste (The Sad Night, June 30, 1520) and in the main site of Tenochtitlán, the Otomi became allies of the Spanish and provided them logistical and military support. After that, they were regularized under the systems of economic exploitation called encomienda and repartimiento. Meanwhile in a spiritual order, the Franciscan friars evangelized them.

During the 16th century, they made a territorial expansion to the Bajío (parts of the states of Querétaro, Michoacán, Guanajuato, and Jalisco). Between 1551 and 1550, they became allies of the Spanish again in their armed struggle against the Chichimeca nations. Their *caciques* (chiefs) obtained prestige, privileges, and lands in exchange of the defense of the roads by which the silver was transited from mines of Zacatecas and Guanajuato to Mexico City.

Marta Martín Gabaldón

See also: Aztec, or Mexica; *Corregidores*; Cortés, Hernán; Encomienda; Encomenderos; La Noche Triste; Mexico, State of prior to Spanish Conquest; Nahuatl Language; Repartimiento; Tenochtitlán, City of.

Resources

Carrasco, Pedro. *Los otomíes, cultura e historia prehispánica de los pueblos mesoamericanos de habla otomiana.* México D.F.: Instituto de Historia, Universidad Nacional Autónoma de México-Instituto Nacional de Antropología e Historia, 1950.

Diehl, Richard A. *Tula, the Toltec Capital of Ancient Mexico.* London: Thames and Hudson, 1983.

Wright Carr, David C. "El papel de los otomíes en las culturas del Altiplano Central: 5000 a.C.–1650 d.C." *Relaciones, Estudios de Historia y Sociedad* 72 (1997): 225–242.

Ovando, Fr. Nicolás de

Born to a noble family in 1460, Nicolás de Ovando was from the Spanish region of Extremadura that produced so many of the explorers and conquistadors of the New World. As a young man and soldier, Ovando's religious zeal prompted him to join the military religious Order of the Alcantara. There he rose to the level of Commander of the Lares, where he came to the attention of the Catholic monarchs of Spain. As disenchantment increased with the Columbus brothers as administrators in the Caribbean, Queen Isabella appointed Fray Nicolás de Ovando to the position of governor of the Indies in 1501.

Arriving in the colony in 1502, Governor Ovando was ironically accompanied on the voyage by Bartolomé de Las Casas—the later defender of the Indians, and carried with him sweeping orders to establish a just and efficient system of Spanish government under the Catholic Monarchs. Ovando's goal was to restructure the economy into one that was productive and sustainable. The royal instructions he carried contained the typical contradictory demands to see to the welfare of the native population while simultaneously collecting tribute from the same natives and compelling them to labor in the mines for gold. Queen Isabella's Real Cedula of 1503 further justified the use of Indian labor—to the point of virtual enslavement—on the basis of providing an environment favorable to their conversion to the Catholic faith. These written policies set the stage for Ovando's treatment of the Indians as subhuman beings, and the abuses that ensued in the Spanish-controlled Caribbean. While the Crown may well have believed they established a system that benefitted all—natives, conquerors, and the Crown—in reality the system enabled the conquering Spanish in America to use the Indians to any extreme in the pursuit of wealth and power—to include working the natives to death.

The policies of Ovando ran into direct opposition to the newly arrived Dominicans in 1510. Initially these missionaries sought to serve the native and to instruct the local Spanish in proper Christian treatment of the Indians. However, resistance to their efforts by the individual island governors and by the Spanish settlers who had benefited from the policies and practices used for the past decade created the opening salvo to an extended conflict over the rights of conquering Spanish and the rights of subjugated natives. Though Ovando, who returned to Spain in 1509 and died in 1518, did not live to see the extended conflict play out between such noted Dominicans as Las Casas and the colonial governors, his policies and actions had a lasting impact on the treatment of the natives for decades to come and the original use of African slave labor in the colonies.

Under Ovando's governorship, the island of Hispaniola was thoroughly explored and numerous cities established. Each of these centers of Spanish authority claimed lands previously owned and inhabited by the native Tainos. Between the resettlement of the natives and their harsh treatment as virtual slaves at the hands of the increasing numbers of encomenderos, a rapid decline in the native population was recorded in the first two decades of Spanish settlement. Desperate for more labor, Ovando approved the exploration of neighboring islands and the capture of neighboring tribes to labor for gold as well as in agricultural production.

Ovando's harsh interpretation and implementation of the Real Cedula ensured success of the new Spanish settlers as readily as it guaranteed the decimation of the local native populations. Efforts to counter the declining labor force eventually led to the importation of Ladinos, African slaves born in Spain. Though only numbering in the hundreds for the first two decades of the 16th century, Spanish-born African slaves, not labor reforms, were soon viewed as the answer to the declining native population and increasing demand for laborers on the Spanish islands.

Nicolás de Ovando's roots in the impoverished Extremadura region of Spain, and his early experiences fighting and serving as a soldier and leader of a militant order of priests during the violent final years of the Reconquista, shaped his life and temperament for governing in the Indies. The costly wars against the Moors, followed by expensive early exploration of the Caribbean, drained Spanish coffers and prompted severe policies designed to recoup losses at the cost of the native Tainos on Hispaniola and neighboring islands. Arriving on the same ship as Las Casas who went on to defend the rights of natives in America over Spanish claims, it was Ovando's policies that shaped the Spanish treatment of natives on a daily basis in the New World for the first century of contact.

Rebecca M. Seaman

See also: Encomenderos; Hispaniola; Las Casas, Bartolomé de.

Resources

Castro, Daniel, Jr. "Another Face of Empire: Bartolome De Las Casas and the Restoration of the Indies." PhD diss., Tulane University, LA, 1994.

Las Casas, Bartholomé de. *The Spanish Colonie.* London: Williams Brome, 1583; Reprint, Ann Arbor: University Microfilms, Inc, 1966.

Palencia-Roth, Michael. "The Cannibal Law of 1503." In *Early Images of the Americas: Transfer and Invention,* edited by Merry M. Williams and Robert E. Lewis. Tucson: University of Arizona Press, 1993.

Lockhart, James, and Stuart B. Schwartz. *Early Latin America: A History of Colonial Spanish America and Brazil.* Cambridge: Cambridge University Press, 1999.

P

Pacarina

Pacarina (paqarina) were sacred places to the Andean peoples that marked where the first human ancestors emerged from the earth. These were often caves, such as the one at Pacarictambo outside of Cuzco.

According to Inca creation mythology, Viracocha, their creator god, made all of the world's tribes and gave them life and a soul. These human ancestors then descended into the earth and came out wherever the creator ordered: from lakes and springs, valleys, trees, rocks, and caves. For the Inca, Tiwanaku (Tiahuanaco), located at the southeastern edge of Lake Titicaca, marked the place where humans first emerged and was also the origin of the universe.

The Incas believed in reincarnation and mummified the prominent members of their society. They also practiced ritual sacrifices and placed these mummies as offerings to the gods in high-altitude places where they were naturally desiccated. Each mummy, or *malquis,* was provided with an assortment of grave goods, which might include figurines of gold and silver. These were taken to the *malquis* final resting place in the pacarina, where it was usually left in a sitting position.

The Inca treated their mummified royalty as though they were still alive, clothing and caring for them and even offering them food. They were consulted on important issues and even taken out of their shrines and included in religious processions. It was believed that once the *malquis* were placed in the paca-rina they could converse with other ancient ancestors.

Karen S. Garvin

See also: *Malquis*; Religion, of Pre-Conquest Inca.

Resources

Molina, Cristóbal de. *Account of the Fables and Rites of the Incas.* Translated by Brian S. Bauer. Edited by Brian S. Baurer, Vania Smith-Oka, and Gabriel E. Cantarutti. Austin, TX: University of Texas Press, 2011.

Moseley, Michael E. *The Incas and Their Ancestors: The Archaeology of Peru.* New York: Thames & Hudson, 2001.

Reinhard, Johan. *The Ice Maiden: Inca Mummies, Mountain Gods, and Sacred Sites in the Andes.* Washington, DC: National Geographic Society, 2005.

Pachacutin

Pachacutin (Pachacutec), the Inca ruler whose reign begun circa 1438, is credited with single-handedly restructuring the empire to sustain the growing state, including its belief system. Historian John Rowe asserts that much of what is known of Inca origin legend was absorbed from various societies already residing in the region prior to the rise of the Inca, and then manipulated to serve the agenda of the state by Pachacutin. Certainly, the Sapa Inca's reign occurred at a point in time when the Inca kingdom emerged as an empire to dominate a broad region.

Pachacutin (Pachacutec), Inca Emperor, ca. 1438.
(Bettmann/Corbis)

Known to the Inca chroniclers as Inca Yupanqui, Pachacutin may well have been the legitimate heir to Viracocha. However, his brother, Urco, seems to have been the favored son whom Viracocha intended to succeed his rule. Other interpretations portray Pachacutin and his father coruling for a time. Whatever the route to the throne, by 1438 Pachacutin emerged as the Sapa Inca, thus began a period of great consolidation, expansion, and reform.

A turning point toward imperial expansion began with the defeat of the traditional enemies of the Inca, the Chancas. Near the end of Viracocha's reign, the Chancas formed a confederation with Quechua-speaking people on the border of the Inca kingdom. Fearful of a defeat, Viracocha fled the city, as did his favored son, Urco. Meanwhile, Pachacutin countered the threat by organizing Inca generals, neighboring rulers, and their forces into a defense of the city of Cuzco. Legend credits Pachacutin for raising warriors out of stone who also assisted in defending the city.

Once Chanca was defeated, the Sapa Inca had the ability to bestow lavish gifts from war plunder upon the scattered *kurakas* that oversaw their own *ayllus* and local communities. The Inca and Andean concept of reciprocity helped ensure these gifts would be rewarded with allegiance to Pachacutin. But to ensure long-term allegiance, the emperor needed to undertake building projects. Storage facilities, used to house excess goods for future times of need, helped create a system whereby the *kurakas* gathered goods through the use of the *mita,* which were in turn used to grant needed goods or more gifts to maintain loyalty.

Storage facilities were only part of this building process. The reconstruction of Cuzco, and in particular the temple to the Sun, Coricancha, helped Pachacutin establish his revised version of the Sun cult, one with the Sapa Incas representing the Sun god, Inti, as his representatives on earth. Again, Pachacutin was instrumental in taking an element of ancient Inca practice and shaping it into a system that supported and perpetuated the state under Inca rule. According to some historians, the emperor disinterred the bodies of previous Incas that were buried in the temple. Placing these mummies on thrones, he helped create the complex ancestral worship of the Sapa Incas, and establish the lineage branches to support the maintenance and immortalization of the mummies, the panacas. He even used his newly acquired wealth to provide lands and servants for the panacas of the past emperors. Some historians also assert that Pachacutin enhanced the already existent Inca worship, tying the concept to the cult of the creator god, Viracocha (interestingly the name of his own father). The connection of the Viracocha cult and the Inca faith with the Lake Titicaca region, where the creator god was believed to first emerge, was of recent origin—coinciding with Inca expansion into that region during Pachacutin's reign.

Once Pachacutin began the process of expansion, and connected this expansion with ensuring loyalty of the Inca *kurakas* through lavish gifts, it became necessary to continue the expansion in order to sustain the reciprocity relationships. Conscription of newly conquered people into the Inca army maintained the necessary forces for continued conquest. The example of the Chancas serving in the forces that went on to defeat the Soras of the Huamanga area is typical of the strategy employed by Pachacutin.

The relocation of groups of people also helped maintain control. Incas by privilege, loyal supporters of the royal Incas, whose desire for rank and status near that of the royal family, obtained such privileges through service to the emperor. Often these high-placed Incas were relocated to regions outside of the Cuzco area, providing a link between the royal Incas and the rural communities of the empire. Likewise, newly conquered people were often relocated to regions where the populace was devoted to the Sapa Inca.

Eventually, the great emperor Pachacutin shared his throne with his son, Túpac Inca. Expansion under his son and later grandson, Huayna Cápac, continued largely unchecked. By the time the Spanish arrived in the region at the time of Huayna Cápac's death, the Inca Empire was the largest empire in the Western Hemisphere. While the Inca kingdom had already existed, and even begun to expand out of Cuzco prior to his rise to power, the process of establishing the extensive empire began with Pachacutin. Without a written language intelligible to the conquering Spanish, and with the Inca understanding of history and chronology differing from that used by Old World chroniclers, it is difficult to separate the fact from the fiction of the Inca past, especially the past of such a impressive historical figure as Pachacutin.

Rebecca M. Seaman

See also: *Ayllus*; Chanca; Huamanga; Huayna Cápac; *Kuraka*; *Mita*; Religion, of Pre-Conquest Inca; Sapa Inca; Túpac Inca Yupanqui.

Resources

Davies, Nigel. *The Incas*. Niwot: University of Colorado Press, 1995.

Hemming, John. *The Conquest of the Incas*. New York: Harcourt Brace Jovanovich, 1970.

Kosiba, Steven Brian. "Becoming Inka: The Transformation of Political Place and Practice during Inka State Formation (Cusco, Peru)." PhD diss., University of Chicago, 2010.

Stern, Steve J. *Peru's Indian Peoples and the Challenge of Spanish Conquest: Huamanga to 1640*. 2nd ed. Madison: University of Wisconsin Press, 1993.

Paullu Inca

In 1534, Manco Inca II was designated the Sapa Inca (unique emperor) by the Spanish. Convinced by the conquistador and governor Francisco Pizarro, the *adelantado* Diego de Almagro and *corregidor* Hernando de Soto that the Spanish wished to live peacefully with the Sapa Inca in control, the young Manco Inca accepted the role. He was supported in his decision by his half-brother, Paullu Inca. Over the next two years, the Spanish internal divisions occurred alongside the increasing subjugation of the Inca, leading to the complete breakdown in relations between the two natives and Europeans and the eventual rift between the two brothers.

By the summer of 1535, the old conflict between Pizarro and Almagro peaked over control of land, wealth, and authority in Peru.

Control of Cuzco, the Inca capital and the official center of the empire, was central to this conflict. Manco and Paullu sided with Almagro, from whom they sought protection. Meanwhile more distant claimants to the throne, the *yanaconas* (lifelong servants of the Inca elite), and the *mitmaes* (dispersed native rebels who had been removed from their home provinces by the Inca) sided with Pizarro. When Almagro undertook an expedition to Chile, Paullu was sent by Manco to accompany the conquistador. Pizarro also left to establish coastal ports to protect shipments of gold, silver, and supplies. The Inca again seemed in control of Cuzco, with only a handful of encomenderos left to maintain a Spanish presence. Manco Inca, probably only 19 years of age, hoped for traditional powers of the Sapa Inca. What he experienced was the corrupt abuse of power under Pizarro's youngest brother, the new *corregidor*, Gonzalo Pizarro. Gonzalo's abuse of the Inca people extended to Manco Inca and his primary wife and sister, whom Gonzalo took as his mistress. In the wake of these conditions, Manco called for the elite Inca from all four *suyus* (regions) of the empire to unite in a siege upon Cuzco.

In the midst of the siege, Almagro returned from Chile with Paullu, now a close ally and supporter of the conquistador. However, the alliances within the Spanish and Inca structure at Cuzco had shifted perceptibly. An older and wiser Manco Inca finally realized the Spanish had no intentions of ever leaving Peru and continued a guerilla war for eight years. Almagro discovered his grant from the king was poor and the only hope of wealth was to recover Cuzco, which he attacked with a vengeance. Pizarro and his brothers were determined to maintain control of the northern kingdom, the coastal ports, Cuzco, and the wealth of the Andes. Meanwhile, Paullu threw his support

behind his constant ally, Almagro, severing the close ties he had shared with his own brother, Manco Inca. In reward for Paullu's loyalty, Almagro crowned him Paullu Inca, the new emperor.

Like Manco Inca, Paullu Inca was older and wiser by 1536. He incorporated the lessons learned on the long, difficult expedition with Almagro. He was keenly aware that Manco's force of 200,000 warriors had been unable to defeat approximately 200 Spanish in the besieged and devastated city of Cuzco. A realist, Paullu accepted the title of "unique emperor" proffered by Almagro. As the rift between Almagro and the Pizarro family deepened into renewed civil war, Paullu Inca employed the same pragmatism. He initially supported Almagro's forces. When the *adelantado* fell ill and his forces were outnumbered, the new Sapa Inca ordered his men to give support to the Hernando Pizarro's soldiers.

Over the course of the next few years, Manco Inca continued to control considerable native armies, who still viewed him as the legitimate Sapa Inca. Paullu Inca continued to serve as Inca and collaborator with the Spanish. Increasingly, he shifted his role from one of native support to one directly opposing and fighting his brother, Manco. Even the Spanish capture and execution of Paullu's half-sister, the wife and sister of Manco Inca, did not compel Paullu Inca to betray his new allegiance with the Pizarro faction. Paullu Inca even went so far as to convert to Christianity, taking the name of Cristoval. In 1545, seven Spanish renegades, befriended by the Sapa Inca, killed Manco Inca. Within a year, Paullu Inca also died at approximately 31 years of age. According to Spanish records, he died of natural causes. The Inca people believed otherwise, and reported that the Sapa Inca was poisoned by the Spanish. With both powerful brothers dead, the title of Sapa Inca again fell to a sole native leader, the 9-year old, easily influenced, Sayri Túpac Inca.

Rebecca M. Seaman

See also: Almagro, Diego de; Manco Inca Yupanqui; Pizarro, Francisco; Pizarro, Gonzalo; Sayri Túpac.

Resources

Gamboa, Pedro Sarmiento de. *History of the Incas.* Translated and Edited by Sir Clements Markham. Cambridge, UK: Hakluyt Society, 1907.

Lamar, Curt. "Hernando de Soto before Florida: A Narrative." *The Hernando de Soto Expedition: History, Historiography, and "Discover" in the Southeast.* Lincoln: University of Nebraska Press, 2005.

MacQuarrie, Kim. *Last Days of the Inca.* New York: Simon & Schuster, 2007.

Peru, State of after Spanish Conquest

The Spanish under Francisco Pizarro defeated the armies of the Inca emperor Atahualpa in 1533, resulting in the capture of Cuzco and the installation of Manco Inca as a puppet emperor under Pizzaro's control. Yet the conquest was not complete. The Spanish became divided under the mismanagement of Hernando and Gonzalo Pizzaro and the jealous quest for control of Cuzco by Diego de Almagro. Instead of a strong Spanish presence and centralized control, the once great empire devolved into rival factions; Spanish fighting Spanish, Inca fighting Inca, Spanish and Inca collaborating against the same. Not until 1572, with the death of the last powerful Sapa Inca, Túpac Amaru II, did the Spanish gain effective control of the Peruvian Empire of the Andes.

Following the execution of Atahualpa, Pizzaro resorted to creating puppet emperors who could serve the Spanish by uniting the indigenous population to supply the Spanish with needed labor, provisions, and wealth. Recent internal conflicts between Atahualpa and his brother, Huáscar, provided the division needed to leverage factions within the Inca Empire against one another. The long practice of the Inca rulers moving loyal elements of the population to regions recently conquered or resisting control created internal divisions within the Inca society across the empire. This was further complicated by the practice of designating loyal foreigners as "Incas of privilege," promoting them to positions of authority within communities, above less loyal Incas—or simply rewarding them with the rights of the Inca elite, such as fine clothing and the use of cacao. These traditional methods of ruling, while effective in extending Inca power over vast regions, left an empire wracked with internal jealousies and ripe for Spain to foster further divisions.

The Spanish managed to split the Inca leadership and encourage disaffected Incas to join the Spanish in taking wealth and power from the Sapa Incas. Once Pizzaro's forces managed to acquire control of strategic Inca cities, rapid changes ensued for the entire societal structure. With the execution of the last great Inca, Túpac Amaru II, in 1572, the structure of government shifted to one controlled by governors approved by the Spanish Crown. The traditional economy was centered on the farming of a wide variety of crops, which included potatoes and cacoa. It also included the raising of llamas and alpacas and the conducting of extensive trade. The Spanish disrupted this economic system while they were simultaneously dependent upon it.

Spain's conquerors and the Crown viewed the great mineral and gem wealth of Peru as the colony's primary asset. To this end, the traditional labor system of the Inca, the *mita,* was merged with the Spanish practice of encomiendas to harness needed laborers for the numerous mines. As increased numbers of Incas professed to accept the Catholic faith, forced labor was discouraged. In its place the Crown instructed the colonial governors to pay the indigenous labor for working the mines. Unfortunately for the Spanish, harsh working conditions deterred many Incas from volunteering. Despite royal edicts to the contrary, the local population was pressed into involuntary service in gold, silver, and mercury mines.

Compulsory labor in the mines not only took a toll on the native health, but it additionally alienated the Inca and Spanish. The initial Neo-Inca movement of resistance was the result of the Spanish seizing power and stealing the wealth of the Inca treasury and temples. A later resistance movement was more complex. The Taki Onqoy was a religious rebellion that called for the Inca to turn away from all things Spanish: Catholicism, clothing, names, and goods. This nativist movement also called for a return to the traditional worship of the huacas, in hopes that the spirits would be pleased with the Inca faithful and destroy the unfaithful and the Spanish foreigners. Both movements emerged out of Spanish abusive authority and the desire of the Inca to return back to a more traditional lifestyle. Unfortunately for the Incas, both movements failed, leaving the rebelling Incas devastated by the Spanish retribution.

Typical of Spanish conquest and restructuring of indigenous societies across the Americas, in Peru, the Inca cities were largely destroyed. In place of the extensive Inca stone structures, the Spanish built Churches, fortresses, and other buildings in a more familiar European style. Catholicism was pushed on the Inca, but traditional native rites were still tolerated. The result was the blending of both cultures, such as the Catholic celebration of All Soul's Day in early November coinciding with the Inca parading of their mummified Inca leaders from several past generations. Blending of the Inca and Spanish population also took place as conquistadors married into the Inca elite. While some of the Inca culture was retained through these acculturation methods, the first century of Spanish conquest saw a rapid deterioration of the Inca faith, Inca government, language, Inca urban structures, wealth, and population.

Rebecca M. Seaman

See also: Atahualpa; Encomienda; Huacas; Huáscar; Manco Inca Yupanqui; *Mita*; Neo-Incas; Pizzaro, Francisco; Pizzaro, Gonzalo; Pizzaro, Hernando; Taki Onqoy; Túpac Amaru.

Resources

Davies, Nigel. *The Incas.* Niwot: University of Colorado Press, 1995.

MacQuarrie, Kim. *The Last Days of the Incas.* New York: Simon & Schuster, 2007.

Stern, Steve J. *Peru's Indian Peoples and the Challenge of Spanish Conquest: Huamanga to 1640.* 2nd ed. Madison: University of Wisconsin Press, 1993.

Peru, State of prior to Spanish Conquest

The Incas trace their roots back to peoples who found their way to the rugged regions of western South America thousands of years before the Common Era. As Andean cultures evolved from the Early Horizon (800 BCE to 100 CE) to the Early Intermediate Period (700–1000 CE), researchers observe the evolution of cultural traits that were representative of the later Inca society. This period was marked by the creation of religious iconography, increasingly oriented around sacred cults. It was also characterized by a significant growth in the production of advanced technological crafts—metallurgy that allowed for soldering and silver-gold alloying, and, most probably during this period, the creation of exquisite Andean textiles. Researchers also observed the appearance of the first true state and urban communities. Archaeological evidence from sites like Moche suggests that priestly, political, military, and social roles were woven together without the people of the community defining distinct administrative positions. Moche was also home to the greatest adobe pyramid ever raised in the Americas, containing as it did 143 million bricks. Pyramid structures like that at Moche were extremely important in Andean communities, as they represented some of the most elaborate burial sites found in South America.

Around the same time two other important cities emerged in the Peruvian highlands. Wari came to power in the Ayacucho Basin between 500 and 750 CE, expanding its influence by constructing centralized settlements through which it could control the transportation of goods and communications. By this time the *quipu*, or "knot-record," was already being used in Wari as a precise way to store data. Centuries later, the Incas adopted this knot-record storage system, as well as some of the Wari principles of statecraft. They even appropriated some of the roads built by the people of Wari. In addition to this regional center, the city of Tiwanaku, which lies to the south of Lake Titicaca, became fully urban around 375 CE. It extended its influence on the coast, in the Bolivian lowlands, and into northwest Argentina. In this capital city, archaeologists have discovered temples, a pyramid, and a sizeable residential area. Tiwanaku, and its companion Lake Titicaca, were revered by the Inca, as the latter believed that the Creator God, the sun, the moon, and the stars all emerged from the lake.

The development of unique Andean cultures, such as those at Moche, Wari, and Tiwanaku, was significant for the future of the region around Cuzco, the eventual capital of the Incas. By 1000 CE, the political environment in the region was extremely fragmented and diverse; and as late as 1200 CE, war raged from southern Ecuador to Argentina. In order to protect themselves from these conflicts, many peoples in the region settled in isolated villages well above the best valley farmlands. A number of the most powerful of these societies, such as the Lopaqa and the Qolla, established themselves in the areas around Lake Titicaca, though it is doubtful that these societies ever attained a state level of organization. Groups that settled in the populous region of the Peruvian sierra may have produced village communities with as many as 4,500 domiciles, housing up to 10,000 people. However, most of the villages in the area of the southern Andes probably contained no more than 1,000 residents, with the largest regional centers consisting of perhaps 20,000 people. By 1200 CE, Cuzco may have already integrated the land surrounding it into an organized state society, setting the scene for the meteoric rise of the Inca.

It was in later part of the Late Intermediate Period that the Inca rose to a prominent role as the dominant society in the region around Lake Titicaca and soon thereafter in Cuzco. Historians debate whether the first four Sapa Incas, Manco Cápac, Sinchi Roca, Lloque Yupanque, and Mayta Cápac, were mythical or historical figures. Yet it is from these founders that much of the later Inca religion and political structure originated, from the incestuous relations of the Inca rulers to the belief that the Sapa Inca was divinely linked to the Sun god, Inti. The ninth Sapa Inca, Pachacutin, became the empire builder, even constructing four sectors within the capital Cuzco that corresponded to the four quadrants of the rapidly expanding Inca Empire. This same Sapa Inca, and his successor Túpac Inca, also initiated what became the common practice of relocating loyal allies and Incas to distant, newly acquired lands as a means of solidifying control over the largest empire in the Americas.

By the Late Horizon Era, immediately preceding the colonial era, the Inca had developed an intricate culture based on elements of the varied people within the empire. The economy, primary agricultural and self-sustaining, provided for large centers like Cuzco and Quito, and used stores of centrally collected foods to sustain the empire in periods of crop failure, wars, and famine. Under Huayna Cápac, who reigned most of the Late Horizon period, the construction of extensive roads and bridges was undertaken to connect the vast empire. By his death in the later 1520s, over 25,0000 miles of roads spanned the mountainous empire. Via this intricate road system, ruling Incas collected great quantities of foods and mineral wealth. It was along these roads that disease also traveled throughout the Andes, killing the Sapa Inca and leaving the empire in the midst of a civil war as the Spanish invaded the region in 1532.

Philip C. DiMare

See also: Huayna Cápac; Inca Civil War; Inca Roads; Manco Inca Yupanqui; Pachacutin; *Quipu*.

Resources

Bernand, Carmen. *The Incas: Empire of Blood and Gold.* London: Thames & Hudson, 1994.

D'Altroy, Terence N. *The Incas.* Malden, MA: Blackwell, 2003.

DiMare, Philip C. "The Amerindian World." In *Cliffs World History,* edited by Fred N. Grayson. Hoboken, NJ: Wiley, 2006.

Fagin, Brian M. *Kingdoms of Gold, Kingdoms of Jade: The Americas before Columbus.* New York: Thames and Hudson, 1991.

Gamboa, Pedro Sarmiento de. *History of the Incas.* Translated by Clements Markham. Cambridge, UK: The Hakluyt Society, 1907.

Karsten, Rafael. *A Totalitarian State of the Past: The Civilization of the Inca Empire in Ancient Peru.* Port Washington, NY: Kennikat Press, 1970.

MacQuarrie, Kim. *The Last Days of the Inca.* New York: Simon & Schuster, 2007.

Philip II of Spain

Philip was the son of Charles V, the Holy Roman Emperor, and Isabella of Portugal, born in 1527. He reigned as king of Spain from 1556 and king of Portugal from 1580 until his death in 1598. His was the world's first global empire, encompassing lands in Europe, South America, the western coast of Africa, and the Pacific Ocean.

"Philip the Prudent" was an intelligent, hardworking man. Devoutly Catholic, Philip saw himself as the defender of Catholicism against the Protestants and Ottoman Turks. He promoted the Catholic Counter-Reformation, uniting his secular empire through the force of arms and his religious empire through the powers of the Spanish Inquisition.

Nonetheless, Philip's administration was rife with corruption from the sale of offices and regional bickering.

As the hereditary monarch of the Habsburg Empire, Philip received instruction in politics and military training. His first experience with war was in 1542 during the Siege of Perpignan in southern France. Recognizing Philip's skill with statesmanship, Charles V began to entrust the regency of Spain to Philip during his absences.

In 1555, Charles V turned control of the Netherlands over to Philip, who already had the duchy of Milan and the kingdoms of Naples and Sicily. On January 16, 1556, Philip ascended to the throne of Spain, inheriting the Spanish Empire, and shortly thereafter, the Franche-Comté. Over the years of his rule, he attempted to expand authority to Portugal and England. Philip and his brother Ferdinand split the family's Habsburg lands in Germany. Spain's growing colonial empire complicated Philip's widespread focus on European issues.

Philip also inherited the empire's economic woes. Between 1559 and 1598 he increased the tax rate more than 400 percent to pay for almost constant wars, the Armada, and the Escorial, his palace near Madrid. Yet Philip still needed loans to finance his empire. Spain became ever more dependent on the revenue generated by its American possessions, but the flood of bullion from the New World contributed to inflation and made matters worse. Philip depleted the treasury and forced Spain into bankruptcy four times.

Friction between Christians and Moriscos in Andalusia erupted into the 1558 Rebellion of Alpujarras after reforms were enacted to enforce earlier decrees prohibiting the use of Arabic, traditional Arabic dress, and other customs. This targeting of negative attention on Arabic-speaking communities was reversed in Philip's policies for New Spain. There, he urged the study of indigenous languages by the Catholic priests. Unlike the Spanish intellectuals at the height of its Golden Age, who called for the use and spread of Castilian as the proper lingua franca, Philip hoped to increase religious instruction by evangelizing through native vernaculars. The impact of this policy shift did not benefit the indigenous populations until the latter half of the 16th century. It was at that time that Philip's desire for promulgating evangelization through the use of native vernacular coincided with the impact of such scholarly leadership in New Spain as Fray Bernardino de Sahagún and the increased Nahuatlized Christian instruction at the College of Santa Cruz of Tlatelolco.

Philip was determined to rid his empire of Protestants and other heretics. By 1568 a nascent Spanish Protestant movement had been crushed, and Moriscos were forcibly converted to Christianity or driven into exile. Spanish students were forbidden to study outside of Spain. In New Spain, the Inquisition finally arrived under Philip's rule. The determination of those wishing to root out heresy in the colonies resulted in inquiries of family lineages of the Peninsulars and Creoles. Many of the initial conquistadors had joined the movement toward the colonies not only for the possibility of wealth and status, but also to flee the accusations of their family having Jewish roots. No longer did conversion to Christianity satisfy the Inquisitors. In the New World, descendants of these conquistadors now felt the impact of the investigations on their lives.

Meanwhile, Philip was fighting on two fronts. By 1575 Spain was bankrupt and could not support a military presence in the east. Philip's need for money to fund attempts at expansion and influence in Europe resulted in the streamlining of the government and economics of the American colonies. It was during Philip's rule that the process of amalgamation was discovered, using mercury to rapidly separate silver and gold from other useless elements. Within 10 years, the impact in New Spain and Peru was felt as new mines of mercury were added to those of silver and gold, stimulating the economies of the colonies and Spain. The negative ramifications of using mercury were also felt, as the already rapidly declining native populations were affected by the mercury poisoning.

As mining improved in the colonies and the use of mercury allowed for enhanced accounting of mining production, it became increasingly apparent that reforms were needed in the colonial leadership. Philip actively replaced the old colonial conquistador leadership with newly appointed governors, *audiencias,* and *visitadors*—all in an effort to ensure the proper functioning of the colonies as producers of valuable ores and agricultural products. The removal of the Pizarros in Peru was a prime example of these efforts. While Francisco Pizarro was already dead by the time Philip came to power, the Pizarros and their supporters still controlled the colony. In reality, the focus of the old conquistadors upon gaining and retaining wealth and power pitted Spaniards against Spaniards and added to the instability of colonial governments. Again in Peru, the internal conflict between warring factions of Spaniards, as well as the rebellion under the resisting Incas of the Neo-Inca and religious Taki Onqoy movement, continued until Philip successfully replaced a series of leaders, leaving a reformed colonial structure in place.

Philip II died on September 13, 1598, in El Escorial, after a decade of ill health that left him crippled with pain and confined to a specially made orthopedic chair. His policies of economic and political reform had lasting impacts on the colonies of New Spain and Peru, with the expansion and productivity of mining. However, the promoting of evangelization of the indigenous population through use of the native vernacular was thwarted by the increased efforts to spread the Inquisition and to root out perceived heresies.

Karen S. Garvin

See also: Almagro, Diego de; *Audiencia*; Mercury; Mines, Role in Mexico; Mines, Role in Peru; Nahuatl Language; Neo-Incas; Pizarro, Francisco; Sahagún, Bernardino de; Santa Cruz of Tlatelolco, College of; Silver; Taki Onqoy.

Resources

Burhart, Louise M. Encounter of Religions: The Indigenization of Christianity; the Nahua Scholar-Intepreters. Occasional Papers in Latin American Studies. 1991.

D'Olwer, Nicolau. *Fray Bernardino de Sahagún.* México: Instituto Panamericano de Geografía e Historia, 1952.

Kamen, Henry. *Philip of Spain.* New Haven, CT: Yale University Press, 1999.

Kelsey, Harry. *Philip of Spain, King of England: The Forgotten Sovereign.* London: I.B. Tauris, 2012.

MacCulloch, Diarmaid. *The Reformation: A History.* London: Penguin, 2003.

Parker, Geoffrey. *The Grand Strategy of Philip II.* Wiltshire, UK: Redwood Books, 1998.

Wasserman-Soler, Daniel I. "Language Policy and Religious Instruction in Spain and Mexico, c. 1550–1600." PhD diss.,University of Virginia, 2012.

Williams, Patrick. *Philip II.* New York: Palgrave, 2001.

Pipiltin

One of two free social classes in Aztec society, the *pipiltin* included the wealthy or noble elements of the populace. The origin of this class traced its ancestry back to the original *tlatoani,* or king, Acamapichtli, who was actually a Toltec nobleman. The father of many children, these descendents formed the core of the nobility for the Aztec society, known as *pipiltin* or *pipii* (singular).

The *pipiltin* were accorded many benefits not allowed to the lower classes, or *macehualtin.* Provided a better education, this class boasted such notables as the priests and important governing officials. Though not all *pipiltin* held high government positions, they did have coveted roles in society. Some were craftsmen, such as the extremely skilled goldsmiths of Aztec society. Others even held the roles of servants in the royal palace. Ruling positions were not guaranteed by inheritance. Those *pipiltin* who served in government, as scholars, craftsmen, or royal servants could move upward in the ranks. All royal positions came from this elite Aztec class.

Pipiltin also owned land in their own names and controlled estates that were often farmed by slaves, or *mayeques.* Unlike the commoners, the elite classes were allowed to decorate their houses and property elaborately. They also could wear expensive clothing and were permitted to wear elaborate makeup and jewelry. Remarkably, the *pipiltin* class did not include the merchants, despite their wealth. Indeed, these merchants were required to dress in the plain garb of the commoners as a signal that they were from the lower class. When Cortés conquered Tenochtitlán and the people fled the city with whatever wealth they could carry, many *pipiltin* disguised their class by dressing in the clothes of commoners. The attempt failed, as the Spanish greed drove them to search all fleeing Aztecs for possible gold or jewels.

Rebecca M. Seaman

See also: *Macehualtin; Mayeques*; Tenochtitlán, Siege of.

Resources

León-Portilla, Miguel, ed. *Broken spears: The Aztec Account of the Conquest of Mexico.* With Foreword by J. Jorge Klor de Alva. Boston: Beacon Press, 2006.

Schwartz, Stuart B., ed. *Victors and Vanquished: Spanish and Nahua Views of the Conquest of Mexico.* Boston: Bedford/St. Martin's, 2000.

Pizarro, Francisco

Francisco Pizarro was one of the conquistadores to arrive in the Americas in the early 16th century. Although he participated in the conquest of Panama and discovery of the Pacific Ocean, he is best known for his conquest of the Inca Empire in Peru in the 1530s. Assassinated by his enemies in 1541, he has since come to symbolize, along with Hernán Cortés and his conquest of Mexico, the Spanish conquest of the Americas.

Francisco Pizarro was born sometime between 1471 (the most agreed upon date) and

Portrait of Francisco Pizarro. (Library of Congress)

1476, in the city of Trujillo in the region of Extremadura, Spain. The illegitimate son of Gonzalo Pizarro Rodríguez de Aguilar and Francisca González Mateos, Pizarro passed the first quarter century of his life tending pigs, never learning to read or write. This changed, however, as news of Christopher Columbus's discovery and early colonization of the Americas began pouring into Spain and Europe during the waning years of the 1490s.

In 1501 Francisco Pizarro is reported to have sailed for the Indies (the Americas), arriving there in 1502. Becoming a lieutenant in the ranks of Hispaniola, by the end of the decade he set off with Alonso de Ojeda to establish the settlement of San Sebastian de Urara in modern northwestern Colombia (established January 20, 1510).

That same year he, along with Vasco Núñez de Balboa, helped to establish the colony of Santa Maria la Antigua del Darién in Colombia. He was also present on the expedition of Balboa when he first sighted the Pacific Ocean on September 25, 1513. In 1519, Pedrarias Dávila (Pedro Arias de Ávila) founded the city of Our Lady of the Assumption of Panamá (Panama City) and appointed Pizarro a *regidor*, or councilman, on the municipal council, as well as encomendero. The system of encomienda was the granting of Indian labor to specific conquistadores in return for promises of protection and Christianization.

By then news of Cortés's conquest of Mexico and plunder of huge sums of wealth reached the settlement in Panama. From the south, rumors of an El Dorado, or a city of gold, began to waft up as well. Pizarro was determined not to miss out on the plunder. Forming an alliance with Diego de Almagro, a fellow conquistador, and Father Hernando de Luque, a priest from Panama who financed the venture, possibly on behalf of a third party, Pizarro set sail with two ships on November 14, 1524. For six weeks they searched for the source of the rumored wealth. Initially, Almagro stayed behind to recruit more resources and men. He belatedly followed Pizarro, losing an eye from an Indian attack, but neither explorer discovered the golden empire. Disheartened, the two and their crew of 80 returned to Panama.

Pizarro and Almagro's second expedition of 1526 included twice as many men and, while still failing in its goal of acquiring wealth, nonetheless received enough proof of its existence to justify the expense. It was at this time that the Spaniards encountered an ocean-going raft, replete with cotton sails and carrying much wealth. After further inquiry they were told about an Inca city known as Tumbes on the Gulf of Guayaquil in modern-day Ecuador.

Running low on supplies, Almagro returned to Panama to collect more. When Pizarro's men began to threaten mutiny if not allowed to return as well, Pizarro reportedly, in dramatic fashion, drew a line in the sand with his sword, stating that those who wished to return should stand on one side, but that those who wished to continue on, as he would, were to cross over and join him. For the few who remained with Pizarro, hunger and misery would be their lot, but so too would unimaginable wealth.

For Pizarro, luck was on his side. Shortly after, Almagro returned with fresh reinforcements in his relief ship. Together they were able to sail southward to the city of Tumbes, where men believed to be Inca nobility came out to meet them. Richly adorned and sturdily built, this city was proof enough for the two men that a golden empire did indeed exist. They sailed back to Panama to prepare an invasion force.

Once back in Panama, Luque and Almagro sent Pizarro to Spain to request official recognition for their planned conquest from Charles V, king of Spain and emperor of the Holy Roman Empire. Promising equal recognition for each of the three partners, he set sail, arriving in Spain in the spring of 1528. Unfortunately for Pizarro, however, he was recognized by one of his Panamanian creditors who happened at that time to be in Spain as well, and was thrown into debtor's prison.

Hernán Cortés, cousin to Pizarro, also happened to be in Spain as well and convinced Charles V of the merits of listening to Pizarro. Ordering his release, Charles listened to Pizarro and then gave his assent to the proposal before setting off for an eastern campaign in Europe. It was therefore left to Queen Isabella of Portugal, wife of Charles V and regent during his absence, to draw up the capitulation, or royal grant, known as the *Capitulacion de Toledo*. With this, Pizarro was granted the titles of governor, *adelantado*, captain general, and alguacil mayor for life, as well as and the rights of discovery and conquest within 200 leagues south of Panama. And for his descendants, he received a coat of arms and membership in the prestigious Order of Santiago. In contrast, Almagro only received the right to be commander of Tumbes and Luque and the spiritual advisor for the region. Thus the seeds of discord in the Americas were at that moment being sewn in Spain.

Nonetheless, the Capitulation, issued July 26, 1529 and signed on August 27, granted the triumvirate and their company—the Company of the Levant—the exclusive rights to conquer and colonize Peru. It offered generous aid in the form of guns, horses, supplies, etc., and granted the right to bestow encomiendas on fellow conquistadores. Ironically, while in Spain Pizarro found it difficult to get enough volunteers to join him. That, he discovered, appeared to be Almagro's forte. According to his Capitulation,

he was to recruit 300, but he could only get 200, including his four brothers. Nonetheless, he set sail anyway, arriving in Panama in early 1530. With less than the numbers, Pizarro set off on December 27, 1530, on his third expedition. He had by now a reduced crew of a mere 180 men, so, once again, Almagro offered to stay behind to recruit more men.

Arriving in Tumbes in the spring of 1532, Pizarro stayed but a short while then in May, headed off. They next established and remained for some time in the town of San Miguel de Piura. By now, perhaps when he was still in Tumbes, Pizarro had received reinforcements, which, subtracting for diseases then taking a toll on his men, brought his effective force up to 200. While in San Miguel, Pizarro learned the Inca ruler, recently victorious from a civil war of succession that had been raging throughout the empire, was at that moment in the town of Cajamarca, about 10 to 12 days' distance.

On September 24, 1532, the band set off, reaching the valley of Cajamarca on November 15. The city itself was deserted, although Atahualpa and his army were encamped some three miles to the north. Sending a few horsemen, including the future explorer of Florida Hernando de Soto, to convince Atahualpa to meet, they were told that he would meet them in the city the following day. This gave the Spaniards enough time to prepare an impromptu ambush.

When Atahualpa arrived the following day, he left his army outside in the valley and brought a group of 6,000 unarmed retainers inside instead. With his men concealed in buildings and behind columns, Pizarro sent his chaplain, the Dominican friar Vincente Valverde and de Soto to meet with the Inca ruler. Unfamiliar with the foreign language spoken by the Spanish priest and lacking a writing system that approximated that used by the Spanish, Atahualpa was unimpressed with the Bible presented in the exchange. When he reportedly tossed the book aside, the emperor was caught unawares as a pre-arranged shout from Valverde called for the hidden soldiers who proceeded to massacre the Indians. Pizarro reported to have been the only one to receive a wound, when he was struck on the hand by a sword while defending Atahualpa from being killed. The emperor, having just imprisoned his brother and enemy, Huáscar, now found himself in a similar fate.

It quickly became obvious that what the Spaniards were after was gold and previous metals. With such a realization came Atahualpa's promise that the room in which he was being kept would be filled with gold as far as he could reach, along with an adjoining room filled with silver. All this, he stated, was ransom to ensure his release. Not only did Pizarro quickly agree but had it written up and notarized as well. In April 1533, Diego de Almagro and his reinforcements of 150 to 200 soldiers arrived, too late to participate in the capture of the Inca ruler.

In all, approximately 1.5 million pesos worth of treasures were delivered to Pizarro and his men. Once melted down, one-fifth was set aside to be sent to Charles V and the rest divvied out. A horseman received 180 pounds of gold and 180 pounds of silver, and Pizarro seven times that. For Almagro and his men, however, only a token amount was given. The seeds of discord grew into stalks of hatred, soon to flower in to violence.

Many advisors urged Pizarro to execute Atahualpa as the ruler had, from prison, just ordered the execution of Huáscar. The main cause for concern was rumors that an army was soon to arrive under the leadership of the capable Rumiñahui to secure the ruler's release. Thus on July 26, 1533, Pizarro ordered

Atahualpa's execution. Originally sentenced to death by being burned alive, Valverde convinced Atahualpa to accept a Christian baptism and be executed by garroting instead, to which he quickly acceded. Three days after, Pizarro defended his actions to Charles V in a letter, arguing that it was carried out because Atahualpa had "ordered a mobilization of fighting men to come against [him] and against the Christians who went there and were present at his capture."

With Atahualpa dead, Pizarro now made Huayna Capac's (Huáscar and Atahualpa's father) oldest legitimate, surviving son Túpac Huallpa the new ruler of the Inca Empire. Crowned in October of 1533, he had just began to feel the power of empire beneath his feet when he died as well, although of what it is not known. Pizarro put the crown on the head of yet another son of Huayna Capac, Manco Inca Yupanqui (December 1533). His reign proved to have more longevity than the previous ones.

Pizarro next set his sights on capturing the capital of the Inca Empire, Cuzco. He and Almagro and their men set off on August 11, 1533, arriving on November 15. While there, word reached Pizarro that Pedro de Alvarado, successful captain under Hernán Cortés, had just landed on the coast with a huge group of Spaniards. Afraid of what this might mean to his monopoly over the conquest of the Inca Empire, Pizarro sent Almagro to get rid of Alvarado. This he did with a huge bribe.

Two important events now occurred in 1535. The first involved the establishment by Pizarro of the City of the Kings (Ciudad de los Reyes), or Lima. Much of the remainder of the conquest for Pizarro was spent either there or in another city soon to be built as well: Trujillo. The second important event began as a rumor. Although the northern part of the empire had been granted to Pizarro with the *Capitulacion de Toledo,* this new rumor stated that the southern portion—south of 200 leagues from Panama—was being granted to Almagro. This meant, Almagro believed, that Cuzco, the capital of the Inca Empire, now belonged to him.

Pizarro had just given command of the city to his brothers Juan and Gonzalo. Francisco evidently believed the rumor had at least a little bit of validity as that spring he ordered his brothers to hand control over to his partner. But Pizarro then reversed himself and ordered the city not be handed over. Faced with a disgruntled Almagro, Pizarro convinced him to take an expedition south to conquer Chile. From July 1535 to March 1537, Almagro remained out of the picture as he endeavored to explore the new territory. Pizarro also left the Inca capital, founding the city of Trujillo. In October 1537 he received the title of marquis.

Back in Cuzco the new puppet Inca emperor Manco Inca, who seemed so compliant when Pizarro first chose him to rule, grew tired of the abuse by the Pizarro brothers and fled the city. Soon after he began an uprising in February 1536 and besieged the capital of Cuzco the following month. Upon hearing of this, Francisco Pizarro sent his brother, Hernando, to attempt a pacification of the region. Unfortunately, Hernando's failure was compounded by an indigenous attack on Lima as well. Appealing to Panama for more reinforcements, he stripped Manco (in absentia) of his office and named his half-brother, Paullu, newly returned from accompanying Almagro to Chile, the new ruler. Out of desperation, or perhaps merely revenge, Hernando Pizarro ordered Mancos's wife, Cura Ocllo, stripped, tied to a pole, and executed by firing arrows into her body.

When Almagro had returned from Chile in 1537 and witnessed the siege of Cuzco, he quickly set about dispersing it. He expected to march in and take command of the city. Hernando Pizarro, however, refused to allow it. Ignoring the Pizarros, Almagro marched in anyway and arrested Hernando and his brother Gonzalo. Gonzalo later escaped, but after negotiations with Francisco Pizarro, Almagro agreed to let Hernando go on the proviso that within six weeks he would leave the country.

Not only did Hernando not leave, but he marched an army against Almagro on July 7, 1538, capturing him and, reportedly on orders of Francisco Pizarro, had him executed the following day. The flower of violence had now exploded across the land, with Manco Inca's Neo-Inca rebellion coinciding with the Spanish civil war between the Pizarros and Almagristas. As news of the agitation crossed the Atlantic and reached the ears of Charles V, Francisco Pizarro set out for Cuzco, founding the town of San Juan de la Frontera en route on January 9, 1539. Emperor Charles, meanwhile, sent Vaca de Castro, lawyer and judge, to confer with Francisco Pizarro and restore peace amongst the conquistadors, even going so far as ordering that he become the next governor if Pizarro were to meet an untimely demise.

Charles had not misjudged the situation. On Sunday June 26, 1541, the followers of the fallen Almagro, still embittered at their slight since the initial Battle of Cajamarca and with their leader martyred, rallied behind Almagro's son of the same name and attacked the governor's palace in the city of Lima. Twenty Almagristas, led by Juan de Herrada, carried out the assassination of Francisco Pizarro, then proclaimed Diego de Almagro el Mozo (the younger) as governor and captain general of Peru. Of course, Vaca de Castro's arrival soon changed this course of events.

Following Francisco Pizarro's death at the hands of the Almagristas, all the major players suffered violent deaths within a short period of time, with the exception of Hernando Pizarro. This brother of Francisco returned to Spain and, after surviving a long imprisonment of 20 years, lived to an old age as the sole survivor of the leading conquistadors of Peru. Francisco Pizarro's body, buried separately from his head, was interred in the cathedral courtyard.

Kim Richardson

See also: Almagro, Diego de; Almagro, Diego de (el Mozo); Alvarado, Pedro de; Atahualpa; Cajamarca, Battle of; Charles V (HRE) or Carlos I of Spain; Cortés, Hernán; Cuzco; Huáscar; Las Salinas, Battle of; Lima; Manco Inca Yupanqui; Paullu Inca; Pizarro, Gonzalo; Pizarro, Hernando; Sapa Inca; Túpac Huallpa.

Resources

Brading, David. *The First America: The Spanish Monarchy, Creole Patriots, and the Liberal State, 1492–1867*. Cambridge: Cambridge University Press, 1993.

Hawthorne, Julian. *World's Best Histories: Spanish America, From the Earliest Period to the Present Time*. New York: The Cooperative Publication Society, 1899.

Hemming, John. *The Conquest of the Incas*. New York: Harcourt Brace Jovanovich, 1970.

Howard, Cecil. *Pizarro and the Conquest of Peru*. New York: Harper and Row, 1968.

Kirkpatrick, F. A. *The Spanish Conquistadores*. 2nd ed. New York: Macmillan, 1946.

Lockhart, James. *Spanish Peru: A Colonial Society*. Madison: University of Wisconsin Press, 1968.

Means, Philip Ainsworth. *Fall of the Inca Empire and the Spanish Rule in Peru, 1530–1780*. New York: Gordian Press, 1964.

Prescott, William H. *The Conquest of Peru*. New York: Harper and Brothers, 1847.

Smyth, Clifford. *Francisco Pizarro and the Conquest of Peru*. New York: Funk & Wagnalls, 1931.

Varón Gabai, Rafael. *Francisco Pizarro and his Brothers: The Illusion of Power in Sixteenth-Century Peru*. Trans: Javier Flores Espinoza. Norman: University of Oklahoma Press, 1997.

Verrill, A. Hyatt. *Great Conquerors of South and Central America*. New York: The New Home Library, 1929.

Pizarro, Gonzalo

Gonzalo Pizarro was born in 1502 in Trujillo, Spain, in the region of Extremadura. He was the half-brother of the conquistador Francisco and Hernando Pizarro as well as the brother of Juan Pizarro. He participated in the capture and death of Atahualpa (1533) in the conquest of the Inca Empire and explored the lands east of Quito (1541–42). He is known for his defiance of the New Laws of the Indies of 1542 and the viceroy who arrived to enforce these ordinances. This directly led to his execution in 1548.

In 1528, Francisco Pizarro traveled to Spain to secure royal permission from the Emperor Charles V for the conquest of the Inca Empire. While there, he enlisted the services of his brothers and half-brothers, including Gonzalo Pizarro. The brothers landed on the coast of Peru, at Tumbes, in 1532 and, by mid-November, captured the Inca ruler, Atahualpa. After ransoming the emperor for a large quantity of gold, Francisco Pizarro executed the Sapa Inca. With their taste for further wealth wetted by the ransom, the conquistadores marched to and captured the capital, Cuzco, where Gonzalo and seven others became the *regidores* (councilmen) of the city.

Problems between the Pizarros and followers of Diego de Almagro, Francisco's partner, quickly developed. Almagro believed Emperor Charles V granted the area of Cuzco to him, but in 1535 Gonzalo and

Hernando both received orders from Francisco to prohibit Almagro's occupation of the city. Violence was delayed when Almagro was ordered to march south to conquer Chile. Upon his return, Almagro discovered the city of Cuzco under siege by Manco Inca, former puppet emperor appointed by Francisco Pizarro. Almagro snuck into Cuzco and arrested both Gonzalo and Hernando; the former escaped and Almagro freed the latter through negotiations with Francisco.

Shortly thereafter, on April 16, 1538, Gonzalo participated in the defeat of the Almagristas on the plains of Las Salinas. Following Almagro's execution, Ferdinand sent Gonzalo to capture the intransigent Inca ruler, Manco Inca. Though unsuccessful in capturing Manco Inca, Gonzalo was appointed governor of Quito with the order to explore the lands to the east. Rumors had been spreading of rich sources of spices and the fabled lands of El Dorado farther inland in the territory referred to as the Land or Province of Cinnamon. Gonzalo set off in February 1541 along with approximately 2,310 Spaniards and 4,000 indigenous auxiliary forces. By November the expedition had reached the Coca River and depleted all stores of food. Gonzalo sent his second-in-command, Francisco de Orellana, to continue on in hopes of finding additional sources of food. Whether he did so or not has been argued, but what occurred next was Orellana's voyage all the way to the Atlantic Ocean, the first European to have made that voyage across South America. Gonzalo, meanwhile, made it to the Napo River, which connects to the Coca, and limped back to Quito.

Arriving in August or September 1542, Gonzalo had failed to find either a lucrative source of spices or the kingdom of El Dorado. Upon his return, he discovered his brother Francisco had been assassinated and Diego de Almagro's son of the same name

was now ruling in his stead. When Spain sent Vaca de Castro to assess the situation in Peru, Gonzalo proclaimed his loyalty to the new governor and retired to his encomienda near Lake Titicaca in the area known as Charcas.

On November 20, 1542, Charles V issued the New Laws of the Indies, which eventually abolished the encomienda system or the tributary system in which Indians contributed goods to the Spaniards in exchange for protection and the provision of religious services. To enforce the Laws, Charles sent Blasco Núñez de la Vela as the new viceroy. Landing at the coast at Tumbes in March of 1544 and Lima in May, he found the encomenderos rising up in opposition.

Initially the new viceroy believed he could compromise with the encomenderos, sending requests to Spain to seek modifications of the Leyes Nuevas. His actions toward the encomenderos became more severe when his ideas met with resistance. He imprisoned the former viceroy and had him returned to Spain. Eventually many neutral Spanish turned toward the rebels who supported Gonzalo Pizarro as their leader. A succession of events occurred that spelled the end of the Pizarro's hold on Peru. After a brief imprisonment, De la Vaca managed to secure his release at Tumbes and launched a counter-revolt. In August, Gonzalo wrote to Charles V asking him to rescind the New Laws. In October, Pizarro forced the *audiencia* of Lima to name him governor. Gonzalo Pizarro, in March 1545, marched north against de la Vela, although the battle between the two forces was not fought until January 16 or 17, 1546. Victorious, Pizarro ordered de la Vela's execution the following day.

Charles V, frustrated with the upheaval in Peru, sent an ecclesiastic, Pedro de la Gasca, to serve as president of the *audiencia* of Panama and reimpose imperial control. With authority granted him by the emperor, Gasca suspended the New Laws and began heading south in February 1547 to end the rebellion. Armed with royal pardons he landed at Tumbes in June. He sent a Captain Diego de Centeno to recapture Cuzco but was defeated at the battle of Huarina, fought sometime between then and October 1547.

After defeating Centeno, Gonzalo returned to Cuzco. The following April in 1548, Gonzalo Pizarro and his army marched out to meet the viceroy at Sacsahuana. Whether due to the prolific use of pardons or the suspensions of the encomienda, the soldiers under Pizarro deserted him en masse, forcing his surrender. The following day, April 10, 1548, Garza had Gonzalo executed. His death marked the end of an era, being the last of both the Almagros and the Pizarros to die in Peru. The only surviving Pizarro who had assisted in conquering Peru was Gonzalo's half-brother, Hernando, who was then pining his time away in a Spanish prison.

Kim Richardson

See also: Almagro, Diego de; Almagro, Diego de (el Mozo); Atahualpa; Charles V (HRE) or Carlos I of Spain; Leyes Nuevas 1542–1543; Manco Inca Yupanqui; Orellana, Francisco de; Pizarro, Francisco; Pizarro, Hernandez; Sapa Inca; Tumbes.

Resources

Hawthorne, Julian. *World's Best Histories: Spanish America, From the Earliest Period to the Present Time.* New York: The Cooperative Publication Society, 1899.

Kirkpatrick, F. A. *The Spanish Conquistadores.* 2nd ed. New York: Macmillan, 1946.

Lamana, Gonzalo. *Domination without Dominance: Inca-Spanish Encounters in Early Colonial Peru.* Durham, NC: Duke University Press, 2008.

MacQuarrie, Kim. *The Last Days of the Incas.* New York: Simon & Schuster, 2007.

Moore, Robert T. "Gonzalo Pizarro's Trail to the Land of Cinnamon and its Denizens." *Condor* 36, No. 3 (May–June 1934): 97–104.

Prescott, William H. *The Conquest of Peru.* New York: Harper and Brothers, 1847.

Varón Gabai, Rafael. *Francisco Pizarro and his Brothers: The Illusion of Power in Sixteenth-Century Peru.* Translated by Javier Flores Espinoza. Norman: University of Oklahoma Press, 1997.

Pizarro, Hernando (ca. 1478–1578)

Hernandez Pizarro (Hernando Pizarro y de Vargas) was a Spanish conquistador instrumental in the Spanish defeat of the Incas and the conquest of Peru. Hernando was born in the city of Trujillo in Extremadura, the western part of Spain. The exact date of his birth is unknown. Hernando was the only legitimate son of Gonzalo Pizarro y Rodriguez de Aguilar, an infantry colonel in the Spanish army. Hernando had two full sisters and three illegitimate half-brothers. He was also a second cousin to Hernán Cortés.

Hernando Pizarro, unlike his brother Francisco, received a good education and military training. He was active at the Spanish court, where he managed to cultivate royal contacts that later proved helpful to his family. Hernando's military experience included fighting in the series of wars between Spain and France. On July 27, 1521, Hernando was appointed as infantry captain during the siege of Logroño.

In 1530, Hernando accompanied his half-brothers Francisco Pizarro, Gonzalo, and Juan on a voyage to the New World. Francisco Pizarro had already made two unsuccessful expeditions to Peru in 1524 and 1526, aimed at conquering the Incas and acquiring rumored wealth. Francisco Pizarro appealed directly to King Charles V, and in 1528, the king signed the *Capitulation de Toledo*, which licensed Francisco to mount a third expedition. The document also gave him absolute authority in any lands that he would discover and conquer.

The brothers sailed from Seville on January 18, 1530, bound for Panama. On December 27, 1530, their three ships sailed from Panama for Peru. They landed at Tumbes, in northwestern Peru, and found that the city had been destroyed during a civil war between the Inca emperors (and half-brothers) Huáscar and Atahualpa.

Hernando Pizarro accompanied the expedition inland, where, in July 1532, Pizarro established the town of San Miguel de Piura, the third Spanish settlement in South America and the first in Peru. After reinforcements arrived, the Spaniards marched toward the Incas, bent on conquest.

Having recently defeated and captured his brother Huáscar, the emperor Atahualpa was camped atop a hill near Cajamarca and sent a man to spy on the Spaniards. Deciding that they were not a threat, Atahualpa invited them to meet with him, and the Spaniards proceeded to Cajamarca and set up camp. Pizarro, far outnumbered, set up an ambush and then dispatched an emissary to the Incas. He also sent a group of 20 horsemen led by his brother Hernando to do reconnaissance.

On November 16, 1532, the Battle of Cajamarca took place, marking the beginning of a prolonged conflict between the Spaniards and the Incas. Atahualpa left his encampment with 80,000 men (reported numbers by the Spanish were probably exaggerated as was typical at the time) and approached the Spaniards. Hernando used his diplomatic skills to invite the Inca into Cajamarca before nightfall to meet Pizarro. Atahualpa left most of his army outside the city, and, in a show of goodwill, proceeded with his unarmed retinue into Cajamarca. The Spaniards had been hiding in buildings and launched a surprise attack, routing the Incas. Francisco Pizarro captured Atahualpa and demanded a huge ransom for his release. Upon receipt of the ransom, Atahualpa was executed.

Hernando Pizarro returned to Spain in 1533 to deliver the *quinto real* to King Charles V (a tax amounting to one-fifth of the spoils) and to report on the conquest of the Inca Empire. He petitioned the king for additional powers and also attempted to resolve the dispute that had arisen between Francisco Pizarro and Diego de Almagro (Pizarro's partner) over the division of Peru.

In 1536 Hernando Pizarro was back in South America, helping to govern Peru alongside his brothers Juan and Gonzalo. Hernando ordered the release of Inca ruler Manco Inca from prison in exchange for promises of great treasure. However, Manco Inca took the opportunity to flee Cuzco and the abusive treatment at the hands of the Pizarro brothers. The Sapa Inca returned to the capital city with an army of 200,000 men. During the 10-month-long siege that followed, Hernando Pizarro defended and held Cuzco despite the size of the enemy's forces.

The rift between Diego de Almagro and Francisco Pizarro widened when Almagro returned from a failed mission to Chile seeking more wealth. In the resulting civil war that broke out between the Spaniards, Almagro seized Cuzco in 1537 and captured Hernando and Juan Pizarro. Hernando was released after negotiations in which he promised to leave for Spain. Instead, he returned to Cuzco with his brother Gonzalo and an army to confront Almagro.

On April 26, 1538, Hernando Pizarro initiated the Battle of Las Salinas. Gonzalo led the infantry and Hernando divided the cavalry into two groups, taking command of one group himself. The battle lasted an hour, with Pizarro's forces winning. Almagro fled the battlefield, but Hernando Pizarro caught up with him and condemned him to death. Almagro was executed on July 8, 1538.

Hernando went to Spain in 1539 as a diplomat to argue on behalf of the Pizarro brothers' South American claims. In spite of bribing officials, he was imprisoned at La Mota for 20 years.

While still in prison, in 1552 Hernando married his 17-year-old niece Francisca Pizarro Yupanqui. They had five children. The marriage may have been made to cement Hernando's estate and prevent the Spanish Crown from confiscating his properties in Peru, as they had done with his brother Gonzalo's.

Hernando was freed in 1560 and faded into obscurity. The date of his death is unknown, but he reportedly lived to be 100 years old.

Karen S. Garvin

See also: Almagro, Diego de; Atahualpa; Cajamarca, Battle of; Charles V (HRE) or Carlos I of Spain; Cortés, Hernán; Huáscar; Las Salinas, Battle of; Manco Inca Yupanqui; Pizarro, Francisco; Pizarro, Gonzalo; Sapa Inca; Tumbes.

Resources

Davies, Nigel. *The Incas.* Niwot: University of Colorado Press, 1995.

Hemming, John. *The Conquest of the Incas.* London: Macmillan, 1970.

MacQuarrie, Kim. *The Last Days of the Incas.* New York: Simon & Schuster, 2007.

Prescott, W.H. *History of the Conquest of Peru.* New York: Random House, 1998.

Varón Gabai, Rafael. *Francisco Pizarro and His Brothers: The Illusion of Power in Sixteenth-Century Peru.* Norman, OK: University of Oklahoma Press, 1997.

Pochtecas

The Pochteca were elite guilds of armed merchants, some of whom collected intelligence information across Mesoamerica for the Aztec state. These guilds occupied their own neighborhoods in the Aztec capital of Tenochtitlán and 11 other important cities in the Valley of Mexico. Guild membership was hereditary, and the guilds were organized into different categories, ranging from elite merchants to intelligence collectors, slave traders, and ordinary merchants. Pochteca had legal oversight of Aztec markets, as well as their own independent law courts.

The Pochteca specialized in buying and selling high status trade goods—ranging from valuable raw materials such as jade, gold, turquoise, bird feathers, seashells, and cacao beans, to luxury items, including jaguar skins, clothing, jewelry, stone carvings, ceramics, and hand-painted manuscripts. Much of the material they sold in Aztec markets was obtained during extended long-distance trading expeditions through foreign states as far south as Guatemala and possibly as far north as the American Southwest.

During these expeditions, the Pochteca, who were trained warriors, carried weapons for protection. Chief among their weaponry was the sword-like wooden *macuahuitl,* which was inset with obsidian blades and used as a slashing weapon. There were no draft animals or wheeled vehicles in Mesoamerica, so the Pochteca had to move on foot or by water in canoes. Groups of merchants traveled together and were accompanied by low-class porters who carried their goods in backpacks consisting of large woven cane containers mounted on carrying frames. The success of these merchants, despite limits in transportation, is evident in the variety and extent of their trade in the Mesoamerican region and beyond.

Glenn E. Helm

See also: Artisans, Mexica; Mexico, State of prior to Spanish Conquest.

Resources

Hassig, Ross. *Trade, Tribute, and Transportation: The Sixteenth-Century Political Economy of the Valley of Mexico.* Norman: University of Oklahoma Press, 1985.

Smith, Michael E. *The Aztecs.* 3rd ed. Chichester: Wiley-Blackwell, 2012.

Smith, Michael E. "Long-Distance Trade under the Aztec Empire: The Archaeological Evidence." *Ancient Mesoamerica* 1 (1990): 153–169.

Ponce de León, Juan

A Spanish soldier and explorer, Juan Ponce de León was born sometime in 1460 in San Sérvas de Campos, Spain, the illegitimate son of a noble family of modest means. As a young man, he became a soldier, and in the early 1490s he fought against the Muslims (Moors) in the southern part of Spain. In 1493, Ponce de León set sail for the New World on Christopher Columbus's second voyage to the Americas. He did not return to Spain with Columbus but stayed in the Caribbean and in 1502 settled on what is now Hispaniola. In 1504, he became the governor of Salvación de Higuey province on Hispaniola. There he made a comfortable profit by selling cassava bread to passing ships headed for Spain seeking fresh food.

In 1508, Ponce de León, while purportedly searching for gold, began the conquest of the island now called Puerto Rico. He went on to serve as its governor beginning in 1509, in the process amassing a fortune via gold and land speculation. Initially well received by the native population, Ponce de León gained a notorious reputation there for him and his dog, which was credited with discerning between friendly and unfriendly Indians. His ensuing brutal treatment of the natives in Puerto Rico resulted in his ouster in 1511. That same year, the natives of the island rose up against Ponce de León's lieutenant, Cristóbal de Sotomayor. While the uprising failed, the indigenous people managed to kill Sotomayor and his son. Meanwhile, the Spanish Crown granted Ponce de León the right to find, explore, and conquer the island of Bimini (in the Bahamas) in 1512.

Ponce de León's interest was captured by reports of the island of Bimini to the north. What he sought in this new opportunity is debated. Tales of a fountain of youth have little to sustain them. It is more likely that, with his plantation declining in profits and his previous sources of indigenous slave labor depleted, he was looking for new sources of cheap laborers. Certainly, his later actions of capturing Florida Indians for use as slaves helps support this rationale.

With the support of the king, Ponce de León set sail to the northwest from Puerto Rico with three ships. He first sighted the Florida Peninsula on March 27, 1513, naming it Pascua de Florida (Feast of Flowers) because of its discovery on Easter Sunday. Seeking further profits in gold and native slaves on what he presumed to be an island, Ponce de León made landfall on the Atlantic coast of Florida. There, he took possession of the peninsula for the Crown. He continued south along the Florida coast, making landfall and meeting the Ais Indians who attacked his men. He charted the Florida Keys (which he named the Martyrs), and then sailed up the Gulf Coast of Florida. Again he met with hostile natives, this time the Calusas. Both tribes resided in the southern

Juan Ponce de León, Spanish explorer best known for his quest of the fabled Fountain of Youth in Florida, also accompanied Columbus on the second expedition in 1493. (Library of Congress)

portion of the peninsula and had fallen prey to earlier slave expeditions by previous conquistadors. On his return trip from his exploration of the Florida coast, Ponce de Leon's expedition landed along the Yucatán coast.

Following this expedition in search of Bimini, Ponce returned to Spain for what he had intended to be a brief visit, during which the king appointed him a captain general. Ponce de Leon received a grant by King Ferdinand to explore and settle in Florida, even bestowing the title of *adelantado* upon

the explorer. The conquistador delayed his return to the New World for a few years, however, burdened by his wife's recent death and with the raising of his daughters. With the news of Cortés's success in Mexico, the lure of potential wealth and prestige proved too much to ignore, and Ponce again traveled to America.

Between 1519 and 1521, Ponce made several trips to Florida. He eventually charted most of peninsular Florida by 1521, though not enough to determine the land was part of a greater continent. He also discovered the Gulf Stream, a warm current of water that passes through part of the Caribbean and parallels the southeastern coast of North America. This current proved crucial to Spanish cross-Atlantic shipments of gold and other goods from the Americas.

Still believing Florida was an island, Ponce de León left for Florida from Puerto Rico on February 20, 1521, determined to reach Bimini. His expedition of some 200 men instead landed on the western coast of Florida. Ponce de León hoped to establish a Spanish colony there, but the fledgling settlement soon fell under attack by hostile natives, and the Spaniards abandoned the site in short order. Wounded during one of the skirmishes, Ponce de León died soon after arriving in Havana, Cuba, from an infection inflicted by a Calusa arrow in July 1521.

Dixie Ray Haggard, Paul G. Pierpaoli, Jr., and Rebecca M. Seaman

See also: *Adelantado*; Columbus, Christopher; Conquistador.

Resources

Fuson, Robert H. *Juan Ponce de Leon and the Spanish Discovery of Puerto Rico and Florida.* Blacksburg, VA: McDonald & Woodward, 2000.

Galloway, Patricia, ed. *The Hernando de Soto Expedition: History, Historiography, and "Discovery" in the Southeast.* Lincoln: University of Nebraska Press, 2005.

Stefoff, Rebecca. *Accidental Explorers: Surprises and Side Trips in the History of Discovery.* New York: Oxford University Press, 1992.

Thomas, Hugh. *Conquest: Montezuma, Cortés, and the Fall of Old Mexico.* New York: Simon & Schuster, 1993.

Weber, David J. *The Spanish Frontier in North America.* New Haven: Yale University Press, 1992.

Popocatepetl

Mount Popocatepetl and Mount Iztaccihuatl are two volcanic mountains that were sacred to the Aztec people of Mexico. They are located some 45 miles southeast of Mexico City and what was the capital of the Aztec Empire, Tenochtitlán. Popocatepetl, the "smoking mountain," reaches upward some 17,800 feet. It has been active in recent history and frequently releases clouds of smoke from its summit. Iztaccihuatl, the "sleeping lady," is an extinct volcano some 17,400 feet in height. Historical records of the mountains and activity around them date to the Spanish arrival at the city of Cholula and the 1519 invasion by the conquistador Hernán Cortés (1485–1547). However, evidence of human habitation in the area goes back to 700 BCE.

One pre-Spanish tale related to the mountains recounts the relation of the warrior Popocatepetl and his great love Iztaccihuatl. Their marriage depended on Popocatepetl winning an upcoming battle. He won, but while away, a rival spread a false rumor that he had died. Iztaccihuatl died of grief before he returned. Upon his return, Popocatepetl placed her body atop the mountain range west of the mountain named for his love, which now has the shape of a sleeping woman. Popocatepetl then climbed the mountain named for him where, torch in hand, he kept vigil.

Both the height and the activity of Popocatepetl made it an object of attention. Bernardino de Sahagún, a Franciscan friar who observed and recorded the activities of Native Mexicas at the time of the Spanish conquest, noted that Popocatepetl and Iztaccihuatl derived some of their sacred status because rain clouds tended to gather around them. Believers would climb the mountains to venerate the water deities. Unfortunately,

Sahagún failed to identify either the deities associated with the mountains or the mythology that surrounded them. At Chocula is a pyramid, Tlachihualtepetl (man-made hill), the largest in the Americas. It appears to have been constructed as a smaller Popocatepetl, possibly in reaction to the major eruption of 90 CE.

Volcanic eruptions have driven people away, while the rich soil around the mountain attracts people back. Traditional rituals designed to keep Popocatepetl calm were still being observed as late as the 1980s, but seemed to have disappeared as the 21st century began.

J. Gordon Melton

See also: Sahagún, Bernardino de; Tenochtitlán, City of.

Resources

Gruzinski, Serge. *The Aztecs: Rise and Fall of an Empire*. New York: Harry N. Abrams, 1992.

Plunket, Patricia, and Gabriela Uruñuela. "Appeasing the Volcano Gods." *Archeology* 51, no. 4 (July–August 1998). http://www.archaeology.org/9807/abstracts/volcano.html (accessed May 17, 2013).

Pohl, John. *Aztecs and Conquistadores: The Spanish Invasion and the Collapse of the Aztec Empire*. Oxford: Osprey Publishing, 2005.

Potonchan, Battle of

The Battle of Potonchan was the first major battle fought by Cortés and his forces upon landing on the Yucatán Peninsula in March 1519. Far outnumbered, the Spanish gradually transferred men from his ships offshore as he played a game of negotiation and political diplomacy with the local Chontal Mayas. The Mayas also delayed the initial clash with the Spanish, using the time to remove their families and valuables from the city while bringing inadequate food supplies to the Spanish. The Mayas claimed they had no more gold, when such was demanded by the *caudillo*. They also claimed insufficient food to feed the growing number of Spanish camped on the shore.

While the conquistador and the Mayas sparred verbally for three days, Cortés sent reconnaissance forces under Pedro de Alvarado and Alonso de Ávila to approach the town from upriver. When the battle finally began, it was in response to the *caudillo* having the *Requerimiento* read to the native population, demanding the acceptance of Charles V of Spain as supreme ruler, and acceptance of the Catholic faith. The sudden onslaught of spears, arrows, and stones pushed the Spanish into the river. Still refusing to divulge the presence of horses, Cortés nonetheless had his artillery brought to shore. The firing of the cannon frightened but did not disperse the Mayas. It was the arrival of Alvarado and Ávila, attacking the Mayas from the rear, that convinced the natives to flee into the marshes.

The Spanish suffered injuries to 20 of their forces, and the loss of a native interpreter who used the battle to escape back to his home on the Yucatán. From this battle of Potonchan, Cortés gained far more than he lost. He became aware of the ability to win conflicts with the native population, even when greatly outnumbered. He discovered the value of the quilted cotton armor of the Maya, allowing greater flexibility and less of a burden for his own forces. He saw the benefit of using artillery, though also noted the limitations of that weapon in dealing with the Mayas. Most importantly, the defeated Maya presented Cortés with gifts of women, one of who was Malinche (later baptized Doña Marina), a Mexica captive who spoke fluent Mayan as well as her native tongue of Nahuatl. Communications between the various native communities remained awkward at first as Malinche translated Nahuatl into Mayan, and the castaway Fr. Gerónimo Aguilar translated Mayan into Spanish. However, this discovery of Malinche's linguistic abilities later enabled the conquistador to communicate effectively with the Aztec as he continued his journey inland toward the Mexica capital of Tenochtitlán.

Rebecca M. Seaman

See also: Alvarado, Pedro de; Aguilar, Fr. Gerónimo de; Ávila, Alonso de; Cortés, Hernán; La Malinche, "Doña Marina"; Nahuatl Language; Tenochtitlán, City of.

Resources

Díaz del Castillo, Bernal. *The Conquest of New Spain.* Translated by J. M. Cohen. New York: Penguin Books, 1963.

Levy, Buddy. *Conquistador.* New York: Bantam Dell, 2008.

Schwartz, Stuart B., ed. *Victors and Vanquished: Spanish and Nahua Views of the Conquest of Mexico.* Boston: Bedford/St. Martin's, 2000.

Restall, Matthew. *Seven Myths of the Spanish Conquest.* New York: Oxford University Press, 2003.

Thomas, Hugh. *Conquest: Montezuma, Cortés, and the Fall of Old Mexico.* New York: Simon & Schuster, 1993.

Potosí

Potosí is a historically important silver mining district and city in southern Bolivia. Spaniards became aware of the Cerro Rico (Rich Hill) of Potosí in 1545, and the discovery sparked a mining boom. For nearly 20 years, Andean miners exploited rich surface ores and refined them in indigenous smelters (*guayras*). However, by the 1560s the surface deposits were gone, and miners began to extract more complex ores from the interior of the hill. Production costs rose, and smelting no longer yielded profitable results.

At that point the Spaniards introduced amalgamation, a new refining technique developed in Mexico and adapted to conditions at Potosí. Amalgamation required grinding of the ore and its mixture with mercury, which formed an amalgam with silver. Workers then washed away the dross, leaving the amalgam, which they heated to volatize off the mercury.

The new technology transformed Potosí. Vast existing dumps of low-grade ore could now be refined, and Cerro Rico seemed to contain limitless quantities of silver ores. To promote amalgamation, the Spanish viceroy Francisco de Toledo committed the government to supply mercury from the Crown's mines at Huancavelica and also to provide cheap forced labor (*mita*) if Spaniards would build refining mills. The onset of underground ore extraction and the substitution of amalgamation for smelting required large capital investments, and Spaniards took control of operations from indigenous miners and smelters, leaving the indigenous population no longer controlling the mining or its proceeds. To supply *mita* labor for the mines and mills, Toledo conscripted workers (*mitayos*) from 16 highland provinces, stretching almost to Cuzco, and obligated them to work one year in every seven years at Potosí.

By 1600, Potosí was officially producing about seven million ounces of silver per year, from which the Crown collected a 20 percent tax (the royal fifth). Contraband undoubtedly pushed the overall output significantly higher. Much of the economic life of colonial Peru subsequently centered on Potosí.

Its silver monetized the economy, and the city constituted the greatest market in Spanish South America. All goods, from basic necessities to luxury items, had to be imported because of the city's location at an altitude of over 13,000 feet above sea level. Nonetheless, the city's population reached 150,000 in the early 1600s, making it the largest in the New World at the time. Rich churches and mansions graced the city center, while huts housed the thousands of indigenous workers. Near the cathedral, a great mint converted silver bars into coin.

After 1620, Potosí's silver output gradually declined, a trend that lasted until the 1730s, when the Crown halved the mining tax. The *mita* continued to supply cheap labor, which permitted the extraction and processing of ores too poor to be profitable without such a subsidy. The levies of workers dropped from 13,000 per year in the 1570s to 3,000 or 4,000 in the 18th century. With the drop in silver production and lower profits, Potosí's population also began to decline, reaching as few as 10,000 in the early 19th century. By the end of the colonial period, Potosí was a mere shadow of its former grandeur, although it continued to inspire Spaniards' imaginations. It remains a mining center and administrative center in modern Bolivia.

Kendall W. Brown

See also: Huancavelica; Mines, Role of in Peru; *Mita*; Silver; Toledo, Francisco de.

Resources

Bakewell, Peter J. *Miners of the Red Mountain: Indian Labor in Potosí, 1545–1650.* Albuquerque: University of New Mexico Press, 1984.

Tandeter, Enrique. *Coercion and Market: Silver Mining in Colonial Potosí, 1692–1826.* Albuquerque: University of New Mexico Press, 1993.

Punta Quemada, Battle of

The Battle of Quemada, a brief skirmish between Spanish forces and Indians of the kingdom of Quito, took place in January 1525 in modern-day Columbia. It concluded Francisco Pizarro's first expedition down the South American Pacific coast in search of fortune.

In 1522, the return of Andagoya's expedition south of Panama fueled speculation of a wealthy kingdom hidden in the Cordilleras in South America. However, the inhospitable landscape deterred serious exploration of the Pacific coast. Francisco Pizarro, an experienced cavalier who had crossed the Isthmus of Panama with Balboa, resolved to make his fame and fortune through conquest like his distant cousin, Cortés.

Pizarro partnered with Diego de Almagro, a soldier of fortune, and Hernando de Luque, a vicar who controlled funding in a small community where he resided. Pizarro took charge of the enterprise, while Almagro equipped the ships, and Luque provided the bulk of the financing. After recruiting nearly 100 men and garnering the consent of the governor, Pizarro and his crew departed Panama in November 1524.

Pizarro's vessel stopped at the Isle of Pearls off of Panama, crossed the Gulf of St. Michael, and headed for Puerto de Piñas. After an unsuccessful voyage on the river Biru, Pizarro guided the ship back to the open ocean, heading southward along the unchartered coast. Low on food and water, the vessel put ashore. The swampy, thicketed landing yielded so little nourishment that Pizarro sent his vessel commanded by Lieutenant Montenegro back to the Isle of Pearls for supplies. Weeks passed before the starving soldiers found an inland Indian village whose inhabitants fled when the Spanish approached. Eventually, Montenegro returned with the stocked vessel and found Pizarro and his crew, less 20 men who had died of starvation.

Pizarro kept a southerly course and put ashore at a point he named Punta Quemada. Pizarro led his men through openings in the thick mangroves and spied a village in a defended position on the edge of an eminence. Discovering that the natives had fled to the hills to protect their women and children, Pizarro occupied the village and his men confiscated food and gold trinkets.

Pizzaro ordered Montenegro to reconnoiter the area and begin communication with the natives. However, the warrior Quito tribe planned to attack both Spanish groups before they could rejoin forces. While Montenegro navigated his men through the defiles of the hills descending from the Cordilleras, the natives waited patiently. Suddenly, war cries and arrows pierced the air, killing three Spaniards and wounding several others. The Spanish rallied, firing crossbows and charging the natives. After driving the enemy back, Montenegro countermarched in the direction of Pizarro.

However, the natives arrived at the village first, firing arrows at the Spaniards, who left the safety of their fortifications to fight in the open. The natives targeted Pizarro, who was wounded in seven places despite wearing armor. Pizarro retreated down a hill and was quickly surrounded by the enemy, but his soldiers rescued him. At this crucial point of battle, Montenegro appeared and hit the enemy in the rear, sending them into the mountains. The tactical Spanish victory left five Spaniards dead and several wounded. An unknown but greater number of native warriors perished.

With a battered ship and wounded men to care for, Pizarro decided to return to Panama with items of gold, hoping to convince the governor to approve another expedition. The Battle of Punta Quemada was the expedition's first violent encounter with the natives. The Spanish victory provided Pizarro and his allies with confidence to launch future larger and deadlier campaigns.

Jeff Ewen

See also: Almagro, Diego de; Pizarro, Francisco;.

Resources

Gabai, Rafael Varón. *Francisco Pizarro and His Brothers: The Illusion of Power in Sixteenth-Century Peru.* Translated by Javier Flores Espinoza. Norman: University of Oklahoma Press, 1997.

Prescott, William. *History of the Conquest of Peru.* Vol. 1. London: Richard Bentley, 1850.

Quechua Language

Quechua, Runa Simi, or runasimi, is a primarily oral indigenous language family spoken principally in the central Andes of South America, including the countries of Argentina, Bolivia, Chile, Colombia, Ecuador, and Peru. Alongside Spanish, it is one of the official languages of Bolivia and Peru. The Incas called their language Runa Simi or runasimi that was later renamed Quechua by colonial Spanish settlers in the 1500s. This was an adaption from the indigenous word *qicwa*, meaning "temperate valley" and referring to areas in the Andes used for maize cultivation. There are an estimated 10 million speakers of the Quechua language, making it the mostly widely spoken indigenous language in the Americas.

The oldest forms of Quechua were used in Cajamarquilla, Lima. The oldest written records of the language, referred to as *quichua,* are written by missionary Domingo de Santo Tomás (1499–1570) in Peru in 1538 after he had previously learned the language in Lima. He later compiled the first Quechua grammar guide, *Grammatica o arte de la lengua general de los reynos de Perú,* and the first book printed in the language. Santo Tomás's works perpetuated the mythical and incorrect origin of the language with the Quechua-speaking people from modern Andahuaylas. Rather, from Lima, the use of the language grew and it was actively employed as a means to unify the Inca Empire. This means that Quechua existed prior to the Incas. Though Quechua consisted of a diverse group of dialects, many of which still

exist, its use grew and spread, shaping other indigenous languages such as Mapudungun. Following the Spanish conquest, Quechua was used as the main means of communication between the incoming Spaniards and the Indigenous population, including clergy of the Roman Catholic Church. This adoption as the lingua franca led to the continued expansion and use of the language. Some other written forms of the language include plays, poems quoted in predominantly Spanish texts, and the *Huarchiri Manuscript* written in 1598, describing the mythology and religion of the valley of Huarchiri. Quechua was banned from public use in Peru in the late 1700s in response to the Túpac Amaru II rebellion in 1780.

Because of Quechua's many dialects, it is considered a language family as opposed to a single language. Classification of all the different kinds of Quechua is complicated, particularly as it lacks written materials and remains a primarily oral tradition. However, Quechua 1, or Quechua B, or Central Quechua of Waywash is spoken primarily in central Peru and along its coast, from Ancach to Huancayo. Varieties include Conchucos, Huaylas, and Huayalla Wanca. Quechua II, or Quechua A, or Peripheral Quechua or Wanp'una, meaning "traveler," can divided into more subsections where Yungay Quechua or Quechua II A is spoken in the mountains of Peru featuring Cajamarca as its most widely used dialect. This second division also featured Northern Quechua, also known as Runashimi, or Quechua II B spoken in Columbia (referred to as Inga Kichwa), Ecuador (referred to there as Kichwa), and northern Peru. The most used dialects of this division are Chimborazo Highland Quichua and Imbabura Quichua. The final division in this particular linguistic system is Southern Quechua, or Quechua II C, spoken in Argentina, Bolivia, Chile, and the south of Peru. The dialectics most used from this final division are Ayacucho, Cuzco, Puna, and South Bolivian. This final division encompasses the largest number of speakers and most of the limited written sources of the language that do exist. Though linguists sometimes disagree on where various dialects should fall in any given classification system, most do adhere to a basic division of central and peripheral largely based on geographical branches of the language. Since the Spanish conquest of the Inca Empire in the mid-1500s the limited writing of Quechua has been done using the Roman alphabet. Unlike many colonial romance languages, like Spanish, Quechua's adjectives are not gendered and used to describe people like a possession as opposed to an identity.

Quechua words appear in languages like Aymara and Spanish because of extensive long-term contact. These languages bear many similarities, including only having three vowel sounds of a, i, and u. Some Spanish has also been added to the Quechua vocabulary such as "bwenu" from "bueno" and "burru" from "burro." Contemporary Quechua features about 30 percent Spanish words. Further, some Quechua words have worked their way into English via Spanish including, but not limited to, coca, jerky, llama, and quinoa.

Mary Shearman

See also: Lima; Santo Tomás, Domingo de.

Resources

Adelaar, William F.H. *The Languages of the Andes (Cambridge Language Surveys).*
Cambridge: Cambridge University Press, 2007.

Nuckolls, Janis B. *Lessons from a Quechua Strongwoman: Ideophony, Dialogue and Perspective.* Tucson: The University of Arizona Press, 2010.

Quetzalcoatl

Worshipped by at least three Mexican civilizations—the Teotihuacán, the Toltec, and the Aztec—Quetzalcoatl was one of the most important gods of Mesoamerica. The god's name has many different meanings. For example, one translation of Quetzalcoatl is "feathered serpent," as a colorful bird called a quetzal inhabits Mexico and Guatemala. However, the word *quetzal* can be translated as meaning feathered or precious. An alternative translation of the deity's name is "precious twin," as the word *coatl* translates as both serpent and twin. This variety of meaning reflects the many different forms by which Quetzalcoatl was worshipped, including a green-feathered serpent and an emperor-priest. Quetzalcoatl is also associated with wind and rain, agriculture and fertility. Comparable to Jesus in Christian teaching, Quetzalcoatl was born to a virgin, Chilmalman, who conceived when God, in the form of Citlallatonac, breathed upon her. From birth Quetzalcoatl was endowed with adult qualities of speech and wisdom and grew up to be beautiful and cultured, educating his peoples in the arts, originating their calendars and providing the knowledge to grow grain.

One of the most popular incarnations of Quetzalcoatl was as an Aztec creator-god. In the Aztec cycle of creation the current world was the fifth to be created. It was believed that Quetzalcoatl made the previous world, which was destroyed by a great flood

Carving of Quetzalcoatl, dominant Aztec and Mayan deity, depicted as a plumed serpent. (Corel)

as punishment for its avaricious inhabitants. Another myth tells how Quetzalcoatl created humans to populate the fifth world, for he stole corn from the ants in order to feed his people and then traveled to Mictlan, the underworld, where he stole skeletal remains. Quetzalcoatl then pierced his penis with the bones and used his blood to fashion the remains into living humans.

In a third myth Quetzalcoatl joined with the god of the heavens, Tezcatlipoca, to create the world. The story tells how the two deities pulled apart the monstrous goddess Tlaltecuhtli, with her head and shoulders becoming the earth and her body the sky. However the best-known myth involving Quetzalcoatl sees him at the mercy of the sinister Tezcatlipoca. This myth tells how Quetzalcoatl took the form of an emperor-priest among the people of the Toltec city of Tula. There he taught the people many

useful things including farming, weaving, and writing. Also, as a benevolent god, Quetzalcoatl prohibited human sacrifice. Tezcatlipoca opposed Quetzalcoatl's rule and in revenge planted in Quetzalcoatl's heart a fear of aging, encouraging the god to imbibe an intoxicating elixir of rejuvenation. Under the influence of this liquor, Quetzalcoatl raped his sister. One version of the myth says that after this transgression, Quetzalcoatl committed suicide by jumping upon a funeral pyre. An alternative version tells that Quetzalcoatl remained as ruler of Tula only for Tezcatlipoca to destroy the Toltec people. With his subjects dead Quetzalcoatl razed his lands and ordered birds to leave the realm.

Both versions of the myth agree that Quetzalcoatl then left Tula, vowing to return, bringing with him peace and light. Subsequently Quetzalcoatl journeyed to the

Atlantic Ocean and sailed toward the sun where his body was consumed by fire with his heart ascending heavenward to become the planet Venus, also known as the Morning Star. As Venus, Quetzalcoatl became a figure of ambivalence, for the Aztecs believed that the sun and stars opposed each other for the sun rose only when the stars faded. Thus the Aztecs feared that one day the stars might overcome the sun, depriving them of sunlight. However, the Aztecs also thought that the Morning Star was benevolent in that it lifted the sun into the sky.

It has been suggested that Quetzalcoatl may have been a real Toltec ruler, for around 950 CE the emperor-priest Topiltzin adopted the name Quetzalcoatl and relocated the Toltec capital to Tula where he instigated a moral way of life. Another mortal said to have been taken to be Quetzalcoatl incarnate was Hernán Cortés, a Spanish conquistador. Aztec seers expected Quetzalcoatl to return from the dead but did not know when this would happen, only understanding that the resurrection would occur in a *Ce Acatl* or One Reed, that is, a year in the Mexican calendar that arrives once in every 52 cycles. Cortés happened to land on the Gulf Coast in a One Reed and was taken by some, including the emperor Montezuma II, to be the reincarnation of Quetzalcoatl. This interpretation of Quetzalcoatl's return was not uniform among the Aztec imperial family, as Montezuma II's brother and successor, Cuitláhuac, rejected connections between the Spanish conquerors and the return of Quetzalcoatl.

Victoria Williams

See also: Aztec, or Mexica; Cortés, Hernán; Montezuma II; Tezcatlipoca.

Resources

Haase, Donald, ed. *The Greenwood Encyclopedia of Folktales and Fairy Tales: Volume One A–F.* Westport, CT: Greenwood Press, 2008.

Leeming, David Adams. *Mythology: The Voyage of the Hero.* Oxford: Oxford University Press, 1998.

Portilla, Miguel León. *Native Mesoamerican Spirituality: Ancient Myths, Discourses, Stories, Doctrines, Hymns, Poems from the Aztec, Yucatec, Quiche-Maya and Other Sacred Traditions.* Mahwah, NJ: Paulist Press, 1980.

Scott Littleton, C., ed. *Gods, Goddesses, and Mythology.* Vol. 11. New York: Marshall Cavendish Corporation, 2005.

Quiahuiztlan

Quiahuiztlan is a fortified archaeological site located on the flanks of the eastern terminus of the Sierra Madre Oriental in central Veracruz, Mexico. Specifically, Quiahuiztlan is situated on a volcanic hill that is known locally as the Cerro de los Metates. Quiahuiztlan was occupied as early as the Epiclassic period (ca. 850) and through the arrival of Spanish conquistadors in 1519. During the Late Post-Classic period (ca. 1200–1519), Quiahuiztlan was incorporated within the Aztec imperial province Cempoallan, governed from the nearby Totonac center of Zempoala. In addition to serving as a frontier post for Cempoallan, Quiahuiztlan provided some protection for the salt-producing estuaries along the coast.

The archaeological site was constructed on a series of natural and artificial terraces. Site components at Quiahuiztlan included residential structures, agricultural fields, and a ceremonial complex. The latter contained a ball court, one- and two-story temple platforms, plazas, and several stucco and stone tombs in the form of miniature temples. These tombs contained secondary burials placed in ceramic vessels. Few other sites in the region have similar tombs, leading some archaeologists to suggest that these represent native imitations of Spanish-style mausolea. Such Spanish burials were observed during the first years of the encounter and were used to inter the Totonac elite who died during the initial wave of smallpox to hit the Gulf coastal population.

Apart from these miniature temple tombs and its spectacular view of the coast, Quiahuiztlan is perhaps best known for hosting events that proved pivotal in the Spanish conquest of Mexico. It was at Quiahuiztlan that Hernán Cortés convinced the native Totonacs to imprison the Aztec officials who oversaw imperial activities in the province. It was on the beach just northeast of Quiahuiztlan that the Spanish established the 16th-century settlement, Villa Rica.

Marcie L. Venter

See also: Cortés, Hernán; Totonacs, Alliance with Spanish; Zempoala.

Resources

Berdan, F. F. et al., eds. *Aztec Imperial Strategies.* Washington, DC: Dumbarton Oaks Research Library and Collection, 1996.

Diaz del Castillo, Bernal. *The Discovery and Conquest of Mexico: 1517–1521.* Translated by A. P. Maudslay. New York: Da Capo Press, 2003.

Evans, Susan Toby, and David L. Webster, eds. *Archaeology of Ancient Mexico and Central America, an Encyclopedia.* New York: Garland Publishing, 2001.

Hassig, Ross. *Mexico and the Spanish Conquest.* Norman: University of Oklahoma Press, 2006.

Quipu

The Inca population, though often considered a civilization lacking a written language, possessed a complex system of recording records and information. The system, known as *quipus* (khipus), consisted of threads of Llama wool died a variety of colors and tied into a series of knots. The rows of threads, knots and loops each represented arithmetical units and other categories that enable the interpreter to recall specific data. The Spanish never understood this difficult system of cataloging data and eventually banned its usage.

Pre-Columbian record keeping of the Inca and non-Inca people of Peru utilized this novel system of recording data and historical information. From the analysis of Spanish clerics such as Cristóbal Molina who knew the Quechua language well, the system noted phrases, sounds, and symbols, but in a manner never mastered by the Spanish. Indeed, while the usage of *quipus* was

A *quipu* made in Peru circa 1430–1532, used by Inca to record information and data. (Werner Forman/Corbis)

widespread, mastery of the system was limited to a select few known as *Quipocamayos* (*quipu* masters). In Pre-Columbian Peruvian society, these skilled specialists were part of a privileged class, responsible for compiling and reciting data on crop yields, storage, mine productivity and other resource records for the entire Inca Empire. Even the quantity of available men for armed service in each village was immediately available through the *Quipocamayos*. José de Acosta, a Jesuit Priest in post-conquest Peru, asserted that the complex writing system was also employed by women, who utilized the "threads" or system of simple *quipus* to record their sins for recitation in the confessional, and elders studying the new Catholic faith used the method to document elements of the catechism.

In the first century following the arrival of the Spanish, *quipus* were used as an integral part of record keeping. When combined with the oral traditions of historical and public record keeping, the end result was phenomenally accurate. Damage to crops and homes, perpetuated by the Spanish in the armed conflict between the invaders and the indigenous population, was documented through the *quipus*. With the Spanish rise to power, *quipus* were used to help gather and transfer data regarding tributes, demographics and productivity throughout the Empire.

In the process of accomplishing his tasks of removing the influence of the Pizarros, restoring the economy, and undermining the authority of the Inca emperors, Toledo employed the services and records of *Quipocamayos*. The Viceroy lifted these indigenous record keepers to the status of assistant scribes. The precision of the native records in the form of *quipus* resulted in their use by Toledo's judges and in his accounting records for tributes as he restructured the Spanish bureaucracy. Under Toledo, the *quipus* were

regulated, with indigenous administrators required to maintain specific types of records through the use of the cords. In this, his theorist and assistant, Juan de Matienzo, guided Toledo's policy. Every six months the native or Spanish supervisors were required to send reports, either in writing or through *quipus*, of all the recent numbers of deaths, births, new eighteen year olds eligible for tribute and fighting, as well as records of any indigenous people who fled Spanish districts. The efficiency of the system assisted the Spanish in documenting the revenues and potential of Peru as a continued Spanish colony.

Toledo's official court historian, Pedro Sarmiento de Gamboa, interviewed some *quipu* masters for the construction of his *History of the Incas,* designed to justify the conquest and control of the Spanish and undermine the legitimacy of the Inca imperial claims to power. However, there is little evidence that Gamboa sought or used the data from the *quipus* so much as he sought specific answers to questions regarding the longevity of Inca rule in the region, as well as any abusive, oppressive or questionable practices (incestuous relations within the royal Inca families) that would rationalize the transfer of authority from the indigenous Inca rulers to the new Spanish conquerors. This subjective method of research was quite effective when using the collective knowledge of the *quipu* masters. The Inca method of recording focused more on numerical data and statistics that were of great concern to the Incas—not on a chronological, calendric record of governance that was sought by the Spanish to document the recent ascent of the Inca to power.

While Toledo and his administration made widespread usage of the *quipus* for their assessment and restructuring of Spanish bureaucracy in Peru, the system soon fell out of favor. The inability for the Spanish to comprehend and control the data and records, combined with the need for increased revenues to reduce the crushing debt experienced by Spain, contributed to a decision to diminish colonial dependence on this native method of record keeping. The declining reliance upon *quipu* masters correlated to the rise in Spanish scribes and notaries within the colonial bureaucracy. The final blow to the usage and survival of *quipus* came with the decision of the Third Council of Lima whose fears of non-Christian Incas use of *quipus* to track offerings to their pagan deities resulted in the order to discontinue their use in record keeping and to destroy *quipus* in the colony of Peru.

Rebecca M Seaman

See also: Quechua Language; Sarmiento's *History of the Incas;* Toledo, Francisco de.

Resources

Davies, Nigel. *The Incas.* Niwot: University of Colorado Press, 1995.

Hemming, John. *The Conquest of the Incas.* New York: Harcourt Brace Javonovich, Inc., 1970.

Lockhart, James and Stuart B Schwartz. *Early Latin America: A History of Colonial Spanish America and Brazil.* Cambridge: Cambridge University Press, 1999.

Salomon, Frank. *The Cord Keepers: Khipus and Cultural Life in a Peruvian Village.* Durham, NC: Duke University Press, 2004.

Quizquiz

A well-trusted general of the Sapa Inca Atahualpa, Quizquiz was one of three dominant military leaders among the Inca at the time of Francisco Pizarro's expedition into Peru in 1533. At that period in Inca history, the empire was recoiling from the sudden death of Huayna Cápac and the ensuing civil war over who would succeed him as the Sapa Inca. The elder of the two heirs, Huáscar, had support from the more southerly region of the empire. After a period of almost five years, he lost the contest for power and the younger brother, Atahualpa, was recognized as the new Inca. Atahualpa's military experience, from years of fighting along the northernmost frontiers near Quito, and the excellent services of his loyal general, Quizquiz, brought him success in the civil war.

It was into this situation that the Spanish brought further division. Initially, they captured Atahualpa and held him hostage, demanding large quantities of gold. When the requested ransom was paid, the Spanish insisted the Sapa Inca had used his influence to turn the Inca population against Pizarro's men. With this justification, Atahualpa was executed. The act reignited the struggle for power in Peru, and placed Quizquiz firmly on the side opposed to the Spanish. Descendants of Huáscar contested the seat of authority over Cuzco from the northern supporters and descendants of Atahualpa. Additionally, the remaining sons of Huayna Cápac—brothers to both Huáscar and Atahualpa—also desired to control the royal fringe. Pizarro played all sides of the equation in an effort to divide the numerically superior Incas and provide an opportunity for the Spanish to acquire wealth and influence.

Following Atahualpa's death, Quizquiz transferred his loyalty to the heirs of his dead monarch, in particular to Atahualpa's little brother, Paullu. Though the Spanish were vastly outnumbered, the internal division among the Inca and the novelty of Spanish horses, military weaponry and strategies swung the contest in the direction of the invaders. Not until the battle of Vilcaconga did the Inca under Quizquiz's leadership effectively use the rugged terrain to exploit the vulnerability of the Spanish and their horses. Even then, Quizquiz neglected to trap Pizarro's forces at the numerous river crossings, narrow valleys, and steep inclines. Additionally, when the Spanish retreated from effective military attacks under the Inca general, the advantage was lost because Quizquiz suspected the withdrawal was a deception.

During the first year of struggles between the Spanish and Incas, Pizarro recognized the need to keep the Incas unified who had opposed Atahualpa and any of his heirs ascending the seat of authority. To this end, Pizarro presented a gathering of Inca leaders from the area of Cuzco with the plausible suggestions of Túpac Huallpa, eldest surviving son of Huayna Cápac. With a compliant Inca on the throne, Pizarro was able to isolate the forces of the dead Atahualpa. This act also effectively ended Quizquiz's attempts to destroy the house of Huáscar, since that house was no longer in contention for the Inca royal fringe. With an acknowledged Inca providing a unifying point for the empire, Pizarro used Quizquiz's military defense of Cuzco as justification to "liberate" the city from its northern occupation.

Once Pizarro held the capital city of Cuzco, his strategy of dealing with the resisting opposition changed. One of Quizquiz's fellow generals, Chalcuchima, had died in the struggle. Only Quizquiz and his "invaders" from the more northerly region of Quito posed a serious threat to rising Spanish influence. To increase his influence, Francisco Pizarro took advantage of the sudden death of Túpac Huallpa to recognize another son of Huayna Cápac, Manco Inca Yupanqui, for the royal fringe, appointing him as a puppet emperor. The new ruler was encouraged by Pizarro to use his newfound authority to raise an army of Incas and allies for the purpose of expelling the Quitan invaders that threatened Cuzco.

No longer possessing vastly superior numbers in opposition to the scattered forces of Pizarro, Quizquiz was compelled to retreat into the mountainous western region of the empire, the Contisuyu. Though Quizquiz's forces were better led, the shifting tides and repeated defeats took their toll. Years of centralized stores of goods, scattered around the empire, were depleted from the civil wars. While the extensive stores of the capital city remained well provisioned, those along the more distant frontiers were exhausted, leaving little to provide for Quizquiz's forces.

With the start of 1534, the Spanish held Cuzco, Jauja, and the coastal city of San Miguel de Piura. Meanwhile, Quizquiz's forces were divided, with approximately half in Quito to the far north, and the other half, under Quizquiz, in the mountains of Contisuyu. The victorious armies that had defeated Huáscar under Atahualpa just a year previous now numbered 20,000—but had lost the momentum of victory. Instead, with his army clamoring to return home to the region of Quito, all Quizquiz could muster was a half-hearted attack on Jauja as they traveled northward toward their homes.

Even in defeat Quizquiz displayed excellent leadership abilities. Covering over 1,000 miles of exceedingly rugged terrain, the general managed to retain a fighting force of well over 12,000 men. He additionally oversaw the escort of camp followers, herds of llamas and other animals, food stores, and other necessities for a traveling force. Meanwhile, his forces effectively practiced a scorched earth policy designed to slow the pursuit of Manco Inca and his Spanish allies. Instead, the Spanish and their southerly Inca allies blocked Quizquiz's route of escape toward Quito. His final attempts to rally his forces backfired. Rebellious officers, desiring nothing more than to return to their homes, refused to fight. One struck Quizquiz with a lance, while others followed up by attacking the fallen general with their clubs and other weapons. His death ended the initial phase of Spanish conquest over the Incas, and provided a model for later resistance movements in years to come.

Rebecca M Seaman

See also: Atahualpa; Contisuyu; Cuzco; Huáscar; Huayna Cápac; Manco Inca Yupanqui; Paullu Inca; Pizarro, Francisco; Sapa Inca; Túpac Huallpa.

Resources

Davies, Nigel. *The Incas.* Niwot: University of Colorado Press, 1995.

Eakin, Marshall, C. *The History of Latin America: Collision of Cultures.* New York: Palgrave MacMillan, 2007.

Hemming, John. *The Conquest of the Incas.* New York: Harcourt Brace Jovanovich, Inc., 1970.

MacQuarrie, Kim. *The Last Days of the Incas.* New York: Simon & Schuster, 2007.

Sanchez, Pedro. *An Account of the Conquest of Peru.* New York: The Cortes Society, 1917.

R

Reconquista, Impact of on Spanish Policy in America

Reconquista is an eight-century-long conflict in Spain between Spaniards and Moors, which had implications for the later Spanish conquest of the Americas. In 711, Muslim Moors from North Africa crossed the Strait of Gibraltar and invaded Spain, driving Christian Spaniards to the far north of the peninsula. For nearly 800 years, Spanish forces slowly fought their way south. The Spanish Reconquest, or Reconquista, was completed when Spaniards captured Granada in January 1492, the last Moorish stronghold in Spain.

Later in that same year, Christopher Columbus sailed west, funded by the Spanish Crown, and seemingly discovered the Americas. The momentum created by centuries of fighting in Spain carried over to the Western Hemisphere as Spanish explorers and settlers followed Columbus's path and colonized the New World. Many scholars believe the experience of the Reconquista had significant impact socially, economically, politically, and religiously on Spanish policy in the settling of the Americas.

The Spaniards' Reconquista strategy was to quickly populate areas occupied by Moors as they pushed south. Similarly, Spaniards set to work building cities in the New World to control the areas seized by conquest from the Native Americans. The social conditions were similar in both cases, as the Spanish did not remove the previous residents, and thus had to learn to live alongside people of a different ethnicity and religion. During the long Reconquista, Spaniards developed a severe dislike for non-Spaniards, and this experience affected their opinion of indigenous peoples in the Americas, whom most Spaniards viewed as inferior.

During the Reconquista, Spanish knights did much of the work of retaking Spain, hoping to make a name for themselves and claim the economic rewards of land and labor. Two systems of labor were particularly important: slavery and encomiendas. Many Spanish commanders enslaved captured Moors or acquired slaves through other means to farm the land, which Spaniards viewed as lowly work. The other choice was the encomienda, a grant of labor given to a noble by the Crown, allowing that noble the services of a certain number of free workers. After the Reconquista, many Spaniards continued their quest for financial gain in the New World, replicating both labor systems there.

For most of the Reconquista, the Spanish political system consisted of a number of small independent Christian kingdoms, and thus there was no centralized effort to reclaim the entire peninsula. Monarchs authorized Spanish knights to recapture much of the land in exchange for paying royal taxes. Moorish leaders were sometimes allowed to stay after their defeat, but as vassals. In the Americas, similar political arrangements were made. Spanish colonizers, authorized by the Crown, did much of the exploring and settling, paying taxes on what they acquired. Eventually, the Crown established viceroyalties in the Americas, but these operated with a great deal of independence. Native cities remained, but as vassals to the Spanish.

Though economic motivations dominated, the Reconquista and the conquest of the Americas were conducted with the understanding that Christianity was being spread, at least in theory. To make sure religious integrity was maintained, the Inquisition, a trial to root out heresy, was introduced on either side of the Atlantic. Also in both cases, religious orders and monasteries often preceded other Spaniards in settling a new area.

The Reconquista ended in 1492. Nonetheless, the Spanish conquest of the New World occurred within the context of that centuries-long struggle, perpetuating the same policies and ideals for another three centuries.

John Laaman

See also: Columbus, Christopher; Encomienda; Jesuit Order, Role of; Slavery, Role of; Tribute, Paid to Spain; Viceroyalty System.

Resources

Elliott, J.H. *Spain, Europe, and the Wider World, 1500–1800.* New Haven, CT: Yale University Press, 2009.

Hassig, Ross. *Mexico and the Spanish Conquest.* 2nd ed. Norman: University of Oklahoma Press, 2006.

McCreery, David J. *The Sweat of Their Brow: A History of Work in Latin America.* Armonk, NY: M. E. Sharpe, 2000.

Religion, of Pre-Conquest Aztec

The religious system of beliefs, practiced by the Aztecs in central Mexico before the Spanish arrived, affected absolutely all spheres of life. The Aztec belief system regulated the actions and behavior of all strata of the population. The ancient Mexica religion belonged to a common system of beliefs practiced in Mesoamerica, which had common cosmogonic vision, rituals, myths, gods, and calendars. The different cultures incorporated certain peculiarities to make each version slightly unique.

The Aztec culture was theocratic, so, both the political administration and the legislation that guided social life were based on divine principles. Religion did not manifest itself in an unitarian way. Instead, it could be divided into two main sectors: the official or public, and the popular or private. To the first one corresponded the great public ceremonies, the prestigious priesthood, the temples, the sacrifices, the myths, and the calendar. These explained the world—its origin, composition, and operation—and served to perpetuate the hierarchical social order.

Conversely, private religiosity manifested itself in the presence of figurines of gods in each house, in the consultations of the priests who read the calendars to guess the character of the days and the daily prayers to propitiate different actions. One difference between the two areas lay in the belief in multiple gods. Ordinary Aztec citizenry tended to exaggerate polytheism because of the belief in magic, in occult and impersonal forces, and therefore conceived these forces as various gods. These same diverse forces were considered by priests as invocations of the same god.

The Mesoamerican world was composed of various elements that combined to form both an horizontal and a vertical understanding of the universe. The horizontal universe was composed by the directions north, south, east, and west, as well as the center. Each direction was associated with gods, trees, birds, and colors. The vertical universe was formed by the surface of the Earth, the Heavens, and the Underworld. The last two were understood to be staggered in 13 and 9 floors, respectively. Each level of Heaven was associated with a god, and each of the Underworld with a proof that the deceased had to overcome to get to *Mictlan* (the place of the Dead).

The primordial god was *Ometeotl* (God two), composed by *Ometecuhtli* (Lord two), and *Ometecihuatl* (Lady two), and resided in *Omeyocan*, the Place of Duality. This pair represented the primordial duality, a fundamental principle in Mesoamerica. The creator couple had four children, called the four *Tezcatlipocas* (Red, White, Black, and Blue).

The fate of the people in the Underworld was characterized by the way in which each one died rather than by their behavior in life, because the misconduct of citizens was punished by a strict penal code. Those who died of natural death went to *Mictlan*, after passing severe challenges on the different floors of the Underworld. Warriors killed in combat, the sacrificed, and women who died in childbirth went to the Paradise of the Sun. Those elected by *Tlaloc*, the god of waters, who were drowned, were struck by lightning, or died of diseases related to water (such as leprosy), went to *Tlalocan*, the closest place to Christian paradise. There was also a place similar to Limbo where the children, under the age where they could eat corn, went. Life for the Aztecs was ephemeral, so they did not conceive the idea of an eternal afterlife.

The natural world was well known by the Aztecs and was also related to the religious sphere. Most gods were associated with terrestrial phenomena and stars visible in the sky. The Sun and the Moon were also the primordial couple, and they were given different names according to their functions. The Sun was male, and was called *Tonatiuh, Nahui Ollin, Nanahuatzin, Huitzilopochtli,* and *Tezcatlipoca*. The Moon was female and was named *Metztli* or *Tecuziztecatl*. The third star in importance was Venus, called *Hueycitlalin* (Big Star) or *Tlahuizcalpantecuhtli* (Lord of the House of Dawn).

The psychic functions of humans were also interpreted within the Aztec worldview. People had a *tonalli,* light or heat, associated with a calendar date and a fate, which could be counteracted by their actions. The *tonalli* was a force involving gods, animals, plants, and things. This force seemed to be represented in what appears to be a breath, located in the head. When *tonalli* "had escaped," it could cause serious illness and death. A second force was the *teyolia* (what makes people live), identified with the "soul," which went to the abode of the dead. This second force was related to the heart. The third force, or the *ihiyotl,* was located in the liver, where the life, vigor, passion, feeling, craving, desire, and greed resided in Aztec people.

A special feature of Aztec religion was the integration of differing belief systems. The different peoples accepted the local gods of others, and built temples and worshipped them. Consequently, the pantheon grew as they conquered new territories. The gods were represented in anthropomorphic form, with specific attributes and attires. An important feature of Aztec deities was their multiplicity: each god was one and at the same time two or more, young and old, male and female, good and bad. For this reason, it is very difficult to classify the gods of the Aztec pantheon into a group.

Some of the most important deities included Creator gods, Sun gods, as well as gods of water, earth, fertility, and others. The Creator god, *Ometeotl,* split into *Ometecuhtli* and *Omecihuatl,* or with other names like *Tonacatecutli* (Lord of our sustenance) and *Tonacacihuatl* (Lady of our sustenance). The Sun gods included *Tezcatlipoca* with its many aspects. The *Black Tezcatlipoca* (Smoking Mirror) ruled over the night sky, associated with death and the north, and he is the patron of sorcerers. The *White Tezcatlipoca* is Quetzalcoatl (Feathered Serpent), god of civilization, of the west, of the air (under the *Ehecatl* form) and of life. The *Blue Tezcatlipoca* was called Huitzilopochtli and was the tribal Aztec god, associated with the south. He was the god of Sun, war, and sacrifice. The *Red Tezcatlipoca* was *Xipe Totec,* associated with the east, with fire, and with fertility and renewal. *Tonatiuh* (He who gives heat) was the Sun as the solar disk, and *Cihuacoatl* (Snake Woman) was the goddess of the growers of medicinal herbs.

Aztec gods of the waters referenced differing forms of water in the environment. *Tlaloc* was one of the oldest gods in Mesoamerica, and although he traditionally was considered "God of Rain," he was a deity of water and earth. His female counterpart was *Chalchiuhtlicue* (the skirt of jade), associated with surface water. Also, there were many gods of the different aspects of water, such as the rain, running water, stagnant water, rivers, and springs.

Among Aztec gods of fertility, *Cinteotl* (God of Maize) was one of the main gods. The various gods of fertility presided over the singing and playing, embodying the awakening of nature, beauty, and love. The gods of earth were tied to the gods of water, vegetation, and fertility, but had warrior characteristics. Among the other important deities, *Coyolxauhqui* (The one with rattles in the face) was a female part of the Moon who was associated with birth and fertility, with the things than renew themselves periodically, with menstruation and drunkenness. *Mixcoatl* (Snake of Clouds) was the god of the North Star, representing the Milky Way, related to the warriors killed in battle or sacrificed.

The Aztec religious life was manifested by external acts or rituals. The ceremonies were very elaborate and had different levels. Whether public or private, communal or personal, such rituals were held in large temples, or in temples of neighborhoods or houses.

In everyday life, the Aztecs were aware of multiple signals related to the behavior of the gods, signals often enshrined in the sphere of superstition. The good or bad omens also were associated with animals and with cooking practices. The Aztecs also believed in different types of ghosts appearing at night. To mitigate the negative results of these phenomena, they had to perform little rituals. Frequently such acts consisted in sweeping the floor and making offerings of fire and *copal* (a type of incense). They also fasted, abstained, and performed acts of self-sacrifice, offering up their own blood and the blood of animals. Human sacrifice was performed at great fiesta and special moments and took place in the main temples. Music and dancing accompanied every celebration.

Religious and civil life was governed by the calendar called Calendar Round. It consisted of two cycles: *tonalpohualli* ("count of the days" or "fate account"; a divinatory calendar consisting of 260 days, the result of combining the numbers from 1 to 13 with 20 names of days) and *xiuhpohualli* ("account of the year"; the ritual or solar calendar consisting of 365 days divided into 18 months of 20 days plus a short cycle of five days). According to this system, there were two types of religious festivals: the "fixed" festivals related to the *xiuhpohualli* and the "mobile" festivals linked to the *tonalpohualli*. Each of the months was associated with one or more gods, to which were made several elaborate ceremonies, especially when professional groups worshipped their patron gods.

In the private sphere, every moment of the life cycle was commemorated with a ceremony, which counted with the presence of relatives and friends. Priests of different types and range took part in all of these ceremonies.

Marta Martín Gabaldón

See also: Aztec, or Mexica; Calendar System of Aztec; Huitzilopochtli; Mexico, State of prior to Spanish Conquest.

Resources

Aguilar-Moreno, Manuel. *Handbook to Life in the Aztec World.* New York: Facts on File, 2006.

Batalla Rosado, Juan José y José Luis de Rojas. *La religión azteca.* Madrid: Editorial Trotta and Universidad de Granada, 2008.

Burland, Cottie A. *The Aztecs: Gods and Fate in Ancient Mexico.* New York: Galahad Press, 1980.

Nicholson, Henri B. "Religion in pre-Hispanic central Mexico." In *Handbook of Middle American Indians,* Vol. 10, edited by Robert Wauchope, 395–446. Austin: University of Texas Press.

Sahagún, Bernardino de. *Florentine Codex: General History of the Things of New Spain.* 12 books. Translated and edited by Arthur J. O. Anderson and Charles E. Dibble. Santa Fe, NM, and Salt Lake City, UT: School of American Research and the University of Utah Press, 1950–1982.

Smith, Michael E. *The Aztecs.* Oxford: Blackwell, 1996.

Religion, of Pre-Conquest Inca

The Incas had a polytheistic belief system and worshipped an immense number of gods, spirits, and deities. They believed their gods lived in heaven, as well as some on earth and in nature. Each deity had a specific purpose, which determined its position in the spiritual hierarchy. The Inca practiced an anthropomorphic faith, imbuing some of their gods with human behavior, as well as feelings of love, hatred, compassion, and other human emotions. The Incas also believed that their gods caused natural phenomena; therefore it was essential to keep these powerful beings happy so that natural disasters could be avoided.

As an animistic faith system, the Incas practiced a form of ancestral worship, which is understood best through the application of panacas. Descendents of the Incas formed family groups, known as panacas. The members of these extended family units were tasked with maintaining the achievements, stories, and holdings of the deceased Inca. Part of this process included the care for the Inca's mummy *(malquis).* Normally housed in cool caves or special structures, the mummies were brought out and paraded in public on important occasions. Members of the panacas dressed these mummies, carried them on platforms, and kept them safe. The lands of the mummies were tended by the panacas servants and slaves, and helped support the continued existence of the Inca's family for the purpose of continuing to immortalize his life.

Huacas, sacred elements of the Inca faith, are another complex component of Inca spirituality. The huacas included holy places or temples where the Incas made offerings to their gods in an effort to please or appease them. The breadth of meaning for this term resulted in a variety of identified sacred objects. Geological features such as oddly formed rocks, streams, and mountains were included in the huacas classification. Sites associated with human activity, such as ruins and battlefields, also qualified as huacas. In the central capital of Cuzco, over 330 huacas were worshiped. Diagrams of radiating lines mapped the location of the sacred sites, radiating outward from the central temple of Coricancha in Cuzco, which was dedicated to the Sun god of the Incas.

Religion of the Inca was dominated by ritual offerings to the sun. (Bettmann/Corbis)

There were two major deities worshipped by the Inca: Inti, also known as Apu-Punchao, and Viracocha. Inti, the Sun, was the supreme god and was honored with the most important feast days in the Inca civilization. Inti was the father of the Sapa Inca, or unique Inca/emperor, who represented the Sun god in human form on earth and shared his sacredness. Indeed, the Sapa Inca confessed his sins directly to Inti, though this was to seek intercession before Viracocha. Symbols associated with the sun, like a huge golden solar disk, were carefully guarded and displayed by the Sapa Inca, capturing the sun's light, on special feast days and important occasions. During these ceremonies, the presiding priest was always the priest of Inti.

Viracocha, meaning "sea foam," was thought to be the creator, another supreme god, and the most powerful of the Inca deities. Though no name or direct power outside of creation was associated with Viracocha, this creator god was distinctly the primary Inca deity. This deity appeared in the inland site of Tiahuanaco at the beginning of time. Most myths of the creation god speak of an emergence out of Lake Titicaca, where he turned previous beings into stone and then created the sun and moon. New people, ostensibly the Inca, were formed from stone and placed at varying locations around what became the Inca Empire, including at the central city of Cuzco. Since evidence indicates the existence of Cuzco before the arrival of the Inca population, historians postulate that existing "primordial" mythology was manipulated by the Inca state to serve the needs of creating and controlling the empire.

Most scholars agree that the Sapa Inca Pachacutin (Pachacutec) was the architect of most strategic mythology regarding creation and Inca heroes noted at the time of the Spanish conquest. It was Pachacutin who ordered the construction of golden statues of the former Sapa Incas that were displayed in Coricancha. He also ordered the live burial of numerous boys and girls in front of the solar disk that was central to celebrating Inti. An additional statue of a boy, cast in gold, also resided in the Sun temple. It was this statue that was venerated by the Sapa Incas, and that presumably spoke to the emperors on occasion.

Sacred ceremonies were a major aspect of the Inca religion. One of the most unique aspects of the religious faith was the use of human sacrifices. These sacrifices were only performed during specific important events in the life of the Inca emperor, such as his illness, death, or the succession of a new emperor to the throne. In these instances, it was customary to perform sacrifices similar to that performed by Pachacutin in dedicating the Sun temple, namely the live burial of young children. More commonly, llamas were sacrificed on special feast days. White llamas were preferred for sacrifices to Inti. In all ceremonies, ritual fine textiles were used. To produce these materials, large numbers of *mamaconas,* or select females were employed in weaving fines cloth and robes, including the use of thread made of gold.

Certain religious ceremonies within the Inca faith contributed directly to the attempts to strengthen the political-economic system. Examples of this included the ceremonies associated with the worship of the thunder god, Illapa. Inclement weather patterns were interpreted as a sign that the local communities, specifically the *ayllu* lineages, had not proffered proper reverence and/or tribute to Illapa. As a consequence, the thunder god would punish the local *ayllus* with drought or torrential rains. Efforts to ward off such potential catastrophes required the presentation of offerings and participation in accepted rituals at the appropriate huacas for the regional *ayllus.* Each *ayllus* had its own huaca that was seen to preserve the members of the *ayllu.* Among the huacas worshipped were the mummies or *malquis* of the local population.

Also associated with local religious practices were the concepts of reciprocity relationships. These practices were quite complex and integrated the ideas of caring for the community through sharing, as well as confessing and forgiving of wrongs meted out by individual members of the *ayllus* over the course of the year. The community leaders or *kurakas* would oversee the gathering of goods intended in part to become offerings and gifts at a ceremony, but also as part of a collection system designed to provide for the needs of the community in times of need. The offerings were in the form of grains, cloth, beer, food, and other items of importance. During ritual ceremonies, offerings were made to a hierarchy of huacas and *malquis* of the *ayllu.* The daylong celebrations included feasting, dancing, targeted fasting (e.g., no salt or no sexual relations), storytelling, and other communal activities. As the celebration reached a peak, public confessions were made of sins committed by the various *ayllu* members. In return for acknowledging the error of one's ways, the expectation was for a designated "confessor" to symbolically forgive the sin. In so doing, rifts within the *ayllus* were mended and unity within the close-knit communities was preserved.

Collectively, religion played a dominant role throughout Inca society. The socioeconomic functions of religion were woven throughout the political economy. The power of the gods regarding material goods was seen in the hierarchical ranking of the ruling elites, and through the privileges bestowed upon those same elites.

Rebecca M. Seaman and
Monae S. Merck

See also: Christianity, Impact of on the Inca; Huacas; Human Sacrifice; Pachacutin; Sapa Inca.

Resources

Davies, Nigel. *The Incas.* Niwot: University of Colorado Press, 1995.

Hemming, John. *The Conquest of the Incas.* New York: Harcourt Brace Jovanovich, 1970.

MacQuarrie, Kim. *The Last Days of the Incas.* New York: Simon & Schuster, 2007.

Sancho, Pedro. *An Account of the Conquest of Peru.* New York: The Cortes Society, 1917.

Sarmento de Gamboa, Pedro. *History of the Incas.* Translated and edited by Sir Clements Markham. Cambridge: Hakluyt Society, 1907.

Stern, Steve J. *Peru's Indian Peoples and the Challenge of Spanish Conquest: Huamanga to 1640.* 2nd cd. Madison: University of Wisconsin Press, 1993.

Repartimiento

A labor system employed by the Spanish, the term repartimiento literally refers to the distribution or allotment of native laborers for use by landholders, miners, and others. With regard to the Spanish American colonies, the term originally applied to the official assignment of native laborers to Spanish colonial encomenderos. Within two decades of Spanish claims to the West Indies, the term was used interchangeably with encomienda. These terms eventually became legally distinct with the enactment

of Carlos I's New Laws in 1542. The New Laws placed increased restrictions on the use of native labor systems (enslavement, encomiendas, and repartimientos). By 1550, repartimiento became the dominant method of acquiring native laborers. The term was sometimes replaced with localized terms, such as *coatequitl* in New Spain and *mita* in Peru. Changing demographics from disease and abuses eventually made the practice virtually obsolete by 1632.

Originally repartimiento was the labor system employed for allocating Indian labor to the various encomenderos. The initial use of native laborers was deemed essential for the survival of the Spanish colonies. Queen Isabella's interest in the success of her colonies was balanced by her sincere interest in regulating better conditions for the Indians and better relations between the natives and Spanish. With her death, little effort was made to protect Native Americans from abusive treatment. Large numbers of natives were assigned as laborers, forced to work in fields and mines with little food. The exposure to diseases, harsh treatment, and conditions caused a massive decline in the indigenous population.

Dominican missionaries were sent to Hispaniola in 1510 to investigate increased evidence of inhumane conditions. Dominicans petitioned the courts for legal reforms to protect the Indians. In 1512, the Laws of Burgos were designed to restrict and control the abuse by encomenderos of their native laborers. These laws initiated the official use of the old Spanish term of encomienda for compulsory labor in America. The premise of the new laws was that, without them, the Indians would continue to live in "idleness and vice, and have no manner of virtue or doctrine" (Laws of Burgos). The laws dealt with a wide variety of regulated issues—from the number of days natives could be made to work, to types of work they must do, where they should be housed, the nominal education of one Indian educated for every 50 forced to labor, and even the indoctrination of the Indians in the Catholic faith. Under this legal structure, each native aged 15 or older officially served at least three weeks per year. In reality, up to 50 percent of village members often served the encomenderos each year. Repartimiento, as set forth in these laws, guaranteed the apportionment of needed labor for the Spanish encomenderos as well as the acculturation and control the native population.

Unhappy with the outcome of the Laws Burgos, Dominican friars such as Bartolomé de Las Casas struggled for years to document and petition the king for further reforms. Meanwhile, the Laws of Burgos proved ineffective in restricting abuse of the native population. Encomenderos, governors, and conquistadors often ignored the repeated instructions to limit or ban repartimiento allotments of specific conquered natives. The eventual success of Las Casas's efforts was realized with the enactment of the Leyes Nuevas of 1542–1543 (New Laws).

In practice, according to the New Laws, Spanish colonists in need of workers applied through local officials for grants of native laborers. Specific numbers of laborers, amount of time laborers were required, and the particular tasks to be undertaken were included in the requests. According to the policy, the leaders of each native community had to provide up to 2 percent of male taxpayers to be used as laborers in any given week. Often the special servants, semislaves or slaves of community elites were excluded from the pool of potential laborers targeted by the repartimiento allotments. A class known as the *yanaconas* lived as serfs in Peru, where they were exempt from the allotment. Free Inca eventually attempted to

be classified as *yanaconas* in order to escape assignment in the mines through the repartimiento allotments. In New Spain, special servants of community elites fell into the semislave class, or *mayeque,* of the Aztec. Only when the number of eligible workers was decimated by repeated deadly epidemics were these elements of the population incorporated into the repartimiento workforce.

Theoretically, no natives were to work for more than four weeks per year under the new repartimiento guidelines. In return, encomenderos were to reimburse laborers. In reality, the number of laborers demanded over the years increased, and the number of available men and women in the native communities decreased as disease and abuses took their toll and birthrates declined. Workers in some regions like Florida were removed from their homes for an entire year at a time. Meanwhile, compensation for labor provided to Spanish colonists was typically in the form of gifts to the village leaders, not to the laborers.

The combination of increased abuses and decreasing native populations eventually prompted the Crown to regulate the practice and encourage other labor alternatives. Unfortunately, colonial enforcement of the new restrictions was irregular at best. When the declining population created serious shortfalls in labor demands, Spanish colonists began to comply with instructions regarding the paying of native laborers and with suggestions to increase the usage of African slaves. In the 1500s, encomenderos and hacienda owners protested attempts to regulate the repartimiento. By 1632, demographics and available labor shifted enough to ensure the general compliance of encomenderos with the abolition of the repartimiento.

Rebecca M. Seaman

See also: Charles V (HRE), or Carlos I of Spain; Encomienda; Encomenderos; Las Casas, Bartolomé de; Leyes Nuevas 1542–1543; *Mayeques; Mita; Yanaconas.*

Resources

Charles I, Hapsburg King of Spain. "De La Libertad De Los Indios." *Recopilacion De Leyes de Los Reynos de Las Indias.* 2nd ed. Madrid: Por Antonio Balbas, 1756.

Ferdinand II, of Aragon. "The Laws of Burgos: 1512–1513." http://faculty.smu.edu/bakewell/BAKEWELL/texts/burgoslaws.html (accessed July 19, 2011).

Gibson, Charles. *Spain in America.* New York: Harper & Row, 1967.

Nutini, Hugo G., and Barry L. Isaac. *Social Stratification in Central Mexico, 1500–2000.* Austin: University of Texas Press, 2009.

Weber, David J. *The Spanish Frontier in North America.* New Haven, CT: Yale University Press, 1992.

Requerimiento

The *Requerimiento* (Requirement) was the formal document of the 16th-century *Spanish Conquest of the Western Hemisphere.* The document informed the hemisphere's indigenous peoples they must accept Christian missionaries and Spanish imperial dominion or be justly conquered. Read to hundreds of indigenous groups, the *Requerimiento* presented the Spanish Crown's theological and judicial justification for its overseas empire. The document was created in 1512 when the Spanish Empire's only external holdings were a few islands in the Caribbean and a few small coastal settlements on the American mainland. Reflecting the Crown's desire to take possession of the New World in an orderly and legal manner, the document was created to validate the Spanish Empire's Indian policy, which began on the island of Hispaniola (today, the nations of the Dominican Republic and Haiti).

The Spanish conquistadores desired to become New World encomenderos, people who held encomienda rights to extract labor and tribute from conquered peoples. The term encomienda stems from the Reconquista, Christianity's medieval struggle against Islam in the Iberian Peninsula (today, the nations of Portugal and Spain). This centuries-long struggle ended with Christian Spain's victory over Muslim Granada in the southern Iberian Peninsula in 1492, just months before Columbus first sailed across the Atlantic Ocean with a commission from the Spanish monarchs, King Ferdinand of Aragón and Queen Isabella of Castile. During the Reconquista, it became the practice for Christian soldiers to receive jurisdiction over the people who lived in villages they captured from Muslims. Columbus's grants in the New World were patterned after this medieval encomienda system in the Iberian Peninsula.

Due to the cruel treatment and excessive economic demands made by Spanish encomenderos, the indigenous population of Hispaniola suffered a massive decline. Dominican friars who arrived in Hispaniola in 1510 began raising concerns about the encomenderos' callous and inhuman behavior. During Advent in 1511, the Dominican priest Antonio de Montesinos preached a fiery sermon to Diego Colón and other encomenderos, warning them of damnation due to their mistreatment of Hispaniola's indigenous population. The encomenderos subsequently complained about the Dominicans to the court of King Ferdinand, who responded by asking theologians and jurists to examine the Spanish Empire's overseas policy.

As a result, King Ferdinand passed a legal code to regulate the relations between

Spaniards and the indigenous people of the Western Hemisphere known as the Laws of Burgos. In addition to the issue of the treatment of indigenous people, the tension between the Dominicans and the encomenderos that led to the Laws of Burgos raised the even larger question of the very legality of Spain's claim to possession of the New World. The Spanish Crown defended their possession on the basis of the Bulls of Donation, especially *Inter caetera divinae,* issued in 1493 by Pope Alexander VI granting the Spanish Crown jurisdiction over all the world's territory it had encountered or would encounter that was not already possessed by another Christian ruler. The following year, the Portuguese Crown and the Spanish Crown signed the Treaty of Tordesillas, a diplomatic agreement approved by the pope that divided the non-Christian world between them.

One of the men whose opinion the king solicited before enacting the Laws of Burgos was Juan López de Palacios Rubios, a distinguished jurist whose treatise *Of the Ocean Isles* defended the Spanish Empire's rule in the Western Hemisphere. Citing the work of the 13th-century canonist Cardinal Hostiensis, Palacios Rubios upheld that the pope could annul political jurisdictions of non-Christians and allocate them to Christian rulers, as Pope Alexander VI had done in his 1493 bulls of donation. Pleased with Palacios Rubios's work, the Spanish Crown assigned him the task of writing up the *Requerimiento.* To satisfy the royal conscience, the Crown ordered that the document be carried by all conquistadores and read to indigenous populations before employing military force against them. Reading the *Requerimiento* aloud became a protocol of the Conquest. Prior to the commencement of any hostilities, the indigenous populations were thus given the opportunity to agree to the terms of the document.

The text of the *Requerimiento* began with a Christian account of the history of the world, followed by an explanation of the foundation of the Church. Accordingly, God had given charge of all the world's nations to Saint Peter, the first pope. After this selective lesson in biblical history, listeners were informed that Pope Alexander VI, a Spaniard, had recognized the Spanish Crown's authority overseas. The *Requerimiento* called on the people listening to acknowledge the pope as ruler of the world and the Spanish Crown as sovereign over their land by virtue of the papal donation of 1493. Indigenous populations were notified that they would be received as vassals if they accepted these pronouncements.

The complex message of the *Requerimiento,* rarely delivered audibly and in a language intelligible to the indigenous peoples, asserted that the Spaniards would not be responsible for the resultant devastation if they resisted. In practice, the reading of the *Requerimiento* often illegally followed skirmishing with the indigenous peoples rather than preceding it. The message of the document shifted the responsibility for the conquest from the perpetrators to the victims.

The *Requerimiento* was first read on June 14, 1514, by the Pedro Arias Dávila expedition on the Isthmus of Panama. The chronicler Gonzalo Fernández de Oviedo was the royal notary who certified the reading of the *Requerimiento* on the Dávila expedition. According to Oviedo, this first attempt to use the *Requerimiento* failed because the expedition entered a deserted village. Nevertheless, the document was read aloud. Oviedo then declared in the presence of his fellow Spaniards, "My Lords, it appears to me that these Indians will not listen to the theology of this Requirement. . . ."

The *Requerimiento* was first successfully read by Martín Fernández de Enciso, a lawyer on the Dávila expedition. In his *Suma de Geografía,* written in 1519, Fernández de Enciso explained the reaction to this initial hearing of the *Requerimiento* from indigenous leaders of the Cenú. According to Enciso, the natives mocked the pope for giving land that was not his to give and the king for taking land he knew belonged to others. A fight ensued, killing two Spanish soldiers.

The *Requerimiento* reflected medieval Christian notions of what constituted a just war, as well as Islamic notions of what constituted a proper holy war. Conquistadores generally began their ventures by taking possession, ceremonially reading the *Requerimiento,* and founding a settlement as a base of operations and a sign of their presence. The reading of the *Requerimiento* was generally derided. The Spanish priest and indigenous rights advocate Bartolomé de Las Casas, who denounced the Spanish Empire's use of war to propagate Christianity in the Western Hemisphere, did not know whether to cry or laugh at the document.

The Spanish Crown formally abolished the *Requerimiento* in 1556. By this time, the Spanish had subjugated most of the major indigenous groups and controlled most of the desirable territories in the Western Hemisphere. Whether or not the indigenous peoples understood the *Requerimiento* or the ultimatum it offered, the Spanish Crown relied on the document to officially legitimate its conquest and rule in the Western Hemisphere. In the conquest, political obedience and religious obedience went hand in hand. The *Requerimiento*'s call to Christian faith and political submission was thus the means by which Spanish power was extended over most of the Western Hemisphere in the first half of the 16th century.

David M. Carletta

See also: Colón, Diego; Columbus, Christopher; Conquistadores; Dávila, Pedro Arias; Encomienda; Fernández de Oviedo, Gonzalo; Hispaniola; Las Casas, Bartolomé de; Laws of Burgos; Ovando, Fr. Nicolás de; Philip II of Spain; Reconquista, Impact of on Spanish Policy in America; Tribute, Paid to Spain.

Resources

Hanke, Lewis. *The Spanish Struggle for Justice in the Conquest of America.* Dallas, TX: Southern Methodist University Press, 2002.

Hoffer, Peter C. *Law and People in Colonial America.* Baltimore, MD: Johns Hopkins University Press, 1998.

Kadir, Djelal. *Columbus and the Ends of the Earth: Europe's Prophetic Rhetoric as Conquering Ideology.* Berkeley: University of California Press, 1992.

McAlister, Lyle N. *Spain and Portugal in the New World, 1492–1700.* Minneapolis: University of Minnesota Press, 1984.

Muldoon, James. *Popes, Lawyers, and Infidels: The Church and the Non-Christian World, 1250–1550.* Philadelphia: University of Pennsylvania Press, 1979.

Seed, Patricia. *Ceremonies of Possession in Europe's Conquest of the New World, 1492–1640.* New York: Cambridge University Press, 1995.

Welton, Jerry. "The Policies of Hernan Cortes, as defined in his letters." PhD diss., University of Illinois at Urbana-Champaign, 1954.

Williams, Robert A. *The American Indian in Western Legal Thought: The Discourses of Conquest.* New York: Oxford University Press, 1990.

Rivalry, Intra-Andean

The competition and conflict that permeated the Inca Empire in the 16th century evolved out of the complex relationships within and structure of the empire itself. Kinship relationships, methods of tracing lineage, especially for the governing Incas, and the assimilation of divergent cultures all contributed to the internal rivalries present throughout the empire. The growing size of the empire and the ruling family also contributed to internal conflicts that were prevalent throughout the 16th century.

The basic kinship unit in the Inca Empire was the *ayllus* system. An intimate version of *ayllus* referred to the close family relatives while small, individual communities were centered on the larger version of the *ayllus,* which was the communal form of the kinship system. With the growth of the empire and the relocation of various ethnic groups, the individual communities were tasked with incorporating other *ayllus* or ethnic groups within the existing system, resulting in conflict at the local level.

The ruling Inca family had their own intimate kinship system. This system, which was comprised of more than just the family, including also servants of the family, was known as the panaqa, encompassing everyone within the Sapa Inca's family (except the Inca himself), including future descendants. The panaqa was responsible for supporting the Inca, and caring for his mummy, upon his death, for generations to come. New Sapa Incas formed a new panaqas from out of the old structure of which they used to be part. In this manner, the *ayllus* of the ruling Inca elite was continually fracturing, especially in the years immediately prior to the Spanish arrival and immediately following.

The fracturing of the panaqas and the growth of the empire heightened the intra-Andean rivalry. The panaqa of each Inca ruler received lands commensurate with their noble status. The structuring of new panaqas for each emerging Inca ruler created

the need to assign more estates of value. Competing for status within the empire, the various panaqas and their individual members often used a variety of means to ensure their own status and estates retained value and/or dominance within the empire. These means included anything from service to the new emperor to use of poison to eliminate competing individuals or panaqas, civil wars, and even cooperation with the invading Spanish.

To further complicate matters, another system of division within the Incas Empire, commonplace in many Andean cultures, split the society into two distinct moieties, known as the Hanan (upper) and Hurin (lower). In the Inca culture, the old center of power was designated Hurin Cuzco, and the new seat of authority, with the more recent panaqas and their lavish new palaces, was known as the Hanan. The latter typically retained close ties with the military, and thus were responsible for the great expansion and power of the empire. The Hurin retained strong connections with the Inca priests, and thereby retained the support of vast numbers of Inca and non-Inca people who had assimilated into the Inca society.

By the time of the Spanish conquest in 1533, the competition between varying panaqas was inflamed by the extension of the empire. Internally, many new cultures were relocated and assigned to different communities and *ayllus,* in an attempt to assimilate and control conquered peoples. Allied societies, which merged with the Inca Empire without the need for war and conquest, were rewarded with the status of Inca by privilege. They were also given positions of authority within the empire and estates to retain their loyalty. As the Hanan branch of Inca rulers extended the empire further north, the competing interests for estates and influence among the Inca panaqas, *ayllus,* and conquered peoples also grew. To control the distant, newly conquered regions, and to ensure the holding of large estates by newly formed panaqas, the Hanan relocated much of the power of the empire to the northern region around Quito. This shift in logistics increased the angst of the Hurin-based panaqas, whose influence in the region of Cuzco remained strong, but whose influence over the empire diminished.

A real threat to this tenuous system of competing panaqas was the rapid succession of Incas to the throne. The threat became reality in the late 1520s. Huallpa Cápac, the existing emperor whose extended panaqas included wives and children belonging to both the Hanan and Hurin branches within the empire, died suddenly from smallpox. Ninan Cuyochi, his designated heir, died within days from the same disease. Unsure of how the seat of power should be distributed, the ruling military elite gave their support to Atahualpa, another son who held the support of the Hanan branch. Meanwhile, the priests and common support of the people around Cuzco went to Huáscar, of the Hurin branch.

The ruling Inca practice of endogamy and polygamy resulted in a convoluted system of determining status among the rulers' offspring. Greater status fell to children of Inca who married one of his sisters. Lesser status fell to offspring of an Inca who married from outside of the ruling family. Even less status fell to those whose mothers were not ethnically Inca. In the case of Atahualpa, while he was associated with the dominant Hanan, his mother was not Inca by ethnicity. Huáscar descended from the Inca Huallpa Cápac and one of his sisters, placing him high in status, despite his association with the lower Hurin branch.

The rapid succession of claimants to the throne, complicated by the endogamy practices and competing panaqas, led to jealousy

and eventually civil war. It was this war that the Spanish observed evidence of as they approached inland toward the center of the Inca Empire. The extreme death toll resulted in confusion among the Inca people as to who was the rightful divine ruler. The success of Atahualpa in the civil war might have solidified the empire again, but his own death at the hands of the Spanish conquerors created a new crisis of leadership. The Spanish exploited the division and confusion, shifting support from one branch of the ruling Inca elite to another, and turning the different panaqas against one another. In the end, the internal rivalries proved far more effective in destroying the extended empire than did the handful of Spanish conquerors with their weaponry.

Rebecca M. Seaman

See also: Atahualpa; *Ayllus;* Hanan; Huallpa Cápac; Huáscar; Hurin; Ninan Cuyochi; Sapa Inca.

Resources

Diez Canseco, Maria Rostworowski de. *History of the Inca Realm.* Translated by Harry B. Iceland. Cambridge: Cambridge University Press, 1999.

Hemming, John. *The Conquest of the Incas.* New York: Harcourt Brace Jovanovich, 1970.

Henson, Sändra Lee Allen. "Dead Bones Dancing: The Taki Onqoy, Archaism, and Crisis in Sixteenth Century Peru." MA Thesis, East Tennessee State University, 2002.

Stern, Steve J. *Peru's Indian Peoples and the Challenge of Spanish Conquest: Huamanga to 1640.* Madison: University of Wisconsin Press, 1993.

Rodriguez de Fonseca, Juan

Juan Rodriguez de Fonseca functioned as the unofficial minister of colonial affairs

324 | Rodriguez de Fonseca, Juan

from the time of Columbus's second voyage through the conquest of Mexico by Cortés. As a trusted advisor to Isabella and Ferdinand, Fonseca directed the development of policy toward the New World and created the Casa de Contratacion (House of Trade), which controlled the imports and exports of Spanish territory in the Americas. Fonseca's long-term of office was marked by controversies and disputes with many leaders of the Spanish expansion.

Fonseca was born in 1451 into a noble family in the province of Zamora in Castile. His ancestors migrated from Portugal nearly a century before. As a younger son, Fonseca was destined for a career in the Roman Catholic Church, following in the footsteps of other male members of the extended family. During the dispute between Joan of Castile and Isabella of Castile over who should rule the kingdom, Fonseca's family came down in support of Isabella. This loyalty was rewarded throughout Fonseca's career.

Isabella asked her confessor, Hernando de Talavera, to take Fonseca under his wing when the young man first came to court. He was ordained a priest on April 6, 1493, and quickly advanced through the ranks of the clergy. In 1494, Fonseca became bishop of Badajoz, followed by increasingly important bishoprics at Cordoba (1499), Palencia (1504), and Burgos (1514). He also held the office of chaplain to Isabella.

Fonseca's value to Isabella and Ferdinand was clear from the diplomatic missions he undertook. In 1497, he was one of the ambassadors who traveled to Burgundy to arrange a double marriage between the children of Emperor Maximilian and children of Isabella and Ferdinand. Fonseca later arranged the English marriage of Catherine of Aragon with Arthur, Prince of Wales.

Fonseca's greatest contribution to history, however, was his influence on the Spanish exploration and settlement of the Americas. In 1493, he was ordered by the king and queen to make arrangements for Columbus's second voyage to the Americas. Speed was essential because they feared other European powers would attempt to stake a claim to the newly discovered lands. Fonseca hired 17 ships and organized over 1,000 people to accompany Columbus back to the Americas. Some historians believe that conflict arose between Fonseca and Columbus over their respective authority and that Fonseca purposely delayed the sailing of the fleet. However, the records indicate that difficulties in obtaining the necessary supplies and funds had more to do with the delays than personal conflicts.

The successful organization of the expedition caused Isabella and Ferdinand to give Fonseca increasing responsibility for matters involving the Americas. He functioned as an unofficial minister with responsibilities for the new lands. As a result, Fonseca came into conflict with Columbus again. The explorer was determined to protect the authority he believed granted him to control the lands he discovered. He was also anxious to control arrangements, shipping, and exports from the Americas to Spain. Fonseca, on the other hand, was determined to maintain the authority of his sovereigns and believed that Columbus was usurping royal powers. This conflict over policy toward the indigenous population in the Indies and ownership of the resources of the New World led Fonseca to develop a bureaucracy that controlled Spanish affairs in the Americas for 300 years.

In 1499, Fonseca convinced Isabella to remove Columbus as governor of the newly found territories. He also began authorizing other captains to undertake expeditions to the West Indies. Most were former associates of Columbus, such as Alonso de Ojeda, who now became his competitors. As a result, more territories were discovered and claimed by Spain and imports from the New World began to flow into Spain, with particular emphasis on gold. Fonseca instituted strict control over these products. Unregistered gold was seized when it arrived in Seville, the sole port for expeditions to and from the New World.

In 1503, Fonseca convinced the monarchs to establish the Casa de Contratacion, or House of Trade, in Seville. He served as the head of the Casa. This agency was given authority to oversee the purchase, transport, warehousing, and sale of merchandise exported to and imported from the Americas. As more lands were discovered in the next two decades, the flow of products to and from the New World increased greatly and income received by the Crown from this traffic became more significant. Fonseca's power increased in 1504, when Isabella died. Ferdinand delegated virtually complete control over the Casa to Fonseca.

The Casa de Contratacion became the only government agency dealing with American affairs. It regulated the passage of individuals to the New World, trained navigators for the voyages, prepared maps and charts of the new lands, administered the property in the New World of Spaniards who had died, and resolved legal disputes over trade. The Casa established policy toward indigenous peoples, including their enslavement and the need to convert them to Catholicism. In 1512, Fonseca convened the Junta of Burgos, which developed a theology on the rights of the Native Americans, leading to an official policy of how they were to be treated—the Laws of Burgos. In 1524, the Case de Contratacion was merged into the Council of the Indies. The Council of the Indies was the central administrative and judicial agency for the Spanish overseas empire.

It had jurisdiction over legislative, financial, judicial, military, ecclesiastical, and commercial matters in the New World. For the next 300 years, the Council was the governing agency for Spanish America. Fonseca was one of the moving forces in the council's creation and served as its first president.

Contemporaries viewed Fonseca as haughty, proud, and jealous of his own power. His strict policies brought many enemies. Columbus and his supporters blamed Fonseca as the cause of their downfall. Other Spanish conquistadors came into conflict with him, such as Hernán Cortés, who conquered the Aztec Empire. When Fonseca believed Cortés was exceeding his authority over Mexico, the Bishop of Badajoz, Cordoba, Palencia, and Burgos arranged to have him removed as governor in 1523. Bartolomé de Las Casas, a bishop who came to support the rights of the Native Americans, believed that Fonseca was responsible for the many cruelties inflicted on them by the Spanish. Fonseca's influence waned following the capture of Tenochtitlán by Cortés. Reprimanded for keeping information about Cortés from King Charles V, a special committee was formed to advise the king regarding Cortés— and the Bishop of Burgos was not included. Fonseca died in Burgos on March 4, 1524.

Tim J. Watts

See also: Charles V (HRE) or Carlos I of Spain; Columbus, Christopher; Cortés, Hernán; Las Casas, Bartolomé de; Laws of Burgos; Ojeda (Hojeda), Alonso de; Tenochtitlán, City of.

Resources

Haring, Clarence Henry. *Trade and Navigation between Spain and the Indies in the Time of the Hapsburgs.* Cambridge, MA: Harvard University Press, 1918.

Mann, Charles C. *1493: Uncovering the New World Columbus Created.* New York: Knopf, 2011.

Phillips, William D., and Carla Rahn Phillips. *The Worlds of Christopher Columbus.* New York: Cambridge University Press, 1992.

Thomas, Hugh. *Conquest: Montezuma, Cortés, and the Fall of Old Mexico.* New York: Simon & Schuster, 1995.

Rodriguez de Villafuerte, Juan

Juan Rodriguez de Villafuerte was one of Hernán Cortés's lieutenants during the conquest of the Aztec Empire and the western part of the New Spain. Villafuerte was described as young, impetuous, and bold. He helped create the first Spanish shipyard on the Pacific coast and later made Acapulco the gate to trade with Asia.

Villafuerte was born 1497 in Salamanca in the Medellin region of Spain. His parents were Gonzalo de Villafuerte and Caralina Ortiz, members of the lower nobility. Like many young men of his generation, Villafuerte was drawn to the New World by the opportunity to make his fortune. By 1518, he was in Cuba. Villafuerte joined Cortés's expedition to the mainland when it left in 1519. Although a young man, his eagerness and obvious loyalty attracted Cortés's attention. Villafuerte became one of Cortés's inner circle. When Cortés and his army landed at Vera Cruz, he appointed Villafuerte his *maestre de campo,* an office in which Villafuerte served as Cortés's chief of staff. As such, the young man had the responsibility of overseeing the day-to-day operations of the army, insuring supplies of food and other essentials.

Villafuerte accompanied Cortés on the march to Tenochtitlán, capital of the Aztecs. During the long period in which the Spanish conquistadors imprisoned Montezuma, Villafuerte was by Cortés's side. According to religious tradition, Villafuerte had brought a small wooden statue of the Blessed Virgin holding the Christ Child as protection on the expedition. When Cortés ordered the idols in the Great Pyramid of Tenochtitlán destroyed and the temples purified for Christian use, Villafuerte's statue was set up to aid in Christian worship. When Montezuma died and the Spanish were compelled to flee Tenochtitlán in the disastrous La Noche Triste, on June 30 1520, Cortés prayed to the Blessed Virgin for success. Villafuerte then took the statue to protect it from the Aztecs. Villafuerte was wounded and hid the statue. It was later recovered and installed in a shrine in Cholula dedicated to the Blessed Virgin under the title of Our Lady of Remedies.

Following La Noche Triste, Cortés gathered allies and supplies for a siege of Tenochtitlán. An important part of the plan was the building of 13 brigantines. Villafuerte assisted with building the brigantines at Tlaxcala, a native city allied with the Spanish. Once the materials were gathered and shaped, they were moved to Tetzcoco by Lake Texcoco, where the final construction took place. When Cortés was ready to attack Tenochtitlán, Villafuerte commanded one of the brigantines that sailed down the human-made channels to the lake. The crew consisted of sailors, 25 soldiers, and artillerymen to fire the one cannon assigned to each ship. The attack on Tenochtitlán, fought through the spring and summer of 1521, was a long drawn-out affair. The Aztecs did not surrender until August 13. Villafuerte and his men were in the thick of the battle. After the Spanish victory, Cortés named Villafuerte temporary governor of Tenochtitlan with a Spanish garrison of 300 men.

Villafuerte was soon employed by Cortés to help subdue other Native American groups. He accompanied an expedition to Michoacan, near the Pacific coast of Mexico, in 1522. The leader was Cristóbal de Olid, one of Cortés's main captains during the conquest of Tenochtitlán. Olid was recalled by Cortés, and Villafuerte was placed in charge of the Spanish and indigenous forces. In November 1522, Cortes ordered Villafuerte and his men to march to Zacatula on the Pacific coast, to complete a shipyard and built ships to explore the Pacific. Villafuerte was not widely regarded as a suitable commander for this mission, due to his youth and lack of experience. Some regarded him as a foolish young man who needed a guardian instead of being placed in an office of authority. Villafuerte quickly proved his critics correct. Instead of marching directly to Zacatula, he attacked Colima, hoping to conquer it. Villafuerte was badly beaten and forced to retreat. On the way, some of his native allies looted from indigenous cities allied with the Spanish. Cortés repaid the losses and replaced Villafuerte as commander of Spanish forces with Gonzalo de Sandoval.

Despite his mistakes, Villafuerte was rewarded with an encomienda in western Mexico. Villafuerte's territory included Zacatula, where the first shipyard was built. Four Spanish ships were soon constructed under Villafuerte's direction, but Zacatula proved to be unsuitable for a shipyard. He moved further operations down the coast to Acapulco, which became the only authorized port for Spanish ships going to and coming from Asia.

Villafuerte married or had as a mistress Doña Juana, a noblewoman of the Mexica, with whom he had a son and a daughter. Following her death in the La Noche Triste, he later married Doña Juana de Zuniga, who was related to Cortés's wife. Their daughter, Aldonza, married Garcia de Albornoz. Aldonza inherited the encomienda in the 1540s, after the death of her parents. Villafuerte also had two brothers who followed him to the New World and were among the Spaniards who settled New Spain.

Tim J. Watts

See also: Brigantines, Use by Cortés; Cortés, Hernán; La Noche Triste; Olid, Cristóbal de; Tenochtitlán, Siege of.

Resources

Grunberg, Bernard. *Dictionnaire des Conquistadores de Mexico.* Paris: Harmattan, 2001.

Himmerich y Valencia, Robert. *The Encomenderos of New Spain, 1521–1555.* Austin: University of Texas Press, 1991.

Thomas, Hugh. *Conquest: Montezuma, Cortés, and the Fall of Old Mexico.* New York: Simon & Schuster, 1995.

Warren, J. Benedict. *The Conquest of Michoacan: The Spanish Domination of the Tarascan Kingdom in Western Mexico, 1521–1530.* Norman: University of Oklahoma Press, 1985.

Ruiz, Bartolomé

A pilot, recruited by Hernán Cortés, became the first Spaniard to encounter Manta and Inca peoples at the trade city of Jocay, 1526. Bartolomé Ruiz served under Francisco Pizarro as a navigator, pilot, and explorer. The expedition sailed southward out of Panama to the coastal city of Jocay in modern-day Ecuador. The venture was comprised of two ships and 160 men. After Pizarro disembarked and Almagro returned to Panama for more resources, Ruiz sailed further south. There he encountered a large raft with indigenous merchants from the Inca Empire. According to eyewitness accounts, the raft, sailed by natives, bore a lateen sail and was conducting trade along the coast in fine cloth out of wool.

Rebecca M. Seaman

See also: Almagro, Diego de; Cortés, Hernán; Pizarro, Francisco: Almagro, Diego de; Cortés, Hernán; Pizarro, Francisco

Resources

Hemming, John. *The Conquest of the Incas*. New York: Harcourt Brace Jovanovich, 1970.

Smith, Cameron. "On the Vessel Sailed by Bartholome Ruiz in 1526: Characterization and Significance for the Pre-Columbian Archaeology of Northwestern South America." Academia.edu. http://www.academia.edu/228489/On_the_Vessel_Sailed_by_Bartholome_Ruiz_in_1526_Characterization_and_Significance_for_the_Pre-Columbian_Archaeology_of_Northwestern_South_America (accessed on December 2, 2012).

Ruiz de Guevara, Antonio

Fray Antonio Ruiz de Guevara accompanied Pánfilo de Narváez in 1520 on his expedition to capture and possibly kill Hernán Cortés. Upon arriving at San Juan de Ulúa, just south of Cortés's newly founded city of Villa Rica de la Vera Cruz, Narváez sent three diplomats to Vera Cruz to deliver a message. The diplomats, a notary (Alfonso de Vergara), a priest (Antonio Ruiz de Guevara), and a soldier (Antonio de Amaya), carried messages from Narváez to several of the leading personnel of Vera Cruz, whom he had been lead to believe were dissatisfied with Cortés.

Guevara and his companions entered the city and were taken to Gonzalo de Sandoval, loyal supporter of Cortés and leader of the community's military defense. When Guevara attempted to convince Sandoval of the need to submit to Narváez as the duly appointed Spanish captain general, and that Cortés was a traitor and enemy of Spain, the conquistador cut him off, threatened to beat them, had the friar and his companions arrested, and sent them off to Tenochtitlán to give the same message directly to Cortés.

Cortés, made aware of Narváez's presence on the coast, used a different approach to the diplomats. Greeting them outside of the city of Tenochtitlán, Cortés placed the diplomats on horses, gave them tours of the city and its grandeur, making sure that he lavished them with gifts of gold and other items of beauty. By the time he sent the diplomats back to Narváez with his own welcome and encouragement for the conquistador to join Cortés (as his subordinate) in the conquest of the wealthy Aztec Empire, the three men were firmly under Cortés's influence, especially Fray Ruiz de Guevara.

Guevara is an excellent example of the shifting allegiances by many of the Spanish in the complex and rapidly changing environment of colonial New Spain. Awed by the wealth and potential of the Aztec Empire, Guevara went back to Narváez with official communications from the *caudillo,* where he spread the wealth, given him by Cortés, among Narváez's own men. This strategy, while used extensively between both conquistadors, resulted in the greatest success for Cortés. With many of Narváez's forces secretly collaborating with the *caudillo,* including Narváez's priest Guevara, it is not surprising that the eventual conflict resulted in such a one-sided victory. Following the battle between the two Spanish forces at Zempoala, most of Narváez's men were incorporated into Cortés's ranks.

Notwithstanding his willing embrace of Guevara and other newcomers to his army of invaders, Cortés was quick to distrust those that seemed to betray his trust. Questions by Narváez's men regarding the distribution of wealth among the expedition were rewarded with being sent back to Cuba at the first opportunity. When Cristóbal de Tapia, protégés of Juan Rodriguez de Fonseca, bishop of Badajoz, Palencia, and Burgos—as well as arch nemesis of Cortés—arrived with instructions to investigate charges against the *caudillo* and to take over the government of New Spain, several individuals demonstrated deference to the royal inspector. Even close supporters of Cortés were banished for seemingly harmless courteous welcomes for Tapia. However, Antonio Ruiz de Guevara, either due to a strong sense of loyalty, the attraction of potential wealth, or because of his service in spreading the Catholic faith that was so important to Cortés, remained among those followers whose loyalties were constant and who stayed service to the *caudillo* in New Spain.

Rebecca M. Seaman

See also: Cortés, Hernán; Narváez, Pánfilo de; Sandoval, Gonzalo de; Tenochtitlán, City of; Villa Rica de la Vera Cruz; Zempoala.

Resources

Diaz, Bernal. *The Conquest of New Spain.* Translated with Introduction by J.M. Cohen. London: Penguin Books, 1963.

Levy, Buddy. *Conquistador: Hernán Cortés, King Montezuma, and the Last Stand of the Aztecs.* New York: Bantam Books, 2009.

Thomas, Hugh. *Conquest: Montezuma, Cortés, and the Fall of Old Mexico.* New York: Simon & Schuster, 1995.

Rumiñahui

Rumiñahui (Rumiñavi or Rumiñagui) was one of the ablest Inca generals during the empire's final days. A supporter of Atahualpa during the Inca civil war between Atahualpa and Huáscar, Rumiñahui was largely responsible for Atahualpa's success. Rumiñahui later battled the Spanish invaders and destroyed the northern Inca capital of Quito rather than see it fall into their hands. For his ability, strength of character, and his defiance against European invaders, Rumiñahui remains a hero to many modern Ecuadorians.

Rumiñahui is a nickname; his real name was Ati II Pillahuaso and he was born in Quito around 1490. He was a member of the nobility, as evidenced from the positions he held. He was possibly a half-brother to Atahualpa. His presumed father, Inca emperor Huayna Cápac, took Rumiñahui's mother as a concubine.

Huayna Cápac and his apparent heir died unexpectedly ca. 1527, and power was divided between two of Huayna Cápac's other sons—Huáscar, the eldest, and Atahualpa, son of Huayna Cápac's favorite concubine from Quito. Neither brother was willing to share power. A rivalry already existed between the traditional Inca capital of Cuzco and the frontier capital of Quito, so the conflict was not just a personal one between Huáscar and Atahualpa. Huáscar sent an army to assert his authority over Quito. Atahualpa was captured but soon escaped. Several leading generals, including Rumiñahui, went over to Atahualpa, who had served as a general during his father's military conquests around Quito.

The civil war that followed helped weaken the Inca Empire. In 1531, Atahualpa's army defeated Huáscar's forces at the battle of Chimborzo. In the final battle of Quipuaypan in 1532, Atahualpa's generals completely defeated Huáscar and took him prisoner. Unfortunately, a Spanish force of approximately 160 men under Francisco Pizarro had landed on the Pacific coast, seeking booty. They marched into the Andes and arrived at Cajamarca, where Atahualpa and his army are camped. On November 16, the Spanish seized him in an ambush and massacred several thousand courtiers and servants. The stunned Inca army failed to respond.

Over the next few months, the Spanish expanded their influence throughout the Inca Empire, awaiting payment of a ransom in gold and silver for Atahualpa's release. Most of the treasure came from the southern regions, but Rumiñahui claimed to collect treasure from the northern provinces. When Pizarro ordered that Huáscar be brought to Cajamarca, the deposed emperor was killed along the way, probably on Atahualpa's orders. Pizarro realized that, if Atahualpa were freed, he would be a dangerous enemy. After receiving the ransom, Pizarro refused to release the emperor, condemning him to death for ordering Huáscar's death.

Atahualpa, knowing he would soon be executed, sent another brother, Quilliscacha, to Quito to bring his sons to their father. Rumiñahui refused to release the boys and went so far as to kill and desecrate the body of Quilliscacha. When Rumiñahui learned of Atahualpa's death at the hands of the Spanish, he withdrew his troops to Quito and prepared to defend the city against the Spanish.

Pizarro believed rumors of wealth Atahualpa removed to Quito and sent Sebastian de Benalcázar to attack Quito. Another Spanish expedition, under Pedro de Alvarado, a rival of Pizarro's who had served under Hernán Cortés, landed in Ecuador at the same time, with the goal of capturing Quito and its wealth. The two expeditions were more interested in beating each other than they were with defeating Rumiñahui. Benalcázar brushed aside weak Inca opposition on his march and reached the city of Tumebamba in April 1534. The Cañari people, enemies of the Inca who lived in the area, joined Benalcázar against Rumiñahui. On May 3, 1534, Rumiñahui attacked Benalcázar at the battle of Teocajas. He hoped the high altitude and marshy ground would affect the Spanish. However, the Spanish horses and armor were too much for Rumiñahui to overcome. Thousands of Quito warriors were killed, but only four Spaniards and four horses died. Nonetheless, Rumiñahui refused to give up and continued to attack the Spanish all day.

At the end of the day, Rumiñahui withdrew. He realized that he could not defeat the Spanish in open battle. As he withdrew slowly to Quito, Rumiñahui continued to skirmish with Spanish. He burned most of Quito before the Spanish arrived. All of the valuables that could be gathered from the city were hidden, possibly thrown into a volcano's crater. Quito's people were evacuated into the higher mountain areas. By the time Benalcázar arrived, Quito offered little reward.

Rumiñahui continued to harass the Spanish for another year. While using effective tactics and with superior numbers of forces, the Spanish advantage of horses and the assistance of thousands of Cañari allies proved too much for the Inca general. Unable to unite his forces with the forces under Quizquiz or Zope-Zopahua, he was eventually captured and tortured in an effort to reveal where he had hidden the treasure from Quito. Rumiñahui refused to reveal the hiding place and was executed on June 25, 1535. In 1985, the Ecuadorian Congress recognized his courage by making December 1 a day of remembrance for Rumiñahui.

Tim J. Watts

See also: Cañari; Cortés, Hernán; Pizarro, Francisco; Quizquiz.

Resources

Cieza de Leon, Pedro de. *The War of Quito; and, Inca Documents.* London: Hakluyt Society, 1913.

Davies, Nigel. *The Incas.* Niwot: University of Colorado Press, 1995.

Hemming, John. *The Conquest of the Incas.* London: Macmillan, 1970.

Restall, Matthew. *Seven Myths of the Spanish Conquest.* Oxford: Oxford University, Press, 2004.

Sarmiento de Gamboa, Pedro. *The History of the Incas.* Austin: University of Texas Press, 2007.

S

Sahagún, Bernardino de

The classic Aztec study of the 1600s was written by Bernardino de Sahagún. Born in Spain in 1499, the Franciscan friar spent 60 years in missionary work in Central Mexico. Sahagún became quite knowledgeable of the Aztec culture, customs, and society. His grasp of Nahuatl, the Aztec language, enabled him to undertake work on the *Historia General de las Cosas de Nueva España,* an encyclopedic work encompassing the history of the Aztec civilization.

Sahagún, a product of his time, used his skill in Nahuatl to help spread the Catholic faith to the Aztec and to bring European style civilization to the same. The friar sought to capture the meaning and core of the Aztec culture, thereby assisting the missionaries who indoctrinated the natives. While serving as a missionary, he became aware of the practice of the Aztec to adopt elements of the Catholic faith, not as a sign of rejecting their old beliefs, but instead to disguise their continued polytheistic faith practices. The Virgin of Guadalupe replaced the shrine at *Tonantzin;* St. John replaced *Tezcatlipoca;* and Santa Ana replaced *Toci.* Though the Christian saints were introduced to the Aztec as part of the new Christian faith, elements of old beliefs and rituals remained in the religious practices by the local people. To accomplish the task of beginning conversion from old beliefs and cultural practices to the Christian based culture of Spain, Sahagún recorded the cultural attributes and history of the Aztec in Nahuatl. However, he used Latin characters, thereby preserving historical information of the people while simultaneously introducing the Nahua/Aztec to the writing system of the Spanish.

In his first years in America, Sahagún taught Aztec children. He struggled with a lack of understanding his students linguistically or culturally. Within a decade, he graduated to teaching higher education to aristocratic Aztec youth, including Latin, history, and philosophy. He went from there to working as a missionary in the small villages where Catholicism had yet to be introduced. The failure to rapidly spread the faith in Middle America led to his initial translation of portions of the Bible and Christian songs into Nahuatl. From there, Sahagún progressed on to study the Aztec culture and histories, preparing for his eventual lifelong work of the history of the region.

In his *Historia General,* Sahagún compared Aztec historical figures and events with European classical figures. Tula of the Aztec past was compared to Troy; the Aztec god, Quetzalcoatl, was likened to King Arthur of English antiquity; and Aztec mythologies were often compared with the Greek and Roman legends. In the process of defending the Aztec part in the history of mankind for the purpose of winning their souls, the friar portrayed the Mexican people as childlike in comparison to their Spanish overlords. Sahagún attempted to capture the Aztec society prior to Spanish conquest. His revelation of the impacts of the perceived cultural achievements, followed by death due to conquest, disease, and decline, elicited sympathy but also perceptions of native inferiority. Maintaining the perception of European superiority not only vindicated the Spanish conquest of the Aztec but also justified the perception of Spanish Catholicism as the true faith.

Despite portrayals of the Mexican people as a declining people with inferior pagan faiths—or maybe because of this portrayal—Sahagún's writings about the Aztec and their culture were deemed dangerous for years. Following the Council of Trent and the implementation of the Inquisition in Spain, the Crown reversed its policies on writings about Pre-Columbian societies. This led to the confiscation order of Phillip II in 1578. Sahagún was deprived of further manuscripts. Nonetheless, much of his material for the *Historia General* escaped destruction. His work was not rediscovered until the late 18th century. Public access to his writings was not available until 1888, when Paso y Troncoso and Eduard Seler published their works on the translated writings of Sahagún. In addition to providing early insights into the lives of the Aztec people, the *Historia General* illuminates the trials faced by Aztecs and Franciscan missionaries as the two cultures clashed and transformed each other in the first century of contact.

Rebecca M. Seaman

See also: Nahuatl Language; Quetzalcoatl.

Resources

Gibson, Charles. *Spain in America.* New York: Harper and Row, 1967.

Spieker, Susanne. "An Early Research in the Field of Education: Bernardino de Sahagún in Sixteenth-Century Mexico." *History of Education* 37, no. 6 (November 2008): 757–772.

Sandoval, Gonzalo de

Born in Medellín in 1497, Gonzalo de Sandoval was a Spanish noble and conquistador

in Mexico, where he was one of the closest collaborators of Hernán Cortés. He was even entrusted with the position of cogovernor of the Mexico when Cortés was away from the capital city of Mexico (March 2 to August 22, 1527). He died unexpectedly of some sickness at Palos de la Frontera in 1528, which he either acquired en route, or in an inn in Spain upon landing there. He was interred in La Rábida Monastery.

Gonzalo de Sandoval made his way to the New World as a young boy. About 1511, as a 14-year-old, he is said to have worked as a squire for Diego Velázquez, the governor of Cuba. Possibly he also took part in the conquest of the island. Yet his most important adventure started in 1518/19, when he was recruited by Hernán Cortés in Trinidad to take part in the Mexico expedition. They were kinsmen, born in the same region in Spain. Sandoval became the youngest and one of the most trusted Cortés's lieutenants during the conquest of the Aztecs.

When Cortés's forces started a direct march toward Tenochtitlán, Sandoval was one of the chief commanders of the troops. His extreme youth resulted in him being despised at times by the older and more experienced soldiers. Nevertheless, Cortés trusted and considered the young Gonzalo a close friend and collaborator. As such, Sandoval took part in the whole march and most of the battles and skirmishes against the local Indians. He also took part in various meetings, feasts, and ceremonies. At one such ceremony, the baptism of a selected group of Indian aristocrats, which included local women, one of the women was offered to young Sandoval as a partner.

On November 8, 1519, Sandoval participated in the celebrative entry of the Spanish into Tenochtitlán. He was also in the group which soon after met with the Aztec emperor, Montezuma II, and took part in talks with the Indian monarch. One week later he helped imprison the Aztec. At this time, Sandoval was entrusted with the command of the garrison Villa Rica de Vera Cruz as *alguacil mayor* to prevent any treacheries being born against Cortés. As the commander of Vera Cruz, Sandoval supplied materials for the construction of brigantines in Mexico.

Soon after, Sandoval proved his loyalty to Cortés when he seized the envoys of a newcomer to the Mexican shores, Pánfilo de Narváez. Sent by the governor of Cuba, Diego Velázquez, Narváez was spreading news demanding the subjugation of Cortés to himself and giving up Tenochtitlán. Messengers were arrested and transported in wooden cases to Cortés. Though Sandoval used his position and authority to assist his mentor, the conflict between Cortés and Narváez could not be solved peacefully, and the two groups clashed in a battle on May 28/29, 1520. Sandoval took part in the battle, which took place on a pyramid, and had great share in defeating and capturing Narváez.

Soon after, Sandoval joined Cortés in the Aztec capital of Tenochtitlán. There he was among the officers opening the Spanish retreat from the city on June 30–July 1, 1520. During this so-called La Noche Triste, Cortés and his army had to fight their way out of the Mexican capital, losing people, horses, and arms.

Afterward, Sandoval conducted military operations against Indians in the region of Tepeaca, forcing most inhabitants to accept peace and pay homage to the king of Spain, even if they had no idea what it meant. Sandoval utilized various measures, not rejecting military force and violence. In January 1521, he conducted the Spanish troops against Indians in several skirmishes at Chalco. He also took vengeance on Indians in Calpulalpan, where the indigenous population had killed and sacrificed to their gods

45 Spaniards. Having secured peace in the region in February 1521, he was ready to transport (with Indian help) the built brigantines to Tenochtitlán.

In the first quarter of 1521, Sandoval worked tirelessly on the eastern and southern banks of the lake surrounding the capital city, subduing and converting for Cortés's use various local Indian tribes. Through his efforts, Sandoval helped to build an anti-Aztec confederacy the provided the Spanish backing in the region, in particular the Tlalhuic province.

By late May, the ground was prepared for an attack against Tenochtitlán, and Sandoval was one of the three commanders of foot divisions attacking the Aztec capital. The siege and attack against the huge Aztec capital lasted almost three months and was rich in dramatic and tragic events. Sandoval had a huge share in the final victory and also prevented disaster on numerous occasions. He was among those who captured *tlatoani* Cuauhtémoc, the monarch of Aztecs, and brought him to Cortés. The capital city Tenochtitlán surrendered in mid-August. By that time most of the city was in ruins, yet Cortés's Indian allies continued the destruction and assassination of hated Aztecs.

Like Cortés's other officers, Sandoval was sent to neighboring provinces to pacify and colonize the region for the benefit of Spain. Thus he went to the region of Coatzacoalcos, where he pacified the cities of Huatusco, Tuxtepec, and Oaxaca. He founded the town of Medellín in Tatatetelco, near Huatusco and south of present-day Veracruz, as well as the port of Espíritu Santo along the Coatzacoalcos River, as Spanish cities. Two years later, in 1523, he founded the city of Colima and established one of the first Spanish governments there. He also completed the pacification of Coatzacoalcos and consolidated the subjugation of Centla, Chinantla, and Tabasco. In many cases, Sandoval's method of pacification employed ruthless treatment of the indigenous population.

In 1524, Gonzalo de Sandoval undertook an expedition to Honduras with Cortés. During this expedition Sandoval gained new favors from Cortés. In the new territories, he was made *alguacil* and granted some encomiendas, such as Xacona. When the expedition ended, Sandoval returned with Cortés to Mexico, where he was entrusted with the governance of the whole province. He became *justicia mayor* of New Spain, replacing Marcos de Aguilar in the governing council of the colony between March 22 and August 22, 1527, during Cortés's absence.

In March 1528, Sandoval embarked for Spain with Cortés. They were returning to their home country to regain the favors they had lost in the Spanish court, favors that would allow them to successfully rule over the vast territories of New Spain. After 42 days at sea, they reached Palos. Almost immediately Gonzalo de Sandoval fell ill, so weak, that he could not even prevent being robbed of 13 bars of gold. Before his death, the youthful friend and loyal supporter of Cortés was visited one last time by his mentor.

Jakub Basista

See also: Coatzacoalcos; Cortés, Hernán; Cuauhtémoc; La Noche Triste; Montezuma II; Narváez, Pánfilo de; Tenochtitlán, Siege of; Velázquez, Diego (de Cuéllar); Villa Rica de Vera Cruz.

Resources

Diaz del Castillo, Bernal. *The Conquest of New Spain*. Edited by Janet Burke and Ted Humphrey. London: Hackett Publishing Company, 2012.

Gardiner, C. Harvey. *The Constant Captain: Gonzalo de Sandoval*. Carbondale: Southern Illinois University Press, 1961.

Thomas, Hugh. *The Conquest of Mexico*. London: Pimlico, 2004.

Thomas, Hugh. *Who's Who of the Conquistadors*. London: Cassell & Company, 2007.

Santa Cruz of Tlatelolco, College of

On January 6, 1536, during the feast of Epiphany, a dramatic inaugural ceremony composed of a procession, three sermons, mass, and meal marked the official start of the Imperial College of Santa Cruz of Tlatelolco, in the barrio of Santiago in today's Mexico City. Functioning under the protection of Emperor Charles V (Carlos I), the institution was the first school for superior studies following the European tradition in the Americas. Throughout the years, it went through several transformations, serving as the site for indoctrination, for empowerment of indigenous scholars, a space where pre-Hispanic knowledge would be recorded, a center for new intellectual production, an impressive library, printing press, and a more sedate—but significant—primary school. The school at once worked to impose Spanish-Christian norms and made space for indigenous representations, turning into a dynamic nexus of interactions, a space that helped create the Nahuatlized Christianity that Louise Burkhart theorized in her work.

Under a Royal Cédula dated December 8, 1535, Viceroy Mendoza financed the building of the school, and set up rules to gather 80–100 students, allegedly children of indigenous nobles, aged 10 to 12 years (later 8 to 12). Students learned Latin, rhetoric, logic, philosophy, and music, as well as indigenous medicine, as the school participated in the effort to fight the terrible pestilences that overwhelmed the city. Its location in a contact zone, plagued by misunderstandings, social struggles, cultural warfare, and population attrition, created periods of apogee and decay for the school. Broadly, the school experienced the following stages. A root period began with contact in the Americas, as ideas and laws about the education of indigenous boys were formed, discussed, and debated and Fray Pedro de Gante's school of *San José de los Naturales* firmly established formal colonial teaching of indigenous children in the valley of Mexico. Fray Arnaldo de Basacio, who taught Latin in San Jose in 1532, later moved to Santa Cruz de Tlatelolco as its first Latin teacher. In addition, between 1534 and 1535, Fray Jacobo de Testera sent two friars to start the educational project in Tlatelolco proper. Over time, indigenous students taught at local Franciscan schools, who proved themselves "the most capable," became part of the School of Tlatelolco's student body.

The Formative Period (1536–1546) covered the school's foundation, passing through 1539 when the children would have been exposed to the trial and death of Don Carlos, cacique of Tetzcoco, accused of being a "dogmatizing heretic." This period ended when the Franciscans, suffering from too low numbers to do their work in the field, entrusted the school to indigenous teachers and guardians (graduates of the school). The convent remained under Franciscan guardianship, and the finances of the school remained at the hands of Spanish *mayordomos.* The third stage, or Period of the Colegiales (1546—1566), saw the school in serious decline thanks in large part to corrupt Spanish overseers, plague decimations, loss of funding and support, and the scholars' difficulties running an institution over which they had no financial control, nor final say. The school struggled and became the center of debates about the value of educating indigenous

subjects, the rights of indigenous men to hold the priesthood, etc.

In the textual period (1566–1590), Fray Bernardino de Sahagún, greatest protector of the school and its students, assumed control of the school, shifting it toward a center for research, translation, and textual production. However, Sahagún's death in 1590 heralded the school's decline. Slowly it became a primary school, enduring a number of ghostly years. The convent and the new seminary for Franciscans—the Colegio de San Buenaventura y San Juan Capistrano—appropriated funds for this educational undertaking, a project approved in 1661. Finally, there was a rebirth stage in the early 18th century. Attempts to bring the school back point to the attachment of the people of Tlatelolco, members of the church, and indigenous scholars, all of whom viewed the college as an unfinished project to which they all laid claim.

Life at the school was intense. The day started at 4:00 in the morning during summers and 4:30 in winters. Wearing their proper school garb, the boys studied until 6:30, breaking only to attend mass. At 6:30, they drank chocolate for breakfast. Between 7:00 and noon students were busy in successive sets of study and lessons. At noon, older students read as the newer kids served supper. From 2:15 until dinner at 8:00, students had study and lessons with a pause to pray the rosary. At the end of their day the boys learned their obligations for the next day. They slept in one long room with beds placed in rows at either side. Throughout the night a light was left on, as older men guarded them, "as much for the keeping of quiet and silence as for the sake of chastity." Each boy had a box, with its key for their books and clothes. No one was allowed to come to the door, or leave without proper dispensation by the Padre Rector and Vice-Rector, a practice that severed the boys from their families.

As students became grown scholars, the success of the school was manifest. Graduates included notable men like Governor Antonio Valeriano, teachers such as Pablo Nazareo, Gerónimo de Medina, and Bernaldino Jerónimo, translators and authors such as Agustín de la Fuente and Juan Badiano, among others. The school also housed outstanding teachers, both European, such as Fray Bernardino Sahagún, and indigenous doctors like Martín de la Cruz and Antón Hernando. The school also created the environment that made the *Florentine Codex*, the *Libellus de Medicinalibus,* and many original texts and translations possible. Without the school, much of our knowledge of the indigenous world would have been meager, and the cultural exchanged would have taken yet another disastrous hit.

SilverMoon

See also: Charles V (HRE) or Carlos I of Spain; *Florentine Codex*; Nahuatl Language; Sahagún, Bernardino de; Sahagún's *Historia General de las Cosas de Nueva España*; Tlatelolco, or Tlateold.

Resources

Burhart, Louise M. Encounter of Religions: The Indigenization of Christianity; the Nahua Scholar-Intepreters. Occasional Papers in Latin American Studies. 1991.

Burhart, Louise M. *Holy Wednesday: A Nahua Drama from Early Colonial Mexico.* New Cultural Studies Series. Philadelphia: University of Pennsylvania Press, 1996.

Burhart, Louise M. *The Slippery Earth: Nahua-Christian Moral Dialogue in Sixteenth-Century Mexico.* Tucson: University of Arizona Press, 1989.

D'Olwer, Nicolau. *Fray Bernardino de Sahagún.* México: Instituto Panamericano de Geografía e Historia, 1952.

Fondo Franciscano. Bibioteca Nacional de México. Exp. 1312. Cuaderno 5. Fol. 27–30.

Mendieta, Geronimo de. *Historia Eclesiastica Indiana.* Mexico: Editorial Porrúa, 1971.

Puga, Vasco de. *Provisiones, cédulas, instrucciones para el gobierno de la Nueva España.* Madrid: Cultura Hispánica, 1945. Fol. 96.

Sahagun, Fr. Bernardino de. *Historia General De Las Cosas De Nueva Espana.* Vol. 3. Madrid: Ediciones José Porrua Turanzas, 1964.

Vetancurt, Agustín de. *Teatro Mexicano.* México: Editorial Porrúa, 1971.

Santo Tomás, Domingo de (1499–1570)

Spanish Dominican friar and linguist Domingo de Santo Tomás was the author of the first Quechua grammar and dictionary. Born in Seville, Spain, in 1499, Santo Tomás traveled to Peru in 1540 as part of Spanish missionary endeavors in South America. Fray Domingo was a strong advocate for local Native language and culture, acting as an intermediary between the Spanish and Peruvians on socioeconomic and political matters. A contemporary of fellow Dominican Bartolomé de las Casas, Fray Domingo campaigned against the perpetuity of the abusive encomienda system for much of his life.

Fray Domingo, the great Dominican associate of Las Casas and later bishop of Charcas, was in Peru in the 1540s and took a vocal and active part in the struggle to define the relationship between the Andean people and Spaniards. Santo Tomás founded the city of Yungay, and established a convent there on August 4, 1540. In 1542, Domingo de Santo Tomás founded another Dominican convent of Chincha, as well. For the purpose of evangelization, he learned the Quechua language spoken along the coast near Lima. He is also credited with the collection of information discussing landholding and the distribution of labor in Chincha under the Incas.

In 1545, he was elected head of the Convento del Santísimo Rosario in Lima. Increasingly, Fray Domingo became a spokesman for native interests in Peru. In 1550, he complained that the Spanish often divided a polity, which he called a province, into as many as three or four encomiendas. He railed about the injustices against human and divine law, which was done by taking away vassals and towns of a central authority or supreme indigenous lord. The native populace was instead divided among as many lords as there were Spaniards receiving an encomienda. Under this system, each of the leaders who were once subject to the supreme lord became independent lords, and neither he nor his Indians obeyed the supreme indigenous lord any longer. This decentralization of the previously centralized Inca system of governance and economy had a major impact upon the population, allowing for the Spanish to control the region and to more easily assimilate the indigenous people into the Spanish culture.

As an advocate of the indigenous population, Fray Domingo believed the Quechua language to be as refined a language for the interpretation of the Christian mysteries as Latin. He also believed since the natives were ready to learn about the faith, he could bridge the gap using their language. In 1560, Domingo published the first lexicon and grammar of Quechua, the language that the Incas had employed as the lingua franca of their empire. These volumes were not merely monuments of meticulous ethnographic investigation and linguistic scholarship. In declaring that Quechua was as elegant, ordered, and articulate a language as Latin and Spanish, and that it could be described according to the same grammatical concepts, Fray Domingo was entering a plea for self-government, with minimal interference from the Spanish.

The lexicon abounds in vocabulary denoting levels of authority that range from the Inca words for king or emperor, to the simple master of servants. The lexicon also provides terminology for professional specializations of merchants, weavers, embroiderers, potters, and many others. Thus, Santo Tomás assembled a point-by-point linguistic portrait of a many layered and ordered society that easily matched its European counterparts.

In 1562, Fray Domingo was appointed Bishop of La Plata o Charcas, in modern-day Bolivia. In the same year, leaders of a large number of ethnic groups, some of which were traditional enemies, met at San Pedro Mama near Lima. It was at this gathering of divergent indigenous representatives that the *kurakas* gave power of attorney to eight Spaniards, one of whom as Domingo de Santo Tomás. The *kurakas* desired that the selected Spanish spokesmen represent their interests in Madrid. Leaders of the Andean communities agreed to act together to convince Spaniards to stop the project of resettling and reorganizing local communities.

The best example of local Andean attempts at negotiation with the Spaniards was in 1560 when *kurakas,* through the intermediary of Santo Tomás, offered a donation of 800,000 pesos if the Crown would reject efforts of encomenderos to turn the encomienda into perpetual grants. Fray Domingo and other clerics initially supported efforts of *kurakas* to enlist Spaniards in preserving and reinforcing their authority. Clerics saw the *kurakas* as a basis of local social order, and the Church went so far as to use the confessional to reinforce chiefly authority as they say it. However, the *kurakas'* meetings and the efforts of clerics failed to reverse Spain's policies in Peru.

Fray Domingo was a champion of the native Peruvian people. He was personally responsible for setting free a number of Indians in the province of Chucuito, who had been imprisoned for sorcery by Dominican friars missionizing the area. His actions were partly out of a conviction that conversion to Christianity was an organic and slow process that must be voluntary. Domingo de Santo Tomás died in December 1570 at La Plata o Charcas.

Justin Pfeifer

See also: Encomienda; Encomenderos; *Kurakas*; Las Casas, Bartolomé de; Quechua Language.

Resources

Hemming, John. *The Conquest of the Incas.* New York: Harcourt, 2003.

McCormack, Sabine. *Religion in the Andes: Vision and Imagination in Early Colonial Peru.* Princeton: Princeton University Press, 1993.

Salomon, Frank, and Stuart Schwartz. *The Cambridge History of the Native Peoples of the Americas.* Volume 3, South America. Cambridge: Cambridge University Press, 2008.

Sapa Inca

The term Sapa Inca means "unique Inca" or emperor and was a reference to the supreme political and spiritual leader of the Inca people and their empire. The Inca nobility typically were relatives of the Sapa Inca. This kin group maintained their power and divinity (claiming descent from the main Sun god, Inti) by carefully controlling the *ayllus* or kinship group of the emperors.

Origin stories indicate that the Sun god Inti designated who would be the Sapa Inca. According to legends, the first dynastic founder, Manco Cápac, was either the son of the Sun god, Inti, or the son of Tici Viracocha, the creator of all things, including the sun. In both legends, the leadership of the Inca populace ends up resting with one, unified, spiritual and political leader, the Sapa Inca. From this comes the belief in the divine connection between the Sapa Inca and the Sun god Inti, as well as the lineage of all Sapa Inca through the same *ayllu.* The *ayllu* of the emperors was the most revered Andean kin group. This helped justify an endogamous line of kin relations that protected the claims of divinity and power of the ruling family. Nonetheless, the *ayllus* incorporated entire households, to include numerous concubines, making the royal lineage much broader than a strictly endogamous system.

Roca Cápac was presumably the first emperor to use the term Sapa Inca in the mid-14th century, though the concept is recognized and applied retroactively to the founder, Manco Cápac. The power of the Sapa Inca reached its height in the 1400s, under Pachacutin, who extended the empire to its greatest limits. The impact of foreign diseases and the conquest by the Spanish weakened the emperor's position. In 1534 the Spanish appointed Manco Inca Yupanqui as emperor, who rebelled against their authority. He successfully established the authority of the Sapa Inca. He governed from the fortress of Vilcabamba, and even managed to temporarily reclaim Cuzco.

Gradually the Spanish managed to gain control of three of the former four kingdoms except Vilcabamba. This lone kingdom continued under the rule of the Sapa Inca Manco Inca Yupanqui and, following his death, by his sons. After Manco Inca's capture and execution in 1544, his nine-year old son, Sayri Túpac, governed through a series of regents until crowned Sapa Inca at age 22. Even then, he was not the sole "unique emperor," as the Spanish simultaneously acknowledged his uncle, Paullu Inca, as the emperor. During Sayri's rule, the power of the Sapa Inca waned. Vilcabamba remained independent but weak. Lured to move back to Cuzco by the Spanish upon Paullu's death, Sayri Túpac held the official title of Sapa Inca, but without the traditional power. Within a year he died, either from illness or poisoning, and was succeeded by his brother, Titu Cusi Yupanqui.

Titu Cusi, captive of the Spanish at a young age and witness to his father's execution, returned the center of Inca authority to Vilcabamba, where he revived the guerrilla wars against Spain. His influence as Sapa Inca spread far beyond the tiny kingdom, fomenting rebellion in Chile and Peru. He fell suddenly ill and died in 1570 and was replaced as Sapa Inca by his younger brother, Túpac Amaru. Very religious and conservative in the practice of native Inca traditions, the new Sapa Inca was determined to protect Vilcabamba from any Christian or Spanish influences. Yet that same year, the new Spanish viceroy, Francisco de Toledo, was equally determined to squelch the Inca rebellion and spread the Christian faith. Believing the Inca had no right to rule the region, Toledo decided to end the rebellion by ridding the Inca of their "unique emperor." Toledo ordered the invasion of Vilcabamba and offered rewards for Túpac Amaru's capture. The emperor was compelled to convert to Christianity. Despite this conversion, he was tried and executed for blasphemy because he had been worshipped as the false god, Inti. In 1572, the last Sapa Inca was killed and the Inca fell completely under Spanish control.

Rebecca M. Seaman

See also: *Ayllus;* Manco Cápac; Manco Inca Yupanqui; Pachacutin; Sayri Túpac; Toledo, Francisco de; Túpac Amaru; Vilcabamba.

Resources

Gamboa, Pedro Sarmiento de. *History of the Incas.* Translated by Clements Markham. Cambridge: The Hakluyt Society, 1907.

MacQuarrie, Kim. *The Last Days of the Inca.* New York: Simon & Schuster, 2007.

Stern, Steven J. *Peru's Indian Peoples and the Challenge of Spanish Conquest: Huamanga to 1640.* 2nd ed. Madison: University of Wisconsin Press, 1993.

Sarmiento's *History of the Incas*

Pedro Sarmiento de Gamboa was born in Spain in 1532, the same time the Inca Empire was being conquered by Francisco Pizarro. He served in the Royal military and eventually set out to explore the New World. After encountering difficulties in Mexico, he migrated to Peru. Following an exploratory voyage of the South Pacific, where he eventually was credited with discovering the Salomon Islands, he returned to Peru. There, in 1572, he was recruited by Viceroy Francisco de Toledo to write a history of the Inca Empire.

The purpose of Toledo commissioning the historical work by Sarmiento de Gamboa underlies the eventual work produced. Viceroy Toledo was tasked with wresting control of the colony from the Pizarros and restructuring the administration in a manner that reflected traditional Spanish authority. Politically, increased pressure of Las Casas to return control of Peru and its wealth to the Incas provided motivation to justify Spain maintaining authority over the colony. The continued resistance of the Incas under Titu Cusi Yupanqui and then Túpac Amaru impeded Toledo's agenda. To justify a new strategy of dealing with the rebel Inca leaders, Toledo sought to portray the Incas as recent and violent conquerors of the traditional inhabitants of Peru and Ecuador. Part of the stratagem included the viceroy personally conducting a *visita* that sought to gather data from allied Inca royalty, often those with close Spanish relations and spouses. Once the data was gathered that supported Toledo's tactics, the next step was to formulate the data in a structure that justified Spanish conquest and even the execution of the rightful Sapa Inca, Túpac Amaru.

Sarmiento's militant support of Spain, as well as his education and experiences, fit the viceroy's purpose. The soldier-turned-explorer was commissioned to take the voluminous data collected through three years of *visitas* and construct a history of the Incas. It is not surprising that the resulting history produced portrays the Incas as recent conquerors of the region—in part because the greatest extensions of the empire had occurred in the last 100 years prior to Spanish conquest. Historical assertion that the Inca emperors employed militaries and violence to conquer their new territories also has support from other histories and archaeological evidence. However, the emphasis placed on the military conquests, and the violent nature of these conquests, reveals the partiality of the author and his employer.

Other aspects of Sarmiento's *History of the Incas* that raise questions about the authenticity of the data are the extreme details Sarmiento included regarding individuals and events from the early years of the empire. While the Inca use of *quipus* to record data were considered quite accurate, the types of data recorded did not align well with the Spanish desire for a chronological history. The use of *quipus* by the Incas was to assist with accounting records at the local level as well as to share and inform regional and central administrative officials of the recorded goods, trade, and population from across the empire. Exceedingly precise for this purpose, the *quipu* masters were also adept at associating this data with societal details for relatively recent times, and legendary feats and traditions from more distant times. *Quipus* were not designed to provide historic

and logographical records from previous centuries. Yet, despite these incongruences, Sarmiento's work incorporates this very type of detail, presumably acquired through interviews with Incas using *quipu* records.

Sarmiento de Gamboa's *History of the Incas* provides a valuable historical understanding of Spanish views concerning the Incas in the late 16th century. It additionally incorporates Inca and non-Inca information regarding the structure and history of the empire. However, students of Inca history should balance this work with other resources that incorporate more impartial accounts of the Inca pre-conquest past.

Rebecca M. Seaman

See also: Pizarro, Francisco; *Quipu*; Titu Cusi Yupanqui; Toledo, Francisco de; Túpac Amaru; *Visitas*.

Resources

Davies, Nigel. *The Incas*. Niwot: University of Colorado Press, 1995.

Salomon, Frank. *The Cord Keepers: Khipus and Cultural Life in a Peruvian Village*. Durham, NC: Duke University Press, 2004.

Sarmiento de Gamboa, Pedro. *History of the Incas*. Translated by Clements Markham. Cambridge, UK: The Hakluyt Society, 1907.

Sayri Túpac

Sayri Túpac, the 14th Inca of Peru, was one of the last emperors of the Inca Empire. He watched his country be subjugated to the will of Spanish conquerors. By the time of his birth, the Spanish were already firmly entrenched in Peru, leaving the Incas to deal with the new lords of the country. Sayri Túpac's life, although short, coincided with a crucial time in the subjugation of the Inca Empire, a period of successive puppet Incas, placed on the throne by the Spanish.

Sayri Túpac was born in 1535, the eldest son of Emperor Manco Inca Yupanqui. Though he initially sought to appease the Spanish, Manco Inca turned against them when his wife and son were captured, and his wife later killed by Pizarro and his men. Manco escaped from the Spanish and fought for independence of the Inca Empire. Meanwhile, the Spanish recognized Manco's brother, Paullu, as the emperor. After years of fighting a guerilla war, and the failed siege of Cuzco, Manco Inca established a kingdom in exile at Vilcabamba. In 1544, Sayri Túpac saw his father murdered before his eyes. Sayri Túpac ascended to the throne, but regents governed the kingdom. The child emperor was essentially left alone in the town of Vilcabamba because of the continuing fighting amongst the Spanish.

When fighting between the Spanish forces of Almagro and Pizarro ended in 1548, and with the death of Paullu, the Spanish reached out to Sayri Túpac in an attempt to get him out of the mountains where he was in hiding. Sayri Túpac allowed the Spanish to see him, especially a man named Diego Hernández. He showered the Spanish with warmth and gifts, presenting them with gold and treating them to many banquets. He finally agreed to acquiesce, leaving Vilcabamba to return to Cuzco, the Inca capital, in 1558. He left behind the royal fringe, symbol of the powers of the Inca, with his half-brother Titu Cusi. The Spanish received Sayri Túpac warmly, along with his wife (and sister) Cusi Huarcay. The viceroy provided the Inca and his wife with accommodations, Spanish servants, and great estates. The Inca people were also happy for Sayri Túpac's return, showering him with gifts.

Sayri Túpac embraced the Catholic religion and was baptized with the new name of Diego de Mendoza in 1559. The issue of his being married to his sister caused somewhat of a concern. In a show of Spanish support for the Sapa Inca, the Church gave them a special dispensation in order for them to marry within the faith.

Sayri Túpac did not live long after his religious conversion, dying just one year later in 1561. It is alleged that he was poisoned. Although many sources point out this has not been verified, the rumor was widely accepted among the Inca people, including his half-brother and successor, Titu Cusi. Nonetheless, ties of the royal Inca family with the ruling Spanish continued. Sayri's daughter Beatriz Clara Coya, considered Sayri Túpac's only legitimate child, later married Martin Garcia de Loyola, who later became the governor of Chile.

Following Sayri Túpac's death, the Spanish realized the folly of their relocating the Inca ruler in Cuzco. Instead of truly removing effective powers from the Inca, the action allowed the continued existence of those in resistance to Spanish control. Left undisturbed during Sayri Túpac's period as puppet emperor, the state of Vilcabamba remained independent and continued to experience the guidance of strong native leaders. Peruvian resistance to the Spanish continued after Sayri Túpac's death from this independent location. The last emperor Túpac Amaru continued to wage war out of Vilcabamba against the conquerors until his own execution in 1572.

Mitchell Newton-Matza and
Rebecca M. Seaman

See also: Almagro, Diego de; Manco Inca Yupanqui; Paullu; Pizarro, Francisco; Túpac Amaru; Titu Cusi Yupanqui; Vilcabamba.

Resources

Bernand, Carmen. *The Incas: Empire of Blood and Gold.* London: Thames & Hudson, 1994.

MacQuarrie, Kim. *Last Days of the Incas.* New York: Simon & Schuster, 2007.

Means, Philip A. *The Fall of the Inca Empire and the Spanish Rule in Peru, 1530–1780.* New York: Gordian Press, 1971.

Sciences and Arts of Pre-Conquest Aztec

The sciences and arts in the Mexica society prior to the Spanish conquest were comprised of uniquely Mexica attributes and a blend of cultural influences from the Mesoamerican region. In the area of the sciences, the Aztec demonstrated unique agricultural innovations with their chinampas (floating fields), botanical gardens, and the dykes that helped retain freshwater supplies even within lakes that collected mineral- and saline-rich waters. The advancements in architectural engineering, math, and astronomy were displayed in the temples and calendar rounds that the Aztec incorporated from Mayan influences. Artistically, the Aztec produced phenomenal woven cotton cloth as well as intricate jewelry and valuable tools and weapons from the metals and gems of the region.

The Aztec calendar, a blend of Aztec cultural concepts and Mayan Calendar Round structure, is a great example of the astronomical and mathematical knowledge of the Mexica. Using important Mexica names and events, the calendar round was set up to reflect key events and issues evident in the Aztec culture. This complex calendar system was actually numerous calendar systems of varying levels of complexity. The purpose of the system was to help the priests guide general members of society in planting, harvesting, and sacrifices. In this manner, the Aztec gods would be appeased and society would thrive.

Closely related to the calendar and the religious events was the architecture of the Aztecs, in particular the temples. As a polytheistic people, the Mexica professed a belief in a wide range of gods. Giving obeisance to these gods, as a means of preventing harm and ensuring bountiful harvests and military victories, was an important part of Aztec life. While individuals and families claimed their own preferred sets of deities for private ceremonies, the public ceremonies dedicated to the dominant Aztec gods were carried out on the monumental temples of the cities.

The temples found in Aztec cities were designed to link directly to the religious precepts that were interwoven within the calendar system. Directly aligned with the cycles of solar "movement," the temples were far more than just architectural wonders. Symbols representing the various deities were found etched into altars or displayed as sculptures at crucial levels in the temple structure.

Similar figures were found in the metallurgy art that was so prominent in the Mexica society. These luxury craft items were highly valued, whether a piece of jewelry made from gold/silver and gems, or a bronze or copper tool or weapon, the craftsmanship of the toltecs (luxury artisans) was superior to any similar work produced in Spain at the time of initial contact. Goldsmiths, or *teocuitlahuaque,* were considered an artisan class to themselves. They even had their own tutelary god to maintain their standards and skills.

One of the most novel forms of art produced by the Mexica was not fully appreciated by the Spanish upon their initial contact. Feather artisans, who produced feather mosaics, especially of the peacock feathers, were highly sought after by members of the *pipiltin* (upper class). So valued was the work from the feather workers that they had their own society ranking system and lived in their own communities within cities like Tenochtitlán.

Other crafts that could be considered arts but were often practical in nature included pottery, tools, and items of daily usage. Pottery was the most plentiful craft. Griddles, used for making corn cakes or tortillas, were other common items in demand by craftsmen. Tools and weapons made out of the extremely hard obsidian also were key market items.

Outside of the skilled craftsmen of the large cities, those who practiced their arts fulltime, most craftsmen combined their technical skills with knowledge of farming. The Aztec farming techniques, while not scientific in the manner of horticultural scientists today, were nonetheless quite adept at supporting their highly populated society. A unique method of farming that was developed by the Mexica was the use of chinampas. These floating fields were created by weaving and piling brush and then the wet earth drudged up from the lake bottoms. To secure the floating fields, trees were planted on the corners of the individual fields, thereby also serving to "wick" up moisture into the field system. All Aztecs farmed to some extent. The city of Tenochtitlán had a myriad of chinampas that helped feed its extensive population. Many used these to grow necessary and desirable crops for their sustenance. However, others diversified, planting flowers and other items of beauty.

Crucial to the successful farming of the chinampas was the availability of freshwater. Unfortunately, the center of the Mexica Empire was is a valley that collected drainage, high in salt content. In an effort to preserve freshwater for their crops, the Mexica developed a series of dykes that kept the salt water at bay, and gradually led to the presence of freshwater sections of the series of lakes surrounding the various Mexica cities. These dykes also provided access across the lakes, something the Spanish made use of in their siege of Tenochtitlán in 1521.

The varied forms of arts and the scientific developments of the Aztecs helped create their distinct society. While the Mexica blended many ideas—both artistic and scientific in nature—from their neighbors, the weaving of those foreign elements into the Mexica culture created unique forms of artistic and scientific expression. It was these novel and advanced elements that amazed the Spanish at the time of first contact in 1519.

Rebecca M. Seaman

See also: Agriculture and Economy, Pre-Conquest Mexico; Artisan, Mexica; Aztec, or Mexica; *Pipiltin*; Tenochtitlán, City of; Tenochtitlán, Siege of.

Resources

Díaz del Castillo, Bernal. *The Conquest of New Spain.* London: Penguin Books, 1963.

Levy, Buddy. *Conquistador: Hernán Cortés, King Montezuma, and the Last Stand of the Aztecs.* New York: Bantam Books, 2008.

Sahagún, Bernardino de. *Florentine Codex: General History of the Things of New Spain.* 12 books. Translated and edited by Arthur J. O. Anderson and Charles E. Dibble. Santa Fe, NM, and Salt Lake City, UT: School of American Research and the University of Utah Press, 1950–1982.

Smith, Michael E. *The Aztecs.* Oxford: Blackwell, 1996.

Soustelle, Jacques. *Daily Life of the Aztecs on the Eve of the Spanish Conquest.* Stanford, CA: Stanford University Press, 1961.

Thomas, Hugh. *Conquest: Montezuma, Cortés, and the Fall of Old Mexico.* New York: Simon & Schuster Press, 1993.

Sciences and Arts of Pre-Conquest Inca

The sciences and arts of the pre-conquest Inca can be seen in a variety of elements within the society. The engineering sciences used in developing the numerous suspension bridges and in the construction of palaces, aqueducts, food storage facilities, and irrigation ditches are just some examples that stand out from the pre-conquest Inca accomplishments. The *ceques,* lines radiating outward from the Temple of the Sun in Cuzco, linked the huacas of the various *ayllus* to the central worship of Inti, the Sun god. Over 300 huacas were connected through this radiating system meant to resemble the rays of the sun. Likewise, the artistic abilities of the Inca can be observed in the elaborate goldsmith work, pottery, and fine weaving.

Living in the rugged Andean Mountains, engineering feats became a necessary part of Inca life during the pre-conquest and even post-conquest era. The building of extensive rope suspension bridges was essential to the efficient functioning of transportation and communication in the rugged terrain. All rope bridges were feats of engineering. However, the large bridges required special support. Stone platforms at the ends of the bridges not only provided stable anchors for the bridge cables, but also helped reduce the length needed for some of the extremely wide gorges and rivers being spanned. Additionally, the stone platforms provided stable entrances and exits from the bridges, reducing the swaying inherent in rope bridges. So advanced was the technology found in these bridges that most chroniclers of the early colonial period provided detailed descriptions, and sometimes drawings of these feats of engineering.

While the Incas may not have perceived agricultural science in the same fashion as horticulturalists today, the diversity of crops developed by the society, and the intricate terraced farming with its accompanying irrigation and aqueduct systems is a testament to their advanced knowledge. The Inca are often given credit for the development of potatoes. However, few understand the variety of potatoes developed by the Incas over the years. Hundreds to thousands of minor varieties have been developed, ranging from fingerling to sweet potatoes, and numerous others. Likewise, the Inca developed Quinoa, a grain that is still considered to be the highest in protein found on earth. These and other nutritious crops were raised throughout the empire. So efficient was the farming system, with terracing used to maximize the potable lands and irrigation channels and aqueducts designed to modify the flow of water, that the Inca *kurakas* (local community/*ayllus* leaders) were able to collect surplus on a regular basis. Large stone facilities were created to store excess and tribute for times of need. When drought did occasionally impact productivity, the stores of foods were distributed to help sustain those in need.

The mining ability of the Incas produced large quantities of gold, silver, and other valuable gems. Artisans worked the precious metals and gems into intricate designs in statues, dishware, ornaments, jewelry, and other artwork. The finer craftsmen produced items for the Inca nobility to wear or use, while common artisans produced jewelry and everyday ware for the general market. Comments from the Spanish upon seeing the beauty of the craftsmanship always acknowledge the superior skills of the indigenous artisans. Sadly, in an effort to transport these items more easily across the rugged terrain, the Spanish often melted down these valuable pieces of art. While the value of the metal was preserved, the value of the art was lost.

An art form found in most ancient societies is the use of pottery. Inca pottery of the Imperial period fell into one of two categories: it was either mass produced, exhibiting standards found throughout the empire, or it was individually produced, making it unique and valuable. In Peru, the Mochica pots incorporated effigies of nature, people, and their deities. Warfare and even sexual practices were popular themes portrayed on household and ritual pots.

A popular, though remote, example of Inca architecture that reflects the scientific developments of the Incas exists still in Machu Picchu. This elaborate, mountainous city was built as a summer refuge of the Sapa Incas. Despite the rugged terrain, immense stones, perfectly shaped for assemblage without mortar and without gaps, formed the basis of the beautiful city. Rarely used, and occupied mainly by the elite Inca classes, Machu Picchu still stands as an example of the lasting quality of Inca stonemasonry. Additionally, the Inca often used their knowledge of astronomy to orient their important temples and buildings, in line with solar solstices and equinox movements.

Rebecca M. Seaman

See also: Agriculture and Economy, Pre-Conquest Inca; Artisans, Inca; *Ayllus;* Huacas; *Kuraka*; Machu Picchu; Religion, of Pre-Conquest Inca; Sapa Inca.

Resources

Bauer, Brian S. *The Sacred Landscape of the Inca: The Cusco Ceque System.* Austin: University of Texas Press, 2011.

D'Altroy, Terence N. *The Incas.* Malden, MA: Blackwell, 2002.

Hemming, John. *The Conquest of the Incas.* New York: Harcourt, Brace, Jovanovich, 1970.

Isabell, William H., and Helaine Silverman. *Andean Archaeology III: North and South.* New York: Springer, 2006.

McEwan, Gordon. *The Incas: New Perspectives.* New York: W. W. Norton and Company, 2006.

Stone-Miller, Rebecca. *Art of the Andes from Chavín to Inca.* New York: Thames & Hudson, 2002.

Suarez, Ananda Cohen, and George, Jeremy James. *Handbook to Life in the Inca World.* New York: Facts on File, 2011.

Sepúlveda's *De Orbe Novo (Historia del Nuevo Mundo)*

Juan Ginés de Sepúlveda was a leading Spanish humanist and scholar in the mid to late 16th century. Educated in Italy, Sepúlveda blended his humanistic thinking and scholastic views while remaining devoted to his Christian faith. He is best known, in relation to the Spanish in the New World, for his *De Orbe Novo* (Latin) or *Historia del Nuevo Mundo* (Spanish).

As early as the 1520s, Dominican friar Bartolomé de Las Casas, a former colonist, spoke and wrote vehemently against the Spanish treatment of the indigenous population in Spain's new colonial holdings. Las Casas argued that the only justification to conquer and settle the New World was to convert Indians. However, he ardently asserted that such conversion should be accomplished without force. Instead, Las Casas believed the conversion of Indians should be carried out through educating the natives about the Catholic faith.

Legalistically, the Crown initially embraced Las Casas's argument. In 1542–1543, Carlos I issued the Leyes Nuevas (New Laws), forbidding the abusive use of encomiendas and repartimientos. Though these New Laws also provided caveats that allowed the continued use of encomiendas as a means of securing Spanish interests in the colonies, the clear intent was to reduce abuses of the Indians and create a process whereby they could be brought into the Catholic fold.

By 1550, Las Casas's arguments in favor of gentle conversion and protection of the new Spanish subjects were being challenged by Juan Ginés de Sepúlveda. The resulting debates between these influential men became known as the Valladolid controversy. King Carlos I orchestrated a jury of eminent scholars (theologians and other learned doctors) to carefully consider both sides of the dispute. Las Casas argued in favor of peaceful education of the natives as a means of conversion. Sepúlveda countered Las Casas, using Aristotle and Aquinas as philosophical and theological authorities. Sepúlveda asserted that the Spanish dealings with the Indians were in essence a conflict of superior (Spanish/Catholic) versus inferior (Native Americans/pagans) beings. At the end of the debates, neither side won, since the goals of both Sepúlveda and Las Casas were not achieved.

With Las Casas's death in 1566, influences impacting Spanish control of Peru swayed the government to lean slightly in favor of Sepulveda's argument. The rebellion of the Neo-Incas, holding out against complete Spanish control of Peru, as well as the desire of the Crown and colonial administration to retain control of Peru and its valuable resources in silver and other minerals, convinced many of the need to continue enslaving the natives as a means of converting and controlling the seemingly inferior population. Yet Spanish losses, revelations of colonial corruption under the Pizarros, and reports of atrocities against the Indians increased lent support for Las Casas's arguments concerning the use of education and peaceful persuasion to convert the Incas. In the late 1560s, Bishop Toledo was sent to govern the colony. Though limitations on encomiendas continued, spurred by the teachings of Las Casas, support for Spanish retention and control of Peru was buttressed by the *History of the Incas* commissioned by Toledo, as well as the *History of the New World* penned by Sepúlveda.

Bishop Toledo developed his biased history of Peru from extensive research and interviews with select elite Incas who supported Spain's presence and opposed a return to traditional Inca rule. Unfortunately, Sepúlveda's history of the Spanish New World was far less scientific and far more biased. Having never been to the Americas, the Dominican relied primarily on writings, letters, and documents regarding the New World that supported his perceptions of Spain's rightful authority over the "inferior, pagan" populace. Despite Sepúlveda's limited success in pushing his views upon Spanish colonial policies in the 16th century, his authorship of *De Orbe Novo* swayed opinions and practices for centuries to come. In this work, Sepúlveda glorified the actions of Cortés, including his enslavement of indigenous populations. Sepúlveda's historical account indicated the Indians should be reduced to slavery and serfdom to punish them for what he considered crimes against nature. To rationalize such harsh treatment, Sepúlveda argued the process would result in the potential for conversion of the Indians, and thereby justified the violence needed to subdue them.

Rebecca M. Seaman

See also: Charles V (HRE) or Carlos I of Spain; Encomienda; Las Casas, Bartolomé de; Leyes Nuevas 1542–1543; Neo-Incas; Repartimientos; Toledo, Francisco de.

Resources

Adorno, Rolena. "Discourses on Colonialism: Bernal Diaz, Las Casas, and the Twentieth Century reader," *MLN,* 103 (March 1988): 239–258.

Brunstetter, Daniel R. *Tensions of Modernity: Las Casas and His Legacy in the French Enlightenment.* New York: Routledge Press, 2012.

Charles I, Hapsburg King of Spain. "De La Libertad De Los Indios." *Recopilacion De Leyes de Los Reynos de Las Indias.* 2nd ed. Madrid: Por Antonio Balbas, 1756.

Hanke, Lewis. *All Mankind is One: A Study of the Disputation Between Bartolomé de Las Casas and Juan Ginés de Sepúlveda on the Religious and Intellectual Capacity of the American Indian.* DeKalb: Northern Illinois University Press, 1995.

Hanke, Lewis. *Bartolomé de Las Casas: An Interpretation of His Life and Writings.* Hague: Martinus Nijhoff, 1951.

Hemming, John. *The Conquest of the Incas.* San Diego: Harcourt, Inc., 1970.

Lockhart, James, and Stuart B Schwartz. *Early Latin America: A History of Colonial Spanish America and Brazil.* Cambridge: Cambridge University Press, 1999.

Sarmiento de Gamboa, Pedro. *History of the Incas.* Translated by Clements Markham. Cambridge, UK: The Hakluyt Society, 1907.

Silver

Silver (chemical symbol Ag) is a naturally occurring metallic element, highly reflective, but easy to oxidize, which has since ancient times been used as a method of monetary exchange. Conquistadors during the early years of the Spanish conquest were more interested in gold as a precious substance than in silver. Yet it was the abundance of silver, and the discovery of several mines by Spanish conquistadores during the course of the 16th century, which financed the rise of Spain as a political and military power. The first silver mines were discovered in Mexico in the 1530s. Subsequent discoveries across northern Mexico were to follow, with mines in Zacatecas (1546), Guanajuato (1550), Pachuca (1552), Santa Barbara (1567), and San Luis Potosí in around the year 1592. In Peru mines were discovered at Porco in 1538 and at Potosí in 1545. Historians place the amount of bullion produced in the Americas from the conquest to the end of the colonial era at a number between 3 and 3.5 billion ounces of silver.

The discovery of the silver mines in Mexico and in Peru made silver the principal export of precious metal from the Americas into the European markets. At first indigenous production's smelting techniques were common for extracting silver from raw ore. The Incas used a more advanced method of processing silver, the *wayra* (Quechua for "air"). However, the increase in demand shifted production to methods that relied on European technology and methods of processing. As a result, by the 1550s, the introduction of mercury as a means of extracting the silver became the primary method used by the Spanish in Mexico and two decades later in Peru. The swell in silver production was enhanced by this introduction of the amalgamation process into Mexican mining in 1556, and subsequently in the Andean region by the 1570s. Amalgamation made it possible to obtain higher outputs of silver from less pure ores, leading to increases in bullion production. Unfortunately, it also introduced deadly toxins from mercury to the native population that conducted the amalgamation process and that was also tasked with mining mercury for use in the process.

Silver was profitable for the Spanish Crown beyond the acquisition of the royal fifth. The silver mined from the colonies was taxed by the Spanish Crown at several points, from mining to refining and minting. The Spanish Crown also controlled the supply of mercury, an essential ingredient in amalgamation.

Jesús E. Sanabria

See also: Mercury; Mines, Role in Mexico; Mines, Role in Peru.

Resources

Bakewell, Peter J., ed. *Mines of Silver and Gold in the Americas. An Expanding World.* Vol. 19. Aldershot, UK: Ashgate Variorum, 1997.

Bakewell, Peter J. *A History of Latin America: c. 1450 to the Present. The Blackwell History of the World.* 2nd ed. Malden, MA: Blackwell, 2004.

Garner, Richard L. "Long-term Silver Mining Trends in Spanish America: A Comparative Analysis of Peru and Mexico." *American Historical Review* 93 (October 1988): 898–936.

Sluiter, Engel. 1998. *The Gold and Silver of Spanish America, c. 1572–1648: Tables Showing Bullion Declared for Taxation in Colonial Royal Treasuries, Remittances to Spain, and Expenditures for Defense of Empire.* Berkeley: University of California, Bancroft Library, 1998.

Tracy, James D., ed. *The Rise of Merchant Empires: Long-Distance Trade in the Early Modern World, 1350–1750.* New York: Cambridge University Press, 1990.

Slavery, Role of

Slavery existed in the Americas long before the arrival of Europeans in the late 1400s and early 1500s. However, in comparison with the form of slavery that emerged out of Europe and the Old World, namely a form of chattel slavery where the person was completely owned as a property, could be bought and sold as such, and whose children were also considered slaves upon birth, traditional slavery in the New World appeared less harsh.

In the Aztec Empire, slaves, or *tlatlacotin,* were allowed to own their own property. These same slaves were capable of purchasing their own freedom from their masters. A male or female *tlatlacotin* was allowed to marry outside of their social class, thereby enabling slaves to marry free men and women. Additionally, offspring of slaves were born free, unlike the chattel practice of perpetuating the slave condition generation to generation. An unusual aspect of Mexica slavery was the practice of allowing a slave who successfully fled to the royal palace to then be proclaimed free.

The relatively mild conditions of Mexica slavery did have a harsher reality. Slaves were often selected to serve as sacrifices in the religious practices of Aztec society. Indeed, it was common for slaves to serve as slave temporarily and then be executed in ritual sacrificial ceremonies. The extensive wars of the Aztec against their neighbors and even tributary tribes supplied the slaves for needed labor and eventual offerings at the regular religious sacrificial ceremonies.

The labor systems of the Inca in Peru proved more complex. The *mita,* a sort of tributary tax in the form of labor, hardly constituted slavery. However, the *yanas,* or *yanaconas,* which were fulltime servants, were nonetheless subject to the payment of taxes. In this aspect, the *yanaconas* appear closer to European serfs than slaves. That slavery of some form existed is clear through accounts of captive maidens being presented as valued gifts to rulers.

The Mayan practice of slavery centered upon captives of war, much like the Mexica. From those slaves, some were sacrificed to the gods (only noble captives met this fate), while the male slaves were exported in trade and the women and children served locally. The traffic in male slaves especially captured the Spanish attention in the first decades of the 1500s, as it promised to supply an economical answer to labor demands.

The Spanish first practice of enslaving American Indians occurred with Christopher Columbus in the 1490s. By 1503, the encomienda, or granting the Spanish rights to native labor, was implemented. As the Spanish extended their control over more territories in America, they also extended their practice of slavery and encomienda. It was not uncommon for the Spanish to acquire thousands of slaves from conquered societies in the wake of battles. As the number of available indigenous laborers declined in the Caribbean, the Spanish raided the coast of the Americas to acquire new slaves. The various native populations did not accept their new conditions passively, but instead rebelled against the Spanish—though with relatively little success. Some newly acquired slaves served the Spanish conquerors, while others were transported back to the Caribbean. Eventually, the export of the Indians for sale as slaves declined with the need for laborers along the expanding frontiers.

Some of the worst stories of indigenous peoples compelled into the service of the Spanish occur with the mining camps. In the first years following the impact of Las Casas's petitions to end the abuse and enslavement of the various native populations, the Spanish used wages and other compensations to lure native laborers for work in the mines. However, the conditions in the mines were horrific, especially the mercury mines, and the increased injuries, illnesses, and death toll of miners, discouraged volunteers. Lacking sufficient numbers of volunteers, the Spanish began to coerce native laborers. As the abuse and coercive nature of compelling labor increased with regard to Spanish mining operations, the Spanish also encountered native resistance movements such as the Taki Onqoy and the Neo-Inca.

Other forms of labor used by the Spanish were employed throughout Mexico, the Caribbean, the isthmus, and South America. While some of these labor practices were intended to prevent the practice of abusive chattel enslavement, the oversight of the labor practices was lax. An example of such a situation included the repartimiento. This practice was similar to the *mita* labor requirements of the Inca in Peru. According to the Spanish practice, temporary labor allotments were required of local native societies, and gifts were given in exchange for the allotment of laborers. While in theory the communities were compensated for the use of their labor force, the reality was that, over time, the distribution of gifts failed to reach the people providing the labor. Additionally, as the Spanish colonial authority became more entrenched, the practice and enforcement of encomenderos complying with the gifting requirements waned. Eventually, the period of labor demands increased from one or two months to a year or more. Simultaneously, the compensation for the labor decreased until no gifts were exchanged for the tributary laborers. At that point, the system became virtual slavery.

Another impact of the practice of slavery was the accompanying mortality of the various Native American peoples. The constant contact of the native peoples with Spanish missionaries, soldiers, settlers, and officials increased their exposure to European diseases. Smallpox, various forms of the plague, and other more common illnesses among the Spanish proved deadly for the Inca, Maya, and Aztec people. Additionally, the tendency for the Spanish to require native populations to abandon more distant villages and to coalesce around central urban centers increased the exposure to disease and the decline in healthy diets. The combination was lethal and contributed to the rapid decline of the indigenous population over the course of the first century of contact.

As the original local populations were decimated, and the demands for silver, gold, mercury, and other ores continued unchecked, alternate forms of labor became a necessity. In the early years of Spanish conquest and settlement, a small number of African slaves and servants accompanied the expeditions, often as personal servants. With the decline of the native labor systems, the demand for African slaves increased. Although the use of Africans as the dominant labor force did not occur in the first century of Spanish conquest, the origins of the slave practices and the decline in indigenous populations that precipitated the increased usage of Africans as slaves began in the first decade of Spanish conquest of the New World.

Rebecca M. Seaman

See also: Encomenderos; Encomienda; European Diseases, Role of; Las Casas, Bartolomé de; Mercury; *Mita*; Neo-Incas; Repartimiento; Silver; Taki Onqoy; *Yanaconas*.

Resources

Arias, Santa. "Empowerment Through the Writing of History: Bartolomé de Las Casas." In *Early Images of the Americas: Transfer and Invention,* edited by Jerry M. Williams and Robert E. Lewis. Tucson: University of Arizona Press, 1993.

Clendinnen, Inga. *Ambivalent Conquests: Maya and Spaniard in Yucatan, 1517–1570.* 2nd ed. Cambridge Latin American Studies. Cambridge: Cambridge University Press, 2003.

Davies, Nigel. *The Incas.* Niwot: University of Colorado Press, 1995.

Palencia-Roth, Michael. "The Cannibal Law of 1503." In *Early Images of the New World: Transfer and Creation.* Edited by Jerry M. Williams and Robert E. Lewis. Tucson, AZ: University of Arizona Press, 1993: 21-64.

Prager, Carolyn. "Early English Transfer and Invention of the Black in New Spain." In *Early Images of the New World: Transfer and Creation.* Edited by Jerry M. Williams and Robert E. Lewis. Tucson, AZ: University of Arizona Press, 1993: 93-110.

Thomas, Hugh. *Conquest: Montezuma, Cortés, and the Fall of Old Mexico.* New York: Simon & Schuster, 1993.

Soras

The Soras was a native society in Peru whose people lived in the region of Huamanga. This society was known in part for their large herds of llamas, as well as productive mines of gold and silver. At the start of the 15th century, they existed as vassals of the Chanca. Under the Inca ruler Pachacutin, the Soras were defeated and incorporated into the Inca Empire, which included the Inca practice of creating two distinct ranks within society.

Inca and pre-Inca societies employed systems of duality in class or status. Within the Inca society, this dual system of ranking was referred to as the Hanan (upper) and Hurin (lower) class. One example of this division of local people existed in the Huamanga region. There, the Inca divided the Soras population into two distinct classes, the Hanansora and the Hurinsora.

Many examples of the dual ranking of Incas and non-Incas have murky origins, making it hard to determine if the system was in existence prior to Inca dominance. However, in the case of the Hanansora and Hurinsora, historical records indicate the Inca introduced the class divisions in the Soras population when they conquered the region in the early 15th century. The Inca compelled other elements of cultural assimilation upon their new subjects. Unlike the Inca, the Soras did not originally speak Quechua, but instead spoke Aymara. The redesign of the social classes and language base was a method of controlling the resistant Soras.

The local government of the Soras was also replaced with an Inca structure, with close oversight. Additionally, archaeological evidence demonstrates a strong Inca influence in the buildings of the Soras, as well as their irrigation systems and other aspects of the infrastructure. The resistance to Inca rule displayed by the Soras, and their attempt to draw the Chanca into the region to defeat the Inca, helps explain why the Inca demanded the Soras assimilate such a wide variety of Inca cultural traits.

Rebecca M. Seaman

See also: Chanca; Hanan; Huamanga; Hurin; Pachacutin.

Resources

Abraham, Sarah. "Provincial Life in the Inca Empire: Continuity and Change at Pulapuco, Peru." PhD diss., University of California, Santa Barbara, 2010.

Davies, Nigel. *The Incas.* Niwot: University of Colorado Press, 1995.

Soto, Hernando de, in Peru

Hernando de Soto was born near Badajoz, Spain, in the late 1490s. He sailed to America in 1514, landing in Darién (Panama). Soto rapidly moved up the ranks and was promoted to captain over cavalry forces by 1519. He accompanied an expedition that same year. Soon after, he joined Licenciado Gaspar de Espinosa's expedition, commanded by Francisco Pizarro. Soto's party was tasked with scouting the territory ahead of Pizarro, where he encountered and helped rescue Espinosa's main force from a native attack. When Avila sent an expedition into the region (Nicaragua) under Francisco Hernandez de Córdoba in 1524, Soto's previous success earned him a noted position in the expeditionary force.

It is at this point that Soto experienced his first active involvement in political struggles within colonial administration. Córdoba's success in Nicaragua resulted in his challenging Ávila's authority, seeking an appointment as governor from the king, Charles I. Soto refused to support Córdoba's grab for power. His refusal resulted in Soto's arrest. Released by his fellow captains, he returned to Darién and reported events to Ávila. Soto's reward for his loyal support of Ávila was an appointment as captain of the guards and extensive encomienda grants. By 1530, he was appointed *alcalde mayor* of Nicaragua's major town. Discontent with the sedentary role, Captain Soto was recruited to participate in Francisco Pizarro's third voyage planned for the exploration of Peru.

Pizarro had already attempted two expeditions to Peru. His original informal partnership with Diego de Almagro lost its funding and external support. To guarantee financing, Pizarro returned to Spain to ask support from Charles I. Receiving royal support, Pizarro returned to America, where tensions with his partners and brothers continued to grow.

Soto was recruited early on by Bartolomé Ruiz, Pizarro's navigator. Eager for adventure, he nonetheless delayed committing to the venture, not wishing to serve in a subordinate role to other participants. Aware that by financing his own forces he might obtain a more significant position in the expedition, Soto recruited his own men and horses. He then negotiated terms with Pizarro that placed him in the role of an attached commander, though he had hoped to be appointed second in command of the expedition.

Soto finally arrived at Isla Puná in December 1531, with 100 men and horses under his command. The timing was excellent, as Pizarro had suffered losses from disease and attacks by the indigenous population. Pizarro proceeded to move inland, using Soto as the vanguard, partly due to his cavalry skills and party because Pizarro viewed Soto as expendable. Soto's reconnaissance role placed him in a position to meet the first emissary sent by Atahualpa, the leading contender for the position of Sapa Inca (unique emperor) in the Inca civil war. Soto brought the emissary back to Pizzaro, where the Spanish learned that Atahualpa was at Cajamarca with a sizeable, well-armed force. The emissary invited the Spanish to be the guests of the emperor.

Upon arrival at Cajamarca, Soto was assigned the role of meeting with Atahualpa. Taking 15 horsemen and an interpreter, he rode into the Inca encampment. Soto, along with Hernando Pizarro and the interpreter,

met with Atahualpa. The Spanish retained their position on their horses the entire time, hoping to awe the emperor and his forces. Displaying no sign of fear or alarm in the presence of the mounted Spaniards, Atahualpa agreed to meet with Pizarro on the following day.

Soto reported the number of well-armed Inca forces at 40,000 men. Pizarro divided his inferior numbered forces, placing horsemen and foot soldiers in buildings surrounding the main square of Cajamarca. When Atahualpa finally entered, he was greeted by an interpreter and a sole priest, Father Vicente de Valverde. The priest read Atahualpa the *Requerimiento* and presented

Hernando de Soto, though best known for his entrada through the southeastern region of North America, was one of Francisco Pizarro's officers. This is an artistic rendering of Soto's efforts to intimidate the Sapa Inca, Atahualpa, with his horsemanship. (Library of Congress)

the emperor with a Bible, which was tossed to the ground by the Inca. Immediately the Spanish attacked, massacring thousands of unarmed Inca forces. Pizarro captured Atahualpa, holding him as a hostage. Then, with several thousands of armed Inca outside the city walls, Pizarro sent Soto to inspect Atahualpa's campsite. Surprisingly, the emperor's forces surrendered to Soto or fled to the surrounding hills.

The Spanish had control of the emperor but not the empire. Over the next two years, Soto scouted and launched military missions against various Inca armies and cities. Typically sent on reconnaissance missions in conjunction with larger forces, Soto repeatedly exceeded his instructions, often to great reward, but occasionally narrowly escaping complete disaster. By 1534, Soto was appointed lieutenant governor of the capital city, Cuzco. During his one year as acting governor, the old rift between Pizarro and Diego de Almagro peaked, resulting in Charles V dividing Peru into a northern (Pizarro's) and a southern district (Almagro's). Both parties immediately claimed Cuzco. Soto, beholden to Almagro for rescuing him from one of his near disasters, initially supported the inclusion of the capital in the southern district.

Soto backed Almagro partially due to his own ambitions. The governor of Cuzco wished to join in Almagro's planned expedition into Chile, as a partner or expedition leader. When Almagro selected another for that role, Soto decided to leave Peru. After receiving his considerable share of Inca wealth in August 1535, Hernando de Soto returned to Spain, prior to his later entrada through the North American Southeast.

Rebecca M. Seaman

See also: Almagro, Diego de; Atahualpa; Cajamarca, Battle of; Cuzco; Encomienda; Pizarro, Francisco; *Requerimiento*; Ruiz, Bartolomé.

Resources

Lamar, Curt. "Hernando de Soto before Florida: A Narrative." *The Hernando de Soto Expedition: History, Historiography, and "Discovery" in the Southeast.* Edited by Patricia Galloway. Lincoln: University of Nebraska Press, 1997.

MacQuarrie, Kim. *The Last Days of the Incas.* New York: Simon & Schuster, 2007.

Stern, Steve J. *Peru's Indian Peoples and the Challenge of Spanish Conquest.* Madison: University of Wisconsin Press, 1993.

Spain, Imperial Goals of

The Spanish Empire, which spanned from 1492 to the 1970s, had specific short-term and long-term aims in its overseas colonization efforts. Spain's imperial period began in the 15th century during the reigns of King Ferdinand II of Aragon and Isabella I of Castile. The completion of the Reconquista in 1492 drove the last Moorish king from the Iberian Peninsula, allowing for a period of stability and for imperial expansion to begin abroad. Ferdinand and Isabella negotiated with Genoese sailor Christopher Columbus on a bold plan to compete with the Portuguese Empire in the Far East by sailing west around the globe. Columbus's discoveries in the Americas began Spain's imperialist expansion westward.

Despite Spain's inability to compete with the Portuguese in Asia, the Spanish conquest of the Americas proved to be an equally lucrative venture. Spain's claim to lands in the Americas was solidified with the Treaty of Tordesillas of June 7, 1494, in which the Spanish and Portuguese divided the globe into two hemispheres of imperial domination. King Ferdinand desired to create a Spanish overseas empire to gain material wealth, increase military power, and to spread Catholicism. The successful settlement of

Hispaniola in the late 15th century led to aspirations of colonial exploitation of other territories as well. Juan Ponce de Leon conquered Puerto Rico in 1508 and ruled there as provincial governor until 1511. Another conquistador, Diego Velázquez, led the conquest of Cuba in 1511, further solidifying Spain's imperial holdings in the Caribbean.

On the Caribbean islands, the Spaniards were largely frustrated in their search for precious metals, spices, and other valuable commodities. Most of the *hidalgos* were quickly disappointed with the lack of gold and silver and were not taken with the idea of farming. Instead, as early as 1499 these aristocratic colonists began to employ the exploitative repartimiento, later associated with the encomienda system. This adapted form of medieval feudalism utilized the natives as a cheap supply of labor. While the monarchy had ultimate title to the land, certain Spanish subjects—called an encomenderos—were given use of parcels of land along with control over the inhabitants. The encomenderos owed loyalty and tribute to their sovereign, as well as a promise to protect and spread the Catholic faith.

The Spanish desire for continued conquest in the Americas stemmed from want of riches, lands, and converts. Between 1519 and 1550, conquistadors driven by a desire to serve king and God, as well as to fill their pockets with riches, won for Spain a huge empire in the New World. One of the most famous of the conquistadors was Hernán Cortés, who departed from Cuba in 1519 with a mere 400 soldiers in order to conquer the great Aztec Empire in Mexico. In less than three years, Cortés reduced the vast Aztec Empire to vassalage for Carlos I (Charles V of the Holy Roman Empire) and Spain. Cortés kidnapped the Aztec monarch Montezuma II and ransomed him for gold and silver. In July 1520, Cortés began a siege of the Aztec capital of Tenochtitlán, resulting in its eventual capitulation in 1521. The Spaniards were assisted by the outbreak of smallpox amongst the Aztecs, as well as the support of Indian allies for the Spanish from rival states. Cortés's victory won for Spain vast territory as well as gold, silver, and precious stones.

The Spanish zeal for power, land, and wealth compelled them to conquer another New World civilization in Peru. The Inca Empire was the largest in the New World, spanning more than 3,000 miles, and consisting of over a million people. Conquistador Francisco Pizarro secured a *Capitulacion* from Carlos I in July 1529, making him governor of New Castile in South America. By 1531, Pizarro sailed from Panama with only 180 men, but in conquering the Incas he utilized many of the same techniques of Cortés. Pizarro arrived in Peru during the time of an immense smallpox outbreak, which preceded Pizarro's forces. By the time he arrived, the disease had ravaged the Incas and even killed their emperor, Huayna Capac. A civil war ensued between the emperor's heirs, and only ended in 1532 with the victory of Atahualpa. Pizarro, using the strategy of Cortés, kidnapped the Inca king, Atahualpa, and held him as ransom for a year. Once he had outlived his usefulness, Atahualpa was executed. In the ensuing chaos, Pizarro's forces captured the Inca capital of Cuzco. By 1535, the Inca lands around Cuzco were firmly in the hands of the Spanish, though the reigning Sapa Inca rebelled against Spanish abuses and began a decades long uprising that thwarted Spanish objectives for the region until the 1570s.

The conquest of Central and South America by the Spanish created an enormous overseas empire. Spanish monarch Carlos I attempted to extract the maximum amount of profit from the conquered lands with the minimum amount of effort. He sent royal agents to Mexico and Peru to establish the basis for Crown rule and reassert monarchical authority. Between 1525 and 1600, the Spanish Habsburgs set up a complicated administrative system headed by the king and the Council of the Indies, made up of legal experts who had complete legislative control regarding policy in the empire. The Council of the Indies decided issues of law and order, treatment of the Indians, economic policy, and even town planning. In order to administer Central and South America, the council established the viceroyalties of New Spain and Peru. The viceroyalties utilized *audiencias,* or royal courts, for administrative and judicial functions, and all of the judges came from Spain.

While the Treaty of Tordesillas had established spheres of influence for Portugal and Spain, imperial ambitions came into conflict with these dictums. The Treaty of Zaragosa (1529) forbade Spain any claims to the Spice Islands in Asia, but by the 1560s, the Spanish were poised to seize the Philippines. In 1571, Miguel Lopez de Legaspi transferred the capital from Cebu to Manila, which was an excellent harbor and possessed rich agricultural lands. The Spanish monarch, Philip II, ordered the Christianization of the new Spanish conquests, which slowly took place with the arrival of Catholic missionaries. The viceroyalty of New Spain held direct control over the Philippines colony. Politically, the viceroy and *audiencia* in Mexico City exercised control through the local governor general. The most important economic role of the Philippines for the Spanish imperial system was as a corollary between the New World and China. Trade between the Spanish America and the Philippines mirrored the Atlantic treasure fleet system, with cargoes of silk, porcelain, and other goods changing hands in exchange for Spanish silver. Estimates indicated that as much as one quarter of New World silver went to China during the 17th century. Spain profited admirably during this period, compensating the empire for its vast expenses incurred due to warfare with other European powers.

The hierarchical control was officially mandated by the monarchy for its American empire. The House of Trade in Seville, which was heavily involved in gold and silver mining, controlled commerce. By 1650, 181 tons of gold and 16,000 tons of silver had been mined from Spain's New World Empire. The encomienda system was another source of economic strength, with mining, animal husbandry, and plantations as the most profitable sectors. Tobacco was a major cash crop in the 17th century, requiring large-scale slave labor to produce the harvest. The interchange of goods between Europe and the Americas involved a convoy system of armed fleets of ships. However, the risk on the seas of pirating was great, especially with growing competition from the English, Dutch, and French.

One of the biggest issues facing the Spanish Empire concerned the treatment of the indigenous Indian population. Dominican friar Bartolomé de Las Casas was a major critic of Spanish abuses against the Indians, believing that the indigenes deserved the same rights and privileges granted to the king's subjects. The Leyes Nuevas of 1542–1543 attempted to prohibit certain abuses, restricting enslavement of the Indians unless specifically approved by the Crown. By 1550, Carlos I had determined that the Indians were indeed subjects of the Crown, allowing them to own property, sue in courts, and to be accepted in the local bureaucracy. Yet despite this paternalism, the encomienda system still allowed Spanish colonists to employ laborers from the Indian populace, provided that there was an appropriate wage rate. These caveats to royal decrees were intended to guarantee the security and economic success of the Spanish colonies in America.

Religion was an issue of great priority within the Spanish Empire. The monarchy enjoyed the unique privilege of *Patronato Real* by the papacy, allowing for the spreading of the Catholic faith and appointment of bishops. Missionary orders such as the Franciscans, Dominicans, Augustinians, and the Jesuits proceeded to spread Catholicism throughout the New World. By 1600, there were roughly 300 monasteries in New Spain alone, with at least 1,500 clergy in them. The religious orders came to control huge tracts of lands and wealth, often coming into conflict with the encomienda holders. Yet the Church continued to receive immense financial and material support from the Spanish monarchy, ensuring the entrenchment of Catholicism in Latin America.

The Spanish Empire managed to survive despite increased attacks by imperial rivals England, France, and the Netherlands. The ruling family, of the Hapsburg line, struggled with internal divisions. Dynastic continental wars in Europe and abroad threatened the stability of the Spanish monarchy, though they managed to maintain formidable holdings in South America well into the 19th century. Nonetheless, Spain's importance as a commercial power began its decline in the 17th century due to a drop in the output of silver mines, increasing debts of the monarchy, and competition from the European powers.

Justin Pfeifer

See also: Atahualpa; *Audiencia*; Charles V (HRE) or Carlos I of Spain; Cortés, Hernán; Encomienda; Encomenderos; Gold, Role of in Spanish Expeditions; Las Casas, Bartolomé de; Leyes Nuevas 1542–1543; Pizarro, Francisco; Reconquista, Impact of on Spanish policy in America; Repartimiento; Silver.

Resources

Ames, Glenn Joseph. *The Globe Encompassed: The Age of European Discovery, 1500–1700.* Upper Saddle River, NJ: Pearson Prentice Hall, 2008.

Kamen, Henry. *Empire: How Spain Became a World Power, 1492–1763.* New York: HarperCollins, 2003.

Maltby, William S. *The Rise and Fall of the Spanish Empire.* New York: Palgrave Macmillan, 2009.

Parry, John Horace. *The Spanish Seaborne Empire.* New York: Knopf, 1966.

Prescott, William. *History of the Conquest of Peru: With a Preliminary View of the Civilization of the Incas.* Philadelphia: J. B. Lippincott, 1876.

Thomas, Hugh. *Rivers of Gold: The Rise of the Spanish Empire 1490–1522.* London: Orion Books, 2004.

Spanish, Division within during the Conquest of Mexico

Disagreements generated between Diego Velázquez, Pánfilo de Narváez, and Hernán Cortés during the conquest of Mexico between 1518 and 1521 highlight the divisions among the Spanish in the New World. The confrontation between the two captains, Narváez and Cortés, led to the formation of factions, which were involved in diverse incidents, and largely determined the course of the war of conquest.

Hernán Cortés (1485–1547) participated in the expedition for the conquest of Cuba led by the *adelantado* and later governor Diego Velázquez de Cuéllar (1465–1524), in 1511. In 1515 he became mayor of Santiago de Cuba. Velázquez organized a third expedition to explore the coast of Yucatán, after the previous two attempts by other explorers failed. On October 23, 1518, he signed the capitulations where Hernán Cortés was appointed captain of the expedition, predating King Carlos I's approval. At the last minute, Velázquez decided to dismiss the ambitious Cortés and appointed a new captain, Amador de Lares. Aware of Velázquez's vacillating support, Cortés decided to leave Santiago in November 1518, prior to receiving orders removing him from command. Sailing to western Cuba, Cortés stopped to recruit soldiers and get supplies before venturing on toward the Yucatán.

Cortés left Cuba with 11 ships, 11 captains, and 550 Spanish. Meanwhile, on November 13, 1518, the king signed the document authorizing Velázquez to make the expedition. With official royal support, the governor made an attempt to stop and arrest Cortés through emissaries. Some of the emissaries delivered the governor's message but then joined Cortés's expedition. Unaffected by the shift in official support for his venture, the conquistador left Cuba on February 18, 1519, for the Mexican coast.

After visiting the island of Cozumel and the coast of Tabasco, the Spanish reached Veracruz, where they founded San Juan de Ulua and the Villa Rica de la Vera Cruz in July 1519. The latter town was erected in order to establish a council to obtain autonomy from Governor Velázquez, following the Castilian laws. Cortés made a pretence of wanting to go back to Cuba, asserting the objectives agreed to with Velázquez at the start of the expedition had already been reached. The strategy of Cortés, who knew most of his captains supported him, was to resign from the position of main captain of the governor of Cuba and to have his men make him the "elected" main captain of a new expedition.

In this manner, he was obligated to show obedience only to the king of Spain. When Velázquez heard the news of this act, he organized an army to capture Cortés. Meanwhile, Admiral Diego Columbus, governor of the island of La Española (Dominican Republic and Haiti), asked the king to support neither side, because he claimed for himself the rights of the Capitulations of Santa Fé (signed in 1492 between the Catholic Kings and Christopher Columbus, his brother).

Having been elected as the captain of the expedition, Cortés proceeded inland, where he sealed an alliance with the Totonac in Zempoala and Quiahuiztlan (Veracruz). He left at Villa Rica de la Vera Cruz a dissatisfied group of Velázquez's supporters, who decided to return to Cuba. Unwilling to be hampered by those who would undermine his efforts, Cortés nonetheless did not wish to allow Velázquez's allies to return to Cuba. Instead, he presided over a court-martial to stop them, and the rebels were severely punished. As a precaution, Cortés decided to sink most of his ships to avoid the desertion of the men.

Cortés turned inland from his coastal conflict with his own people. After he defeated the Tlaxcaltec, commanded by Xicoténcatl Axayacatzin, he sealed an alliance with the powerful native kingdom. With his new allies, he continued his progress inland, and arrived in Tenochtitlán, the seat of Aztec power. There Cortés took the emperor, Montezuma II, hostage to prevent a rebellion against his insufficient forces. Meanwhile, in April 1520 in Spain, the Council of Castile convened to listen to the *procuradores* (solicitors) of the Villa Rica de la Vera Cruz who had managed to return home to report on events. The council had to decide about the dispute between Cortés and Velázquez.

Without waiting for a decision by the Council of Castile, Diego Velázquez confiscated the properties of Cortés in Cuba, and ordered an army, led by Pánfilo de Narváez (1470–1528), to arrest or kill him. This did not please the *juez de residencia* (judge of residence) of La Española, Rodrigo de Figueroa, who tried to stop Narváez. Failing to stop the punitive expedition, the judge sent Lucas Vázquez de Ayllón to Villa Rica de la Vera Cruz to negotiate an agreement between the opposing captains.

Narváez arrived in Cempoala, and from there he kept a secret correspondence with the captive Montezuma to lure him against Cortés. Having his advice ignore by Narváez, Ayllón began to shift his initially anti-Cortés sentiments to a more favorable view of the conquistador. Narváez viewed Ayllón's opposition to his actions as a betrayal, accused Ayllón of speaking well of Cortés, had the mediator arrested, and along with some supporters, sent Ayllón back to Cuba. Ayllón convinced the ship captain to head for La Española, where he informed Spain about the violent behavior of Narváez.

When Cortés was informed about the arrival of Narváez, a series of messages with offers, negotiations, insults, and threats were exchanged between the two Spanish captains. Cortés decided to face his enemy, leaving Pedro de Alvarado in charge of the Spanish troops in Tenochtitlán. Cortés had 260 soldiers against the 800 men of Narváez. However, Cortés had bribed the Spanish artillery to prevent them from opening fire on his forces. During the conflict, Narváez suffered many wounds and lost an eye. Defeated, his men laid down their arms and swore loyalty to Cortés; their defeated captain was sent to Veracruz as a prisoner.

Afterward, Cortés returned to Tenochtitlán, where a rebellion between the Mexica was underway. Shortly before starting the final siege of Tenochtitlán, in mid-1521, Captain Antonio de Villafaña, still loyal to Diego Velázquez, hatched a plan to kill Cortés. Unsuccessful, Villafaña was caught and executed. Back in Spain, after much discussion, the Council of Castile settled the lawsuit between Velázquez and Cortés in 1522, proclaiming Cortés *adelantado*, captain general and governor of New Spain. Despite this obvious vindication, Cortés was forced to return the money invested by Diego Velázquez in the venture against the Aztec Empire in Mexico. In so doing, the rift between the competing Spanish leaders in New Spain was effectively brought to a close, though conflicts between conquistadors competing for riches and status continued for years.

Marta Martín Gabaldón

See also: Alvarado, Pedro de; Ayllón, Lucas Vázquez de; Charles V (HRE) or Carlos I of Spain; Montezuma II; Narváez, Pánfilo de; Olid, Cristóbal de; Ordaz, Diego de; Velázquez, Diego (de Cuéllar); Velázquez de León, Juan.

Resources

Prescott, William H. *The History of the Conquest of Mexico.* Edited by Harvey Gardiner. First published in 1847. Chicago, IL: The University of Chicago, 1966.

Pohl, John, and Charles M. Robinson III. *Aztecs and Conquistadores: The Spanish Invasion and the Collapse of the Aztec Empire.* Oxford: Osprey Publishing, 2005.

Sánchez Sorondo, Gabriel. *Historia oculta de la Conquista de América.* Madrid: Ediciones Nowtilus, 2009.

Thomas, Hugh. *The Conquest of Mexico.* London: Pimlico, 2004.

T

Tahuantinsuyu

Also written Tawantinsuyu (modern), the term means "four regions" of the Inca Empire and was used by the Incas when referring to their people and society. Cuzco, the seat of what became the Inca Empire, started as a single village. In the later 14th and early 15th century, the city and its immediate surrounding conquests were organized into four precincts to facilitate effective governance. Some historians theorize that this organization is founded on religious teachings regarding the creator god of the Inca, Viracocha, who initially divided the world into four sections. This is the basis of what became the Tahuantinsuyu—both the organization into quadrants and the empire itself.

The Inca Empire, originating in the valley of Cuzco, expanded greatly in the 15th century under the leadership of Pachacutin (Pachacuti-cusi Yupanqui or Pachacutec) and Túpac Inca Yupanqui, reaching throughout modern-day Ecuador and Peru in the Andes. It was under Pachacutin that the empire was divided into four distinct quadrants or *suyu*. The four sections of the extended empire radiated outward from Cuzco, designated by *ceques* lines that connected ancient sanctuaries and huacas of the Inca and neighboring tribes. Each *suyu* was accessed by principal roads, which extended out of Cuzco into the four quadrants. The *suyus* were assigned military commanders, or Apos, by the Inca government as a means of extending Inca authority outward into each section.

The *suyu*, or quadrants, became the basic physical structure for organizing the Inca leadership over diverse peoples in exceedingly rough terrain. The four regions included the Antisuyu in the northeast, the Collasuyu in the southeast, Chinchaysuyu in the northwest, and the Contisuyu (Condesuyu) in the southwest. In addition to the four major *suyus*, the empire was further divided into provinces, each with its own villages and districts. These smaller units often were based upon tribal orientations from pre-Inca times. Central government for these provinces was assigned to Incas of high status known as t'oqrikoqs. Incas by privilege, consisting of Quechua-speaking tribes, also served in the role of *kurakas* to help govern the scattered tribal societies.

Access to and distribution of wealth was directly related to the expansion and method of controlling the quadrants, provinces, and villages. In the 15th century, wealth and power was viewed as the control of resources—specifically foodstuffs and certain luxury items. The Incas used tributes of goods to gather stores of resources controlled by the administrators of the *suyus*, as well as the internal provinces and villages. As the empire expanded into regions capable of producing needed foodstuffs for the widespread empire, emperors offered the leaders of the potential allies rewards, including luxury items that made governing as a subject of the Inca more beneficial than continued independence. In this manner, the size and productivity of the four *suyus* continued to expand.

Historical records differ on the method and timing of expansion. Those favoring a long tradition of Inca expansion, combining organization, administration, shared wealth, and warfare fall in the school of thought headed by Garcilasco de la Vega. Countering this view, Viceroy Toledo's official historian Pedro Sarmiento de Gamboa, and others of the same era, asserted wars of conquest were the dominant method of expansion. This later school of thought places the bulk of these expansionary conflicts in the last half of the 15th century, asserting they were responsible for the rapid, recent, and extensive holdings of the Incas.

Whatever the interpretation of how the Incas spread and held their empire, the division of that empire into four distinct *suyus* for administrative purposes, during the preconquest era, is unquestioned. Like the Inca before them, the Spanish control of the empire began with the conquest and administration of Cuzco. The Spanish then attempted to extend their power north and south, into Ecuador and Chile. The northern section provided years of resistance, as the rebel Incas continued to govern and to raid the Spanish holdings and supply lines from the remote Antisuyu region.

Rebecca M. Seaman

See also: Antisuyu; Chinchaysuyu; Collasuyu; Contisuyu; Cuzco; *Kuraka*; Pachacutin; Quechua Language; Sarmiento's *History of the Incas*; Toledo, Francisco de; T'oqrikoq; Túpac Inca Yupanqui; Vega, Garcilaso de la.

Resources

Davies, Nigel. *The Incas.* Niwot: University of Colorado Press, 1995.

Hemming, John. *The Conquest of the Incas.* New York: Harcourt Brace Jovanovich, 1970.

MacQuarrie, Kim. *The Last Days of the Incas.* New York: Simon & Schuster, 2007.

Taki Onqoy

The conservative, religious reaction of the Inca, known as the Taki Onqoy, was an attempt to undermine the threat Spanish colonialism presented for the native cultural beliefs. Meaning "dancing sickness" or "dance of disease," the term refers to the convulsions demonstrated by members of the spiritual sect as they danced and entered a form of trance.

Millenarian in nature, the Taki Onqoy held that its members should reject all things European. In doing so, it was believed that the Inca would be restored to their more traditional order. *Taquiongos,* or messengers of the native deities, taught that the unified Andean spirits would defeat the Christian god and kill the Spanish through disease, war, and other calamities. Militarily, the *taquiongos* preached that two armies, led by native gods, would battle the Christian god and reverse the calamity brought upon the Inca by Pizarro's victory almost 30 years prior. Additionally, diseases, like those the Spanish brought, would destroy the Europeans. A flood would rise up and destroy the Spanish cities, removing all trace of the Spanish culture. To ensure the success of the Andean gods, and to avoid falling victim to the fate of the Spaniards, devoted Incas were instructed to worship and dance to the merciless huacas (sacred spirits, beings, or totems). Those Inca gods who opposed ethnic independence were excluded from the message of regeneration.

The religious revival movement seems to have originated in the region of Huamanga around 1560. Typical of Andean belief systems, the gods were instrumental in any major catastrophes that beset the society. The decade of calamity that fell upon the region was therefore seen as inherently religious in nature, and a consequence of the Inca betraying their traditional beliefs. The angry huacas, abandoned by natives who no longer worshiped them or fed them their ritual sacrifices, wandered the empire, in search of Spaniards and disloyal natives to kill. Only with the return of the natives to their traditional beliefs would the people of the Andes experience a true paradise, free from disease and full of prosperity.

The *tanuiongos* (leaders among the Taki Onqoy) brought huacas and idols to welcoming villages, encouraging the people to worship them and make confession to them. They also collected, in return, their own wealth in the form of religious offerings of llamas, cloth, ceremonial beer, and other tributes to the gods. Incorporated into their messages were exhortations to fast and to completely abandon all elements of Hispanic life, especially the Catholic faith. The success of the messengers, who attracted followers from all ranks of society, bore witness to the frustration of the general population under Spanish dominance. Even new converts to Christianity returned to their former deities. Fears arose that the anti-European movement would undermine all Spanish control, and alienate the newly cooperating *kurakas*. Such a shift would risk a general rebellion of the *ayllus* against the distant rural encomiendas. The movement helped create a Pan-Indian movement, even pulling in the Sapa Inca, Túpac Amaru.

Ironically, the revival movement that sought to alienate Spanish Catholic influences was initially betrayed in the Catholic confessional to a Spanish priest, Luis de Olivera, in 1564.

In response, an intense, detailed inspection, undertaken by curate Cristóbal de Albornoz, revealed the breadth of the anti-European religious revival. Albornoz conducted an intensive anti-idolatry campaign, confiscating stashed weapons and condemning more than 8,000 Indians. The millenarian movement was suppressed and most natives returned to Spanish control and the Catholic fold. The participating leaders, like the *tanuiongos* and Túpac Amaru, were called to account with their lives, while Spanish clerics like Albornoz furthered their careers.

Rebecca M. Seaman

See also: Albornoz, Cristóbal de; *Ayllus*; Encomienda; Huacas; Huamanga; *Kurakas*; Túpac Amaru.

Resources

D'Altroy, Terence N. *The Incas.* Malden, MA: Blackwell, 2003.

Henson, Sändra Lee Allen. "Dead Bones Dancing: The Taki Onqoy, Archaism, and Crisis in Sixteenth Century Peru." MA Thesis, East Tennessee State University, 2002.

MacQuarrie, Kim. *The Last Days of the Incas.* New York: Simon & Schuster, 2007.

Stern, Steve J. *Peru's Indian Peoples and the Challenge of Spanish Conquest: Huamanga to 1640.* Madison: University of Wisconsin Press, 1993.

Tapia, Andres de

Born approximately in 1498, Andres de Tapia was a prominent conquistador who accompanied Hernán Cortés on his invasion of the Aztec Empire. Although a young man at the time, Tapia was often cited in various contemporary accounts of the expedition for his bravery and skills. Tapia spent most of the remainder of his life with Cortés before returning to New Spain. He wrote a short history of the invasion, which offered a unique participant's account.

Little is known of Andres de Tapia's early life. He was apparently born in Medellin, Spain, around 1498. Cortes was also born in Medellin, which undoubtedly helped Tapia to establish a strong relationship with him. Tapia worked as a groom for Diego Colón, the first-born son of Christopher Columbus. Tapia probably accompanied the Second Admiral of the Indies to Haiti in 1509, seeking his fortune in the New World. In December 1518, he arrived at Santiago de Cuba. Tapia had learned that Cortés was recruiting men for an expedition to the mainland, and decided to accompany his neighbor from

Medellin, in an effort to gain riches. Cortés and his fleet had already sailed in November, before Tapia arrived, but information indicated Cortés planned to stop in Havana to complete outfitting his army. Tapia hurried to that city and arrived in time to join the expedition on its way to Mexico.

Tapia was familiar to Diego de Velázquez, governor of Cuba. Velázquez had commissioned Cortés to undertake the voyage of exploration and trade to the Yucatán, but over time, did not trust the explorer to follow his orders. Velázquez arranged for the young Tapia to keep tabs on Cortés, providing him with money to purchase the supplies and weapons he needed to participate in the expedition. Velázquez recruited others he expected to remain loyal, for the purpose of ensuring that the conquistador would not overstep his bounds and deviate from the instructions provided by the governor. Tapia, like many others recruited by Velázquez, was impressed with Cortés and became his avid supporter. Unlike some others in the expedition who were either initially reluctant to follow Cortés or later questioned the *caudillo*'s actions and decisions, Tapia remained loyal to Cortés for the rest of his life.

Despite Tapia's youth, evidence indicates he was a brave and resourceful soldier by the time he sailed for Mexico. During the expedition, he distinguished himself repeatedly. When most of the ships first made landfall at the island of Cozumel, the men had their first contacts with the Native Americans. While on the island, Tapia led a small group that met three approaching men. One of the men spoke to Tapia in Castilian, asking if they were Christians. The man was Gerónimo de Aguilar, a shipwrecked Spanish sailor who had been among the Native Americans for 10 years. Aguilar had been accepted into the local people and learned Mayan. Tapia quickly took him to Cortés. Aguilar was an important addition to the expedition because he could speak to most of the people who lived along that part of the coast. Soon afterward, Cortés led his ships down the coast to Vera Cruz. There he founded a permanent settlement. After a battle in which Tapia participated, Cortés made peace with the local residents. The leaders of the town gave him supplies and 20 women that the conquistador distributed among his captains and Extremadura friends. One of these females, Malinche (Doña Marina) proved instrumental to Cortés for her linguistic ability in Nahuatl and Mayan.

Tapia's account of Cortés's decision to scuttle his ships and march on the Aztec capital of Tenochtitlán shows a shrewd side to the conquistador. Cortés offered to send everyone who did not want to accompany him back to Cuba on a single ship. After those who wanted to go home had shown themselves, Cortés sank all the ships. He could then keep surveillance over those who were against him. Though originally recruited by Velázquez to spy on Cortés, Tapia showed himself to be a loyal supporter of the *caudillo*.

Tapia's growing military reputation, and the esteem with which Cortés regarded him, were evident in the battles that occurred during the march to Tenochtitlán and afterward. He was among the Spaniards who captured an Aztec leader Cuauhpopoca who opposed the Spanish. Later, Tapia led a reconnaissance force that scouted the positions of the expedition under Pánfilo Narváez sent by Governor Velázquez to bring Cortés back to Cuba. During a night attack on the rival expedition, Tapia was part of the group that captured Narváez. Later, Tapia distinguished himself during the long and violent siege of Tenochtitlán.

As a reward for his loyalty and military skill, Cortés rewarded Tapia in 1521 with an encomienda of Cholula and its people. Tapia received income from the city and appointed its indigenous rulers. However, Cortés took Cholula away from Tapia in 1523 and gave it to another conquistador. Instead, Tapia received a number of smaller territories, as well as several offices in the government of New Spain.

In 1528, Tapia accompanied Cortés back to Spain, to defend the conquistador's actions in the New World. Cortés received the title of Marqués del Valle Oaxaca, along with much territory. However, even after Cortés and Tapia returned to New Spain in the 1530s, Cortés was not able to regain control over the land. Tapia accompanied him on other expeditions, which failed to achieve riches or fame. Tapia spent years in Spain, trying to regain control over Cholula. He returned to New Spain in 1548 and held a number of minor offices. His fortunes continued to decline and Tapia died in poverty in October 1561.

During his later years, Tapia set out his experiences in a short book. Entitled *Relation of Some of the Things that Happened to the Very Illustrious Don Hernando Cortés, Marqués del Valle . . .* , the book tells Tapia's views of the events from the departure out of Havana to the defeat of the expedition sent by Velázquez to capture Cortés. Although written in the 16th century, Tapia's account was not published until the 19th century. Historians have used Tapia's work to complete the accounts set out by other participants in the conquest.

Tim J. Watts

See also: Aguilar, Gerónimo de; Colón, Diego; Columbus, Christopher; Cortés, Hernán; Cozumel; La Malinche, "Doña Marina"; Nahuatl; Narváez, Pánfilo de; Tenochtitlán, Siege of; Velázquez, Diego (de Cuéllar).

Resources

Fernandez del Castillo, Francisco. *Tres Conquistadores y Pobladores de la Nueva Espana: Cristobal Martin Millan de Gamboa, Andres de Tapia, Jeronimo Lopez.* Mexico: Talleres Graficos de la Nacion, 1927.

Levy, Buddy. *Conquistador: Hernán Cortés, King Montezuma, and the Last Stand of the Aztecs.* New York: Bantam Books, 2009.

Schwartz, Stuart B. *Victors and Vanquished: Spanish and Nahua Views of the Conquest of Mexico.* Boston: Bedford/St. Martin's, 2000.

Tapia, Andrés de. "Relation of Some of the Things that Happened to the Very Illustrious Don Hernando Cortes, Marques del Valle." In *The Conquistadors,* edited by Patricia de Fuentes. New York: Orion Press, 1963.

Thomas, Hugh. *Conquest: Montezuma, Cortés, and the Fall of Old Mexico.* New York: Simon & Schuster, 1993.

Tarascans

The Tarascan kingdom, located to the west of the Aztec state and bordering the Pacific Ocean, was the second largest empire in Mesoamerica when the Spanish arrived in Mexico. The pre-conquest kingdom and its people were known as *Purhépecha*. Centered around the imperial capital of Tzintzuntzan on the shore of Lake Pátzcuaro in the modern Mexican state of Michoacán, the multiethnic kingdom dated back to the 13th century. *Purhépecha* or Tarascan warriors were equipped with clubs, bows and arrows, lances, poison darts, shields, and cotton armor. The kingdom was considered quite prosperous, for its fishing, diverse agriculture, and mines.

Following a period of imperial expansion in the 14th and 15th centuries, the Tarascans came under repeated attack by the Aztecs between the 1470s and 1518. The most notable Tarascan victory was at Matlatzinco, during the campaign season of 1479–80, when an Aztec army and its allies overextended their supply line and fought a larger Tarascan force. Of the 24,000 Aztec-led troops, only about 2,100 escaped the battlefield.

The Tarascan state was badly weakened by smallpox that originated in Europe prior to the arrival of the Spanish in Tarascan territories in 1521. The Tarascan king, Tzintzicha Tangaxoan, sought to escape the fate of the Aztec monarch and did not resist the Spanish invaders. Spanish colonists began to effectively occupy and exploit the kingdom in 1524. Mistaking the *Purhépecha*'s disrespectful reference to the Spanish (*tarascué*) as the indigenous identity, the Spanish appellation of Tarascan became the designation for the kingdom in historical documents. In 1530 the Tarascan state was politically extinguished when the king was executed, following a trial in which he was convicted of charges ranging from planning to attack the Spanish, to dancing while wearing the flayed skin of a sacrificed Spaniard.

Glenn E. Helm

See also: Ahuitzotl; Montezuma II.

Resources

Craine, Eugene R., and Reginald C. Reindorp, trans. and ed. *The Chronicles of Michoacán.* Norman: University of Oklahoma Press, 1970.

Pollard, Helen Perlstein. *Tariácuari's Legacy: The Prehispanic Tarascan State.* Norman: University of Oklahoma Press, 1993.

Schmall, John P. "Michoacán: A Struggle for Identity." *History of Mexico.* Houston Institute of Culture. www.http://www.houstonculture.org/mexico/michoacan.html (accessed September 9, 2012).

Warren, J. Benedict. *The Conquest of Michoacán: The Spanish Domination of the Tarascan Kingdom in Western Mexico, 1521–1530.* Norman: University of Oklahoma Press, 1985.

Tecuichpo ("Doña Isabel")

Tecuichpo, also known by her baptismal name of "Doña Isabel," was the daughter of the Aztec emperor, Montezuma II, with his official wife. Eleven years of age at the time of her father's death, Tecuichpo is said to have undergone a ritual marriage to Cuitláhuac, brother of Montezuma. Though the marriage was considered legitimate, it seems to have been one of political expediency and was not consummated.

Tecuichpo adopted the Christian faith of the Spanish, accepting the honorary title of Doña for her noble status, and Isabel in honor of the Spanish queen. As an adult, she married three times, first to Alonso de Grado who died in 1527. She was married soon after to Pedro Gallega de Andrade, who died suddenly in 1530. While still married to Gallega she had a daughter, believed to have been a child of Hernán Cortés. With her last husband, Juan Cano, she produced five children. As a child of Montezuma, she was awarded encomienda to maintain her status. She appears to have lived a contented life with Cano until her death in 1551.

Rebecca M. Seaman

See also: Cortés, Hernán; Cuitláhuac; Montezuma II.

Resources

Restall, Matthew. *Seven Myths of the Spanish Conquest.* Oxford: Oxford University Press, 2003.

Thomas, Hugh. *Conquest: Montezuma, Cortés, and the Fall of Old Mexico.* New York: Simon & Schuster, 1993.

Tenochtitlán, City of

Built on an island in Lake Texcoco, on the site of present-day Mexico City, Tenochtitlán was the capital city of the Aztec Empire. Tribute from conquered peoples made the city prosperous and it grew rapidly to become a heavily populated urban center; in the early 16th century, Tenochtitlán's population of about 400,000 was the largest in Mesoamerica. After Tenochtitlán's destruction in 1521, the Spanish built Mexico City on top of the Aztec ruins. Tenochtitlán remained largely hidden until 1790, when two sculptures, the famous Aztec Calendar Stone and a statue of the earth goddess Coatlicue, were unearthed. Valuable finds continued to be made during construction projects in Mexico City throughout the 19th and 20th centuries. Recent archaeological excavations and the analysis of Aztec texts have provided further insight into Tenochtitlán's brief but dramatic history.

According to tradition, Tenochtitlán was founded in the first half of the 14th century (some scholars give the date 1325) by the Aztec (or Mexica) people on the site where they found an eagle perched on a cactus devouring a snake. The earliest settlement was sited on two marshy islands in Lake Texcoco. This territory was quickly enlarged by the construction of habitable floating platforms between the islands and the mainland shore. Among the site's advantages was access to the lake's natural resources as well as strategic defense against the more powerful peoples on the mainland. Built on a grid plan, the city was orderly and fairly symmetrical in layout. It grew rapidly in size and population and became even larger after conquering and incorporating the nearby city of Tlatelolco, which became the site of Tenochtitlán's enormous, busy marketplace. Tenochtitlán's territory also included extensive agricultural and residential areas on the mainland near the lake, and the area covered by greater Tenochtitlán was administered as four distinct wards. Canoes

provided transportation around the city and floated goods to market.

Intensive agricultural practices supported Tenochtitlán's large and concentrated population. Not only were lakeside fields farmed, but crops were grown on the water as well. *Chinampas,* cultivated fields created on platforms on the lake's surface, were the basis of Tenochtitlán's highly productive agriculture. Most of the farmers who cultivated the *chinampas* and the mainland fields lived not within the city proper but rather in the surrounding suburban and cultivated areas on the mainland. Canals and dikes kept the freshwater that springs fed into Lake Texcoco separated from the lake's own salty water, and terracotta aqueducts conveyed more fresh water into the city. Three broad causeways linked Tenochtitlán to the community on the mainland; a Spanish account claimed that these causeways were wide enough for 10 horses to cross abreast.

Tenochtitlán in a 16th-century painting, probably based on Hernán Cortés's sketches. British Museum. (Jupiterimages)

Within the main part of the city the population was composed mostly of priests, warriors, administrators, and craftspeople that produced, among other goods, pottery, textiles, featherwork, and stonework. Tenochtitlán's vast whitewashed palace complexes included hundreds of rooms, offices for bureaucrats, libraries, justice halls, and workshops. The emperor and other nobles maintained luxurious gardens, aviaries, and zoos on their properties, which were located near the main religious sanctuary. The common people resided in distinct, relatively self-contained neighborhoods called *calpulli*. As the population grew and Tenochtitlán became the region's economic and political center, its administrative structure expanded and was divided into specialized departments for such interests as the military and taxation. Very little is known, however, about the specific procedures of the government's operation.

Nine Aztec emperors ruled from Tenochtitlán, including Acamapichtli, the founder of the Aztec imperial dynasty, and Itzcoatl, who allied Tenochtitlán with Texcoco and Tlacopan. Montezuma I is credited with improving the administrative and judicial systems at Tenochtitlán and overseeing many architectural projects. In 1487, the emperor Ahuitzotl consecrated Tenochtitlán's Great Temple with tens of thousands of human sacrifices. His successful military campaigns brought in vast quantities of tribute to the capital, and it developed rapidly during his rule. Among Ahuitzotl's additions to the city was its much-needed second aqueduct to accommodate the growing population. In 1503, a huge flood that struck Tenochtitlán included Ahuitzotl among its victims.

The city contained hundreds of temples and many religious complexes, including two major ones located in Tenochtitlán itself and in Tlatelolco. At the Tenochtitlán complex, walls measuring 1,200 feet in length surrounded a variety of religious structures, including pyramids painted red and blue, courtyards, living quarters for priests, a ball court, and a holy pool and grove. The main pyramid, called the Great Temple, stood 100 feet high and was decorated with giant serpents carved in stone. It was consecrated to the war god Huitzilopochtli and the rain god Tlaloc. Atop the pyramid were two separate temples dedicated to each god. Such offerings from Tenochtitlán's vassals as pottery, jade, shells, and textiles were buried within the pyramid's precincts. Near the Great Temple was the huey tzompantli, an enormous rack that displayed the skulls of sacrificial victims on horizontal poles.

When Hernán Cortés and his Spanish conquistadores entered Tenochtitlán in 1519, they were astounded by the size and complexity of the city as well as by its clean streets, great marketplace, and efficient public sanitation system. In 1520, the city was unable to hold out against a siege leveled by a combined force of Spaniards and Tlaxcalans (a local Aztec enemy). By 1521, probably less than 200 years after its founding, the Spanish and their allies captured and largely destroyed Tenochtitlán.

ABC-CLIO

See also: Ahuitzotl; Cortés, Hernán; Tlatelolco, or Tlateold.

Resources

Broda, Johanna, David Carrasco, and Eduardo Matos Moctezuma. *The Great Temple of Tenochtitlan: Center and Periphery in the Aztec World.* Berkeley: University of California Press, 1989.

Henderson, Keith, and Jane Stevenson Day. *The Fall of the Aztec Empire.* Denver, CO: Roberts Rhinehart, 1993.

Smith, Michael Ernest. *The Aztecs.* Malden, MA: Blackwell, 2002.

Tenochtitlán, Siege of

The city of Tenochtitlán, capital of the Aztec Empire, appeared impervious to an attack by the limited number of Spaniards accompanying Hernán Cortés in his invasion of 1519. The city was located on an island in the middle of a large lake that was surrounded by allied cities. Access to the city was limited by the use of either boats or causeways that could easily be lifted to stop unwelcome visitors. Nonetheless, by August 13, 1521, the city was defeated and burned by the conquering Spanish forces.

The victory of the Spanish in the face of overwhelming numbers of Mexica is understood best when examining specific factors. The participation of native allies under the Spanish, the use of brigantines, the impact of disease, and the use of a blockade all played important roles. It was through the combination of these factors that the Spanish were able to defeat the Aztec Empire.

Cortés achieved a position of authority within Tenochtitlán by December 1519. He held hostage the emperor Montezuma II as well as members of his family and council. However, complete control over the city and empire remained elusive. By April 1520, news reached the *caudillo* of an expedition by Pánfilo Narváez, sent by Governor Diego de Velázquez de Cuéllar to arrest Cortés. Fearing this news would turn the tide against the outnumbered Spanish and possibly serve to draw his native allies either into Narváez's camp or to the Aztecs, Cortés determined to split his forces, leaving some under Pedro de Alvarado in Tenochtitlán while he took the remainder to deal with the Spanish threat from the coast.

Siege of Tenochtitlán, portraying Hernán Cortés's capture of the capital in 1521. (Wildside Press)

Cortés was successful in not only defeating Narváez's forces, but also in integrating most of them into his own army—including at least one who carried the smallpox virus. Thus reinforced, he returned to the Aztec capital, only to discover the city in rebellion against the Spanish. The *caudillo*'s forces, along with those under Alvarado who was responsible for the uprising, fought desperately but were expelled from the city in the disastrous La Noche Triste (the Sad Night) of June 1520. The Spanish left behind several soldiers who were then sacrificed to the Aztec gods and reportedly eaten, which also included the Spaniard with smallpox.

Aware of the wealth to be had should he conquer the Aztec Empire, and determined not to return to Cuba until he was victorious, Cortés set about designing a strategy that would employ his small numbers and his allies. Unaware that smallpox was spreading within the Aztec capital and already resulted in the death of the new emperor Cuitláhuac, the *caudillo* used the city of Tlaxcala as a base for planning the siege. That fall he ordered the construction of brigantines under the Spanish carpenter Martín Lopez for use in attacking the island city of the Mexica.

On December 27, 1520, the *caudillo* set out from Tlaxcala to Texcoco, his new base until the fleet of brigantines and canal were ready. Accompanying him was a vast army of Tlaxcala warriors and carriers, numbering somewhere between 10,000 and 20,000 strong. As Cortés approached Texcoco, worries about resistance increased. The *tlatoani* of the city-state, brother of Cacama who had been allied with Montezuma and executed by the Spanish, seemed to indicate they would be welcomed, but instead fled with his population to Tenochtitlán. Meanwhile, his remaining brother, Ixtlilxochitl, pledged his support to the Spanish. At Texcoco the numbers of

forces under the *caudillo* increased, with Ixtlilxochitl and his remaining forces joining the fight against the Mexica. The increased numbers of warriors convinced other neighboring towns to abandon their allegiance to the Aztec and join the forces supporting Cortés.

With enhanced numbers came the dilemma of feeding his allies. Cortés undertook a risky strategy to accomplish this, one that also provided him with additional information and disguised the preparations of a naval attack. A series of reconnaissances were made around the great lake, locating food and apprising the Spanish of the territory and resources laid out against them. Where possible, the towns encountered along the perimeter of the lake were encouraged to ally themselves with the Spanish, this reducing the imbalance of forces and tightening Cortés's hold on the island city. His objective was to cut off provisions for the great capital city, thereby weakening them for the impending attack.

By the end of January, Cortés ordered Gonzalo de Sandoval to carry the secret brigantines overland from Tlaxcala to Texcoco. Meanwhile, he also ordered the digging of several channels from the now allied city of Texcoco to the lake, allowing for the relatively secret construction and then sailing of these same boats at the time of the attack. The *caudillo* also used the first few months of 1521 to conduct a number of forays around the lake, securing further allies, as well as training the Spanish and Tlaxcalan forces to fight effectively together.

On April 28, 1521, the siege of Tenochtitlán began in earnest. Already deprived of expected tribute, and running short of provisions from the numerous Spanish forays and alliances surrounding the great lake, the Aztec emperor Cuauhtémoc attempted once again to lure his former subjects back under his control, promising a reduction in tributes. Instead, the offer signaled the weakening of the Aztec, convincing more towns to shift their allegiance to the Spanish. Further evidence of the waning power of the empire included the order to cast the imperial treasure into the lake ahead of the Spanish invasion. Increased sacrifices, shifted from the traditional planting feasts to cries for help in war, were conducted by lessening numbers of priests as the smallpox epidemic within the city walls increased its silent but deadly attack upon the Aztec.

By the first of June, the numbers of allied native auxiliaries supporting Cortés ranged anywhere from 220,000 to 500,000 strong. Having sent foot soldiers overland earlier, the *caudillo* ordered the brigantines to set sail on June 1. With Sandoval attacking and holding Iztapalapa by land, Cortés set off with his brigantines. The first triumph was against the small island of Tepepulco, housing the important temple of Tlacochcalco. Cortés killed all male inhabitants and then proceeded on to temples at Xoloc. Meanwhile, Alvarado took his foot soldiers, cavalry, and native auxiliaries along the Nonoalco causeway approaching the capital. Another captain of Cortés, Cristóbal de Olid, held Coyoacán.

The complete blockade of Tenochtitlán still eluded Cortés, with the causeway between Tlatelolco and the capital serving as a channel for provisions. Intent on isolating the emperor in his capital, Cortés ordered Sandoval to secure the route and close Tenochtitlán from further supplies. The fight then became one of urban warfare, with the once beautiful city of Tenochtitlán besieged from within and outside. Mexica under the emperor ravaged the city for stones that were thrown from the rooftops, while the Spanish set fire to the buildings lining the main thoroughfares to eliminate future assaults from above. The continued resistance from the Mexica eventually forced Cortés to order the complete destruction of the city. The entire city was set ablaze, followed by incursions ordered each day, probing further into the city each time.

By the end of June, the city was beginning to starve, freshwater was at a premium, the small *chinampas* or family farms were destroyed, and fishing was impossible. By July, Cuauhtémoc relocated to the allied city of Tlatelolca. Instead of the fighting declining at this point, the intensity increased, with street-to-street warfare resulting in higher and higher death tolls. The Mexica, in defensive positions, began to contemplate victory, a possibility assisted by Cortés again splitting his forces into three groups. Repulsed, the Spanish and their allies again lost captives to the Aztecs, who sacrificed them in full display of the invading force.

The tides of the siege again shifted back to the Spanish in July, and though the Mexica proved determined and brave, the ravages of the war, blockade, fires, and disease eventually won out. On August 13, 1521 Cuauhtémoc personally conducted the final sacrifices of prisoners held in Tlatelolco, an attempt to deny that privilege to the Spanish or their native allies. Realizing that surrender was necessary, the emperor nonetheless planned to flee. His attempt was thwarted as he was captured and ceremonially presented to Cortés. The fate of the Mexica population was far from ceremonial, as their traditional Tlaxcalan enemies exacted years of vengeance upon them.

Rebecca M. Seaman

See also: Alvarado, Pedro de; Cacama; Cortés, Hernán; Coyoacán; Cuauhtémoc; Cuitláhuac; Ixtlilxochitl II; La Noche Triste; Narváez, Pánfilo; Olid, Cristóbal de; Sandoval, Gonzalo de; Tenochtitlán, City of; Texcoco, Alliance with Tenochtitlán; Tlatelolco, or Tlateold; Velázquez, Diego (de Cuéllar).

Resources

León-Portilla, Miguel. *The Broken Spears: The Aztec Account of the Conquest of Mexico.* Foreword by J. Jorge Klor de Alva. Boston: Beacon Press, 2006.

Levy, Buddy. *Conquistador: Hernán Cortés, King Montezuma, and the Last Stand of the Aztecs.* New York: Bantam Dell, 2008.

Restall, Matthew. *Seven Myths of the Spanish Conquest.* New York: Oxford University Press, 2003.

Schwartz, Stuart B., ed. *Victors and Vanquished: Spanish and Nahua Views of the Conquest of Mexico.* Boston: Bedford/St. Martin's, 2000.

Thomas, Hugh. *Conquest: Montezuma, Cortés, and the Fall of Old Mexico.* New York: Simon & Schuster, 1993.

Tenochtitlán, Spanish Rule of

On November 8, 1519, Hernán Cortés and his forces arrived in Tenochtitlán, where they met with King Montezuma II (Moctezuma). The vast size of the city impressed the conquistadors. It was the largest in the Aztec Empire, divided into four districts with a population ranging from an estimated 200,000–350,000.

Roughly a week after their arrival, the Spanish captured the Aztec king Montezuma, making him their hostage. A series of fierce battles and a lengthy siege for possession of the city soon followed. In August 1521, the last of the Aztec rulers surrendered, placing Tenochtitlán firmly in control of Cortés. The conflict took a massive toll on the city, in lives and architecture, and is ranked one of the costliest in the history of warfare. However, the aftermath of the fighting ushered in the greatest changes for the former Aztec capital.

In reward for adding to the imperial lands, Emperor Charles V named Cortés governor, captain general, distributor, and chief justice of this new land called New Spain and its subjects within. In 1522 Cortes oversaw construction of a new city originally called Mexico-Tenochtitlan, built upon the ruins of the old Aztec capital. The new Spanish rulers systematically destroyed most of the remaining native architecture existing in Tenochtitlan following the destruction of the conquest. Mexico City became a second capital, this time to New Spain.

The center of the new city was designated as la traza, a 14-block zone intended strictly for settlement of Europeans, their servants, and slaves. Displaced Aztecs were moved in large numbers into the southern Cuauhtémoc borough of Mexico City, which is referred to today as San Juan Tenochtitlan. In a sense, Mexico City quickly became two cities: the European zone, and the barrios that were overseen by native leaders who were permitted a measure of control over the remaining indigenous areas. Cortés appointed Pedro de Alvarado the first Alcalde, or magistrate of Mexico City. Both areas, and the surrounding barrio settlements, operated as an altepetl, a self-governing community, with native and European leaders.

On the encouragement and supplications of Cortés, friars made a pilgrimage into Mexico City to begin the conversion of the Mexica to Christianity. Their arrival heralded the end of the old temples and religious structures. Those "pagan" places of worship still standing were torn down, replaced by churches dedicated to the Catholic faith. The four main districts of the Aztec capitol were renamed in honor of patron saints.

Culturally there was a massive shift. European tools, plants, animals, clothing and art fashions, literature, and music were gradually introduced into New Spain. This interchange worked both ways, flowing from Mexico City back to Spain. Ancestry began to become intertwined as Europeans and Natives married and started families.

Labor and material for the new civic works was drawn from the indigenous populations. Early Spanish rule was marked by a series of severe epidemics that further ravaged the native population, uprisings that protested Spanish treatment and policies, and political intrigue. A near civil war broke out inside the city in 1525, but was prevented by the timely return of Cortés. Spanish rule of Mexico City was marked by several turbulent periods over the next three centuries. The culmination of a decade-long struggle gained the Mexican Empire its independence on September 27, 1821.

Mexico City continued to develop atop the Aztec ruins, further erasing traces of its past. Archaeologists have been able to excavate beneath the streets, salvaging artifacts. These relics, along with study of surviving native texts and period accounts, have been used to gain insight on the former glory of the Aztec capital.

Michael D. Coker

See also: Alvarado, Pedro de; Charles V (HRE) or Carlos I of Spain; Cortés, Hernán; Montezuma II; Tenochtitlán, Siege of.

Resources

Levy, Buddy. *Conquistador.* New York: Bantam Dell, 2008.

Kinsbruner, Jay. *The Colonial Spanish-American City: Urban Life in the Age of Atlantic Capitalism.* Austin: University of Texas Press, 2005.

O' Hara, Matthew. *A Flock Divided: Race, Religion, and Politics in Mexico, 1749–1857.* Durham, NC: Duke University Press, 2010.

Texcoco, Alliance with Tenochtitlán

The city-state of Texcoco, located beside the lake that also bordered Tenochtitlán and Tlacopan, was one of the major cities of central Mexico at the time of the Spanish conquest in 1519–1521. Spanish records indicate that there were approximately 80,000 to 100,000 houses in the city, making it a major metropolitan area for that era.

The people of Texcoco were allied with the city of Tenochtitlán in a sort of triple alliance. The three cities included in this alliance were not evenly matched in authority, however, with the Aztec, or Mexica, of the capital in Tenochtitlán dominating the coalition. Cementing the alliance was accomplished through the perpetuation of marital ties between the imperial family out of Tenochtitlán and the siblings and offspring of other royal families from Tlacopan and Texcoco.

Such a marital alliance existed shortly before the arrival of the Spanish under Hernán Cortés. Nezahualpilli, the *tlatoani* or ruler of Texcoco was married to the sister of Montezuma II. One of numerous wives of this particular *tlatoani,* the relationship soured and he had his wife executed. Upon the death of Nezahualpilli, his sons, the offspring of numerous marriages, jockeyed for positions in the city-state. Cacamatzin (Cacama), the maternal nephew of Montezuma through his long-deceased mother, received support for the position of *tlatoani* from the Aztec emperor. The result was a civil war between supporters of Ixtlilxochitl, a younger brother, and Cacama over authority in Texcoco.

It was in the midst of this internal struggle that Cortés advanced from the coast of Mexico toward the capital of Tenochtitlán. Encouraged by the "fat cacique" of Zempoala to secure an alliance with the alienated brother, Ixtlilxochitl, the Spanish gained a sizeable allied force prior to even entering the Aztec capital. This Spanish encroachment on the Triple Alliance drove the official *tlatoani* of Texcoco, Cacama into a closer relation with his uncle, Montezuma. Records indicate that he was repeatedly present at the council meetings called by the emperor to discuss how to deal with the Spanish. Indeed, Cacama was sent as a dignitary to approach Cortés, possibly to broker a deal that would result in the Spanish withdrawing from the region.

Despite the long-held alliance between the capital city and Texcoco, the internal division within the city-state over which brother should rule and the increasing support by other native cities for the Spanish created a rift between the partners. Cacama eventually pulled his allegiance to his uncle and returned to Texcoco, where he was captured and turned over to the Spanish. The city-state came under the authority of the new *tlatoani,* Ixtlilxochitl, whose animosity toward the Mexica drove him willingly into an alliance with the Spanish.

Rebecca M. Seaman

See also: Cacama; Cortés, Hernán; Ixtlilxochitl II; Montezuma II; Tenochtitlán, Siege of; Zempoala.

Resources

Gillespie, Susan D. *The Aztec Kings: The Construction of Rulership in Mexica History.* Tucson: University of Arizona Press, 1989.

León-Portilla, Miguel. *The Broken Spears: The Aztec Account of the Conquest of Mexico.* Foreword by J. Jorge Klor de Alva. Boston: Beacon Press, 2006.

Schwartz, Stuart B., ed. *Victors and Vanquished: Spanish and Nahua Views of the Conquest of Mexico.* Boston: Bedford/St. Martin's, 2000.

Thomas, Hugh. *Conquest: Montezuma, Cortés, and the Fall of Old Mexico.* New York: Simon & Schuster, 1993.

Tezcatlipoca

One of the four sons of the dual-gendered deity Ometeotl, Tezcatlipoca was an Aztec and Toltec god of warriors, rulers, and sorcerers as well as an omnipotent and omnipresent god of punitive justice and fate. Tezcatlipoca was also the embodiment of conflict. The name Tezcatlipoca translates as Dark Mirror Lord or Smoking Mirror, for Tezcatlipoca was said to have a magic mirror that could predict the future as well as show him the way into the hearts and minds of people. In codices, this mirror appears on Tezcatlipoca's head or as a substitute for one of the god's feet. Tezcatlipoca was also depicted as a jaguar for he is associated with earth, with the jaguar acting as his companion spirit.

Tezcatlipoca is sometimes considered the rival of another Mesoamerican deity, Quetzalcoatl, with whom he features in a number of myths. One Toltec-Aztec myth tells that

Tezcatlipoca, the god of warriors, rulers, and sorcerers for the Aztec, Toltec, and other Mesoamerican people. (Julioaldana/Dreamstime.com)

Tezcatlipoca beat Quetzalcoatl in a ritual ball game, then transformed into a jaguar, and chased Quetzalcoatl from Tollan. Another Aztec story tells that Tezcatlipoca ruled the first world until it was devoured by tigers. At that point in the story, the god Quetzalcoatl became the dominant deity, ruling the second world in place of Tezcatlipoca. The rivalry between the two gods also features in the myths of Tollan in which Tezcatlipoca tricks Quetzalcoatl into violating his own sister. However, in other myths the two deities unite to create life. For instance, according to some Aztec myths, it is believed that the present world, or sun, was co-created by Tezcatlipoca and Quetzalcoatl. This interpretation asserts the two deities united to pull apart the monstrous goddess Tlaltecuhtli, with her head and shoulders becoming the earth and her body the sky.

Tezcatlipoca is indeed a contradictory figure for, despite his association with a range of subjects and concepts inclined toward darkness and death, he is often viewed as a creator as much as he is a destructive force. This is evident in some versions of the Mesoamerican creation myths in which Tezcatlipoca is the chief creator-god, a composite figure consisting of the Four Tezcatlipocas, that is, the four creators of the created suns. The composite Tezcatlipoca was made up of Tezcatlipoca himself, Quetzalcoatl, Huitzilopochtli, and Xipe Totec.

Victoria Williams

See also: Aztec, or Mexica; Quetzalcoatl.

Resources

Aguilar-Moreno, Manuel. *Handbook to Life in the Aztec World.* Oxford: Oxford University Press, 2006.

Leeming, David Adams. *The Oxford Companion to World Mythology.* Oxford: Oxford University Press, 2005.

Scott Littleton, C., ed. *Gods, Goddesses, and Mythology.* Vol 11. New York: Marshall Cavendish Corporation, 2005.

Titu Cusi Yupanqui

Titu Cusi Yupanqui was the penultimate Inca emperor during the Spanish conquest. He ruled the rump Inca state of Vilcabamba for a decade. During that time, he coexisted with the Spanish-controlled territory nearby. With crafty negotiations, Titu Cusi Yupanqui managed to appear to accommodate the Spanish without actually giving anything up. Had Titu Cusi Yupanqui lived, he might have been able to arrange for the survival of an Indian state within the Spanish Empire. During his reign, he dictated his memoirs to a Catholic priest, providing the only record of the Spanish conquest from the view of the indigenous people.

Titu Cusi Yupanqui was born in 1530, the son of Manco Inca and grandson of Huayna Cápac, the last undisputed ruler of the Inca Empire. He was born just before the Inca-Spanish War, and his name meant "magnanimous and fortunate." The Spanish conqueror Francisco Pizarro named Manco Inca emperor, but soon thereafter the "puppet" Inca organized an army and attacked the Spanish at Cuzco in 1536. After a relieving Spanish army broke the year-long siege, Manco Inca set up his rule in the remote Vilcabamba Andes. The Inca forces continued to wage a guerrilla war against the Spanish, however. Manco Inca ruled for eight years before seven Spaniards who he had befriended stabbed and killed him. They were later caught and executed by his heirs.

Manco Inca was succeeded by his younger son, Sayri Túpac, even though leading nobles preferred the older Titu Cusi Yupanqui. King Philip II of Spain granted a pardon to

Sayri Túpac for any crimes committed during Manco Inca's siege, and the five-year-old Sayri Túpac went to live in Cuzco under a peace treaty with the Spanish. He received the traditional estates of his father and other Inca emperors. Sayri Túpac was baptized and became a Christian. Unknown to the Spanish, the Inca nobles and Titu Cusi Yupanqui observed from a distance how Sayri Túpac was treated to decide if the Spanish could be trusted. Just as all seemed to be going well, Sayri Túpac died suddenly in 1561, possibly poisoned by the Spanish or by radicals from Vilcabamba who did not want peace.

Leading Incas named Titu Cusi Yupanqui emperor. He had been captured by the Spanish as a boy and ransomed for gold. He had no love for the Spanish and suspected they had killed his brother. Nonetheless, he was a clever ruler who realized that accommodation with the Spanish was preferable to war. He initially renewed the raids on Spanish territory and encouraged revolts by other Indians against the Spanish. One Spanish writer reported that no one could travel without a strong escort. The Spanish responded by confiscating all horses and gunpowder weapons from Indians. They also openly threatened to conquer Vilcabamba. Titu Cusi Yupanqui changed his tactics. He opened negotiations again and allowed Spaniards to enter Vilcabamba. In 1566, the treaty of Acobamba was signed, establishing peace between the two sides.

In 1567, Titu Cusi Yupanqui declared his allegiance to the king of Spain. On July 9, he performed rites to the sun and, placing his hand on the ground, declared that, of his own free will, he placed himself under the king. As agreed by the treaty, Titu Cusi Yupanqui also allowed two Augustine monks and a royal administrator into Vilcabamba. He dictated his memoirs to one of the monks, providing the only recorded example of Inca views of the Spanish conquest. As revealed in his memoirs, Titu Cusi Yupanqui was an exuberant, good-natured, friendly, and thoughtful person. His main concern was for the well-being of his subjects and for the preservation of the Inca state and his dynasty.

Titu Cusi Yupanqui's son, Quispe Titu, was baptized a Christian in 1567. He received a special dispensation to marry his cousin, the daughter of Sayri Túpac, to strengthen his claim to the Inca throne. By 1570, Friar Diego Ortiz had become a close companion to Titu Cusi Yupanqui. In 1571, Titu Cusi Yupanqui suddenly fell ill and died. Friar Ortiz was accused of poisoning him and was tortured and killed. After Titu Cusi Yupanqui's death, Túpac Amaru became emperor. Unlike his brother Titu Cusi Yupanqui, Túpac Amaru would not negotiate with the Spanish. Within a year, Vilcabamba was conquered, and the last Inca state was destroyed.

Tim J. Watts

See also: Manco Inca Yupanqui; Phillip II of Spain; Sayri Túpac; Túpac Amaru; Vilcabamba.

Resources

Hemming, John. *The Conquest of the Incas.* London: Pan Macmillan, 1970.

Markham, Clements R. *The Incas of Peru.* New York: Dutton, 1912.

Metraux, Alfred. *The History of the Incas.* New York: Pantheon, 1969.

Tlamatimine

Also known as *tlamacazque* or priest-teachers, the *tlamatimine* were the teachers found in pre-conquest Mexica schools for the noble classes. Not all *calpulli* possessed these specialized schools or *calmecac,* most of which existed in larger cities and were housed within or immediately adjacent to *calpulli* temples. It is not surprising that these upper-level educational institutions fell under the protection of the god Quetzalcoatl.

These *calmecac* schools and the teachers were designed to prepare the *pipiltin* (nobility) for their proper roles in society. The *tlamatimine* were strict disciplinarians in a system of tight regulations and controls. The use of structured curriculum was accentuated by harsh punishments such as beating recalcitrant students with maguey thorns, forcing them to inhale chili smoke, and other abusive reprimands.

The *tlamatimine* teachers were not only responsible for teaching the customs of Mexica society, but also taught their students the complex pictographic written language needed to study other aspects of theology, astronomy, history, and rhetoric. The *tlamatimine* taught their noble students the intricate complexities of the Aztec calendar system. Even geometry and other forms of math were included in the *calmecac*.

Special training was provided by the *tlamatimine* for young men, preparing them for the military. Additionally, the teachers structured religious worship into the daily schedule, including having student rise at midnight to pray to the gods. As a result of this intense focus on military and religious training, many of the young *pipiltin* pupils eventually became priests and military leaders of the Mexica. The *tlamatimine* also prepared future teachers, healers, codes painters, and other societal leaders. Indeed, one of the primary purposes of the *tlamatimine* and the *calmecac* was to produce leaders for the entire Mexica society.

Rebecca M. Seaman

See also: Aztec, or Mexica; Calendar System of Aztec; Education, Pre-Columbian Mexico; *Pipiltin*.

Resources

Gruzinski, Serge. *The Conquest of Mexico: The Incorporation of Indian Societies into the Western World, 16th-18th Centuries.* Translated by Eileen Corrigan. Cambridge, MA: Polity Press, 1993.

Kobayashi, José María. *La Educación Como Conquista: Empresa Franciscana En México.* 2nd cd. México: El Colegio de México, 2002.

Sahagún, Bernardino de, Alfredo López Austin, and Josefina García Quintana. *Historia General De Las Cosas De Nueva España.* 3 vols. México: CONACULTA, 1988.

Tlatelolco, or Tlateold

A subordinate municipality of Tenochtitlán, Tlatelolco was populated by Mexica. Indeed, the island city was the original city of the Mexica and boasted the largest market in all of the Americas. According to the Spanish who first visited the market, it was more impressive than those of Europe.

Tlatelolco had its origins in the mid-15th century. Founded by Cuauhtlatoa, the city became the original center of trade in the fine cottons for which the Mexica were so well known. Following the devastating war with the larger Mexica city of Tenochtitlán, Tlatelolco was incorporated into the capital city. The city's main temple was closed in acknowledgment of the defeat of the people and their deity; the market, essential to the regional economy, remained open.

Following the conquest and absorption of Tlatelolco by Tenochtitlán, the city was made to pay tribute to its conqueror. The relation between the two cities remained frigid, with the Tlatelolco residents asserting they were treated as second-rate citizens. However, with the invasion of the Spanish under Hernán Cortés, Tlatelolco took on greater importance. This portion of the island was the last to fall to the Spanish conquest, falling prey to the successful blockade of food to support the sizeable population. Following the Spanish victory, the people of Tlatelolco blamed the Mexica-Tenochca and Montezuma for the defeat.

In the years after their defeat, the Tlatelolco provided informants for the Franciscan historian, Bernardino Sahagún, when he was revising his earlier version of the *Florentine Codex*. It is not surprising, therefore, that the revised version portrays Montezuma II in a negative light. The former emperor of the Aztec was described therein as vacillating, frozen with fear, and incompetent.

According to an Aztec account of the Spanish conquest, the defeat of Montezuma was linked to Mexica mysticism. Cortés reported that Montezuma had himself indicated a "lord" had left Tlatelolco and the Mexica believed his descendants would return one day to subjugate them. The initial version of the *Florentine Codex* by Sahagún made no reference to Cortés in connection to the god, Quetzalcoatl. However, the later version, and the Aztec account, is replete with references to Mexica mysticism, apparitions, and prophets that foretold the coming of Cortés and the burning of the greater city of Tenochtitlán.

Reconstruction of the capital region began shortly after the conquest. The all-important market was re-created. Repopulated and led by Mexica chiefs, the city of Tlatlelolco endured, but with its new appellation, Santiago Tlatelolco.

Rebecca M. Seaman

See also: Aztec, or Mexica; Cortés, Hernán; Montezuma II; Sahagún, Bernardino de; Tenochtitlán, Siege of.

Resources

León-Portilla, Miguel. *Broken Spears: The Aztec Account of the Conquest of Mexico.* Foreword by J. Jorge Klor de Alva. Boston, MA: Beacon Press, 2006.

Restall, Matthew. *Seven Myths of the Spanish Conquest.* New York: Oxford University Press, 2003.

Thomas, Hugh. *Conquest: Montezuma, Cortés, and the Fall of Old Mexico.* New York: Simon & Schuster, 1993.

Tlaxcala, Battle of

The Battle of Tlaxcala is a series of skirmishes in September 1519 between the Spanish invasion force and their indigenous allies versus the Aztec. In this battle, the forces of Conquistador Hernán Cortés gained a decisive edge in their campaign against the Aztec Empire.

Cortés departed Cuba in February 1519 with two ships loaded with horses, cannons, and several hundred soldiers. The expedition's first contact with the outlying Aztec settlements occurred in April 1519. Shortly after this initial landfall, Cortés quelled an internal revolt among his own forces. As part of the mutineers' plans involved returning back to Cuba, Cortés ordered their naval transports sunk. The decision, along with a shortage of supplies, increased the Spanish dependence on allying with Natives. The local kingdom of Cempoala (Zempoala) hosted the Spanish during this early period of exploration and conquest. Using translators, Cortés was able to gain insight into the scope and shaky political state of the Aztec Empire.

Cortés not only learned of the divisions within the Aztec structure, but he also learned of the Tlaxcalans. This federation of four districts had fiercely resisted Aztec expansion, most notably in the "flower war," also called the "war of flowers." The Aztec emperor, Montezuma II, sent forces twice—both of which had been bested trying to subdue the rebellious domain of the Tlaxcalans.

This success against the larger and militaristic Aztecs earned the Tlaxcalans the distinction of resolute enemies to the Aztecs. While it is unlikely Cortés received a detailed blow-by-blow report, it is clear he gathered enough to know this kingdom would make excellent allies and possibly present a challenge to the Spanish conquerors.

After marshaling influence and resources in Cempoala, Cortés moved through the province of Zautla, which provided indifferent cooperation. On the outskirts of the city of Tlaxcala, Cortés, now with over 400 native auxiliaries, tried to open diplomatic channels. The initial Spanish attempt was rebuffed and the Spanish were compelled to engage a superior force, yet emerged victorious. A second similar skirmish occurred a day after the first; with similar results, the Spanish held the field despite being outnumbered. At the end of the second day Cortés ordered the small Tlaxcala village of Teocacingo fortified.

Cortés left behind in Teocacingo a contingent of men to hold the position, and then sallied forth into the interior in search of provisions. Five or six nearby villages were destroyed, and approximately 400 prisoners were taken in the following days. For two weeks Cortés held in this position and engaged in sporadic skirmishing. A large host of Tlaxcala warriors gathered, intent on wiping out the Spanish. One account numbered the Tlaxcala at 150,000 and another at 40,000; the actual number was actually likely far lower. Cortés's secretary Francisco López de Gómara wrote after the fact that the Tlaxcala did not attack immediately, but instead sent food over to the Spanish. This gesture, according to Gómara, was done only so the claim they had beaten their foes only because they were starving and tired could not be used to blemish their victory. A larger third engagement followed and concluded with the Tlaxcala in full-retreat.

This victory had not come without a cost. Forty-five Spaniards were killed and dozens wounded in these engagements. Several irreplaceable horses were lost, and a considerable quantity of powder and shot were expended. Nonetheless, the Tlaxcalans were impressed with the performance of the vastly outnumbered Spanish. Although small in number, the technological advantage their muskets, mounts, armor, and weapons brought to the battlefield was considerable. Concentrated musket, crossbow, or cannon fire could pierce massed formations of opponents who had no way to counter the attack. The alien horses provided scouting and offensive measures unfamiliar to the Aztecs. These strange animals and foreign technology that produced loud noises and cast off black clouds of smoke on an unprepared foe could also deliver a severe psychological impact. Having witnessed all of this first-hand, the Tlaxcalans made the decision to unite their forces with the Spaniards. The Tlaxcalans also brought their own Native allies into the alliance, further increasing Cortés's manpower.

Had Tlaxcala not supported Cortés it is unlikely he would have been able to proceed through neighboring Cholula lands successfully. Capture of Tenochtitlán and the Aztec emperor, Montezuma II, would have been impossible. Standard histories often stress Cortés's wisdom in recruiting the Tlaxcala for his own ends. Another perspective to consider is that the Tlaxcala saw the alliance with the Spanish as a means to achieve their political goals. The alliance with between the Tlaxcala and Cortés can clearly be seen as a turning point in the Spanish domination of the Aztec Empire.

Michael D. Coker

See also: Cholula Massacre; Cortés, Hernán; López de Gómara, Francisco; Guns, Impact of; Horses, Impact of; Montezuma II; Zempoala.

Resources

Kirkwood, Burton. *The History of Mexico.* Westport, CT: Greenwood Press, 2004.

Thomas, Hugh. *Conquest: Montezuma, Cortés, and the Fall of Old Mexico.* New York: Simon & Schuster, 1993.

Wood, Michael. *Conquistadors.* Los Angles: University of California Press, 2002.

Toledo, Francisco de

Born in Oropesa, Spain, in 1515, he was a third cousin of the Emperor Charles V (HRE). At age 20, he joined the religious military Order of Alcantara and eventually became the Count of Oropesa. By the 1550s Spain was suffering under crushing military debt and governed by Philip II of Spain. In 1569 Philip appointed Toledo as the fifth viceroy of Peru in an effort to standardize policies from the initial colonial period (1532–1569) known mainly for invasion, warfare, haphazard administration, and occasional temporary alliances between the Pizarros and the Inca Indians. Philip sought a close ally he could trust not only to stabilize the colony of Peru, but also to counter Frey Bartolomé Las Casas's arguments that Spain should release control of the colony to the Incas as rightful rulers.

Toledo, as the newly appointed viceroy of Peru, was tasked with bringing a semblance of stability and prosperity to the Spanish colony. His appointment was in part a reaction against the abuses and extremes of the Pizarrian period of governance in the land of the Incas. Toledo was expected to not only remove the remaining influences of the Pizarros and their associates, but to also provide a new economic and governing structure. Ten years of declining productivity of Hernando Pizarro's mines and estates and the 30 to 40 years of constant wars and rebellions in the distant colony reduced the revenues expected from the mineral-rich region while they simultaneously increased royal expenditures needed to sustain a strong Spanish presence.

The new viceroy carried with him papers providing papal approval of the marriage of the Inca emperor, Titu Cusi Yupanqui, to his first cousin, Beatrice Clara Coya. This approval was part of a long-negotiated Treaty of Acobamba between the previous governor and captain general of Peru, Don Diego de Castro, and Titu Cusi. Castro attempted to increase the influence of the Spanish through the expansion of missionary outreach as well as negotiating a truce with the isolated Inca kingdom in Vilcabamba. In particular, Castro hoped to lure the Inca emperor out of his mountainous refuge and establish an Inca kingdom within the Spanish Empire in Peru. Despite the acceptance of Augustinian and Franciscan missionaries and the eventual papal approval of his marriage to his cousin Beatrice, Titu Cusi still refused to come out of Vilcabamba.

The arrival of Francisco de Toledo in 1569 soon spelled the end to further attempts to seriously negotiate a mutually agreeable truce between the Spanish and Incas that would leave the Inca controlling an internal kingdom. Instead, Toledo set about following his instructions to remove the economic and political influence of the Pizarros, restructure the government and economy, and bring peace to the region. While his administrative duties were assisted by royal support to retract the original Capitulacion of Toledo, granting extensive authority and revenues to Pizarro, his brothers and associates, Francisco de Toledo's duties were hampered by the years of rebellion and the recent emergence of the Taki Onqoy movement.

Soon after his arrival, Toledo declared Hernando Pizarro's repartimientos vacant and reappointed administrators over mines and other holdings of the Pizarros, then overseen by the state. In this manner the viceroy was able to access more resources for his own viceroyalty court, but also was able to recoup over 50,000 pesos of debt owed to the Crown. Devoid of further income from the colony, the Pizarros withdrew from Peru. Meanwhile, Toledo used some of the recovered repartimientos to negotiate with the Inca, Titu Cusi. He also negotiated with Vasco de Guevara to provide cattle to help sustain the Inca in return for additional repartimientos. While he still failed to lure the Inca emperor out of Vilcabamba, he managed to win the approval of increasing numbers of Inca and non-Inca people in the region around Cuzco. A grandson of the Sapa Inca Atahualpa, Carlos Inca, praised Toledo for the unequaled zeal with which he undertook his administrative duties for the good of the empire.

An early decision of the new viceroy, to personally travel throughout the colony to investigate the state of the government and colony on a general *visita,* immediately sent the signal of a fresh approach to Spanish administration of Peru. Toledo's visit to Cuzco, the first by any viceroy, initiated an investigation of more than just the Pizarro holdings and accounts. The viceroy sought to firmly establish the role of the Spanish Crown as the rightful authority, and to diminish the legitimacy of the Incas to rule the region.

The method Toledo used to affirm Spanish hegemony in Peru was a series of investigations. Different lists of questions were used to interview Incas loyal to the Spanish, relatives of the ruling Inca elite, and non-Incas. The questions varied based on the information the viceroy hoped to extract. Much of the information was gleaned directly from personal interviews—often of people with limited knowledge of past events. At other times, Inca records supplemented Toledo's

inquiries, recorded using the indigenous system of *quipus.* Such knowledge was especially requested of non-Incas and the Incas who were aware of the more recent expansion of the Inca Empire in the century immediately prior to the Spanish conquest.

Following his acquisition of data and interviews supporting an account of recent imperial conquest of the Peruvian lands by the Incas, Toledo sent a series of reports to Spain justifying Spanish control of the region and his eventual execution of the last Inca emperor, Túpac Amaru, in 1572. He then set about creating a history of the region that supported his account. The viceroy provided the interview and *visitas* data to Pedro Sarmiento de Gamboa, Toledo's official court historian, and ordered the construction of a history that clarified the short-lived status of the Inca as rulers of the region and the underlying animosity the original inhabitants held for the Incas. While the history acknowledged the prosperity of the Incas, it simultaneously portrayed their rule as one of force and based on idolatry and cheap theatrical tricks to ensure the populations' adoration of the Inca elite as Sun gods. Instead of Spain relinquishing central control of Peru to the Incas, or even sharing governance with the indigenous population, Toledo's report and subsequent history of the Inca reaffirmed Spain's determination to maintain domination over the colony.

Francisco de Toledo's service as viceroy was relatively short-lived, from 1569 to 1581. Nonetheless, the impact of his term in office influenced Peru down through the centuries. The removal of the influence and abuses of the Pizarros, the execution of the last Inca emperor, and restructuring of the economy immediately impacted the rising Spanish control and declining Inca power. The construction of a history that undermined the Inca's authority and supported

Spanish dominance had a lasting influence upon Peruvian society and the perception of Peru's history to this day. Nonetheless, Toledo's decision to execute the Sapa Inca Túpac Amaru destroyed the confidence Phillip II placed in him. The success of Toledo's reforms earned him several enemies. In 1581 he was recalled from his post as viceroy and returned to Spain where he spent the rest of his life in prison, dying in 1584.

Rebecca M. Seaman

See also: Pizarro, Hernando; *Quipus*; Repartimiento; Sapa Inca; Sarmiento's *History of the Incas*; Taki Onqoy; Titu Cusi Yupanqui; Túpac Amaru; Vilcabamba; *Visitas*.

Resources

Davies, Nigel. *The Incas.* Niwot: University of Colorado Press, 1995.

Gabai, Varón. *Francisco Pizarro and His Brothers: The Illusion of Power in Sixteenth-Century Peru.* Norman: University of Oklahoma Press, 1997.

Hemming, John. *The Conquest of the Incas.* San Diego: Harcourt, 1970.

Lockhart, James, and Stuart B Schwartz. *Early Latin America: A History of Colonial Spanish America and Brazil.* Cambridge: Cambridge University Press, 1999.

Salomon, Frank. *The Cord Keepers: Khipus and Cultural Life in a Peruvian Village.* Durham, NC: Duke University Press, 2004.

Sarmiento de Gamboa, Pedro. *History of the Incas.* Translated by Clements Markham. Cambridge, UK: The Hakluyt Society, 1907.

T'oqrikoq

Part of the hierarchy of governmental leaders in the Inca Empire, the t'oqrikoqs were officials whose positions were a blend of provincial administrator and judicial authority. The empire had a series of hierarchical positions, with the Sapa Inca and his family at the apex. The next level of administrative posts was those positions whose function was to oversee the four quadrants of the empire, the Contisuyu, Antisuyu, Chinchaysuyu, and Collasuyu. These administrators were typically experienced generals who served as loyal supporters of the emperor. The four quadrants, with their military overseers, were then divided up into several smaller provinces.

The provinces within the individual quadrants were administered by members of the royal family or by Inca by privilege of a rank equal to the royal family. These important provincial administrators were known as t'oqrikoqs. Essentially the position of t'oqrikoq was the Inca forerunner to what the Spanish later referred to as provincial governors. These authorities were responsible for governing and administrating justice over a specific province within the empire.

While t'oqrikoqs were responsible for the government and judicial systems of their assigned provinces, and commonly resided within the same provinces, their responsibilities went beyond this limited arrangement. The governors also served as traveling representatives of the ruling Inca, much in the manner of circuit justices.

The authority and prestige of the t'oqrikoqs gave rise to a virtual class within the government and the Inca society. To keep this powerful class in check, a subordinate class of tucuyricoc, or inspectors, were designated as judicial officials. The task of these inspectors was to report directly to the imperial government on the administration of justice throughout the varying provinces. In this manner, the powerful t'oqrikoqs retained their status and authority, yet were prevented from becoming a threat to the empire or its people.

Rebecca M. Seaman

See also: Antisuyu; Chinchaysuyu; Collasuyu; Contisuyu; Government, Pre-Conquest Inca; Tahuantinsuyu.

Resources

Davies, Nigel. *The Incas.* Niwot: University of Colorado Press, 1995.

Keen, Benjamin, and Keith Haynes. *A History of Latin America.* 8th ed. Boston: Houghton Mifflin Harcourt, 2009.

Totonacs, Alliance with Spanish

The Totonac people currently inhabit the north-central portion of the Gulf lowlands and adjacent highlands of the modern Mexican states of Veracruz and Puebla. They have occupied this region since well before the arrival of Hernán Cortés and the Spanish in the spring of 1519. At the time of Spanish arrival, the Totonacs lived in several large centers and fortified towns along the coast and in the interior mountains. Two of their best-known centers were Zempoala (Cempoallan) and Quiahuiztlan. The large earlier center El Tajín is also attributed to the Totonacs. Much of the Totonac territory had been incorporated into the Aztec Empire.

There is little agreement about the origin and meaning of the name Totonac. The term *totonaco* was a derogatory referent used by the Aztecs (Mexica specifically) when expressing what they considered to be the backwardness of other people. It may also mean "people from the land of heat," "people from where the sun rises," or literally "three hearts" or "three honeycombs." The latter meanings come from the Totonac language and may figuratively represent the three city-states that made up pre-Hispanic Totonacapan. However, it is uncertain if the name is derived from the Totonac language at all, or from Nahua.

The Totonacs have shared the Gulf lowlands and adjacent highlands with Nahua speakers since at least the Early Post-Classic period (ca. 1000 AD).

The earliest Western depictions of the Totonacs were written by Bernal Diaz del Castillo, one of the chief chroniclers of the Spanish conquest of Mexico who provided eyewitness accounts of Totonac-Spanish introductions and subsequent alliances against the Aztecs. Despite their early arrival and investment along the central Gulf lowlands, the Spanish encountered several other indigenous Mesoamerican groups before the Totonacs. The Totonacs were different from the groups of the Yucatán, Campeche, Tabasco, and southern Veracruz Gulf Coasts in that they were the first to eagerly ally with the Spanish against another indigenous group—the Aztecs. One Totonac ruler (from Zempoala) indicated to Cortés that he had acquiesced to Axayacatl (ruler from 1468 to 1482), not out of loyalty but out of fear.

This attitude toward the Aztecs signaled to Cortés that cleavages existed within the Aztec network that he could exploit to the Spanish advantage. In response to the Totonac leader's complaints, Cortés promised to relieve the burdens of the people of Zempoala, achieving in exchange their loyalty and important logistical aid. Cortés garnered subsequent cooperation from the leader of nearby fortified Quiahuiztlan. Because of the situational character of alliances between Mesoamerican city-states, the Totonac leaders may have viewed this pledge of fealty to Cortés and the Spanish monarch more fleetingly than Cortés had imagined.

Marcie Venter

See also: Aztec, or Mexica; Cortés, Hernán; Diaz del Castillo, Bernal; Nahuatl Language; Quiahuiztlan; Zempoala.

Resources

Diaz del Castillo, Bernal. *The Discovery and Conquest of Mexico: 1517–1521.* Translated by A.P. Maudslay. New York: Da Capo Press, 2003.

Hassig, Ross. *Mexico and the Spanish Conquest.* Norman: University of Oklahoma Press, 2006.

Valderrama Rouy, Pablo. "The Totonac." In *Native Peoples of the Gulf Coast of Mexico,* edited by Alan R. Sandstrom and E. Hugo García Valencia. Tucson: University of Arizona Press, 2005.

Toxcatl Massacre

The Toxcatl Massacre (either May 10 or May 16, 1520) refers to the slaughter of Aztec nobles by order of Pedro de Alvarado during the Spanish occupation of the Aztec capital, Tenochtitlán.

Hernán Cortés arrived in what is now Mexico in 1519 in order to acquire reported wealth and to conquer the Aztec Empire. Due to confusion about the true identity and motivations of the Spanish, as well as the fact that he had managed to kidnap the Aztec emperor, Montezuma II, Cortés was able to initially occupy Tenochtitlán with no violence. He and his small force of Spanish soldiers, along with their numerous Indian allies, took up residence in one of the city's palaces and stayed there for the winter of 1519–1520. Despite the fact that the Aztecs brought them food and water, the Spanish and their allies quickly became unwanted guests.

In 1520, Cortés had to leave Tenochtitlán to confront a second Spanish expedition sent by Governor Diego de Velázquez to arrest him (Cortés had begun his conquest illegally, when Velázquez pulled his support of the expedition), he left his second-in-command, Pedro de Alvarado, in charge of the city. The captured emperor, Montezuma, requested permission from Alvarado for the Aztecs to celebrate the upcoming Toxcatl festival, an important annual event honoring one of the major gods of the Aztec pantheon. Alvarado granted him permission, and preparations began.

However, as preparations continued, Alvarado became increasingly fearful that the celebration was a cover for an impending Aztec uprising against the Spanish. Evidence of the purported plot came in two forms. First, the Aztecs stopped bringing the Spanish food or water, resulting in the need for Alvarado's men to travel outside the palace compound to purchase these things in the market. Second, as Alvarado traveled around the city, he saw strange things that his Indian allies (traditional enemies of the Aztecs) convinced him to interpret in the worst possible ways. For example, they told him that the large stakes being raised in the center of the city were to sacrifice him and his men and that the Aztecs were preparing large cooking areas in order to eat the Spanish soldiers. Whatever truth there might have been to such rumors or the interpretations of the Spanish's Indian allies, Alvarado became convinced that an attack was imminent.

Rather than wait for the Aztecs to attack, Alvarado decided to strike first. Alvarado and his men advanced on the city's main temple and took control of the gates leading in and out of the building in order to prevent any escape. Then, on Alvarado's command, his men slaughtered over 100 unarmed Aztec nobles participating in the celebration inside. Not surprisingly, this led to open, armed conflict between the Spanish, their Indian allies, and Aztec warriors in the city. Cuauhtémoc, nephew and son-in-law of the captured emperor Montezuma, rallied the Aztecs against the Spanish. Alvarado and his men soon found themselves besieged within the palace complex and only survived because of the return of Cortés from the coast. Cortés's forces regrouped with the others in the palace complex, where they fought for over a week against the city's warriors before finally escaping Tenochtitlán during the disastrous events of La Noche Triste. Eventually, however, Cortés returned to reconquer the city and, in time, the entire Aztec Empire.

John Gram

See also: Alvarado, Pedro de; Cortés, Hernán; Cuauhtémoc; La Noche Triste; Montezuma II; Tenochtitlán, Siege of; Totonacs, Alliance with Spanish.

Resources

Bakewell, Peter. *A History of Latin America.* 2nd ed. Malden, MA: Blackwell, 2004.

Diaz del Castillo, Bernal. *The Conquest of New Spain.* Translated by J. M. Cohen. Baltimore: Penguin Books, 1963.

Thomas, Hugh. *Conquest: Montezuma, Cortés, and the Fall of Old Mexico.* New York: Simon & Schuster, 1993.

Tribute, Paid to Mexica

Tribute represents the type of tax paid prior to the Spanish conquest in the center of Mexico, consisting of both goods and services. Under the Mexica there were two levels of taxes: a local tribute and a royal tribute. In both cases, the tribute was organized and controlled by the ruling classes and nobility, indicative of the both the social and political structure of the Mexican society and government.

Peasants, or *macehuales,* paid the local tribute. This socioeconomic class served as craftsmen and traders inside specific localities. The local tribute was directed toward maintaining the *macehuales*' nobility (*pilli,* pl. *pipiltin*), rulers, priests, and warriors. The local tribute basically consisted of services inside lords' homes, working in their fields, and supplying food, water, firewood, and other resources. It was one of the fundamental mechanisms that enabled the correct running of society based on social stratification and the division of labor.

The royal tribute was an obligatory payment to the ruling cities of the Aztec Empire, or Triple Alliance, by the subjugated cities and towns. In this manner, the royal tribute helped maintain the power and status of the victors. The royal tribute arose primarily as the fruit of the victory of one group over another in war, and constituted the manner in which the imperial state was organized. The resulting empire, built out of conquests and sustained by compulsory taxes, was more of a tributary empire than a political one. The payment was made in a quantity and frequency established by the victor and consisted primarily of set measures of cocoa beans, food, raw materials, manufactured luxury goods, personal services, and building materials. It was through these collected tributary goods that the state, the palaces, and public constructions were maintained.

On the whole, tribute-paying people recognized their subordination to those who dominated them and therefore paid. Depending on the level of collaboration or resistance exhibited by people during the Mexica conquest, the tributary levels were more or less demanding. Frequently certain rights were established, such as being allowed to continue with their own social and political organization. The practice of demanding goods from far away ecosystems has also been documented. Thus, the insubordination of the most rebellious people resulted in compelling them to import products from places such as the Central American jungles.

Once the quantity, substance, and frequency of payment was established (monthly, every three months, or every six months, among others), a *calpixque* or tax collector was assigned to the conquered city and placed in charge of administering the collection and sending the products to Tenochtitlán, the capital. There, the tributary goods were stored in the warehouses of the ruler's palace (*tlatoani*), next to the tributes paid by those who were subjugated to his direct rule.

The two main pictographical sources concerning this subject are the *Matrícula de Tributos* and the *Mendoza Codex,* which mention the tributes that 35 or 38 provinces paid to Tenochtitlán during the rule of Montezuma Xocoyotzin ("The Young", or Moctezuma II, a.k.a. Montezuma II, 1502–1520). These resources speak of how the major and heaviest materials came from the provinces closest to the city, while rare and valuable products were sent from far away places. Porters, or *tamemes,* transported the merchandise from the conquered provinces. Some had to pay an extra tax in order to gain entrance to the capital. Many of these goods came from a commerce that already had stable routes established before the Aztec military invasions.

Marta Martín Gabaldón

See also: Artisans, Mexica; Aztec, or Mexica; *Macehualtin*; Mexico, State of prior to Spanish Conquest; Montezuma II; *Pipiltin*; Tenochtitlán.

Resources

Berdan, Frances F. *The Aztecs of Central Mexico: an Imperial Society.* New York: Rinehart and Winston, 1982.

Berdan, Frances y Jacqueline de Durand-Forest. *Matrícula de Tributos, Museo de Antropología, México (35–52).* Graz, Austria: Akademische Druck und Verlangsanstalt, 1980.

Hicks, Frédéric. "Subject States and Tribute Provinces: Aztec Empire in the Northern Valley of Mexico." *Ancient Mesoamerica* 3, no. 1 (1992): 1–10.

Tribute, Paid to Spain

The type of tax paid by indigenous people to the Spanish during the colonial era was designated as "tribute" and consisted of both goods and services. More clearly used in the viceroyalty of New Spain than in Peru, the Spanish organized the tax following the same model as the pre-Hispanic tribute system, although quantity, types of products, and the manner in which the collection was undertaken were altered throughout the 16th century.

The so-called *tributo real* (Royal tribute), paid to the Crown, was diversified. Through the institution of the encomienda, the king gave a Spanish encomendero the right to receive part of the tributes that the indigenous people, as vassals, had to pay to the Crown. The encomendero agreed with the indigenous elites of each village (called caciques in Mexico and *kurakas* in Peru) on the quantity of tribute they had to hand over to him. In exchange, he had to insure the wellbeing of the indigenous people, in spiritual and worldly aspects, protecting and indoctrinating them. The said tribute was handed over in the form of labor upon the lands and home of the Lord, and in goods: chilies, beans, cocoa, honey, corn, tortillas, firewood, cotton fiber, domestic animals, gold, and silver, among other products.

In Mexico, those villages that were not under an encomienda regime were considered in *corregimiento,* which is under direct jurisdiction of the Crown. In these cases, the tribute collected became part of the royal estate, and from there, some part was diverted to maintaining the work of religious institutions. Both in Mexico and in Peru, one-fifth of the metal extracted from mines, called royal fifth, also went directly to the royal chest.

In New Spain, the so called *tributo local* (local tribute), paid to the nobleman upon which one depended or to the local lord, was maintained during the colonial period in a very similar fashion to that existing in the pre-Hispanic era. In each *barrio* (quarter) there was a principal, called *tequitlato,* in charge of the tax payers, and at the same time the commoners *(macehuales),* organized into groups of twenty, were under the care of a government employee called *centecpanquixqui;* five groups of these were controlled by another, known as *macuiltecpanpixqui.* The public treasury of the indigenous nations was closely tied to the tributary system. The income that formed part of the *caja de comunidad*—community chest, a common money reserve—was a part of the collected tax, stemmed from cultivating community *milpas* (maize fields), from income taxes, and sometimes from profits made through selling common land and also from benefits achieved with community herds. The funds were dedicated to paying salaries, defraying the expenses of lawsuits or transport, and maintaining religious cults, amongst other things.

The colonial tributary system introduced large changes in the circulation of funds, in the final destination of the goods and in the indigenous labor, as well as introducing money as a new form of payment. All of this occurred in order to guarantee the growth and prosperity of the Spanish Empire. Some tributary goods demanded were needed for creating manufactured goods while others were targeted for exportation. The tribute, in form of labor, was employed after the second half of the 16th century, thereby creating new economical sectors (haciendas, mines, and mills). Tax money represented the Crown's wish to establish a solid means of payment, consolidating its circulation and thus introducing the huge benefits gained in America into the international markets.

From the decade of 1560 onward, the Crown reformed the tributary system, adjusting it to the new socioeconomic situation. This was undertaken in New Spain during the government of the viceroy Luis de Velasco, "The Father" (1550–1564), and in Peru with the viceroy Francisco de Toledo (1569–1581). It was expected to achieve a European rational order, resulting in exhaustive valuations that employed *visitas* and indigenous censuses. From then on, the functionaries known as *corregidores* took the Royal tribute, paid by indigenous people in order to avoid the abuses committed by encomenderos. Some of the modifications introduced by the Spanish administration included a specific fee paid by each person and the gradual shift of taxes in the form of goods to money. In Mexico, they imposed an annual payment consisting of one peso and a half *fanega* (bushel) of corn or of an equivalent grain. The Spanish also organized the taxation of almost every administrative aspect, state, church, and village taxes. Additionally, personal service in benefit of encomenderos was legally abolished. In Peru, the Spanish imposed the colonial *mita* system, inspired by the ancient Andean one. This system consisted in tribute in the form of community work carried out in mines, mills or state infrastructures, as bridges and roads.

Marta Martín Gabaldón

See also: *Corregidores;* Inca Elite; *Macehualtin*; Maize; Mines, Role of in Peru; *Mita*; Peru, State of after Spanish Conquest; Toledo, Francisco de; Tribute, Paid to Mexica.

Resources

Coatsworth, John H. "Political Economy and Economic Organization." In *The Cambridge Economic History of Latin America,* Vol. 1, *The Colonial Era and the Short Nineteenth Century,* edited by Victor Bulmer-Thomas, John H. Coatsworth, and Roberto Cortés Conde. New York: Cambridge University Press, 2006.

Gibson, Charles. *The Aztecs under Spanish Rule: A History of the Indians of the Valley of Mexico, 1519–1810.* Stanford, CA: Stanford University Press, 1964.

Hassig, Ross. *Trade, Tribute, and Transportation: The Sixteenth-Century Political Economy of the Valley of Mexico.* Norman: University of Oklahoma Press, 1985.

Rojas, José Luis. *A cada uno lo suyo: El tributo indígena en la Nueva España en el siglo XVI.* Zamora, Michoacán: El Colegio de Michoacán, 1993.

Tucuyricoc

One of the lower ranks of the Inca administrative hierarchy, the tucuyricocs were nonetheless important for the role they played. These low-ranked officials were part of the judicial system and often known as visitors. Like their Spanish equivalents of *visitadors,* the tucuyricocs were tasked with investigating particular issues.

The tucuyricocs functioned in one of the lowest positions within the central Inca administration. These minor bureaucrats traveled throughout assigned provinces, basically serving as inspectors whose job was to ensure the proper administration of justice. Any improper legal practices were presumably reported by these judicial officials to the central authorities of the province, military administrator of the particular *suyu* division, or the Inca's central government. In reality, the inspectors were given instructions to report on specific issues or aspects of the provincial government.

Due to the territory covered by each individual tucuyricocs, the amount of information and data gathered was extensive. To facilitate their reports, the investigators employed the use of *quipus* to help them document relevant data. The complexity of this system of recording data necessitated an education system that could train people as not only capable judicial officials, but also as *quipu* masters. At the very least, the Inca society provided an education for descendants of the Incas and certain highly placed Incas by privilege. It also enabled the Inca to present an image of the government as fair and protective of the people.

Rebecca M. Seaman

See also: *Quipu*; Tahuantinsuyu; *Visitas.*

Resources

Davies, Nigel. *The Incas.* Niwot: University of Colorado Press, 1995.

Zuidema, R.T. "Hierarchy and Space in Incaic Social Organization." *Ethnohistory* 30, no. 2 (Spring 1983): 49–75.

Tumbes

Located in the northern end of the Inca Empire, the Tumbes province (Tumbez) fell within the larger quadrant of the empire, Chinchaysuyu. This region was occupied and conquered by the Inca in the 15th century under the rule of Túpac Inca. The city of Tumbes, on the coastal border between modern-day Ecuador and Peru, benefited architecturally and economically from their association with the Inca. Eventually, the people of Tumbes allied their city to the Inca Empire as a vassal state. It was from this location that Túpac Inca continued his wars of conquest.

In 1526, Francisco Pizarro voyaged south along the Pacific coast, where his first contact with the Inca Empire occurred at sea. Aware that this newly encountered society showed signs of advancement and wealth, Pizarro was determined to explore further to discover the source of the wealth. In 1528, with a handful of soldiers and few supplies, his second voyage sailed into the Gulf of

Guayaquil. There Pizarro's men encountered their first Inca city—Tumbes. According to the reports, the city was well structured, and again displayed signs of belonging to a wealthy, advanced society.

Convinced of the potential of his new discovery, Pizarro returned to Panama to provision his expedition and recruit more soldiers. When he finally returned to Tumbes in early 1531, the city lay in ruins, the result of a civil war raging within the Inca Empire between Huáscar and Atahualpa for control of the throne. It was from the ruins of Tumbes that the conquistadors turned inland and eventually met and captured Atahualpa at the city of Cajamarca.

Rebecca M. Seaman

See also: Atahualpa; Cajamarca, Battle of; Chinchaysuyu; Huáscar; Pizarro, Francisco; Túpac Inca.

Resources

Davies, Nigel. *The Incas.* Niwot: University of Colorado Press, 1995.

Hemming, John. *The Conquest of the Incas.* New York: Harcourt Brace Jovanovich, 1970.

Túpac Amaru

Túpac Amaru ("royal serpent") was the last emperor of the Inca Empire and ruled from 1571 to 1572. He was executed by the Spanish but remained an important symbol of resistance in South America.

Túpac Amaru was born around 1554. He was the third son of Manco Inca Yupanqui, who was the half-brother of Atahualpa, the leader of the Inca Empire defeated by Francisco Pizarro and the Spaniards in 1533. The Spaniards quickly vanquished the Incas in the Inca-Spanish War, took control of their territory, and set up puppet Inca rulers

Túpac Amaru, the last Inca Emperor, ruled briefly from 1571 to 1572. (De Agostini Picture Library/G. Dagli Orti)

intended to ensure Spanish hegemony. Resistance, however, continued in the form of a new Inca government and a religious movement known as Taqui Onqoy.

At first, Manco Inca Yupanqui had allied himself with Pizarro and the Spaniards. Upon the death of Atahualpa, he became the puppet ruler of the Incas and cooperated with the Europeans from 1533 to 1536. After several years of poor treatment, however, Manco revolted against the Spaniards. He then led a year-long siege of the city of Cuzco that ultimately failed. Unable to take Cuzco, Manco retreated to Vitcos, located in the province of Vilcabamba in a remote mountain region of southern Peru. There he established Vilcabamba as the last Inca capital. The region was important in that it included a number of key Inca holy sites. During the continued struggle between resistant Inca rulers and the Spanish conquerors seeking complete power, there was a revival of native religion in the secluded capital. The Incas built a temple in their new stronghold and had their golden image of the sun moved there along with the mummies of the emperor's ancestors. In 1544, several Spaniards seeking refuge among the Incas assassinated Manco in the presence of his three sons.

Manco was followed as emperor by three of his sons. The first to rule was Sayri Túpac, who was still a child when his father died. Eventually, he allied himself with the Spaniards and was baptized as a Christian. The Spanish hoped that he would be able to win over the remaining Inca resistance. However, he died under suspicious circumstances, probably from, poisoning in 1560 and was followed by his brother Titu Cusi Yupanqui. Titu Cusi continued the Inca resistance and even planned a general uprising against Spanish rule in 1565. Later, however, he also negotiated with the Spaniards and was baptized. Upon the death of Titu Cusi, Túpac Amaru became the leader of the Inca resistance.

Túpac Amaru was crowned in 1571. Though his rule was short, he returned traditional beliefs and practices to the now small Inca kingdom at Vilcabamba. Unlike his brother Titu Cusi, who was willing to negotiate and had made concessions to the Spaniards, Túpac Amaru vigorously opposed the Spaniards and Christianity. A strong believer in native religion, he rejected Christianity and tried to eradicate all signs of it. He destroyed churches, killed Spaniards who were living among the Incas, and persecuted those natives who had converted to Christianity. In addition, Túpac Amaru closed off the borders of Vilcabamba. Such sentiments could be found in the movement known as Taqui Onqoy, which had begun in the 1560s and was a revival of traditional religion and culture. Those traditions were now transformed into a call for revolt and liberation.

Meanwhile, the new viceroy of Peru, Francisco de Toledo, wanted to subdue the Inca resistance. Toledo did make a last attempt at diplomacy and sent an envoy with a message to the emperor. However, the Incas killed the Spanish emissary. An enraged Toledo then decided to attack Vilcabamba. In 1572, Toledo sent hundreds of Spaniards along with thousands of native allies to subdue Túpac Amaru and the Incas. When the Spaniards took Vilcabamba, Túpac Amaru and his pregnant wife fled into the jungle. A group of Spaniards followed them and found them warming themselves around a campfire. Túpac Amaru and his family were captured and taken to Cuzco, along with the disinterred, mummified bodies of Manco Inca and Titu Cusi.

In Cuzco, the Spaniards instructed Túpac Amaru in Christianity and had him baptized. He was also tried and convicted in a hurried and unfair trial, accused of treason for defending Vilcabamba against the Spanish invaders and for serving as the spiritual leader of a pagan people who worshiped him as a false god. The Spanish additionally accused Túpac Amaru of raids that had actually been conducted by his brother and father before him. Some members of the clergy protested the sentence of death given to the last emperor of the Incas. They claimed he was innocent and should instead be sent to Spain. His inability to speak the Spanish language and the lack of legal representation guaranteed a conviction. Toledo disregarded all protests, and in September 1572, the Spaniards executed Túpac Amaru by beheading him in front of a large crowd in the main plaza of Cuzco. The Spanish authorities had his severed head placed on a pike and put on public display. Active Inca resistance to

Spanish rule came to an end with the death of Túpac Amaru. However, many Incas in Cuzco still revered their dead ruler and went to worship his head at night. In order to end that practice, the viceroy had the head removed and buried.

After Túpac Amaru's execution, his three-year-old son Martín was taken from Cuzco to Lima, where he died several years later. Túpac Amaru's daughter, Juana Pinca Huaco, remained in Cuzco and later married Felipe Condorcanqui, a *curaca* or chief from Tinta to the south of Cuzco. With Toledo firmly in control, the appointment of official Inca emperors was discontinued.

Túpac Amaru remains an important symbol of resistance in South America. In the 1780s, José Gabriel Condorcanqui, the great-great-grandson of Túpac Amaru's daughter, took on the name Túpac Amaru II during a major uprising against the Spanish that included a siege of Cuzco. In the 1980s, a Marxist guerrilla movement in Peru took on the name Túpac Amaru.

Ronald E. Young

See also: Atahualpa; Manco Inca Yupanqui; Sayri Túpac; Taki Onqoy; Titu Cusi Yupanqui; Toledo, Francisco de; Vilcabamba.

Resources

Klarén, Peter F. *Peru: Society and Nationhood in the Andes.* New York: Oxford University Press, 2000.

MacQuarrie, Kim. *The Last Days of the Incas.* New York: Simon & Schuster, 2007.

Means, Philip A. *The Fall of the Inca Empire and the Spanish Rule in Peru, 1530–1780.* New York: Gordian Press, 1971.

Túpac Huallpa

Túpac Huallpa was the son of Huayna Cápac, the last totally independent emperor of the Incas. He briefly served as a puppet emperor for the Spanish conquistadores after they had his older brother, Atahualpa, executed. Túpac Huallpa proved to be a compliant front for the Spanish and may have been poisoned by those who wanted to fight the Spanish.

Túpac Huallpa's birth date is unknown. His name meant "royal cock." As a younger son of a lesser wife, Túpac Huallpa was not expected to succeed to the throne, although the Incas did not practice a set rule for succession. Túpac Huallpa had the misfortune of coming of age at the time of the Spanish invasion. Huayna Cápac spent most of his reign expanding the empire to the north. He heard rumors of strangers, but had not received any Europeans at his court when he died suddenly of smallpox in 1527, well in advance of the first contact by Spaniards with the Incas.

Huayna Cápac was briefly succeeded by his eldest son, Ninan Cuyochi, and then his son Huáscar Inca. Huáscar, the son of Huayna and his primary wife, also did not last long on the throne. Civil war broke out between Huáscar and his half-brother Atahualpa (son of a non-Inca mother). Atahualpa eventually won the war and imprisoned his brother. Thus, it was Atahualpa who was emperor when Francisco Pizarro led an expedition into Inca lands. Because the Spanish numbered less than 200 men, Atahualpa believed he had nothing to fear. This overconfidence, coupled with the Spanish use of gunpowder weapons of guns and canon, steel armor, and horses, proved the undoing of Atahualpa's forces. The Spanish weapons, armor, and strategies were all unknown to the Incas. Under the pretense of giving gifts to the emperor, the Spanish attacked the unarmed escorting forces of the emperor, and the Inca warriors were routed with great slaughter. The Spanish, under Pizarro, took

Atahualpa prisoner. He was still not greatly concerned, since he did not believe such a small group could do more than raid the empire. Atahualpa negotiated a huge ransom, after which he was to be released.

After receiving the ransom, Pizarro suspected an attack by forces loyal to Atahualpa. In response, he had Atahualpa executed on August 29, 1533. He then needed a candidate for the throne to unify Incas not in allegiance with the recent emperor. He began to promote good relations with those who had supported Huáscar. He realized, however, that Túpac Huallpa was the eldest remaining legitimate son of Huayna Cápac and could make a good case to be named emperor. Pizarro called together all the chiefs of the Incas in Cajamarca. He presented Túpac Huallpa, and the chiefs agreed that he would be acceptable as emperor. The following day, Túpac Huallpa was coronated according to Inca custom, with great feasting and dancing. Each chief presented a white feather to Túpac Huallpa as a token of his vassalage. Túpac Huallpa then spent three days in a house, shut up and fasting, to honor the memory of Atahualpa. After that, he emerged in the robes of the emperor. Túpac Huallpa presented a white feather to Pizarro, in token of his submission to him. The following day, the Spanish had the Inca chiefs pledge their submission to the king of Spain. Many of the Indians present seemed to view Túpac Huallpa's coronation as the restoration of their legitimate ruler.

Pizarro soon completed preparations to move on the Inca capital of Cuzco. The distance was 750 miles, but the army was able to use the excellent Inca roads. The first part of the journey was uneventful. Many of the people were not opposed to the Spanish and turned out to see them and the new emperor. For his part, Túpac Huallpa believed that the Spanish would restore him to the royal throne at Cuzco. He helped make arrangements for

their journey, including supplies along the way. When the army reached Jauja in October, they were faced with the first opposition. An army of Incas attempted to block their route. A sudden attack by the Spanish with horses and firearms soon dispersed the Incas. They were so demoralized that they offered no more opposition, although they greatly outnumbered the Spanish.

At Jauja, Pizarro rested his army from October 12 to October 27, 1533. While he was there, Túpac Huallpa suddenly died. He had been weakening from a disease ever since they left Cajamarca. Although some suspected he was poisoned, the evidence seemed to indicate Túpac Huallpa died of the disease he had been battling. His death was a great inconvenience for Pizarro, who had benefited from the emperor's compliant accommodations to Spanish wishes.

Tim J. Watts

See also: Atahualpa; European Diseases, Role of; Guns, Impact of; Horses, Impact of; Huayna Cápac; Huáscar; Inca-Spanish War, Causes of.

Resources

Bernand, Carmen. *The Incas: Empire of Blood and Gold.* London: Thames & Hudson, 1994.

Hemming, John. *The Conquest of the Incas.* London: Pan Macmillan, 1970.

Means, Philip A. *The Fall of the Inca Empire and the Spanish Rule in Peru, 1530–1780.* New York: Gordian Press, 1971.

Túpac Inca Yupanqui

Túpac Inca Yupanqui, the 10th emperor of the Inca Empire in South America, ruled from 1471 to 1493. He reigned at the height of the empire after a period of formation and expansion and was known as a great conqueror.

Túpac Inca Yupanqui, 10th emperor of Inca who governed at the height of the empire, 1471–1493. (Bettmann/Corbis)

The exact year of Túpac Inca's birth is unknown. The son of Inca emperor Pachacutin Inca Yupanqui, Túpac showed great promise as a youth. He was raised to be a strong leader. His father often trained him personally. In addition, Túpac Inca sometimes accompanied Pachacutin's trusted generals on their campaigns.

During his father's rule, Túpac Inca helped to greatly expand the Inca Empire to the north. While earlier groups sometimes raided those areas, the Incas made conquest more permanent. Túpac Inca subdued the lands of the Quechuas and the Chancas, and he reached present-day Quito, Ecuador. He then completed the conquest of the Chimús, the largest and most important group in Peru before the appearance of the Incas, as well as their last serious rival. Túpac Inca was able to conquer the Chimú capital after the long Battle of Chan Chan. Following their victory over the Chimús, the Incas not only took over Chimú territory, but they also absorbed much of Chimú culture, especially in the area of art. Túpac Inca also learned political organization, irrigation, and road building techniques from the Chimús.

Sometime in 1471, Pachacutin abdicated in favor of his son, who inherited a large and rich empire. During his rule, Túpac Inca greatly enlarged the Inca Empire through war and conquest, often at great cost. His first military campaign involved the tropical rainforest near the Tono River. Túpac Inca and the Incas had always been attracted to the rainforest and its products. However, the campaign was not an easy one, as the Incas never perfected military operations in the difficult environment of the rainforest.

At times, Túpac Inca faced stiff resistance to his rule. He had to interrupt his campaign in the rainforest because there was a major rebellion of the Colla and Lupaca peoples in the Lake Titicaca region. The rebels were encouraged by rumors that Túpac Inca had perished in the rainforest expedition. The Inca leader was forced to capture the mountaintop forts of the Collas around Pucará. He then moved against the Lupacas, who had retreated to the southwest corner of the Titicaca Basin and made an alliance with the Pacasas. Once again, however, the Inca armies were triumphant, and the revolt ended.

After putting down the rebellion in the Titicaca region, Túpac Inca continued to expand the empire to include highland Bolivia, northwestern Argentina, and the desert coast of Chile. The Chilean campaign in particular was a major undertaking that went over mountains and across coastal deserts. Due to the fact that there were few local people in the mountains to aid the Inca armies, Túpac Inca sent specialized engineering corps to prepare the way and build suspension bridges. Upon conquering Chile, he set the southern boundary of the empire at the Maule River.

The final phase of Túpac Inca's imperial expansion was to incorporate the southeastern coast of Peru. In 1476, he launched a major campaign in the region. Most of the area's inhabitants surrendered peacefully or put up only minimal resistance. Túpac Inca did meet stiffer resistance in the Cañate Valley, where it took nearly three years to conquer the inhabitants.

Túpac Inca excelled at organizing his vast empire and took a great personal interest in running its affairs. At the same time, he knew how to effectively delegate authority, a necessity for governing such widespread territories. To that end, he issued many new laws. He reorganized problem areas like the Titicaca region after the Colla rebellion there. He introduced the *mita,* a system of classifying the adult male population into units that were then used for labor assignments or military service. Túpac Inca also started the system of tribute in which each province contributed "chosen women" to serve in religious shrines or to become the wives of distinguished soldiers. In addition, he perfected the practice of incorporating the religious shrines and views of conquered peoples, as was the case in Titicaca and Koati. He often reworked their stories in order to include aspects of Inca dominance.

Túpac Inca was probably responsible for building the Temple of the Sun on the Isla del Sol (Island of the Sun) on Lake Titicaca in the eastern Andes Mountains. The temple marked the spot where the Inca Sun god sent Manco Cápac and Mama Ocllo, the founders of the Inca Empire, to Earth. Túpac Inca also occupied the Pilco Kayma, or Inca's Palace, a two-story building surrounded by fountains and gardens.

Túpac Inca traveled often during his reign. He visited many towns throughout the provinces of the Inca Empire. He journeyed as far south as the Maule River in present-day Chile. On those trips, he stayed in palaces especially built for his ceremonial visits. Oral tradition even says that Túpac Inca traveled on the Pacific Ocean, visiting various islands.

Túpac Inca died unexpectedly in about 1493. He originally wanted his son Huayna Cápac to follow him, but he seems to have later changed his mind and preferred another son named Cápac Huari. In the power struggle that ensued, Huayna Cápac won and became emperor.

Ronald E. Young

See also: Huayna Cápac; Pachacutin; Manco Cápac; *Mita.*

Resources

Bernand, Carmen. *The Incas: Empire of Blood and Gold.* London: Thames & Hudson, 1994.

Karsten, Rafael. *A Totalitarian State of the Past: The Civilization of the Inca Empire in Ancient Peru.* Port Washington, NY: Kennikat Press, 1970.

V

Vázquez, Martín

Martín Vázquez was a well-known member of Hernán Cortés expedition to Mexico, one of a number of Extremeños surrounding the *caudillo*. Bernal Díaz del Castillo described him as a native of Olmedo, a rich and prominent man who resided in Mexico City, and who died of natural causes. In testimony given decades after the conquest, Vázquez claimed that he, in fact, came from the village of Martín Muñoz in the region of Segovia. Other sources indicated that he came from the region near Olmedo, also in Segovia. Vázquez declared that he traveled to the New World in the early years of settlement and participated in the expedition of Pedrarias Dávila to settle Panamá in 1514, at the colony of Castilla del Oro. He married before the conquest of Mexico while in Cuba. Some sources indicate that his wife was a native woman from Cuba. He eventually had three sons and a daughter.

Vázquez sailed to Mexico for the first time in the company of Hernández de Córdoba, and later joined the Cortés excursion. He was a crossbowman in these expeditions. At the establishment of the colony at Villa Rica de la Vera Cruz, Vázquez was purportedly present and participating in electing the council and other authorities, to include the designation of Cortés as chief justice and captain of the king's armies.

As one of the Extremeños trusted by Cortés, Vázquez was given positions of importance. He served as both horseman and crossbowman for most of the conquest. In later testimony, Vázquez claimed to have been one of the guards of Moteuctzoma (Montezuma II), the Aztec emperor at the time of Cortés's initial occupation of Tenochtitlán. He participated in many of the important battles in the conquest of Mexico, and was present in the disastrous defeat of the Spanish best remembered as La Noche Triste, on June 30, 1520. The Extremeño reported later that 600 Spaniards were lost through death or capture that night. The Mexica sacrificed most of those soldiers who were captured. Vázquez also testified to having received numerous wounds during the various battles, and was certainly injured during the escape from Tenochtitlán.

Consistently loyal to his benefactor, Cortés, Vázquez later provided testimony regarding the king's gold that was lost in the retreat from Tenochtitlán during the La Noche Triste, attesting to the efforts of the *caudillo* to protect and transport the gold out of the city. There is some conjecture that Vázquez's extreme loyalty is in part due to an incident during the siege of the Aztec capital in 1521. Almost a year after the defeat of La Noche Triste, Vázquez was again fighting among Cortés's forces in the four-month long siege of the city. In the heated struggle to wrest the last defensive position from the Aztec emperor, Vázquez was rescued from capture and certainly death at the hand of the Mexica.

For his years of service in battle, Martín Vázquez received the village of Tlaxiaco in encomienda. In fact, Vázquez initially received Xilocingo, Chicuautla, and Mixtepec in encomienda. These were taken from him during the period following Cortés's departure for Spain and struggles for political authority in New Spain. Later he was compensated for the loss of these holdings with the grant of Tlaxiaco. He settled in Mexico City by 1525 and became a legal resident there. Others reported that his house in Mexico City became a center for card games and gambling. He was active in the local economy, owned slaves, bought and sold some items of gold and precious stones, and possibly was a mine owner. He died of natural causes sometime around 1550.

John Schwaller

See also: Cortés, Hernán; Dávila, Pedro Arias; Díaz del Castillo, Bernal; Hernández de Córdoba, Francisco; La Noche Triste; Montezuma II; Tenochtitlán, Siege of; Villa Rica de la Vera Cruz.

Resources

Díaz del Castillo, Bernal. *The History of the Conquest of New Spain.* Edited by David Carrasco. Albuquerque: University of New Mexico Press, 2008.

Grunberg, Bernard. *Dictionnaire des conquistadores de Mexico.* Paris: L'Harmattan, 2001.

Thomas, Hugh. *Conquest: Montezuma, Cortés, and the Fall of Old Mexico.* New York: Simon & Schuster, 1993.

Thomas, Hugh. *Who's Who of the Conquistadores.* London: Cassell & Company, 2000.

Vega, Garcilaso de la

Garcilaso de la Vega, sometimes known as El Inca, was one of the great chroniclers of the life, history, and culture of the Incas. Drawing on sources unavailable to earlier Spanish historians, he portrayed the Incas as an advanced and classical society and provided a multitude of detail to prove his point. He also wrote an account of the Spanish conquest of Peru, which endorsed rule by the mestizo offspring of conquerors and native nobility. Vega's lyrical works have had a powerful effect on historical interpretations of Peru beginning in the 17th century and continuing through succeeding generations.

Vega was born as Gómez Suárez de Figueroa on April 12, 1539, in the ancient Inca capital of Cuzco. All of his subsequent philosophy and historical writing would be tied to questions of heritage. He was descended from the royalty both of Europe and America and consistently sought to elevate these bloodlines in the political philosophy of 17th-century Peru. His mother, Isabel Suárez Chimpu Ocllo, was a concubine of his father, Sebastian Garcilaso de la Vega. She was an Inca princess, the granddaughter of the great Túpac Inca Yupanqui. His father had served under such famous figures in the conquest of America as Hernán Cortés

Garcilaso de la Vega, or El Inca, was a great chronicler of the life, history, and culture of the Incas, who he portrayed as an advanced, classical society. (*Obras de Garcilaso de la Vega,* 1804)

in Mexico, Pedro de Alvarado in Guatemala, and Francisco Pizarro in Peru.

At first Vega lived with his mother and then became his father's secretary and traveling companion. Throughout his youth, he gathered information about Peru before the Spaniards came, as well as recollections about the conquest under Pizarro and the immediate results. When his father died in 1559, Vega was familiar with both sides of his ancestry, the Spanish and the Inca.

Vega was recalled to Spain in 1560 by order of King Philip II, and he settled among his distinguished paternal relatives in Extremadura, a region in the southwest of Spain. Under the protection of his uncle, Alonso de Vargas, Vega later settled in the Andalusian village of Montilla. There, he continued his education, aided by the learned clergy and supported by a trust established by his father. Vega served under John of Austria against the Moors at Granada, as well as other military operations in Europe. After the demands of a 30-year military career, he settled in Córdoba, a city in the south of Spain that was the headquarters of the royal chronicler Ambrosio de Morales and a group of learned historians known as the Córdoba savants. It was in this atmosphere, in the later part of his life, that Vega began to produce the writings for which he is most remembered.

Vega's first literary achievement was the translation from Italian of Leon Hebreo's *Philosophy of Love.* Hebreo was a Portuguese Jew whose philosophical explanation of both divine and human love was condemned by the authorities. The Inquisition in 1564 forbade the Latin version, although scholars admired its dialogues. Vega was encouraged by his friends to undertake the translation, which he apparently did to occupy hours of enforced leisure. Vega also appreciated the challenge of expanding a source of knowledge. Aided by his extraordinary linguistic skills, in 1590,

Vega produced the finest Spanish translation of the *Philosophy of Love.* It was an auspicious start to his literary career.

After a decade and a half of hard work, in 1605, Vega published *The Florida of the Inca,* the exhaustive account of the expedition of Hernando de Soto to Florida, more than 60 years before. Vega was forced to rely primarily on oral testimony and personal recollections from common soldiers who accompanied the expedition, though he also used most of the written sources available. His primary source was his old friend Gonzalo Silvestre, who lived near Montilla and had been a soldier on the expedition. Vega's work was noted for its literary elegance, as well as its thoroughness. Later historians questioned the historical accuracy of *The Florida,* but readers in Vega's day accepted it without question, and the royal chronicler Antonio de Herrera used it extensively in his own accounts of the expedition.

Vega's masterpiece was his history of the Inca Empire and its conquest by the Pizarros. The first part was published in 1609, printed by the famous presses of Pedro Crasbeeck in Lisbon and dedicated to Catalina of Portugal, Duchess of Braganza. The title was *Primera parte de los comentarios reales, que tratan del origin de los Yncas . . . Escritos por el Inca Garcilasso de la Vega, natural del Cozco, y capitan de su Magestad* (*First Part of the Royal Commentaries, Which Deal With the Origin of the Incas . . . Written by the Inca Garcilaso de la Vega, Native of Cuzco and His Majesty's Captain*).

In the first part of the *Commentaries,* Vega described the geographic setting of the Inca Empire, its history, and cultural heritage. Information about social and political institutions, dynasties, costumes, religious beliefs, mythology, and languages were all included. Vega drew upon his knowledge and experiences growing up, taking pride in his distinguished family heritage. He made no pretense about being a mestizo. On the contrary, Vega's whole point in constructing his history was that it was precisely mestizos like him, descended from Inca royalty and conquistadores, who should rule in Peru.

Vega claimed to be correcting the mistakes of earlier Spanish historians. Drawing on his knowledge of Quechua, the language of the Incas, he was able to provide new perspectives. In his effort to rehabilitate the image of the Incas, Vega described them as bringing enlightenment to the more primitive Andean peoples who inhabited the region before the Incas came to power. The Inca Empire was described as having a civilizing effect, preparing the way for Christianity and the assimilation of European culture.

The second part of the *Commentaries* was prepared by 1616 and published after Vega's death (April 23, 1616) by the presses of Andres Barrera's widow. Against Vega's wishes, it appeared as the *Historia general del Peru* (*General History of Peru*). In this part, Vega described the Spanish conquest. Though he endorsed what he narrated as the glorious achievements of the conquistadores, he also discussed its disruptive effect and the bloody events that followed. Again, Vega made a case for the importance of the mestizo and the Indian nobility. Yet conservative Spanish critics saw Vega's work as the foundation of a program that could be used to overturn Spanish rule. Eventually, the Spanish Crown forbade Vega's works in Peru.

Tim J. Watts

See also: Alvarado, Pedro de; Cortés, Hernán; Phillip II of Spain; Pizarro, Francisco; Quechua Language; Túpac Inca Yupanqui.

Resources

Anadon, Jose, ed. *Garcilaso Inca de la Vega: An American Humanist.* South Bend, IN: University of Notre Dame Press, 1998.

Delaney, John J., and James Edward Tobin. *Dictionary of Catholic Biography.* Garden City, NY: Doubleday, 1961.

Varner, John Grier. *El Inca: The Life and Times of Garcilaso de la Vega.* Austin: University of Texas Press, 1968.

Vega, Garcilaso de la. *The Florida of the Inca.* Translated by John and Jeannette Varner. Austin: University of Texas Press, 1996.

Velázquez de Leon, Juan

Juan Velázquez de Leon (?–ca. July 1, 1520) came from the same prominent Castilian family in Cuéllar as the governor of Cuba, Diego Velázquez. He proved to be a capable fighter with a distinctly harsh, stuttering voice. Though from a noble family, like many nobles in Spain, Velázquez was not wealthy. He journeyed to Santo Domingo to seize opportunities in the New World, but after killing Altasi Rivas, he moved on to Cuba. His relationship with the governor failed to secure him significant patronage or an encomienda grant of natives and consequently he joined Hernán Cortes's enterprise to Mexico. When Governor Velázquez wrote to him to delay Cortes's expedition, Velázquez de Leon chose not to act.

Once in Mexico, Velázquez and others connected to the Cuban governor criticized Cortés's leadership, particularly the practice of trading gold without setting aside the royal fifth. During these troubles Cortés dispatched several forces to scout the land, locate potential settlement sites, and to search for gold. Manned by Cortés's critics, these expeditions proved useful in reducing opportunities for Cortés's opponents to send unfavorable reports. With this in mind and suspicious of the governor's cousin, Cortés regularly dispatched Velázquez on such missions. Cortés took advantage of the temporary absence of his critics to found Vera Cruz. He then had the city's officials elect him as the *justicia mayor* and captain general of the territories.

Juan Velázquez was one of several men arrested by Cortés over a plot to seize control of a ship to sail to Cuba in order to apprize Governor Velázquez of the situation, and potentially to allow him to intercept the treasure that Cortés planned to send to the king. Cortés destroyed the remaining ships and sentenced the primary suspects to be lashed and the pilot's feet cut off. However, Cortés eventually pardoned Velázquez and others, and many of these men henceforth became his strongest supporters.

Velázquez won a degree of Cortés's trust, as he was selected to lead one of the six companies when the expedition advanced toward Tenochtitlán. Like many of the Spanish leaders of the expedition, Velázquez was presented with an elite young woman, the daughter of Maxixcatl, in order to secure the alliance with Tlaxcala. He was one of four captains, along with Cortés, to meet Montezuma II after the Spanish arrival in Tenochtitlán. Given the small number of Spaniards within the city, Velázquez urged Cortés to seize the Aztec emperor. Consequently, Cortés demanded that Montezuma come as a guest (captive) of the Spaniards. Cortés blamed the necessity of this not on his own distrust, but that of the other Spaniards. After hours of negotiations with the emperor, Velázquez insisted that either Montezuma accompany them or be killed.

Velázquez served as the head of Montezuma's guard. Eventually the two men grew friendly, given their close proximity and frequent hunting expeditions. In 1520, Cortés imprisoned Velázquez over a disagreement with Gonzalo de Mexia, the treasurer of the expedition, who insisted that the royal fifth be charged over several gold plates that Velázquez ordered made. Velázquez maintained that he received the gold as a gift from Cortés, and that thus the tax had been paid. The two men fought, resulting in wounds on both sides, and their imprisonment. Montezuma urged Velázquez's release, purportedly after hearing him in chains on the floor above. This sort of personal interest and lobbying for mercy was uncharacteristic of Montezuma and indicative of the friendship that had developed. Cortés released him and charged him with further sorties to locate gold, and to accompany Diego de Ordaz on an expedition to found a settlement.

When Velázquez's brother-in-law, Panfilo de Narváez, led an expedition to apprehend Cortés, he sent entreaties for Velázquez to join him, which Velázquez then turned over to Cortés. Given his connection to Narváez, Cortés dispatched Velázquez to negotiate a peaceful settlement. Narváez countered with an offer that if Cortés could be killed, Velázquez would be placed in command of Cortés's men. During these negotiations, Velázquez fell out with one of his kinsman in Narváez's force, the younger Diego Velázquez, effectively ending the negotiations. Before he left, he reportedly paid a gunmaster to plug Narváez's cannons with wax. Velázquez then led one of the five companies in the victorious attack against Narváez.

The attack on Narváez significantly reduced Spanish power within the capital city of Tenochtitlán and the Aztecs mounted a rebellion, which besieged the small garrison under Pedro de Alvarado. When Cortés's force arrived back in the capital, they found the situation untenable. Cortés pulled out of Tenochtitlán on the night of June 30, 1520, referred to as La Noche Triste. Juan Velázquez de Leon and Pedro de Alvarado commanded the rearguard, entrusted with the king's fifth of the treasure. Alvarado survived the fighting, but Velázquez de Leon was not seen again. If captured alive, the Aztecs may have sacrificed him.

Michael Beauchamp

See also: Alvarado, Pedro de; Cortés, Hernán; La Noche Triste; Montezuma II; Narváez, Panfilo de; Tenochtitlán; Velázquez, Diego (de Cuéllar).

Resources

Diaz del Castillo, Bernal. *The Conquest of New Spain.* New York: Penguin Classics, 1973.

Prescott, William H. *History of the Conquest of Mexico.* New York: Harper and Brothers, 1843.

Thomas, Hugh. *Conquest: Montezuma, Cortés, and the Fall of Old Mexico.* New York: Simon & Schuster, 1993.

Velázquez, Diego (de Cuéllar)

Diego Velázquez was born in 1465 in Cuéllar in the region of Segovia, Castile. From a noble family, he and two brothers made their way to the Caribbean to seek wealth and influence. Along with several other famous explorers and conquerors, Velázquez arrived in the Caribbean in 1493 on Christopher Columbus's second voyage. Velázquez became a member of Bartolomé Colón's household and, through his service to Governor Fr. Nicholas de Ovando, became extremely wealthy. While in this role, Velázquez helped lead the massacre of Xaragua on Hispaniola. He also participated in the attack against Hatuey, a resisting Tainos chief who managed to safely flee to the island of Cuba.

In 1511, Velázquez led an invasion of the island of Cuba and was declared lieutenant governor and *repartidor* or distributor of the encomienda assignments. He was accompanied to Cuba by Pánfilo de Narváez and Hernán Cortés, both of whom went on to achieve fame for their violent conquests. Employing tactics that included the use of arquebusiers, crossbows, and war dogs, Velázquez's forces pursued the Tainos population across the island. Within a decade he had established seven Spanish outposts across Cuba, which eventually all became permanent cities.

Despite the violent tactics that resulted in the burning death of Chief Hatuey and the rapid decline in the native Cuban population, Velázquez was considered moderate in his treatment of the Indians. Even Fr. Nicholas de Ovando, defender of the natives, portrayed the governor in a favorable light. The increasingly Spanish population of the island supported Velázquez, authorizing him to deal directly with the government in Spain, and thereby bypassing the ineffectual leadership of Diego Colon. Despite this honor, Velázquez continued to seek the title of governor, and eventually did receive the title of *adelantado*.

As Lt. Governor of Cuba, Velázquez was privy to rumors about powerful kingdoms and great wealth to be found further west. Raids for slaves along the coast of Central America yielded more than just laborers. Evidence built up regarding possible riches and a dense population available to enslave on the mainland, compelling Velázquez to investigate. In 1517, he sent three of his friends to reconnoiter Central America: Ochoa de Caicedo, Hernandez de Cordoba, and Cristobal de Morante. Velázquez's primary objective was to capture slaves for use on the island of Cuba while the three selected leaders of the excursion sought land and wealth. To ensure the legality of the slave-raiding expedition in light of the 1513 regulation of such missions, Velázquez obtained a license from the Jeronymite priors who had helped push through the restrictive legislation known as the Laws of Burgos.

The expedition provided mixed results. The discovery of new lands provided further evidence of dense populations and mineral wealth, yet the loss of Spanish lives and the absence of the desired slaves tempered the find. Velázquez recognized the potential of the failed excursion and sought not only permission to undertake another attempt, but also sought authority for the new lands in the form of the title of *adelantado*. Upon receiving approval to send another expedition to the Yucatán, Velázquez funded the venture and appointed his nephew, Juan de Grijalva to lead it. The small fleet sailed in 1518 and, though the Spanish met with some violent resistance, was able to establish friendly trade with the people of Tabasco (Mayan) and Ulúa (Mexica), including trade in gold.

From this more successful voyage under Grijalva, Velázquez determined to send an even larger expedition to explore the interior and establish trade in slaves and gold. Outfitting several ships with food and trade goods, he appointed Hernán Cortés as the captain general. Initial announcements proclaimed the purpose of the voyage was to establish a Spanish settlement in the Yucatán and search for a possible strait to access trade with China, but the later instructions to Cortés belied the governor's desire to trade for gold and slaves. Timing was crucial, as it was rumored other expeditions had sailed from Puerto Rico the same year.

Once Cortés set sail from Cuba, Velázquez shifted his sentiments toward the captain general. He ordered messengers to follow the fleet with instructions to imprison Cortés and replace him with the leadership of Vasco Porcallo. Aware that relatives of Velázquez desired his replacement, the Captain General Cortés outmaneuvered them and continued on. While he was able to escape the initial attempts to block his voyage, the expedition's ranks contained loyal supporters of Velázquez who contributed to divisions within Cortés's command.

In November 1518, the same month Cortés sailed from Santiago de Cuba to complete his preparations, the Council of Castile met at Saragossa and granted a license for Velázquez to seek "islands and mainland territory which had . . . not been discovered," but which failed to grant Velázquez the full title of governor or that of *adelantado*. Velázquez's representative in Spain continued to negotiate for the desired titles and authority. The designation of *adelantado* was finally granted in May 1519, though news of the honor did not arrive in the Caribbean for several months.

In the months following Cortés's departure, Velázquez seized the property of his captain general, as well as other conquistadors under Cortés's command. The new *adelantado* of Yucatán's initial fears and anger toward Cortés began to fade, as was his natural inclination. The economy and political state in Cuba was stable, though a shortage still existed for indigenous laborers. News that his ally among Cortés's forces, Francisco de Montejo, had returned with a ship full of gold and other valuables seemed to offer great hope for the future. This was countered by the realization that Cortés sent the gold under Montejo directly to the Crown, circumventing Velázquez. Intent on restoring his authority, the *adelantado* sent messengers to waylay Montejo; but the attempt failed.

Frustrated, Velázquez decided upon two avenues of reclaiming his influence. He conducted an enquiry in Cuba, seeking to condemn Cortés. The results from this partial proceeding were then sent to Spain to initiate proceedings there, intended to condemn Cortés and his supporters of defrauding the king of his royal fifth. Velázquez's efforts were supported by Juan Rodriguez de Fonseca, the previously influential Bishop of Badajoz and Burgos and leading figure on the Council of the Indies. However, Fonseca was less influential in the court of Charles I, newly designated Holy Roman Emperor Charles V. Instead, the emperor recognized the importance of Cortés's contributions to the Crown and delayed indefinitely any decision regarding the condemnation of Cortés or his status in Mexico.

Velázquez's other approach was to personally conduct an expedition to follow and capture Cortés. The latter plans collapsed in the wake of the first major smallpox epidemic in the Caribbean. Forced to remain in Cuba, Velázquez sent Pánfilo de Narváez in his place. Narváez sailed from Cuba in 1520, accompanied by Lucas Vázquez de Ayllón. The presence of Ayllón was required by the *Audiencia* of Santo Domingo in an effort to prevent hostilities between the Spanish conquistadors. Narváez managed to alienate Ayllón, redirecting a potential ally toward support of Velázquez's target, Cortés.

The Narváez expedition was doomed from the outset. Manned with many supporters of Cortés, and carrying the smallpox epidemic with them, Narváez set out to disrupt Cortés's efforts to conquer Tenochtitlán. Narváez even proclaimed his intent to restore the Aztec Empire to Montezuma's control. In the end, Cortés defeated Narváez's forces, incorporated the remnants into his own armies, and blamed Narváez and Velázquez for the Spanish defeat at La Noche Triste that occurred during his absence from Tenochtitlán. Narváez's treatment of Ayllón resulted in a scathing report to the *Audiencia* and to the Royal Council of Castile, a report that was directed toward Narváez and his patron, Velázquez.

The combination of Cortés's success and Velázquez's violation of the *Audiencia*'s orders regarding Ayllón helped secure Cortés the titles of *adelantado*, repartidor, captain general and governor of New Spain.

Velázquez's charges against Cortés were reduced to the status of a civil lawsuit. In 1524 Diego Velázquez died in Cuba before a *residencia* targeting his actions over the previous decade could be completed.

Rebecca M. Seaman

See also: *Adelantado*; *Audiencia;* Ayllón, Licenciado Lucas Vázquez de; Charles V (HRE) or Carlos I of Spain; Cortés, Hernán; Cuba; Grijalva, Juan de; La Noche Triste; Montejo, Francisco de; Montezuma II; Narváez, Pánfilo de; Ovando, Fr. Nicolás de; Rodriguez de Fonseca, Juan; Xaragua Massacre.

Resources

Diaz, Bernal. *The Conquest of New Spain.* Translated with Introduction by J.M. Cohen. London: Penguin Books, 1963.

Eakin, Marshall C. *The History of Latin America: Collision of Cultures.* New York: Palgrave Macmillan, 2007.

Landa, Diego de, Fr. *Yucatan: Before and After the Conquest.* Translated with Notes by William Gates. New York: Dover Publications, 1978.

Thomas, Hugh. *Conquest: Montezuma, Cortés, and the Fall of Old Mexico.* New York: Simon & Schuster, 1993.

Viceroyalty System

The system of political organizational units used by the Spanish Crown to administrate the American colonies was known as the viceroyalty system. Following the Spanish conquest of the Aztec and Inca Empires, Spain sought to guarantee royal control over the region. The size of the new territory, its distance from Spain, and the threat of conquistadors wielding unregulated power all led the Spanish monarch, Carlos I (Charles V HRE), to create a colonial viceroyalty system, which mirrored the political organization of Spain itself. In 1535, the Crown formed the viceroyalty of New Spain, headquartered in Mexico City, which contained territory from the old Aztec Empire. In 1542, the viceroyalty of Peru followed the same pattern, with Lima as the capital, managing lands of the former Inca Empire.

Over the course of the colonial period, the appointment of viceroy was almost always given to European-born Spanish bureaucrats or military officers. The rationale for this practice was partly because it was hoped that, as outsiders, the Spanish viceroys would be more impartial in administrating the colonial holdings. For most, the extremely prestigious position of viceroy was a reward for a career of service to the Crown. However, the position was usually not meant to be permanent, and thus the average term of office was relatively short, typically around five to eight years.

The viceroyalty system as a whole was organized hierarchically and bureaucratically. The Crown stood alone at the top of the imperial government. Below the monarch was the Council of the Indies, located in Spain, which oversaw colonial administration. In the New World, the colonies were divided into viceroyalties, which were themselves divided further into smaller units. Bureaucrats appointed by the Crown staffed each level of this system, strengthening the hierarchical character of the government.

Although the viceroyalty system was a hierarchical bureaucracy, it was also defined by decentralization. Only in the Crown and the Council of the Indies was power mostly centralized. Bureaucrats on the other side of the Atlantic operated in a decentralized fashion with multiple hierarchies of frequently overlapping responsibilities and jurisdictions. Viceroys governed alongside, and often coordinated, three other administrative hierarchies: the judicial *audiencia*, the Church, and the fiscal administration.

Despite the complexities of these multiple hierarchies, viceroys enjoyed a certain amount of flexibility in their governing. Their main responsibilities included collecting taxes, internal and external defense, managing public works, and general administrative duties, which were usually fairly straightforward. However, they also had to uphold Spanish laws, which were many and frequently contradictory. Early in the colonial period, viceroys began to approach the impossible task of enforcing these laws with the response of "I obey but do not execute." This practice acknowledged the authority of the Crown, but delayed obeying an order until the Crown was made aware of local circumstances. Since the Spanish court was not always up to date on conditions in the colonies, this response was allowed to continue, which added to the decentralization of policymaking for Spanish America. However, administrative flexibility also existed alongside methods of maintaining imperial authority. Of these, the most important were the *residencia,* an end-of-term judicial review, and the *visita,* a secret investigation that could be instigated at any time. Each of these was used to guarantee the viceroys were diligent in their duties and did not take too many liberties.

Toward the end of the colonial period, two new developments affected the viceroyalty system. First, as Spain fell into financial troubles in the 17th and 18th centuries, the court looked for ways to make the empire more profitable. Starting in the early 17th century, the Crown began selling important bureaucratic appointments in the colonies. By the end of the century, even viceroy positions were sold. This allowed more American-born Spaniards to gain these offices. Second, by the 18th century the empire had grown substantially in the Western Hemisphere. As a result, two new viceroyalties were created: the viceroyalty of New Granada in 1739 and the viceroyalty of the Rio de la Plata in 1776, located in northern and southern South America, respectively.

The viceroyalty system was the Spanish response to the problem of colonizing the New World and preserving Spanish rule over the distant colonies. Through multiple bureaucratic hierarchies, an emphasis on decentralization, and systems of authority and flexibility, Spain was able to maintain control over its American holdings for three centuries.

John Laaman

See also: *Audiencia;* Charles V (HRE) or Carlos I of Spain; Government, Pre-Conquest Aztec; Government, Pre-Conquest Inca; Mexico, State of after Spanish Conquest; Peru, State of after Spanish Conquest; Spain, Imperial Goals of; *Visitas.*

Resources

Burkholder, Mark A., and Lyman L. Johnson. *Colonial Latin America.* 7th ed. Oxford: Oxford University Press, 2009.

Elliott, J.H. *Spain, Europe, and the Wider World, 1500–1800.* New Haven, CT: Yale University Press, 2009.

Phelan, John Leddy. "Authority and Flexibility in the Spanish Imperial Bureaucracy." *Administrative Science Quarterly* 5, no. 1 (June 1960): 47–65.

Vilcabamba

In 1537, the emperor Manco Inca Yupanqui fled from the Spanish dominated city of Cuzco, fearing for his life and the destruction of his empire. He set up a base in the city of Ollantaytambo, which he used to launch raids against the forces of Hernando and Gonzalo Pizarro and Diego de Almagro. Eventually, Manco Inca realized his location was untenable. Too close to the Spanish in Cuzco, he was forced out of Ollantaytambo. He established a new capital in a more distant and isolated ancient city of Vitcos. Eventually he was forced to flee even further to the remote mountains of the Antisuyu region.

Known as Vilcabamba, or "sacred valley," the new capital sat in a mountainous and forested location. The city was approximately 100 miles north and west through rugged terrain from Cuzco, and at approximately 5,000 feet in elevation. Sheltered in a valley, the city lay between the Chontabamba and Concevidayoc rivers. Manco Inca's new refuge experienced a temporary period of peace and security as the Spanish struggled with internal conflicts and defining the legal authority over the city of Cuzco.

Vilcabamba was the largest settlement in the remote region of the same name, with over 400 structures. The new capital was located in the Andes mountains, but along the edge of the Amazonian rain forest region. The Neo-Inca rebel followers of Manco Inca were initially few in number, but were joined by warrior forces from other Inca communities, *mitmaq* populations (colonized Incas and Incas by privilege) from the Pilcosuni who were loyal to the Sapa Inca, and even warriors from the Amazon region. From this isolated capital, the rebelling Inca and allies reorganized under their emperor. The Neo-Inca guerrilla fighting force learned to ride Spanish horses they had captured, as well as how to fire muskets. Following the conflict between Diego de Almagro's forces and the forces of the Pizzaro brothers, the Neo-Incas were joined by a few Spaniards such as Diego Méndez, stragglers who fought under Almagro and were associated with the assassination of Francisco Pizzaro.

With a growing loyal following, the emperor's new capital rapidly took shape. Traditional stone houses and storage shelters surrounded a plaza. The city received water through aqueducts, and was surrounded by coca fields and other crops that helped sustain the city. As the years passed and power in the capital passed from Manco Inca to his sons, the city became the center of a widespread trade network that reached deep into the Amazon to the Vilcabamba highlands. The Sapa Incas used the same trade routes to acquire information and send communications outward from the remote capital in an effort to regain control over the traditional Inca Empire. Effectively, the Sapa Incas governed the majority of the Antisuyu region and a large portion of the Collasuyu region.

Despite their initial success, increasing numbers of Spanish colonists, combined with the divisions and resentment toward the Inca power among the indigenous population, gradually eroded the authority of the Sapa Incas during this period of exile and seclusion. By 1572, with the arrival of Viceroy Francisco de Toledo, the capital of Vilcabamba came under attack. The final emperor, Túpac Amaru, was captured and executed. The remote center of Inca power was destroyed. With the population removed by the Spanish to a new location under a similar name, the city was lost to history until the late 20th century.

Rebecca M. Seaman

See also: Almagro, Diego de; Antisuyu; Collasuyu; Neo-Incas; Manco Inca Yupanqui; Pizzaro, Francisco; Pizzaro, Gonzalo; Pizzaro, Hernando; Túpac Amaru.

Resources

Davies, Nigel. *The Incas.* Niwot: University of Colorado Press, 1995.

MacQuarrie, Kim. *The Last Days of the Incas.* New York: Simon & Schuster, 2007.

Stern, Steve J. *Peru's Indian Peoples and the Challenge of Spanish Conquest: Huamanga to 1640.* Second Edition. Madison: University of Wisconsin Press, 1993.

Vilcashuamán

A strategic outpost in the Incan Empire, the city of Vilcashuamán was an administrative center west of Cuzco, on a main Incan road leading to the coast. The city sits on a plateau that overlooks the Vischongo River that runs through a deep gorge. The location was important for the control of the road from Cuzco to the coast, as well as control of the bridge spanning the river and gorge. Additionally, the lands above and immediately around the city provided grazing land for llamas and rich fields for farming.

In 1533, Pizarro and his men surprised the small contingent of Inca holding the fortress at Vilcashuamán. The supplies and families of the Incas under the general Quizquiz were eventually released by the Spanish, though the city was secured by a small force left by Pizarro as he ventured further to capture Cuzco. This stronghold at a strategic crossroad remained an important outpost to the Spanish for years to come.

In 1536, Vilcashuamán again proved tactically important during the uprising of Manco Inca Yupanqui. With Cuzco under siege, Pizarro sent reinforcements to the Vilcas region to secure the crossroads for Spanish travel to and from the coast. Additionally, Pizarro attempted to retain the local population around Vilcashuamán as a means of ensuring continued agricultural supplies for the Spanish. He was able to retain the crossroads, but goods shipped over the roads to and from the Vilcas region constantly came under attacks by the resistant Incas. It was not until the 1560s, with increased relocation and restructuring of native communities, that the Spanish were able to secure more of the empire and to successfully withstand the constant raids of the Neo-Inca movement. Throughout this early colonial period, however, Vilcashuamán remained in Spanish hands and an important military and administrative outpost securing the route to Cuzco from the coast.

Rebecca M. Seaman

See also: Manco Inca Yupanqui; Neo-Incas; Pizarro, Francisco; Quizquiz.

Resources

Davies, Nigel. *The Incas.* Niwot: University of Colorado Press, 1995.

Hemming, John. *The Conquest of the Incas.* New York: Harcourt Brace Jovanovich, 1970.

Villa Rica de la Vera Cruz

The city was the first such town established by Hernán Cortés and his able lieutenants Francisco de Montejo and Alonso Hernández Puertocarrero along the coast of Mexico in 1519. Established presumably to honor the king of Spain, it was named for the wealth in the region and in honor of their landing on Good Friday. The *caudillo* used the founding of Vera Cruz to remove himself from the authority of the governor of Cuba, Diego Velázquez de Cuéllar, who initially ordered the expedition to Mexico and funded much of the venture. In establishing a cabildo (council) for the newly designated town, Cortés circumvented his benefactor and appealed directly to a higher authority, the king. He did this by going beyond Velázquez's initial orders of exploration and to return with any gold, adding settlement and conquest to his achievements, and all in the name of the king. His men elected Cortés as the *justicia mayor* and captain general of the settlement.

Cortés's establishment of Villa Rica de la Vera Cruz initially alienated the Aztec emperor, Montezuma II. Prior to founding the town, Cortés encountered people from about 20 villages, known as the Totonacs. Approached by the leading cacique from the city of Zempoala, Cortés negotiated a treaty, promising protection of the Totonacs. Under the authority of the Aztecs, these people were compelled to pay tribute to the Emperor Montezuma. The Totonacs related how their best young women and men were taken to serve as slaves or for sacrifices to the Aztec War God. In Cortés, the "fat cacique" saw a way out from subjugation by the Aztec Empire in the form of an alliance with the Spanish.

While visiting with the Totonacs at Zempoala, the Spanish were approached by emissaries from Montezuma II. The emperor gave gifts to the Spanish, including gifts of gold, and requested that they leave his empire and abandon their plans to build a city. Instead, Cortés asserted that, in order to honor his own emperor the king of Spain, he must personally meet with the Aztec leader. As the emissaries returned to Tenochtitlán with the message, the Spanish set about establishing their new city near the fortress of Chiahuitzla, naming the structure Villa Rica de la Vera Cruz.

The construction of Vera Cruz was rapid, with all levels of the Spanish force joining in the labor. News of the progress reached Montezuma, already smarting from reports of the Totonacs' refusal to pay their annual tribute. In a flurry of exchanged messages, Cortés's persuasive manner and insistence on an audience with the emperor—when all would be resolved—calmed Montezuma. The Spanish were invited to Tenochtitlán, though some remained on the coast at Vera Cruz under the leadership of Gonzalo de Sandoval. It was during Cortés's absence that a series of ships, sent by Diego Velázquez, were lured ashore by Sandoval and their crew added to the forces of the city. Eventually, the expedition of Pánfilo de Narváez landed slightly south of the settlement, pulling Cortés's Zempoalan allies temporarily into the camp of Narváez and threatening Vera Cruz's existence. The conflict between the Spanish forces of Cortés and those of Narváez, at the Battle of Zempoala, resulted in the loss of Narváez and the further assimilation of forces into the Cortés expedition, reinforcing the coastal city and assisting the *caudillo* in his future siege of Tenochtitlán.

By the end of the 16th century, the Spanish linked roads from Vera Cruz to other wealthy mining towns further inland, thereby providing a quality port from which to export gold and silver back to Spain. Located on the coast, the city served as the major port of the region for centuries.

Rebecca M. Seaman

See also: Cabildo; Cortés, Hernán; Montejo, Francisco de; Narváez, Pánfilo de; Sandoval, Gonzalo de; Tenochtitlán, City of; Totonacs, Alliance with Spanish; Velázquez, Diego (de Cuéllar); Zempoala.

Resources

Diaz, Bernal. *The Conquest of New Spain.* Translated with Introduction by J. M. Cohen. London: Penguin Books, 1963.

Levy, Buddy. *Conquistador: Hernán Cortés, King Montezuma, and the Last Stand of the Aztecs.* New York: Bantam Books, 2009.

Pagden, Anthony, trans. and ed. *Hernan Cortes: Letters from Mexico.* New Haven: Yale University Press, 1986.

Restall, Matthew. *Seven Myths of the Spanish Conquest.* Oxford: Oxford University Press, 2003.

Thomas, Hugh. *Conquest: Montezuma, Cortés, and the Fall of Old Mexico.* New York: Simon & Schuster, 1993.

Visitas

Typically a reference to an inspection or inspection tour of parishes or territories under an *audiendia*'s jurisdiction, *Visitas* carried great weight for the indigenous populations in the century immediately following the Spanish conquests. Thanks to the wealth of information these inspections collected, they continue to carry great weight with students of the era to this day.

Visitas were a process of gathering information on colonial holdings, religious and secular. To an extent, the purpose of such inspections was in the interest of efficiency and standardization of the various provinces. An example of a common *visita* function was the guarantee of timely tythes by the encomenderos or sufficient tributes by the local indigenous population. At times the *audiencia,* archbishop or other governing official ordered a general inspection, as a means of determining operational strengths and weaknesses. At other times, rumors of abuses or problems prompted more specific, targeted *visitas.*

The inspection was conducted by an appointed *visitador.* That individual was to gather census data, conduct interviews, take down statements made by local Spaniards and Indians, and occasionally even to hold hearings. *Visitadors* were supposed to be objective in their assessments, but individual visitadors sometimes used their inspections and findings for personal benefit. Cristóbal Albornoz, a secular priest, provides an example of such a self-motivated *visitador.* The conundrum presented by such ambition was that the posts of *visitadors* were typically appointments made to people outside of a targeted district. Lacking close friends and allies, *visitadors* stood little chance of gaining popular support for advancement from the local residents, who sought to reduce their tithe and tributary obligations. Meanwhile, superiors making appointments to the positions of *visitador* were seldom motivated to promote inspectors who failed to increase tributary and tithe incomes.

The common usage of *visitas* was to gather demographic information regarding the local indigenous population as a means of maximizing the tributes collected by the Spanish. Though the inspectors appointed were still often from outside of the region in question, the *visitadors* who oversaw *mita* or tribute payments were typically sympathetic to Spanish recipients of encomiendas, repartimientos, and other forms of labor and tribute incomes.

Spanish extended control over territories in Middle and South America had devastating effects upon the local populations. Extensive overuse of labor, wars, disease, and relocation of indigenous peoples dramatically reduced population censuses. Without regular adjustments to the tithe and tributary obligations, local native households experienced heavier and heavier burdens. Appeals for new counts were often the prompts for ordering a *visita*.

Even in areas with drastic reductions in native populations, the resulting calls for a new tributary count did not necessarily result in adjusted encomienda or repartimiento tributes. Even tithing amounts often remained stationary despite evidence substantiating massive drops in the population. Sometimes *visitadors* sympathetic to encomenderos were to blame. At other times, self-motivated *visitadors* who sought support for their own advancement bore responsibility. Whether or not the findings of the *visitas* resulted in adjusted tributary or tithe payments, the demographic data, detailed reports, and accounts gathered provides an excellent source of primary documents for researchers today.

Rebecca M. Seaman

See also: Albornoz, Cristóbal; *Audiencia;* Encomiendas; Encomenderos; *Mita;* Repartimiento.

Resources

Brooks, A.M., comp. *The Unwritten History of Old St. Augustine: Copied from the Spanish Archives in Seville, Spain.* Translated by Annie Averette. St. Augustine: 1909.

Villamarin, Juan A. Villamarin and Judith E. Villamarin. *Indian Labor in Mainland Colonial Spanish America.* Newark: University of Delaware, 1975.

Wernke, Steven A. and Thomas M. Whitmore. "Agriculture and Inequality in the Colonial Andes: A Simulation of Production and Consumptions Using Administrative Documents." *Human Ecology: An Interdisciplinary Journal.* Aug 2009, Vol. 37 Issue 4 (August 2009): p421–440.

War, Customs of among Aztec

Aztec customs of warfare are rooted in the Aztec culture and history. Origin stories of how the Aztec came to live in the Valley of Mexico are replete with stories of conflict with other societies. Even when they arrived and settled in the valley, the Mexica established communities on marginal lands where the existing inhabitants of the region chased them.

In the first 100 years of the Aztec presence in the Valley of Mexico they participated as mercenaries in the constant warfare that riddled the region. The Mexica established their city of Tenochtitlán on an island. There they built up floating fields that enabled them to grow foods to feed their people in a hostile environment. Using their agriculture as a base for trade with the other societies in the valley, the Mexica gradually forged alliances based on economics and military services.

For the Mexica people, warfare was not just a tool used to gain and hold power, it was engrained within the society. The religion of the Mexica was woven with ceremonies that highlighted acts of war. Human sacrifices, sometimes massive in their nature, were provided mainly through the ceremonial deaths of captured enemies. Warriors of great status, earned from feats of battle, belonged to distinguished military organizations, held high positions in society and in the political structure. While all males were expected to serve in the military if the need arose, the armies were led by distinguish warriors who were typically members of the war societies,

such as the eagle warriors, jaguar warriors, and others.

Like Europeans of the time, the Aztec were capable of mobilizing large armies, but were hampered by the limitations of supplying these militaries. Consequently, warfare was traditionally reserved to the dry monsoonal season, when peasant farmers were free from agricultural labor and roads were more passable. The forces raised by the Mexica, a combination of their own people and of allied cities who lived in fear of the Mexica, dwarfed the abilities of other societies, even those capable of forming limited coalitions that occasionally opposed the Mexica.

As all males were expected to serve in the military, and military service provided increased status, distinguished service became a means of rising in social status. Young boys were trained from an early age to learn the art of war. *Macehualtin* or commoners were not allowed to own land held in their own names. However, *macehualtin* who distinguished themselves in battle sometimes were awarded grants of land, had their tribute requirements removed, and even were permitted to wear the cotton clothing reserved for the noble classes.

Males of the *pipiltin* or noble class were given a strong education from an early age. This education not only prepared *pipiltin* males to serve as administrators in the government, but also drilled them in military skills. Distinguished military service for *pipiltin* could result in a rise in status, the gain further lands, and the acquisition of *mayeques* or slaves from captives. Additionally, those who distinguished themselves in war were permitted to wear elaborate clothing, jewelry, and the much desired feathers of the high nobility and great warrior classes.

Military weaponry of the Aztec employed various materials. The armor worn by the *pipiltin* warriors was comprised of quilted cotton. So superior was this armor that the Spanish soon abandoned their metal armor in favor of the lighter, more flexible and cooler cotton. Obsidian points, for arrows, spears, knives, and short swords, were also valued weapons. Capable of cutting through Spanish metal armor, these weapons were nonetheless quite brittle and broke easily in battle. Spears were given greater range through the use of atlatls. Consequently, the effective distance of the Mexica warriors using arrows and spears was superior to that of a Spanish arquebus in rapidity and accuracy of fire. However, the Spanish countered with their use of accurate, rapid firing crossbows. Another weapon, one that was easily used by the farmers-turned-warriors, though less effective, was the common stone. As the Spanish advanced through Mexica cities, they discovered the danger of stones slung, thrown, or dropped from roofs lining the thoroughfares.

No discussion of Aztec warfare, especially war customs in the region in and around Tenochtitlán, would be complete without considering their canoes. With the capital city located in a lake, and farming being conducted on a system of floating fields, it is no wonder that the Aztec population was adept at the art of canoeing. This skill became an effective tool in the war customs used to defend the capital, and one that initially ably defeated the Spanish under Cortés. In order to counter this Mexica advantage, Cortés was compelled to develop a navy of brigantines, carried overland in pieces, put together in secrecy, and sailed down a series of manmade channels. Even then, the brigantines

would not have succeeded without the small artillery also used by the Spanish to defeat the hordes of Aztec warriors surrounding the Spanish boats in the native canoes.

The Aztec societal structure, based on a militaristic system, and honed by years of warfare with neighboring societies, dominated the Valley of Mexico and the lands extending outward from their capital Tenochtitlán. The value placed on military leadership and skills, the traditions in Aztec origin stories, as well as the religious practices, contributed to the dominance of the Mexica as a militarily powerful society in Mesoamerica at the time of the Spanish conquest in the early 16th century.

Rebecca M. Seaman

See also: Aztec, or Mexica; *Macehualtin*; *Mayeques*; *Pipiltin*; Religion, of Pre-Conquest Aztec; Tenochtitlán, City of.

Resources

Barghusen, Joan D. *The Aztecs: End of a Civilization.* San Diego, CA: Lucent Books, 2000.

Berdan, Frances F. *The Aztecs of Central Mexico: An Imperial Society.* Florence, KY: Wadsworth, 2004.

León-Portilla, Miguel, ed. *The Broken Spears: The Aztec Account of the Conquest of Mexico.* With Foreword by J. Jorge Klor de Alva. Boston: Beacon Press, 2006.

Schwartz, Stuart B., ed. *Victors and Vanquished: Spanish and Nahua Views of the Conquest of Mexico.* Boston: Bedford/St. Martin's, 2000.

Thomas, Hugh. *Conquest: Montezuma, Cortés, and the Fall of Old Mexico.* New York: Simon & Schuster, 1993.

War, Customs of among Inca

During the period of the Inca Empire, from ascendancy in the mid-15th century to conquest in the 1530s, warfare remained constant. The causes and purposes of wars were to acquire additional territories for the Inca state, although conflicts over royal succession also frequently led to bloodshed.

Conquest was the major cause of warfare. A ruling Sapa Inca, upon his death, would designate his heir but would not pass on any acquired wealth. Instead, all of his accumulated possessions as well as his mummified remains or *malquis* would be taken care of by a group of his descendants known as *panaca*, the royal lineage and cult. Every so often, they would be brought out and consulted on important issues. Occasionally, the *panacas* of deceased Incas competed for lands, titles, and positions of authority that helped to guarantee their continued sustenance.

The new designated heir found that, while inheriting the mantle of authority, he was left with little else. He now needed to embark on a period of conquest in his own right in order to acquire lands, ingratiate himself with the nobility, and, perhaps most importantly, build up to have his own panaca in preparation for his own death. Of necessity the Inca ruler and empire was in a constant state of warfare. For example, when Pachacutin became ruler in 1438, his father, Wiracocha, left him nothing. So he conquered the region from Central Peru to the region of Lake Titicaca. Likewise, when Huayna Cápac, Pachacutin's grandson, became ruler he too marched to war, expanding the Inca Empire all the way into the territory of Ecuador. The main purpose for war in his case was expansion.

When Huayna Cápac died suddenly, and his intended successor died shortly thereafter, a succession crisis arose between his two sons Huáscar and Atahualpa. The resulting civil war led to the weakening of the empire and assisted in the eventual conquest by

the Spaniards. An Inca ruler had numerous wives, and generally designated his heir as one of the sons of his principal wife, which was, during the latter part of the period of Inca rule, generally his sister. No set rule for succession existed, and when Huayna Cápac succumbed unexpectedly to smallpox and his initially designated heir died soon after, he left the door open to differing contestants. This was not the first instance of such a crisis, but it proved to be the most significant. The *panacas* of Huayna Cápac and Ninan Cuyochi (designated heir) competed for the same lands, titles, and positions of authority. To make matters worse, Atahualpa and Huáscar desperately needed the same resources to sustain their civil wars. When the Spanish captured Atahualpa, then executed him for having his own brother killed, two more *panacas* struggled for resources to honor their deceased Incas and to maintain a level of existence that would enable them to immortalize their ancestors. The rapid succession of Incas and the simultaneously competing *panacas* created internal turmoil beyond mere civil war seeking control of the empire.

Whether the war undertaken was that of expansion or internal wars of succession, the practices remained the same. Once the Inca made the decision to go to war, divinations and consultations with oracles occurred, lest anything be left to chance. The Inca ruler generally led soldiers into battle. Less frequently he handed the job off to a close relative, such as in 1463 when Pachacutin gave command of the army to his son, Topa Inca.

No professional, standing army existed in the Inca Empire, as all soldiers were called up when needed. They were arranged according to *ayllus,* or clans, as they marched to war. However, the Sapa Inca's bodyguard was permanent and the royal families all had members contained officers who desired to lead the rank and file into battle. In that sense, the Inca did indeed have a professional core to their military machine.

Once conquest occurred, then came pacification. The Inca military came up with an ingenious method wherein recently conquered peoples were uprooted and relocated closer to the centers of power at Cuzco, and more loyal subjects took possession of the lands of the conquered "Non-Incas." Moreover, the ruling class in the conquered region remained in power, but their children were brought to Cuzco to be educated. These children also served as hostages to thwart, it was hoped, possible uprisings.

In sum, unlike the Aztec and other contemporaries, wars by the Incas were not fought to acquire hostages, sacrificial victims, nor to establish a tributary empire. They were fought principally to expand the empire and, secondarily, as a result of the weak system of succession.

Kim Richardson

See also: Atahualpa; *Ayllus*; Huáscar; Huayna Cápac; *Malquis*; Ninan Cuyochi; Pachacutin; Sapa Inca.

Resources

Bennett, Wendell C., and Junius B. Bird. *Andean Cultural History: The Archaeology of the Central Andes from Early Man to the Incas.* Garden City, NY: Natural History Press, 1964.

Brundage, Burr Cartwright. *Lords of Cuzco: A History and Description of the Inca People in their Final Days.* Norman: University of Oklahoma Press, 1967.

Mann, Charles C. *1491: New Revelations of the Americas Before Columbus.* New York: Alfred P. Knopf, 2006.

Mason, J. Alden. *The Ancient Civilizations of Peru.* Baltimore, MD: Penguin Books, 1961.

Moseley, Michael E. *The Inca and their Ancestors of Peru.* London: Thames and Hudson, 1992.

Von Hagen, Victor Wolfgang. *Realm of the Incas.* Rev. ed. New York: Mentor, 1961.

Wanchope, Robert, ed. *The Indian Background of Latin American History: The Maya, Inca, and their Predecessors.* New York: Alfred A. Knopf, 1970.

War, Customs of among Maya

Maya warfare, much like the Maya themselves, is ancient and variable. Warfare in the Maya world took place in the form of village against village, or of city versus neighbor, as the societies forged different hegemonic territories through battle and conquest. All histories of warfare included components of ethnic strife and distrust, and affected not only political and warrior classes, but also the lives of the general population. Our understanding of Maya warfare, despite evidence of its proliferation, remains vague given our limited understanding of ancient Maya political institutions and the deployment of organized violence as a political activity.

The cultivation of maize made possible the rise of Maya civilization. If the rise of maize is similar to other agricultural examples, than warfare in Mesoamerica must have been rare or absent for hundreds, perhaps thousands, of years while maize domestication began and until it flourished. Prehistoric peace also must have accompanied the rise and consolidation of early centers in Mesoamerica. Maize cultivation in Mesoamerica contributed to the rise of stratified societies occupying territories with well-defined and defended boundaries. These new polities sought domination in relationships and competed for resources. As complex societies emerged throughout Mesoamerica, long-distance trade relationships grew, as did cultural exchange. The militaristic Zapotec of Oaxaca, whose rulers emphasized military authority and success in battle, and the cult of militarism at Teotihuacán each left powerful legacies on Maya political leaders who combined those influences with their own ideas of divine kingship. Like all Mesoamerican civilizations, Maya society included a warrior class and nobility supported directly by conquest and control.

Evidence from the Pre-Classic period indicates that warfare increased along with the proliferation of developed centers. An increase in ritualized violence in the form of human sacrifice accompanied increased organized violence. Both human sacrifice and warfare demonstrated the strength of the *ahau* to his rivals while simultaneously nurturing the threat of violence at home. Defensive features such as stone walls at El Mirador, moat-like features at Edzna and Cerros, as well as walls and ditches at Becan suggest conflicts between Pre-Classic centers. Such features were more prominent in the Pre-Classic than in the Classic period, and although war was a frequent occurrence during the Classic period, defensive fortifications were rare until the end of the Late Classic period.

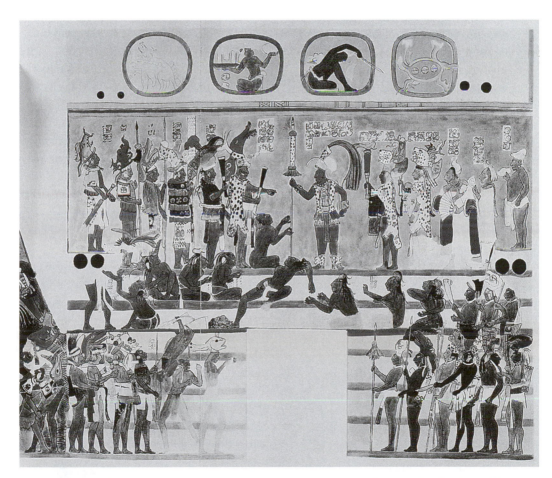

War customs of the Maya, as depicted in a wall painting from Bonampak. (Peabody Museum, Harvard University, Cambridge, MA/The Bridgeman Art Library)

Classic period warfare among the Maya was neither of a large scale nor was it utterly destructive. Instead, it was waged with the limited strategic motive of dominance over another ruler. Competition for resources occurred among individuals or groups and a combination of self-interest, honor, prestige, and even self-aggrandizement may be ascertained in the Classic period record of "captive counts" and prisoner tallies. Monuments at numerous sites depict the primary activity of Maya warfare during the Classic period in the form of bound captives, often prostrate beneath the feet of an *ahau,* to be used as participants in the ballgame, or as sacrificial victims or slaves for labor. The ballgame, itself a form of preparation for, or result of, warfare, along with other metaphorical forms of warfare like the hunt, meant that Maya warriors entered the deadly serious activity of seizing captives, engaging in battle, and subjugating rival cities and their leaders.

The capture of the foreign *ahau* was the most dramatic result of battle, and long-term imprisonment led to pride in victory while simultaneously disabling the rival city. When Double Bird, the *ahau* at Tikal, was captured by Caracol in 562 AD, Tikal descended into instability, uncertainty, and chaos for nearly a century. Stelae contain the histories of military exploits and victories. For example, Stela 31 at Tikal tells that, "Smoking Frog demolished and threw down the buildings in Uaxactún" in 378 AD. Experts believe that the war between Tikal and Uaxactún was one of conquest, and not just for captives or resources. Altar Q at Copán documents the installation of Kuk Mo in 426 AD, the new *ahau* depicted in full Teotihuacán regalia. Kuk Mo's was buried with his Teotihuacán style helmet and his remains include a number of severe, healed wounds consistent with those of a warrior. The most graphic extant evidence of Maya warfare is the murals at

Bonampak. The mural in Room 2 contains a battle scene and captives, and demonstrates that the history and practices of Maya warfare ran deep and from early in Maya Classic period. Venus, the guiding constellation of Maya warfare, appears prominently in the celestial bands above the battles scene.

While a Late Classic period increase in warfare may indicate a stylistic shift in the inscriptions, and while carved monuments chronicling military conflict are less common in the north than in the south, there is no doubt that Chichén Itzá dominated the northern Yucatán as military power during the Post-Classic period. Chichén Itzá's militaristic culture is visible in the site's imposing architecture. Influences from Tula and Teotihuacán are observed through the graphic murals and grim skull racks. In its quest for control (possibly in order to regain control of trade routes of valued elite commodities), Chichén Itzá played a role in the decline of many northern Yucatán cities. Evidence such as a low defensive wall at nearby Uxmal and an apparently hastily constructed wall at neighbor Cobá may indicate conflict with expansionist Chichén Itzá.

All imperial declines and collapses have involved warfare to a degree, but it is usually a symptom and not the cause of the collapse. The question of Maya collapse is too complex to be elucidated by only one factor or perspective. Maya warfare dates to the Pre-Classic period; its manifestations, like in other empires, may take place between rival polities, or between internal rivals. The motives and actors varied across time and region. From the Late Classic period onward, Maya warfare became less an organized state action than violence at all societal levels. The incomplete Maya historical record adds to the complexity.

Charles Heath

See also: Chichen Itza.

Resources

Carmean, Kelli, and Jeremy A. Sabloff. "Political Decentralization in the Puuc Region, Yucatán, Mexico." *Journal of Anthropological Research* 52, no. 3 (Autumn 1996): 317–330.

Houston, Stephen D., and Takeshi Inomata. *The Classic Maya.* New York: Cambridge University Press, 2009.

O'Mansky, Matt, and Arthur A. Demarest. "Status Rivalry and Warfare in the Development and Collapse of Classic Maya Civilization." In *Latin American Indigenous Warfare and Ritual Violence.* Tucson: University of Arizona Press, 2007.

Otterbein, Keith F. "Warfare and Its Relationship to the Origins of Agriculture." *Current Anthropology* 52, no. 2 (April 2011): 267–268.

Stuart, David. *The Order of Days: The Maya World and the Truth About 2012.* New York: Harmony Books, 2011

Women, Status of Inca

The atmosphere for women in Inca society was not demeaning. However, the climate also did not provide ready opportunities for women to advance in society. While women of royal lineage were different from those of common birth, both groups of women experienced the same subservient roles to Inca males.

Women were individuals of the realm and, like the males, were meticulously registered and had a special place in the advancement of society. Women were important in harvesting crops. Produce from those efforts was divided so that one-third supported the ruling dynasty, another one-third supported the religion, and the final third supported the family. Consequently, the labor of women in the fields was instrumental in providing food not only for their families but for others throughout the realm. Women also worked in their homes, cared for their families, spun yarns, and wove fabric. The Inca women's other major contribution, as mothers, was to the growth of the Inca population.

Pregnant women's daily tasks were not lessened because of their state of health. Women were just as likely to give birth in a field as in their own homes. Male children were desired above female children, and the realm granted twice as much land to the family for the birth of a baby boy. Between the fifth and 12th birthday, young girls went through a naming ceremony in which they were no longer considered a suckling baby. At that stage, girls began helping their mothers in the home and in the field. Within this time range, young girls matured physically to the point of becoming a woman in the eyes of society.

Around the age of 18, woman could marry. Virginity, instead of being counted as a badge of honor, was usually considered a blemish. Indeed, some marriages were performed on a trial basis, in which either the husband or the wife could leave their spouse. Most marriages, some arranged prior to the ceremony, were not religious in nature and simply administrative. Marriage was the equal duty of both men and women, in order to further the economic and military power of the Inca realm through increasing the population. Consequently, divorce was possible in those cases where a woman did not conceive a child. However, men and women were treated equally in the eyes of the law when it came to fidelity. Adultery resulted in the same punishment of death for male and female individuals of society.

Women of royalty, and queens (Coya) lived different lives than those of common birth. These women sometimes achieved positions of authority over the entire realm, typically during the rare absence of a male leader. The Coya always led the female pillar of society; this included some priestesses of the state religion that were associated with the planting of the fields. The Coya also sometimes mediated peace in the midst of war. Royal women also had their own personal wealth and lands for their use.

One institution of the Inca that involved women was the Aclla, also known as "the house of the chosen" and the "Virgins of the Sun." These women were primarily chosen from common birth, though some royal women became a part of this group. The Aclla, chosen because of their beauty and rank in society, were sent to the capital where they served at religious ceremonies. These women were selected around the age of eight to ensure that they were virgins throughout the rest of their lives. Punishment for Aclla women whose virginity

was lost resulted in death by being buried alive. Sometimes these women were taken by the emperor or given to civil and military leaders as rewards. These women could then break their vow of virginity and act as concubines to these men for the rest of their lives. Women of royal birth who were Aclla were never given as rewards and had to remain chaste. These Acllas, though they had no political authority, were honored as virgins in a society where virginity was usually a blemish.

The status of women in the Inca Empire was that of important contributors to the society. She did not exactly have as many rights as her male counterpart yet she was integral in the continuance of the Inca realm and recognized as such. The Inca woman, though not recognized above the man, was not abused or degraded and was recognized for her important work.

Matthew Blake Strickland

See also: Inca Elite; Incas; Peru, State of prior to Spanish Conquest

Resources

Anton, Ferdinand. *Woman in Pre-Columbian America.* New York, NY: Abner Schram, 1973.

Bingham, Marjorie Wall, and Susan Hill Gross. *Women in Latin America—From Pre-Columbian Times to the 20th Century.* Vol. 1. St. Louis Park, MN: Glenhurst Publications, 1985.

Cobo, Bernabe. *Inca Religion and Customs.* Edited and translated by Roland Hamilton. Austin: University of Texas Press, 1990.

Graubart, Karen B. *With Our Labor and Sweat: Indigenous Women and the Formation of Colonial Society in Peru, 1550–1700.* Stanford, CA: Stanford University Press, 2007.

Powers, Karen Vieira. *Women in the Crucible of Conquest: The Gendered Genesis of Spanish American Society, 1500–1600.*

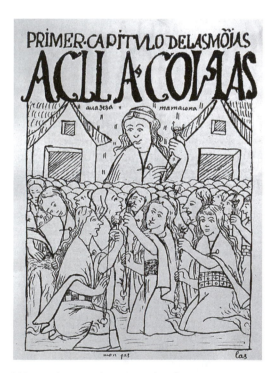

Women's status among the Inca was epitomized by the Accla, or chosen virgins. (Private Collection/The Bridgeman Art Library)

Albuquerque: University of New Mexico Press, 2005.

Silverblatt, Irene. *Moon, Sun, and Witches: Gender Ideologies and Class in Inca and Colonial Peru.* Princeton, NJ: Princeton University Press, 1987.

Women, Status of Mexica

In Mexica society, the status of women was usually traditional and their roles of wife and mother were strictly proscribed. As daughters and wives, they were subjects to both fathers and husbands. They were responsible for the efficient maintenance of the household, early socialization of children, and training of young girls. This norm was the ideal image and as such, women were considered to have positive characters.

The socialization process into this traditional status began with birth. The baby girl's destiny was symbolized in ritual. During her first bath, for example, the midwife would put the baby into the vessel intended for the girl to be bathed for the next few years, along with her spindle, carton, spinning bowl, sweeper, and broom. This practice served to symbolize that a female child was bound to the house. Near the grinding stone, at the edge of the family hearth, the midwives would bury the umbilical cords of female babies, thus placing the newborn's original source of life near the object that most represented her domestic status: the hearth.

As described in the Codex Mendocino, their mothers taught female children the appropriate activities of women. These activities included the preparation of food, maintenance of the house, and weaving. At 12 years of age, daughters were required to sweep the house and the street, as well as serve the evening meal. At age 13, girls were taught the techniques of grinding corn and making tortillas and other food. Fourteen-year-old girls were taught how to weave. By the age of 15, the typical Mexica female was considered a woman, with all the requisite skills and training to keep her own house. As a maiden she was to be modest, pleasing in appearance, and reserved in manner.

Sahagún recorded long orations by the parents of young women, which describe the ideal behavior of a woman, including the importance of sexual virginity. When a young woman was ready for marriage, representatives of the intended husband, or the young man himself, would go to negotiate the marriage and present offerings to the girl's parents. Once the intended bride's parents approved the marriage, the woman had no choice in the matter. After marriage, the next stage was motherhood, which was ideally fulfilled when a woman became pregnant. If the woman died in childbirth, she became mocihuaquetzque ("woman warrior") or cihuapipiltin ("deified woman") and was considered comparable to a brave male warrior who had died on the battlefield. This was typically the only time a woman gained any equality status with men in the Mexica society.

In addition to these traditional roles, some women achieved a prominent status in the history and development of the Mexica society. They provided, for example, important kingship links and many of these women appeared at turning points in the history of the Mexica people. In the Codex Xototl, a series of marriages to sisters and daughters of important and influential leaders depicted women as playing a pivotal role in the consolidation of the Mexica reign. A sister of Huitzilihuitl married Ixtlilxochitl of Texcoco and was the mother of Nezahualcoyotl. Acamapichtli, the first Mexica king, was the offspring of parents from Mexica and Culcuacan nobility. As the Mexica became the leading power of the

Valley of Mexico, Mexican princesses were important in strengthening the solidarity of the reign. Royal Mexica women who married tributary rulers automatically became the first wife and their children would be considered legitimate heirs to rulership.

Despite traditional roles as mothers and keepers of the home, women played important public roles in Mexica society as well. Chief among these roles were positions as doctors, merchants, and priestesses. Leading mythological figures and deities of the Mexica society included females, as well. Itzpapalotl, Mectli, and Coatlicue are prominent women at turning points in the history of the Mexica. Itzpapalotl appears in the semi-mythical historical accounts of the wanderings of the Chichimeca (ancestors of the Mexica) and provides the Mexica with the techniques of sedentary life. She taught the Chichimeca hunting and agricultural techniques and other basics of non-nomadic life. Mectli means "grandmother Maguey" and is a variant of Mextli, which means "heart or navel of Maguey." Mextli also provides the name "Mexica." The cult dedicated to this woman focused on the earth and her high priest was called "lord of the earth." Similarly, Coatlicue gave birth to the Mexica god, Huitzilopochtli, and later reminded the Mexica of their beginnings.

Whether serving important roles as mothers, wives, merchants or priestesses, women in the Mexica society filled prominent positions. The private nurturing and public civilizing influences impacted the Aztec people at all levels of society.

Fernando Ortiz

See also: Aztec, or Mexica; Mexico, State of prior to Spanish Conquest; Sahagún, Bernardino de.

Resources

Durán, Diego. *Historia de las Indias de Nueva Espana e Islas de la Tierra Firma.* Dominico en el siglo XVI. Mexico: Editorial Porrua, 1967.

Garibay, Angel Ma. *Teogonia e Historia de los Mexicanos.* Tres Opusculas del Siglo XVI. Mexico: Editorial Porrua, 1973.

Nash, June. *The Aztecs and the Ideology of Male Dominance.* Chicago, IL: The University of Chicago Press, 1978.

Sahagún, Fray Bernardo. *Historia general de las cosas the Nueva Espana.* Mexico: Editorial Porrua, 1969.

X

Xaragua Massacre

The Xaragua massacre in 1503 helped to break Taino resistance to Spanish colonization of Haiti. The leading cacique of Xaragua, Anacaona, was forced to witness the murder of most of her subordinate chiefs, along with hundreds of her people. She was later executed under the charge of plotting a revolt. Although the Taino were nearly exterminated, Anacaona became a symbol of their resistance to Spanish rule.

When Columbus landed in Haiti in 1492, the island was populated by the Taino people and divided into six provinces or kingdoms ruled by chiefs known as caciques. Each province had subordinate chiefs and had distinctive hierarchies of authority. The southwest peninsula of Haiti included two significant provinces, Xaragua and Maguana. The cacique of Maguana was a chief named Caonabo, a respected leader who was apparently not a Taino. He was married to Anacaona, sister of Behecio, cacique of Xaragua. Anacaona, whose name meant "golden flower," was respected for her beauty, intelligence, and artistic ability.

The Spanish quickly demanded tribute from the Taino. Resistance was met with violence. Columbus took Caonabo as a prisoner when the two met under the guise of friendship. Caonabo died en route to Spain when the ship he was on sank. Anacaona returned to Xaragua. In January 1497, Columbus's brother Bartolomé visited Behecio and Anacaona to arrange for them to pay a quarterly tribute to the Spanish. Bartolomé Colón noted that the brother and sister were treated as equals by the indigenous population and were regarded by their people as co-rulers.

By 1502, the Spanish governor of Haiti was Fr. Nicolás de Ovando. An authoritarian leader, Ovando arrested his rivals and put down any resistance by Taino groups. By the summer of 1503, he was ready to move against Xaragua, the strongest remaining Taino province. Ovando announced he would pay a friendly visit to Anacaona to negotiate the tribute owed to Spain. During his visit, 300 Spanish infantry and 70 cavalry accompanied him on the voyage.

Expecting a diplomatic visit, Anacaona invited the lesser caciques and leaders of Xaragua to her village for the festivities. Several days of festivities followed the Spanish arrival, with feasts and displays of Taino music and dancing. Ovando invited the leading Tainos, including Anacaona to a display of Spanish horsemanship in return. When they gathered in the central square of the village where the Spanish cavalry was assembled, the infantry surreptitiously sealed off the area and moved in. Ovando gave the signal for the massacre to begin when he touched the cross hanging on his chest. The cavalry turned on the unarmed crowd and began to slaughter them. At least 80 of the leading caciques were captured and taken into a thatched building. They were tortured into confessing that Anacaona planned an uprising against the Spanish. The building was burned, killing the leaders. The massacre continued over the next few weeks, with Xaragua's inhabitants being hunted down and killed or enslaved.

Anacaona herself was taken to the Spanish capital of Santo Domingo. She was tried for treason and hung. Her death marked the virtual end of any Taino resistance to the Spanish colonization of Haiti. Between forced labor and slaughter, nearly all the Taino were soon exterminated.

Tim J. Watts

See also: Columbus, Christopher; Ovando, Fr. Nicolás de.

Resources

Keegan, William F. *Taino Indian Myth and Practice: The Arrival of the Stranger King.* Gainesville: University Press of Florida, 2007.

Redmond, Elsa M. *Chiefdoms and Chieftaincy in the Americas.* Gainesville: University Press of Florida, 1998.

Rouse, Irving. *The Tainos: Rise and Decline of the People Who Greeted Columbus.* New Haven, CT: Yale University Press, 1992.

Yanaconas

The term *yanaconas*, or the Quechua *yana*, refers to full-time retainers with a lifelong commitment. Members of this element of the Inca society broke away from the traditional *ayllus* clan or community structure to serve their Inca masters. Often referring to craftsmen, semiskilled workers, personal servants, and also farmers and miners, the *yanaconas* worked directly for the elite *coya* of Inca society or for the priests of various Inca deities.

Yanaconas often were required to relocate great distances from their home communities. As a result, they did not contribute tribute or *mita* payments through their local *kuraka*. *Yanaconas* were exempt from these payments, both in the pre-conquest and post-conquest periods. This made belonging to this specialized class attractive. The fragmentation of the loyal, community-based *ayllus* also endangered the internal unity of the Inca system, and made the empire susceptible to rebellion.

With the arrival of the Spanish, many of the *yanaconas* shifted their allegiance from the *coya* Incas to the Spanish invaders. Serving as personal retainers, the *yanaconas* provided valuable information about the location of Inca strongholds, as well as stored wealth the Spanish so desperately craved. In return for their valuable service, the Spanish extended the exemptions from paying tribute, as well as bestowed the right of some *yanaconas* to own lands.

In the midst of the immediate conquest, the *yanaconas*, referred to as native auxiliaries, were allowed and even encouraged to participate in the plunder of the Inca elites. This practice not only helped augment the numbers of personal servants in the Spanish service, but also contributed to widespread looting of a variety of forms of wealth—as the native auxiliaries coveted items that the Spanish did not initially recognized as valuable. The benefits accrued by the *yanaconas* under Spanish rule not only increased the size of the class and impacted the loss of valuable Inca relics, it additionally disrupted the traditional structure of the society, which was based in recognizable communities centered around *ayllus*.

Rebecca M. Seaman

See also: *Ayllus; Kuraka; Mita.*

Resources

Hemming, John. *The Conquest of the Incas.* New York: Harcourt, Brace, Jovanovich, 1970.

Stein, Steve J. *Peru's Indian Peoples and the Challenge of Spanish Conquest: Huamanga to 1640.* 2nd ed. Madison: University of Wisconsin Press, 1993.

Titu Cusi Yupanqui. *An Inca Account of the Conquest of Peru by Titu Cusi Yupanqui.* Translated, Introduced and Annotated by Ralph Bauer. Boulder: University Press of Colorado, 2005.

Yucatán Peninsula

The Yucat n Peninsula, the heart of ancient Mayan civilization, separates the Caribbean Sea from the Gulf of Mexico. It lies east of the Isthmus of Tehuantepec, which geographically divides the Central American region from the North American continent. As the ancient center of Mayan civilization, many archaeological sites, such as Chichén Itzá, Tulum, and Uxmal, remain. Maya and people of Mayan descent comprised much of the population at the time of the Spanish conquest as they still do to this day. Today, the peninsula mostly lies in southeastern Mexico, but it also comprises parts of Belize and Guatemala.

The Yucatán Peninsula's natural vegetation is comprised of short and tropical jungles. The area where the Mexican, Belizean, and Guatemalan boundaries meet is occupied by the largest continuous tract of Central American tropical rainforest. Heavily forested at the time of Spanish conquest, it is undergoing deforestation today. The peninsula lies within the Atlantic hurricane belt. Strong, short-lived storms called nortes have historically plagued the peninsula.

Mayan ruins remaining at Tulum, on the Yucatán Peninsula, Mexico. (PhotoDisc, Inc.)

The origin of name "Yucatán" is debated. Mayans called the peninsula *ma'ya'ab,* or "a few." One popular explanation claims the Spanish asked the natives the place's name and interpreted their response as "Yucatán" when it was "I don't understand you" in their language. Another explanation claims "Yucatán" derives from the Nahuatl (Aztec) word *Yokatlān,* or "place of richness."

Important Mayan sites developed in the Yucatán Peninsula around 800 BC. Mayan city-states flourished there during the Classic period (250–900 AD) before mysteriously beginning to decline. Early 16th-century Spanish conquistadors, having taken control of Puerto Rico and Cuba, began to explore areas west of these islands. Francisco Hernández de Córdoba's expedition, while exploring the Yucatán Peninsula, became the first of several Spanish excursions to encounter the Maya. Francisco de Montejo, an associate of Hernán Cortés, was first charged with subduing the peninsula. Spanish control was finally achieved in the 1540s. The Maya often rebelled unsuccessfully against Spanish control over the centuries.

The perception of the Yucatán Peninsula as a place of wealth owes much to its geographic location. Though heavily forested with tropical forests, the towns and villages on the peninsula had a flourishing agriculture, with fields of maize, squash, beans, and yucca. The region's agriculture was not only sustained the local population but also facilitated trade with the inland Mexica and the island people of the Caribbean. It was supplemented by domesticated animals such as ducks and turkeys, as well as hunting and fishing. Trade was extensive throughout the region of Central America, with the Yucatán Peninsula falling in the center of the regional trade networks. It was through this trade, and the profitable exchange of captured slaves, fine fabrics and gold, that the initial Spanish conquistadors mistakenly assumed that mineral wealth originated in the peninsula. It was later realized that the source of the gold found in the Yucatán was from the Aztec Empire and other Central American locales.

Eric Martone

See also: Aztec, or Mexica; Chichen Itza; Montejo, Francisco de; Nahuatl Language; Yucatán, State of prior to Spanish Conquest.

Resources

Lockwood, C. C. *The Yucatán Peninsula.* Baton Rouge: Louisiana State University Press, 1989.

Jones, Grant, ed. *Anthropology and History in Yucatán.* Austin: University of Texas Press, 1977.

Kintz, Ellen. *Life under the Tropical Canopy: Tradition and Change among the Yucatec Maya.* New York: Holt, Rinehart and Winston, 1990.

Rider, Nick. *Cancun and the Yucatan.* New York: DK Publishing, 2010.

Yucatán, State of after Spanish Conquest

After their arrival to the Yucatán Peninsula, the conquerors organized the territory politically according to certain Spanish institutions, but on the basis of Mayan indigenous organization. There were at least 18 major political centers in the northlands of the peninsula. They were called *cuchcabal* in the Mayan language. A governor, who resided at a place comparable to the "capital" ruled those spaces. It was the most important political-territorial institution during the 16th century, and the Spanish referred to it as *cacicazgo.*

Within the *cuchcabal* structure, the *cuchteel* (pl. *cuchteeloob*) was the basic unit, composed of clusters of houses that housed extended family groups. Each residential unit was identified by a place name. *Cuchteeloob* also included areas for the farming activities of the family. There, families developed systems of cooperation and mutual aid. The administrative officer was the *ah cuch cab,* who oversaw the collection of tribute to the crown. The *cuchteel* also was the basis of a military unit and the *ah cuch cab* gathered people for war.

The cluster of three to five *cuchteeloob* was known as a *batabil* (pl. *batabiloob*). The authority over the clustered units was a figure called *batab,* who lived in one of the village units. The operating range of the authority of the *batab* provided the demarcation of the *cuchteeloob*. This feature made the *batabil* similar to a Spanish seigniory.

As the political centers, *cuchcabaloob* served as the capital towns and controlled the surrounding dependant areas. Rulers received the name of *halach uinic* (pl. *halach uinicoob*). These political figures resided in the main towns and were the supreme power for the larger political units.

The Spanish used this set of categories to organize the indigenous territory. They alluded to the *batabil* as *pueblo,* and sometimes as *señorío* (seigniory), to refer both to the social community and the territorial extension. *Cabecera* (administrative center) was applied to name the place of residence of the *halach uinic* and *batab; sujeto* (subject) was used to describe two types of hierarchical subordination: the village under the authority of the *cuchcabal* and the *cuchteel* under the *batabil. Parcialidad,* barrio (neighborhood), estancia, *colación, anexo* (annex), and *milpería* were used to refer to the *cuchteel.* All of these terms also were applied to categorize the new towns founded according to different levels of subordination.

The Spanish settlements were placed in important places with favorable conditions.

For example, in 1541, Campeche was founded in the Mayan capital Can Pech. Similarly in 1542, Mérida was founded in T'ho, and in 1543, Valladolid in Sací. These villas or cabildos (councils) divided the peninsula of Yucatán into small territories more or less regular in size, called jurisdictions or districts.

In the beginning, the organization did not affect the integrity of the *cuchcabaloob* because the cabildos of the Spanish had no power over them. The Spanish, encomenderos included, lived in the cabildos so-called *villas cabecera.* The main royal officer, supreme power in Yucatán, lived in Mérida.

The Spanish authority on Mayan society was led at first by the figure of the *adelantado* (title given to a particular personage to discover, conquer, and populate a territory). Francisco de Montejo occupied this post since 1526, and between 1546 and 1549, he was appointed as *adelantado*, governor, and captain general of Yucatán. In 1550, the figure of *alcalde mayor* (main mayor) was established as a royal representative. Don Diego de Quijada served as *alcalde mayor* between 1550 and 1565, after being appointed directly by the Spanish king, Philip II. He designated *tenientes de alcaldes mayores* (deputies of main mayors) in Valladolid and Campeche. This way, politically, the jurisdictions of the *villas* became subjects of Mérida. They exerted political and administrative functions, and thus, the ancient prerogative of *halach unic,* to intervene in disputes when *batabiloob* could not do it, was displaced. The power of the *cuchcabaloob* was questioned.

Due to the remoteness of Yucatán with respect to Mexico City and the difficulties encountered in its conquest and colonization, the *Capitanía General de Yucatán* (general captaincy of Yucatán) was created in 1565 as an administrative area belonging to the viceroyalty of New Spain. It was under the direct governance of the king for military and government issues. The *gobernador* (governor) was the highest authority. However, having no *audiencia real* (royal court), these governors had to appeal to the one in Mexico City to resolve legal matters.

In Yucatán, vast territories were given to encomenderos under the encomienda system. These encomenderos sometimes confronted other civil and religious authorities in the region. This conflict was characteristic to the decentralized and overlapping authority system structured by the Spanish Crown in its American colonies.

The religious organization also helped to organize the state of Yucatán. The Franciscan friars founded convent houses, which were *cabeceras de doctrina* (heads of doctrine) of villages called *visitas* (visits) or *pueblos bajo campana* (villages under bell). For the rational organization of the *pueblos de indios* (villages of Indians), in order to exercise better political economic and religious control, congregations or reductions were made. Spatially, these concentrated the subject villages under their administrative centers and redistributed the space to centralize economic and religious activities. Thus, *cabeceras de guardanía* were created as centers of religious and political influence, and also served to help collect alms and labor to sustain the centers.

Within villages, the activities were centralized through the creation of churches, *cajas de comunidad* (community banks), administrative institutions, and government bodies. Meanwhile the Spanish-imposed *corregidores,* the *batab,* became the governor.

Marta Martín Gabaldón

See also: *Adelantado*; Cabildo; *Corregidores*; Encomienda; Encomenderos; Montejo, Francisco de; Phillip II of Spain.

Resources

Farriss, Nancy M. *Maya Society under Colonial Rule: The Collective Enterprise of Survival*. Princeton, NJ: Princeton University Press, 1984.

Quezada, Sergio. *Pueblos y caciques yucatecos (1550–1580)*. Mexico D.F.: El Colegio de México, 1993.

Restall, Matthew. *The Maya world: Yucatec culture and society, 1550–1850*. Stanford, CA: Stanford University Press, 1997.

Yucatán, State of prior to Spanish Conquest

The Yucatán, a peninsula protruding out from Central America into the Caribbean, contained a tropic environment prior to Spanish conquest, much as it maintains to this day. The constantly warm temperatures contributed to a scarcity of freshwater, which contributed to dissention within the region. Heavily forested, the region was often beset by hurricanes, common in the Gulf of Mexico.

According to the oral traditions of the Maya communicated to the Spanish, the Maya dominated the region for over 1,000 years. The center of power and religion was Chichen Itza until the 1200s when civil war broke out. Mayapan became the capital, and retained that position until the ruling Cocom family was toppled in the 1441 revolt. This civil war resulted in the dispersion of the kingdom into lesser states that were scattered throughout the peninsula. According to Fr. Diego de Landa's recording (1566) of Mayan traditions, the fall of Mayapan was succeeded by intervals of peace and prosperity that were occasionally disrupted by hurricanes, plagues, and wars.

At the time of the first Spanish explorers, the region remained divided into separate states and scattered communities with related yet independent political structures. According to the testimony of Friar Geronimo de Aguilar, a captive of different Mayan communities in the second decade of the early 1500s, some of these communities were quite hostile to foreigners, either enslaving them or sacrificing them to their gods. Meanwhile others allowed captives to merge into their communities, like Aguilar and his Spanish companion, Gonzalo Guerrero, did in differing fashions.

Though the scattered villages and communities appeared autonomous units, in reality there existed approximately 16 different provinces or territories. The people of each province gave loyalty to their local community leaders, but owed allegiance to the provincial head, or *halach uinic*. The relatively autonomous towns aligned with neighboring towns within the region when confronted with threats from the outside. It was not uncommon for these autonomous communities to initially make decisions regarding new trade or foreign contacts, only to have pressure exacted by their neighbors that caused the town to shift its original actions and trade commitments.

At the time of the Spanish arrival in the Yucatán, the people of the area sustained themselves through agriculture, with fields of maize, squash, beans, and yucca, among others. They also supplemented their diets with fishing and hunting, in particular rabbits and deer. Large hens, usually ducks and turkeys, were domesticated and used in the diets of the people. Flourishing trade, with neighboring communities and with the Mexica further inland, accounted for much of the gold present in the Yucatán region. Other items imported through trade included cloth and slaves. Trade was conducted through the use of cacao, red shells, and stone "counters."

The use of servants and slave labor was common. Typically captives of wars, these laborers were exchanged through a substantial slave trade network throughout the region. Servants had varying ranks among them, with the personal servants of high officials sometimes having their own underservants. Slaves could expect a harsh existence; many were purchased to serve as human sacrifices commonly conducted in the Yucatán's multiple temples.

Typical housing in the Yucatán was spread out. Large yards contained small planting areas and housed the plentiful servants and slaves. Buildings on the peninsula's interior were of wattle and daub, while buildings in the coastal areas were comprised of baked clay, with a plaster covering the brick walls like a sort of whitewash. The whitewashed or plastered walls of the chiefs were covered with beautiful frescoes. Roofing material was from a rough thatching material or from the leaves of local palms. The roofs were very steep to redirect the heavy rains off and prevent leakage. In areas where stone was available, important buildings such as temples, and sometimes the homes of high officials were built from stone masonry. Houses of high officials typically contained a series of patios that gave an airy quality to the rooms.

Cultural origins of the people of the Yucatán at the time of conquest can be traced through the Maya, as well as the Chiapas from the south and west. By the time Spanish explorers arrived on the peninsula, the Maya and Chiapas people shared much in common, including great similarities in their languages. The Mexica, who were increasing their foothold in the western and northwestern fringes of the peninsula, spoke a distinctly different tongue, resulting in translation problems for the local populations in the Yucatán and later for the Spanish.

Rebecca M. Seaman

See also: Aguilar, Geronimo de; Aztec, or Mexica1;Chichen Itza; Mayas.

Resources

Clendinnen, Inga. *Ambivalent Conquests: Maya and Spaniard in Yucatán, 1517–1570.* 2nd ed. Cambridge: Cambridge University Press, 2003.

Diaz, Bernal. *The Conquest of New Spain.* London: Penguin Books, 1963.

Landa, Friar Diego de. *Yucatán: Before and After the Conquest.* Translated with Notes by William Gates. New York: Dover Publications, 1978.

Schwartz, Stuart B. *Victors and Vanquished: Spanish and Nahua Views of the Conquest of Mexico.* Boston: Bedford/St. Martin's, 2000.

Z

Zempoala

Zempoala (Cempoallan, Cempoala) is an archaeological site that was a coastal city-state capital near the mouth of the Actopan River in central Veracruz, Mexico. Located within Totonacapan, Zempoala, and between 30 and 50 villages, towns, and fortifications made up the Cempoallan province of the Triple Alliance (Aztec Empire).

The province of Zempoala was only tenuously incorporated into the empire, however. Its initial conquest was by Motecuhzoma Ilhuicamina, with subsequent reconquests made during the reigns of Axayacatl and possibly Motecuhzoma II (Montezuma II). The instability in this region may have been exacerbated by the leaders of Tlaxcala, who often interfered in the affairs of their neighbors to the east, inciting rebellion against the Triple Alliance. Zempoala was governed by a native *tlatoani* (lord) known as the "fat cacique." He told Cortés that an imperial agent traveled throughout the province collecting tribute in young people for sacrifice and personal service. Early Spanish descriptions of contact period Zempoala indicate that the local leader arbitrated matters that affected the inhabitants of the center and its hinterland, even though it was sometimes at the direction of the imperial authorities.

Zempoala is one of the first cities that hosted Hernán Cortés and accompanying Spaniards after they made landfall on the Gulf Coast in the spring of 1519. When the Spanish entered the center, they called it "Sevilla" and were astonished by the large population of the city (ca. 80,000), its bustling plazas surrounded by white plastered buildings, its lush irrigated fields, and its canals. The principal compound at the center was the setting for several historically significant events during the first year of the conquest. It was from Zempoala that Cortés assembled Spanish troops, native allies, artillery, and porters for their long trek inland to Tenochtitlán, the primary capital city of the Triple Alliance. Like many other places in Mexico, within the first century of the arrival of European diseases, the population of Zempoala was devastated.

The urban architectural core of Zempoala consists of large, irregularly shaped temple-plaza compounds that sprawl along the riverbank. Several intensive archaeological projects at the site have revealed a lengthy occupational history, but the apogee of settlement and monumental construction date to the Late Postclassic period (ca. 1250–1521 CE). The architectural styles at the site are generally characteristic of the Central Mexican highlands, suggesting that considerable construction occurred after the center was incorporated into the Triple Alliance.

Marcie L. Venter

See also: Cortés, Hernán; Montezuma II; Tenochtitlán, City of

Resources

Berdan, F. F., Blanton, R. E., Boone, E. H., Hodge, M. G., Smith, M. E., and Umberger, E., eds. *Aztec Imperial Strategies*. Washington, DC: Dumbarton Oaks, 1996.

Brüggemann, Jürgen. K., ed. *Zempoala: el estudio de una ciudad prehispánica*. Mexico City: Antropología e Historia, 1991.

Diaz del Castillo, Bernal. *The Discovery and Conquest of Mexico: 1517–1521.* Translated by A.P. Maudslay. New York: Da Capo Press, 2003.

Durán, Fray Diego. *Historia de las Indias de Nueva España e Islas de la Tierra Firma.* Translated by Angel Ma. Garabay. Mexico: Editorial Porrua, 1967.

Evans, Susan Toby, and David L. Webster, eds. *Archaeology of Ancient Mexico and Central America, an Encyclopedia.* New York: Garland Publishing, 2001.

Maya-Spanish War Timeline

250–800 Maya of the Yucatán experience their Golden Age. The calendric rounds (long and short) are employed. The center of religious and pseudo-political control is located in Chichen Itza. The Mayan vegecimal math system using zero as a place holder enables the Maya to have a calendar system far in advance to any in the world, and architectural engineering feats far beyond those simultaneously found in Europe.

800–900 Major upheaval breaks up the relative unity of the Maya, leaving authority once again in the hands of local "holy lords" with religious and political authority.

1000–1200 Central Mexico united under the Toltec. The Mayan societies experience periods of unification and devolution within the region.

1250 The Aztecs (Mexica) arrive in the Valley of Mexico, which is already densely populated.

1250–1450 Mayapan develops into the city and sociopolitical center of the Northern Yucatán region, beginning to decline under the Cocom family rulers of the mid-1400s.

ca. 1325 The Aztecs found the city of Tenochtitlán on Lake Texcoco.

1376–1395 Movements by the Aztec under Acamapichtli spreading their authority, infringing on independence of the Maya of southwestern and western regions of the Yucatán.

1395–1417 Reign of Huitzilihuitl, second Aztec emperor.

1417–1426 Reign of Chimalpopoca, third emperor of the Aztecs.

1426–1440 Reign of Itzcóatl, fourth Aztec emperor. During this time, the Aztecs form an alliance with the peoples of Texcoco and Tlacopan, further threatening Mayan trade independence.

1428 The Triple Alliance of Tenochtitlán, Texcoco,

and Tlacopan conquers Atzcapotzalco.

1440–1469 Reign of Montezuma I expands Aztec authority beyond Valley of Mexico, accompanied by the waning of authority in Mayan centers like Mayapan, opening region to Aztec domination and demands for tributary payments in the form of labor and captives for human sacrifices.

1492 Christopher Columbus's initial arrival in Caribbean. Subsequent exploration of region makes tentative contacts with Maya of Mesoamerica.

1502 Montezuma II becomes the ninth emperor of the Aztecs.

1511 Cuba invaded and settled under Diego Velázquez de Cuéllar. Fr. Gerónimo de Aguilar and his companion Gonzalo Guerrero are shipwrecked and stranded on the Yucatán coast among the Maya.

1515 Bartolomé de Las Casas returned to Spain to gain support for his mission to the Indians, appointed priest-procurator to the Indians.

February 8, 1517 Conquistador Francisco Hernández de Córdoba departs Cuba with a mission to explore rumors of rich lands to the west. His expedition includes the future chronicler Bernal Díaz del Castillo

who records initial Spanish perceptions of Maya.

February 20, 1517 Hernández de Córdoba sights Isla Mujeres off northeastern Yucatán. Despite an initially friendly greeting from the Maya natives and gifts of gold, his party is attacked numerous times over the next few weeks. Hernández de Córdoba flees back to Cuba in April, with tales of new lands wealth.

April 8, 1518 Cuban governor Diego Velázquez's nephew, Juan de Grijalva, sets sail for Mexico.

May 3, 1518 Grijalva sights the island of Cozumel (northeastern Mexico), which he explores for four days before heading south and discovering Ascensión Bay. He then rounds the Yucatán Peninsula, following Hernández de Córdoba's earlier route.

May 26, 1518 Grijalva comes ashore near Champotón. The Mayan natives allow him to draw water and present him with some gold gifts before ordering the Spaniards to leave. Grijalva refuses and indecisive battle results.

June 17, 1518 Grijalva names island Sacrificios Island for signs of human sacrifice. The local Totonac Indians, an offshoot of the Mayas, offer him an elaborate welcome, hoping to use Spanish to overthrow Aztec rule and reestablish strong Mayan city states.

June 24, 1518	Grijalva receives a minor embassy from the distant Aztec emperor Montezuma II, lays claim to the island of San Juan de Ulúa, detaching Alvarado with report and booty. Grijalva presses deeper into the Gulf of Mexico before returning.
October 23, 1518	Governor Velázquez organizes another expedition, headed by Hernán Cortés. Governor is soon disconcerted by the speed and scope Cortés's preparations and decides to replace him at the last minute with Luis de Medina.
November 18, 1518	Cortés sets sail from Santiago de Cuba, gathering more recruits and supplies while openly defying Velázquez's repeated recalls.
February 21, 1519	Cortés's expedition lands at Cozumel.
March 13, 1519	Cortés is joined by a Spanish castaway, Gerónimo de Aguilar, who has been living among the Indians of the Yucatán for eight years. Aguilar will prove an invaluable translator.
March– April 1519	Spanish victories against Poonchán and Cintla convince Mayas to submit to Spanish rule. Offer Cortés 20 Indian slave women, including Malinche who interprets Nahuatl to Maya.
April 21, 1519	Spaniards approached at San Juan de Ulúa by emissaries of Aztec administrator Teutliltzin, inquiring as to their intentions, fearful of the increased resistance by the Maya to paying their tribute.
April 24, 1519	Cortés is met by Teutliltzin and a large Aztec retinue. Cortés sends overtures of friendship to Montezuma but continues encouraging the Mayan city-states to refrain form paying tribute to the Aztec.
May 1, 1519	Teutliltzin returns with an embassy sent by Montezuma discouraging the strangers from visiting the Aztec capital. Cortés receives a delegation of Totonac Indians from nearby Cempoala, revealing Mayan tribes are resentful of Aztec rule.
May–June 1519	Cortés founds a new Spanish settlement in Totonac territory, which is to be called Villa Rica de la Vera Cruz. He is elected as its "mayor," a legal fiction that will allow him to sever ties with Velázquez, report directly to the king in Spain, and take credit for claiming this Mayan region for Spain.
June 1519	Mayan cacique, Xicomecoatl, of Cempoala, proposes Cortés form an alliance with the inland tribes of Tlaxcala and Huejotzingo to help overthrow the Aztecs.
June 28, 1519	Cortés completes his journey to Quiahuiztlan and secretly encourages its inhabitants

to seize a score of Aztec tribute-collectors.

June 30, 1519 Cortés continues to covertly encourage the local Mayan natives to refuse paying tribute to the Aztecs.

July 1, 1519 A single caravel with news that Velázquez is authorized to take possession of any new lands discovered west of Cuba prompts Cortés to gather all wealth gleaned from conquest and trade with the Maya and interior Aztecs, and to ship it with messages directly to the king, in hopes of winning approval for his independent campaign.

August 8, 1519 Cortés begins marching inland for Cempoala, the dominant city of the Totonacs, accompanied by 800 Cempoalan auxiliaries.

August 16, 1519 Having reached Cempoala and renamed this city Nueva Sevilla, Cortés resumes his advance inland. Most Indian tribes prove hospitable, and he marches uncontested through Jalapa, Xicochimalco, Ixhuacán, Zautla, and Ixtacamaxtitlán.

1519–1524 Cortés continues his march on the inland Aztec while he leaves his subordinate, Gonzalo de Sandoval and a small number of his forces to hold the coastal Mayan region.

April 1520 Velázquez sends Pánfilo de Narváez to capture and kill Cortés. Narváez's presence on the Mayan coast upsets the alliances Cortés negotiated with the cacique of Cempoala.

Early May 1520 Cortés departs for Cempoala, leaving Pedro de Alvarado to hold Tenochtitlán.

May 29, 1520 Using stealth, Cortés and his native allies capture Narváez at Cempoala before a general alarm can be raised. Narváez's army, never particularly loyal, surrenders and is incorporated into that of Cortés.

June 24, 1520 Cortés returns to Tenochtitlán. He leaves mostly Narvaristas whom he doesn't trust to hold Villa Rica de la Vera because the friendly relations with the Mayan did not necessitate a large retinue along the coast.

September 1520 the first news of smallpox spreading among the indigenous population reaches Cortés. The disease kills friendly and foe Indians alike, but leaves the Spanish remarkably untouched. This fact results in the perception of the Maya and other indigenous people that the Spanish have a power god who protects them.

August 1521– August 1522 In the year following the fall of Tenochtitlán, Cortés and his soldiers consolidate their holdings throughout Mesoamerica. Disease, starvation, and increased Spanish presence at news of wealth made any Mayan resistance weak. Cortés requests for Franciscans to be sent to New Spain to help convert and as-similate the indigenous population. The indigenous population is assigned to serve in encomiendas as rewards for the service of Spanish soldiers and for Mayan and other allied caciques.

1524 Spain creates the Council of the Indies to oversee all aspects of colonial administration in the New World. Cortes encounters the aloof Mayan people known as the Itza, the last Mayas to hold out against the Spanish.

1524–1542 Several conquistadors are assigned positions of authority for the purpose of extending Spanish authority and securing further wealth from the New World.

1528 Cortés travels to Spain to defend himself in front of King Charles I (Holy Roman Emperor Charles V) against allegations that he had organized his conquests to create his own personal empire and that he had abused the Indians. He is successful in convincing the king of his allegiance to the Spanish Crown.

1535 Spain creates the viceroyalty of New Spain. Centered at Mexico City, it eventually encompasses all of present-day Central America, Mexico, and elsewhere.

1541 The last of the Mayan people are subdued in Mesoamerica.

1542 King Carlos I of Spain (Charles V—HRE) enacts the Leyes Nuevas, or New Laws of 1542–1543. Designed to reduce and eventually eliminate the abusive practices of encomienda and repartimiento, Spanish governors and encomenderos largely ignored the new policy.

1520s–1560s The Maya experience rapid decline in the face of diseases and heavy compulsory labor requirements. The Spanish establish a capital city at Mérida, in the Yucatán Peninsula.

Inca-Spanish War Timeline

ca. 1200 The Inca people appear in the Cuzco Valley.

ca. 1410–1438 Reign of Viracocha Inca, who took his name from the Inca deity Viracocha.

1437 The powerful Chanca tribe conquers most of the Quechua peoples.

1438 At the Battle of Cuzco, Incas defend capital Cuzco from Chancas under leadership of Pachacuti Inca, the bloody victory establishes the Inca as the dominant Andean highland power.

1438–1471 Reign of Pachacuti Inca Yupanqui. Pachacuti uses victory at Battle of Cuzco as a springboard to seize title of emperor from his brother, greatly expanded the territory of the Incas.

1468 Battle of Chan Chan, Incas conquer the powerful Chimú culture.

1471–1493 Reign of Túpac Inca Yupanqui, 10th emperor of the Inca Empire.

1476 Major campaign to subjugate the southeastern coast of Peru.

1493–1526 Reign of Huayna Capac. Inca Army was used to quell a number of rebellions throughout the large empire. Huayna Capac focuses on the northern frontiers of the empire, setting up Quito as a secondary capital. Divides his empire between two of his sons.

1500 Pachacuti and Túpac Inca expand empire to most of present-day Peru and parts of Ecuador, Chile, Argentina, and Bolivia.

November 14, 1524 Francisco Pizarro forms a partnership with Diego de Almagro and Fr. Hernando de Luque. Pizarro leaves Panama City to explore southward.

April 14, 1525 Pizarro's expedition reaches Candelaria, base camp attacked by a band of hostile Quilian warriors, expedition retreats to Chochama to recuperate.

Spring 1526	Pizarro and Diego de Almagro conduct second reconnaissance. Notice impressive signs of wealth and civilization. Sends pilot Bartolomé Ruiz farther south to reconnoiter and Almagro back toward Panama for reinforcements.
September 1526	Almagro reaches Panama, Pedrarias Dávila has been replaced as governor by Pedro de los Ríos.
October 18, 1526	Ruiz, traveling south, sights San Lucas.
December 3, 1526	Ruiz's expedition reaches Cape San Antonio, captures native vessel.
January 8, 1527	Almagro leaves Panama with 40 additional soldiers to rejoin Pizarro.
June 1527	Lands at Terapulla, attacked by hostile natives, Spanish retreat to Gallo Island. Almagro leaves for Panama to raise additional reinforcements.
July 1527	Upon reaching Panama, Almagro is detained by Governor de los Ríos.
August 28, 1527	De los Rios detains Ruiz, just arrived in Panama seeking reinforcements for Pizarro.
September 14, 1527	De los Rios sends his own subordinate, Pero Tafur, to recall Pizarro, who refuses to return to Panama.
March 1528	Ruiz is able to rejoin Pizarro, brought only a small ship

	to reinforce forces at Gallo Island.
Late 1528	Pizarro returns to Panama. Heads toward Spain to secure royal backing, promises to represent all three partners equally.
July 26, 1529	Pizarro signs a charter at Toledo with the Crown. Receives knighthood in the Order of Santiago and allowed to rule as "governor and captain-general" of the new territory.
January 18, 1530	Pizarro departs Spain with brothers and additional men.
January 31, 1531	Pizarro sets sail from Panama City, recruits forces under Hernando de Soto, promising the young conquistador the position of second in command. Cavalry are disembarked San Mateo Bay.
April 1531	Spaniards reach abandoned city of Coaque. Pizarro establishes a base ashore, dispatches Bartolomé de Aguilar for more volunteers, bearing gold and precious stones as proof of this new land's wealth.
September 1531	The first of these reinforcements—30 men from Nicaragua under Sebastián de Velalcázar—arrive, just as Pizarro is preparing to march still farther south.
October 1531	Expedition reaches Portoviejo, refreshed and reinforced. Chief Tumbalá and

17 of his lieutenants arrested, handing over to their mortal enemies by Spanish.

March 1532 Hernando de Soto arrives from Nicaragua with more men, and the expedition begins rafting across to Tumbes. Chief Cacalami is obliged to sue for peace, Pizarro installs a 50-man garrison.

May 16, 1532 Pizarro marches inland. En route he learns that the Inca Empire is in the midst of a civil war between Huáscar and Atahualpa. Evidence of the population having recently been devastated by disease—possibly smallpox.

Mid-September 1532 The Spaniards reach Tangara (renamed San Miguel de Piura).

September 24, 1532 Pizarro marches out of San Miguel.

November 6, 1532 Pizarro reaches Saña, greeted by an embassy from Atahualpa (who has recently defeated and imprisoned Huáscar).

November 15, 1532 Spanish come within sight of Cajamarca, where emperor Atahualpa is encamped with a large army.

November 16, 1532 Battle of Cajamarca, Atahualpa is seized, stunned Inca army fails to retaliate.

November 17, 1532 At Pizarro's command, the captive Atahualpa orders the army to disperse.

Late 1532 Atahualpa offers to pay ransom for his release. Pizarro accepts, uses Atahualpa's authority to keep Peru calm. Huáscar brought as a prisoner from Cuzco, murdered en route.

January 5, 1533 Hernando Pizarro investigates rumors of Inca army massing at Huamachuco. Approaches great temple of Pachacamac to search for treasure.

February 15, 1533 Spaniards depart Cajamarca for Cuzco with Inca envoys to speed the gathering of Atahualpa's ransom.

Early March 1533 Hernando Pizarro meets with the Inca general Chalcuchima at Jauja on March 17, convinces Chalcuchima to join the Spanish.

April 14, 1533 Almagro arrives at Cajamarca with 150 Spanish troops and 50 horses.

April 25, 1533 Hernando Pizarro treats Chalcuchima as a captive and tortures regarding whereabouts of treasure.

June 12, 1533 Hernando Pizarro departs Cajamarca for the coast, taking 100,000 *castellanos* and a report for the king of Spain.

July 16, 1533 Francisco Pizarro makes a massive distribution of booty to his followers in Cajamarca.

July 26, 1533 Pizarro accepts ransom for Atahualpa's release then has him garroted and burned for fear that General Rumiñahui is approaching with a vast army.

Early August 1533 Pizarro and Almagro invest Huáscar's younger brother Túpac Huallpa (whom they also hold prisoner) as the new emperor.

August 11, 1533 The Spaniards march southward out of Cajamarca toward the distant Inca capital of Cuzco.

Mid-September 1533 The Spaniards reach Recuay, rest for 12 days before resuming their progress toward Cuzco.

October 11, 1533 Spaniards greeted as liberators by inhabitants of Jauja, Quitan army withdraws, Pizarro's cavalry slaughters them when attempt is made to fire the city. Remaining Quitan army joins Quisquis's forces near Cuzco.

Late October 1533 Puppet emperor Túpac Huallpa dies in Jauja of a mysterious disease.

October 24, 1533 Pizarro sends de Soto ahead with 70 riders to secure bridges along royal highway to Cuzco.

October 27, 1533 Pizarro installs 80-man garrison in Jauja under Alonso Riquelme, then departs.

October 29–30, 1533 De Soto's flying column surprises Yucra Hualpa's retreating army at Vilcas, Quitans launch a furious counterattack, de Soto obliged to release captives in order to withdraw.

November 8, 1533 De Soto surprised by Quisquis's forces at Vilcaconga, retreats, but then recovers next day.

November 13, 1533 Pizarro overtakes Almagro and de Soto at Vilcaconga. Manco Inca selected as next puppet Inca, has Chalcuchima burned alive for collaborating against Spaniards.

November 14, 1533 Flying column is sent ahead to beat Quitan forces from destroying Cuzco, repelled in a clash at a pass outside that city.

November 15, 1533 Pizarro and Manco enter Cuzco together without opposition, as Quisquis's army retires.

November 16, 1533 Manco officially proclaimed as Emperor Manco Inca Yupanqui.

December 1533 de Soto's attempts to pursue the retreating Quitan army prevent by rugged terrain.

January 23, 1534 Conquistador Pedro de Alvarado (Mexico) learns of wealth in Peru and sets sail from Poseción, Guatemala to take part.

Late January 1534 Pizarro sends Almagro and de Soto with 50 riders and 20,000 Cuzcan allies to reinforce Jauja's 80-man Spanish garrison under Riquelme.

February 1534 Jauja attacked by Quisquis. The Spanish garrison defeats Quitans and forces them to retreat.

February 25, 1534 — Alvarado lands at Portoviejo, mistreats coastal tribesmen before striking inland toward Guayaquil.

Early March 1534 — Pizarro's lieutenant Sebastián de Velalcázar sets out from San Miguel de Piura to conquer Quito before Alvarado can intervene.

April 1534 — Pizarro and Manco reach Jauja, collaborate to drive Quisquis out of entrenched positions farther north.

April 7, 1534 — Almagro reaches Saña, attempts to overtake and assume command of Velalcázar's contingent to head off Alvarado but is driven back by native opposition.

Late April 1534 — Velalcázar's column scatters Chiaquitinta's Quitan warriors near Zoro Palta.

May 3–4, 1534 — Anti-Incan forces reinforce Spanish at Tumibamba, Velalcázar's army encounters the main Quitan army under General Rumiñahui, compelling them to withdraw.

May 8, 1534 — Almagro writes to Charles V, complaining of Alvarado's incursion.

Mid-May to Early June 1534 — de Soto, Gonzalo Pizarro and their allies pursue Quisquis's army as far north as Huánuco, fighting a series of engagements, before returning to Jauja.

May 21, 1534 — Emperor Charles V issues a royal decree subdividing South America among its various conquistadores, disputes still remain over Cuzco.

June 22, 1534 — Almagro and Velalcázar's army fights its way into Quito, deserted and burned by Inca. Rumiñahui's army badly beaten, native chieftains switch allegiance to Spanish.

July 1534 — Velalcázar vainly searches for Incas' vanished treasure, massacring women and children of Quinche. Almagro and Velalcázar abandon Quito.

August 1534 — Spanish armies confront each other. Deal struck on August 26, Almagro buys Alvarado's ships and equipment and the latter returns toward Guatemala, leaving his men behind. Armies' morale under Quisquis collapses and he is murdered by dissatisfied officers.

February 1535 — Velalcázar sends his lieutenant Diego de Tapia to pacify the Quillacinga Indians on the Angasmayo River.

March 1535 — Fighting almost erupts between pro-Pizarro and pro-Almagro factions, both claiming Cuzco falls under their jurisdiction according to royal decree.

Late May 1535 — Pizarro mediates deal with Almagro, latter leads new expedition farther south to conquer Chile—reputedly even richer than the Inca Empire—allowing Spanish Crown to resolve dispute over Cuzco.

July 3, 1535 Almagro begins his expedition into Chile. Pizarro returns to coast to found Lima. Hernando Pizarro sails for Spain. Gonzalo and Juan Pizarro remain in Cuzco where they reportedly abuse Manco Inca and his sister/wife.

Early November 1535 Manco attempts to flee Cuzco, imprisoned by Juan and Gonzalo Pizarro. Pizarro brothers lead punitive expedition against Ancocagua.

January 1536 Hernando Pizarro returns from Spain, releasing Manco who is covertly manufacturing weapons and marshaling troops to attack Cuzco when rainy season ends.

April 18, 1536 Manco leaves Cuzco with Hernando Pizarro's permission, supposedly to attend religious ceremonies in the Yucay Valley and to bring back gold.

April 21, 1536 News of Manco's plot reaches Cuzco and Juan Pizarro is immediately dispatched to disperse the assembling Incas.

Late April– Early May 1536 Juan Pizarro fights his way into Calca and captures part of the Inca forces, Pizarro's contingent recalled with word of native army bearing down upon Cuzco under General Inquill. The Incas besiege Cuzco, trapping the Spaniards in two buildings.

May 1536 Francisco Pizarro sends two relief columns toward Jauja, one is ambushed by Quizo Yupanqui's army, which annihilates the trapped Spaniards with rock-slides. Quizo Yupanqui continues northward and destroys a second Spanish contingent under Diego Pizarro.

May 16, 1536 Although dying in the attempt, Juan Pizarro leads 50 riders in a wild dash that succeeds in circling out into the countryside to the fortress of Sacsahuaman.

Late May 1536 Hernando and Gonzalo Pizarro are eventually able to capture the Sacsahuaman citadel. Approximately 2,000 Inca defenders are killed or commit suicide.

July–Early August 1536 Francisco Pizarro dispatches relief column under Francisco de Godoy to reinforce Jauja but Quizo Yupanqui's army arrives first, slaughtering Spanish defenders.

August 1536 Quizo Yupanqui descends onto the coastal plateau with a huge army to take Lima, surprise sally by Pizarro's hidden cavalry breaks the warrior ranks, Quizo Yupanqui eventually killed along with most of his officers, army disperses.

Late August 1536 Hernando Pizarro attacks Manco at new headquarters in fortress of Ollantaytambo. Stalemate develops with both sides remaining exhausted within their bases during rainy season.

November 8, 1536	Alonso de Alvarado marches from Lima to reconquer the interior of Peru.
January 1537	After being reinforced at Jauja by Gómez de Tordoya, Alonso de Alvarado resumes his slow drive toward Cuzco.
Early April 1537	Almagro returns to Cuzco from Chile, sends peace embassy to Manco. Attacked by an Inca army, Almagro fights way to Cuzco by April 18, deposes and imprisons Hernando and Gonzalo Pizarro, assumes overall command of the city.
July 12–13, 1537	Almagro dispatches his lieutenant Rodrigo Orgóñez with 10,000 native auxiliaries to subdue Alonso de Alvarado's relief force, overwhelms it almost without bloodshed.
Late July 1537	Manco abandons siege of Cuzco and relocates to Vilcabamba. Orgóñez attempts to pursue the fleeing emperor. Paullu is crowned the new puppet emperor.
September 1537	Almagro opens negotiations with Francisco Pizarro over ownership of Cuzco. Fighting erupts between both factions, and Hernando Pizarro leads an invasion of the central highlands.
April 6–26, 1538	Battle of Las Salinas between Spanish forces. Orgóñez is wounded, captured, and beheaded, Cuzco is then occupied and Almagro imprisoned.
July 8, 1538	A vengeful Hernando Pizarro has Almagro tried and garroted.
Late July 1538	Manco urges the Lupaca tribe to attack its traditional foe the Colla, now vassals of the Spaniards. Hernando Pizarro and Paullu defeat the Lupaca in battle.
Autumn 1538	The Conchuco tribes rise against Spanish rule, Manco uses his army to threaten Spanish communications between Cuzco and the coast. Francisco Pizarro fails to capture or kill Manco but compels rebellious natives to retire by December 22.
December 1538–February 1539	Gonzalo Pizarro's and Paullu's fight way into Cochabamba Valley. The Spaniards, reinforced by strong contingents under Hernando Pizarro and Martín de Guzmán, help to subdue all of Cochabamba's tribes.
April 1539	Gonzalo Pizarro and Paullu track down Manco at his remote new capital of Vilcabamba, force Manco to flee Vilcabamba, which the Spaniards destroy temporarily.
July 1539	Vilcabamba expedition returns to Cuzco with numerous captives, including Empress Cura Ocllo.
Late September 1539	Francisco Pizarro returns into Cuzco from Arequipa hoping to negotiate Manco's surrender.

October 1539	After a fierce eight-month campaign in Condesuyo Province by Captain Pedro de los Rios, the Inca high priest Villac Umu submits to the Spaniards.
November 1539	Manco slaughters Pizarro's envoys. Pizarro has Cura Ocllo stripped, beaten, killed, and her body being floated down the Yucay River to be found by Manco's men. Guerrilla warfare persists for a number of years, yet Peru is largely subdued.
June 26, 1541	Assassins hired by Almagro's son break into Francisco Pizarro's lavish palace near Lima and stab the conquistador to death.
1542	The Spanish Crown establishes the viceroyalty of Peru, with its capital at Lima. The same year, the Crown issues the New Laws (urged by Bartolomé de Las Casas), designed to prevent Spanish abuse of the natives in the New World, laws largely ignored.
1544	Manco is murdered by Spaniards involved in the murder of Pizarro, whom he had given refuge to at Vilcabamba. His young son, Sayri Túpac, becomes emperor of the rebel Inca state.
1558	The Spanish reach out to Sayri Túpac, convincing him to leave Vilcabamba and return to the traditional Inca capital of Cuzco.
1559	Sayri Túpac embraces Catholicism and is baptized Diego de Mendoza.
1561	Sayri Túpac dies, possibly poisoned either by the Spanish or by radicals from Vilcabamba who did not want peace. His half-brother, Titu Cusi Yupanqui, is named emperor in Vilcabamba.
1564	The native religious movement, known as the Taki Onqoy, is revealed in the confessional to Luis de Olivera, a Spanish priest, movement is deemed a heresy for its rejection of all things Spanish and the embracing of nativist huacas.
1566	After unsuccessfully attacking the ever-increasing number of Spaniards from his fortress of Vilcabamba, Titu Cusi agrees to the Treaty of Acobamba, nominally establishing peace between the two sides.
July 9, 1567	Titu Cusi agrees to submit to the authority of the Spanish king, but still refuses to leave Vilcabamba.
1569–	Curate Cristóbal de Albornoz uses his authority to gather evidence about the Taki Onqoy, discovering its spread through much of the Huamanga region and affecting many converted Incas.
1571	Titu Cusi dies suddenly, allegedly poisoned by a Spanish friar. His younger

brother, Túpac Amaru becomes the last Inca emperor, vigorously opposes Christianity and accommodation with the Spanish, carrying on a brief struggle for Inca independence.

Summer 1572 Angered by Túpac Amaru's policies, Viceroy Francisco de Toledo sends an expedition to capture Vilcabamba. Túpac Amaru, his pregnant wife, and family are captured while trying to flee through the jungle.

September 1572 Túpac Amaru is tried and beheaded in Cuzco. Toledo uses his office to conduct a *visitas,* putting down the Taki Onqoy movement and gathering testimony from non-Incas and Incas who favor Spanish rule. Information used for official history portraying the Incas as newcomers who had no right to rule Peru.

Aztec-Spanish War Timeline

ca. 1250   The Aztecs (Mexica) arrive in the Valley of Mexico.

ca. 1325   The Aztecs found the city of Tenochtitlán on Lake Texcoco.

1376–1395   Reign of Acamapichtli, first emperor of the Aztecs.

1395–1417   Reign of Huitzilíhuitl, second Aztec emperor.

1417–1426   Reign of Chimalpopoca, third emperor of the Aztecs.

1426–1440   Reign of Itzcóatl, fourth Aztec emperor. Aztecs form an alliance with Texcoco and Tlacopan.

1428   The Triple Alliance of Tenochtitlán, Texcoco, and Tlacopan conquers Atzcapotzalco.

1440–1469   Reign of Montezuma I, fifth emperor of the Aztecs. Aztec Empire expands beyond the Valley of Mexico.

1469–1481   Reign of Axayacatl, sixth Aztec emperor.

1481–1486   Reign of Tizoc, seventh emperor of the Aztecs. Significant weakening of the Aztec Empire.

1486–1502   Reign of Ahuitzotl, eighth Aztec emperor.

1502   Montezuma II becomes the ninth emperor of the Aztecs.

1511   Cuba invaded under Diego Velázquez de Cuéllar

1515   Bartolomé de Las Casas appointed priest-procurator to the Indians.

February 8, 1517   Conquistador Francisco Hernández de Córdoba departs Cuba to explore rumored rich lands to the west.

February 20, 1517   Hernández de Córdoba sights Isla Mujeres off northeastern Yucatán. Returns to Cuba after being attacked, tales of wealth spark considerable interest.

April 8, 1518   Cuban governor Diego Velázquez's nephew, Juan de Grijalva, sets sail for Mexico.

May 3, 1518   Grijalva explores island of Cozumel before heading south and discovering Ascensión Bay.

May 26, 1518   Grijalva lands near Champotón where he is confronted by Maya warriors. Indecisive

	battle, Grijalva sails farther west.
June 17, 1518	Grijalva names island Sacrificios Island for signs of human sacrifice. Spanish welcomed by Totonac Indians in hopes of alliance to overthrow Aztec rule.
June 24, 1518	Grijalva receives emissaries from Aztec emperor Montezuma II, claims island of San Juan de Ulúa, sends Alvarado to Cuba to report wealth. Grijalva explores as far north as Cape Rojo before turning back.
October 23, 1518	Governor Velázquez organizes another expedition, headed by Hernán Cortés. Decides to replace him at the last minute with Luis de Medina.
November 18, 1518	Cortés sets sail from Santiago de Cuba, gathering more recruits and supplies along Cuba coast while openly defying Velázquez's repeated recalls.
February 21, 1519	Cortés's expedition lands at Cozumel.
March 13, 1519	Cortés is joined by a Spanish castaway Gerónimo de Aguilar, serves as Mayan translator.
March–April 1519	Spanish victories against Potonchán and Cintla convince Mayas to submit to Spanish rule. Offer Cortés 20 Indian slave women, including Malinche who interprets Nahuatl to Maya.
April 21, 1519	While at San Juan de Ulúa, the Spaniards approached by Aztec emissaries inquiring as to their intentions.
April 24, 1519	Cortés met by Aztec, Teutliltzin, who sends a request for Spanish to meet Montezuma.
May 1, 1519	Teutliltzin returns from Montezuma with gifts for Cortés, and message discouraging a visit to the Aztec capital. Cortés meets with Totonac Indians from Cempoala, revealing subject tribes are resentful of Aztec rule.
May 10, 1519	Teutliltzin reappears with more presents, plus emperor's final rejection for a meeting with Spaniards.
May–June 1519	Cortés founds a new Spanish settlement called Villa Rica de la Vera Cruz. He is elected as its "mayor" and starts sending reports directly to the king in Spain.
June 1519	Spaniards received by Xicomecoatl of Cempoala, proposes to Cortés an alliance with the inland tribes of Tlaxcala and Huejotzingo to help overthrow Aztecs.
June 28, 1519	Cortés secretly encourages Mayas to seize a score of Aztec tribute-collectors, releases two in a false gesture of friendship.
June 30, 1519	Montezuma send gifts in thanks for release of two captives, Cortés allowed to visit Tenochtitlán but might

not be received by Mont-
ezuma. Cortés covertly en-
courages local natives to
refuse paying Aztecs tribute.

July 1, 1519 Francisco de Saucedo arrives
from Cuba with additional
men and news that Velázquez
authorized to take possession
of any new lands discovered
west of Cuba. Cortés sends
three ships with messages
and gifts directly to king.

August 8, 1519 Cortés marches toward
Cempoala with 800 Cempoa-
lan auxiliaries.

August 16, 1519 Renames Cempoala as Nueva
Sevilla, Cortés resumes his
advance inland, uncontested
through Jalapa, Xicochi-
malco, Ixhuacán, Zautla, and
Ixtacamaxtitlán.

August 31–September 12, 1519 Battle of Tlaxcala. Victory
paves way for important
alliance with Tlaxcalans.

October 12, 1519 Cortés resumes march inland,
reinforced by Tlaxcalans.

October 15, 1519 The expedition arrives at
Cholula, major Aztec satellite.

October 18, 1519 Convinced Cholultecans are
plotting with Montezuma,
Cortés slaughters over 6,000
in the Cholula Massacre.

November 1, 1519 Cortés's army departs
Cholula for Huejotzingo.

November 8, 1519 Spanish army reaches the
shores of Lake Texcoco,
marches along a six-mile
causeway, personally wel-
comed into Tenochtitlán by
Montezuma.

November 14, 1519 Cortés learns of attack on
garrison by Aztecs, uses
incident as excuse to confront
Montezuma and moves him
into the Spaniards' under
Spanish guards.

Early December 1519 Cualpopoca offending Aztec
officers ordered tortured and
burned alive by Cortés, who
then places Montezuma in
irons.

December 1519–April 1520 The Spaniards remain in
Tenochtitlán, gathering
tribute and information from
empire.

March 5, 1520 Governor Velázquez
launches an expedition under
Pánfilo de Narváez to arrest
and execute Cortés.

April 1520 Word reaches Cortés of the
Narváez Expedition.

Early May 1520 Cortés departs Tenochtitlán
to confront Narváez at Cem-
poala, leaves 120 behind in
Tenochtitlán as an occupation
force under Pedro de Alvarado.

May 16, 1520 Alvarado orders the massacre of a large group of na-
tive celebrants, precipitates
rebellion.

May 29, 1520 Cortés captures Narváez at
Cempoala. Narváez's army
surrenders and is incorporated into that of Cortés.

June 24, 1520 Cortés returns to Tenochtitlán where garrison is isolated
and shunned by the Aztecs.

June 25, 1520 Cortés releases Montezuma's
brother Cuitláhuac in at-
tempt to open markets for

provisions, move backfires. In the ensuing battle, several Spaniards killed, Cortés and his men retreat back into their quarter of the city.

Late June 1520
Spaniards force Montezuma to address mob to stop attack, emperor stoned by own people, dies, leaving Cuitláhuac the 10th emperor of the Aztecs.

June 30–July 1, 1520
La Noche Triste, Cortés and his men attempt to sneak out of the capital, are discovered, and forced to fight their way out of Tenochtitlán.

July 2, 1520
A series of pitched battles leave Spaniards and Tlaxcalans fleeing through Tepotzotlán and other deserted towns.

July 7, 1520
The Spaniards and their allies are almost overwhelmed by a large Aztec force at Otumba, emerge victorious after fierce hand-to-hand combat.

July 8–11, 1520
Cortés's men reach the safety of the Tlaxcalan town of Hueyotlipan, recover from their week-long flight from Tenochtitlán. The king's royal fifth portion of the wealth from Tenochtitlán discovered missing.

August 1, 1520
Cortés carries out a punitive expedition through Huejotzingo, Cholula, and Acatzingo against the province of Tepeaca.

August 7, 1520
The Spaniards reach Tepeaca, killing some 400 warriors, cruelly ravaged city,

prompting many other Aztec satellites to refrain from attacking or begin to ally with the invaders.

September 7, 1520
Cuitláhuac is officially elected emperor in Tenochtitlán, but takes no offensive steps against the foreign enemies.

September 1520
The first news of smallpox spreading among the indigenous population reaches Cortés.

Mid-September 1520
Cortés arrives in Huaquechula, whose leaders immediately present him with 40 high-ranking Aztec captives.

Early October 1520
Cortés seizes Aztec garrison town, Izúcar. Aztec troops offer heavy resistance before being annihilated.

Mid-October 1520
Cortés instructs his shipwright Martín López to build a fleet of brigantines to recapture Tenochtitlán.

November 25, 1520
Emperor Cuitláhuac dies of smallpox, thousands of indigenous people die while Spanish are mysteriously unaffected.

Early December 1520
Gonzalo de Sandoval marches northward from Tepeaca to secure supply route from the Gulf Coast, defeating Aztec vassal-states at Zautla and Xalacingo, chieftains switch allegiances.

December 29, 1520
Cortés begins offensive against the Aztec capital.

January 1, 1521
The expedition reaches Coatepec, scattering a small Aztec force.

January 2, 1521	Cortés's army is greeted by its frightened rulers of Texcoc, who offer their allegiance. Discovers most of populace fleeing into the Aztec capital, Spaniards sack the city.		before returning to Texcoco. Additional Spanish reinforcements arrive at Veracruz.
		March 14, 1521	The Spaniards and their allies fight their way into Oaxtepec.
January 5, 1521	Cortés approached by the chieftains of Cuautinchán, Huejutla, and Atengo, agree to switch sides and fight with the Spaniards.	**March 16, 1821**	Sandoval overruns the hilltop Aztec fortress of Yecapixtla.
		April 3, 1521	After receiving the submission of the chieftains of Tuxpan, Mexicaltzingo, and Nautla, Cortés disperses a huge new Aztec army gathered to threaten Chalco.
January 9, 1521	Cortés leaves Sandoval in command of fortified garrison at Texcoco then leads attack on the nearby city of Ixtapalapa. The retreating Ixtapalapans breach city's causeway so the ruined city is suddenly flooded.		
		April 4–5, 1521	Cortés clashes with a large body of enemy soldiers from Tlalmanalco, who agree to abandon the Aztec cause.
January 10, 1851	Aztec columns close in on the waterlogged Spaniards and Tlaxcalans at Ixtapalapa, driving them back into Texcoco.	**April 8, 1521**	The Spaniards destroy the Aztec garrison that has reoccupied Oaxtepec.
		April 13, 1521	The Spaniards descend upon the seemingly impregnable city of Cuernavaca, defenders submit that same afternoon to Cortés.
Late January 1521	Aztec emperor, Cuauhtémoc, leads his army down the eastern shores of Lake Tenochtitlán to compel resubmission to Aztecs. Cortés sends Sandoval to fetch brigantines that Martín López has constructed.		
		April 15, 1521	Expedition storms the strongly fortified lakeside city of Xochimilco, taking it by nightfall after very heavy fighting.
February 15, 1521	Sandoval returns to Texcoco with 10,000 Tlaxcalan bearers, carrying the pieces of wood that will be assembled to form López's vessels.	**April 16, 1521**	A fleet of 2,000 canoes bearing 12,000 Aztec warriors appears from Tenochtitlán. Three days of combat ensue.
Mid-to-Late February 1521	Cortés circles around Lake Texcoco, burning and assaulting cities, testing outer defenses of Tenochtitlán	**April 20, 1521**	Cortés marches six miles into Coyoacán, finding it deserted, probes Tenochtitlán's outer defenses.

April 22, 1521	Returning to Texcoco finds more Spanish volunteers have arrived.
April 25, 1521	Four days of ceremonies begin within Aztec capital to celebrate Cuauhtémoc's official coronation as 11th emperor of the Aztecs.
April 28, 1521	López's brigantines are launched at Texcoco.
April 29, 1521	Cortés dispatches messages to all allied cities, urging them to send as many men and supplies to Texcoco for one final offensive against Tenochtitlán, 60,000 rally to the Spanish.
May 7, 1521	Cortés divides forces, under himself, Cristóbal de Olid, and Sandoval. Three of the four causeways leading out of Tenochtitlán are severed, leaving one open to furnish the Aztecs with a tempting avenue of escape.
May 10, 1521	Alvarado's and Olid's contingents depart Texcoco, reaching the deserted city of Jilotepec the next day.
May 12, 1521	Alvarado and Olid march into empty Tacuba, Spaniards begin fortifying while a Tlaxcalan column probes up its causeway, fighting the defenders of the Aztec capital until sundown.
May 13, 1521	Olid presses on to Chapultepec, destroys aqueducts emanating from the spring there, cutting off Tenochtitlán's water supply before proceeding to Coyoacán.
May 31, 1521	Sandoval's unit departs Texcoco for Ixtapalapa.
June 1, 1521	Terrified inhabitants of Ixtapalapa flee at Sandoval's approach, uncontested column enters and burns city before fortifying the area. Cortés encounters stiff resistance near Tepeapulco.
June 2, 1521	Cortés pushes almost into the outskirts of Tenochtitlán, cuts Ixtapalapa causeway so four of his brigantines can penetrate into the inner lake.
June 3–9, 1521	A week-long lull in major fighting allows both sides to skirmish against each other's lines.
June 10, 1521	Cortés orders Alvarado and Sandoval to attack from their bases while he launches a major thrust up the Ixtapalapa causeway. Spanish retreat at nightfall.
June 15, 1521	Cortés fights way back into Tenochtitlán, with support from Xtlilxóchitl, native auxiliaries fill causeway. Assault column lights fires and levels houses in Tenochtitlán. Aztec counterthrusts throw the invaders back at nightfall.
June 16, 1521	Cortés resumes his assault up the Ixtapalapa causeway, discovers breaches reopened. Spanish recapture two gaps but retire again at nightfall.
June 17–18, 1521	Cortés shifts his strategy, attacking up the Tacuba causeway. The Spanish advance seizes three bridges

on its first day. By June 18, the remaining four are secured, establishing contact with Alvarado's force.

June 30, 1521
Cortés launches major assault under two columns, both columns fight their way deep into the city before becoming bogged down, both columns retire.

July 2, 1521
Emissaries from Cuernavaca inform Cortés that warrior priests of Malinalco and Couixco attacking their district, Cortés detaches a contingent under Andrés de Tapia to assist against the warrior-priests.

Early–Mid-July 1521
Cortés receives a similar request from the Otomí inhabitants of the highlands regarding their Matlatzincan neighbors. He detaches Sandoval to their aid.

Mid–Late July 1521
Spanish victories restore the besiegers' prestige, increasing Cortés's native auxiliaries. Arrival of a ship at Veracruz brings gunpowder, crossbows, and more soldiers.

July 24, 1521
Spaniards surprise Aztec civilians creeping out of beleaguered Tenochtitlán in search of food, massacring 800 of them.

July 25, 1521
Three-quarters of the city now controlled by the invaders.

July 29, 1521
Alvarado's contingent fights its way into the very center of Tlatelolco, plants flag atop the city's twin towers.

August 3, 1521
Cortés and Alvarado resume their assaults, slaying 12,000 more civilians. Cortés estimates only an eighth of Tenochtitlán remains under Aztec control.

August 12, 1521
Another major assault occurs, thousands of noncombatants are massacred.

August 13, 1521
Emperor attempts to flee, captured. Emperor's surrender marks end of Tenochtitlán's conquest by Cortés; at least 100,000 people have perished.

August 1521–August 1522
Cortés and his soldiers consolidate their holdings. Disease, starvation, and the fall of capital city weakens native resistance. Cortés requests for Franciscans to help convert and assimilate the indigenous population.

1522–1525
Numerous officers under Cortés undertake similar conquests throughout Mesoamerican region.

1524
Spain creates the Council of the Indies to oversee all aspects of colonial administration in Mexico and elsewhere in the New World.

1528
Cortés travels to Spain to successfully defend against allegations he organized his conquests to create his own personal empire.

1535
Spain creates the viceroyalty of New Spain.

Bibliography

Abercrombie, Thomas. *Pathways of Memory and Power: Ethnography and History among and Andean People.* Madison: The University of Wisconsin Press, 1998.

Abraham, Sarah. "Provincial Life in the Inca Empire: Continuity and Change at Pulapuco, Peru." PhD diss., University of California, Santa Barbara, 2010.

Adelaar, William F. H. *The Languages of the Andes (Cambridge Language Surveys).* Cambridge: Cambridge University Press, 2007.

Adorno, Rolena. "Discourses on Colonialism: Bernal Diaz, Las Casas, and the Twentieth Century reader," *MLN* 103, no. 2 (March 1988): 239–258.

Allen, Heather. "Literacy, Text, and Performance in the Histories of the Conquest of Mexico." PhD diss., University of Chicago, 2011.

Almazán, Marco. "Hernán Cortés: Virtù vs. Fortuna." *Journal of American Culture* (June 1, 1997): 131–137.

Ames, Glenn Joseph. *The Globe Encompassed: The Age of European Discovery, 1500–1700.* Upper Saddle River, NJ: Pearson Prentice Hall, 2008.

Anadon, Jose, ed. *Garcilaso Inca de la Vega: An American Humanist.* South Bend, IN: University of Notre Dame Press, 1998.

Andrien, Kenneth. *Andean Worlds: Indigenous History, Culture, and Consciousness under Spanish Rule, 1532–1825.* Albuquerque: University of New Mexico Press, 2001.

Apffel-Marglin, Frédérique, and Proyecto Andino de Tecnologías Campesinas (Peru). *The Spirit of Regeneration?: Andean Culture Confronting Western Notions of Development.* London/New York: Zed Books, 1998.

Austin, Alfredo López, and Leonardo López Luján, *Mexico's Indigenous Past.* Translated by Bernardo R. Ortiz de Montellano. Norman: University of Oklahoma Press, 2001.

Aveni, Anthony F. *Stairways to the Stars: Skywatching in Three Great Ancient Cultures.* New York: Wiley, 1999.

Bakewell, Peter J. *Mines of Silver and Gold in the Americas.* Aldershot, UK: Variorum, 1997.

Barghusen, Joan D. *The Aztecs: End of a Civilization.* San Diego, CA: Lucent Books, 2000.

Batalla Rosado, Juan José y José Luis de Rojas. *La religión azteca.* Madrid: Editorial Trotta and Universidad de Granada, 2008.

Baudez, Claude F., and Sydney Picasso. *Lost Cities of the Maya.* New York: Harry N. Abrams, 1992.

Bauer, Brian S. *The Sacred Landscape of the Inca: The Cusco Ceque System.* Austin: University of Texas Press, 2011

Bauer, Brian S. Bauer, Lucas C. Kellett, and Miriam Aráoz Silva, with contributions from Sabine Hyland and Carlo Socualaya Dávila. *The Chanka: Archaeological Research in Andahuaylas (Apurimac), Peru.* Los Angeles: Cotsxen Institute, 2010.

Beezley, William, and Colin MacLachlean. *Latin America: The Peoples and Their History.* 2nd ed. Belmont, CA: Thompson Wadsworth Publishers, 2007.

Berdan, Frances F. *The Aztecs of Central Mexico: An Imperial Society.* Florence, KY: Wadsworth, 2004.

Berghaus, Günter, ed. "Performance Research: On Ritual." *Center for Performance Research* 3, no. 3 (Winter 1998): 65–73.

Bernand, Carmen. *The Incas: Empire of Blood and Gold.* London: Thames and Hudson, 1994.

Bingham, Marjorie Wall, and Susan Hill Gross. *Women in Latin America—From Pre Columbian Times to the 20th Century.* Vol. 1. St. Louis Park, MN: Glenhurst Publications, 1985.

Boone, Elisabeth H. *Cycles of Time and Meaning in the Mexican Books of Fate.* Austin: University of Texas Press, 2007.

Brading, David. *The First America: The Spanish Monarchy, Creole Patriots, and the Liberal State, 1492–1867.* Cambridge: Cambridge University Press, 1993.

Bremmer, Jan ed. *Studies in the History and Anthropology of Religion 1: The Strange World of Human Sacrifice.* Leuven: Peeters, 2007.

Bricker, Victoria Reifler. *The Indian Christ, the Indian King: The Historical Substrate of Maya Myth.* Austin: University of Texas Press, 2009.

Broda, Johanna, David Carrasco, and Eduardo Matos Moctezuma. *The Great Temple of Tenochtitlan: Center and Periphery in the Aztec World.* Berkeley: University of California Press, 1989.

Brooks, Francis J. "Motecuzoma Xocoyotl, Hernán Cortés, and Bernal Díaz del Castillo: The Construction of an Arrest." *Hispanic American Historical Review.* 75 (May 1995): 149–183.

Brotherson, Gordon. *Book of the Fourth World: Reading the Native Americas through Their Literature.* Cambridge: Cambridge University Press, 1992.

Brown, Kendall W. *A History of Mining in Latin America: From the Colonial Era to the Present.* Diálogos Series. Albuquerque: University of New Mexico Press, 2012.

Brown, Robert McAfee. "Review: *Witness: Writings of Bartolome de las Casas.*" *Christian Century,* 109 (July 1, 1992): 655–656.

Brüggemann, Jürgen. K., ed. *Zempoala: el estudio de una ciudad prehispánica.* Mexico City: Antropología e Historia, 1991.

Bruhns, Karen Olsen. *Ancient South America.* Cambridge: Cambridge University Press, 1994.

Brumfield, Elisabeth M. "Aztec State Making: Ecology, Structure, and the Origin of the State." *American Anthropologist* 85, no. 2 (1983): 261–284.

Brundage, Burr Cartwright. *Empire of the Inca.* Norman: University of Oklahoma Press, 1985.

Burger, Richard L., and Lucy C. Salazar. *Machu Picchu: Unveiling the Mystery of the Incas.* New Haven, CT: Yale University Press, 2008.

Burhart, Louise M. *Encounter of Religions: The Indigenization of Christianity; the Nahua Scholar-Intepreters.* (Occasional Papers in Latin American Studies). Storrs: Center for Latin American and Caribbean Studies, University of Connecticut, 1991.

Burkholder, Mark A., and Lyman L. Johnson. *Colonial Latin America.* 7th ed. Oxford: Oxford University Press, 2009.

Burland, Cottie A. *The Aztecs: Gods and Fate in Ancient Mexico.* New York: Galahad Press, 1980.

Carmack, Robert, et al. *The Legacy of Mesoamerica: History and Culture of a Native American Civilization.* Upper Saddle River, NJ: Prentice Hall, 1996.

Carmean, Kelli, and Jeremy A. Sabloff. "Political Decentralization in the Puuc Region, Yucatán, Mexico." *Journal of Anthropological Research* 52, no. 3 (Autumn 1996): 317–330.

Carrasco, Pedro. "Cultura y sociedad en el México Antiguo." In *Historia General de México,* 153–233. México D.F.: El Colegio de México, 2000.

Castro, Daniel, Jr. "Another Face of Empire: Bartolome De Las Casas and the Restoration of the Indies." PhD diss., Tulane University, Los Angeles, 1994.

Chamberlin, Russell. "Charles V: Europe's Last Emperor?" *History Today* 50, no. 2 (2000): 2–3.

Christenson, Allen J. "Maize Was Their Flesh: Ritual Feasting in the Maya Highlands." In *Pre-Columbian Foodways: Interdisciplinary Approaches to Food, Culture, and Markets in Ancient Mesoamerica,* edited by John E. Staller and Michael Carrasco, 577–600. New York: Springer, 2009.

Christensen, Mark Z. "The Use of Nahuatl in Evagelization and the Ministry of Sebastian." *Ethnohistory* 59, no. 4 (Fall 2012): 691–711.

Clayton, Thomas. *Bartolomé de las Casas and the Conquest of the Americas.* Malden, MA: Wiley-Blackwell, 2011.

Clendinnen, Inga. *Ambivalent Conquests: Maya and Spaniard in Yucatan, 1517–1570.* 2nd ed. New York: Cambridge University Press, 2003.

Coatsworth, John H. "Political Economy and Economic Organization." In *The Cambridge Economic History of Latin America. Vol. 1. The Colonial Era and the Short Nineteenth Century,* edited by Victor Bulmer-Thomas, John H. Coatsworth, and Roberto Cortés Conde. New York: Cambridge University Press, 2006.

Cobo, Bernabe. *Inca Religion and Customs.* Edited and translated by Roland Hamilton. Austin: University of Texas Press, 1990.

Coe, Michael D. *Mexico: From the Olmecs to the Aztecs.* New York: Thames and Hudson, 1994.

Cole, Jeffrey A. *The Potosi Mita, 1573–1700.* Stanford, CA: Stanford University Press, 1985.

Collier, George Allen, Renato Rosaldo, and John Wirth. *The Inca and Aztec States, 1400–1800: Anthropology and History.* New York: Academic Press, 1982.

Cook, Jeannine, ed. *Columbus and the Land of Ayllon: The Exploration and Settlement of the Southeast.* Darien, GA: Lower Altamaha Historical Society, 1992.

Cook, Noble David. *Born to Die: Disease and New World Conquest, 1492–1650.* Cambridge and New York: Cambridge University Press, 1998.

Cook, Noble David, and W. George Lovell, eds. *"Secret Judgments of God": Old World Disease in Colonial Spanish America.* Norman: University of Oklahoma Press, 1991.

Conrad, Geoffrey W., and Arthur A Demarest. *Religion and Empire: The Dynamics of Aztec and Inca Expansionism.* Cambridge: Cambridge University Press, 1984.

Corbett, Bob. "Pre-Columbian Hispaniola—Arawak/Taino Indians." *The History of Haiti.* http://www.hartford-hwp.com/archives/43a/100.html (accessed July 22, 2011).

Córdova Tello, Mario. *El convento de San Miguel de Huejotzingo, Puebla.* Mexico City: INAH, 1992.

"Cortés's Inland Expedition." *Military History* 24, no. 3 (May 2007): 64–65.

Covey, R. Alan. "Multiregional Perspectives on the Archaeology of the Andes During the Late Intermediate Period (c. A.D. 1000–1400)." *Journal of Archaeological Research* 16 (September 2008): 287–338.

Crandall, John. "The Inca and Their Roads." *Latin American History.* http://suite101.com/article/the-inca-and-their-roads-a8761 (accessed October 23, 2012).

Crosby, Alfred. *Ecological Imperialism: The Biological Expansion of Europe, 900–1900.* Studies in Environment and History Series. Cambridge, UK: Cambridge University Press, 2004.

D'Altroy, Terence N. *The Incas.* Malden, MA: Blackwell, 2003.

Davidson, Miles H. *Columbus Then and Now: A Life Reexamined.* Norman: University of Oklahoma Press, 1997.

Davies, Nigel. *The Ancient Kingdoms of Mexico: A Magnificent Re-creation of Their Art and Life.* London: Penguin Books, 1982.

Deans-Smith, Susan. "Culture, Power and Society in Colonial Mexico." *Latin American Research Review.* 33, no. 1 (1998): 257–277.

Diamond, Jared M. *Guns, Germs, and Steel: The Fates of Human Societies.* New York: W. W. Norton, 2005.

Díaz del Castillo, Bernal. *The True History of the Conquest of New Spain.* Translated with an Introduction and Notes by Janet Burke and Ted Humphrey. Indianapolis, IN: Hackett Publishing, 2012.

Diehl, Richard A. *Tula, the Toltec Capital of Ancient Mexico.* London: Thames and Hudson, 1983.

Diel, Lori Boornazian. "Manuscrito del aperreamiento (Manuscript of the Dogging): A "Dogging" and Its Implications for Early Colonial Cholula." *Ethnohistory* 58, no. 4 (Fall 2011): 585–611.

Diez Canseco, Maria Rostworowski de. *History of the Inca Realm.* Translated by Harry B. Iceland. Cambridge: Cambridge University Press, 1999.

Di Giovanni, Mario. *Christopher Columbus: His Life and Discoveries.* San Gabriel, CA: Columbus Explorers, 1991.

DiMare, Philip C. "The Amerindian World." In *Cliffs World History,* edited by Fred N. Grayson. Hoboken, NJ: Wiley, 2006.

Douglas Cope, Robert. *The Limits of Racial Domination: Plebeian Society in Colonial Mexico City, 1660–1720.* Madison: University of Wisconsin Press, 1994.

Eakin, Marshall C. *The History of Latin America: Collision of Cultures.* New York: Palgrave Macmillan, 2007.

Elliott, J.H. *Spain, Europe, and the Wider World, 1500–1800.* New Haven, CT: Yale University Press, 2009.

Erickson, Clark L. "The Lake Titicaca Basin: A Precolumbian Built Landscape." In *Imperfect Balance: Landscape Transformations in the Precolumbian Americas,* edited by David L. Lentz, 311–356. New York: Columbia University Press, 2000.

Evans, Susan Toby, and David L. Webster, eds. *Archaeology of Ancient Mexico and Central America, an Encyclopedia.* New York: Garland Publishing, 2001.

Fagan, Brian M. *Kingdoms of Gold, Kingdoms of Jade: The Americas before Columbus.* New York: Thames and Hudson, 1991.

Farriss, Nancy M. *Maya Society under Colonial Rule: The Collective Enterprise of Survival.* Princeton, NJ: Princeton University Press, 1984.

Fisher, Andrew B., and Matthew D. O'Hara, eds. *Imperial Subjects: Race and Identity in Colonial Latin America.* Durham, NC: Duke University Press, 2009.

Fuson, Robert H. *Juan Ponce de Leon and the Spanish Discovery of Puerto Rico and Florida.* Blacksburg, VA: McDonald & Woodward, 2000.

Gabai, Rafael Varón. *Francisco Pizarro and His Brothers: The Illusion of Power in Sixteenth-Century Peru.* Translated by Javier Flores Espinoza. Norman: University of Oklahoma Press, 1997.

Gallenkamp, Charles. *Maya: The Riddle and Rediscovery of a Lost Civilization.* 3rd rev. ed. New York: Viking Penguin, 1985.

Garner, Richard L. "Long-term Silver Mining Trends in Spanish America: A Comparative Analysis of Peru and Mexico." *American Historical Review* 93 (October 1988): 898–936.

Gillespie, Susan D. *The Aztec Kings: The Construction of Rulership in Mexica History.* Tucson: University of Arizona Press, 1992.

Gitlitz, David M. *Los Arias Dávila de Segovia: entre la sinagoga y la iglesia.* San Francisco: International Scholars Publications, 1996.

Graubart, Karen. "Indecent Living: Indigenous Women and the Politics of Representation in Early Colonial Peru." *Colonial Latin American Review* 9, no. 2 (2000): 213–235.

Graulich, Michel. *Myths of Ancient Mexico.* Translated by Bernard R. Ortiz de Montellano and Thelma Ortiz de Montellano. Norman: University of Oklahoma Press, 1997.

Griffiths, Nicholas, and Fernando Cervantes, eds. *Spiritual Encounters: Interactions between Christianity and Native Religions in Colonial America.* Lincoln, NE: University of Nebraska Press, 1999.

Grunberg, Bernard. *Dictionnaire des conquistadores de Mexico.* Paris: L'Harmattan, 2001.

Gruzinski, Serge. *The Conquest of Mexico: The Incorporation of Indian Societies into the Western World, 16th–18th Centuries.* Cambridge: Polity Press, 1993.

Guitar, Lynne. "Boiling It Down: Slavery on the First Commercial Sugarcan Ingenios in the Americas (Hispaniola, 1530–45)." In *Slaves, Subjects, and Subversives: Blacks in Colonial Latin America,* edited by Jane G. Landers and Barry M. Robinson. Albuquerque: University of New Mexico, 2006.

Haase, Donald, ed. *The Greenwood Encyclopedia of Folktales and Fairy Tales: Volume One A–F.* Westport, CT: Greenwood Press, 2008.

Hakim, Joy. *The First Americans.* New York: Oxford University Press, 1993.

Hanke, Lewis. *The Spanish Struggle for Justice in the Conquest of America.* Dallas, TX: Southern Methodist University Press, 2002.

Hassig, Ross. *Mexico and the Spanish Conquest,* 2nd ed. Norman: University of Oklahoma Press, 2006.

Hastorf, Christine Ann. *Agriculture and the Onset of Political Inequality before the Inka.* New York: Cambridge University Press, 1993.

Headley, John. *The Emperor and His Chancellor: A Study of the Imperial Chancellery under Gattinara.* Cambridge: Cambridge University Press, 1983.

Heath, Ian. *Armies of the Sixteenth Century: The Armies of the Aztec and Inca Empires.* Vol. 2. Guernsey, UK: Foundry Books, 1999.

Heilman, Jaymie. "A Movement Misconstrued: A Response to Gabriela Ramos's Interpretation of Taki Onqoy." *Colonial Latin American Review* 11, no. 1 (2002): 123–138.

Henderson, Keith, and Jane Stevenson Day. *The Fall of the Aztec Empire.* Denver, CO: Roberts Rhinehart, 1993.

Henson, Sändra Lee Allen. "Dead Bones Dancing: The Taki Onqoy, Archaism, and Crisis in Sixteenth Century Peru." MA Thesis, East Tennessee State University, 2002.

Hicks, Frédéric. "Subject States and Tribute Provinces: Aztec Empire in the Northern Valley of Mexico." *Ancient Mesoamerica* 3, no. 1 (1992): 1–10.

Himmerich y Valencia, Robert. *The Encomenderos of New Spain, 1521–1555.* Austin: University of Texas Press, 1996.

Hoffer, Peter C. *Law and People in Colonial America.* Baltimore, MD: Johns Hopkins University Press, 1998.

Hoffman, Paul E. *A New Andalucia and a Way to the Orient: The American Southeast during the Sixteenth Century.* Baton Rouge: Louisiana State University Press, 2004.

Houston, Stephen D., and Takeshi Inomata. *The Classic Maya.* New York: Cambridge University Press, 2009.

Hudson, Rex A., ed. *Peru: A Country Study.* Washington: GPO for the Library of Congress, 1992. http://countrystudies.us/peru/5.htm (accessed on July 22, 2011).

Hunt, Stephen. *Christian Millenarianism: From the Early Church to Waco.* Bloomington: Indiana University Press, 2001.

Hyslop, John. *The Inka Road System.* Orlando, FL: Academic Press, 1984.

Isabell, William H., and Helaine Silverman. *Andean archaeology III: North and South.* New York: Springer, 2006.

Jackson, Sarah E. "Continuity and Change in Early Colonial Maya Community Governance: A Lexical Perspective." *Ethnohistory* 58, no. 4 (Fall 2011): 683–726.

Jacobs, James. "Tupac Amaru: The Life, Times, and Execution of the Last Inca". *The Andes Web Ring.* http://www.jqjacobs.net/andes/tupac_amaru.html (accessed May 20, 2012).

Johnson, Robert W. "The Irony of the Capac Nan." *The Social Studies.* 83 (1992): 21–24.

Jones, Mary Ellen. *Christopher Columbus and His Legacy: Opposing Viewpoints.* San Diego, CA: Greenhaven, 1992.

Jones, Oakah L., Jr. "Rescue and Ransom of Spanish Captives from the indios barbaros on the Northern Frontier of New Spain." *Colonial Latin American Historical Review* 4, no. 2 (Spring 1995): 128–148.

Julien, Catherine. *Reading Inca History.* Iowa City: University of Iowa Press, 2009.

Kadir, Djelal. *Columbus and the Ends of the Earth: Europe's Prophetic Rhetoric as Conquering Ideology.* Berkeley: University of California Press, 1992.

Kalyuta, Anastasia. "The Household and Estate of a Mexica Lord: "Información de doña isabel de Moctezuma", México: FAMSI, 2007. http://www.famsi.org/reports/06045/06045Kalyuta01.pdf (accessed November 14, 2012.)

Kamen, Henry. *Empire: How Spain Became a World Power, 1492–1763.* New York: HarperCollins, 2003.

Keegan, William F. *Taino Indian Myth and Practice: The Arrival of the Stranger King.* Gainesville: University Press of Florida, 2007.

Keen, Benjamin, and Keith Haynes. *A History of Latin America.* 8th ed. Boston: Houghton Mifflin Harcourt, 2009.

Kelsey, Harry. *Philip of Spain, King of England: The Forgotten Sovereign.* London: I.B. Tauris, 2012.

Kelton, Paul. *Enslavement & Epidemics: Biological Catastrophe in the Native Southeast 1492–1715.* Lincoln: University of Nebraska Press, 2007.

Kessell, John L., ed. *Remote Beyond Compare.* Albuquerque: University of New Mexico Press, 1989.

Kicza, John E. "Indian Freedom: The Cause of Bartolome de Las Casas, 1484–1566, A Reader." *Hispanic American Historical Review* 76 (November 1996): 774.

Kinsbruner, Jay. *The Colonial Spanish-American City: Urban Life in the Age of Atlantic Capitalism.* Austin: University of Texas Press, 2005.

Kintz, Ellen. *Life under the Tropical Canopy: Tradition and Change among the Yucatec Maya.* New York: Holt, Rinehart, and Winston, 1990.

Kirby, I. E., and C.I. Martin. *The Rise and Fall of the Black Caribs.* Kingstown: St. Vincent & the Grenadines National Trust, 1998.

Kirkwood, Burton. *The History of Mexico.* Westport, CT: Greenwood Press, 2004.

Klarén, Peter F. *Peru: Society and Nationhood in the Andes.* New York: Oxford University Press, 2000.

Kobayashi, José María. *La Educación Como Conquista: Empresa Franciscana En México.* 2nd ed. México: El Colegio de México, 2002.

Koch, Peter O. *The Spanish Conquest of the Inca Empire.* Jefferson, NC: McFarland & Co., 2008.

Kosiba, Steven Brian. "Becoming Inka: The Transformation of Political Place and Practice during Inka State Formation (Cusco, Peru)." PhD diss., University of Chicago, 2010.

Lamana, Gonzalo. *Domination without Dominance: Inca-Spanish Encounters in Early Colonial Peru.* Durham, NC: Duke University Press, 2008.

Lamar, Curt. "Hernando de Soto before Florida: A Narrative." In *The Hernando de Soto Expedition: History, Historiography, and "Discovery" in the Southeast.* Lincoln: University of Nebraska Press, 2005.

Landa, Diego de. *Yucatan: Before and After the Conquest.* Translated with Notes by William Gates. New York: Dover Publications, 1978.

Lane, Kris, and Matthew Restall. *The Riddle of Latin America.* Boston, MA: Wadsworth, 2012.

Lanyon, Anna. *The New World of Martín Cortés.* Sydney: Allyn & Unwin Press, 2003; Reprint, Cambridge, MA: De Capo Press, 2004.

Lee, Jongsoo. *The Allure of Nezahualcoyotl: Pre-Hispanic History, Religion and Nahua Poetics.* Albuquerque: University of New Mexico Press, 2008.

León-Portilla, Miguel, ed. *The Broken Spears: The Aztec Account of the Conquest of Mexico.* Translated by Angel Maria Garibay with Foreword by J. Jorge Klor de Alva. Boston: Beacon Press, 2006.

Levy, Buddy. *Conquistador: Hernán Cortés, King Montezuma, and the Last Stand of the Aztecs.* New York: Random House, 2008; Reprint, New York: Bantam Books, 2009.

Lippy, Charles, Robert Choquette, and Stafford Poole. *Christianity Comes to the Americas: 1492–1776.* New York: Paragon House, 1992.

Littleton, C. Scott, ed. *Gods, Goddesses, and Mythology.* Vol. 11. New York: Marshall Cavendish Corporation, 2005.

Lockhart, James. *The Nahuas after the Conquest: a Social and Cultural History of the Indians of Central Mexico, Sixteenth trough Eighteenth Centuries.* Stanford, CA: Stanford University Press, 1992.

Lockhart, James, ed. *We People Here: Náhuatl Accounts of the Conquest of Mexico.* Berkeley: University of California Press, 1993.

Lockwood, C. C. *The Yucatán Peninsula.* Baton Rouge: Louisiana State University Press, 1989.

Lovell, W. George. "'Heavy Shadows and Black Night': Disease and Depopulation in Colonial Spanish America." *Annals of the Association of American Geographers.* (September 1992): 426–443.

Lowry, Lyn Brandon. "Forging an Indian Nation: Urban Indians under Spanish Colonial Control." PhD diss., University of California, Berkeley, 1991.

MacCulloch, Diarmaid. *The Reformation: A History.* London: Penguin, 2003.

MacLachlan, Colin M., and Jaime E. Rodriguez. *The Forgings of the Cosmic Race: A Reinterpretation of Colonial Mexico.* Berkeley: University of California Press, 1980.

MacQuarrie, Kim. *The Last Days of the Incas.* New York: Simon & Schuster, 2007.

Malpass, Michael A. *Daily Life in the Inca Empire.* Westport, CT: Greenwood Press, 1996.

Maltby, William S. *The Rise and Fall of the Spanish Empire.* New York: Palgrave Macmillan, 2009.

Mann, Charles C. *1493: Uncovering the New World Columbus Created.* New York: Knopf, 2011.

Martin, Cheryl E. "Institutions and Society in Colonial Mexico." *Latin American Research Review* 25, no. 3 (1990): 188–198.

Martin, Cheryl, and Mark Wasserman. *Latin America and Its People.* 3rd ed. Boston, MA: Prentice Hall, 2012.

Matthew, Laura E., and Michel Oudijk. *Indian Conquistadors: Indigenous Allies in the Conquest of Mesoamerica.* University of Oklahoma Press, 2007.

Mauss, Marcel. *The Gift: The Form and Reason for Exchange in Archaic Societies.* New York: W. W. Norton, 2000 (reprint).

McAlister, Lyle N. *Spain and Portugal in the New World, 1492–1700.* Minneapolis: University of Minnesota Press, 1984.

McCormack, Sabine. *Religion in the Andes: Vision and Imagination in Early Colonial Peru.* Princeton: Princeton University Press, 1993.

McCreery, David J. *The Sweat of Their Brow: A History of Work in Latin America.* Armonk, NY: M. E. Sharpe, 2000.

McEwan, Gordon. *The Incas: New Perspectives.* New York: W. W. Norton and Company, 2006.

McKeever-Furst, Jill Leslie. "Codices." In *Encyclopedia of Latin American History and Culture,* edited by Jay Kinsbruner and Erick D. Langer. 2nd ed. Vol. 2. Detroit: Charles Scribner's Sons, 2008.

Medina, José Toribio, ed. *The Discovery of the Amazon.* New York: Dover, 1988.

Méndez, Cecilia. *The Plebian Republic: The Huanta Rebellion and the Making of the Peruvian State, 1820–1850.* Durham, NC: Duke University Press, 2005.

Mena García, Carmen. *Pedrarias Dávila o "La ira de Dios": una historia olvidada.* Sevilla: Universidad de Sevilla, 1992.

Miller, Mary E. *Maya Art and Architecture.* London: Thames and Hudson, 1999.

Millones, Luis. "The Time of the Inca: the Colonial Indians' Quest." *Antiquity* 66, no. 250 (March 1, 1992): 204–216.

Mills, Kenneth, William B. Taylor, and Sandra Lauderdale Graham. *Colonial Latin America: A Documentary History.* Wilmington, DE: Scholarly Resources, 2002.

Morris, Arthur. "The Agricultural Base of the Pre-Incan Andean Civilizations." *The Geographical Journal* 165 (1999): 286–95.

Morris, Craig, and Adriana Van Hagan. *The Incas: Lords of the Four Quarters*. London: Thames and Hudson, 2011.

Moseley, Michael. *The Incas and Their Ancestors: The Archaeology of Peru*. New York: Thames and Hudson, 1993.

Mumford, Jeremy. "The Taki Onqoy and the Andean Nation: Sources and Interpretations." *Latin American Research Review* 33, no. 1 (1998): 150–165.

Muñoz Camargo, Diego, Luis Reyes García, and Javier Lira Toledo. *Historia de Tlaxcala: Ms. 210 de la Biblioteca Nacional de París*. Tlaxcala, México: Gobierno del Estado de Tlaxcala; Centro de Investigaciones y Estudios Superiores en Antropología Social; Universidad Autónoma de Tlaxcala, 1998.

Nesvig, Martin. "Spanish Men, Indigenous Language, and Informal Interpreters in Postcontact Mexico." *Ethnohistory* 59, no. 4 (Fall 2012): 739–764.

Niles, Susan. *The Shape of Inca History. Narrative and Architecture in an Andean Empire*. Iowa City: University of Iowa Press, 1999.

Norris, Jim. *After the "Year Eighty": The Demise of Franciscan Power in Spanish New Mexico*. Albuquerque: University of New Mexico Press, 2000.

Nuckolls, Janis B. *Lessons from a Quechua Strongwoman: Ideophony, Dialogue and Perspective*. Tucson: The University of Arizona Press, 2010.

Nutini, Hugo G., and Barry L. Isaac. *Social Stratification in Central Mexico, 1500–2000*. Austin: University of Texas Press, 2009.

O' Hara, Matthew. *A Flock Divided: Race, Religion, and Politics in Mexico, 1749–1857*. Duke University Press, 2010.

O'Mansky, Matt, and Arthur A. Demarest. "Status Rivalry and Warfare in the Development and Collapse of Classic Maya Civilization." In *Latin American Indigenous Warfare and Ritual Violence*. Tucson: University of Arizona Press, 2007.

Otterbein, Keith F. "Warfare and Its Relationship to the Origins of Agriculture." *Current Anthropology* 52, no. 2 (April 2011): 267–268.

Palencia-Roth, Michael. "The Cannibal Law of 1503." In *Early Images of the Americas: Transfer and Invention,* edited by Jerry M. Williams and Robert E. Lewis. Tucson: University of Arizona Press, 1993.

Pardo, Oxvaldo F. *The Origins of Mexican Catholicism: Nahua Rituals and Christian Sacraments in Sixteenth-Century Mexico*. Ann Arbor: University of Michigan Press, 2009.

Parker, Geoffrey. *The Grand Strategy of Philip II*. Wiltshire, UK: Redwood Books, 1998.

Pearce, Adrian J. "Huancavelica 1700–1759: Administrative Reform of the Mercury Industry in Early Bourbon Peru." *Hispanic American Historical Review* 79, no. 4 (November 1999): 669–702.

Phillips, William D., and Carla Rahn Phillips. *The Worlds of Christopher Columbus*. New York: Cambridge University Press, 1992.

Pizzigoni, Caterina. "Conclusion: A Language across Space, Time, and Ethnicity." *Ethnohistory* 59, no. 4 (Fall 2012): 785–790.

Pohl, John, and Charles M. Robinson III. *Aztecs and Conquistadores: The Spanish Invasion and the Collapse of the Aztec Empire*. Oxford: Osprey Publishing, 2005.

Pollard, Helen Perlstein. *Tariácuari's Legacy: The Prehispanic Tarascan State*. Norman: University of Oklahoma Press, 1993.

Powers, Karen Vieira. *Women in the Crucible of Conquest: The Gendered Genesis of Spanish American Society, 1500–1600*. Albuquerque: University of New Mexico Press, 2005.

Prem, Hans J. *The Ancient Americas: A Brief History and Guide to Research*. Translated by Kornelia Kurbjuhn. Salt Lake City: University of Utah Press, 1997 [1989].

Quezada, Sergio. *Pueblos y caciques yucatecos (1550–1580)*. Mexico D.F.: El Colegio de México, 1993.

Rabasa, José. *Franciscans and Dominicans under the Gaze of Tlacuilo: Plural-World Dwelling in an Indian Pictorial Codex*. Morrison Library Inaugural Address Series 14. Berkeley: Doe Library, University of California at Berkeley, 1998.

Ramirez, Susan E. *To Feed and be Fed: The Cosmological Bases of Authority and Identity in the Andes.* Stanford: Stanford University Press, 2005.

Raudzens, George. *Technology, Disease, and Colonial Conquests, Sixteenth to Eighteenth Centuries: Essays Reappraising the Guns and Germs Theories.* History of Warfare Series, Vol. 2. Leiden, Netherlands /Boston: Koninklijke Brill NV, 2001.

Read, Kay A. *Time and Sacrifice in the Aztec Cosmos.* Bloomington: Indiana University Press, 1998.

Redmond, Elsa M. *Chiefdoms and Chieftaincy in the Americas.* Gainesville: University Press of Florida, 1998.

Reinhard, Johan. *The Ice Maiden: Inca Mummies, Mountain Gods, and Sacred Sites in the Andes.* Washington, DC: National Geographic Society, 2005.

Restall, Matthew. *Seven Myths of the Spanish Conquest.* Oxford: Oxford University Press, 2004.

Restall, Matthew, and Kris Lane. *Latin America in Colonial Times.* Cambridge: Cambridge University Press, 2011.

Richardson, Glenn. "Charles V 'Universal Soldier.'" *History Review* 38 (2000): 42–47.

Rider, Nick. *Cancun and the Yucatan.* New York: DK Publishing, 2010.

Rinehart, James. *Apocalyptic Faith and Political Violence: Prophets of Terror.* New York: Macmillan, 2006.

Rivera, Luis N. *A Violent Evangelism: The Political and Religious Conquest of the Americas.* Louisville, KY: Westminster/John Knox Press, 1992.

Rostworowski de Diez Canseco, Maria. *History of the Inca Realm.* Translated by Harry B. Iceland. New York: Cambridge University Press, 1999.

Rouse, Irving. *The Tainos: Rise and Decline of the People Who Greeted Columbus.* New Haven, CT: Yale University Press, 1992.

Sabloff, Jeremy A. "It Depends on How We Look at Things: New Perspectives on the Postclassic Period in the Northern Maya Lowlands." *Proceedings of the American Philosophical Society.* 151, no. 1 (March 2007):11–26.

Sallnow, Michael. *Pilgrims of the Andes: Regional Cults in Cuzco.* Washington, DC: Smithsonian Institute Press, 1987.

Salomon, Frank. *The Cord Keepers: Khipus and Cultural Life in a Peruvian Village.* Durham, NC: Duke University Press, 2004.

Salas Cuesta, Marcela. *La iglesia y el convento de Huejotzingo.* Mexico City: Universidad Autónoma de México, Instituto de Investigaciones Estéticas, 1982.

Sánchez, Carlos Serrano. "Mestizaje y Características Físicas de la Población Mexicana." *Arqueologia Mexicana* 11, no. 65 (February 2004): 64–67.

Sánchez Sorondo, Gabriel. *Historia oculta de la Conquista de América.* Madrid: Ediciones Nowtilus, 2009.

Schele, Linda, and David Freidel. *A Forest of Kings: The Untold Story of the Ancient Maya.* New York: William Morrow and Company, 1990.

Schwaller, John F. "The Expansion of Nahuatl as a Lingua Franca among Priests in Sixteenth-Century Mexico." *Ethnohistory* 59, no. 4 (Fall 2012): 675–690.

Schwaller, John F. "The Importance of Mextizos and Mulatos as Bilingual Intermediaries in Sixteenth-Century New Spain." *Ethnohistory* 59, no. 4 (Fall 2012): 713–738.

Schwarz, Stuart B., ed. *Victors and Vanquished: Spanish and Nahua Views of the Conquest of Mexico.* Boston: Bedford/St. Martin's, 2000.

Seed, Patricia. *Ceremonies of Possession in Europe's Conquest of the New World, 1492–1640.* New York: Cambridge University Press, 1995.

Sharer, Robert. J. *The Ancient Maya.* Stanford, CA: Stanford University Press, 2006.

Silverblatt, Irene. *Moon, Sun, and Witches: Gender Ideologies and Class in Inca and Colonial Peru.* Princeton, NJ: Princeton University Press, 1987.

Smith, Michael Ernest. *The Aztecs,* 3rd ed. Malden, MA: Wiley-Blackwell, 2012.

Spieker, Susanne. "An Early Research in the Field of Education: Bernardino de Sahagún in Sixteenth-Century Mexico." *History of Education* 37, no. 6 (November 2008): 757–772.

Staller, John E., Robert H. Tykot and Bruce F. Benz. *Histories of Maize in Mesoamerica. Multidisciplinary Approaches.* Walnut Creek, CA: Left Coast Press, 2010.

Stark, Barbara L., and Philip J. Arnold, III. *Olmec to Aztec: Settlement Patterns in the Ancient Gulf Lowlands.* Tucson: University of Arizona Press, 1997.

Stefoff, Rebecca. *Accidental Explorers: Surprises and Side Trips in the History of Discovery.* New York: Oxford University Press, 1992.

Stern, Steve J. *Peru's Indian Peoples and the Challenge of Spanish Conquest: Huamanga to 1640.* Madison: University of Wisconsin Press, 1993.

Stewart, Paul. "The Battle of Las Salinas, Peru, and Its Historians." *The Sixteenth Century Journal* 19, no. 3 (Autumn 1988): 407–434.

Stockel, H. Henrietta. *On the Bloody Road to Jesus: Christianity and the Chiricahua Apaches.* Albuquerque: University of New Mexico Press, 2004.

Stuart, David. *The Order of Days: The Maya World and the Truth About 2012.* New York: Harmony Books, 2011.

Suarez, Ananda Cohen, and George, Jeremy James. *Handbook to Life in the Inca World.* New York: Facts on File, 2011.

Tandeter, Enrique. *Coercion and Market: Silver Mining in Colonial Potosí, 1692–1826.* Albuquerque: University of New Mexico Press, 1993.

TePaske, John Jay, and Kendall W Brown. *A New World of Gold and Silver.* Leiden, Netherlands; Boston: Brill, 2010.

Terraciano, Kevin. "Three Texts in One: Book XII of the Florentine Codex." *Ethnohistory* 57, no. 1 (Winter 2010): 51–72.

Thomas, Hugh. *The Conquest of Mexico.* London: Pimlico Press, 2004.

Townsend, Camilla. *Malintzin's Choices: An Indian Woman in the Conquest of Mexico.* Albuquerque: University of New Mexico Press, 2006.

Townsend, Richard F. *The Aztecs.* London: Thames and Hudson, 1992.

Valderrama Rouy, Pablo. "The Totonac." In *Native Peoples of the Gulf Coast of Mexico,* edited by Alan R. Sandstrom and E. Hugo García Valencia. Tucson: University of Arizona Press, 2005.

Vilches, Elvira. *New World Gold: Cultural Anxiety and Monetary Disorder in Early Modern Spain.* Chicago: University of Chicago Press, 2010.

Villela, Khristaan D., and Mary Ellen Miller, eds. *The Aztec Calendar Stone.* Los Angeles: The Getty Research Institute, 2010.

Warren, J. Benedict. *The Conquest of Michoacán: The Spanish Domination of the Tarascan Kingdom in Western Mexico, 1521–1530.* Norman: University of Oklahoma Press, 1985.

Wasserman, Daniel I. "Language Policy and Religious Instruction in Spain and Mexico, c. 1550–1600." PhD diss., University of Virginia, 2012.

Webster, David. "Surplus, Labor, and Stress in Late Classic Maya Society." *Journal of Anthropological Research* 41, no. 4 (1985): 375–399.

Wells, E. Christian. "Recent Trends in Theorizing Prehispanic Mesoamerican Economies." *Journal of Archaeological Research* 14, no. 4 (December 2006): 265–312.

Wernke, Steven A., and Thomas M. Whitmore. "Agriculture and Inequality in the Colonial Andes: A Simulation of Production and Consumptions Using Administrative Documents." *Human Ecology: An Interdisciplinary Journal.* 37, no. 4 (August 2009): 421–440.

Williams, Patrick. *Philip II.* New York: Palgrave, 2001.

Wilson, Samuel M. *The Indigenous People of the Caribbean.* Gainesville: University Press of Florida, 1997.

Woodrow, Alain. *The Jesuits, A Story of Power.* New York: G. Chapman, 1995.

Wright Carr, David C. "El papel de los otomíes en las culturas del Altiplano Central: 5000 a.C.–1650 d.C." *Relaciones, Estudios de Historia y Sociedad* 72 (1997): 225–242.

Yannakakis, Yanna. "Introduction: How Did They Talk to One Another: Language Use and Communication in Multilingual New Spain." *Ethnohistory* 59, no. 4 (Fall 2012): 667–674.

Zadik, Benjamin Joseph. "The Iberian Pig in Spain and the Americas at the time of Columbus." M.A. Thesis. Berkeley: University of California, 2000.

Zuidema, R. T. "Hierarchy and Space in Incaic Social Organization." *Ethnohistory* 30, no. 2 (Spring 1983): 49–75.

Zulawski, Ann. *They Eat from Their Labor: Work and Social Change in Colonial Bolivia.* Pittsburgh: University of Pittsburgh, 1994.

Contributors

John H. Barnhill
Independent Scholar

Jakub Basista
Professor of History
Jagiellonian University, Krakow, Poland

Michael Beauchamp
Visiting Assistant Professor of History
Texas A&M University—Qatar

Amy H. Blackwell
Independent Scholar

Norbert Brockman
Professor Emeritus of International
Relations
St. Mary's University, San Antonio, TX

Kendall W. Brown
Professor of History
Brigham Young University

David Cahill
Professor, School of Humanities
University of New South Wales
Sydney, Australia

Rev. David M. Carletta, Ph.D
The Church of St. Matthew & St. Timothy
New York, NY

Christopher Alex Chablé
Regional Arts Commission
St. Louis, MO

Jill M. Church
Serials & Electronic Resources Librarian
Montante Family Library
D'Youville College, NY

Michael D. Coker
Assistant to the Director
Old Exchange and Provost Dungeon
Charleston, SC

Lisa L. Crutchfield
Assistant Professor of History
LaGrange College, GA

Scott R. DiMarco
Director, Library and Information
Resources
Mansfield University of Pennsylvania

Philip C. DiMare
Lecturer, Department of Humanities and
Religious Studies
California State University

Mark Dries
Graduate Student, Department of History
University of California-Davis

Rick Dyson
Information Services Librarian
Missouri Western State University

Emily A. Engel
Assistant Professor of Art History
Herron School of Art and Design
Indiana University

Thomas Edsall
Independent Scholar

Jeff Ewen
Senior Adjunct Professor
Terra Haute, IN

Marta Martín Gabaldón
Library Center for Research and Studies in
Social Anthropology
Tlalpan, Mexico

Karen S. Garvin
Independent Scholar

Ryan Gillen
Graduate Student, Department of History
Valdosta State University, GA

John Gram
Graduate Student, Department of History
Southern Methodist University, TX

Ryan Hackney
Harvard Center for Hellenic Studies

Dixie Ray Haggard
Assistant Professor, Department of History
Valdosta State University, GA

Charles Heath
Assistant Professor, Department of History
Sam Houston State University, TX

Glenn E. Helm
Library Director

Navy Department Library
Naval History & Heritage Command
Washington Navy Yard

Erika R. Hosselkus
Assistant Professor, Department of History
Southeast Missouri State University

Burton Kirkwood
Professor of History
University of Evansville, IN

John Laaman
Graduate Student, Department of History
Auburn University, Alabama

Covadonga Lamar Prieto
Assistant Professor
Hispanic Studies, College of Humanities,
Arts, & Social Sciences
University of California—Riverside

Jeffrey Kent Lucas
Associate Professor, Department of History
Coordinator, Undergraduate Social Studies
Education
University of North Carolina at Pembroke

Eric Martone
Assistant Professor of History & Social
Studies Education
Mercy College, NY

J. Gordon Melton
Distinguished Professor of American
Religious History
Institute for Studies in Religion
Baylor University, TX

Monae S. Merck
Graduate Student, Department of History &
Political Science
Elizabeth City State University, NC

Mitchell Newton-Matza
Independent Scholar

Fernando Ortiz
Consultation, Education, & Research Staff
Saint John Vianney Treatment Center,
Downingtown, PA
Director Counseling Center
Gonzaga University, Spokane, WA

Justin Pfeifer
Department of History
University of Toledo, OH

Paul G. Pierpaoli Jr.
Fellow
Military History, ABC-CLIO, Inc.

Charles V. Reed
Assistant Professor, Department of History
& Political Science
Elizabeth City State University, NC

Annette E. Richardson
University of Alberta

Kim Richardson
Assistant Professor, Department of
History
University of South Carolina—Lancaster

Anna Rulska
Assistant Professor, Department of Political
Science
North Georgia College and State Unive-
rsity

Jesús E. Sanabria
Assistant Professor-Librarian
Bronx Community College Library and
Learning Center, NY

John Schwaller
President
SUNY Potsdam, NY

Rebecca M. Seaman
Professor of History

Chair of the Department of History &
Political Science
Elizabeth City State University, NC

Jessica Sedgewick
Independent Scholar

Mary Shearman
Department of Gender, Sexuality and
Women's Studies
Simon Fraser University, British Columbia,
Canada

Debra J. Sheffer
Associate Professor, Department of History
Park University, MO

SilverMoon
Lecturer, Native American Studies
West Virginia University

John Howard Smith
Assistant Professor
Texas A&M University–Commerce

Matthew Blake Strickland
Department of History
Valdosta State University, GA

Angela T. Thompson
Assistant Professor, Department of History
Eastern Carolina University, NC

Spencer C. Tucker
Senior Fellow
Military History, ABC-CLIO, Inc.

José Valente
Independent Scholar

Marcie L. Venter
Center for Archaeological Research
Missouri State University

Nicole von Germeten
Associate Professor
Oregon State University

Tim J. Watts
Subject Librarian
Kansas State University

Victoria Williams
Independent Scholar

Jason Yaremko
Associate Professor, Department of History
Coordinator, History Programme, Bachelor
of Education Access Programme
University of Winnipeg, Manitoba,
Canada

Ronald E. Young
Canterbury School
Fort Myers, FL

Index

Note: Page numbers in **boldface** reflect main entries in the book.